A SOCIAL AND RELIGIOUS
HISTORY OF THE JEWS

Ancient Times: Volumes I–II

VOLUME II

CHRISTIAN ERA: THE FIRST FIVE CENTURIES

A SOCIAL
AND RELIGIOUS
HISTORY OF
THE JEWS

By SALO WITTMAYER BARON

Second Edition, Revised and Enlarged

Ancient Times: Volumes I–II
VOLUME II
CHRISTIAN ERA: THE FIRST FIVE CENTURIES

Columbia University Press
New York and London

The Jewish Publication Society of America
Philadelphia

COPYRIGHT 1937, 1952 BY COLUMBIA UNIVERSITY PRESS, NEW YORK

SECOND EDITION 1952
ISBN 0-231-08839-6

PRINTED IN THE UNITED STATES OF AMERICA

15 14 13 12 11 10 9 8 7 6

CONTENTS

A SOCIAL AND RELIGIOUS HISTORY
OF THE JEWS

Ancient Times

High Middle Ages

CHRISTIAN ERA: THE FIRST
FIVE CENTURIES

NEW HORIZONS

Political, social and economic differentiation of Jewry, in Palestine and in the Diaspora, was matched by the enormous variety of its religious beliefs and observances. The main factors are easily discernible. Extensive religious syncretism went hand in hand with sectarianism. Clearly, some syncretistic ingredients penetrated even the purely Jewish sectarian movements, while the formation of sects gave added stimulus and furnished new subject matter for doctrinal fusion. On the whole, the communities of Syria and Asia Minor were most exposed to foreign ideas and subsequent syncretistic identification, whereas in Palestine the deeply rooted social and economic contrasts resulted chiefly in sectarian divisions.

In that most syncretistic age of all recorded history, millions of Jews were drawn into the whirl of facile synthesis of the most disparate religious doctrines and rituals. While the corrosive forces of Hellenism had long been undermining the well-established creeds and cultures of the Orient, growing political and economic uniformity tended to reintegrate the elements into a new unity. The more homogeneous the Roman Empire became, the more urgent became the quest for a new all-embracing culture. The Jews lived in the most focal centers and in an exposed social and intellectual situation. Although firmly rooted in their ancestral creed, they showed unusual capacity for absorbing foreign ingredients and adjusting themselves to their environment. More than any other population group, they seem to have served as the yeast in this fermenting world.

HUMANITARIANISM

Wealthy and educated, poor and illiterate equally shared in the movement. There were outright renegades of the type assailed by the author of Third Maccabees. One of them, Antiochus, son of a Jewish elder, caused much suffering to the Antioch Jewish community in the days of the Great War. After completely severing their ties with Judaism, members of the Herodian dynasty sat on the thrones of Armenia and Chalcis and finally brought forth a full-fledged Roman, Gaius Julius Alexander Berenicianus, recorded as Roman consul in 117 and proconsul of Asia in 132. Even orthodox Jews saw no objection to dedicating synagogues to pagan dignitaries in recognition of specific benefactions or in order to place the buildings under their protection. More significantly, the masses adopted not only the mores, but much of the folklore of their environment. Some found Greek mythology superior to the biblical sagas. To such people the myth of the sons of Aloëus in the *Odyssey* had a much greater appeal than the biblical story of the Tower of Babel. The otherwise orthodox author of the Testament of Abraham had no compunctions about incorporating in his narrative some of Plato's eschatological myths (for instance, that of Er in the *Republic*). The rabbis themselves, often unconsciously, adopted such widespread Hellenistic tales (frequently of Indian or other oriental origin) as the ring of Polycrates or the parable of the lame and the blind. Through the latter they tried to explain the joint responsibility of soul and body for sins committed before their separation. Familiarity with such folktales, as well as with some popular legal practices, could be taken for granted even with average Palestinian audiences, and rabbinic preachers alluded to them so briefly that their hints often became cryptic to subsequent generations.[1]

Growing sentiment for human brotherhood added force to these attempts at harmonizing the diverse cultural and religious heritages throughout the Mediterranean world. While Plato still considered war against barbarians a natural necessity—only internal conflicts among the Greeks were to be shunned—Alexander the Great opened a new era in international relations. His famous banquet at Opis, in 324, symbolized the new approach. "When he prayed," says W. W. Tarn, "for a union of hearts and a joint commonwealth of Macedonians and Persians, he proclaimed for the first time, through a brotherhood of peoples, a brotherhood of man." Even in the days of Lysias we hear of men who, for materialistic reasons, were prepared to regard "any country in which they have their business" as their true fatherland. *Ubi bene ibi patria* became, long before the Roman "melting pot," the watchword of many idealistic or uprooted individuals. Before long, Panaetius (the first to formulate a consistent theory of humanitarianism) had to warn the various peoples to adhere to their national cultures and not to pretend to be Greeks. To be sure, his pupil Poseidonius was not prepared to extend the same degree of toleration to Judaism. He, Cicero, and others were inclined to view the Jewish religious observances, as did Tacitus two centuries later, as "opposed to those of all other religions." Their humanitarian teachings, nevertheless, fascinated many thoughtful Jews, who saw in them a basic acceptance of their own age-old blend of universalism and particularism.[2]

These teachings reflected, moreover, the general political optimism which, although coupled with incipient cultural despair, led the dominant groups during the centuries of Hellenistic and Roman expansion to believe in the approach of eternal peace and glory. Graeco-Roman messianism, reflected in the beautiful "messianic" eclogue of Virgil, written in 40 B.C.E., approximated the old messianic dreams of the Jewish people. Whether or not the Roman poet was directly influenced by the Bible or the Jewish Sibylline Oracles, many Jewish readers must have seen in his and other Graeco-Roman utopias signs of the approaching end of days. They readily overlooked the difference between the idea of the world's political pacification through Roman power and their own preëminently spiritual messianic hope. It required the great menace of Caligula's insistence on emperor worship to stir the conscience of all but the most tenuous Jews. In a pagan world which, as Pliny said, numbered more gods than men, or, as R. Isaac phrased it, "If the name of every idol were to be specifically mentioned, all skins [parchments] in the world would not suffice," it was natural to deify above all the emperor as the personification of the unity of empire, or the entire *oikoumene*. But many other nuances of hero worship could more readily be reconciled with the Jewish tradition. Moreover, philosophic reinterpretation of the Greek and Roman creedal and cultural traditions in the direction of monotheism and ethics lastingly influenced the Hellenistic Jews, to whom ethical monotheism was hereditary.[3]

In the face of this general ethical monotheism, Jews sometimes even forgot their own "historical monotheism." Philo, in particular, although a strictly Jewish monotheist, in many respects took the road to philosophical compromise. His messianism, in particular, was, as we recall, as close to the Graeco-Roman brand as to the intrinsically Jewish. To be sure, he adduced belief in a forthcoming age of eternal peace as one of the main aspects of the superiority of monotheism over polytheism, as the unity of God may be said to include the idea of the unity of mankind and, therefore, of world amity. But even here we find more of Platonic idealism and of the actual *pax Romana* than of the idea of miraculous redemption at a certain historical moment. Certainly Philo's messiah was a leader, saint, prophet, priest and, at the utmost, a pacific ruler, rather than a conquering hero. Indeed, his writings are permeated with Hellenistic rather than Jewish cosmopolitan "philanthropy." The expression *kosmopolites* occurs in nine passages, the word *philanthropos* in thirty-three, *philanthropia* in fifty-one, throughout his extant works, but the famous "Thou shalt love thy neighbour as thyself" (Lev. 19:18) is never stressed as the chief motivation. As compared with the Alexandrian philosopher, even the Hellenistic writers of the New Testament sparingly used the expression *philanthropia,* usually intending to convey nothing more than simple loving-kindness. In the Greek and Philonic meaning of general humanitarianism, in accordance with the usual contemporary Latin translation *humanitas,* it is used once only. In fact, as Heinemann points out, Philo in his emphasis upon cosmopolitanism surpasses the cynic philosophers, the very inventors of this term. To thousands of educated Jews, however, especially in the northeastern corner of the Mediterranean, even Philo must have appeared much too Jewish.[4]

GRAECO-ORIENTAL ART

Unsophisticated masses must have been even more deeply impressed by the contrast between the austerity of the Jewish synagogue ritual and the fascinating pageantry of the Greek and oriental temples. Only on his rare visits to the Temple in Jerusalem could a Diaspora Jew satisfy his craving for elaborate and picturesque ceremonies. But in his own home town he must often have resented the glaring disparity between his own humble and austere house of worship and the monumental pagan temples adorned with mosaics and wall paintings and filled with impressive statuary. Certainly the more ambitious or artistically minded Jews were not always prepared to shrug off this conspicuous inferiority by a contemptuous reference to "idolatry." Many must also have wondered whether the negligible and largely honorary role played by the priesthood in synagogue worship and the exclusive control vested in local elders, often wealthy but poorly educated and little trained in ceremonial, were not too high a price to pay for the "democratization" of their synagogue. The rabbinate, which in Palestine now assumed the ritualistic supervision, was still in its early stages in the Graeco-Roman dispersion.

Congregational recitation of Hebrew prayers doubtless was another source of discomfort to some Jews. Even if translated into his vernacular language, these were not always sufficiently intelligible or personally relevant to satisfy the individual worshiper's pious yearnings; nor were they secretive enough to arouse his curiosity about some hidden mysteries. Certainly the quest for the secret meanings (*kavvanot*) of the traditional Hebrew prayers, extensively indulged in by later kabbalists, was still in its infancy then. To be sure, such wavering Jews could observe that the very simplicity of their ritual often attracted Gentiles tired of the "empty" display of heathen ceremonials and looking for an escape from the glamorous but to them meaningless, if not immoral, rites of their temples and gymnasia. But it would have been amazing if there had not also been numerous Jews to whom the alien pastures seemed greener, and whose individual temperaments made them long either for the grandeur of Greek art or for the sexual satisfactions of the orgiastic mystery cults.

So strong, however, was Judaism's appeal to its adherents and the leaders' control over the masses, at least as long as the Palestinian center was more or less intact, that we learn of but few outright conversions. Realizing its own limitations, rabbinic leadership displayed considerable tolerance with respect to ritualistic diversity. Even in neighboring Jericho, the Mishnah informs us, there developed six local customs at variance with prevalent Palestinian usage. Only three of these were found objectionable by the rabbis. They did not mind approving, for instance, a certain different way of reciting the *Shema'* that was apparently so old that second-century opinions were divided on some of its essential features (M. Pesaḥim IV, 8; j. 31b). In such older centers of Jewish life as Egypt and Babylonia local customs went very far in meeting the peculiar requirements of their communities. In Egypt, particularly, the Temple of Onias, the great synagogue of Alexandria, and such special holidays as the Purim of Pharos offered some worth-while substitutes for the Palestinian Temple. Babylonia's ritualistic divergences were soon to become a major source of an independent legal tradition coloring the outlook of the Babylonian sages throughout the first millennium after 70. But in the younger communities of Syria and Asia Minor the

Palestinian patterns were long followed more or less blindly. We never hear of Palestinian visitors having any difficulty in participating in, or even leading, local services there. More than one community seems to have tried to live up to the ideal (later formulated in regard to *Shema*ʿ by a third-century Palestinian teacher) that the entire congregation recite its prayers "with the same careful attention, the same voice and the same intonation" (Cant. r. VIII, 15).

We know too little, however, about the Diaspora liturgy and music to be sure of the extent of this self-imposed uniformity. There doubtless remained some room also for local or even individual deviations. "By the Greeks of the Aristotelian school," says Eric Werner, "music was considered a servant of the state, by the Jews an instrument of either holy ecstasy or unholy temptation, by the Church Fathers a handmaid of the Church." It would appear that, however successful Palestinian resistance may have proved to the infiltration of the official music of Greek temples, many Diaspora individuals and communities did not equally well withstand the "unholy temptation" of pagan tunes, especially if they appeared in a more innocuous secular garb. Such adaptations must have increased as the so-called melismatic and hymnic songs, current in first-century Palestine, gradually disappeared from the synagogue after 70. Protracted mourning for the loss of the Temple was hardly the chief reason. Being technically more difficult, these songs were probably neglected even earlier in the more distant Diaspora communities which did not have at their disposal Temple-trained experts. Certainly levites of the type of R. Joshua, who could use his experience at Temple chanting for teaching his fellow worshipers in the synagogue, were rarely available in the dispersion. Out of respect for the Sabbath and holiday rest, the recitation of psalms was doubtless conducted there without accompaniment by musical instruments. That is why there is no mention of instrumental music in Philo's graphic description of a typical Sabbath service which, incidentally, shows that congregational singing, even responsoria, played but a minor role in the Egyptian synagogues. Such elimination of instruments from the outset reduced the original Temple psalmody to a faint echo. Simplification progressed further when the responsive antiphony was dropped in favor of general unison. This constant impoverishment in the variety and quality of synagogue music must have opened the gates ever more widely for the influx of non-Jewish musical motifs. Musical borrowings, evident in the later history of the Diaspora, must have been doubly frequent in the ancient, more formative period of Jewish liturgy.[5]

Less irresistible was the impact of the Greek theater and drama. Biblical tradition had sufficient elements of dramatic dialogue and action to inspire Jewish playwrights and actors to imitate the great achievements of the Greek drama. The fact that Palestinian Jewry did not yield to that temptation was owing not so much to the general deterioration of the Hellenistic theater as to its constant associations with pagan doctrines of "fate" and the physical intervention of heathen deities. After 70, especially, the Palestinians showed reluctance even to visit Greek theaters, both because of these pagan associations and because of the frequent derision of Jewish types. Both these motives appear clearly in the controversy between R. Meir and other rabbis. But all of them agreed that Jews should not attend Gentile spectacles. No traces of such aversion can be found in Diaspora Jewry, however. Philo, for instance, saw no objection to attending theatrical performances. Another Alexandrian, Ezechielos, actually wrote a Greek drama on a biblical theme. In Puteoli a Jewish actor, Aliturus, befriended Josephus on his early journey to Rome. Later, the Jewish community of Miletus had a reserved section in the municipal theater, inscribed "Place of the Jews." By no means a sign of segregation, this fact reveals the keen interest of Diaspora Jews in dramatic arts.[6]

While our information on the influence of Hellenistic music and theatrical arts on the Jews is very limited and can at best be conjectured from scanty evidence, there is no question about the impact of Greek architecture on Jewish life. So rigid an expounder of Jewish law as R. Eliezer ben Hyrcanus lived in Palestine in a house built in the Greek style. The very Temple, when rebuilt by Herod into one of the world's marvels, closely followed traditional patterns and yet revealed the unmistakable imprint of Greek design and architectonic harmony. Of course, statues and human figures in bas reliefs were totally banned. Modern excavators have been astonished by the paucity of extant sculptures even in the "Greek" cities of Palestine. Nor are the numerous explanations hitherto offered wholly convincing. One certainly cannot attribute it principally to the removal of many statues by foreign conquerors and the destruction of many others by Muslim fanatics in later centuries, since the same factors did not prevent the survival of a mass of statuary in other Near Eastern lands. The nondurability of local limestone, combined with the high cost of foreign marble, must have served as a more permanent deterrent. But we know that there was enough marble available for the construction of those sumptuary mausolea uncovered in the relatively small Galilean community of Beth She'arim. In Jewish Palestine at least, statues, especially if associated with any form of ritual, appeared as the very embodiment of idolatry. The mere attendance by Rabban Gamaliel II at a bath adorned by the statue of Aphrodite in Acco caused widespread resentment, which could not entirely be laughed off by a humorous remark.[7] Otherwise, however, the Palestinians evidently accepted most of the technological and stylistic improvements of the Hellenistic age which was dominated everywhere by an unprecedented passion for building. How much more must Hellenistic Jewry have been subject to the influence of the architectural beauties of "Japheth!"

Graeco-Oriental decorative arts penetrated even the synagogue and the cemetery. For a long time official Jewry had strenuously objected to plastic representations of men and animals. The Roman general, Vitellius, respected Jewish feelings to the extent of choosing a roundabout way, lest he offend the inhabitants of Jerusalem by the sight of Roman standards. Other Jews in Palestine, however, even more in the Diaspora, had no such feelings. In many recently excavated Palestinian synagogues, although dating from a somewhat later and more rigidly observant age, have been found remarkable specimens of mosaic floors with animals and human figures. It stands to reason that the synagogue art which Hillel, Jesus or Josephus contemplated did not materially differ from these later specimens.

Of equal significance have been the discoveries in Diaspora lands. The remains of the Delian synagogue (?) of the second pre-Christian century have long been considered the oldest thus far known. The synagogue of Stobi (near Monastir in Yugoslavia), whose inscription was first published in 1932, is most remarkable as an evidence of geographic expansion about 165 C.E. Structures and internal decorations of most of these Jewish houses of worship so greatly resembled those of non-Jewish buildings that our ability to differentiate between them depends largely on our interpretation of names or particular phrases preserved in extant inscriptions. This type of evidence obviously leaves much to be desired. In fact, a good case has been made against the identification of the Delos remains with a synagogue, while Claudius Tiberius Polycharmus, the founder of that in Stobi, may have been but a recent convert to Judaism.[8]

All these finds were overshadowed by the significant Franco-American discovery of a synagogue, dating from 245 c.e. in Dura-Europos. Not only has the existence of a fairly affluent Jewish community in that city on the Euphrates been definitely established, but also important manuscripts and, most astoundingly, frescoes have been brought to light, revealing a hitherto unknown early style of painting. The affinities with the early Christian art of the Santa Maria Maggiore in Rome and the Vienna manuscript of the Greek Genesis now enable us to trace back the history of Christian art to these Jewish models. The missing link, long postulated by such art historians as J. Strzygowski, has thus been found. We also understand why Christians long continued using Old, rather than New Testament, iconography, as it had evidently been developed before them by Jewish illuminators of the Septuagint, and why they depicted, for example, Jesus as holding the rod of Moses. Dura also gives us an inkling of the extent and depth of the artistic assimilation by Jews of alien motifs and techniques. Some of the painters, as well as Jewish elders for whom they worked (for example, Samuel the "priest") obviously were pious Jews. The frescoes are filled with Jewish traditions and beliefs and offer a sort of pictorial sketch of Jewish history, as narrated by Scripture and embellished by the Aggadah. These artists mourned for the fall of Jerusalem and fervently looked forward to the coming of the Messiah and the resurrection of the dead. And yet they seem completely unaware of any sinful imitation.[9]

Rome's Jewish catacombs are even more syncretistic. The candelabrum of seven branches (*menorah*), the horn (*shofar*), the palm-branch (*lulab*), and other Jewish symbols are common. Several specimens of such emblems of Judaism as the hexagram of David, the pentagram of Solomon, and even the swastika have also been found in both the older and the more recently uncovered Villa Torlonia tombs. But strictly pagan decorative motifs, such as winged genii (holding a candelabrum!) and other mythological figures are also plentiful. Some of these sarcophagi may have been previously owned by pagans; in one case the central figure, probably an objectionable pagan symbol, was blotted out by the new Jewish owner and replaced by the candlestick. In some cases, however, the sarcophagi must have been made, or at least ordered, by Jews. One inscription actually records the passing of a Jewish professional animal painter (*zographos*) named Eudoxios. No such plastic representations have been unearthed in Leontopolis. But the Jews of that district (to which the temple of Onias lent more than local distinction) cremated bodies, a custom elsewhere regarded as so un-Jewish that the Roman community, in order to avoid it, introduced the use of those subterranean cemeteries, the catacombs.[10]

Some Roman customs, to be sure, may have had a purely local character, and one should avoid too easy generalizations for all of Jewry. For example, in the Roman community the seven-branched candelabrum seems to have assumed a symbolic importance unequaled by any other Jewish emblem. It undoubtedly always was a purely Jewish symbol. Modern excavations have shown that, in its essential form, it was found in Palestine during the early Iron Age and not afterwards, which disproves its supposed Babylonian or Persian origin. But only for Roman Jews does it appear to have become almost what the cross was for Christians. One wonders whether Titus' triumphal arch, constantly reminding the Jewish passers-by of the temple trophy carried to Rome, did not help strengthen their pious reverence for that ancient emblem.[11]

Various figures of angels (victories) bearing crowns, have been confirmed, however, by finds as far away as Carthage and even in Palestinian synagogues. Despite his extremist formulation, E. R. Goodenough is not altogether wrong in explaining the ubiquity of this "crown of victory":

Whether the Jews who put this symbol on their graves and synagogues were profoundly mystical, or were only hoping that Judaism would take them to immortality after death, the symbol itself must, for Jews as for pagans and Christians, have represented the fulfillment of their religious aspirations, their hope in Judaism. . . . [From paganism] the symbol went over into Judaism and Christianity and, though all its former explanations were indignantly repudiated, it still meant at the end what it had meant at the beginning, the coming, in one sense or another, into divine and immortal life.

In the same period, other Palestinian Jews were troubled when handling current coins on account of the plastic representations upon them! [12]

True, the crown symbol as such probably no longer carried any of these deep religious connotations in the consciousness of most

Jews using it. The same holds true for the various representations of the vine, palm, and olive trees found on all sorts of Jewish monuments. Whatever one thinks of the connection, in Philo's symbolism, between "the beautiful and glorious crown which no human assembly has ever bestowed" and the palm tree (*tamar*), symbol of victory and virtue, to which the killer of the serpent (evil spirit) is wedded, one need not look for any mystic significance in the palm tree of ancient Jewish iconography. This holds true despite, or perhaps because of, the prevalence of such sacred uses among the other Near Eastern peoples. In preëxilic times the official opposition to the *asherah* worship reduced such representations among Israelites to a minimum. At the same time pictures of animals like the lion or the cock on the seals of Shema, servant of Jeroboam, and Jaazaniah, apparently elicited no objections. During the Maccabean age and later, on the other hand, the *asherah* was no longer a menace and Jews could readily reproduce their Palestinian trees as national emblems, without any compunctions about their possible mystic meanings to others. A colossal golden vine adorned the very entrance to the Temple. Another bearing the inscription, "From Alexander, the King of the Jews," which had been donated by Aristobulus II to Pompey, was estimated by Strabo (who had seen it at the Temple of Jupiter Capitolinus) to have been worth five hundred talents. It is possible that this vine, or rather entire "garden," had previously been placed at the Temple by the Jewish king who found it necessary to placate the Roman general by presenting him with this impressive gift. It would be utterly surprising, however, if some Jews, particularly in the dispersion, had been completely unaffected by the symbolic interpretations of sacred trees among their neighbors.[13]

The contrast between the literary sources, with their reiterated emphasis upon the prohibition of imagery, and the actual use of animal and even human figures (painted but not sculptured) in synagogue decorations, has long puzzled modern scholars. This widely prevalent usage cannot be explained even by the discovery of a Leningrad fragment of the Palestinian Talmud, stating that R. Abun, a Palestinian teacher of the early fourth century (or was it his posthumous son?), "did not hinder" his contemporaries from drawing designs of mosaics, and that a century earlier, in the days of R. Johanan, the rabbis did not interfere with painting murals. The talmudic teachers certainly did not encourage the

painting of nude women on synagogue walls, as was done in Dura
(the Egyptian princess personally fetching Moses from the river).
The text indicates, on the contrary, that the practice, under the
impact of Graeco-Roman mores, had become so deep-rooted that
the rabbis could not avoid legalizing it, even for Palestine. Similarly, their protest against crowning brides proved unavailing.
Though doubtless an older oriental custom, such crowning seems
now to have connoted something akin to the mystic "crown of
victory." The Tannaim prohibited it by stressing the need of
mourning for the Temple. The Babylonian, R. Ḥisda, found even
scriptural backing for the contention that so long as the "high-
priest's mitre is removed, everyone's crown shall also be taken
off." Nevertheless, this rabbinic prohibition was so widely disobeyed that late in the fourth century Mar bar R. Ashi himself
prepared a wreath for his daughter.[14]

Equally futile was the rabbis' attempt to discourage the erection of mausolea and the writing of tombstone inscriptions to
perpetuate the memory of the deceased. So deeply ingrained was
the Jewish belief in resurrection that the mausoleum itself came
to be called *nefesh* (soul), or by its Greek equivalent, *psyche*. M.
Schwabe has made it plausible that the use of this Greek term for
tombstone was probably owing to Jewish influence. The only
other instance of such designation is found on the *psyche* in the
Adjlun of one Zenodorus who, however, may likewise have been
a Jew. In vain did R. Simon ben Gamaliel teach, "One does not
make mausolea [*nefashot*] for the righteous, their words are their
memory." Fortunately for our knowledge of the past, even Palestinian Jewry paid no heed to that advice. Not only the Jewish
necropolis of Jaffa, but also the cemetery of Beth She'arim has
preserved many a Jewish *psyche* erected or inscribed by local
Jews as well as foreign visitors. Ultimately, the rabbis themselves
had to allow the use of excess receipts from charitable collections
for the erection of tombstones for deceased indigents. Advocates
of these "souls" could readily invoke the biblical record replete
with such memorials made of stone as Rachel's tomb. They could
also point to the existing tombs of ancient kings in the very heart
of Jerusalem, as well as to the more recent funerary monuments
of Hasmonean rulers or the converted Queen Helena of Adiabene.
Aided by the popular desire to lend visible expression to filial
piety, the more liberal view espoused by R. Nathan (otherwise
the spokesman for the conservative and aristocratic school of

Shammai) prevailed over the austerity preached by the Hillelite, Simon ben Gamaliel.[15]

Unfortunately, most of the extant monuments of Jewish art and epigraphy date from the second century or later. One might argue, therefore, that they reflect a stage of evolution posterior to the destruction of the Temple and the ensuing relaxation of centralized controls. The passage of time, too, doubtless heavily favored the assimilatory forces. Much of what appeared forbiddingly alien at first, became a familiar sight and, before long, an ingrained habit. However, we need but recall the iconoclastic fervor of the Zealots during the Great War, and the vengeance they wreaked on the palace of Herod Antipas in Tiberias merely because it had been adorned by representations of animals. Even the "assimilationist" Josephus, after living in Rome for more than twenty years, still blamed King Solomon for the cherubs and lions in his Temple and palace. Obviously, this was a burning issue long before 70. So strong, however, was the pressure of the Graeco-Oriental environment that the attack quickly spent itself on the destruction of works of art then existing, which may in part explain why so few of them have survived. But it could not stem the tide of ever new absorption of alien patterns by Jewish artists and patrons in Palestine. In the dispersion not even the nationalistic author of Third Maccabees ventured to voice serious objections. Orthodox Philo defended, of course, the Decalogue's prohibition of imagery, but he did it through the rather forced humanitarian argument that the Gentiles' high appreciation of works of art had not prevented the latter's gifted creators from growing "old in poverty and disesteem." [16]

MAGIC AND RITUAL

Another bridge between the Jewish and Gentile worlds was built by the growing popular indulgence on the part of both in the obscure arts of astrology and magic. We have ample contemporary evidence for the extent to which the Chaldaean astral religion, whose influence had made itself felt in early postexilic Judaism, had now become a dominant and expansive force throughout the Mediterranean world. Appealing only to the masses at first, it soon became fashionable in the upper classes.

Astrology, in particular, began to satisfy the general absorption in the unknown and mysterious. The impact of astral mythology and the mysterious rites which developed along with it also had profound justification in the uncontested achievements of such Babylonian astronomers as Kidenas (fourth century B.C.E.). At any rate, their astronomic computations concerning the duration of the world sounded more convincing, at least to the educated, than did the Parsee and Jewish chronology covering only a few thousand years. Cicero, Diodorus, and Seneca were not alone in finding the short life accorded the cosmos by the Graeco-Roman, Jewish, and other computations less plausible than the estimate of about 470,000 years for the period from the creation to the death of Alexander, or the estimate that between Alexander and the end of the world more than 50,000 years would elapse.

To these Babylonian astral and astrological influences were added powerful Egyptian models, particularly those of the Hermetic religion. For the Jews, Egypt was the foremost center of magic and sorcery, the Talmud declaring that of the "ten measures [qabbim] of magic which were given the world, nine were taken by Egypt and one by the rest of the world." Typical of many folktales current among Palestinian Jews is the remarkable story of what happened to a naive later rabbi, Ze'iri. Having acquired a donkey in Alexandria, we are told, the rabbi wished to give the animal some water, whereupon it turned into a piece of lumber. He got his money back, but was told, "Were you not Ze'iri, we would not have returned the money to you, for who buys anything in this city [known for its magic] without testing it in water?" [17]

Like all others, the Jews, especially if living in Egypt, felt the strange attraction of the mysterious Egyptian practices. Artapanus did not hesitate to make Abraham Pharaoh's teacher in astrology, while the Samaritan Pseudo-Eupolemus extended Abraham's contribution to all astral sciences, in which the patriarch had allegedly instructed both Egyptians and Phoenicians. Even the less outspoken Palestinian rabbi, Eleazar of Modein (about 100 C.E.) extolled Abraham's profound knowledge of stars, which caused "the kings of East and West to foregather early at his door." These and other Jews could well invoke the biblical phrase of God as the "Lord of hosts" (sebaot) and envisage the heavenly stars ranged behind the Almighty in a sort of battle formation to combat the forces of evil. From this point it was only one step to believing that each star was inhabited by an angel doing the command of the Lord, and thence another step, to seeing in falling meteors the embodiment of fallen angels or demons. This notion, current also in Zoroastrian circles, was ascribed to King Solomon by the author of the so-called Testament of Solomon.[18]

Official Judaism had long denounced sorcery under any form, the Pentateuch repeatedly decreeing the penalty of capital punishment for its exercise. The interpenetration of Irano-Chaldaean demonology and angelology in the later phases of the Jewish religion, however, necessarily fostered the atavistic aspirations to master, for the uses of man, the hidden, often inimical forces of the universe. The apocalyptic literature, some parts of which were highly esteemed even by the rabbis, is filled with references to supernatural relations between man and the spirit world. Against this elemental upsurge of the irrational the rabbis could fight only a sort of delaying action. They, finally, tried to take it under their own aegis and to cleanse it of all its polytheistic ingredients.[19]

Continued stubborn rejection certainly would have proved unavailing. Did not even the mighty Roman triumvirs, with all the state power at their disposal, bow to the insistent popular demand and erect an Egyptian temple in Rome? Marcus Agrippa's subsequent expulsion of all foreign magicians and astrologers (33 B.C.E.), although part of a powerful Western reaction, was intrinsically a confession of weakness. It underscored the futility of attempting to preserve an official monopoly in that tenuous realm of foretelling the future, which often also served as a powerful weapon in contemporary partisan struggles.

This is not the place to analyze more fully the ramified angelology and demonology of the apocryphal, pseudepigraphic, and early rabbinic literatures. Suffice it to say that, just as his heathen neighbor had populated the world with gods, the ordinary Jew saw the universe inhabited by a vast array of good and evil spirits. Precisely because he staunchly adhered to his monotheistic credo he doubly required some mediating agents between himself and his Creator, whose very name he no longer dared to utter. By the end of the Second Commonwealth and later, some Jews even feared to transliterate the name of God into another alphabet, often copying the four Hebrew letters in a Greek context. This practice, referred to by the Church Fathers, is illustrated by some Greek fragments of Aquila recovered from the Genizah palimpsests by Taylor, Burkitt, and others. In Aquila the word is written in the ancient Hebrew script, while in the Hexapla it sometimes appears as WHWH in its archaic form. At any rate the Greek reader was expected to pronounce it *Kyrios*, the Greek equivalent and, according to Baudissin, also the prototype of the Hebrew *Adonai*. Many Jews were now beginning to refrain even from casually using the accepted circumlocution of *Adonai* or *Kyrios*.[20]

Biblical reminiscences added force to this quest for intermediaries. The more rationalistic Sadducees, who endeavored to minimize the belief in angels, had considerable difficulty in explaining such clear-cut Pentateuchal passages, as, "Behold, I send an angel before thee, to keep thee by the way, and to bring thee into the place which I have prepared. Take ye heed of him and hearken unto his voice." Most Pharisaic and Diaspora Jews doubtless read with enthusiasm Ezekiel's vivid descriptions of the Chariot and pondered over the role of Satan in the speculations of Job and his friends or in the visions of Zechariah. They certainly appreciated the aid which their people was receiving, according to Daniel, from its particular "great prince," the archangel Michael. The more deeply they delved into the apocalyptic writings, the more puzzled, as well as stimulated to further elaboration, they became by such descriptions of the seven archangels as are still extant in the evidently pre-Maccabean section of the book of Enoch:

And these are the names of the holy angels who watch. Uriel, one of the holy angels, who is over the world and over Tartarus. Raphael, one of the holy angels, who is over the spirits of men. Raguel, one of the holy angels, who takes vengeance on the world of the luminaries. Michael, one of the holy angels, to wit, he that is set over the best part of mankind [Israel] and over chaos. Sarqael, one of the holy angels, who is set over the spirits, who sin in the spirit. Gabriel, one of the holy angels, who is over Paradise, and the serpents and the Cherubim. Remiel, one of the holy angels, whom God set over those who rise.[21]

Not that they were altogether convinced of the angels' friendship. Later rabbinic legends, echoing popular apprehensions, often depicted the reputedly strong undercurrent of hostility, even envy, toward man among these celestial beings. It was believed that the angels, allegedly created on the second day in order not to lend them a semblance of having had a share in the world's creation (the contention of "heretics" that God had a "partner" was sharply repudiated), opposed the creation of man on the sixth day. Later on they objected to the revelation of the Torah to

Moses and the divine presence at the Temple. Supposedly they constantly harped on the psalmist's query, "What is man that Thou art mindful of him, and the son of man that Thou thinkest of him?" At the same time, they were often forced, on God's orders, to intervene in favor of man, and particularly Israel. The author of Second Maccabees, for example, described the Jews' victory over Lysias as having been achieved with the aid of a rider who "appeared at their head, in white apparel, brandishing weapons of gold." Each of the "seventy" nations, moreover, had its appointed guardian angel, who constantly pleaded its cause before the Almighty and fought for it in war and peace. Thus the old struggle among the national deities was transformed into a struggle between those secondary powers under the reign of the One and Only God.[22]

Israel, too, had its "advocate" and paraclete before the Lord: Michael, the greatest of archangels. In the Testament of Levi the protective intermediary is quoted as saying, "I am the angel who intercedeth for the nation of Israel that they may not be smitten utterly, for every evil spirit attacketh it" (5:6). Sometimes, however, the pride of chosenness made Jews emphasize their own unique relationship directly with the Deity. Echoing the well-known Deuteronomic assertion, many of them heartily repeated after Sirach, "For every nation He appointed a ruler, but Israel is the Lord's portion" (17:7). But this conviction could readily be harmonized with the belief in a special "spokesman" or "spokesmen" who interceded between Israel and God, as God's prophets had long been thought of doing. Ultimately, the belief spread that each individual, too, had his guardian angel who accompanied him all the time and defended him against the unceasing onslaught of evil spirits. Jews agreed that this world of demons was created by God and was doing his will. Nevertheless, behind the powerful figure of Satan or Asmodaeus (together with his feminine counterpart or counterparts, the *Lilith* or *Lilin*) there often lurked the fearsome awe of the Evil Principle itself to which the spread of dualistic propaganda from Iran added constant nourishment.

From the practical angle it became increasingly important for the individual to enlist the support of friendly spirits and to render harmless those of evil design. There developed a whole pseudo-science of incantations and exorcisms. It was believed that through the proper, extremely precise use of certain words and formulas, man could force a particular spirit to do his bidding. The knowledge of a demon's name, or the expert manipulation of divine names, could go very far in controlling one's destiny as well as that of one's friends or enemies. In the Apocalypse of Abraham (20–21) God Himself was said to have promised to inscribe his holy Name on the foreheads of the pious to assure their inviolability.

A whole array of amulets (*qemi'ot*) was used for protective purposes, and such warnings as were implied in the story of the fallen Maccabean warriors who had concealed under their shirts "amulets of the idols of Jamnia" proved unavailing. Like Josephus, most rabbis began viewing the traditional religious implements of *tefillin* (phylacteries) and *mezuzot* (doorpost emblems) as protective charms. Judah the Patriarch himself is said to have sent a *mezuzah* to King Artabanus (IV?) of Parthia assuring him that the Scriptural passages contained therein would "guard you while you sleep." R. Jeremiah was confident that so long as he wore phylacteries he need fear no evil spirits. Although historically of little value, it is characteristic that several magical formulas were handed down by tradition in the name of R. Joshua ben Peraḥiah, an early Pharisaic teacher. Talismans of all kinds had become so common that a fourth-century rabbi (Ḥanina ben Isaac) could use them in picturesque metaphor. Expatiating on Gen. 32:26 he explained the "angel's" inability to overpower Jacob by the latter's five talismans (*qemi'im*), namely, his own merits and those of his parents and grandparents. Because of these protective merits God also warned every nation wishing to attack the Jews, "Your lord could not prevail over Israel, how much less can you hope to do so!" [23]

Merits of the Fathers and other biblical heroes were often invoked in various other ways. We are told, for example, by the first-century (?) author of the apocryphal *Lives of the Prophets* that the Egyptians held in high honor the prophet Jeremiah, "for at his prayer, the serpents which the Egyptians call *ephoth* departed from them; and even at the present day the faithful servants of God pray on that spot [Jeremiah's grave, the former site of a royal palace], and taking off the dust of the place they heal the bites of serpents." The colorful story of Jonah, elaborated in subsequent legends, likewise lent itself to extensive magic use. If inscribed on a scroll, it instantly converted the latter into an effective amulet.[24]

Many magic books, instructing the readers in the use of formulas and other devices, were circulating among Jews and non-Jews. Some of them were attributed to King Solomon, who was frequently eulogized as the king of magicians. It is not impossible that the rabbis' wish to counteract this popular acceptance of Solomon's mastery over demons contributed to their decision to canonize the book of Ecclesiastes which reputedly expressed the wise king's more genuine skeptical and worldly convictions.

Use of magic aids cut across national and religious lines. Before his deposition, the Jewish King Archelaus consulted "Chaldaean" soothsayers. The Roman procurator Felix, on his part, greatly honored a Jewish magician from Cyprus who succeeded in enticing the Herodian princess Drusilla to leave her converted husband (King Azizus of Emesa) and to join Felix. Another Jewish magician, Josephus tells us with considerable elation, by his tricks deeply impressed Vespasian and the entire imperial court. Particularly widespread was the use of magic herbs and exorcisms in folk medicine and religious healing. Celsus, an otherwise enlightened apologist for the Graeco-Roman civilization, deeply admired the Egyptians for their intimate knowledge of the names of numerous demons inhabiting the human body. He was astounded by the Egyptian physicians' ability to invoke these names and thereby heal the ailments of particular limbs. On the other hand, Lucian of Samosata (second century) derided the magic healing of podagra "through the incantations of a Jew." [25]

Women, generally more illiterate and superstitious than men, were irresistibly attracted to the magic arts. The Talmud repeatedly speaks of the "majority of women being witches" and says that "the most pious of women is engaged in sorcery." Official Judaism protested vainly. Not even R. Simon ben Shetaḥ's fanatical execution of eighty women in Ascalon, evidently carried out with great difficulty because of Ascalon's independence, could stop a practice rooted in the conditions of the age. Neither were the rabbis themselves without blemish. Soon after 70, R. Joshua ben Ḥananiah boasted of his ability to transform cucumbers and melons into a living deer. Two centuries later, R. Ḥanina and R. Oshaiah reputedly studied the "Book of Creation" every Friday and, with its aid, formed a tender calf whose meat they consumed on the Sabbath. Their Babylonian predecessor, Rab, believed that fully 99 per cent of all diseases were due to an "evil eye." Of course, the effects of such a *jettatura* could best be remedied by the use of magic counterirritants. With their high appreciation of life, the rabbis were doubly willing to make allowances for magic healing. While generally counting magic among the forbidden "Amorite folkways," they ruled that "anything bearing on healing does not fall within" that category. It should also be borne in mind that "in some of the medical passages, if we substitute germs for living demons who bring disease, we have the substance of the passage with a modern ring." [26]

Diaspora Jewry went further along this alluring road. In foreign lands the obstacles which official Jewish leaders could erect were slighter, the example set by the surrounding nations more impelling. In fact, economic considerations added their decisive influence, as magic frequently became a lucrative professional activity. The Jews, increasingly segregated throughout the Mediterranean world, having a religion which, because of the very absence of a visible deity and the strangeness of its customs and observances, doubly attracted superstitious minds, became, along with the Chaldaean priests, the most sought-for magicians. Hadrian's alleged statement about the light-mindedness and instability of the Egyptian population, including its Jews, that "there is no Jewish archisynagogus, no Samaritan, no Christian presbyter who is not an astrologer, a soothsayer or an anointer" (*non mathematicus, non haruspex, non aliptes;* Vopiscus' *Vita Saturnini,* VIII, 3 in *Scriptores historiae Augustae,* III, 398f.) may not be genuine, but it does reflect the actual conditions in many Mediterranean countries.

Since most people had an unreasoning fear of the power of the Word, it was readily believed that a Jew by the mere utterance of the name of God could perform miracles of any kind. Indeed, pagans and Christians, as well as Jews, began to invoke *Jao* (frequently coupled with names like Abraxas, Sebaot, and others) as the god of magic and sorcery. Deep into the Byzantine age, that name was inscribed on amulets and doorsteps, to conjure away headaches, overcome indifference in love affairs and the like. For the few more conscientious Jews who may have hesitated to invoke the divine name itself, the ever more numerous and elaborate names of angels could serve as substitutes. The author of the Abraham Apocalypse actually provided an excellent onomastic alternative in the angel Jaoel, tamer of the Leviathan and the nether world's other dark forces and all-powerful harmonizer between the ever-quarreling "cherubim."

Very widespread, also, was the use of the magic formula, "God of Abraham, Isaac and Jacob." According to Origen, this formula was applied not only by Jews but also by "almost all those who occupy themselves with incantations and magical rites. For there is found in treatises on magic in many countries such an invocation of God." Some "vagabond Jews" in Ephesus tried to exorcise an evil spirit by using the formula, "We adjure you by Jesus, whom Paul preacheth." Luke reports this event by saying that the evil spirit answered, "Jesus I know, and Paul I know; but who are ye?" and adds that, on this occasion, Paul burned a collection of magic books valued at 50,000 drachmas. In Babylonia, particularly after the Sassanian conquest, even official Judaism was increasingly permeated with magic lore. The clear indications in the legendary portions of the Babylonian Talmud are confirmed by many magic bowls bearing Jewish inscriptions, unearthed in the Euphrates Valley. Such bowls were usually built into home foundations or buried in cemeteries to keep off pestilences and evil spirits.[27]

RELIGIOUS SYNCRETISM

Only one more step was required for the completion of religious syncretism. Especially in those countries where a large section of the Jewish population consisted of proselytes or semi-proselytes, the latter inevitably brought to their new religion novel ingredients. Some consciously regarded elements of their previous creeds as worthy of preservation; others synthesized the old and the new credos without too much thought. Influences of soil and climate led even racially pure Jews to deviate from accustomed beliefs. For many, the teachings of mystery cults about the winning of individual salvation through certain rites must have constituted a permanent attraction mixed with repulsion. Finally, the more the individual Diaspora Jew was inclined to propagandize, the more readily did he tend to persuade others, and eventually to persuade himself, that the Jewish God was more or less identical with the supreme local deity.

Hence these frequent identifications with Dionysius and Sabbazius, with the Egyptian Ḥnub and Set, with the Asiatic Asclepius-Glycon, and in general with the "highest God," the *hypsistos* of the whole Graeco-Roman world! Eventually things went so far that many a Diaspora half-Jew could join Celsus in saying, "that it matters nothing whether the highest being be called Jupiter, or Zeus, or Adonai, or Sabaoth, or Ammoun (as the Egyptians term him) or Pappaeus (as the Scythians entitle him)." Two members of the community of Apollonopolis (Edfu) did not hesitate to express their thanks to "God" by placing dedicatory inscriptions in the local temple of Pan. Ironically, one of them may merely have complied with a popular demand that anyone returning from a sea voyage should render thanks to God for saving him from imminent danger.[28]

While these syncretistic forms are found from Carthage and Rome to Mesopotamia, from Egypt to Asia Minor, the northeast was the center of the most crucial contacts. Nowhere else did religious fraternization progress so far as in the cities of the Anatolian and Balkan shores of the Mediterranean and the Black Sea. As early as 150 B.C.E. an "alien" named Nicetas son of Jason, "a Jerusalemite," contributed 100 drachmas to a Dionysian festival in Jasus, Caria, on the Anatolian coast. He may have been a member of the defeated party of Jewish Hellenizers who, escaping the wrath of the victorious Maccabeans, must have seen no more harm in subsidizing pagan festivals than did Herod and others after him. He may also have accepted the identification of Dionysius with Sabbazius, and therefrom, with his Jewish God, an identification which was to mislead so many later writers (Valerius Maximus, Plutarch, and others). Reciprocally, in the days of Nero a synagogue was built in Acmonia with money donated by the most aristocratic Gentile lady of the city, Julia Severa. Although serving as a high priestess of the city's pagan deity she was married to a man who bore the honorary title of "ruler of the synagogue for life," which does not necessarily mean that he professed Judaism. The Apamaean city officials who chose to strike coins associating their city with Noah and his ark, because of age-old associations of Ararat with a neighboring mountain, may also have been more than lukewarm sympathizers with Judaism despite their active participation in the local pagan worship. A Gentile in the Greek island of Euboea stipulated in his will that, to frighten away ghouls, sentences taken from two verses in Deuteronomy be inscribed upon his tombstone. On the other hand, a Hierapolis Jew ordered that at every Passover and Pentecost his tombstone should be adorned with flowers—obviously a pagan custom at that time.[29]

In Asia Minor these syncretistic mixtures were stimulated by the wide acceptance of the Sabbazius worship, evidenced as early as 135 B.C.E. in the interesting letters of King Attalus III to the cities of Cyzicus and Pergamum. Elsewhere, too, Jewish contributions to the syncretism of the age were steadily increasing. On the fringe of every settlement were not only the numerous *sebomenoi*, but many types of syncretistic half-Jews. In a Roman catacomb is the grave of one Vincentius, whose wife Vibia was Jewish, while he himself "belonged to a Jewish pagan sect that admitted neophytes of every race to its mystic ceremonies"! Indeed, both the priest and his wife, living in Rome in the third century, appear to have been simultaneously Jews, Christians, and heathens! Certainly his epitaph enjoining the onlooker, "Eat, drink and play," reminiscent of both Epicureanism and Ecclesiastes, would have seemed to an orthodox Jew an incongruous funerary advice. His designation as "high-priest of the god, Sabazios [*numinis antistes Sabazis*] . . . who with a pious mind had observed the holy precepts of the gods," the remarkable Judeo-Christian-pagan frescoes surrounding his tomb and its very location in a Christian graveyard—all show how vague the distinctions between the individual religious groups had become in the imperial city a few decades before Constantine.[30]

Of course, in dealing with ancient Jewish syncretism one must always bear in mind the great differences of chronology and geography. What it means to juxtapose trends and events of the various parts of this extended area, and, even more, of the various periods from the first century B.C.E. to the fourth century C.E., can best be illustrated in the case of Christianity, which, in the century and a half between Paul and Tertullian, underwent striking transformations. On the other hand, the difficulties of segregating the various elements and assigning to each a definite date and place are enormous. Even when we encounter the widespread cult of the "highest" (*hypsistos*) God, we need some further supporting evidence before we can definitely ascertain Jewish influence. Transitions are so blurred that in many cases, such as that of the Angelos stones of Thera, endless discussions have arisen as to whether a particular historical survival should be ascribed to Judaism, Christianity, or paganism. Even proving mere dependence of one upon another is exceedingly hard because, as G. F. Moore remarks, "borrowings in religion, at least in the field of ideas [not rites or myths], are usually in the nature of the appropriation of things in the possession of another which the borrower recognizes in all good faith as belonging to him." The difficulties are further aggravated by the irrational character of many elements, particularly those belonging to the Hellenistic mystery religions.[31]

There is no doubt, however, that the various shades of half-Jews soon became a tremendous force in shaping sectarian ideologies within and outside Christianity. In Mandaism, Manicheism, and in the various gnostic movements, traces of such semi-Jewish groups are incontestable. Among people of Jewish descent and non-Jewish creeds, among those of Gentile stock who had adopted certain Jewish tenets, or, most commonly, among descendants of former proselytes, there arose men of deep religious feeling and often of great vision and creative power, seeking new religious formulations. Indeed, in the multicolored religious pattern of the first Christian centuries the Jewish element, particularly as derived from semi-Jewish groups, played a preëminent role. Thus, in a way different from that of official Jewry, half-Jewry likewise became a vital factor in the religious life of the eastern Mediterranean.

SAMARITANS

Sectarian movements in Palestine show equally great strength and variety. The Second Commonwealth is without doubt the richest period in the history of Jewish sects. The great intensity of religious feeling and the creative power of religious individuals produced, in an age of irreconcilable social conflicts, an extraordinary medley of attempts to solve the questions of the relation of man to God and the universe.

The earliest Jewish sect, one which still survives, was that of the Samaritans. Although their antecedents reach back to the period of the kings, their separation as a body apart dates from the Second Temple. Indeed, the final break seems not to antedate Alexander the Great. Josephus, our chief source of information, is, as elsewhere, quite hazy about the chronology of the Achaemenid regime. He seems to telescope events recorded by Nehemiah with others which, according to him, took place during Alexander's conquest of Asia, thus bridging a gap of more than a century. He may be right, however, in implying that the final separation came only when the Samaritans succeeded in erecting a temple of their own on Mount Gerizim, which they soon identified with patriarchal Bethel-Luz. In this rivalry between

Jerusalem and Gerizim, which was later called by a Samaritan authority "the House of the Powerful God, the Tabernacle of his angels, the Place of the presence of his majesty, the Place destined for sacrifice," lay the roots of the controversy. Although the formal Samaritan profession of faith of later days shows the unmistakable imprint of the Muslim credo, it well emphasizes this basic issue:

> My faith is in Thee, YHWH; and in Moses Son of Amram,
> Thy Servant; and in the Holy Law; and in Mount Gerizim
> Beth-El; and in the Day of Vengeance and Recompense.

Nothing in this credo, except the fourth article, could have been repugnant to the most orthodox Pharisaic Jew, unless it be the kind of apotheosis of Moses, as distinguished from the exaltation of the Law, which gave him a place akin to that of Mohammed in the Muslim confession. That is why the rabbis were right in saying that once a Samaritan severed his allegiance to Gerizim and acknowledged Jerusalem he might be readmitted to the Jewish fold.[32]

We know today that the denunciations by the author of the book of Kings (II Kings 17), reiterated with many embellishments by the rabbis, were only partly justified. The Jews regarded these sectarians as "Cutheans" pure and simple, namely as descendants of the foreign tribes transplanted into Northern Israel by the Assyrian rulers after the fall of Samaria. These newcomers were said to have accepted the Israelitic creed because of a superstitious dread of "lions," without altogether abandoning their inherited idolatrous concepts. Modern research agrees that, from the seventh century on, this alien influx constituted only a part of the population of northern Palestine. The majority, as before, were descendants of ancient Israelites, only a fraction of whom had been deported by the Assyrians.

Its alienation from the Jews was deepened, however, by the infiltration of ever new alien elements. Both Assyrians and Persians treated Samaria as a district capital and stationed soldiers and officials there permanently. According to Eusebius, Alexander the Great, after suppressing a Samaritan rebellion, rebuilt the city as a Macedonian colony. Once again destroyed by John Hyrcanus (about 107), it was "liberated" by Pompey and reëstablished by Herod as a "Greek" municipality. Almost equally checkered was the career of Beth-shan whose Greek name,

Scythopolis, reminded the ancient writers of the purported Scythian invaders in the days of Jeremiah. Its strange history is now illustrated by the remarkable local finds reviewed by Alan Rowe. After a temporary eclipse old Shechem, too, staged a revival as the "Greek" city of Neapolis and before long it struck pagan coins syncretistically dedicated to Baal-Zeus (158 c.e.).

Nevertheless it was precisely the ancient Israelitic background of the Samaritan majority which accounted for the rise and ultimate separation of this schismatic movement. The Samaritans may be briefly characterized as the survival, both ethnically and religiously, of Northern Israel. Their religion was merely the resuscitated northern religion which, although purified of the strictly pagan ingredients of the "popular" religion, still clung to the territorially bound creedal sublimations of the Palestinian soil. In this sense, the biblical accusations hurled against the *Ashema* worship of the Samaritans were not quite without foundation. Technically, *Ashema* might have been only a substitute for the Tetragrammaton, like the Jewish *Adonai*. But in essence it much resembled the localized deity, the Baal.

For this reason the localized worship on Gerizim, whether or not justified historically by the Samaritans' reading of Gerizim instead of Ebal in Deut. 27:4 and Josh. 8:30, was a serious relapse into the preprophetic religion. It is self-evident that they could not, under these circumstances, accept the writings of the prophets as authoritative. Not only did the prophetic literature, preponderantly composed by Judeans, contain too many outspoken affirmations of the holiness of the Temple at Jerusalem, but its essential separation of Jewish religion and nationality from localized worship could not be accepted by these heirs of the ancient Canaanite-Israelitic earth-bound creed. To them Gerizim meant far more than Jerusalem had ever meant to exilic or Palestinian Jewry. They not only defied overt natural facts by claiming that their sacred hill was taller than Ebal (it is in fact some 200 feet lower), indeed was the tallest of all mountains, but also believed that it had been the original site of the Garden of Eden, that it had towered untouched above the waters of the Flood, that it was the scene of the sacrifice of Isaac and that at the end of days it would become the location of Paradise. Or, as they phrased it, "the Eternal Hill shall be left in the midst of the Garden." In the days of Pilate a local visionary had no difficulty in attracting large crowds to Gerizim by promising to "show

them those sacred vessels which were laid under that place, because Moses had put them there." Until today the Samaritans
turn to Gerizim not only in their prayers, but also on such festive
occasions as the circumcision of newly born boys or the semi-
sacrificial slaughtering of animals.[33]

With astonishing tenacity they revered the sanctity of their holy
mountain, even after the loss of their sanctuary. If we may believe Josephus on this point (a final answer to this moot question can possibly be given only through excavation), they possessed a temple there for only two hundred years. At any rate,
once John Hyrcanus had destroyed it (in 128 B.C.E.), they never
again succeeded in erecting a sanctuary with unhampered priestly
service. Even today, however, they still celebrate Passover by sac-
rificing lambs. Like the Jews, they, too, began worshiping in
synagogues. But if we may take a clue from their recently discovered
fourth-century synagogue at Salbit (ancient Shaalbim, northwest
of Jerusalem), they oriented their prayers toward Mt. Gerizim.[34]

Unfortunately our knowledge of the most crucial aspects of
Samaritan history and religion is based on sources of dubious
authenticity. For the most vital developments down to the Muslim period, we are almost exclusively dependent on the statements
by opponents, such as are included in the Old Testament, Josephus, Epiphanius, and the Talmud. The Samaritans doubtless
had preserved some reliable historical records of their antiquity,
the narrative of Abu'l-Fath (middle of the fourteenth century)
being largely built upon some such older chronicles. But with
the exception of their Scriptures, their Targum and liturgies,
very little can be definitely ascribed to the older periods. For example, the book *Asatir* (probably meaning something like "Legends of the Early Days") is ascribed by its modern editor to the
third century B.C.E., while others think that it was written under
Muslim domination (approximately the ninth century). We possess altogether a few small manuscript fragments and inscriptions
which may be attributed more or less confidently to the period
before Justinian's anti-Samaritan legislation. Palaeographically
reviewing the evidence available in 1941, W. R. Taylor concluded
that only the first and third of the Emmaus inscriptions, published in 1881 by Clermont-Ganneau, are likely to be pre-
Christian, while the first five centuries C.E. have yielded only one
further Emmaus inscription, the Leeds fragment, the Shechem
Decalogue, and another more recently discovered decalogue. The

historic reliability of the entire subsequent literature, moreover, is undermined by its pronouncedly apologetic and polemical aims.[35]

At the beginning of their schism only the Pentateuch had been canonized. That is why the Samaritans adopted it alone as their Scripture. They also accepted the canonical book of Joshua. Notwithstanding some 6,000 minor linguistic variants and a few dogmatically determined deviations, the Samaritan Pentateuch is, in subject matter, practically identical with the Jewish Torah. Unfortunately, despite its fine workmanship, A. von Gall's critical edition of the Samaritan Pentateuch published in 1914 no longer fully satisfies our scientific requirements. Many important new manuscripts have become available during the last decades, which would more than justify a new comprehensive edition.[36]

Being deprived of the living flow of prophetic preachment and hagiographic creativity, at no time enjoying full political sovereignty, wedged in between more powerful, mostly hostile neighbors, these sectarians, however stubborn, could hardly resist the influences of either their immediate Jewish and Gentile environment or of the general Irano-Chaldaean and Greek ideas permeating the entire Near East. Political expediency, too, often dictated their choice of allegiance, as was pointed out by Josephus. When the Jews were powerful, they claimed to be Jewish. But when the fortunes of the Jewish people were at a low ebb, they vociferously disclaimed relationship with Jewry, and demanded recognition of their kinship with the Sidonians, based on their descent from Canaanite-Phoenician stock. Although neither assertion is devoid of a grain of historic truth, the Jews could never forget that, at a most critical moment of their history the "Cutheans" collaborated with Antiochus Epiphanes and, yielding to pressure, temporarily dedicated their temple to Zeus Xenios or Hellenios. The Jewish populace readily believed that the Samaritans worshiped a dove at their sanctuary. This allegation, reminiscent of the supposed donkey worship in Jerusalem, bears all the earmarks of a popular canard. But it may somehow reflect Samaritan hospitality to the intrusion of such alien cults as that of Semiramis-Astarte which was often symbolized by the dove. Needless to say that Jews and Samaritans condemned each other's scriptural deviations as conscious forgeries.[37]

In their Hellenistic Diaspora the Samaritans also produced a Greek translation of the Pentateuch, the so-called *Samareitikon* which, still known to some Church Fathers, is extant today only in a few fourth-century fragments. Their poet Theodotus sang the praises of the "sacred town" of Shechem more ardently than Philo the Elder did those of Jerusalem. But he explained its name "from Sikimios son of Hermes," evidently one of those syncretistic identifications with Shechem son of Hamor (Eusebius' *Praeparatio,* IX, 22). The Samaritan historians, Pseudo-Eupolemus and Malchus Kleodemus, outdid even Artapanus in synthesizing biblical with Graeco-Oriental mythology. By reporting, for instance, that the sons of Abraham from Keturah had spread into many adjoining lands and that the Tyrian Heracles had married one of Abraham's granddaughters, Malchus could claim for his coreligionists physical as well as ideological kinship with almost all nations among whom they then lived.

Curiously, these schismatics were saved from extinction mainly by their borrowings, however reluctant, from their Jewish enemies. Although long rejecting the whole structure of Jewish eschatology and soteriology, they ultimately adopted the Jewish doctrines of reward and punishment after death and resurrection. As late as the talmudic age the rabbis considered a Samaritan's denial of resurrection, next to his allegiance to Gerizim, as the most serious obstacle to his admission to the Jewish fold. But the fourth-century Samaritan poet Marqah could already describe in detail what he believed were his people's long-accepted traditions concerning the Day [*le-yom*] of Vengeance and Recompense predicted, according to their version, in the Blessing of Moses.

It is the Day of Vengeance [he wrote] on the guilty ones and the Day of Reward for all the good ones, the Day of Resurrection, the Day of Comfort, the Day of Reckoning, the Day of Decision, the Day on which the feet will slide, the Day of Fear, the Day of Judgment, the Day of Weeping, the Day of Law, the Day of Gathering, the Day of Truth, the Day of Awe, the Day of Presentation, the Day of Protection, the Day of Rejoicing, the Day of Righteous Judgment.

This strong eschatological belief, reinforced by an ever more fervent messianic hope, helped sustain the people in the days of its recurrent martyrdom for the faith. Of course, the Samaritans had no use for a Messiah of the house of David. Nor were they quite certain about one of their own purported royal ancestry of Joseph. But under the leadership of their high priests they could revert to some early expectations of a Moses *redivivus* serving as the great Redeemer, the *taheb* or *shaheb,* as they later called him.

Particularly after the downfall of the Maccabean kingdom Jewish
concentration on the Davidic redeemer relegated the one of the
tribe of Levi almost entirely to the domain of sectarian groups.
None of these, however, exalted Moses as did the Samaritans.
Emphasizing the eschatological implications of Deut. 18:15–18 and
possibly using Christian terminology, they spoke of the great
lawgiver as the Pure One and the Light on Earth. They also rewrote
Deut. 34:10 to read that "No prophet *shall* arise in Israel like
unto Moses." [38]

Neither could they escape the prevailing trends toward angelology and demonology, which were far stronger than was warranted
by the casual references in the five books of Moses. Even more
important, since social conditions had undergone profound transformation during the centuries after the fall of Samaria, daily
life had to be regulated by many laws in addition to those contained in their Scriptures. Without acknowledging it, they had to
read into the Pentateuch a whole body of oral law to which,
characteristically enough, they gave the name *hillukh,* in direct
analogy to the rabbinic *halakhah.* Both words mean only the
pious man's "way" of life. The Samaritan methods of hermeneutic
interpretation were, despite all divergences, evidently modeled
after those developed by the rabbis. Only in this way were these
sectarians, too, in a position constantly to adjust their law to the
exigencies of life and thus to preserve their basic heritage under
ever-changing external conditions.

The great religious creativity characteristic of the declining
Second Commonwealth affected also the Samaritan community.
The latter, too, soon harbored many heterodox wings. The obscure
personality of Simon Magus, given wide notoriety by the New
Testament account, evidently belongs to the fringe of a half
Samaritan and half Jewish-pagan gnosis. According to the evidently
biased report in Acts, Simon had "used sorcery, and bewitched
the people of Samaria, giving out that himself was some great one
[God]. To whom they all gave heed, from the least to the greatest,
saying, This man is the great power of God [*dynamis tou theou*]."
A century after the event, Justin Martyr, himself a native of
Neapolis-Schechem, claimed that Simon had done "mighty acts of
magic, by virtue of the art of the devils operating in him" in the
city of Rome, where he was honored by a statue reading *Simoni
Deo Sancto.* Nearly all Samaritans, Justin contended, and a few
of other faiths believed in Simon's divine powers. So endowed

he could, of course, release his followers from all obligations toward the Law, teach that evil was a conventional, rather than a natural notion and advocate extreme sexual promiscuity. Another Samaritan heresiarch, mentioned by later Church Fathers, was Simon's alleged teacher, Dositheus. Apparently of Jewish descent, this pseudo-Messiah supposedly gathered a considerable following and introduced creedal and ritualistic deviations which lasted for centuries.[39]

Because of the extreme paucity of reliable records, it is impossible for us to unravel these sectarian strains from what might be called official Samaritanism of the first century. But there is no question that, in action and counteraction, the latter must have received many impulses from its various rebellious offshoots. Probably not until the final consolidation of its doctrine during its fourth-century renaissance under the leadership of Baba Rabba may we speak of a controlling system of beliefs and rituals affecting the entire movement.

Whatever their creed may have been at a particular time, many Samaritans were ready to sacrifice their lives for it. Their will to live and their devotion to their religion helped them survive in an inimical world. After Herod's death Archelaus treated them with great brutality (Josephus' *War* II, 7, 3.111). The Romans frequently shed Samaritan blood, Pilate, for instance, massacring them on a provocation so slight that the Roman governor of Syria recalled him from his post. Rumor, probably magnified by Christian bias, had it that, on his return to Rome, the cruel procurator was executed, or else died a suicide. In the year 67 the Samaritans wished to participate in the Jewish revolt by independent action, but their first move was drowned in blood. Down through the ages they continued to battle against all neighbors, Jews, Romans, Christians, and Muslims. Not even Justinian's declarations of 529 and 531, that they be regarded as a Christian and not a Jewish sect, and the ensuing intensification of intolerance, made them abandon their inherited creed.

Above all they hated the Jews with whom fate so often chained them in common danger, but with whom they generally refused to make common cause. Animosity reached such heights that the Samaritans frequently resorted to puerile methods in interfering with the sacrificial worship at Jerusalem or with the proclamations concerning the calendar which regularly emanated from the central Jewish authorities. On one occasion they allegedly strewed human bones in the Temple precincts, in order to defile the sanctuary and its priesthood. At other times they reputedly raised misleading beacon fires on the mountain tops (the customary Jewish procedure in announcing to the Diaspora the beginnings of a new month) at dates different from those set in Jerusalem. In their own pseudepigraphic Book of Joshua they later gloated over the prank played by two Samaritan youths on a pious Jewish pilgrim. During the night, we are told, these youngsters replaced with mice the pilgrim's sacrificial doves intended for the altar in Jerusalem. This substitution, noticed by the pilgrim only after his arrival in the Jewish capital, in some unspecified way set in motion a long chain of events which resulted in the destruction of the Temple.[40]

Jews reciprocated with hatred and contempt. Sirach's denunciation of the "foolish nation" was echoed by many other writers. To be sure, a Jew could take it for granted that the Samaritans had put aside the tithe. A Samaritan could be counted in the necessary quorum for saying grace. A Jew could even eat unleavened bread prepared by these sectarians, because all these were commandments accepted by them, and "a commandment to which the Cutheans fully adhere, is observed by them more scrupulously than by the Israelites." Against this theoretical tolerance, the hatred of the Jews, enhanced by rabbinical attempts at segregation, eventually succeeded in excluding from use even ordinary bread baked by Samaritans.[41]

At any rate, the Samaritans remained only a minor sect within the Jewish people. Their very attachment to a locality became increasingly a handicap. They seem never to have succeeded in maintaining their Diaspora communities for any length of time, except in Damascus with its strange immemorial ties to northern Palestine. Just as their deported forefathers were unable long to preserve their identity outside Palestine, so all Samaritan settlements in the later Diaspora seem to have been short-lived. In Egypt, particularly, where Alexander and Ptolemy I established Samaritan communities (one of which seems to have been perpetuated in the name of the Egyptain village Samareia, recorded in several papyri of the third century B.C.E.), they often succeeded in annoying the Jews. They brought about a disputation before Ptolemy VI Philometor as to the respective values of their Holy Scriptures, a disputation which resulted in the death of the Samaritan disputants and perhaps also in the Greek translation of the Bible. But they were unable to save their own community from extinction. The same reasons which, throughout the ages, brought about Jewish emigrations from Palestine, also affected Samaritans. Forced repeatedly to leave the Holy Land and to establish settlements abroad, they always saw these settlements vanish after a few generations. Until recently they survived exclusively around Shechem (Nablus), and here in steadily diminishing numbers. The most tenacious vitality could not save on foreign soil a people that had experienced neither the Exile nor the prophetic emancipation of religion from its territorial roots.[42]

PHARISEES AND SADDUCEES

Jewry's rapid expansion in and outside Palestine after the Maccabean revolt stimulated further sectarian formations. To be sure, the new religious currents were not sects in the technical sense. They did not separate from the rest of Jewry, as did the Samaritans. While believing in the superiority of its own teachings, each of them identified itself with the whole people, hoping that eventually its tenets would be universally adopted. In many cases the underlying economic and political divisions were so obvious as to overshadow the creedal disparity itself. Only the overwhelming religiosity of the age forced them to assume a religious coloring. Once religious nonconformity had been established, however, the fierceness of the struggle was intensified by the glow of sectarian fanaticism.

We have seen that political animosity between Sadducees and Pharisees could rise to a high pitch and at times lead to open civil war. Sharp economic and social divisions added to the political controversies. The Sadducees, representatives of the priestly and lay aristocracy, had every reason to resist customs and beliefs evolved by the masses under the leadership of middle-class and "plebeian" intellectuals. On the other hand, the Pharisees, as their name seems to indicate, were also separatists; they segregated themselves from the nations as well as from the rest of the people, especially from the illiterate mass of those who "sit at the corners" (*yoshebe qeranot*). They seem to have organized fraternities (so-called *haburot*), which imposed on the membership more duties than rights, and particularly the most rigid observance of the Law.[43]

Neither the number of such fraternities nor their total membership is known. The figure of 6,000 Pharisees who refused to take an oath of fidelity to Herod, mentioned by Josephus, is certainly far below the true total. Inasmuch as an oath of fidelity by private individuals is nowhere recorded in the Roman or the Hellenistic empires, we may assume that all these 6,000 men were office-holders of a sort. It is conceivable that the Pharisaic elders, soldiers, and fiscal agents, when ordered to take the usual oath of allegiance to their ruler, raised conscientious objections. But there were probably tens of thousands of others who, as private citizens, had no such occasion to suffer for their convictions. In any case, however small a fraction of the population they may have been, the Pharisees none the less enjoyed great popularity and may be said to have represented the large majority of the nation.[44]

Detached from political and territorial bonds, Pharisaism revealed also an astonishing expansive force. In Babylonia and, with modifications, in Hellenistic Jewry it dominated the scene. R. Judah ben Batira, in fact every one of the Babylonian leaders known to us, was a Pharisee, as were in essence also Philo in Alexandria, Paul's father in Tarsus, and Theudas in Rome. In the second century, Celsus, otherwise fairly well informed about Syrian Jewry, knew only of Jews to whom their God promised "to raise them up from the dead with the same flesh and blood" (Origen's *Contra Celsum*, VI, 29), as if that doctrine had never been disputed by Sadducees. The latter movement, on the other hand, remained, like the Samaritan schism, largely restricted to the boundaries of Palestine. Hence the numerous striking, although largely involuntary, resemblances between the teachings of these two groups.

Parallel with these sociopolitical contrasts arose sharp conflicts of purely religious convictions. In their reaction against Hellenism, the Sadducees, consisting chiefly of wealthy and educated Jews, went to the other extreme. Like all newly awakened patriots, they were inclined to overemphasize their national peculiarities and to insist on the rigid application of Jewish law. But once having lost contact with the living currents of their faith, they had no alternative except to revert to sources previously canonized. Just as the early Maccabees used the archaic "Hebrew" script on their coins, although for centuries the people had, for the most part, employed "square" characters, the Sadducees now concentrated on the written law as their authority. Both were expressions of the nationalist revival. But the line of tradition having been broken, artificial return to ancient institutions served as a new point of departure.

On the other hand, the Pharisees, representing the living ethnic body, could appropriately insist on the validity of the oral law as well. This represented the legal evolution of customs and beliefs which had slowly grown out of the imperceptible changes in national realities from generation to generation. The Pharisees could acknowledge the changes brought about through centuries of progressing life as parts of a living tradition, reconciling them with the written law wherever necessary through a continuous hermeneutic reinterpretation of the Torah, rather than through its literal application.

In fact, they believed that certain traditions incorporated in the oral law had, from the outset, been revealed to Moses on Sinai and hence enjoyed coördinate authority with the written law. To be sure, admitting the unreliability of human memory, later rabbis speculated on the 1,700 specific applications of hermeneutic rules and 3,000 individual laws, which had supposedly been forgotten during the days of mourning after Moses' death. But they also believed that an ingenious scholar like Othniel, son of Kenaz among Moses' early successors, could recover such knowledge through a proper, divinely inspired, interpretation of Scripture. Conversely, where memory failed, the observation of actual practice might supply the missing links. As late as the days of Hillel, we are told, leaders of the Sanhedrin, puzzled by a legal problem, invited this relatively unknown foreign student to communicate to them some traditions which he had learned from their own predecessors in office. In the subsequent discussion it turned out that Hillel himself had forgotten a particular legal detail; unperturbed, he advised them to observe how ordinary Jews unconsciously acted according to custom, for "if they are not prophets, they are sons of prophets." We need not be surprised, therefore, by the self-assurance with which, for instance, Nahum the Libellarius or R. Eliezer ben Hyrcanus communicated to their colleagues Mosaic traditions which had reached them through their teachers. In a polemical vein, the Pharisees decided that in some cases the transgression of the words of scribes was more reprehensible than that of the words of the Torah. In this way the Pharisees claimed, according to Josephus, to have excelled "the rest of their nation in the observances of religion and as exact exponents of the Law." [45]

In short, by synthesizing traditions with the revealed words of Scripture the Pharisees acknowledged the supremacy of the time element, of national evolution, of history. The Sadducees, however, adhering to the basis of their political power, had to attach more importance to the space element, to the unchanging and permanent, to the revealed word of God in its most literal sense.

CONFLICTING THEOLOGIES

Immutability pervading all existence also affected the life of each individual. To the Sadducees, therefore, life appeared bounded by and confined to a personal existence, lived here and now. The Pharisees, linking individual life with the great processes in history, believed "that souls have an immortal vigor in them, and that under the earth there will be rewards or punishments, according as they have lived virtuously or viciously in this life; and the latter are to be detained in an everlasting prison, but that the former shall have power to revive and to live again." Josephus, who "writing in Greek and for Greeks, naturally and almost necessarily adapts himself to their terminology and modes of thought," nevertheless here expresses the fundamental conception of Pharisaism: the combination of immortality of the soul with bodily resurrection. The idea of judgment and retribution after death is also of crucial significance. It is pushed so far as to exclude the wicked from resurrection.[46]

Although many passages in apocryphal literature omit mention of this distinction, Pharisaism as a whole insisted upon the resurrection theology. Persian and Hellenistic influences had impressed on the previous generations, at least, a longing for immortality of the soul, and this hope had found expression in some pre-Maccabean writings. But in the Maccabean upheaval, in many senses the first war of religion in history, the Jewish warriors became religious martyrs for whom the idea of a happier existence in the world beyond became more than a psychological compensation. Finding in the accumulated lore of their forefathers clues for a belief in individual immortality, they could no longer be satisfied with the conviction of eternal national continuance. If the individual suffers so severely in this world, they felt, he must personally be rewarded by a life of happiness in the world to come.

The Maccabean revolt thus suddenly helped bring to life a hitherto more or less quiescent idea. As late as 200–180 Sirach referred merely to the "rest" of the departed after death. He preached the enjoyment of life in this world, "for in Sheol there is not delight" (14:16), and urged the mourners not to mourn too long: "Remember him not for he hath no hope . . ." and "When the dead is at rest let his memory rest" (38:21, 23). He was so outspoken that many modern scholars are inclined to regard him as an outright Sadducee. The conflict between the two movements was still latent, however, and he may be regarded as voicing a widespread notion, rather than partisan opinion.

A few years had passed when in the midst of the great national crisis another author arose with a clearly defined concept of resurrection. "And many of them that sleep in the dust of the earth shall awake, some to the everlasting life, and some to reproaches and everlasting abhorrence"—these words of Daniel become from now on the corner stone of the whole Pharisaic lore concerning the Hereafter. The fertile imagination of apocalyptic visionaries soon began depicting graphically the delights of the new life granted at the end of days to the righteous and the humble. The following rather restrained description in the Ethiopic Enoch may serve here as one of the earliest illustrations:

Then shall they rejoice with joy and be glad, and into the holy place shall they enter; and its fragrance shall be in their bones, and they shall live a long life on earth, such as thy fathers lived: And in their days shall no sorrow or plague or torment or calamity touch them.[47]

Such claims appeared preposterous to the Sadducees. Realists in public life, most of them were too rationalistic to acquiesce in these yearnings. Nor did they find any reference to them in the revealed law of Moses and sharply repudiated all hermeneutic attempts to read pertinent, oblique hints into the scriptural texts. The Pharisees countered by condemning the mere denial that the Torah itself teaches the doctrine of resurrection as a sufficient reason for man's loss of a share in the world-to-come.[48]

Sadducee opposition could not stem the tide, however, and the idea of another world gained strength continually. It represented the best solution of the contradictory aspirations of the nation and the individual. It gave a more satisfactory answer to the age-old theodicy than did the question marks left even by so towering a thinker as he of the book of Job. It integrated national as well as individual destinies into the whole process of history. Even this novel idea was, however, not a break with, but merely a new link in the chain of continuity. The contrast between the more other-worldly character of Pharisaic Judaism and the principally this-worldly orientation of the prophetic religion is not so great as has been asserted. "Retribution after death," says Moore, "established itself in Judaism as a complement to the old belief in retribution in this life or in the article of death, not as a substitute for it." More-over, as heretofore, the nation's future and not that of the in-dividual remained the decisive objective. To quote Moore again:

What the Jew craved for himself was to have a part in the future golden age of the nation, as the prophets depicted it. . . . It was only so, not in some blissful lot for his individual self apart, that he could conceive of perfect happiness [*Judaism*, II, 312].

At the end of days—this became the growing conviction—not only the national body then in existence, but Israel of all history, of the generations past as well as of those yet unborn, would participate in the universal reign of God.

In this synthesis of personal resurrection and national escha-tology Palestine, of course, has its singular position. Not only will the new era of the reign of God begin in the Holy Land, some rabbis contended, thirty days earlier than elsewhere, but the bodies of the dead will rise from the dust only in Palestine. Since the days of the royal proselytes of Adiabene many a pious Jew has gone to spend the last days of his life in Palestine, in order to have a resting place for his body there and await the blowing of the trumpet announcing the coming of the Messiah.

At the same time we need no more telling expression of the Pharisees' this-worldly orientation, even in the doctrine of resurrection, than the second benediction of the '*Amidah,* probably introduced by them in the first century B.C.E. The early formulation represents a remarkable belief in God's invisible power in this and in the other worlds, even if it is reduced to "Thou art mighty, Thou quickenest the dead and art powerful to save" (Elbogen) or to "Thou sustainest the living with grace and quickenest the dead with great mercy" (Finkelstein). One is not astonished that in a country as dry as Palestine the quickening of the parched soil by rain awakened associations with the revival of the dead. Hence the combination of both ideas in the second benediction during the winter months, the "rainy season." [49]

This integration of individual life with the whole nation and even with the universe is also consistently pursued by Pharisaism in its teachings concerning personal responsibility. How deep an impression the Hellenistic realities had made upon the Sadducees is nowhere better seen than in their stern affirmation of individualism. Again clinging to the letter of Deuteronomic utterances (which represented merely the first stirrings of individual self-determination in a Jewish world still overwhelmingly corporate), they made the individual fully responsible for his actions which, they said, rest entirely on his independent decision. To cite Josephus' sharp formulation, "The Sadducees . . . do away with Fate altogether, and remove God beyond, not merely the commission, but the very sight, of evil. They maintain that man has the free choice of good or evil" (*War* II, 8, 14.164-65).

Free will thus became another matter of theological difference between the Sadducees and the Pharisees. Of course, the tradition-bound Pharisees could not possibly attempt to turn back the wheels of history and restore corporate responsibility in its erstwhile fullness. Since the days of Deuteronomy and Ezekiel, the principle of individual guilt and punishment had become too deeply rooted in the life of the new, more individualistic society. On all occasions, therefore, the Pharisees and their successors, the rabbis, stressed individual responsibility for actions. The apothegm of a Jewish author of the second century B.C.E., "For he that is just and humble is ashamed to do what is unjust, being reproved not of another, but of his own heart, because the Lord looketh on his inclination," could have sprung equally well from a Pharisaic or from a Sadducean source. Virtue for its own sake was also stressed by the early Pharisaic teacher, Antigonus of Socho, in his well-known dictum concerning the duty of serving God without expectation of reward. Even Aqabiah ben Mahallalel's last injunction to his son, "Your deeds alone will bring you near, or keep you afar" (which must have sounded doubly suspicious, as Aqabiah had previously been excommunicated on account of his legal deviations) was nevertheless included in the Mishnah.[50]

The preponderant majority of Pharisaic teachers, however, linked the fate of the individual to that of the universal whole by the teaching of divine providence. While one wing of the movement, the Essenes, went to the extreme of adopting a belief in unrestricted determinism, the major section kept to the middle road. Their attitude, best known in the formulation of Rabbi 'Aqiba—"All is foreseen; and free will is given" (M. Abot III, 19)— represented a difficult synthesis of predestination and free will which caused considerable difficulty to the more disciplined Jewish thinkers of the Middle Ages. The Pharisees were practical leaders rather than philosophers, and they seem to have worried very little about the philosophic dilemma. Their rabbinic disciples stressed sometimes the one, sometimes the other element, in accordance with changing circumstances, their personal temperaments, or even passing moods.

Here, too, the national element crept in. The duties of a "chosen people" certainly imposed upon each member a much heavier yoke of personal responsibility. On the other hand, the individual's burden was lightened through the "merit of the Fathers" (zekhut abot). Although this doctrine occupies a prominent place only in the lucubrations of the later rabbis, there is hardly any doubt that this ancient survival of corporate responsibility came down in unbroken continuity from the early days of Israel. Even Moses was said to have invoked the deeds of the Fathers to placate God's ire in a most critical moment of Israel's history. The author of II Maccabees, though rewriting the narrative of Jason of Cyrene, is, as often elsewhere, a true spokesman of Palestinian beliefs, too, when he asserts that the appearance of the spirits of Onias and Jeremiah to Judah in a dream did not a little rejoice the Maccabean warriors, and helped stir them up to valor. On the other hand, some Pharisaic teachers tried to blame sin not only on the evil spirit within man, but also on temptation by demons. The same author of the "Testaments" who had stressed virtue for its own sake, also emphasized these machinations by hostile spirits within man which he must learn to combat.[51]

This doctrine of man's eternal vigilance against the irruption of inimical spiritual powers, as well as the idea that the Fathers and other saints or martyrs intervene with God in favor of the people, gained momentum through the growth in importance of the divine mediators in Pharisaic theology. By chance this doctrinal conflict is mentioned only in the New Testament (Acts 23:8) and not in Josephus or the Talmud, but that it existed is hardly subject to doubt. The socially oriented, relatively contented and static Sadducees differed here again from the deeply dissatisfied progressive and dynamic masses. For the Pharisees, the leaders of the discontented, the problem of the relation between a perfect creator and an imperfect world became one of life and death. Hence their emphasis on the inscrutability of God's ways. His transcendence and holiness, already fully formulated during the Exile, became now an even more necessary answer to prevailing perplexities. To be sure, the dominant group within Pharisaism was not of a speculative nature. Their attitude was naive and practical rather than contemplative and doctrinaire. They were not even aware of the essential contradiction between their belief in God's transcendence and the equally strong desire for the assertion of God's immanence. But some wings among them stressed the transcendence of God to a degree previously unknown in Hebrew thought. Especially the large apocalyptic literature of that age, beginning with Zechariah, increasingly separated God's essence from this corrupt world He had created.

Of necessity, the growing gulf had to be bridged. We recall how the combined pressures of contemporary syncretism and of its major constituents, the Chaldaean astral religion, Parsee dualism and angelology, and the Hellenistic mystery cults, had helped develop a whole system of links. The world of the average Palestinian began to be filled with spirits, good and evil, in comparison with which the "gods" of the ancient popular religion were innocent playthings. Like the author of the Book of Jubilees he believed that the universe was crowded with

the angels of the presence, and the angels of sanctification, and the angels [of the spirit of fire and the angels] of the spirit of the winds, and the angels of the spirit of the clouds, and of darkness, and of snow and of hail and of hoar frost, and the angels of the voices and of the thunder and of the lightning, and the angels of the spirits of cold and of heat, and of winter and of spring and of autumn and of summer, and of all the spirits of His creatures which are in the heavens and on the earth, the abysses and the darkness, eventide (and night), and the light, dawn and day, which He hath prepared in the knowledge of His heart [2:2].

With unspeakable horror he contemplated the majority of these "angels" as spirits of evil and darkness.

Moreover, no longer, as in the Persian period, were these demons satisfied with a secondary role. Satan, in particular, in Job and Chronicles merely an instrument of God's will, began to assume a significance almost rivaling that of the Supreme Being. The author of the "Testaments" put into the mouth of Levi a deathbed exhortation to his children, "And now, my children, ye have heard all; choose, therefore, for yourselves either the light or the darkness, either the law of the Lord or the works of Beliar" (19:1).

The Sadducees were horrified. These wealthy and educated rationalists accepted "angels" in the Pentateuchal sense of messengers fulfilling God's will, but they categorically denied the existence of spirits with wills of their own. Sirach had already repudiated the responsibility of outside forces for man's sins. "God created man from the beginning," he declared, "and placed him in the hand of his *Yeṣer* [good or evil spirit]. If thou desirest, thou canst keep the commandment." Hence, "when the ungodly curseth Satan, he curseth his own soul." The Sadducees also objected to any ritual remotely indicative of astral mysticism. When, on one occasion, they observed their Pharisaic colleagues at the Temple subject the seven-branched candelabrum to ritual ablutions, they exclaimed derisively, "Come and watch the Pharisees purify the moonlight." The Pharisees themselves seem not to have been unaware of the foreign origin of their angelology. Simon ben Laqish gave utterance to an old Pharisaic conviction, when he stated hyperbolically that, like the names of the months, "so also the names of the angels were brought home by them [Israel] from Babylonia." The Pharisaic scribes, nevertheless, did not hesitate to acknowledge this foreign importation as an integral constituent of their living tradition. Rejecting the extravagances of apocalyptic literature, however, they integrated it into the total system of Judaism and moved it to a corner of the Aggadah. In the Mishnah, for example, that authoritative legal code of later Pharisaism, there is no mention whatever of angels or demons, not even where these had been discussed in the original sources.[52]

No less wide was the gap between the Sadducees and Pharisees in their views of existing religious institutions. Many Sadducees were members of the priestly class, but this was not the sole reason for their emphasis on the Temple and the sacrifices. There was a strong mutual attraction between a party built upon the affirmation of the state and territory and a priesthood centered in a territorial symbol, the sanctuary. Moreover, the Temple was for them an integral part of the state. The Temple's treasury was the state's main exchequer not only in the times of the ancient kings of Judah or the Maccabees, but in all periods of its existence. One need only consider the annual influx of millions of half shekels, and of the immense voluntary donations from all over the world, to visualize what significance a patriotic group, wielding political power and, through religion, power over these funds, would attach to the existence of the sanctuary.

At the same time the Pharisees strove to develop other institutions essentially ethnic in character. They did not reject the

Temple, its sacrifices, or even the priestly class. Too much sanctity had been attached to these during the Exile and the Maccabean revolt, when their lack was felt as a national catastrophe. The Pharisaic teachers tried, however, to make popular institutions of them. They introduced a great popular festival, the water procession (*simḥat bet hashoebah* or *ha-shobah*, procession with torches), in which the masses participated. They enlarged upon the popular aspects of the Passover sacrifice, as well as upon the duty of making pilgrimages to Palestine. The priests, too, they declared, were merely representatives of the people. According to their tradition, the high priest himself was addressed annually before his greatest function on the Day of Atonement by representatives of the Sanhedrin, "You are our deputy and the deputy of the court, we adjure you by Him who made his name dwell in this house, that you change nothing of what we have told you" (M. Yoma I, 5).

Judaism, however, was to be maintained in Palestine and the Diaspora by other institutions in addition to the priesthood, Temple, and sacrifices. The Pharisees had to consider world Jewry more than the Sadducees, whose horizon was necessarily confined to the boundaries of Palestine. Hence they began to stress those elements in religion and law which were applicable to Jews outside the country as well. The Sabbath was clearly one such institution. Hence the glorification of the Sabbath idea, as in the period of the Exile, and the elaboration of the Sabbath laws in minutest detail. The idea of the synagogue now took definite shape. The foundations laid during the Exile were enlarged and deepened, and upon them a structure erected which rivaled and soon replaced the Temple in significance. The other cornerstone became the Torah in the double meaning of "institution and faith," as Schechter characterized it.

While Sirach still considered the priests as the main teachers of the people, the Pharisaic leaders gradually evolved the doctrine of the three mutually independent crowns of kingdom, priesthood, and Torah. Before long one of their disciples reported God as saying, "The Crown of the Torah is offered to everyone, and I consider him who has won it as if all three had been offered him, and he had won them all; and him who has failed to win it as if all three had been offered him and he had lost them all." Another of their followers, author of the Aramaic Targum, paraphrased the biblical injunction, "Ye shall be unto Me a kingdom of priests and a holy nation," to read "Ye shall be unto my Name kings, priests and a holy nation." It should also be noted that the scribes themselves were fully conscious of their radical innovations. The laws, in particular, concerning the Sabbath, pilgrimages to Jerusalem, festive offerings and the unlawful use of sacred property were all developed largely in this period of a vast Diaspora and intense struggle against abuses by the Sadducean priests. An ancient tradition readily admitted that, with respect to Scriptural antecedents, these laws "are like mountains hanging by a hair." But it was through these very innovations that the Pharisees planted the seeds of a popular educational system, broader and more effective than any other in the ancient world.[53]

LESSER SECTS

Within the organized Pharisaic body and its sphere of influence, however, there appeared diverse currents. As poverty grew and social conflicts became sharper, the social divisions within Pharisaism itself became more marked. Official leaders, Pharisaic as well as Sadducean, took little cognizance of the economic factor. Poverty was not much of a problem for Sirach, nor for the author of the Wisdom of Solomon. The later Pharisees rationalized actual conditions; Rabbi Hananiah (the Pharisaic "lieutenant of the high priests" in the period of the destruction) declared that "he who takes to heart the words of the Torah eliminates many apprehensions" (ARN, xx, ed. by Schechter, p. 70). Finally, Rabbi 'Aqiba took an extreme position, saying that "poverty is as becoming to the daughter of Jacob as a red strap on the head of a white horse" (Lev. r. xiii, 4). So widely accepted was this fate that R. 'Aqiba's saying was quoted a century later as a popular proverb (Hagigah 9b).

Other Jews thought differently. They were not ready to submit quietly to the economic ills gnawing at the very life of the people. Not only fugitive slaves but also miserable free workingmen often organized bands to attack merchants and other wayfarers. Robbery became a permanent feature of Palestinian life. Even the general pacification of the country by the Herodian and Roman armies failed to eradicate the evil. Since the dominant class in Rome was vitally interested in preserving robbery and piracy throughout the Mediterranean as the main source of slave supply, Roman police action was half-hearted. On the other hand, the persistence of economic distress constantly bred new desperadoes.

These social outcasts soon found a rationale of their own. Some took up arms not merely to help themselves but to help the whole people. They saw Roman oppression as the embodiment of all evil. Invoking the ancient prophecies, heeding the preachments of new prophets, Judas of Galilee and his descendants refused obedience to any earthly monarch. As Josephus says, "These men agree in other things with the Pharisaic notions; but they have an inviolable attachment to liberty and they say that God is to be their only Ruler and Lord" (*Antt.* XVIII, 1, 6.23). All means were justifiable to remove Roman oppression.

In this way arose the *Zealotic* faction, which for decades carried on a desperate guerilla warfare against the Romans. In its rationalization, the movement appeared as a special messianic belief that only through an armed uprising, sustained by God, could the enemy be expelled and God's reign of peace and universal prosperity dawn upon mankind. That is why an extremist wing among them, the "assassins" (*sicarii,* as they were called from the use of a short Roman dagger, the *sica*) had no scruples about murdering a Roman official or a Jewish partisan of Rome. Galilee, with its numerous mountain refuges, was the cradle and became the permanent home of the various groups constituting this bellicose sect. The ethnic composition of the province, full of recent converts, and the sharp economic conflicts prevailing there, nurtured an undying revolutionary spirit.

Unfortunately almost all our knowledge of these ancient revolutionaries and "terrorists" is derived from statements by opponents. Their own writings, which may well have appeared in the shape of political pamphlets or, more likely, apocalyptic visions, have not survived. The only pseudepigraphon sometimes ascribed to their movement, the Assumption of Moses, is chronologically and ideologically much too unreliable to warrant any conclusions.[54] Josephus, our main witness, has a special axe to grind in showing the Roman public that the Jewish rebellion had been staged by a conglomeration of irresponsible fanatics and self-seeking criminals.

Pharisaic leaders in general denounced these "brigands" (*biryonim*) for striving by robbery and violence to set up a Jewish state against Rome. For them no armed clash could decide the struggle with the mighty empire, but the power of the spirit alone. In this sense the Zealots may be said to have broken away from the main body of Pharisaism and constituted a separate sectarian movement. To classify them, however, as Josephus does, as a sect along with the Sadducees, may be justified from the sociopolitical, but not from the religious viewpoint. When Judas upbraided his country-men "as cowards for consenting to pay tribute to the Romans and tolerating mortal masters, after having God for their lord," he used accepted religious nomenclature for purely political propaganda. There is no record of any specific Zealot rituals or religious institu-tions. Despite the physical continuity of leadership in Judas' family for over sixty years, it had little sectarian cohesiveness in more quiescent periods. In critical years it attracted a most heterogeneous following, but it often fell apart on the first provocation. Nor is it accidental that at the outbreak of the Great War it found its strong-est, though rapidly shifting, Judaean allies in the Idumaeans. These descendants of former proselytes, fighting side by side with their Galilean brethren, became the radical protagonists of the political principle in Palestine.[55]

ESSENES

Another wing of the Pharisaic movement went to the other ex-treme. It rationalized political weakness and economic poverty as blessings in themselves. The Essenes (probably so-called on account of their leanings toward extreme piety or ritualistic purity) de-clared the ascetic life alone acceptable to a pious Jew. Like their predecessors, the Rechabites, they denounced the vices of urban life, and especially commercial or industrial pursuits. Like the Rechabites, too, they preferred segregated communities in more or less deserted regions where they could devote their life to contem-plation and religious rites, earning a meager living from cattle rais-ing and simple crafts.

In the light of intervening economic developments, however, they accepted agriculture as a legitimate pursuit. Their extreme preoccupation with social justice is well reflected in the "tremen-dous oaths" which they imposed upon every initiate after he had stood the test of three probationary years. According to Josephus he was made to swear,

first that he will practice piety towards the Deity, next that he will ob-serve justice towards men; that he will wrong none whether of his own mind or under another's orders; that he will for ever hate the unjust and fight the battle of the just; that he will for ever keep faith with all men, especially with the powers that be, since no ruler attains his office save by the will of God; that, should he himself bear rule, he will never abuse his authority nor, either in dress or by other outward marks of superiority, outshine his subjects; to be for ever a lover of truth and to expose liars; to keep his hands from stealing and his soul pure from unholy gain; to conceal nothing from the members of the sect and to report none of their secrets to others, even though tortured to death. He swears, moreover, to transmit their rules exactly as he himself received them; to abstain from robbery; and in like manner carefully to preserve the books of the sect and the names of the angels.

Josephus' eyewitness testimony (he had spent three years in the wilderness with Bannus, an Essenian hermit) appears the more credible, as some such initiatory rights are also recorded in the case of admission to the Pharisaic order. The latter's emphasis upon ritualistic pledges, however, underscores the purely ethical content of the Essenian oaths. Philo, too, was greatly impressed by that sect's concentration on ethics, though achieved at the price of an anti-intellectual aversion to logic and physical sciences.[56]

Not all Essenes, however, succeeded in escaping urban civilization. Philo, as well as Josephus, observed that "they dwell in many cities of Judaea and many villages, and in large and populous societies" (quoted from Philo's *Hypothetica*, XI, 1 in Eusebius' *Praeparatio*, VIII, 11; in Gifford's transl. III, 410). But the majority seems to have withdrawn to a rather inhospitable district on the shores of the Dead Sea. They were communists, living in houses owned by the community; their communal meals were regarded as a religious ceremony of prime importance. Not only did their communistic methods of production make slave labor superfluous, but they seem to have objected to the institution on egalitarian principles. They made no effort, however, to propagandize for a new order of society for the world as a whole; indeed the majority of them refused to procreate. Pliny was struck by the strange beauty of the "tribe," which he found

remarkable beyond all the other tribes in the whole world, as it has no women and has renounced all sexual desire, has no money and has only palm trees for company. Day by day the throng of refugees is recruited to an equal number by numerous accessions of persons tired of life and drawn thither by the waves of fortune to adopt their manners [*Hist. Nat.*, V, 15, 73].

Unlike the Samaritans, Sadducees, or Zealots, the Essenes had a very "good press" even in antiquity. The memory of their activities and teachings has come down to us through admirers rather than enemies. We may even possess in some of the apocryphal writings (Enoch, Apocalypse of Abraham, the fourth book of the Sibylline

Oracles) remnants of a literature which, if not part of the Essenian sacred books mentioned by Josephus, was at least influenced by Essenian ideology. One may doubly regret therefore the fact that this sect, which Bousset somewhat exaggeratingly called "the first organized monastic community" and which, in previous generations, had fascinated students in various fields, has attracted much less attention in recent years.[57]

It is obvious, however, that the entire Essenian outlook and way of life had a deep religious coloring. Essenian teachings resemble in many ways the extreme preachments of the prophetic messengers from the desert. The new status of the Jewish people within world religious currents, however, brought about an imperceptible incursion of all sorts of syncretistic ideas. Josephus was amazed by their reverence for the sun. "Before the sun is up," he observed, "they utter no word on mundane matters, but offer to him certain prayers, which have been handed down from their forefathers, as though entreating him to rise" (War II, 5.128). The beauty of sunrise over the mountains of Moab can offer only partial explanation. Rejection of animal sacrifices and devotion to the study of their esoteric literature may have been simply a radical offshoot of tendencies general in all Pharisaism. Many of their rites and ceremonies, however, bear a distinctly alien imprint. Pythagorism, Orphism, Chaldaean astral religion, Parsiism and, apparently, even Buddhism, all may have contributed ingredients much transformed on their way to the Jordan Valley. Age-old Semitic traditions, apparently forgotten by Israel for centuries, came back to life. In the ritualistic conviviality of the order were revived memories of the sacrificial repast of the ancient Semites, symbolizing the communion between the clan and the clan-god.

With all that, the Essenes were Jews, even Pharisaic Jews. They observed the minutest detail of every Pharisaic law. For example, Hippolytus remarked that some of them stayed in bed throughout the Sabbath, apparently in order to avoid the temptation to work. Politically they were, on the whole, also Pharisees. They were extreme pacifists, opposed to war as an evil in itself, and refused to participate in the production of arms. At the outbreak of the Great War, however, they rallied behind their people's leadership. Although on principle opposed to mastery of man over man, "not only as unjust, being a breach of equality, but as impious, since it violates the order of Mother Nature," they readily submitted to military discipline. One of their number, John the Essene, actually served as commander of a strategically important district in the north and west of Judaea. When later the Roman armies approached Jerusalem, 4,000 of them, undoubtedly a majority, were among the most heroic defenders of the besieged city. They fought to the last drop of blood; not one survived the catastrophe.[58]

In contrast to the Samaritans and the Sadducees, this essentially Pharisaic group would have been able to maintain itself in the Diaspora. True, reiterated attempts of New Testament scholars to identify offshoots of Essenism in Rome and Asia Minor as a background for Romans 14–15 and Colossians 2 have not proved successful, but there is nothing intrinsically wrong in the assumption that some Essenes may have established themselves in Jewish communities outside Palestine. There was, indeed, an analogous order in Egypt known as the *Therapeutae*, "the citizens of heaven and of the universe," as Philo characterized them. So striking are the similarities, so slight the differences, that to assume an entirely independent historical evolution appears hardly justified. Philo, whose indubitably authentic *De vita contemplativa* is our chief source, gives us the best clue to the main distinction. As against the antiintellectualism of the Essenes, he stresses here the ardent quest for "wisdom" on the part of the *Therapeutae*. One can readily understand that sophisticated Alexandrian Jews, even if tired of civilization and prepared to seek the calm and solitude of semimonastic life, nevertheless appreciated natural sciences and formalistic logic much more than their counterparts among the Palestinian farmers. Resentful of the Pharisaic-Sadducean squabbles, the latter were also more inclined to repudiate intellectual preëminence as such.

That neither of the two groups fully survived the destruction of the Temple was not so much owing to their lack of vitality, or even adaptability, as to the increasing concentration of Judaism upon the main stream of Pharisaism. In the process of consolidation, all extreme movements were gradually driven to the periphery of Jewish life and finally excluded from it. Whatever elements of Essenism survived, operated under the cover of some obscure Jewish sects of Water Drinkers, Morning Ablutionists, and, possibly, Sun Worshipers, casually referred to in the talmudic literature. They also constantly reasserted themselves in the half-Jewish and half-Christian or half-pagan sects of Nazarites, Sampseans, Elkasites, Mandaeans and others, which, somewhat more fully described by the Church Fathers, filled the history of the eastern Mediterranean peoples with their internal strifes down to the rise of Islam.[59]

"NEW COVENANTERS"

Other trends in Pharisaism also took the shape of sectarian movements. The so-called *Damascus sect*, the subject of great controversy for many years, has been definitely established by L. Ginzberg as an integral part of Pharisaism. Its members observed rituals and laws which clearly originated from the oral tradition (even the Sadducees could not consistently evade the practical observance of their opponents' widely accepted rules and regulations). As a matter of principle they invoked the Deuteronomic phrase, *gebul rishonim* (the landmark which they of old had set) in the Pharisaic sense of a "hedge" built by the leaders of former generations around the written law. They believed in "angels of destruction," in Belial or Mastema, and recognized divine providence and other Pharisaic doctrines. Only, like the Essenes, they went beyond the main body in some tenets.

On rare occasions their more rigid interpretation of the Law agreed with that of the Sadducees. As a rule, however, they merely exaggerated some special point of the Pharisaic Halakhah as, for instance, when they prohibited polygamy and the marriage of a niece to her mother's brother. Like the Essenes (and, apparently, the Pharisaic order) they also required an oath from their initiates. Perhaps originating from a movement among dissatisfied and disestablished priests in Jerusalem and hence assigning to the "priests" a leading position in society, they nevertheless repudiated the Temple and animal sacrifices. Their organization was also somewhat similar to Essenian "monasticism," although they seem to have been concentrated in the city. A supervisor (*mebaqqer* or *episcopos*) controlled all religious life. This branch of Pharisaism also succeeded in long surviving exile. Apparently to escape the intolerance of the authorities, it emigrated to Bet-Zabdai near Damascus, the city which for ages was the most fertile soil for sectarian divergences. Here its adherents awaited the coming of the messiah, hoping to belong to those who would "escape during the period of visitation, while the rest would be handed over to the sword." Although of Palestinian origin, they have become, as a Damascus sect, one of the great curiosities in the history of religion.[60]

From among these sectarians, or some group closely related to them, seem to have come most of those ancient scrolls whose discovery in the 'Ain Fashkha cave has caused such a deep stir in biblical scholarship. E. L. Sukenik, in his first tentative edition of some of these fragments, pointed out both linguistic and ideological affinities between the new texts and Schechter's "Zadokite" documents. The fragment of the epic description of the "War of the Children of Light with the Children of Darkness," in particular, uses terms found in profusion only in the Damascus manuscripts. Perhaps even more pronounced is the resemblance in the martial tone and the description of the decisive victory ultimately to be gained by the "Children of Light," led by their "chief priest." That this victory would ultimately benefit the whole nation may well be expected in this period of great stress. "Zion rejoice greatly," the author exclaims in a climactic passage, "Jerusalem come out in song, be merry all the cities of Judah. Keep your gates open constantly to bring in the wealth of nations. Their kings will serve thee, and all thy tormentors shall bow before thee and lick the dust of thy feet" (Sukenik's *Megillot genuzot,* I, 20; II, 52).

Equally warlike is the tone of the so-called "Habakkuk Commentary," or rather the ancient midrash on the prophecies of Habakkuk:

The Habakkuk Commentary was written [says its recent editor] by a sectarian of the Holy Land who wished to show how the national and religious situation of his day had been foretold by the prophet Habakkuk. His chief interest was in the Righteous Teacher (or Teacher of Righteousness) and in the Wicked Priest who had persecuted the Righteous Teacher and his followers. The role of the Righteous Teacher, as this writer presents it, is to proclaim the New Covenant and to interpret the words of God's servants, the prophets.

In this struggle between the followers of the *moreh ṣedeq* (this term is used also by the covenanters of Damascus) and the entrenched power of *ha-kohen ha-rashaʻ,* however, the social disequilibrium in the country in the late Maccabean and Herodian age comes clearly to the fore. More outspokenly than the writers of the other documents, this homilist correlates the Wicked Priest's fiscal oppression and exploitation of the poor with his general religious and ethical shortcomings. Interpreting, for example, the ancient prophecy of doom for the country's agricultural output (Hab. 2:17), the preacher relates it directly to the abuses of the Wicked Priest, "who had planned to destroy the poor." The writer effectively combines the older and newer religious and social grievances. "It is Jerusalem," he exclaims, "in which the Wicked Priest has wrought abominable deeds. He has defiled the sanctuary of the Lord and robbed the land, that is, the townships of Judaea, where he has plundered the sustenance of the poor." The description of the Wicked Priest who had begun to rule "in the name of truth" but who was spoiled by power and, forgetting the divine commandments, began to squander on women the money squeezed out from his people (on Hab. 2:6) might fit particularly well Aristobulos II. But it could also apply to almost any other Maccabean high priest or, less directly, any high priest officiating in the Herodian era. It would be difficult, however, to find any period in the later history of the Jewish people when these particular accusations, couched in these particular terms and addressed to a Wicked Priest, would have carried equal conviction.[61]

Another fragment directly relating to the organization of the sect seems to indicate that, as in the case of Essenes and members of the Pharisaic order, each initiate had to take an oath to conduct himself in accordance with the ethical principles of the group and to separate himself from "the community of the men of iniquity." More, there is even an intimation that, like the Essenes, the members were expected to share their wealth. They obligated themselves "to love all the Children of Light, each whatever his station by the will of God, and to hate all the Children of Darkness, each in accordance with his guilt and the vengeance of God. All those who volunteer for its [the group's] truth shall offer all their thought and strength and property into the sodality of God." Considering that the Essenes insisted upon the community of goods, this interpretation seems to commend itself. Thus the sharp social conflicts intermingled with the religious controversies to create a state of extreme tension throughout the provinces of Judaea.[62]

QUEST FOR NEW TRUTHS

The declining Second Commonwealth thus offers a multicolored picture of groups of men striving for new religious formulations to solve some of the age-old riddles of existence, as well as to meet unprecedented socio-economic and political challenges of the moment. The acids of Hellenism dissolving the millennial patterns of life throughout the Near East, the constant mixture of races and religions, the spread of literacy to ever larger segments of the population enabling the urban common man, if not yet the slave and village proletarian, to take an increasing part in public life and thinking—all cried out for some new all-embracing religious truths to integrate these disparate elements into a new wholeness.

Jews, scattered throughout the focal centers of the eastern Mediterranean, Italy, and North Africa, and yet retaining their strong spiritual allegiance to their traditional creed, their homeland and Temple, vigorously responded. While accepting much from their environment, they were also prepared to contribute to the new synthesis to the utmost of their capacity. Even before the rise of the virulent forms of classical antisemitism they tried to show to their neighbors the grandeur of their own historic achievement. After the spread of anti-Jewish feeling it became a matter of sheer self-preservation to make their historic record more palatable to the non-Jewish majorities. Just as a romanticizing Egyptian priest, Chairemon, extolled the ancient Egyptian faith in terms attractive to many educated Hellenistic pagans, so did not only Jewish intellectual leaders like Philo, but also the average Jews, endeavor to translate their ancestral beliefs in terms understandable to their neighbors.

In the process they unconsciously absorbed much of what must have proved to be stubbornly alien to their own tradition. In the lower echelons, particularly, many ordinary Jews imitated their neighbors' behavior, partook of the artistic and hedonistic ways of life, cultivated the accepted magic arts and forms of religious healing, without always fully realizing that they thereby deviated into by-paths and dead-end alleys leading away from Judaism's accepted highway to perfection. Before long some more thoughtful individuals sought to rationalize all such syncretistic combinations which they found already deeply rooted in their own communities. But, with few exceptions, most Jews still looked to Jerusalem for authoritative guidance. From there was to come the ultimate decision as to which of the new ingredients were but innocuous accretions, and which must be eschewed completely as dangerous deviations or even as outright idolatry.

Unfortunately, Jerusalem was long unable to supply that guidance. So long as the Sadducees sat in the seat of the mighty, one might have expected these scions of formerly "Hellenizing" groups to evince particular understanding for the difficulties of the millions living in the dispersion. However, these men seemed so wrapped up in the exigencies of their domestic struggles that, apart from political negotiations, they did not evince the necessary solicitude for the needs, particularly the spiritual needs, of the Jewish minorities in other lands. Their very emphasis upon the state idea made them speak even a religious idiom which must have sounded strange to the necessarily nonpolitical masses in the Diaspora. Their effort to turn back the wheel of history, to skip the centuries-old evolution of Oral Law and to revert to the earlier law of Scripture, must also have alienated the common man in the Egyptian, Syrian, and still more in the Babylonian communities. The latter doubtless viewed his long-accepted folkways, themselves the result of that centuries-long evolution, as the very essence of Judaism.

For this reason he listened most eagerly to the voice of the Pharisaic leaders who, from the outset, had world Jewry equally in mind. But for a long time Pharisaic leadership seems to have had no official status as compared to the high priesthood and the Temple hierarchy. The rabbinic "pairs" and later the Hillelites must have fought a constant up-hill battle to persuade the masses in the dispersion that it was they who represented the true spirit of Judaism and not the priests officiating at the Temple. Only the increasingly obvious corruption of the hierarchy after the downfall of the Maccabees made it possible for Pharisaism to become the main form of world Judaism and to gain the substantial adherence of such leaders as Philo in Alexandria or Judah ben Batira in Parthian Nisibis, of Paul's father in Tarsus or Mattiah ben Ḥeresh in Rome.

And yet Pharisaism itself spoke in many tongues. Politically often impotent and economically weak, it had none of those trappings of sovereign power at its disposal which might have helped sustain uniformity in beliefs and conduct, and thus nurture religious conformity. The Pharisaic movement was not only involved in a perennial battle against the powers that were, but at the same time found itself torn by internal sectarian convulsions, which long prevented it from achieving that much-needed singleness of purpose. What was worse, it found its influence undermined by its own ambivalent attitude toward the masses of the "people of the land," who were at once cherished as ardent followers and despised as ritualistically unreliable illiterates. It is small wonder, then, that so many Jews both in Palestine and abroad looked to some sudden supernatural intervention to lead them out of their increasingly staggering difficulties.

X

THE GREAT SCHISM

DEEP-ROOTED pessimism was, indeed, the mood of the age. All other nationalities which had come under the heel of Rome increasingly realized that they had to pay an extraordinarily high price for the genuine benefits of the *pax Romana*. Especially after the honeymoon of the Augustan age had passed, they were prone to forget the wounds of their former internecine wars and to remember only ever more vividly the seamy sides of Roman oppression and haughtiness. The masses of slaves and other underprivileged groups were in a permanent state of unrest, even if they were not always united and organized enough to stage overt revolts. The formerly ruling classes in Rome herself found themselves dispossessed from their position of power by the imperial upstarts and their personal favorites, often recruited from the dregs of provincial society. As early as the first century the growing inner degradation, characteristic of all dictatorial regimes, was emphasized by the irresponsibility of Caligula and Nero and the anarchy which followed the latter's death. Above all there was a pervasive feeling of helplessness which generated widespread and intrinsically interrelated forms of political quietism, grasping hedonism, and mystic escapism, all of which were ultimately to sap the strength of the empire.

No wonder then that even the still fairly intact bourgeoisie of the Graeco-Roman world, unlike its nineteenth-century counterpart, was increasingly filled with evil forebodings. When the semimessianic exuberance over the establishment of the Roman peace by the "savior," Augustus, had worn off, a patriotic Roman like Tacitus began to despair of the future of his civilization. By way of contrast, he not only glorified the healthy simplicity of life among the Teutons but, as we shall see, he even conceded a point to the Jewish messianic expectation by accepting its misapplication to Vespasian. Neither he nor Suetonius found any fault with a whole people acting under the impulse of such an expectation.

Jews belonged, in fact, to the most virile groups in the empire. They consistently refused to surrender to the overwhelming force of Roman aggression or hostile public opinion. Long inured to resisting the forces of nature, deeply convinced that the inner dynamism of their ultimate historic destiny would help them overcome all difficulties, however staggering, they succeeded in coloring their pessimistic outlook on the immediate future with an optimistic hue of the ultimate good which must come from the divine guidance of history generally and God's pledges to their people in particular. The Roman peace, they believed, might be but a caricature of the peace between nations foretold by their ancient prophets. True that the hand of the oppressor lay heavily and unshakably upon their shoulders; that dismal hatreds and suspicions against them raised hydra heads among most of their neighbors; that they themselves were irremediably divided and perennially feuding against one another: nevertheless, all this was but a sign of that internal dissolution of the corrupt old order, which must precede the establishment of the new and ultimate order. The very reign of the "children of darkness" thus seemed to many Jews simply the fulfillment of the numerous dire apocalyptic prophecies and, as such, a necessary prerequisite for the ushering in of the final "day of the Lord."

MESSIANIC EXPECTATIONS

This belief in the approaching end of days and the early appearance of a personal messiah was, indeed, of transcendent importance in the very formation of all heterodox groups. In every case the messianic ideal dominated religious discussions, both in Palestine and in the Diaspora. Not only the apocalyptic literature, but all the Hellenistic and Palestinian writings of the age are permeated with utopian thinking. Even for those who remained closest to the life of the time, like the majority of responsible Pharisaic leaders, messianism was a strong propelling force. There seemed, indeed, to be no other reasonable justification for the persistence of such an extraordinary body politic as the Jewish.

Messianic hopes had many nuances, however. Zealot activists expected the redeemer to appear sword in hand and to lead the people against Rome's military power. Probably Menahem ("the Comforter"!), one of their leaders, was thought to be such a messiah, or, at least, the forerunner of the final messiah like Elijah, or like the messiah, son of Joseph. The latter was always envisaged as a great and victorious general who would lead his people from victory to victory and yet end by falling on the battlefield. Through his death as hero and martyr he would open the gate for the advent of the final redeemer, the son of David. Hence even the repeated execution of the Zealot chieftains, far from being a sign of defeat, could be interpreted as merely a part of the divine scheme of ushering in the messianic era.[1]

Most apocalyptic visionaries, on the other hand, expected redemption in the shape of a cosmic cataclysm, out of which would emerge a new world with the chosen people marching toward final salvation at the head of a transformed mankind. Even before its canonization the tremendous apocalyptic vision of the four evil beasts by Daniel (7:2 ff.), which was to exert such an enormous influence on all future messianic speculations, was reinterpreted to signify the historic succession of the four empires of Babylon, Persia, Greece, and Rome. The Roman Empire "dreadful and terrible, and strong exceedingly," was now to be succeeded by an everlasting dominion, established by "one like unto a son of man [kebar enash]," to whom God would give "dominion, and glory, and a kingdom, that all the peoples, nations, and languages should serve him." The author of Enoch likewise prophesied that "the Son of Man who hath righteousness . . . shall loosen the reins of the strong and break the teeth of the sinners" (46:3–4).

Speaking in picturesque rather than precise language, these and other apocalyptic writers give us but a slight inkling of the profound differences in the messianic outlook of various groups and individuals. Personal tempers and group biases, changing circumstances in national and world affairs, as well as the autonomous operation of hermeneutic interpretations of accepted texts by revered teachers, all affected the endless variations of the messianic theme in the literature of the age. To the more worldly author of the Book of Jubilees, for example, the ultimate catastrophe was to be followed only by an era in which "the children shall begin to study the laws, and to seek the commandments, and to return to the path of righteousness." During that reign of the son of Judah "there shall be no Satan any more nor any evil destroyer. For all their days shall be days of blessing and healing" (23:26, 29; 31:18). The author of the Assumption of Moses, on the other hand, perhaps writing after the fall of Jerusalem, expected the change to come from the rise of men who, like the Maccabean martyrs (not warriors!), would be determined to "die rather than transgress the commands of the Lord of Lords, the God of our fathers." Their leader Taxo, of the tribe of Levi, would through successful exhorta-

tion to religious martyrdom bring about God's personal intervention.

For the Heavenly One will arise from His royal throne, and He will
go forth from His holy habitation, with indignation and wrath on account of His sons. And the earth shall tremble; to its confines shall it be
shaken. . . . And the sun shall not give light and the horns of the
moon shall turn into darkness and be broken, and she will be turned
wholly into blood, and the circle of the stars shall be disturbed. And the
sea shall retire into the abyss, and the fountains of water shall fail, and
the river shall dry up [9:1, 6; 10:3-6, disregarding Charles's emendation
of verse 5].

Imagination often ran riot in depicting the sufferings of Jews
and all men during the final gigantic struggle between Gog and
Magog and the subsequent bliss to all survivors after the ultimate
establishment of the kingdom of heaven. The author of IV Ezra,
perhaps writing under the fresh impression of the fall of Jerusalem,
revels in the description of the unspeakable horrors which will accompany the great transition. "Then shall the sun suddenly shine
forth by night and the moon by day; and blood shall trickle forth
from wood and the stone utter its voice . . . and the birds shall
take to general flight, and the sea shall cast forth its fish." Nor
would, in his opinion, the messianic redemption be truly final.
After four hundred years, the messiah and all living beings would
suddenly die and the universe be turned into "primaeval silence"
for seven days. Only after this final pause would come the new,
definitive messianic era. The author of the Syriac Apocalypse of
Baruch, on the contrary, took delight in describing the blessings
of the end of days when "the earth shall yield its fruit ten thousand-
fold and on each vine there shall be a thousand branches, and each
branch shall produce a thousand clusters, and each cluster produce
a thousand grapes and each grape produce a *khor* [about 120 gal-
lons] of wine." In short, these dreamers envisaged not the mere beginning of a new epoch, but rather the advent of a new cosmic *aeon*,
the complete cessation of the usual historic processes and a fundamental change in the laws of nature.[2]

Others had less high-flown expectations. Without necessarily
denying the eschatological implications of the advent of the redeemer, they viewed its effects primarily from the angle of the
contemporary struggle for power. To the mighty King Solomon,
one of the psalmists attributed only the prayer that God "raise up
unto them their King, the son of David. . . . And gird him with

strength, that he may shatter unrighteous rulers, and that he may purge Jerusalem from nations that trample [her] down to destruction" (Psalms of Solomon 17:23–24). Of course, this redemption would involve the gathering of Jews from all the countries of the dispersion. By bringing back the remnants of the lost Ten Tribes it would also fulfill the old prophecies of reuniting Israel and Judah. Nor could any of these changes occur without God's miraculous intervention. This is, indeed, the tenor of several benedictions in the daily 'Amidah which, despite numerous variations developed in the course of centuries, seem to antedate the fall of Jerusalem.[3]

Whatever their particular interpretations, however, most Jewish groups in the declining Second Commonwealth cherished the belief in the almost immediate coming of the redeemer. The general impatience, particularly of the apocalyptic writers, is well illustrated by their numerous attempts to figure out the exact date of his arrival. But Daniel's well-known computations, referring to his own time, were typical of their general ambiguity, which made it possible for messianic dreamers in subsequent generations to recalculate the same basic data in a way better suited to their own wishful thinking. Only the recurrent disappointments finally induced the rabbis to object to the entire method of "calculating the end."

Belief in the early coming of the redeemer was so universal that the very Herodians, mentioned in the Gospels, seem to have justified the rule of the reigning dynasty by some messianic allusions in Jacob's blessing. Credence was also readily given to individual visionaries who promised to lead the whole nation into its chosen land. Almost anyone could engage the attention of a people brought to despair by the overwhelming power of Rome and the dismal domestic situation. "Deceivers and impostors," writes unsympathetic Josephus, "under the pretense of divine inspiration fostering revolutionary changes, they persuaded the multitude to act like madmen and led them out into the desert under the belief that God would then give them tokens of deliverance." When in 44, after the death of Agrippa I, the country was again taken over by the Romans, a prophet named Theudas was easily able to assemble a large crowd, whom he led to the Jordan, promising to divide its waters. A few years later (52–54) an "Egyptian" messiah appeared and brought 30,000 Jerusalem Jews to the Mount of Olives, declaring "that he would show them from hence how, at his command, the walls of Jerusalem would fall down." Roman soldiers speedily and bloodily suppressed both commotions.[4]

At an earlier date—and not merely through the whim of a Herodian princess—another messianic prophet, John the Baptist, had met a similar tragic end. Allegedly disclaiming all messianic ambitions, he nevertheless clearly intimated that he was performing the function of forerunner, akin to that of Elijah in the prevailing popular anticipation. He evidently succeeded neither in dampening the hopes of the people who "were in expectation" nor in allaying the apprehensions of the authorities (Luke 3:15–20). The southern steppes were, indeed, excellent terrain for guerilla warfare and revolutionary plotting. Herod Antipas was, therefore, fully justified in fearing a revolt. John's influence did not vanish with his death. True, few teachings can reliably be attributed to him. Unless we accept Eisler's theory connecting him with the Damascus sect, we can at best indulge in the hopeless game of trying to unravel some of his sayings from those ascribed in the Gospels to his disciple, Jesus. Scholars also still differ as to whether his followers remained, for generations to come, a clear and prominent Judeo-Christian sect, or were absorbed by the main stream of Pauline Christianity. The tragic figure of the Baptist, in any case, has for centuries been a prime symbol of the irrepressible conflicts, political, economic, and religious, pervading Jewish society in the period of its final loss of political independence.[5]

RISE OF CHRISTIANITY

There arose among the Jews another sect, which soon developed into a great schism and finally into a great independent religion: Christianity. Out of the social unrest in Palestine, out of the national dissatisfaction, out of the differences in outlook between Palestinian and world Jewry, grew that movement which was destined to play such a surpassing role in the history of mankind. Before long it swelled to a powerful torrent, threatening to submerge the whole Jewish people.

Each of the three successive stages in early Christianity—the purely eschatological Palestinian community, the Diaspora Christianity centering in the cult of the Kyrios Christos, and the early Catholic Church—was another step away from Pharisaic Judaism. In its first stage, the new movement was hardly more than a sectarian current within Judaism, no more apart, for instance, than the

Essenes. The second stage began with a definite schism and ended in a new religion, which received in the third stage its definite organization. Evidently the second stage was most decisive. While the protagonists during the first period were Jesus and the Palestinian Judeo-Christians, those of the second were principally Hellenistic Jews of the Anatolian-Syrian variety, until the movement finally came under the predominant control of Gentiles and the impact of Rome.[6]

No attempt can be made here to give an account, however brief, of the history of early Christianity. Not only would the enormity and complexity of the task and the vast divergence of opinion concerning the most fundamental New Testament sources discourage such an attempt, but our concern in this book is primarily with *Jewish* society and religion. The rise of Christianity can, therefore, be treated here merely from the point of view of its role *within* the evolution of Jewish social and religious life and of its influence upon the subsequent destinies of the Jewish people. Nor should the reader expect here another treatment of Jesus and the apostles "from the Jewish point of view." Such a treatment has never appealed to the present author, even in purely theological discussions. In an historical analysis like the present, it would be out of place altogether. It may suffice to state here that in recent years such investigations have emanated from various camps in contemporary Jewry. To be sure, the majority, orthodox and conservative Jews, have clung to the age-old policy of avoiding discussion of the subject. But many "liberal" and nationalist Jews have taken a stand.[7]

Even dismissing as unscientific the recurrent attempts to disprove the historicity of Jesus, one can hardly deny that endeavors to reconstruct the details of his life are doomed to failure by the contradictory nature of the sources. There is practically no archaeological evidence elucidating the strictly biographical data. Sensational news in the world press during the fall of 1945, connected with the discovery near the main Jerusalem-Bethlehem road of eleven new ossuaries, were not borne out by further careful scrutiny. True, two of these ossuaries bore the Greek inscription, *Iesous;* one also a sign of the cross drawn in charcoal on each of its four sides. But the name Jesus was far too common in Palestine to warrant any identification with the founder of Christianity. Nor is the date of these tombs, placed by Sukenik at between 50 B.C.E. and 50 C.E., supported by any reliable evidence.[8]

In fact, we do not even know exactly where and when Jesus was

born. Most critical scholars disregard the tradition pointing to Beth-
lehem, and merely debate whether Nazareth or some place in the
vicinity of Capernaum was Jesus' birthplace. They also agree that
he was born several years *before* the Christian era, although few
accept Olmstead's date of about 20 B.C.E. Even the actual locality
and the exact date of the crucifixion are still hotly debated. Although there is fairly general agreement that the chronology later
accepted by the Western Church and putting the Passion in 29 C.E.
is based on a misunderstanding of Luke 3:1, there is less unanimity
as to which chronological sequence is to take its place. For example,
Olmstead's telescoping of the entire ministry of Jesus into 475 days
from December 18, 28, to April 7, 30, seems decidedly too radical.[9]

As narrated in the Gospels, therefore, the story of Jesus—contemporary German scholars often speak, without disrespect, of the
Jesus Roman—belongs to the second stage in Christian evolution.
Thence come also its numerous inconsistencies. "It is probable,"
writes D. W. Riddle, "that there is as much difference between the
Jesus of Mark and the Jesus of the Fourth Gospel as there is between the Jesus of Case and the Jesus of, say, Bishop Headlam. . . .
In the Gospels, as elsewhere in the New Testament, Jesus has become several things to several men." We may thus understand why,
as Riddle also remarked, many unhistorical or, if we may use that
term, transhistorical (*übergeschichtlich*) treatments of Jesus, being
unconscious approximations of Paul's attitude, appeal so much
more strongly to the mass of nonspecialists than do historically
sounder biographies. That is also why the whole problem of "In
History or Beyond History" has been such a major preoccupation
of New Testament scholars ever since M. K. Haymann's work on
biblical theology published in 1708, and why it has frequently colored certain modern interpretations of the Old Testament as well.
Typical of the existing feeling of insecurity is C. T. Craig's statement of his personal belief

that the older historicism had run into bankruptcy. It tended to forget
that after all it was an enterprise carried on for its human values. But the
present revolt is in grave danger of becoming a retreat to dogma rather
than an advance to a truer insight into the permanent significance of the
events recorded in the Old and New Testaments. That peril can be met
only as men of sound historical training accept the challenge to interpret the meaning of Christian faith.

Nor is it astonishing to find so many modern writings oscillating
between recurrent attempts at outright denial of the historicity of

Jesus and those aimed at "modernizing" episodes of his life and his teachings so as to make them more readily acceptable to the changing tastes of each people and generation.[10]

On the other hand, Schelling's deep insight that Jesus' "biography has been written long before his birth" was borne out by a century of scholarly research. The age-old eschatological-messianic hopes of the Jewish people necessarily furnished Palestinian believers in Jesus with all the integral elements of that "life" as the embodiment and realization of their hopes. Pauline Christianity, on the other hand, was increasingly centered on the worship of the "Lord Christ." Contrary to Old Testament usage, Jesus had become "the Messiah" without a limiting pronoun or genitive (Mark 8:29 and other passages), and his picture was increasingly colored by borrowings from the various mystery religions of salvation. Under these circumstances, many details of his biography belong to the world of ideas rather than to that of historic fact.

Jesus' association with John the Baptist, his brief ministry during two or three years, even the crucifixion, all these outstanding events clearly reveal that he was building solely on the basis of Palestinian Judaism. He is said to have had dealings with a Greek municipality in Palestine only once, when Gadara, prominent as a home of Hellenistic thinkers and writers, expelled him as a Jewish miracle worker. His Jewishness is even more clearly reflected in the numerous sayings attributed to him by the Gospels, which, in view of the reverence for the oral transmission of ancestral teachings, may be regarded as the most authentic part of the early tradition. To be sure, A. Loisy is undoubtedly right in saying that "neither the preacher nor his most faithful hearers dreamed of fixing the tenor of his preaching for the purpose of transmitting it to posterity." In this respect Jesus' audience resembled the general public of his day attending synagogue services and listening to the homiletical expositions of preachers, rather than the disciples of academies especially trained for literal preservation of the legal decisions rendered by their masters. In some respects all early Christian teachings must have shared with the Aggadah its loose, if creative, form of transmission which differed greatly from the more disciplined, and hence more rigid, recording of the halakhic part of Oral Law.[11]

Preservation of these teachings in Greek translation similarly mars the genuineness of their tone. "For a few sheets containing genuine Aramaic sayings of Jesus," declared A. Deissmann, "we would, I think, part smilingly with the theological output of a whole century." The connotations evoked by the apt retranslations into Aramaic of Dalman and Torrey give an inkling of how different a meaning must often have been conveyed by the original. Not only have all the early traditions of the days of Jesus indubitably circulated for a long time only in the language of the Palestinian natives, but there is every reason for assuming that the earliest gospel was composed in Aramaic. This is indeed the meaning of the much-debated statement by Papias (as reported by Eusebius) that Matthew had transcribed Jesus' sayings (*logia*) in the "Hebrew dialect." Nor ought we to discard completely the possibility, frequently discussed in recent generations, that even the present Gospels, or at least those of Mark and John, were originally written in Aramaic and later translated into Greek. Even one who, like the present writer, does not share C. C. Torrey's enthusiastic conviction "that our four canonical Gospels, entire and just as they stand (excepting Luke's prologue, John 21, and the first two chapters of Luke's Gospel, which he rendered from Hebrew) are translations from Aramaic," will concede that at least a great many passages in the Greek Gospels owe their origin to traditions, written or oral, which had long been known to the early Christian community in Aramaic only. The less educated the disciples were, the less likely were they to transmit even authentic Greek conversations, such as the proceedings before Pilate, in their original Greek formulation. But hardly any two scholars will now agree on the exact Aramaic retranslation of most Greek passages.[12]

The modern "formgeschichtliche" method, developed in part along the lines previously employed by E. Norden in classical studies and by H. Gunkel and his school in Old Testament criticism (there called "gattungsgeschichtliche" method), has increased rather than diminished prevailing uncertainties. By correctly assuming the circulation for many decades of individual pericopes in oral form, this school has tried to penetrate behind the written tradition to the underlying oral formulations—a highly important but obviously hazardous undertaking. The battle for and against "form criticism," ferociously raging in the 1930's, was fought to a standstill in the 1940's, with most questions left open. F. Büchsel's remark, is, in any case, as true today as it was a decade ago: "Not *the* picture of Jesus and early Christianity has emerged from historical science to replace that of the New Testament, but many different, indeed strikingly different, pictures." [13]

JESUS THE MESSIAH

At any rate, Jesus appears as an essentially Pharisaic Jew. He was, of course, primarily the spokesman of ideas current among the "people of the land," particularly in Galilee, in so far as they may be in any way distinguished from the whole body of Pharisee sympathizers. From the beginning "he preached in their synagogues throughout all Galilee, and cast out devils." His religious healing, exorcisms, and other miracles were as much taken for granted as was the intervention of angels who are mentioned some 170 times in the New Testament. On one occasion he complained that his disciples' "heart was hardened," because they were not sufficiently impressed by his miraculous feeding of five thousand men on five loaves of bread. Appealing to the common man, he did not hesitate to share meals with publicans and sinners, to the chagrin of the more scrupulously orthodox among his followers who, like other Pharisaic Jews, suspected as being untithed every bit of bread served by an 'am ha-areṣ. As a spokesman of the disaffected masses Jesus attacked the hypocrisy of religious leaders and the materialism of the rich with equal vehemence, coining for the latter the famous simile of the camel's difficulties in going through the eye of a needle.[14]

None of that was unprecedented, however, nor in any way directed against the people as a whole. "Think not that I am come," reads one of Jesus' most genuine declarations, "to destroy the law or the prophets; I am not come to destroy, but to fulfill." The probable Aramaic original, preserved in the Talmud, "I am come not to detract from the Law of Moses, but to add to it," has an even more authentic ring. Numerous Jewish as well as Christian scholars have repeatedly emphasized the fact, that, individually examined, the sayings of Jesus (including that magnificent collection called the Sermon on the Mount) can be traced in similar apothegms in rabbinic literature, many of which must have come down from an age preceding the Christian era. Even such an overtly antinomian utterance as "the Sabbath was made for man, and not man for the Sabbath" has its parallel in R. Simon ben Menasya's interpretation of Exod. 31:14 as saying: "The Sabbath is given to you, but you are not surrendered to the Sabbath." The recurrent fulminations against the "scribes and Pharisees" found throughout the Gospels, even if genuine, reveal only the disillusionment of an impatient (because creative) religious reformer, with the shortcomings of an institutionalized leadership in his own camp. It appears ever clearer, however, that almost all these polemical passages have undergone intensive sharpening in the process of transmission and redaction.[15]

On the other hand, the general tone and color, certain particular emphases, are clearly individual. Nourished by the ideas of Pharisaic Judaism, Jesus stressed the messianic hope, foreseeing its fulfillment in his own time. Immediately upon the imprisonment of John the Baptist, we are told in the earliest Gospel (Mark), "Jesus came into Galilee, preaching the gospel of the kingdom of God, and saying, The time is fulfilled, and the kingdom of God is at hand: repent ye, and believe in the gospel." This formula, or its seemingly more authentic version the "kingdom of heaven" (*malkhut shamaim*) consistently used in Matthew, was consciously equivocal. But it must have conjured up in the minds of Jewish listeners the whole array of messianic and eschatological expectations with which their imagination had been stirred by apocalyptic writers and preachers for many generations.[16]

It is difficult to ascertain, through the haze of sources completely rewritten in the period of an established Christ cult, what conclusions Jesus himself drew from the fact that the era of the kingdom of heaven was drawing near. The evidence hardly supports C. H. Dodd's widely discussed theory that Jesus viewed his own achievement as one of "realized eschatology." It has been suggested that, on the contrary, the "gospel of the kingdom" was more akin to the prophetic than the apocalyptic doctrines of the messianic age; that Jesus never applied to himself the eschatologically fraught Old Testament designation of "Son of man," of the time of whose arrival, he himself declared, "knoweth no man, no, not the angels which are in heaven, neither the Son, but the Father"; and that he appeared to his disciples as but a prophet speaking with "authority," rather than as the messiah. These suggestions seem to go to the opposite extreme. In fact, one must not overstress the distinction between "prophet" and "messiah" in the consciousness of a first-century Palestinian Jew. "In Jesus' day," rightly observes F. W. Young, "there were no Jewish prophets. . . . The next prophet would be one of two individuals: Elijah (or the forerunner of the Messiah) or the Messiah himself." Nor should we underestimate the impact of Jesus' personality on a distraught people which had long clung to its undying hope that some world-shaking supernatural intervention was due at any moment. Although his message may have been interpreted differently by different men in his own entourage, we need not deny that to most of them he must have appeared as a self-avowed messiah, son of David who, through his purely spiritual message, would usher in the kingdom of heaven during the long-awaited end of days.[17]

While such a declaration deviated abruptly from precedent in form rather than in substance, it seems to have led Jesus to a more revolutionary conclusion. With the realization of the messianic expectation, so he taught, nationalism had largely completed its task and should give way entirely to the universalistic aspects of the Jewish religion. In the messianic age, moreover, he or at least some of his immediate disciples concluded, Jewish law need no longer be strictly adhered to. The talmudic statement that even the Sabbath may be disregarded for the sake of man had on the lips of Jesus a different sanction. So had his declaration that he had come to fulfill the law. His elaboration, particularly, "For verily I say unto you, Till heaven and earth pass, one jot or one tittle shall in no wise pass from the law, till all be fulfilled" (Matthew 5:18) must have led many of his disciples to the conclusion that, with the advent of the redeemer, all had been fulfilled. The concept that the law in general is inferior to the "spirit" (*pneuma*) is also part of the prophetic and Pharisaic outlook, but Jesus gave it a much more central position.

This reign of the spirit, however, can be achieved only with the realization of the old prophecies, with the actual "kingdom of heaven" established in this world. In Jesus' preachment of that kingdom, based upon peace between man and man, became articulate the deep yearning of those pacifist elements of the Galilean people of the land, who reacted sharply against the point of view of their brethren, the Zealots. With respect to the empire, remarks F. C. Grant, "Jesus did not go the full length of hearty co-operation —let alone promote an armed revolt (as Eisler and others have supposed)—nor did he, on the other hand, counsel anything like 'passive resistance'—he was neither a Caiaphas nor a Theudas nor a Gandhi. Why should he be? The reign of God was at hand!" In brief, Jesus implicitly, rather than directly, denied both state and nationality, and his kingdom of heaven went beyond the range of both. Not that either state or nationality was to be regarded as an intrinsic evil. Therefore, "Render unto Caesar" what belongs to the state and obey the law representing the national principle; but above both is that supreme sovereignty of the "spirit." [18]

Such an attitude necessarily provoked a sharp reaction from both the Roman administration and the Jewish leaders.

Just as in modern society [writes S. J. Case] if one were to set oneself against an established method of procedure in the realm of medicine, legal practice, or politics, one would immediately be regarded as a menace to the common welfare and, consequently, a proper object for arrest and punishment, so in the situation of Jesus, where religion was the all-embracing interest of society, a vigorous hostile action was the normal consequence of his open non-conformity [*The Social Origins of Christianity*, p. 57].

However pacific, moreover, his aims may have been and however hard he may have tried to infuse purely spiritual meaning into the terms "messiah" and "king of Jews," these were fighting words of the first order. In the existing permanent state of tension any Roman administrator taught by the experience of other messianic commotions must have seen red at the mention of a new movement spreading in both the capital and the provinces. The procurator must have considered it a matter of sheer prudence to suppress the agitation before it got out of hand. Such action took place in a fashion momentous to the history of mankind: Jesus' arrest, trial, and crucifixion.

Whether the details of the Gospel narrative of the Passion are authentic or not is of comparatively little import. Modern scholars tend to agree more and more that, contrary to the Christian tradition, the Roman share in opposing Jesus far exceeded the Jewish. There seems to be historical value only in the narrative concerning the procedure before Pilate (Mark 15), while the alleged earlier sentence pronounced by the high priest (Mark 14) would have been altogether impossible under the Sanhedrin's jurisdictional limitations. The Pharisaic leaders participated directly in the prosecution and trial even less than the Sadducean high priest and his associates, and the execution was an exclusively Roman affair.[19]

However, among the Pharisees there was no friendliness to Jesus. The scene of Golgotha, whose description with such glowing anti-Jewish bias was to become the source of unceasing tribulations for Jewry in the Christian world, may in truth not have occurred in this fashion at all. The bulk of the Jews, nevertheless, had to oppose Jesus. The only question at issue was one of procedure. The Pharisees, pursuing a course repeatedly applied to Christian apostles such as Peter, Paul, and James, opposed harsh internecine means of suppression. Gamaliel's speech against the condemnation of Peter, culminating in the exhortation, "Refrain from these men, and let them alone; for if this counsel or this work be of men, it will come to naught," whether in itself historical or not, well epitomizes the Pharisaic attitude toward sectarian Jews. In essence, however, Jewish resistance turned out to be even stiffer and more enduring than that of the Romans.[20]

JUDEO-CHRISTIAN FOLLOWING

Jesus' crucifixion at first stunned his disciples. Much as they may have cherished the literary recollections of Deutero-Isaiah's suffering Servant of the Lord and believed, with the author of Fourth Maccabees, that individuals could through suffering atone for the sins of their fellow men, they, like most other Palestinian Jews, could not quite divorce their vision of the advent of the messiah from that of a visible final triumph over all enemies. Jesus' execution in a manner reserved for worst criminals must have deeply shocked most of his followers. Probably at that time his opponents began to jeer at the "hanged one" (talui) and applied to him the Deuteronomic phrase, "For he that is hanged is accursed by God" (the Aramaic translation actually paraphrased here "hang him on a tree" by "crucify him on a cross"). Even before the execution Simon-Peter denied being Jesus' disciple. One of the twelve apostles, Judas Iscariot, had so completely lost faith in the new movement that he was allegedly ready, on his own initiative, to betray the master. Not until they had the vision of Christ resurrected did the other apostles regain their composure and resume their mission. They now began to recall every detail of what Jesus had said during their Last Supper with him and to extol the mystic implications of their partaking of the bread and wine. There is no way of ascertaining the authenticity of his sayings reported by Mark, "This is my body," "This is my blood of the new testament which is shed for many," or of the still more pointed injunction quoted by John, "Verily, verily, I say unto you. Except ye eat the flesh of the Son of man and drink his blood, ye have no life in you." But there is no question that from these recollections soon arose the ritual of Eucharist which, wholly unprecedented among Jews, though not among their Gentile neighbors, became profoundly symbolic of the mystic union between the Christian worshiper and his Deity.[21]

Emphasizing above all this combination of Last Supper, Crucifixion, and Resurrection, the early Christian community found an answer to the riddle of its founder's agonizing death, which had become "unto the Jews a stumblingblock, and unto the Greeks foolishness." It still had to go on explaining the difference between Jesus and the various pseudo-messiahs who had tried to incite a Jewish rebellion against Rome. "Much more than Mark," writes E. E. Jensen, "the later synoptics show many evidences of the desire to erase from the record of Jesus' life any suspicion that he had been a pretender king of the revolutionary type common in his day." For this purpose Pilate had to be depicted as doubting Jesus' rebellious designs and merely "willing to content the people." This brief statement in Mark is then increasingly elaborated in Matthew and Luke, until in John the Roman procurator is reputed to have said, "Behold, I bring him forth to you, that ye may know that I find no fault in him." More, Pilate allegedly conceded Jesus the right to be called "King of the Jews" in the spiritual sense. In this connection he even suggested Jesus' release—we possess but dubious external evidence for the reputed custom of the annual release of a prisoner on Passover eve—while the Jews insisted on the liberation of an ordinary criminal, Barabbas. Many scholars have come to the conclusion that this Barabbas, if not altogether a figment of imagination, was an *alter ego* for Jesus himself who, as Jesus Barabbas (Bar Abba = the Father's Son), had been twice brought before Pilate, once as Barabbas and the second time as the messiah. The first time he was discharged; but on the second occasion he was condemned to death for high treason.[22]

These extensions of the original story, which took on an increasingly pro-Roman and anti-Jewish coloring, have come down to us from the Gospels, only one of which (Mark) seems to have been written before the fall of Jerusalem, possibly in Rome itself. Matthew, Luke, and John represent a similar number of stages away from Judaism and toward a synthesis with the prevailing ideas of the Graeco-Roman world. These evangelists were not Jew-baiters in the ordinary meaning of this term. But with the victory of the Pauline interpretation of Christianity and the growing success of the Christian mission among Gentiles, they had to draw an ever sharper line of demarcation between the old and the new dispensations. Hence, their increasing stress on the anti-Jewish elements in the earlier tradition. Luke, himself of Gentile origin, did not even have to overcome any native pro-Jewish bias in either his Gospel or his Acts of the Apostles. Only John, who probably was of Jewish ancestry, at times betrays signs of typical Jewish self-hatred. Nor were their writings immune from later interpolations, since, as we shall see, the major battle between Marcion and the adherents of the Old Testament was yet to be fought. As late as the end of the second century, none of the New Testament writings had been canonized, and Theophilus of Antioch could still regard the Old Testament alone as comprising the official Scriptures of the Church.[23]

Sharing their founder's aloofness from both state and nationality, the leaders of the early Judeo-Christian Church negated the paramount principle of the Graeco-Roman world as well as that of Judaism. In this way they adumbrated a synthesis of both—indeed went beyond both. Their ideal could, however, become real only through the coming of a kingdom of heaven on earth. Jesus and the first group of disciples sincerely believed that this new era was at hand. Jesus himself may have changed his mind in the course of his brief ministry. At first he may have expected the end of days in his own lifetime, while later he seemed to believe in its arrival at his death. But he never doubted its imminence.[24]

Most of his followers, too, even more after the crucifixion than before, believed that they themselves would witness the end of days. The *parousia*, this resolution of the contrasts between this world and the world to come, was their cherished hope for the immediate future. So convinced were they of Christ's momentary return, whether to Galilee (as intimated by Mark and Matthew) or Jerusalem (as implied in Luke), that they did not even indulge in those fantastic "computations of the end" on the basis of Old Testament passages to which their more despairing successors, as well as Jews, were to resort so frequently.

In the meantime they continued to live as did all Palestinian Jewry. The small group around James and Peter, largely Galileans, exulted in the expectation of the forthcoming "restitution of all things, which God hath spoken by the mouth of all his holy prophets." Most Palestinian followers of Jesus did not accept the antinomian view implied in his messianic message, although according to some Jewish convictions, apparently going back to the Maccabean period, Jewish law might be abolished on the advent of the messiah. This view seems not to have been widely held, however. The author of Jubilees, for instance, constantly emphasized the eternal validity and immutability of the Law. Even the oft-quoted talmudic statement, "The commandments will be voided in the world to come," is reported as merely a personal deduction of R.

Joseph, a third-century Babylonian teacher, and really refers only to the days after the resurrection of the dead. The immediate connection of the resurrection with the advent of the messiah had actually been denied by Mar Samuel, R. Joseph's predecessor.[25]

Only Stephen, a Hellenistic Jew, was reported by witnesses to have spoken "blasphemous words" against the Temple and the law and contended that Jesus would "change the custom which Moses delivered us" (Acts 6:13–14). Most of the disciples so strictly adhered to all commandments of Pharisaic Judaism that they were shocked to learn that Peter, after his encounter with Cornelius in Caesarea, had eaten with Gentiles (11:3). Despite Old Testament precedents, they refused to believe "that on the Gentiles also was poured out the gift of the Holy Ghost" (10:45).

Leadership of the entire Christian community long rested with the Judeo-Christian group, as is attested by the New Testament writers themselves, almost all of whom belonged to its Gentile-Christian opponents. "Among their contemporaries," rightly observed F. W. Beare, "Peter and James were accorded greater importance than Paul; but for us the relative greatness of these other Apostles is obscured by the fact that they have left no literary remains and that they found no biographer to tell the story of their labors." Despite such intensive efforts as have gone, for instance, into Dean E. G. Selwyn's voluminous commentary and excursuses on *The First Epistle of St. Peter,* it is still debatable how much of that or the second epistle represents that apostle's genuine thinking. Similarly the most important data of his life, including his reputed crucifixion in Rome, are either unknown or controversial. According to reiterated reports in the world press, recent excavations at the Vatican have yielded sensational finds, including Peter's own earthly remains. However, the full archaeological documentation of these reports has, at this writing, not yet seen the light of day. Even the apostle's traditional identification with Cephas (Kaipha) has been denied by such scholars as Lake and Goguel, while a more recent attempt to identify him with Simon Bar-Jona (Matthew 16:17) and Simon Zealotes (Luke 6:15) and, hence, to make him both a member of the Zealotic party and founder of the Ebionite sect, is more ingenious than sound.[26]

Peter's general espousal of nomistic Judeo-Christianity, however, is not subject to doubt. Nor would any orthodox Jew have gone further than James' alleged exclamation, "For whosoever shall keep the whole law, and yet offend it in one point, he is guilty of all." The Pharisees recognized the allegiance of these apostles and their associates and refused to join in the violent persecution. Even later Jewish legends tried to minimize Peter's share in the rise of Christianity. One such legend actually ascribed to him the authorship of the prominent prayer *Nishmat* in the Sabbath morning service. James' execution by the Sadducees was condemned, according to Josephus, by all "moderate and law-abiding" citizens. Even Papias' report (about 130) that the latter's namesake, James son of Zebedee, was executed "by the Jews" together with his brother John, is controverted by John's longevity, attested in the Gospel named after him, whose priority over Papias can no longer be contested.[27]

In general, these Judeo-Christians' way of living differed from that of the Jewish majority only through their belief that the messiah had already come and the ensuing additional emphasis upon the ceremonies of baptism and the Eucharist. According to a recent reconstruction of "Ebionite Acts of the Apostles," it was in the seventh year after the crucifixion that, in their debates with Jewish sages, the Judeo-Christian leaders stated that "the Jews erred with respect to the first advent [of the redeemer] and this is the sole disagreement between us and them." Far from assuming its later purely sacramental character, baptism and even the Eucharist, glorified because of their connection with John the Baptist–Elijah, the forerunner of the messiah, and Jesus, the messiah son of David, were at that time only sectarian deviations. They probably were no more sharply repudiated by the orthodox majority than were the distinctive rituals of the Essenes or the "New Covenanters." As illustrated by Gamaliel's aforementioned speech, the Pharisaic leaders consistently refused to participate in any violent suppression of the Judeo-Christian "heresy." The masses of their followers seem to have been no less forebearing.[28]

Nor was the peculiar Judeo-Christian community life essentially heterodox. It was communistic, not in the Marxian sense of social control over the means of production, but in the sense of communal consumption, based upon charity and loving-kindness. As such it likewise resembled that of the Essenes and, at the most, was merely the speculative Judaism of men living under the highest tension of preparedness for the second coming of Christ. Would this lofty ideal survive, however, once the end of days was recognized not within sight, but postponed perhaps for an indefinite "millennium"?

PAULINE SCHISM

At this crucial moment Paul assumed the leadership. A great visionary, he was at the same time endowed with a fine sense of reality. He began to adapt Jesus' teachings to actual life. Although his intellectual achievements both in the field of Hellenistic culture, which he acquired in his home city of Tarsus, and in that of Judaism, which he was said to have studied under Gamaliel in Jerusalem, were extremely limited, he became the great theologian and formulator of the new religious outlook. He succeeded in erecting the imposing structure of Pauline Christianity, not through a process of systematic thinking, but by lending expression to his high-strung emotions and by seeking in creative fashion the reconciliation of his own Jewish and Hellenistic heritages. It becomes increasingly evident that, with all his wish to escape, he remained until the end of his life essentially a Hellenistic Jew, thinking in terms of rabbinic allegory and dialectic. The pagan mysteries of salvation furnished him, as has been rightly asserted, "only the mold in which he cast his personal conception of Christianity."

In contrast to Jesus the Galilean, Paul may be classified as the intellectual spokesman of Hellenistic Jewry, particularly of the type prevalent in Asia Minor. He not only spent there the formative years of his childhood and adolescence, but after his conversion (in the late thirties) lived some fourteen years in Syria and Cilicia (Gal. 2:1), pondering over the meaning of his experience before he ventured to publish his first epistle (I Thess., 50–51 C.E.). Apparently a man of fairly independent means, he earned a living as a skilled craftsman. He also enjoyed the privileges of Roman citizenship, which, although granted to the descendant of any slave freed by a Roman master, served him in good stead with the authorities. At a critical juncture it helped him to escape the wrath of the Palestinian Jews by an appeal to the emperor. On his journeys, which he seems to have been able to finance from his own resources, he enjoyed the fine hospitality extended to all Jewish travelers by the local communities. Further intensified among the newly formed Christian brotherhoods, such hospitable reception facilitated missionary efforts of Paul and his followers and the exchange of ideas between visitors and hosts.[29]

From these travels and far-flung connections Paul gained wider horizons than those accessible to his average Palestinian confreres. As a rule, he thought in terms of world Jewry, rather than in those of Palestine. From this standpoint, he was easily induced to abandon many revolutionary and communistic ingredients of the earlier movement. We recall how insignificant the social conflicts within the Diaspora communities were, as compared with their seething turbulence in Palestine. Similarly, as we shall see, there was a deep cleavage between the increasingly rebellious, anti-Roman mood of the Palestinian masses and the strong imperial loyalties of Rome's other Jewish subjects.

Jesus' "Render unto Caesar" was both an evasion of an embarrassing question and a necessary expedient, akin to the daily use of Caesar's coins, which was expected to be abolished in the new eschatological era. Paul not only extended that obligation to the rendering of "fear" and "honour" to whom fear and honor were due, but declared sweepingly,

Let every soul be subject unto the higher powers. For there is no power but of God; the powers that be are ordained of God. Whosoever therefore resisteth the power, resisteth the ordinance of God; and they that resist shall receive to themselves damnation. . . . Wherefore ye must needs be subject, not only for wrath, but also for conscience sake.

Nor did he object to the prevailing economic system. Although constantly reiterating the requirement of charity, he was proud of his ability to provide for his and his family's needs through the labor of his hands, both essentially Jewish doctrines in the dispersion as well as in Palestine. In short, largely accepting the existing social order, he visualized the victory of Christianity merely as a prolongation and crowning of the expansion of Judaism.[30]

Since Jesus' teachings were exclusively oriented toward the "kingdom of heaven" and, hence, essentially indifferent toward this world, they lent themselves to a conservative affirmation of existing realities as much as to their ascetic or revolutionary negation. Very soon Paul discovered wherein had consisted the chief obstacle to the expansion of Judaism. Even full-fledged Jews in his country must have felt the yoke of the law much more heavily than the Jews in Palestine. Those among them who were recent proselytes suffered from it in a still higher degree. It may be taken for granted that many of these Diaspora Jews, like the Galilean 'ame ha-areṣ, could not adhere strictly to the rigid law. Perhaps the poor among them, including slaves and hired workers, often had to disregard dietary laws, the laws of the Sabbath, and other regulations. Such religious transgressors were deeply troubled; their conscience told them that they were sinners.[31] Others belonging to the large class of *sebomenoi* wanted to become Jews, but did not see their way clear to accepting the whole burden of the law.

For all these, probably constituting a majority of the Jewish people in Asia Minor and neighboring countries, Paul found a formula. All of you are Jews, he told them, as long as you believe in the spiritual tenets of Judaism. For a time the ritual law in all its ramifications had been necessary. But with the advent of the messiah, "who had already come," it was nullified. Faith had now taken the place of the law. Surveying the whole history of the Jews, as a development toward this climactic achievement, Paul told his listeners in the synagogue of Antioch in Pisidia, and reiterated on all occasions,

Be it known unto you therefore, men and brethren, that through this man is preached unto you the forgiveness of sins: And by him all that believe are justified from all things, from which ye could not be justified by the law of Moses [Acts 13:38–39].

Using the terminology of Jeremiah and of Philo, he substituted the circumcision of the heart for the circumcision of the flesh. Here was the symbol of the new covenant between man and God. In one word, the law had been abolished, and with it its bearer, the Jewish national group. Israel in the flesh had been replaced by a more universal body of men, Israel in the spirit.

Needless to say, Paul was not always consistent. His was too emotional and creative a personality to allow for mechanical adherence to thoughts previously formulated. Even during the dozen years of his literary activity, E. B. Allo was able to discern four distinct stages of spiritual evolution. It is small wonder, then, that despite his emphatically antinomian teachings, Paul himself seems to have remained all his life a fairly observant Jew. Not only was the entire chronology of his journeys linked to such Jewish holidays as Passover and the Day of Atonement, but, in accordance with Jewish law, he circumcised Timotheus the son of a Jewess, although the father was a Gentile. Moreover, after returning from his preachment to the Gentiles and on his arrival in Jerusalem, Paul did not mind going through the public ceremony of purification, in order to prove, in the words of the local Judeo-Christian leaders, "that thou thyself also walkest orderly, and keepest the law." In the same Epistle to the Galatians in which he coined the famous phrase, "For I through the law am dead to the law, that I might live unto God," he also testified "to every man that is circumcised [a born Jew], that he is a debtor to do the whole law," merely adding that compliance with the law will avail nothing, unless it is combined with "faith which worketh by love." [32]

By this contrast between faith and law, however, Paul, perhaps unwittingly, laid the foundation for a final separation of Christianity from the Jewish people. This he did neither with a joyous heart nor by sudden decision. Like all great religious or social reformers, Paul was impatient to see his preachment realized. His violent temper intensified his anger over the stubborn refusal of the Jewish majority to accept his views. His missionary efforts were often met, as at Pisidian Antioch, by Jews who "spake against those things which were spoken by Paul, contradicting and blaspheming." On five different occasions he was given the prescribed thirty-nine lashes (II Cor. 11:24). No wonder that, frequently discouraged, he reiterated his wrathful exclamation of that moment, "It was necessary that the word of God should first be spoken to you: But seeing ye put it from you, and judge yourselves unworthy of everlasting life, lo, we turn to the Gentiles" (Acts 13:45–46).

Nevertheless, wherever he went he persisted in addressing the Jews first. "Paul tries over and over again to come to terms with the synagogue," says E. Dobschütz, somewhat irreverently, "until sooner or later each one throws him and all his adherents out, whereupon he opens a competitive establishment on his own premises." In Thessalonica (modern Salonica), for example, where he found a well-established Jewish community, he went, "as his manner was," to the synagogue on three successive sabbaths and reasoned with the Jews "out of the scriptures." In neighboring Beroea (modern Verria), which probably included a larger ratio of proselytes and "God-fearing," the congregation displayed a more receptive mood toward his interpretation, until messengers of Thessalonican Jewry "stirred up the people" (Acts 17:2, 11–13; cf. also the two inscriptions of later date analyzed by L. Robert in *REJ*, CI, 82 ff.).

Occasionally, as in Athens, Paul went into the market and disputed with any passer-by. Like other itinerant preachers he doubtless had little difficulty in finding debaters among the argumentative, often rhetorically trained, average citizens of a typical Greek city. But his only venture into philosophic debate with the higher intelligentsia, known as his speech on the Athenian Areopagus, ended in complete failure. So long as he endeavored to present to his sophisticated audience the usual apologetical arguments in philosophic garb, advanced some time before him by Philo and other Hellenistic-Jewish thinkers, he commanded their attention. But the moment he asserted that the redeemer, concerning whom God had "given assurance unto all men," had risen from the dead, his speech was drowned in laughter. He left Athens without being able to organize a Christian community. It stands to reason that once he had decided to take up the gauntlet against the Epicureans and Stoics, Paul made a special effort to approximate their jargon, while retaining the essential beliefs of his Hellenistic-Jewish environment and combining with them his new faith in Christ rearisen. The disastrous outcome of this debate made him turn his back on the formal dialectics of Greek philosophy and concentrate on the more popular homiletical answers to the then fairly universal quest for new religious truths. Among the masses, indeed, his speeches found more attentive listeners. Their deep yearning for salvation, long stimulated by Jewish propaganda, was heightened during the early years of his activity by a severe famine throughout the Mediterranean world (48–51). No wonder that, at the very outset, he found on his journeys nuclei of incipient Gentile Christian communities. Largely consisting of former semiproselytes in different stages of conversion to Judaism, these new Christians must have lent a particularly attentive ear to the comforting words of this "apostle to the Gentiles." [33]

In his general theological outlook, too, Paul still was in many ways a Jew for whom history was the foundation of religion. His interpretation of the past, so prominent in all his writings, is essentially Jewish, even when he turns the point against Jews and Judaism.

One may read in the Epistle to the Romans [says J. Pedersen] how agonizing it was for Paul to reject the claim of his people to its own history. He cannot get rid of his own conviction that the Jews, in so far as they become Christians, have after all a certain precedence in regard to their history.

The history of Israel, so brilliantly described in the Old Testament, furnished him and his successors their most effective means of propaganda. This fact was recognized as early as Tertullian, who harped on the theme of the "antiquity of that divine library" and asserted that Moses had lived "about a thousand years earlier than

the Trojan War, and consequently earlier than Saturn himself."
In Paul's theology, too, the process of revelation was, in its gradual
development toward the messiah, essentially a Jewish historical
motif, as was the belief in a future age after the second coming of
Christ.[34]

In many ways, however, Paul sacrificed history to nature. The external fact, that he so frequently used the word "nature" (*physis*)—
an abstract Greek conception which had found no place in the Old
Testament—may be merely a matter of form. But his way of using
it reveals a basic estrangement from Judaism, of which he seems
not to have been fully aware. For example, when he spoke of the
"vile affections" which were "against nature" (*para physin*) he was
still within the Jewish religious outlook. But when he emphasized
the value of "uncircumcision which is by nature" (*ek physeos*) he
talked to Graeco-Roman Gentiles in their language and not in that
of the Jew. His argument recalls the insistence of Antiochus, reported by the equally Hellenistic Jewish author of IV Maccabees,
that Eleazar eat swine's flesh, "for most excellent is the meat of this
animal which Nature has graciously bestowed upon us, and why
should you abominate it?" [35]

His non-Jewish approval of nature, however, led Paul to the
other extreme of opposing nature by overemphasizing the dualism
of God and the world, of spirit and flesh, with a sharpness surpassing anything to be found in the Judaism of his day. The idea that
the messiah had come already foreshadowed the conception of finality. The belief in the messiah's incarnation and preëxistence, indeed the entire "logos Christology" formulated in the Epistle to
the Colossians, removed the historical personality of the redeemer
still further into the realm of timelessness. Whether Paul's main
objective was to explain Jesus' "sonship," rather than corporeal
generation, or in order to show him as the eternal and preëxistent
instrument of divine revelation, the "Savior's" timelessness necessarily became an integral part of the Pauline theological doctrine.
Paul also began to formulate dogmas in Christianity to replace the
flow of tradition in Judaism. Again we note something final, as opposed to a process in time.[36]

Greek philosophy and Roman legalism thus furnished Paul not
only with external forms. Here, intrinsically, was a reaction of the
static against the dynamic. This attitude, already conspicuous in
Paul, was enlarged upon by such Gentile Hellenistic thinkers as
Clement and Origen.

FORMATION OF THE CHURCH

Palestinian Christianity resented deeply all these deviations from orthodox Judaism. Jewishness, even of the Galilean people of the land, was too deeply rooted for them to give up their allegiance to the chosen people. Peter himself gloried in the fact that the Jews "are the children of the prophets, and of the covenant which God made with our [other texts read: your] fathers, saying unto Abraham, And in Thy seed shall all the kindreds of the earth be blessed." The Palestinians for a long time regarded Paul as an apostate. Helped by the signal success of his mission abroad, however, and by the shortsighted intolerance of the secular authorities at home, he managed to silence a great deal of opposition.[37]

Paul also astutely captivated the benevolence of the Jerusalem leaders by recognizing the spiritual hegemony of the mother community. Arriving in Jerusalem in the famine year of 49, he not only submitted his missionary work among the Gentiles to the judgment of the "pillars" of the Jerusalem community, James, Cephas, and John, but also undertook at their behest to institute on his subsequent journeys regular collections for the poor of the Holy City. In this way, the resources of the Diaspora congregations were to be marshaled for the benefit of the mother church, just as Diaspora Jewry had long been accustomed to support financially the Temple and its affiliated institutions.[38]

For a while a compromise formula was adopted at the Council of Jerusalem, imposing upon Gentile converts the obligation to "abstain from the pollutions of idols, and from fornication, and from things strangled and from blood" (Acts 15:20)—all prohibitions closely resembling the six or seven commandments for the descendants of Noah in Jewish law. But with the increasing shift of the center of gravity from Palestine to the Diaspora, even these limitations had to be dropped. When Agrippa's persecution forced him out of the country, Peter unconsciously strengthened the anti-Jewish elements in the rising Church.

Somewhat later the fall of Jerusalem definitely decided the issue. The Palestinian Christians, in contrast to the Essenes, separated themselves from the rest of Jerusalem's population by emigrating to Pella, thus furnishing ample justification for the recurrent denunciations of their unpatriotic behavior. To be sure, the Christians were not the only ones to quote Deutero-Isaiah's disparagement of the Temple, "The heaven is My throne, and the earth is

My footstool: Where is the house that ye may build unto Me?" We know from Josephus that at the hour of greatest peril the leaders of the besieged Jews, though clinging to the hope that the Temple might yet be saved, argued "that the world was a better temple for God than this one." But when linked to the traditional messianic speculations about the final catastrophe of the Gog and Magog wars, the belief in the coming of the messiah actually presupposed the destruction of the Temple as part and symbol of the people's harrowing experience. There was a persistent tradition that Jesus himself had foretold,

There shall not be left one stone upon another, that shall not be thrown down. . . When ye shall see the abomination of the desolation, spoken of by Daniel the prophet, standing where it ought not, . . . then let them that be in Judaea flee to the mountains.

Facing his accusers Stephen tried to explain, but not to deny, his having said "that this Jesus of Nazareth shall destroy this place." Some of these traditions may have been sharpened into rationalizations of the Christian community's actual behavior during the great crisis of 66–70. Certainly the puzzling "sign," given by Jesus after he had cleansed the Temple of money-changers, "destroy this Temple, and in three days I will raise it up," reported only in the Gospel of John, seems to be such a rationalization after the event. But there is little doubt that ordinary patriotism simply did not fit into the pattern of thought of the apostles and their entire eschatologically aroused community, which expected the immediate second arrival of its redeemer.[39]

The destruction of the Temple transferred Christian leadership to the Hellenistic countries, especially Syria. The disappearance of the unifying center helped widen the breach between Judaism and Christianity. The Christians, moreover, saw in the Temple's destruction a visible realization of earlier announcements of God's ire at the people He had formerly chosen. The non-Jewish cult of the "Lord Christ" thus easily supplanted the purely eschatological Christianity of Palestine. Roman law officially recognized Christianity as a new religion, when Emperor Nerva exempted its adherents from any obligation toward the *fiscus judaicus*.

Paul's astonishing missionary successes among the Gentiles entirely depended on the twilight situation of all the Hellenistic Jewish masses, from Syria to Rome. It is characteristic that his extended journeys never led him to Babylonia nor to Egypt. His failure to cross the imperial frontiers to Parthia, despite his awareness of the multitudes of "Barbarians and Scythians" awaiting conversion, can be explained by the difficulties of such a journey and the tenuous cultural relations between the Greek-speaking western Jews and their Babylonian coreligionists who knew little Greek. But he could not have omitted Alexandria, intellectual and economic metropolis of the Western world at that time, except for important reasons.[40]

His epistles, too, were exclusively addressed to the peoples of Asia Minor, Greece, or Rome. This is true not only of those regarded by modern New Testament critics as authentic, but of almost every one ever ascribed to him. His denunciation of the Jewish people and its external symbol, the law, apparently had little effect in countries of strong national Jewish sentiment. As Paul turned his back on the Jews and traditional Judaism, his realism drove him to the Hellenistic Jews and Gentiles and, consequently, also the Hellenistic and Roman view of life.

No longer could he and his followers limit themselves to a negation, however. More and more the positive elements of the Graeco-Roman world began to replace what had been dropped of Judaism. Greek mystery religions began to furnish Christianity with ceremonies and rites to replace many Jewish observances. It is generally agreed today that, much as Christian ritual in its origins was influenced by Jewish ceremonies (even today any Christian reciting the Lord's Prayer unconsciously repeats in part an ancient paraphrase of the *Qaddish,* a Jewish-Aramaic prayer for mourners), the incursion of alien rites had started even before Paul. Bousset and others have effectively argued that this ritualistic transformation preceded the dogmatic, and that, in essence, the latter was merely a rationalization of the new cult. It was a curious irony of history, when the leaders in the denunciation of Jewish "legalism," from Paul down, were immediately compelled to adopt a new set of ceremonies. But what would an institutionalized religion be without some sort of ritual? Early Christian art also started to cast off the shackles of Jewish imageless worship. We can still trace this transformation in extant monuments; the development was from rejection to tolerance, then support, and finally exaltation of the artistic auxiliaries of worship. This Hellenization of Christian art seems likewise to have preceded the conscious affirmations in literature. While in all these areas early Christianity could build upon solid foundations established by Hellenistic Jewry, Paul went much further than any of his Jewish predecessors in incorporating Graeco-Roman ideas into his theological system. We have also seen how the state of

Rome, banished from sight by the founder, came back with renewed vigor in the system of the disciple.[41]

Clearly, not all departures from Judaism to Hellenism ought to be attributed to Paul. Throughout his active life this apostle to the Gentiles had to struggle against extremists in the Hellenistic camp, as well as against the Judeo-Christian movement. There is even some merit in K. Holl's remark that "Paul had not surrendered Christianity to Hellenism, but rather salvaged it from being completely submerged in Hellenistic culture." He frequently interfered in local affairs of the nascent Christian communities not only to extirpate moral turpitude, but also to combat such "heresies" as those of the *pneumatikoi* (spiritualists). He did not hesitate to apply the extreme penalty which, in the absence of Jewish capital jurisdiction, could be secured only through lynching or assassination. What he meant by delivering "unto Satan" Hymmenaeus and Alexander, "that they may learn not to blaspheme," that is, not to preach their erroneous Greek rather than Jewish doctrine of resurrection, is explained by his reprimand of the Corinthian community for having tolerated in its midst a man who had sinned with his father's wife. Paul ordered it "to deliver such an one unto Satan for the destruction of the flesh, that the spirit may be saved in the day of the Lord Jesus"—a rationale which was to play such a pernicious role at the hands of medieval heresy hunters.[42]

Nevertheless, it was Paul's overpowering personality which, aided by his steering a course between the two extremes, determined the gradual estrangement between the young Church and its mother religion. Paul's epistles, assembled in various local collections by more or less faithful disciples and amplified by many others wrongly attributed to him, soon began to circulate throughout the Christian world. Some of the spurious epistles were written by Christians of Jewish origin and bore the imprint of Hellenistic Jewish teachings even more strongly than the genuine ones. The significant Epistle to the Hebrews, for example, apparently composed by a Hellenistic Jew before the fall of Jerusalem (one passage seems to refer to a still existent Temple), is deeply indebted to Philo in both verbiage and ideas. But other letters were written by Gentile Christians with an increasing anti-Jewish bias. Even Paul's genuine epistles, moreover, written by an impulsive genius over a period of a dozen years to meet ever new challenges, were far from consistent. But for this very reason they could the more readily be misinterpreted by his successors to fit their own needs and outlook, which was increasingly nurtured on Graeco-Roman rather than Jewish conceptions. Genuine or spurious, Paul's epistles soon became a major "literary influence," reaching out to most distant communities and helping cement their unity. They thus left an indelible imprint on the thinking of all subsequent generations.[43]

In short, with Paul, the Christian Church begins. As a church, an organized movement, it had to accommodate itself to life. At the very beginning of his career Paul may have been coresponsible for the name Christians. Despite its Latin form, it appears, the designation was not imposed upon the disciples by the Romans, but was a self-selected name to connote the fellowship of men who had sworn allegiance to Christ. Luke, who reports that "the disciples were called Christians first in Antioch," not by mere coincidence stresses the presence there of Saul of Tarsus who, together with Barnabas, spent "a whole year" teaching and meeting with the other disciples. It certainly would have been in keeping with the great organizer's general outlook to choose a name which conveyed the idea of a spiritual and communal body united in the worship of Lord Christ. To the Roman authorities, however, it increasingly appeared as a secret conspiracy bent upon ultimate world conquest.[44]

By removing circumcision and the other Jewish legal impediments, Paul opened the road to the expansion of Christianity which, in its triumphant progression, combined the old expansionist forces of both Judaism and Rome. The idea of the Roman Empire was thus first inculcated in Christianity. From Paul to later Roman Catholicism was only a step, and a necessary one. For centuries to come the Roman Empire persecuted Christians more vigorously than it did Jews. It was fighting here against a force which opposed it on its own grounds. Jewish propaganda, with its limitations of Jewish law and its insistence on ethnic assimilation, could not compare as a challenge with the unrestricted mission of the Church, that potential state-church and church-state. Even in surrendering, the Roman state finally succeeded in smuggling itself, so to speak, into the Christian system, and recapturing its former position under a new guise. In fact, viewed from the standpoint of Roman history, the gradual unfolding of Roman religion appears as the result of a fusion of the various gods which prehistoric times and the migrations of peoples had established in Italy, of Etruscan and Greek gods, and finally of oriental gods and cults which joined the procession. But invariably "it is the city which impresses upon religion its quasi-juridical and administrative form and eventually lends to the Church, too, its basically political character." In more than one sense, Roman Catholicism thus became the heir of imperial Rome.[45]

TRIUMPH OF DISRUPTIVE FORCES

The rise of Christianity and its separation from Judaism, as well as the destruction of the Second Temple which greatly facilitated it, checked the great expansion of the Jewish people. One of the most remarkable movements of all time thus came to an abrupt end. Precisely when Judaism seemed to be nearing the goal of its history—the reconciliation of its national and universalist ideologies, through a process of inner and outer growth as an ethnoreligious unity beyond the boundaries of state and territory—it suffered a sudden reverse.

Sudden, and yet inherent in the situation. When the Jewish people emerged as a major force in a changed world, after three centuries of quiet preparation through inner concentration, this world reacted not so much through violent opposition as by the sheer force of persistence. Within the enormous body of Jews there arose, under these extraneous influences, so many currents, sometimes assuming the pronounced form of sectarian movements but generally drifting imperceptibly within the main stream, that the break-up was really but a question of time. With keen insight the rabbis later distinctly recognized these reasons for the breakdown. R. Johanan ben Toreta thus expounded his philosophy of history:

Why was Shiloh destroyed? On account of the desecration of the sacrifices which was rampant there. As for the First Temple of Jerusalem; why was it destroyed? On account of idolatry, incest and bloodshed prevailing there. But as to [the Jews of] the Second Temple: we know that they were laboriously studying the Torah and rigidly observing the tithes; why then were they exiled? Because they loved *mammon* and hated one another [T. Menaḥot XIII, 22, 533 f.; cf. b. Yoma 9].

As long as Palestine was a Jewish country, as long as a large part of the people, whether a mere third or even less, lived its own protected life, the centripetal cohesiveness proved stronger. But when new developments in the outside world, superimposed upon these internal difficulties, brought Palestinian Jewry into an irremediable conflict with the world power of Rome, the disruptive forces were bound to prevail. The ensuing loss of the necessary minimum natural base, combined with the resuscitated natural forces operating under cover in the life of the people itself, struck the Jews at a moment when the climax of their achievement appeared close at hand. History was still winning a great victory over nature, but not in such a manner as to appear to the main body of Jewry to be realizing the deep yearning of centuries.

BREAKDOWN AND
RECONSTRUCTION

W HEN the final hour struck, Jews found themselves fighting
Romans with military weapons, in a sphere where they
themselves were weakest and their opponents at the height
of their skill and training. No matter how many victories they had
won in the battle of words and the clash of ideas, they were now
confronted by the whole military might of Rome, made doubly
impregnable by its long tradition of invincibility. Moreover, while
Rome's power, in itself overwhelming by all rational calculations,
was further enhanced by her rulers' singleness of purpose, Jewry
was deeply divided with respect to the very need and aims of the
mortal struggle. There was hardly any Roman in a position of trust
and responsibility who did not agree with the imperial administration that the "rebellion" in Judaea must be crushed swiftly and
ruthlessly. The Jews, internally divided on almost every political,
social, or religious issue, could not fully utilize even their very
limited resources.

In regard to Roman rule itself there was a basic cleavage between
the outlook and interests of the Hellenistic Diaspora and those of
Palestinian Jewry. This was the Jewish counterpart to the aforementioned basic dichotomy between the Roman policies in Judaea
and those in other provinces. The growth of Egyptian and Syrian
antisemitism and the ensuing struggle for civil and economic rights
made the Jews in these and adjacent countries Rome's natural allies. We recall how interlocked anti-Jewish and anti-Roman trends
had become in Egypt during the agitation of the "heathen martyrs." From the days of Julius Caesar and Marcus Agrippa, Roman
privileges often served as the main rampart against which wave
after wave of local Jew-baiting came to grief. The opposite was true
in Palestine, where the Roman policies operated in reverse and
consistently favored the Greek minority against the Jewish majority. This was, indeed, but the application of the same old maxim
of dividing and thus the more effectively dominating the subject
populations. For this and other reasons we find, as H. Dessau rightly

remarked, that "after a century of uninterrupted reign of the Caesars, no region of the vast Roman Empire had become so little reconciled with Roman rule, as was Judaea."

Only the non-Roman Diaspora could, therefore, wholeheartedly side with the Palestinian "rebels." According to Josephus, the revolutionary party indeed "hoped that all their fellow-countrymen beyond the Euphrates would join with them in revolt" (*War* I, 1, 2.5). Of course, not being masters of their own political destinies, Parthian Jews (apart from a few volunteers) could join the struggle only on orders from their king, which were not forthcoming. In Palestine itself, we shall see, the Herodian and Sadducean parties were either pro-Roman or too deeply concerned about the preservation of the existing social order to view with equanimity the unleashing of unpredictable revolutionary forces. The Pharisaic leadership, too, apart from being far more deeply preoccupied with religious and social, than with political, problems was undoubtedly conscious of the interests of world Jewry which, it knew, would be seriously jeopardized by a Judeo-Roman war.

With divided counsel and half a heart the Jewish people thus entered the decisive military phase of its long-simmering conflict with Rome. The most spectacular event in this dramatic sequence was the war of 66–70 (73), with its somber finale: the destruction of the Temple in Jerusalem. This was, however, the beginning, rather than the end, of a long-enduring conflict, and its effects far transcended the sheer loss of a central sanctuary.

THE GREAT WAR

It must not be supposed that the revolt was incited only by religious fanaticism. In its main effort to win freedom, it did not entirely ignore political realities. Superficially, the forces engaged would seem so unequal that little Palestine must be foredoomed. The fact is, however, that the fanatical leaders of the revolt could invoke certain factors favorable to their cause. The great conglomeration of Jews throughout the eastern Mediterranean constituted a power which, if properly marshaled, could perhaps venture to defy the most formidable military nation of history. Even such enemies as Tacitus admitted that the Jews were, as a rule, "healthy and capable of hard work." They had been much sought after as soldiers for centuries. Neither the exemptions from military service granted them out of deference to the Sabbath (such as are recorded in Asia Minor in 49–48 and 43 B.C.E. at a time when the Roman partisan armies were in dire need of recruits), nor the frequent employment of foreign mercenaries by the Herodian kings as more reliable in the suppression of domestic disturbances, sufficed to extinguish the warlike spirit among the Jewish youth. Did not Herod himself engage Babylonian Jewish soldiers, previously enlisted by the Roman governor of Syria, C. Sentius Saturninus? Now with the growing religious fanaticism accompanying the wars with the Romans, the greater zeal and devotion of the Jewish warriors partly made up for the shortcomings of their military training and equipment.[1]

To be sure, the best accoutred Jewish soldiers were in the employ of Agrippa II who, styling himself Marcus Julius Agrippa, ruled over a predominantly pagan kingdom and was an outright Roman collaborationist. He whom the outbreak of the revolt found in Alexandria congratulating the renegade Jew, Tiberius Alexander, on his appointment to the prefecture of Egypt now overtly coöperated with the same official serving as Titus' chief of staff. Among Agrippa's soldiers were many pro-Roman Jews, including the descendants of those Babylonians who had been settled in Palestine by his great-grandfather. The pagan contingents from Sebaste and Caesarea had long evinced such blood-thirsty hatred of Jews that Claudius had seriously thought of transferring them to Pontus. They welcomed the opportunity of lawfully shedding Jewish blood. Nor was guerrilla warfare now as effective as it had been in the Maccabean uprising, because of the greater population density, the strategic importance of larger cities, and the excellent new Roman roads. Only in the sparsely populated southern districts of the Negev could old-type raiders still inflict great damage on the enemy and escape. Hence the survival of such foci of resistance as Masada for three years after the fall of Jerusalem.[2]

Nevertheless, the devotion and ability of the leaders and the self-sacrificing fanaticism of their followers made the first conflict an intermittent seven years' war. It has been suggested that in 68 C.E. the Palestinian Jews, in secret understanding with Egyptian Jewish grain merchants and shippers, decided in Jaffa "on a move such as, since the Punic wars, no enemy of Rome had dared to imagine against her. Their plan aimed at nothing less than a food blockade of the city of Rome herself." This plan was, of course, foolhardy, and Jaffa's second destruction sealed its doom. Yet Vespasian, one of Rome's ablest generals, disposing of a considerable army and using the most advanced methods of warfare, required weeks and months to reduce each fortified town. Modern scholars, struck by the great disparity of forces and forgetful of Rome's numerous commitments on other fronts, have sometimes tried to explain Vespasian's long campaign by the fact that in the troubled days after Nero's death he felt safer in Palestine than as a victorious general in Rome. That this was not the principal cause, however, is evident not only by comparison with the equally arduous campaign against Bar Kocheba at a time when Palestinian Jewry had been greatly weakened by the preceding defeat, but also by the importance which the Flavian emperors themselves attached to their victory. Vespasian, Titus, and even Domitian (as late as 85 c.e.) successively issued coins with the legend of *Judaea Capta* or *Devicta*. If the former two refused to assume the honorific title *Judaicus*, similar to *Africanus* or *Germanicus* assumed by other victorious generals, this was clearly the result of the unique situation of the Jewish people in which the name *Judaicus* could refer equally to the citizen of Judaea and the professing Jew in the dispersion. Certainly neither Vespasian nor Titus wished even remotely to indicate their sympathies for the Jewish faith. Titus had been taunted frequently enough, especially by the Alexandrian Jew-baiters, for his love affair with the Jewish princess Berenice, whom apparently for this reason he was unable to marry.[3]

In any case, for the siege of Jerusalem alone, Titus had at his disposal four Roman legions, a tremendous force, indeed, when one recalls that not long before this three legions had sufficed for the speedy conquest of the whole of Armenia. Titus' legions were reinforced, moreover, by parts of two other legions, twenty cohorts of allied infantry and eight squadrons of cavalry, as well as "a strong contingent of Arabs who hated the Jews with all that hatred that is common among neighbors." Tacitus, from whom these facts are quoted, described the Judaean campaign as a major event in Rome's military history, thus paying unwitting homage to the despised Jews. Josephus feared no public ridicule when, in a book addressed to the Graeco-Roman public, he ventured to speak of "the greatest [war] not only of the wars of our own time, but, so far as accounts have reached us, well nigh of all that ever broke out between cities or nations." [4]

The fierce rage of the Roman soldiers against the inhabitants of Jerusalem when the city finally fell is likewise understandable in view of the unexpectedly protracted defense. Apparently in the decisive moment Titus lost control over the soldiery. Even in antiquity it was a moot question as to who was responsible for the destruction of the Temple. The two historians who might supply the most exact information are not unprejudiced. Josephus, the Jewish friend of the Flavian dynasty, describes at great length the war council of the seven Roman generals, headed by Titus, in which the majority, including Titus and his chief lieutenant the Jewish apostate Tiberius Alexander, voted to spare the Temple. When later, the soldiers, after storming the sanctuary, set it on fire against his orders, Titus himself tried to stop the conflagration. On the other hand, Marcus Antonius Julianus, one of the members of the council who voted for the destruction, apparently reported that Titus had shared his opinion. We must bear in mind, however, that while Josephus' work appeared in Titus' lifetime and doubtless with his approval, Julianus seems to have prepared his memoirs after the emperor's death.[5]

Nevertheless, the Jewish people, instinctively, put the blame upon Titus, feeling that a complete Roman victory required the removal of the central Jewish sanctuary. A few years later Vespasian felt impelled to close even the comparatively unimportant Temple of Onias. Subsequent generations of Jews knew Titus only as the "wicked one." Jewish legend described with relish his unnatural death through a mythical insect which gradually bored into his brain, in accordance with the then widespread belief that such was the punishment meted out to all sanctuary desecrators.[6]

REVOLTS UNDER TRAJAN AND HADRIAN

Even in adjacent countries, the Jewish masses under able leadership seemed to have subdued both natives and Romans with comparative ease. The few available sources do not supply satisfactory answers to the intriguing question as to what type of Jewish soldiers fought in the Hellenistic Diaspora, particularly in Egypt. It made, of course, a great deal of difference whether they had been trained in special Jewish detachments or merely fought as individual members of ethnically and religiously mixed military contingents. We recall the role played by Jewish generals in the late Ptolemaic kingdom. The literary records, particularly Josephus, referring to these commanders, also indicate the presence of separate Jewish units in the second and first pre-Christian centuries. On the other hand, earlier data supplied by Greek papyri reveal the names of numerous Jewish soldiers, but all of them appear dispersed among various non-Jewish ethnic units. Tcherikover's slightly romantic explanation (*Ha-Yehudim be-Miṣrayim*, pp. 44 ff.) that this transition occurred about 150 B.C.E., coincident with the new reputation acquired by Jewish combatants in the Maccabean armies, is controverted by the fact that the first known commander of a large Jewish detachment and founder of the important military colony in the district of Leontopolis was Onias, a Palestinian refugee at the very beginning of the Maccabean revolt.

A better explanation of this contrast between Josephus and the papyri, if it should be confirmed by further discoveries, may perhaps be found in Egypt's loss of control over Palestine after 200. Theretofore the government could freely levy soldiers from among its Jewish subjects in Palestine, as well as in Egypt, and place them in mixed units, only occasionally mentioning their ethnic-religious allegiance. But when Palestine became a Syrian province or an independent principality, its soldiers began forming separate contingents of mercenaries on a par with the Thessalians, Macedonians, and other foreigners. Possibly some Egyptian Jews, too, now preferred to join these "foreign" detachments of coreligionists, rather than be scattered among their Egyptian compatriots of other ethnic and religious origins. After the reunification of Egypt and Palestine under Roman suzerainty these Jewish contingents disappeared again, while the new hostility of most Egyptians (Josephus speaks of "their long-standing hatred of us"; *Ag. Ap.* II, 6.70) seems effectively to have kept out Jews even from mixed detachments. Hence the paucity of references to Jewish soldiers in Roman Egypt. It is doubly astonishing, therefore, that after a century and a half of Roman rule Egyptian Jewry had preserved so remarkable a fighting spirit and ability.

Apart from relatively minor skirmishes in the aftermath of the Great War, the rebellion under Trajan, less than half a century after the destruction of Jerusalem (115–17), proved that the Jewries of Egypt, Cyrenaica, and Cyprus were for a time vigorous enough to dominate large parts of these countries. It appears that the struggle here was directed principally against the "Greek fellow citizens" (Eusebius) rather than against the Romans, although a Milan papyrus mentions in retrospect the "battle of the Romans against the Jews." As in the few disturbances stirred up by some Zealot refugees from the Great War in Alexandria and Cyrene, the local Jews seemed eager to settle old scores with their ancient local enemies, rather than with their erstwhile Roman protectors. In fact, not long before this, Trajan had been blamed by one of the Alexandrian "martyrs" for allowing his council to be dominated by Jews and exhorted "to turn round and help your own people, and not defend the godless Jews." The Roman governor of Alexandria in 115, Marcus Rutilius Lupus, so early and effectively suppressed the Jewish uprising in the city that it could thenceforth serve as a haven of refuge for multitudes of pagan provincials vanquished by their Jewish neighbors. But with equal sternness he also arrested the counterexcesses staged by the Alexandrians against the Jews. Outside the Egyptian capital the Jews were long victorious. A Bremen papyrus, for example, records the total defeat of a detachment of Egyptian peasants, probably in the district of Hermopolis. An Oxyrhynchus writer of about 200 C.E., on the other hand, mentions a local victory against the Jews which, in his day, was still celebrated in an annual festival. In Cyrenaica and Cyprus the Jews evidently succeeded in conquering and devastating the respective capitals of Cyrene and Salamis, before the Romans intervened. Only as an afterthought, it appears, their leaders, particularly their Cyrenian King (Messiah) Lukuas-Andreas, turned against the Romans. From the outset, however, the messianic background of the uprising had grave anti-Roman implications and, after becoming overt enemies, Lukuas and his partisans seem to have invaded Palestine, seeking to liberate it from Roman domination. They were soon joined by the Jews of Mesopotamia, immediately behind Trajan's armies, which had penetrated to the Parthian capital of Ctesiphon.[7]

This far-flung uprising, which in Egypt and Cyrenaica alone required on the Roman side "many battles for a considerable time" under an outstanding commander, Marcius Turbo, showed that Roman domination of the eastern Mediterranean could possibly be shaken. There certainly was a mighty army outside the Roman frontiers which could be counted upon as an ally. Even in its decline the Parthian Empire was a force which the western power was never entirely able to subdue. Once in 40 B.C.E., Parthian armies actually reached Palestine. During the Great War, to be sure, the Parthians had shortsightedly adhered to their treaty with Rome concluded two years before, and their king congratulated Titus on his victory. But the prevention of Rome's complete "pacification" of all her eastern provinces seemed to hold the only rational safeguard for the containment of Rome's ambitions within the frontiers of the Augustan Empire. Even after the days of Bar Kocheba,

Rabbi Simon ben Yoḥai, a radical opponent of Roman rule, hyperbolically expressed this hope, "When you see a Persian [Parthian] horse tied at the graveyards of Palestine watch for the approaching steps of the Messiah." [8]

Like so many of Rome's opponents, however, the Jewish people suffered from lack of coördination. When the Great War broke out in Palestine in 66, neither Parthia nor Diaspora Jewry was ready. The few upheavals launched by the Palestinian refugees in Egypt and Cyrenaica occurred when the rebellion in Palestine had been almost totally suppressed. Later, when Trajan's armies were engaged in a prolonged and difficult campaign against the Parthians, Diaspora Jewry's strong military action from Cyrenaica to Cyprus could have nullified Trajan's whole ambitious enterprise by severing the Asiatic army's lifeline to Italy. At that moment, however, Asia Minor, Syria, and Palestine, with the largest share of Jewish manpower, remained quiescent. The Jews of Palestine had not recovered sufficiently from the wounds of the Great War; and the small revolt (if it can be called a revolt), led by the two brothers Julianus and Pappus distracted the Roman garrison only temporarily. Incidentally, Julianus himself was an Alexandrian, not a Palestinian Jew.[9]

Nevertheless these two Jewish uprisings had some lasting effects on world history. The outbreak of the War, in 66, came at a crucial moment when Nero was working out grandiose plans for world conquest. These had to be postponed until after the suppression of the Jewish "rebellion." In view of the emperor's death and the subsequent period of anarchy until the ascension of Vespasian, they were delayed again until the days of Trajan. When this emperor, after preliminary victories in other parts, finally turned on Parthia, the hereditary enemy, hoping to administer it a mortal blow and at the same time to secure the economically ever more important trade routes to India and the Far East, the Jewish revolt threatened to cut off his armies from their main Italian base. So important was this logistic aspect that, apart from assigning to his outstanding general, Lusius Quietus, the task of subduing Mesopotamian Jewry, Trajan chose Turbo, a naval commander rather than a field officer, for the pacification of the disturbed Mediterranean regions. The difficult struggle for the control over the island of Cyprus showed that he was right. We can understand, therefore, the anger of the Romans who thus saw themselves despoiled of the fruits of their great victory. In Cyprus, for example, they not only wreaked bloody vengeance on the Jewish rebels, justifying it by the usual crop of rumors of preceding Jewish atrocities (uncritically repeated by later chroniclers), but also in a wholly unprecedented fashion permanently excluded Jews from ever again settling on the island. In fact, even a Jew found on a Cypriot shore after a shipwreck was liable to immediate execution.[10]

Such violent repression naturally engendered further bitterness. Hadrian, who succeeded Trajan in 118, had played a prominent role in the eastern campaign and had the opportunity of observing from close range both the weaknesses of the Roman position and the unbroken defiance of the Jewish people. He decided, therefore, to give up the newly conquered provinces, to conclude peace with the Parthians and to devote himself to the consolidation of the vast imperial possessions held before Trajan's eastern expedition. He also sought to pacify the Jewish masses by holding out some vague promises of rebuilding their Holy City and, perhaps, even reconstructing their Temple. He may also have wished to show to Palestinian Jewry that its relatively passive behavior during the latest disturbances was appreciated by the government.

Before long it became apparent, however, that appeasement of Jews was not reconcilable with his main program. Deeply imbued as he was ever since his student days in Athens with the ideals of Greek culture, he increasingly conceived his task of consolidation in terms of achieving greater cultural homogeneity among the peoples of his far-flung empire. Like other metropolitan centers, the new Jerusalem, which he was going to rebuild, was to become a "Greek" city. As such it would help batter down the stubborn Jewish resistance to the adoption of the prevailing mores of the Graeco-Roman world. Ultimately, he sharply alienated the Jews by his outlawry of circumcision. Very likely he did not realize at the time the gravity of this measure, which, in his opinion, was merely suppressing another "barbarian" obstacle to cultural uniformity and mutual amalgamation. His placing of circumcision on a par with castration merely underscored the emperor's general impatience with the perpetuation of unfamiliar customs.

By that time Palestinian Jewry had recuperated sufficiently to organize a new grand rebellion under the leadership of Simon Bar Kocheba (132–35). Egyptian Jewry, however, had been totally disabled by the disastrous outcome of the previous encounter. For a few decades after 117, Egyptian Jewish names disappear even from the extant rolls of taxpayers. Half a century later, under Marcus

Aurelius, the formerly populous Jewish quarter of Edfu seems to have had but one Jewish family of Achillas Rufus, whose three sons bore purely Egyptian names.[11]

Bar Kocheba and his Palestinian followers fought on alone and for three and a half years held out against "the best generals sent by Hadrian." Dio Cassius, from whom this phrase is borrowed, realized the danger that this uprising might have extended over the whole Mediterranean world. Hadrian himself hastened to the scene of battle and spent about a year and a half in Gerasa. He entrusted the actual conduct of the campaign to his outstanding general, Sextus Julius Severus, whom he summoned from Britain. Severus had at his disposal the Tenth Legion and elements of nine other legions, some 35,000 men in all, with auxiliary troops probably double that number. Confronted by these mighty forces, the Jews derived comfort from the memory of the ultimate Maccabean victory against equally overwhelming odds. Bar Kocheba generally looked back to the Maccabean example and struck coins with the legend, "Simon, Prince [nasi] of Israel," reminiscent of Simon, the Hasmonean. Other coins bore such propagandistic watchwords as the year of "the Redemption of Zion," or "the Freedom of Israel." By thus proclaiming his intention to emulate the Maccabean warriors and renew the glory of the Temple, he must have strongly appealed to both Palestinian and Diaspora Jewry. Through the latter he may also have hoped to enlist some outside assistance, particularly from Parthia. Other coins, bearing the legend Eleazar ha-Kohen (the Priest) evidently referred to the priestly head (R. Eleazar of Modein, or ben Azariah?) of the revolt, of which R. 'Aqiba was the intellectual and Bar Kocheba the military and political leader.[12]

INTERNAL DISCORDS

Such division of the three powers formerly united in the hands of the Maccabean commanders underscored the internal differences between the two liberation movements. The world situation was even more different from what it had been in 165 B.C.E. Unlike the Seleucidae, who were kept busy by sharp domestic conflicts, had strong enemies among their numerous neighbors, and faced the rising power of Rome which had already forced Antiochus IV himself out of Egypt, the Roman emperors were now at the pinnacle of their military and political grandeur. Internally rather pacified, confronted by no really expansive enemy on its frontiers, their empire and its constant military growth appeared to them, as it did to most Romans, as the "manifest destiny" of their people. In this sense, their conflicts with the Jews assumed some of the characteristics of religious wars, even if the issues involved appeared to be purely secular.[13]

On the ordinary military level, however, such an empire could not possibly have been overthrown by the Jews alone, even if all of them had acted in unison. As it was, the very large Syrian-Jewish population seems to have kept aloof during all three uprisings. The general effeminacy of Syrian life as well as the successful propaganda of the rising Christian Church, now increasingly centered in Antioch, were doubtless responsible.

Perhaps even more disastrous were the inner dissensions in the rebellious regions themselves. During the Great War not only Palestine's Greek municipalities but even such preponderantly Jewish cities as Sepphoris and Tiberias actively opposed the revolutionary armies. Not even in Judaea did unanimity prevail. The small group of early Christians left Jerusalem at the outset, went across the Jordan to Pella and declared in favor of neutrality. The really influential leaders of the people, whether Sadducees or Pharisees, were sharply opposed to a war with Rome. The Sadducees, weakened and corrupted by a century of foreign domination, abandoned their own age-old affirmation of an independent Jewish state. Reduced to a small group of leaders without a following, they were too realistic to overlook the disparity of forces. Warnings of the futility of resistance against the tremendous power of Rome, such as were assembled by Josephus in the imaginary harangue of King Agrippa II, found a ready response in their hearts. "Are you wealthier than the Gauls," the king allegedly asked, "stronger than the Germans, more intelligent than the Greeks, more numerous than all the peoples of the world?" (*War* II, 16, 4.364). This and other such questions no doubt passed from mouth to mouth among these wise and cautious aristocrats.

From its inception, moreover, the uprising carried revolutionary implications. While at the Temple the priests were still debating the cessation of the daily sacrifices for the emperor, according to Josephus the main signal for the revolt, the infuriated mob burned the archives of Jerusalem which, containing records of indebtedness, had become in the public eye symbols of economic exploitation (*War* II, 17, 2.409 f., 427 ff.). The uprising having thus started as a civil war, its prospective victims understandably enough refused to make common cause with their assailants.

The nonpolitical Pharisees had, by virtue of their whole ideology and past experience, equally good reasons to oppose an armed conflict. They had taken an active part in the revolt against Antiochus, because then the very basis of their ethnic-religious life was impaired. They had been prepared to stand up as one man against Caligula's idolatrous impositions. Again, when Hadrian's legislation touched a vital nerve of that organism, R. 'Aqiba and others (though not all of the rabbis) became leaders of the rebellion. They considered this struggle a *milhemet misvah* (war in behalf of a commandment) and, as such, the sacred duty of each individual and the whole nation. Many of them died the death of martyrs. 'Aqiba, who had unhesitatingly proclaimed Bar Kocheba as the long-expected messiah, was apparently kept in prison for several years before his execution and burial in Caesarea. We are told that the Roman executioner himself was so deeply impressed by the steadfastness of R. Hanina ben Teradyon that he suffered death together with his victim—incidentally, a common motif in the early Christian martyrologies. There were, however, many other Pharisaic leaders who even then objected to armed rebellion. R. Hanina's friend, R. Jose ben Qisma, doubtless was not alone in arguing that, even on religious grounds, one should not overtly defy the government.

Brother Hanina [R. Jose once asked his friend] don't you know that that nation [the Romans] has been given dominion from Heaven? It has destroyed the Lord's house and burned His sanctuary, slain His pious worshipers and exterminated the best among His children, and yet it still exists.

Nor was R. Jose satisfied with R. Hanina's unquestioned reliance upon God's will. "I talk to you reason," he insisted, "and you answer me, 'Heaven will have mercy.' " [14]

No such outright religious martyrdom beckoned to victims of either the Great War or the revolt against Trajan. Under the latter emperor, as under Nero and Vespasian, the Roman oppression was purely political and fiscal. It was not even directed against the Palestinian people as a political entity. The administration merely exploited it, as it did all other subjects, for the benefit of the empire and its ruling caste. To oppose such a political force by another, a rebel army, would, the Pharisees felt, transfer the battle to the domain of statehood and armed forces in which the Romans were so much superior. Under the pressure of patriotic zealots, Rabban Johanan ben Zakkai and other Pharisaic leaders joined half-heartedly for a time a campaign which, even if successful, would have involved sanctioning a principle inimical to their own. Furthermore, whatever they thought of the other arguments allegedly marshaled by Agrippa, the Pharisees doubtless felt keenly the inherent dangers to their coreligionists of the whole Roman dispersion. "All these, if you go to war," the king had reputedly warned, "will be butchered by your adversaries, and through the folly of a handful of men every city will be drenched with Jewish blood" (*War* II, 16, 4.399).

Most significantly, the Zealots themselves, nourished by Pharisaic ideas, refrained from selecting the only course which might have brought success: an offensive against Rome on the whole Asiatic front. After the initial advances against the Roman garrison, they did not pursue the enemy into Syria. Here and in the adjacent countries they might have attracted as allies all the discontented peoples and classes, and set on fire the whole structure of Roman rule in the East. They remained in Palestine, fortifying a few towns and awaiting the arrival of stronger Roman forces to whom they offered heroic resistance. Their few emissaries who reached Alexandria or Cyrene seem to have incited their coreligionists (against the calmer counsels of their local leaders) to settle their old feuds with the Gentile world at large, rather than to make common cause with the oppressed native masses. Bar Kocheba, too, evidently failed to make use of those "outside nations" who, according to Dio Cassius, were ready to join him. Although "the whole earth was being stirred up," he limited his efforts to the conquest of Jerusalem and the reëstablishment of Jewish control over the province of Judaea proper. There seem to have been but minor outbreaks in other parts of the country, which were easily crushed by the Romans within two months (May–July 133). Only a frenzied messianic belief in a forthcoming supernatural intervention may explain this utter disregard of *Realpolitik*.[15]

Even the Zealots thus seem to have felt that not through arms alone would Rome be vanquished, and to have looked forward to some sudden miracle to help them defend the Holy Land. From Judas the Galilean to Bar Kocheba and beyond, courses an unbroken line of revolutionary leaders in whose entire make-up direct revolutionary action was indistinguishably blended with messianic utopianism. It was the tragedy of the Jewish people that, at a most decisive moment, it had to stop its ethnic-religious expansion to take up secular arms in defense of an eminently secular political principle, from which it had long been estranged, and in opposition to the very embodiment of that principle, the Roman Empire.

POLITICAL REVERSES

In each of these wars hundreds of thousands of Jews were killed. In addition to the numerous legends concerning the bloodshed during the Great War, we have the definite statement of Josephus that 1,197,000 of Jerusalem's inhabitants were either killed or captured by Titus. This number is not greatly reduced by the fairly cautious historian Tacitus, who, writing a few decades later, gives an estimate of 600,000 Jewish fatalities alone. The Bar Kocheba war cost Palestinian Jewry, according to Dio Cassius, 580,000 killed in action, in addition to countless others who died of hunger, disease, or fire. All these figures are doubtless highly exaggerated, but they give us an idea of the tremendous impression made on contemporaries by the staggering Jewish losses. "All of Judaea," adds Dio, "became almost a desert." [16] The ravages of the war against Trajan cannot be statistically computed, but the great Egyptian Jewish center never recovered from the shock, while the community of Cyprus was completely wiped out. The sum total of the casualties and victims of malnutrition and disease in the seven decades from 66 to 135 must have been enormous. We may also take it for granted that at least some Jewish captives, sold into slavery, were likewise lost to the Jewish people. Certainly many of the children who were carried off were brought up as Gentiles in a non-Jewish environment.

Apart from such losses, the Jewish people also suffered considerable political reverses. Palestine, the core of the whole Jewish settlement, was now politically paralyzed. Instead of lending moral and political support to Diaspora Jewry, it became economically a liability and politically a handicap. No longer was it considered by the Romans as an allied country, upon whose help they could count against the peoples of western Asia. The Palestinians had proved to be the most recalcitrant of all. Although the Romans were statesmanlike enough not to let their anger over the rebellion mislead them into immediate repressive measures against Diaspora Jewry, such events necessarily increased the reciprocal ill feeling. The revolts in the Diaspora added to the animosity.

General developments in the empire were also unfavorable to the Jews. Until about the middle of the first century the Jews in Palestine and abroad could be regarded by the Roman rulers as a welcome element in the population, although many Roman officials sided with the local Gentiles against the Jews. Scattered in great numbers in settlements the majority of whose population was more or less unfriendly to Rome, they were a cement helping to maintain the structure of empire, especially since they were totally uninterested in irredentist movements. As the empire as a whole grew more and more homogeneous politically, economically, and culturally, however, the Jews, who had retained their ethnic and religious integrity, now began to appear as one of the greatest obstacles to complete uniformity. Under these circumstances, the hostility of local populations was easily communicated to Romans living in the various provinces. The anti-Jewish feeling in Rome and Italy also rose to a considerable height the moment this group of foreigners started to proliferate rapidly. With their special way of life, they were a strange element, even in the cosmopolitan capital. The literature of the age reflects the partly contemptuous and partly inimical attitude prevailing among the educated classes in the imperial city.

All these reasons contributed toward a gradual lowering of the legal and political status of Jewry throughout the empire. There is no evidence, to be sure, for Mommsen's once widely accepted theory that, after 70, the vanquished Palestinian Jews sank to the status of half-free *dediticii*. According to the definition given by the distinguished Roman jurist Gaius, only those were called *dediticii* "who had once fought with arms against the Roman people and, subsequently, when vanquished, had surrendered." This evidently did not apply to Palestine even in 63 B.C.E., when only a small part of the country had resisted Pompey. Hence, the obviously favorable status of its inhabitants in the subsequent generations. Once a country had been incorporated in the empire, no armed uprising of however large a segment of the population could alter the status of the province as a whole. In the case of the Jewish revolt under Nero and Vespasian the Romans knew well enough that most areas of the Jewish settlement itself had remained quiescent, while even in the turbulent districts there was a large pro-Roman faction and a great many others who had not taken any active part in the hostilities. Suddenly to lower, therefore, the status of the entire population as a permanent reprisal for acts of a minority—and it was good governmental policy, reflected by Josephus, to claim that only a small minority had been involved—would not only have been unjust, but an act of sheer folly.[17]

Nor is there a grain of truth in Mommsen's other assertion, likewise frequently quoted, that after the fall of Jerusalem the Jews were no longer regarded officially as a nationality, but only as a religious denomination. This assertion is no more true than Wellhausen's similar theory that the Jews lost their national character after the destruction of the First Temple. All such theories, obviously colored by political and theological biases, have failed to take account of ancient conditions which allowed for little separation between religious and national feelings. Herodotus, for one example, unhesitatingly quoted the Athenians as indiscriminately invoking the "kinship of all Greeks in blood and speech and the shrines of gods and the sacrifices that we have in common, and the likeness of our way of life," all of which transcended their political boundaries. Discussing Domitian's measures about the Jewish fiscal tax, Seutonius does not hesitate to speak of the *imposita genti tributa* (the tribute levied upon their people; *Domitianus,* XII, 2). Clearly, Mommsen's and Wellhausen's theories, which reflect nineteenth-century controversies, not only failed to do justice to Roman concepts of nationality and religion, but also overlooked the peculiar ethnic character of the Jewish people which, whether under Nebukadrezzar, Vespasian, or William I, never completely fitted into the general patterns of national divisions.[18]

Nevertheless, the immediate raising of Palestine to the status of an independent province (it had theretofore merely been a subdivision of Syria), combined with the reappropriation and redistribution of the land and the absence of a central sanctuary, meant a tightening of Roman control. As a reprisal, all Jewish land was declared the emperor's domain. The administration, to be sure, seems to have used its newly acquired powers with considerable discretion. If a few ruthless Jews acquired farms auctioned off by the government, Jewish leaders treated them on a par with other "strong-arm" men, creating in the much-debated "law of *siqariqon*" a (none-too-effective) safeguard for the original owners. On the whole, however, the government itself apparently left not only the "loyalists" but most other farmers in the actual possession of their land. Such Pharisaic leaders as the Hillelite Gamaliel II (despite his father's likely implication in the revolt), R. Eliezer ben Hyrcanus and R. Eleazar ben Azariah, retained their vast landed possessions. Most of the "rebels" had, in any case, either lost their lives or been captured and sold into slavery. The settlement of 800 Roman veterans in Ammaus, the later Colonia Amatha in the vicinity of Jerusalem, injected only one more ethnic element into the heterogeneous population. Of course, theoretically, the Jewish peasants sank from the status of owners to that of more or less hereditary "tenants," although Gamaliel II and others unperturbedly continued to lease their estates to other, real tenant farmers. All of them undoubtedly also paid more in "rent" now than they had previously paid in taxes, which had already been extremely heavy. They also probably suffered more from arbitrary exactions of hostile officials, at least in the first few years. However, life seems to have soon resumed its normal rhythm. Curiously, even the last Jewish king, Agrippa II, was not deprived of his throne, but seems to have been rewarded by the addition of rich and largely undisturbed Galilee to his dominion. Only after his death in 92 did his possessions fall back into direct Roman suzerainty. None the less, morally even more than physically, the heel of the arrogant conquerors now lay heavily on the backs of the downtrodden population.[19]

Of much greater and more enduring consequence was the decree of Vespasian establishing the so-called *fiscus judaicus,* issued after the war. This Jewish "fiscal tax" of a half shekel annually was to be paid in lieu of the previous Temple tax, which the Jews had voluntarily imposed upon themselves in accordance with their biblical law. Like the Temple tax, it rested not only on the rebellious Jews of Palestine, but on all Jews above the age of twenty residing anywhere in the empire. In Egypt it was collected from all men and women from the ages of three to sixty or sixty-two. This extension, at variance with the biblical requirement and probably also with the previous practice of the Jewish communities, was entirely owing to Vespasian's well-known greed. Equally unprecedented was the collection of that tax from slaves of Jews, attested not only in Egypt. Domitian went so far as to try to collect it even from renegade Jews who certainly would not have paid it to the Temple. He did not hesitate to instruct his agents to submit suspected tax dodgers to physical examination. The historian Suetonius (born about 69 c.e.) later reminisced how, as a youth, he had personally witnessed when "a man ninety years old was examined before the procurator and a very crowded court, to see whether he was circumcised." This degrading procedure, which in the hands of over-suspicious or unscrupulous tax collectors must have led to many abuses affecting persons of non-Jewish extraction as well, so deeply aroused public opinion that Domitian's successor, Nerva, abrogated it as one of the first acts of his administration. He even commemorated this fact in a special memorial coin with the legend, *Fisci judaici calumnia sublata* (On the Removal of the Shameful [Extortion] of the Jewish Fiscal Tax). He continued, however, with the more normal processes of collecting this impost, which had by that time become an important item in the imperial budget. In Egypt alone it seems to have yielded some 8,000,000 drachmas annually to the special *procurator ad capitularia Judaeorum* designated for this purpose in Rome. Doubtless in connection with this redefinition of the fiscal obligation as resting only upon professing Jews, the growing Christian community secured from Nerva exemption from the tax and, indirectly, official recognition of the severance of its ties with the Jewish denomination.[20]

According to Vespasian's decree, these contributions were to be collected for the Temple of Jupiter on the Capitol. It is not clear whether the emperor was guided by purely personal avarice or by serious political considerations. This may have been an attempted means of pacifying the restive inhabitants of Gaul and Germany, whose hopes of regaining independence surged higher and higher when their imagination was struck by the symbolic simultaneity of the destruction by fire of Rome's supreme sanctuary on the Capitol during the civil war of 69 c.e. and the great initial success of the Jewish rebellion. Many a Druid on the Rhine and the Loire, Tacitus tells us, inspired by the exaggerated news about the conflagration in the capital, rhapsodized over the approaching downfall of Rome. The idea of presenting to these restless tribes the spectacle of the vanquished Jews paying with their sacred tax for the reconstruction of the Capitoline Temple was not unworthy of a Roman imperator.[21]

The imposition of this special tax, although economically no new burden, constituted a sharp deviation from the principle of civic equality. For the first time, the Jews of the whole empire became a special source of revenue. Here was born the idea of the Jew as the specific taxpayer, to play so important a role in later fiscal history.

If Vespasian's decree represented a violation of the principle of equality, Hadrian attacked his Jewish subjects at an even more vulnerable point, their self-government. The homogeneity of the empire having materially progressed during the century and a half of imperial rule, the alien character of the Jews became more and more obvious. To fight it, Hadrian prohibited circumcision, classifying it, with castration, as a capital crime. While this decree was partly inspired by the emperor's apprehensions over the incipient signs of Rome's depopulation and also applied to several other groups in the population (Egyptian priests and Arabs), these could not be compared in size and importance to the Jewish people. Other edicts of Hadrian were directed against the Jews exclusively. According to rabbinic sources, he prohibited public gatherings for instruction in Jewish law, forbade the proper observance of the Sabbath and holidays, and outlawed many important rituals. We do not know whether the latter prohibitions were directed only against the Jews in Palestine or against those of the whole empire, or whether they included all worship in the synagogue—neither extension seems at all likely—but they constituted such a radical departure from the previous imperial safeguards of Jewish ethnic-religious autonomy that the Jews in Palestine had no course except defiance. Indeed, the revolt of Bar Kocheba, although outwardly smothered, was not fully extinguished until Antoninus Pius, Hadrian's successor, revoked the decree concerning public gatherings and limited the prohibition of circumcision to Roman subjects of non-Jewish extraction. Henceforth only a man born of Jewish parents could be circumcised. With this law Antoninus made Jewish proselytism extremely difficult, thus incidentally playing into the hands of Christian propagandists. The ethnic bonds of Jewry, however, could not fail to be considerably strengthened.[22]

However brief in duration, Hadrian's anti-Jewish measures served as a permanent warning to the Jews that the Romans might, at any moment, again play havoc with their surviving religious institutions. Gone was the punctiliousness of previous administrators. Already in Vespasian's days the Roman legionaires freely displayed their eagles and probably even sacrificed on their altars in the very streets of desolated Jerusalem. When, after clearing up the last foci of Diaspora Jewry's resistance in 117–18, Hadrian was ready to extend the fruits of Graeco-Roman paganism to Jewish Palestine as well, he was but temporarily deterred by the Bar Kocheba revolt. After its sanguinary suppression he proceeded with his plans of building a pagan sanctuary in the city of Jerusalem which, now renamed Aelia Capitolina, completely shut out Jewish settlers.

For a time Jerusalem must have been principally a city of Roman soldiers, with a sprinkling of non-Jewish civilians providing for their needs. Recent excavations indicate the presence there of two different army camps during the second century. Two other large cities likewise felt the impact of Hadrian's dejudaizing efforts. Sepphoris was now renamed Diocaesarea, while in the Adrianeion of Tiberias pagan worship was practiced in the midst of what was rapidly becoming the major center of Jewish life in the country. Antoninus Pius neither revoked nor modified any of these measures. According to St. Jerome's not altogether unbiased account, as late as the fourth century, Jews were allowed to gather only once a year (on the Ninth of Ab) at the sole remnant of their Temple, the Wailing Wall. Here they could loudly bemoan the loss of their two sanctuaries (as well as that of Bethar, some seven miles to the southwest, if they still cared to remember it) on the same fatal ninth day of their eleventh month. At that time it still required considerable bribing of corrupt officials, before any individual Jew was allowed to extend his sojourn for a few days or to pay other visits to that relic of his ancient sanctuary. The new all-Gentile city of Jerusalem thus for many centuries symbolized the permanent deep estrangement of the Palestinian Jews from their imperial masters.[23]

CIVIL RIGHTS

Fundamentally, however, neither Vespasian nor Hadrian endeavored to curtail Jewish rights of citizenship. Apart from the new discriminatory tax, there was nothing in the legislation of these crucial sixty-five years (70–135) which in any way altered the right of any Jewish individual to enjoy whatever type of citizenship he had personally inherited or otherwise acquired. As before, the emperors, even if unfriendly to the Jews, consistently refused to clarify their highly complicated legal status. They evidently were determined to leave matters as they had been during the pre-war period. In fact, the anti-Jewish burghers of Alexandria and Antioch suggested to both Vespasian and Titus that they utilize the Jewish rebellion as an excuse for the rescinding of Jewish privileges. But both roundly refused. Such intransigence, entirely unreasonable in the burghers' opinion, must have added fuel to their old-standing controversy with the empire, as is reflected in the recently discovered "Act of the Heathen Martyrs," dated in 79–81 C.E.[24]

Hadrian, too, although going to extremes in interfering with Jewish religious life, never enacted any discriminatory legislation affecting Jewish rights as citizens. Characteristically, he did not even try to abrogate the old Jewish exemption from imperial worship, although this certainly was an extraordinary privilege enjoyed by Jews alone. Realizing the uncompromising nature of Jewish resistance on this score, he was evidently prepared to tolerate their abstention from overt acts prohibited by their religious law, provided they would not insist on living in a way contrary to the mores of the majority. He whose "melting pot" ideology had made him permit, contrary to deep-rooted Greek traditions, the "citizens" of the newly elevated *polis* of Antinoupolis to intermarry with native Egyptians, must have realized that discriminatory civil legislation would only strengthen the forces of Jewish "separatism." He would have thereby defeated the entire aim of his stringent measures, perhaps taken with serious misgivings, against those peculiarities of Jewish religious observance, like circumcision and the Sabbath, which tended to perpetuate the Jewish *amixia* with their neighbors.

At any rate, in the age of the Antonines Jews seem to have individually enjoyed as many rights as they had in the Claudian period. They undoubtedly even shared in the intervening extension of the rights of all provincials. Many more Jews than previously now enjoyed outright "Roman" citizenship. This still was the most privileged status in the empire, despite the strictures of romanticizing Tacitus that it no longer amounted to much in his day. When, finally, in 212 c.e., Caracalla enacted his famous *constitutio Antoniniana de civitate*, establishing a uniform Roman citizenship for the overwhelming majority of the imperial population, almost all Jews seem to have become such *Aurelian* citizens, a designation frequently found in their Roman catacomb inscriptions during that period. The only class exempted from the operation of the new egalitarian law were the *dediticii*. But there is every reason to believe that few Jews at that time belonged to that "stateless" class, unless they happened to be, according to Segré's very questionable theory, native Egyptian *laographoumenoi* (persons subjected to the census tax). Nowhere even in rabbinic letters, highly articulate though they are in voicing all sorts of grievances against Roman oppression, do we hear of any overt legal discrimination concerning Jewish civil rights. In fact, the only important anti-Jewish legislation recorded in the later Roman legal and historical literature is Spartianus' report about the otherwise rather friendly emperor, Septimius Severus, who "forbade conversion to Judaism under heavy penalties." But this had long been accepted Roman policy from the days of Tiberius, Claudius, and Domitian, except that, as in all other matters, provincials were now assimilated in their status to the inhabitants of Italy.[25]

Like all provincials, Jews were now more readily admitted to public office. Of course, with increasing imperial absolutism, there were fewer and fewer important elective offices. Hence, it mattered little whether or not all the new Roman citizens enjoyed the old *ius suffragii*. Appointment to office also often depended on property qualifications, which may have excluded a disproportionate number of Jews in view of their generally meagre economic resources. On the other hand, unlike the first century when Tiberius Alexander had to change his faith before he could overcome such obstacles as were inherent in the pagan oath of office, the administration now went out of its way in safeguarding Jewish equality of opportunity. Septimius Severus and Caracalla, in particular, specifically considered the Jewish candidates' conscientious scruples. In the words of the jurist Ulpian, "the divine Severus and Antoninus have not only permitted those who adhere to the Jewish superstition to obtain public office [*honores*], but also imposed upon them such formalities [*necessitates*] as would not offend their superstition." [26]

The word "permitted" is a legal euphemism in so far as by that time most Jewish office holders, including members of the municipal councils, were used mainly for collecting, under personal responsibility, various extortionist taxes. Local administrative expenses had to be defrayed, in part, from their own purse. No wonder, then, that a contemporary rabbi, Johanan, advised his fellow Palestinians, "If they elect thee to the council [*boulé*], make the Jordan thy boundary," that is, flee to Transjordan (j. M.Q. II, 3, 81b). Whatever their personal wishes, however, the number of Jewish civil servants now seems to have sufficiently increased to constitute a problem for the later Christian emperors.

MODERATION IN MOURNING

On the fall of Jerusalem, Judaism was so integrated a system of action and belief that not even the need to make a new start was to involve it in vital transformation. Unlike the First Exile, the new Diaspora necessitated adjustments of detail, but not the remodeling of the whole life of the nation on unforeseen patterns. Had not the

First Exile itself furnished that most crucial experience, since which the majority of Jews had lived on foreign soil and amid strange civilizations? All that was required now was the focalization of life on those factors of proved stability, which for ages past had been the source of their great capacity for survival.

Such intensive concentration of effort involved, however, the abandonment of the unparalleled aggressive expansion. Instead of constantly putting out new feelers and entering into ever-new combinations with the outside world, there came a recoil into the inner self. The daughter religion, Christianity, inherited along with the expansiveness of the Judaism of the Second Commonwealth its increasingly variegated sectarian currents. Talmudic Judaism, on the other hand, soon to be unified and consolidated, eliminated all organized "heresies" from the life of the people for centuries to come. As early as the second century, Celsus, an informed writer, knew nothing about the Sadducean denial of resurrection and simply stated that the Jews shared with the Christians the belief in the ultimate resurrection of the dead.

The struggle assumed curious form, the affirmation of convictions rather than explicit negation. Even when negation became imperative, direct polemics were avoided as much as possible. Talmudic literature indicates against what tremendous odds Judaism struggled for survival, but it seldom contains a specific reference to the mighty opponents. Talmudic texts, even after the mutilations of medieval and modern Christian censorship have been repaired, often leave the modern critic in the dark as to whether a particular outburst of rage is aimed at the Christian, pagan Roman, Parsee, or other enemy. This posture of the Jewish leaders was as much an expression of great inner strength as of fear. Did not the author of the first book of Maccabees refrain from mentioning even the names of the "traitors," Jason and Menelaus?

A striking illustration of this attitude lies in the Jews' relation to the outstanding event of the period: the destruction of the Temple. There was, of course, infinite mourning over the loss of the sanctuary, the point of convergence for all the scattered settlements. It had not come as a total surprise, however. A few such leaders as R. Johanan ben Zakkai were filled with evil forebodings of the forthcoming disaster for many years before 70 (Yoma 39b). R. Zadok reputedly fasted for forty years (a round figure for a generation) to stave it off, so that the actual fall of Jerusalem found his body in a state of utter exhaustion (Giṭṭin 56a). Despite these warn-

ings the Jewish people were stunned by the event. They were prepared to believe that, in his wrath, God had sent his angels to help
wreck his sanctuary (Apocalypse of Baruch, 7–8; Lam. r. II, 4), and
that subsequently the very course of nature had been affected. R.
Joshua testified, "Since the destruction of the Temple there has
been no day without some curse, the dew has not fallen to the good
of the crops and the taste of the fruit has gone." R. Jose added,
"Even the juice of the fruit has dried up" (M. Soṭah IX, 12; b. 49a).

Not only on the Ninth Day of Ab, specially set aside for com-
memoration of the vanished glory, but throughout the year, Jews
were to recall, even in the midst of the greatest personal joy, the
deep national sorrow. In that generation certain luxuries, merry-
making and song on festive occasions were prohibited by law. A
special benediction for the restoration was inserted into the main
daily prayer. Other constant reminders were the unpainted spot on
the wall and the omission from the accustomed meal of a particular
dish. Extremists wished to renounce the use of meat and wine altogether, since they could no longer be offered on the altar in Jerusalem. According to an old talmudic tradition, however, at this juncture R. Joshua objected. Consistently carried out, he argued, this
would have meant also abstinence from bread and fruit, both of
which had likewise been objects of sacrificial offerings. R. Joshua's
final declaration, "Not to mourn at all is impossible, because the
fatal decree has already been enacted; to mourn too much is likewise impossible, because one must not issue a prohibition which
society cannot endure," may be regarded as the authoritative view
of Jewish leaders soon after the catastrophe.[27]

Characteristically, no poet of that day, as previously the author of
Lamentations, has dramatized the Second Destruction, and no contemporary elegy, if written, has been deemed worthy of inclusion
in the commemorative services of the Ninth of Ab. Only much later
(according to a tradition ascribed to R. Ḥiyya of Sepphoris) was an
additional prayer for that day inserted in the fourteenth benediction of the 'Amidah. After lamenting over "the city which is in
mourning, destroyed, laid waste and desolate; it is delivered into
the hands of strangers and downtrodden under the feet of tyrants;
legions have possessed her and idol worshipers have despoiled her,"
the benediction voices the hope that "Thou, O Lord, [who] didst
consume her with fire, with fire Thou wilt restore her." It was left
to some Egyptian Jewish poets to make their Sibylla describe with
much pathos the "evil blast of war [which] shall come from Italy

and shall lay in ruin God's great temple" and to predict that no impure Greek would again "run riot" in the land of the Hebrews and the beautiful city, for all would conform with Jewish law.[28]

Curiously, neither the generation of 70 nor the immediately following generations of Jews and Christians seem to have evinced great interest in the whereabouts of the Temple implements carried away by Titus. Only a century later did R. Eleazar, son of the historian R. Jose ben Ḥalafta, avail himself of his official mission to Rome to look over some of these objects. In later discussions with his colleagues he testified that he had seen there the Temple's *parokhet* (curtain), still showing the bloodstains of sacrificial animals, and the high priest's headband which, contrary to opinions at home, he found to have had the words "Sacred unto the Lord" inscribed on a single line. But R. Eleazar doubtless was an exception. Like his father, he evinced unusual historical interests. On his visit to Alexandria he inquired for vestiges of the Jewish sojourn in Egypt in pre-Exodus days. With Samaritans he debated the burning historical issue as to which denomination was responsible for the falsification of those passages in which the Jewish and the Samaritan Bibles disagreed. His interests were so atypical that his observations in Rome were recorded in the rabbinic literature only in connection with some legal debates. It was left, therefore, to modern scholars since Adrian Reeland (1716) to search, none too successfully, for some vestiges left in later records.[29]

As time went on the wounds began to heal and excessive mourning had no longer to be combated. On the contrary, a certain degree of forgetfulness set in, especially in the happier and more distant settlements of Babylonia, whose rabbis often felt obliged to remonstrate against what they thought was, in view of the circumstances, too joyous a mood. Asked by a Palestinian colleague, "Why are the holidays in Babylonia so hilarious?" R. Assi, a Babylonian *émigré*, could say only that the poverty of Babylonian Jewry made them "compensate" their hard daily life with boisterous joy during the festivals (Shabbat 145b). As if Palestinian Jewry were more prosperous at that time!

Rather than blaming the foreign enemy, Jewish leadership followed the old prophetic line of self-accusation and ascribed the downfall to the people's own transgressions. Typical of these rationalizations is a story told about the generation's outstanding rabbi, Rabban Johanan ben Zakkai. When on his journey to Emmaus he noticed on the road Miriam, daughter of Naqdimon ben

Gurion of distinguished parentage, whose marriage contract providing 1,000,000 gold denars for her widowhood he had himself
signed as a witness. Now she had become so poor that, to still her
hunger, she collected grains of barley from excrements left behind
by an Arab rider's horse. R. Johanan was moved to speculate on the
homiletical implications of the verse, "If thou know not, O thou
fairest among women."

You were unwilling to be subject to God [he began preaching], behold
now you are subjected to the most inferior of the nations, the Arabs.
You were unwilling to pay the headtax to God, "a beqa a head"; now
you are paying a headtax of fifteen shekels under a government of your
enemies. You were unwilling to repair the roads and streets leading up
to the Temple; now you have to keep in repair the posts and stations on
the road to the royal cities.   . . Because thou didst not serve the Lord
thy God with love, therefore shalt thou serve thine enemy with hatred;
because thou didst not serve the Lord thy God when thou hadst plenty,
therefore thou shalt serve thine enemy in hunger and thirst. . . .

The Jews' greatest sin, R. Johanan concluded, was that "they were
deficient in the study of the Torah." His disciple, R. Eliezer ben
Hyrcanus, further explained that God himself was deeply grieved
over the loss of the sanctuary, and every night He "roars like a lion"
over his ruined abode. But even He can do nothing about it until
the Jews repent their sins and mend their ways. Were He to deviate
from this principle of justice by a single step, the world would immediately collapse. Neither master nor pupil doubted for one moment, however, that Israel would ultimately repent and, being the
essential goal of all creation, it would endure forever.[30]

Rabban Johanan's harangue must have conveyed to many listeners the old prophetic idea that the Jewish people's recent involve-
ment in power politics had in itself been a departure from the road
laid down for it by its divine master. Not only the general contrast
between surrender to the divine will and subjection to foreign nations, but also the phrasing, "You were unwilling to be subject to
God" (lehishta'abed la-shamaim), must have recalled to many listeners the dire predictions of Samuel the Seer and other antimonarchical preachments by ancient prophets. R. Johanan was even
more directly allusive in a homily concerning the biblical law which
was later recorded among his five outstanding doctrines. The law
required that if a Hebrew slave decided to overstay his term, his ear
must be pierced, because, said R. Johanan, "it had heard the Sinaitic declaration, 'For unto Me the children of Israel are servants,'

and yet it threw off the yoke of heaven and accepted human domination; therefore, let the ear be pierced, for it did not live up to
what it had heard" (T. B.Q. VII, 5, 358, on Exod. 21:6; Lev. 25:55).
Like the prophets of old, R. Johanan did not object to a Jewish
kingdom as such, but he had long been disgruntled with its corrupt
regime which had so sharply deviated from the principles of the
Torah.

Now he and his associates considered it their major duty to restore peace to the country devastated by decades of civil and foreign wars. Pointing out that the Bible had forbidden to lift up an
iron tool upon the stones of the altar, because the stones served to
establish peace between Israel and their Lord, R. Johanan taught,
"How much the more, then, should he who establishes peace between men and his fellow-men, between husband and wife, between city and city, between nation and nation, between family and
family, between government and government, be protected, so that
no harm should come to him!" By insisting that "charity atones for
Gentile nations," he also intimated that even the Romans might be
forgiven, if they expiated their cruelties by a new charitable attitude toward Jews. His colleague, Ḥanina, "lieutenant of [high]
priests," went a step further. He not only taught that "great is
peace, for it is the equivalent of all the works of creation," but also,
taking a clue from Jeremiah, explained, "Thou shalt pray for the
welfare of the kingdom, for were it not for the fear of it men would
swallow one another alive." In its final reformulation at the academy of Yabneh the main daily prayer, the 'Amidah, was made to
conclude on a grand finale: a prayer for peace. In general, the following homily on "I adjure you, O daughters of Jerusalem," although coined a century or two after the fall of Jerusalem, well
reflects the prevailing mood of rabbinic leadership. God imposed
three oaths, declared R. Joseph ben Ḥanina, "one that Israel shall
not scale a wall [fortify its cities], one . . . that they shall not rebel
against the nations, and one which the Holy One blessed be He imposed upon the nations that they shall not subject Israel to too oppressive a regime." [31]

Peace meant, however, not only international, but also domestic
pacification. The priest Ḥanina himself made his objectives perfectly clear, when he interpreted Num. 6:26, The Lord "give thee
peace," by adding: "that is, at home." In fact, "not to increase controversy in Israel" became one of the keynotes of rabbinic policy,
as illustrated, for instance, by R. Gamaliel's apology for his harsh

treatment of R. Eliezer. Even farther reaching was the attempt at reconciling the various ethnic groups in the Palestinian population. As we shall see, this effort extended even to the ancient and most tenacious area of marriage laws. The old biblical prohibitions of admitting Moabites and Ammonites to the fold were now interpreted away by R. Joshua, while R. 'Aqiba extended liberal treatment also to proselytes of Idumaean and Egyptian stock. Peace with the Arab neighbors in Transjordan, now indistinguishably intermingled with the Ammonites and Moabites, as well as the relinquishing of the old feuds with the Herodian and other remnants of ancient Edom, became the more imperative for R. 'Aqiba, as on the eve of the Bar Kocheba revolt he must have realized the paralyzing effect of these internal animosities on Palestine's earlier military campaigns.[32]

On the other hand, to perpetuate the memory of the Temple and to remind their people of its grievous loss in their daily transactions, the rabbis introduced quite early the custom of dating events by the era of its destruction. Curiously, if compared with our other chronological data, the beginning of this era fell in the year 68 rather than 70 c.e., thereby coloring all subsequent Jewish computations. In a typical homily relating to the First Temple, but evidently referring to his own time, R. Johanan ben Zakkai or another early rabbi censured the Jews for not having used the computation based on the building of the Temple, "so they had to count from its destruction. . . . They were not satisfied to count in accordance with their own era—so they had to count according to the era of others." Nevertheless, in documents which required exact dating, both this and the Seleucid eras were expressly discarded by the tannaitic legislation in favor of the one in local use. In private life the era of the destruction was frequently combined with that of sabbatical cycles. For example, a tombstone inscription found at Kasr et-Tuba is dated "on the first of Marheshvan of the first year of the sabbatical cycle in the year 364 since the destruction of the Temple" (432–33 c.e.). Palestine's non-Jewish population, too, usually dated its documents by its local eras. The absence of the latter usage in Jerusalem and its replacement by the years of the respective emperor's reign is, as Alt has pointed out, proof for the utter dependence of this post-Hadrianic Roman colony upon the imperial center. Curiously, no Roman administrator seems to have interfered with the replacement of the imperial era by one commemorating the tragic outcome of a Jewish rebellion.[33]

RETURN TO NORMALCY

Full resumption of the accustomed way of life was another way of combating despair. The general human habit of attending to daily chores in the midst of great upheavals must have maintained a measure of continuity in the life of provincials even while Jerusalem was besieged. It was reinforced now by a studied effort on the part of leaders. A certain reluctance of Palestinian and world Jewry to take cognizance of the finality of the great catastrophe is exemplified by Josephus. Discussing Jewish law three decades after the destruction of the Temple, he referred to its cult as if it still were in force (*Ag. Ap.* II, 22.188). For him the priest, and not the rabbi, still was the leader of the people.

This was not merely a priest's prejudice in favor of his class, for there was, indeed, an inordinate number of priests and levites in the Pharisaic leadership after the Great War. Just as the first fall of Jerusalem had brought to the fore such great prophets-priests as Jeremiah and Ezekiel, and as the first period of reconstruction had borne the indelible mark of the priestly scribe Ezra, so did the second breakdown and rebuilding place in the forefront the great priest-rabbi Johanan ben Zakkai. While Johanan himself had apparently not officiated at the Temple but had lived most of his life as a merchant and judge in a provincial town, he was ably assisted by the high-ranking priest Ḥanina, and by such other scholarly priests as R. Zadok, Jose and Samuel ben Netanel. The greatest of his distinguished disciples were the levites Eliezer ben Hyrcanus and Joshua ben Ḥananiah, and the priest Tarfon (Tryphon). Such extraordinary concentration not only reflected the greater educational opportunities available to the priestly class during the Temple's existence, but also the extent to which its energies had previously been absorbed by the Temple ritual, political intrigues and, at best, Sadducean learning which was ultimately lost to the people. The prolonged unwillingness of the Roman authorities to deal with members of the Hillelite family, whose head, Rabban Simon ben Gamaliel I, seems to have played a certain role in the revolt and become one of its "martyrs," must likewise have strengthened the hand of the priestly faction long allied with the Pharisaic movement.

From the standpoint of Diaspora Jewry, the disappearance of the remote sanctuary brought about even fewer changes in established modes of life. The only contact of practical import, the pilgrimages to Jerusalem, was maintained long after the destruction. Even after Hadrian's rigid exclusion of Jews from permanent sojourn in the city, the pious from all over the world often continued to pay homage to their holy place. Whether or not the Romans consistently permitted the Jews to visit Jerusalem only on the Ninth of Ab, the Talmud constantly lists three pilgrimages, one for each traditional holiday. During the protracted period of governmental disorganization in the third century, particularly, R. Johanan strongly encouraged such pilgrimages. He assured would-be visitors that, in contrast to heavenly Jerusalem which is accessible only to those invited, "anyone wishing to go up to earthly Jerusalem, may do so" (B.B. 75b). Nor is it at all surprising that Diaspora Jewry, including its staunchly orthodox Babylonian segment, never adopted the new era introduced by the Palestinian leaders. The computation "from the destruction of the Temple" was long known in Palestine only, and even there, we recall, never became exclusive. For more than a millennium, Jewry as a whole continued dating its business documents and historical records by the Seleucid era.

More important, pious Jews in Palestine continued to pay tithes and other dues to the priests as when the sanctuary was intact. R. 'Aqiba, for instance, observed this commandment so pedantically that, when a controversy arose between two schools of law, he decided to pay a double tithe on his citrons, to satisfy both (T. Shebi'it IV, 21, 67). That the income derived from these dues was sometimes quite considerable is seen in the example of R. Tarfon who, during a famine, allegedly betrothed three hundred women solely in order to enable them, as wives of a priest, to consume the sacred food (T. Ketubot V, 1, 266). Indeed, the insistence upon the payment of tithes increased, rather than diminished, and for generations to come the rabbis reiterated their extreme condemnation of food which had not been tithed. To stem evasions on the part of landowners acquiring land in the neighboring districts of Syria, which generally was not subject to the "laws attached to the land" of Israel, they now decreed that "A Jew buying a field in Syria is like a purchaser in a suburb of Jerusalem. He must pay on it his regular heave-offering and tithe" (T. Terumot II, 10, 27).

At the same time there grew a new feeling of mutual responsibility, and, with it, a vigorous restatement of the old doctrines of charity. Although recorded only in one source, there is no reason to doubt the authenticity of the comforting words attributed to R.

Johanan ben Zakkai. On leaving the ruins of Jerusalem, we are told, R. Johanan heard his pupil, R. Joshua, bewailing the absence of Temple and sacrifices to expiate for Israel's sins. "My son," the master replied, "do not grieve, we possess a similar means of expiation [loving-kindness, as it is written]: 'For I desire mercy, and not sacrifice' " (II ARN VIII, 22, on Hos. 6:6).

Prayer was an even more direct and time-honored substitution. R. Eleazar ben Pedat's later exclamation, "Prayer is more significant than sacrifice," reinforced by the invocation of the shades of Isaiah, sounded the keynote of rabbinic rationalization. Some rituals were now adopted to reinforce the symbolic link between synagogue and Temple. For example, before 70, only the Jerusalem priests used the *lulab* (festive wreath) at their Temple services during the entire Feast of Tabernacles; laymen did so only on the first day. From now on R. Johanan decided that all of world Jewry should perform the *lulab* ritual on each of the seven days. R. Gamaliel II revised the ancient Passover Haggadah, inserting, in particular, commemorative references to the Passover sacrifice and prayers for the restoration of Jerusalem and its sacrificial system. The well-known priestly blessing, theretofore fully recited at the Temple alone, now became in ever-expanding form a major feature of daily and, later, of holiday services at the synagogue. Some unification, even standardization of prayers became the more necessary, as world Jewry had lost its all-pervading liturgical center in Jerusalem. The *'Amidah,* amplified by the antiheretical benediction and one for the rebuilding of the Temple, now reached its more or less definitive form when R. Gamaliel II supervised its "arrangement" at Yabneh. The benedictions preceding and following the *Shema'* were now clearly arranged for both morning and evening services, although a few minor differences still continued to engage the attention of rabbis for several generations.[34]

The Bar Kocheba revolt and the ensuing dispersal of surviving scholars added stimulus to these unifying efforts. The worshiper was also enjoined to pray with such concentration that, as the rabbis expressed it hyperbolically, "even if a king greets him he shall not reply, even if a snake crawls at his heel he shall not interrupt" (M. Berakhot V, 1). It is small wonder then that, in the eyes of a suspicious ruler like Hadrian, even Jewish gatherings for purposes of worship assumed a subversive character. R. Meir later reminisced, "One day we were sitting before R. 'Aqiba and reciting the *Shema',* but we did not make it audible to our ears because of a *quaestor* [Roman detective] standing at the door" (T. Berakhot II, 13, 4).

Any individual was entitled to add prayers of his own, however. Various rabbis themselves engaged in such liturgical creativity without expecting their prayers to find more general acceptance. Doubtless typical of a great many others is a prayer which R. Eliezer used to recite at the conclusion of the *'Amidah* and which, coming from a man as cantankerous and unable to get along with people as he, is doubly significant:

May it be Thy will, O Lord my God and God of my fathers, that hatred for us shall not enter the heart of any man, nor hatred for any man enter our heart; that no one shall envy us, nor we envy anyone else; that Thy Torah be our preoccupation all the days of our life; and that our words prove an effective petition before Thee.[35]

Above all, the study of the Torah now became the very core of survival. Reminiscent of Simon the Just's old adage, "The world rests on three things: the Torah, worship and loving-kindness," the generations following the fall of Jerusalem concentrated on building up the three institutional pillars of Judaism: the academy, the synagogue, and communal welfare. The talmudic tradition that it was R. Johanan ben Zakkai who had asked Vespasian for "Yabneh and her sages" is reinforced, rather than controverted, by Josephus' similar claim of having secured from Titus freedom for some of his friends and sacred books. To invest the new center of learning with superior sanctity R. Johanan not only took over for its council the venerable name of Sanhedrin, but also rather high-handedly introduced there the blowing of the horn on a New Year's day which happened to fall on a Sabbath—a prerogative theretofore reserved only for Jerusalem.[36]

In order to exercise more complete control over the scholarly class, now slated to play the dominant role in the affairs of the people, the title "Rabbi" began to be conferred on each disciple upon ordination by a qualified master. The supreme title "Rabban" remained the mark of distinction of the head of the academy. We recall that, without fully assuming the later "sacramental" character of the Catholic ordination, such *semikhah* had always involved the conferral of spiritual authority and the maintenance of historic continuity adumbrating the Catholic doctrine of the Apostolic succession. That is why it, too, was outlawed by Hadrian, with reprisals threatened for the whole community in which it was performed. R. Judah ben Baba suffered the death of a martyr because he had ordained five or six disciples, mostly pupils of his halakhic opponent R. 'Aqiba, in a defile near Usha (Sanhedrin 14a).

Prominent sages were encouraged to attend regularly the academy's sessions. Banishment from the seat of learning, as happened to R. Eliezer, became a major calamity, while protracted voluntary abstention led to the loss of contact with the progressive evolution of learning. Remembering the example of R. Eleazar ben 'Arakh, once R. Johanan ben Zakkai's most promising pupil, who upon withdrawing to a smug and comfortable life in Emmaus had lost all his intellectual prowess, R. Nehorai, perhaps R. Eleazar's disciple, advised all students, "Proceed to the place of learning and do not say that it shall follow you, so that thy colleagues may help you maintain it. 'And lean not upon thine own understanding' " (M. Abot IV, 18, quoting Prov. 3:5). Concentration on the Torah was, indeed, considered the main remedy for all private and public ills and as the ultimate antidote to foreign domination. The priest Hananiah's homily on a verse of the psalmist, "He who takes to heart the words of the Torah, eliminates many apprehensions: the apprehensions relating to [the sword], hunger, foolishness, fornication, evil spirit, married woman, vanities and the yoke of human domination" (ARN, XX, 1, 70, on Ps. 19:9), was echoed in many variations by his contemporaries and successors. R. Eliezer taught with even greater abandon that the whole universe was maintained only for the sake of the Torah (Nedarim 32a). We shall see how profound and permanent were the effects of this "intellectualization" of Jewish life on the subsequent destinies of the people.

For a while, to be sure, the people could not reconcile themselves to the final loss of national independence. Messianic hopes surged ever higher, eventually finding expression in the upheavals against Trajan and Hadrian. It was not without reason that, as Hegesippus informs us, the Roman emperors Vespasian, Domitian, and Trajan ordered the hunting out and execution of all who claimed Davidic descent. Controversies as to the personality of the messiah between the Hasmonean and anti-Hasmonean parties were forgotten in the common distress. All united in the hope of approaching redemption. Even R. 'Aqiba, then the recognized intellectual leader of all Jewry, believed, as we recall, in the messiahship of Bar Kocheba.

The bloody suppression of the Bar Kocheba revolt, however, had a sobering effect. Before long rabbis and populace remembered Bar Kocheba (son of a star) only as Bar Koziba (son of a lie) and blamed on him the death of one of that revolt's "real" martyrs, R. Eleazar of Modein who was Bar Kocheba's own uncle. The steady advance of the Christ-cult in the Graeco-Roman world was equally ominous. The rabbis of the following generations consequently regarded the mitigation of belief in the immediate appearance of the redeemer as a positive duty. Without in any way weakening in their faith in his ultimate arrival, they stressed its total unpredictability as to time and circumstances. In a remarkable legend, connected with R. Joshua ben Levi's mission to Rome, we are told that the rabbi was directed by Elijah to one of the Jewish beggars sitting at the gates of the capital as the prospective messiah. Among these dregs of humanity, reminding us of Martial's strictures at Roman Jewry, R. Joshua discovered an individual bandaging his wounds with special dispatch. On inquiry, the rabbi was informed that the beggar-messiah wished to be ready at a moment's notice and also that he expected to come "today." At the end of the day the disappointed rabbi was pacified by Elijah who explained to him the messiah's remark as merely an echo of the psalmist's assertion, "Today, if ye would but hearken to His voice!" Even more sharply the sages reiterated, "The Holy One, blessed be He, said to Israel: You built the Temple and it has been destroyed, so do not build it again until you hear a voice from heaven"; or "The son of David will not come until the Jews will have despaired of redemption." This reconciliation with inescapable reality reached its climax in the famous rationalization of R. Eleazar ben Pedat. This third-century Babylonian-born sage, homiletically expatiating on Ezekiel's "iron wall," exclaimed, "Since the day of the destruction of the Temple an iron wall has been removed between Israel and their Father in heaven." [37]

AFTER BAR KOCHEBA

Through rationalizations like these the Jewish people succeeded in overcoming the traumatic effects of the loss of the central sanctuary and national independence and in establishing a *modus vivendi* with the conquerors. In all essentials this resolution of difficulties was maintained after the fall of Bethar and the abrogation of Hadrian's serious infringements on Jewish autonomy. Continuity of outlook and mode of living was so well maintained that many rabbinic teachings, if handed down anonymously, cannot be confidently dated before or after 135 on internal evidence alone.

Physical ravages, to be sure, were most appalling. Not only had Jerusalem now become a non-Jewish city, but most of Judaea, formerly the core of Jewish settlement, was completely dejudaized. Only in isolated districts along the Jordan, in the south, and near the coast did Jewish farmers cling tenaciously to the soil. "Of seventy-five Jewish settlements in Judaea," notes M. Avi-Yonah, "recorded in ancient sources, not one has preserved vestiges of Jewish life after the fall of Bethar." The center of gravity of Jewish life shifted to Galilee, which now doubtless embraced the majority of the Jewish population in the country. This province not only suffered much less during the campaigns, but apparently was also spared some of the vengeance of Roman administrators after 70. Under Agrippa II's benevolent regime it seems to have quickly healed the wounds inflicted by the Great War. It sustained relatively little direct destruction of life and property during the Bar Kocheba revolt. In fact, its Jewish population succeeded in time in converting the former "Greek" cities of Tiberias and Sepphoris into Jewish strongholds. By the time of Constantine, Epiphanius complained, they had become all-Jewish cities, "no pagan, Samaritan or Christian" being allowed to live there. On the other hand, in the vicinity of Shechem, raised by Hadrian to the rank of a Greek polis and renamed Flavia Neapolis (Nablus), Jews were assimilated by the Samaritan majority. About 300 c.e., R. Abbahu complained that thirteen Jewish villages in that district had been wholly "absorbed by the Samaritans." [38]

In any case, the Jews seem to have become a minority in the Roman province of "Palaestina," which name now replaced that of Judaea in official usage. While most Jews still lived by farming, a greatly increased percentage settled in the larger cities and turned to industrial and commercial occupations. After the restoration of peace there seems to have been a gradual intensification of industrial production. The manufacture of glass, particularly, and of other products requiring special skills made considerable headway. We shall see that later economic developments throughout the empire, tending to promote the self-sufficiency of each province, further stimulated the gradual displacement of foreign by native merchants, including Jews.

Nevertheless, Jewish emigration, a more or less permanent feature of ancient Palestinian demography, now assumed alarming proportions. To stem it the rabbis applied moral suasion reinforced by legal enactments. A characteristic passage in the Tosefta, evidently originating from discussions in the post-Hadrianic period, reads:

A man should live in Palestine, even in a city with a Gentile majority, rather than abroad even in a wholly Jewish city. To wit, living in Palestine is the equivalent of [fulfilling] all the commandments in the Torah, and he who is buried in Palestine is like one buried under the altar. No man shall emigrate abroad unless two *se'ahs* of wheat cost a *sela'* [double the usual price and, hence, a symptom of great economic stringency]. R. Simon says, This applies only to one who cannot purchase it at all, but one who can, must not leave even if one *se'ah* cost a *sela'*. R. Simon further observed, Elimelech [of the story of Ruth] was a great man and communal leader, but because he went abroad he and his sons died of hunger, while the rest of Israel survived on its soil.

R. Simon's equally distinguished colleague, R. Meir not only promised big celestial rewards to anyone "who resides in Palestine and speaks Hebrew," but also expatiated on the great fertility of the country, which promised ample returns to its farmers. With typical oriental exaggeration he reported, "I have seen in the valley of Beth-Shan that a parcel of land requiring one *se'ah* of seed has yielded seventy *khors* of produce," that is, a return of some 2,100 times the investment. Taking a clue from the Deuteronomist's enthusiastic assertions, he also assured his listeners that "Palestine lacks nothing." Furthermore, to curtail emigration and foster the influx of new arrivals, the rabbis gave preference to either husband or wife who wished to stay in the country or settle in it. Regardless of any other marital regulations or agreements, the courts were to force any recalcitrant partner to yield to his or her pro-Palestinian mate.[39]

Equally important was the protection of Jewish holdings within the country and the prevention of their sale to Gentiles. If they were to permit the operation of pure economic laws, the rabbis realized, much Jewish property would sooner or later find its way into Gentile hands, since Gentiles were now in the majority, had suffered less from the wars, commanded greater capital resources, and could always count on governmental support. Alienation of Jewish houses or farms, moreover, by promoting mixed residential living and greater social intimacy, was also endangering the religious loyalties of Jews. Numerous rabbinic restrictions were, therefore, enacted on the sale of a variety of objects to non-Jews. Farthest reaching was R. Meir's decision, "One must not rent them houses in Palestine, still less fields; in Syria one may rent them houses, but not fields; in other countries one may sell them houses and rent fields." By prohibiting land sales R. Meir wished to prevent Jews from permanently losing land and turning away from agriculture even in the dispersion. More realistically, his colleague R. Jose ben Ḥalafta advocated freedom of all real estate transactions in other countries, the prohibition of only the sale of fields to Gentiles in Syria, and even permission to rent but not sell them houses in Palestine. Even he agreed, however, on the complete outlawry of both sales and leases of Palestinian Jewish farms to Gentiles (M. 'A.Z. I, 8).

Reëstablishment of Palestinian controls over world Jewry in the religious sphere was the next most urgent step. One of the most direct means of such control, now that Palestine's exclusive possession of Temple and sacrifices had been replaced by universal synagogue worship, was regulation of the Jewish calendar. From time immemorial Diaspora Jewry had followed the lead of the Palestinian authorities in celebrating the new moons and ensuing holidays. Without a perpetual calendar, there was indeed a great danger to world Jewish unity if each country were allowed to follow its own observations of the rising new moon and, on occasion, set different dates for the beginning of the new month. Even more dangerous were possible variations in the intercalation of an additional month every second or third year, to equalize the lunar with the solar computation. If allowed to go on, such local deviations would, in their cumulative effect, break up the Jewish faith into conflicting groups, even more at variance as to details than are Christian churches today through their respective observance of the Julian and Gregorian calendars.

For this reason, R. Simon ben Yoḥai declaimed, "He who has a chance of proclaiming a leap year and fails to do so, is like one who worships idols" (j. Ḥagigah III, 1, 78d). When Hadrianic legislation had made it impossible to issue such proclamations from Palestine, R. 'Aqiba did not hesitate "to intercalate years and fix months abroad" (Berakhot 63a). He thereby created a dangerous precedent, however. Even when the emergency had passed, R. Ḥananiah, nephew of R. Joshua, who had in the meantime settled in Babylonia, wished to continue this practice in his adopted country, which was rapidly developing into a major center of Jewish life. Reawakened Palestinian leadership immediately intervened, however. Perhaps mindful of the permanent division brought about by their forefathers' assent, during the Maccabean emergency, to the building of the Temple of Onias, they sent messengers to Babylonia who, combining diplomatic suasion with threats of excommunication, nipped in the bud that separatist move.

In the country itself the community was likewise completely reorganized under rabbinic leadership, whose hegemony, as we shall see in fuller detail, now was uncontested. The Samaritan chronicler's assertion that, after the crucifixion of the thirty-six rabbis at Nablus, "there was no imam among them, nor wisdom, nor teaching of Law, nor was anyone able in the days of these kings to give instruction in the Pentateuch; except one in a thousand, and two in a myriad," is true only with respect to the war years and shortly thereafter. As soon as Antoninus Pius revoked or modified the Hadrianic decrees, the disciples ordained by Judah ben Baba and other scholars emerged from their various hiding places or returned from abroad. They speedily reconstituted a "Sanhedrin" in Usha. Strenuous efforts were made to attract as large a number of pupils as possible. A public invitation was issued, "Let anyone who had studied come and teach, and anyone who had not studied come and learn." Despite the crowded living quarters in that small Galilean community and the dismal poverty of most students, this center of learning soon began to rival the older school of Yabneh. Before long R. Simon ben Gamaliel, who had escaped from prison during the revolt and had gone into concealment, was recalled to head the academy. It seems that in its efforts to pacify the country, the new Roman administration collaborated with this Jewish chief, thus laying the foundations for the development of the Palestinian patriarchate which, for several generations, was to guide the destinies of the Jewish people.[40]

POLITICAL ACQUIESCENCE

Permeated with a messianic hope which lent itself equally to secular and spiritual interpretation, the Jewish people emphasized sometimes the one, sometimes the other facet. In the wars of liberation secular messianism came to overshadow all other traditional teachings among the Zealots and reached its climax in R. 'Aqiba's public proclamation of Bar Kocheba as the Messiah, son of David. After their tragic defeats, the Jews fell back on the original prophetic vision of the messianic future, which now appeared the more congenial, as it had been born from similar military travail and political impotence. In fact, R. Eleazar ben Shammua', who for a short time before R. Simon ben Gamaliel's assumption of the presidency seems to have headed the small band of scholars engaged in reconstructing the Jewish community, constantly reminded his associates of this prophetic preachment. Taking a clue from the priestly blessing, "And [the Lord] give thee peace" (Num. 6:26), he declared, "Great is peace, for the prophets harangued the people only about peace" (Sifre on Numbers 42, ed. by Friedmann, fol. 13b).

Concentration on the pacific tasks of reconstruction now became the avowed policy of the leaders. Rebuilding from the ruins what was left of the Jewish communal structure, taking care of the poverty-stricken masses and, particularly, the restoration and expansion of the educational system became the main tasks of the generation after 135. Once again it was R. Eleazar who sounded the keynote. Asked by his pupils what one was to do in order to escape the trials and tribulations which, according to age-old traditions, were to accompany the advent of the messiah—this query was a clear reflection of their own experiences—he replied succinctly, "Let him engage in the study of the Torah and in acts of loving-kindness" (Sandhedrin 98b). In view of the tremendous losses in lives suffered during the revolt there also was a greater appreciation of human life. Strong measures were taken not only to encourage immigration to, and discourage departures from, the Holy Land, but promotion of marriages assumed the character of unprecedented urgency. Assistance to needy brides to enter wedlock, going under the name of *hakhnasat kallah,* now became a focal element in the entire communal scheme of social welfare. Reviewing the staggering casualties of the successive uprisings, another outstanding rabbi of that generation, R. Nehemiah, came to the conclusion that "one man is as important as all the works of creation put together" (ARN, XXXI, 91).

In this mood of quiet resignation, rather than despair, the new generation looked toward the future with unshaken confidence in the righteousness of God's inscrutable ways. Once again Jews blamed themselves, rather than the Romans, for their sufferings. They believed that only through repentance and wholehearted return to the commandments of the Torah, which they had sadly neglected, could they hope to secure the expiation of their sins. They must refrain, in particular, from "hastening the end" before the time appointed by God in his infinite wisdom. In the meantime they would the more obediently fulfill the two oaths which, as one of their sages had assured them, had been imposed upon Israel and refrain from fortifying their cities and rebelling against their foreign masters. They would only hope that the latter would reciprocate by keeping their oath of not oppressing the Jews too severely.

Such self-control, in all essentials postulated by R. Johanan ben Zakkai and his associates after the fall of Jerusalem, became the dominant attitude of the whole people after the fall of Bethar. In this way Jewry succeeded in speedily overcoming the depressing mental effects of the disaster. With renewed confidence it dedicated itself to the main task of inner consolidation.

XII

CLOSING THE RANKS

CLEARY perceiving how much its inner divisions had contributed to its downfall, the Jewish people now concentrated on achieving internal unity under its single-minded rabbinic leadership. Gone was the dream of achieving universal acceptance of the Jewish faith by the gradual processes of persuasion and education. Only some supernatural intervention, Jews believed, to come in an unforeseeable future, would bring about the realization of those prophetic predictions, whose ultimate fulfillment they now doubted even less than before. In the meantime, the people had paid a high price for its overexpansion during the last two centuries of the Second Commonwealth. By growing too fast it had absorbed too many alien elements, physically and culturally, made too many compromises, and flirted with too many alien ways of life and thought. The results were those sharp sectarian and political divisions which had almost brought it to the brink of extinction. By turning its back on the outside world and devoting itself unstintingly to the cultivation of its own millennial heritage, it expected to repair the ravages and renew its strength for the unceasing struggle for survival.

The first to be eschewed was the Sadducean sect, which could not possibly survive the loss of the Jewish state. Not that the tremendous energy which had gone into the formation and development of that great sectarian movement simply vanished into thin air. Many of its teachings were not only perpetuated in the Christian churches but, by indirection or contrast, helped shape some of the rabbinic views as well. A pre-Sadducean Sadducee, if one may call him so, like Sirach, was often directly, but more often tacitly quoted in the Talmud. Several verses are quoted in one talmudic tractate expressly as "written in the book of Ben Sira" and introduced in a form usually reserved for canonical writings, whereas in another tractate they appear anonymously, with the introductory word giving the impression that they were sayings coined in a rabbinic academy.[1] If more of the strictly Sadducean writings were extant, they would undoubtedly help elucidate many another obscure rabbinic passage, whereas today we cannot always be sure whether even one of the relatively few overt talmudic attacks on the *şeduqim* really refers to members of that sect or is aimed at heretics in general. Moreover, the underground survival of some Sadducean teachings within the Jewish fold, until their reëmergence in the related medieval sect of Karaites, can hardly be doubted. Nevertheless, all overt forms of Sadduceeism and its identifiable organized groups ceased immediately after the destruction of the Temple.

Although all the Essenes were dead after their "no surrender" battle at Jerusalem, Essenism was not. Apart from celebrating ever new victories in Christendom, particularly in its heterodox fringes, some of the Essenian ideals found many adherents among Jews in later periods, often among men who had never heard of the existence of the Essene sect. Similarly, such other groups as the "New Covenanters" contributed their share to the permanent heritage of the people, as will doubtless become more evident when the newly discovered documents stemming from their partisans or sympathizers have become more fully assimilated. However, this sect, too, soon disappeared from Jewish public life and its underground survivals, if any, can be detected with even greater difficulty.

While all these divergent movements were now quickly absorbed in the mainstream of Judaism, the growing Christian Church moved further and further away from its mother religion. After 70 even the mediating Judeo-Christian group began to disintegrate, to be totally eliminated from both Judaism and official Christianity after Bar Kocheba. It, too, continued to exert great spiritual influence, particularly on sectarian Christian trends, but it could serve no longer as the great moderating force between the two faiths. Bent on inner consolidation, the Jewish people now eschewed its Judeo-Christian members along with all other sectarians. It began treating all Christians alike, substantially on a par with other non-Jews. In the course of time it became increasingly evident, however, that the two faiths had become too deeply intertwined in their common heritage and, to some extent, also in their common destinies, for the Jews consistently to maintain this attitude of aloofness.

ANTI-CHRISTIAN REACTION

The reticence of the talmudic sages on the subject of the rising tide of Christianity has often attracted attention. The rare and glaringly inaccurate references of the Jewish teachers to Jesus reveal how little they were preoccupied with the new religion during the first century. Even where the rabbis quoted a passage from the Gospels, as in their satirical description of the corrupt Christian judge unmasked by Rabban Gamaliel II and his sister, they evidently knew it from hearsay only. The few later legends centering on Peter are decidedly favorable, whereas Paul, the main enemy, is not once unequivocally mentioned in talmudic literature. Neither has Josephus, writing in Greek for Jewish and Gentile Greeks, more than one indifferent passage on the rise of Christianity. Even if the repeated attempts to prove the authenticity of the entire passage (or that of a much longer one preserved in the Slavonic Josephus) were some day to be crowned with success, the conclusion would only be that a leading Jewish intellectual was able to speak sympathetically, rather than polemically, about the new religion.[2]

In the second century, however, bitterness mounted. Christian traditions concerning Jesus and the apostles were now rewritten in an increasingly anti-Jewish spirit. The Gospels had not yet become canonized and, hence, their texts were still rather fluid. As late as 178, Celsus could point an accusing finger at those Christians who rewrote their Gospels three or four times until they produced a text to suit their purposes. Even Josephus' detached narratives were sometimes reinterpreted in an anti-Jewish vein. His lengthy description, for example, of the prosecution of James essentially confirmed the aforementioned report in the Acts of the Apostles. It showed clearly that the vast majority of Jews had been sharply opposed to the conviction of the leader of the Judeo-Christian faction and that the latter had fallen victim only to the arbitrary proceedings of the Sadducean high priest, Ananus. Jewish public opinion, moreover, had become so deeply aroused that Agrippa I was soon forced to discharge the high priest. By the middle of the second century, however, Josephus' story was totally revised by his paraphrast, Hegesippus. In a long passage, preserved by Eusebius, the trial and execution of James were presented as the direct result of anti-Christian agitation by scribes and Pharisees. Hegesippus wound up his report by saying that soon thereafter Vespasian invaded Judaea and destroyed the Temple. This juxtaposition of the Christian "rewrite man" then gave rise to the idea that Josephus himself had blamed the fall of Jerusalem on this miscarriage of justice. Already mentioned by Origen who incidentally betrays in this connection his ignorance of the "Flavian testimony" concerning

Jesus, this reputed confession of the Jews' collective guilt by Josephus became one of the clichés of patristic literature.[3]

Conversely, Judaism now became more antagonistic to Christianity. The revolts against Trajan and Hadrian and the ensuing destruction of many Jewish communities greatly weakened the Judeo-Christian groups and relegated them to the Church's sectarian fringe. To the Christians the acceptance by most Palestinian Jews of the messiahship of Bar Kocheba appeared as the final and irrevocable Jewish rejection of the Christ Jesus. Jewish patriots, on their part, doubly resented Christian enmity in the midst of their war for survival. They could forgive the Christians' removal to Pella during the Great War, when so many loyal Jews were pro-Roman or pacifist, and when even R. Johanan ben Zakkai was smuggled out of the besieged city. Now, however, such fundamentals of the Jewish faith as circumcision, Sabbath observance, and public assemblies for study were at stake. Much as we may discount Justin Martry's bias in trying to persuade Emperor Antoninus Pius that Christians had not been involved in that uprising, the assertion in his *First Apology* that Bar Kocheba had ordered "that Christians alone should be led to cruel punishment, unless they renounced Jesus Christ," had a fairly authentic ring. It evidently was but a theological reformulation of what had probably been Bar Kocheba's military measure against a dangerous "Fifth Column," easily understandable under the existing emergency. Whether or not they were generally considered spies and Roman partisans, the refusal of all Christians to participate in the struggle, indeed their gloating over the political downfall of Judaea—whose very name soon went into disuse among the Romans, pagan and Christian alike—opened an unbridgeable gap between the mother and daughter religions.[4]

One need remember only another comment (relating to circumcision) by Justin Martyr, a native of Shechem and contemporary of Bar Kocheba, to understand the intensity of mutual hatred.

[It] was given for a sign [the Christian apologist informed his alleged Jewish interlocutor] that you may be separated from other nations, and from us; and that you alone may suffer that which you now justly suffer; and that your land may be desolate, and your cities burned with fire; and that strangers may eat your fruit in your presence, and not one of you may go up to Jerusalem.

All rabbis now agreed that the "gospels and other heretical writings" should not be salvaged from the fire on a Sabbath, despite the divine names included in them. But while on weekdays R. Jose the Galilean advised to excise the names and only confine the rest to the flames, R. Tarfon irately exclaimed, "By the life of my children! If they fall into my hands I shall burn them together with their names. If an enemy should pursue me, I should escape to a temple of an idol but not to their churches, for idolaters deny God out of ignorance, but these men know God and deny Him." His pupil, R. Ishmael added: "They inject hatred, jealousy and rivalry between Israel and their Father in heaven." A generation later R. Meir punned on the Greek term for Gospel, calling it *aven gilyon* (or *gillayon*), the sheet of falsehood, while in the third century, R. Johanan spoke of it as *'avon gilyon,* the sheet of sin.[5]

Yet Jews on the whole, particularly in Palestine, still avoided public debate, although religious disputations had not been uncommon even in Achaemenid Persia or Hellenistic Egypt. We have, for instance, the (rather obscure) record of such a disputation between Jews and Serapists before Trajan in Alexandria (*Oxyrhynchus Papyri*, X, No. 1242). Hence, Papiscus, of the *Altercatio Jasonis et Papisci* (so styled by Jerome), and the better known Tryphon, of Justin's dialogue, need not be altogether fictitious personalities. However, the former reputedly was an Alexandrian Jew, while the latter, though a native of Palestine, was said to have been a refugee of the Bar Kocheba revolt and a resident of Greece. Here he frequently associated with Stoic and other philosophers. Neither man was, of course, in any way typical of the average Palestinian Jew of his time. In any case, the official leaders of Jewry in Palestine and Babylonia viewed public religious controversies with great distrust. At least of two great Babylonian teachers, Rab and Raba, we hear expressly that they shunned religious discussions with Christians (Shabbat 116a), even though in Babylonia, under Persian domination, there was absolutely no danger for a Jewish debater. The rabbis were too well aware of the futility of such intellectual acrobatics.

On the other hand, Jewish leaders regarded it as their duty to instill in their own people all knowledge necessary for resisting propagandists of other creeds. "Know how to refute an Epicurean" became the constant refrain of those who advocated the education of Jewish youth in general sciences, and especially in the Greek language and culture. Of course, many talmudic teachings reveal an evident polemical or apologetical undertone. When the Talmud asks "Has God a son?" (j. Shabbat VI end, 8d), it voices against Christianity the same argument as was advanced by a representative pagan like Celsus. So widespread were these Jewish and pagan objections to the divine character of Jesus that there arose among Christians themselves the great Arian heresy. More subtly R. Eleazar ben Azariah in one of his monthly homilies before the academy of Yabneh expatiated on Deut. 26:17–18 and insisted upon the uniqueness of both God and Israel. "The Holy Blessed be He said to Israel," he declared, "just as you have made me a unique object in the world, so shall I make you a unique object in the world" (Ḥagigah 3a).

Christians, on their part, attacked the relevancy of law to moral behavior, often adducing the argument that, although the Torah had not yet been given in the patriarchal age, the people lived a saintly and pure life. It was to answer this argument that some later rabbis, consciously exaggerating, taught that Abraham was familiar with Jewish law in its totality and observed even such a minute regulation as that concerning the "concoction of dishes" preparatory to cooking on a holiday falling on the eve of a Sabbath (Yoma 28b).

More important were legal enactments against Christianity. Perhaps the oldest such negativistic regulation was the limitation of the fast days to the middle of the week, from Monday to Thursday, by the representatives of the Jewish masses at the Temple (the so-called *anshe ma'amad*). The abstention from fasting on Saturday, and hence also on Friday, appeared quite natural. But at least R. Johanan felt it necessary to explain that the Jews did not fast on Sunday "on account of the Christians." He may well have meant that the Christians should not be led to think that the Jews abstain from work on that day as an acknowledgment of the Christian claim to its sanctity.[6]

Two characteristic liturgical changes likewise reflect the reaction against the new creed. Originally the Ten Commandments were read daily in the synagogue. But when Christian polemists began to impugn the validity of all other Pentateuch laws, the position of the Commandments in the daily service began to be viewed differently. Eventually the Palestinian rabbis eliminated their public recitation from daily prayers, and Babylonia in the days of R. Ashi (*ca.* 400) followed suit. Only Egypt seems to have clung to the older practice for a long period. The abandonment of the cherished custom of publicly reciting what was always regarded as the highest Sinaitic revelation was simply a means of stressing the equal value of the whole Torah as revealed Scripture. To underscore this point the rabbis emphasized that a day before that momentous revelation Moses had already read to the people "the book of the covenant" (Exod. 24:7) which, according to R. Judah the Patriarch, included "the laws commanded to Adam and the children of Noah, the commandments given to the Israelites in Egypt and at Marah, and all other commandments." [7]

The best known anti-Christian liturgical modification is the inclusion in the daily 'Amidah of a special prayer against heretics (minim). Whether this change occurred, as is probable, at the end of the first century, and whether it was enacted merely to keep Judeo-Christians (specifically mentioned in one old text) out of the synagogue, or to proclaim the definite breach between the two religions, is debatable. But there is no doubt that this twelfth benediction represented the formal recognition by official Judaism of the severance of all ties between the Christian and other schismatics and the national body of Jewry. [8]

Very likely immediately upon the insertion of the new benediction Rabban Gamaliel II dispatched letters to the various Palestinian communities and to "our brethren in the dispersion [galuta] of Babylonia, the dispersion of Media and the rest of the Jewish dispersion," informing them of this formal act of divorcement. These letters may have resembled in form the regular messages sent out by Gamaliel I to keep the entire Diaspora informed about changes in calendar. During their journey to Rome in 95 c.e., Gamaliel II and his colleagues also had personal opportunities to acquaint particularly the Jews of the imperial capital of their decision, although it may have been this very journey and the resultant observation of the havoc played by Christian propaganda in the Hellenistic dispersion that gave the impetus to the decisive breach. In Rome R. Gamaliel and his associates preached in the synagogue on the theme that, unlike most earthly lawgivers who enact laws for others to obey, God himself observes all the laws He had given to Israel. Challenged by a heretic (min) who asked why God broke the Sabbath by such work as causing rainfall, they casuistically replied that the whole world being his "private property," God was entitled to move the rain drops from one part of his domain to another. With perfect consistency other rabbis insisted that God was attending synagogue, putting on phylacteries, and performing other religious rituals, unmindful of the gross anthropomorphism of such a view. [9]

HISTORICAL CONTROVERSIES

Attack and counterattack also opened up new historic vistas. In the relatively placid pre-Maccabean period, the Jews were prone to neglect their own history and to confide to almost total oblivion entire generations of Jews after the Babylonian Exile. Under the impact of classical antisemitism, however, Jewish apologists increasingly had to resort to historical arguments to prove the priority of Jewish over the Greek contributions to civilization and, later, to justify the Jewish claims to equality of rights, or the rebellions against Rome. Now they had to deal with an internal enemy who, even after the separation, appropriated the entire realm of Jewish history as its own and increasingly denied it to the Jewish people itself. History, not in its realistic record but in its mutually accepted homiletical and hermeneutic elaboration, became for centuries the main battleground between the rivaling Jewish and Christian denominations. Once again, as in the Hellenistic-Jewish apologias, attention was focused on the generations from Adam to Moses, rather than on later prophets or kings.

It was of vital importance to Christian missionaries to persuade the pagan world that Christianity was not a recent religion, as did, for example, late in the second century Theophilus of Antioch, that storm center of religious controversy. They, therefore, not only claimed for Jesus Davidic descent, but also began dating the beginnings of Christianity further and further back. As early as the last years of Trajan, St. Ignatius, likewise of Antioch, asserted that the Israelitic prophets had lived in conformity with Jesus, rather than *vice versa*. He also coined the paradox that "Christianity did not believe in Judaism, but Judaism believed in Christianity." Later writers placed the Christian origins in the days of Moses, the patriarchs, and even the first generation of man on earth. Tertullian stated explicitly that one particular law "given to Adam, we may recognize as containing all the commandments later given through Moses in such profusion." He thereby laid the foundation for the Christian doctrine of natural law which, though nurtured from Stoic and Philonic ideas, was destined to play such an extraordinary role in the subsequent destinies of the Western world. The North African jurist also intimated that the separation between Judaism and Christianity had taken place in the days of Cain and Abel. Cain was, of course, the older brother whose sacrifice was rejected by God and, hence, he slew (that is, crucified) the younger brother.

This homiletical excursus, too, was to have a strange career in the Middle Ages, in many ways complicating all Judeo-Christian relations.[10]

Without taking direct cognizance of such attacks the rabbis differentiated between the six or seven Noahide and the six hundred and thirteen Jewish commandments, not even bothering clearly to define either computation. They also continued to describe Cain as a prototype of all criminals and shared with Philo the condemnation of this alleged rebellious champion of the supremacy of reason and legitimacy of carnal pleasures. They, of course, rejected the second-century gnostic sect of "Cainites" who glorified such rebellion and indulged in sexual promiscuity. To witnesses in criminal proceedings they also continued to hold out Cain as a warning that miscarriage of justice resulting in bloodshed would cause suffering for countless generations. Incidentally there is an ancient ring to this warning to witnesses: "You shall know that criminal trials are unlike civil litigations; in civil litigations a man pays the money and he is forgiven, in criminal trials his [the condemned man's] blood and the blood of his offspring cling to the witness to the end of the world." It seems to reflect actual practice at the time when Jewish courts still exercised capital jurisdiction and, hence, before the crucifixion of Jesus. Very likely this stereotype warning inspired the Christian tradition that the Jews, present at Golgotha, had taken the curse, "His blood be on us and on our children." Perhaps as a reaction to the Christian assault, however, we find later rabbis occasionally revealing a kindlier attitude to Cain, as when they taught that he was but an accidental slayer who later expiated for his sin through exile. They significantly added, "Exile expiates for sin," or even more broadly, "expiates for everything." [11]

Christian apologists also appropriated to themselves the patriarchs and Moses. Already the first-century author of the Epistle of Barnabas used a typical rabbinic *gematria* to illustrate that "Abraham, who first instituted circumcision, did it looking forward in spirit to Jesus," that is, toward circumcision of the heart. The 318 men servants circumcised by the patriarch represented but the numerical value of the Greek T (symbol of the cross) and IH (the first two letters of Jesus' name). Similarly Joshua was victorious over the Amalekites only as long as Moses held up his hands in a way resembling the cross. Unwittingly, "Barnabas" demonstrated how deeply indebted Christian circles were to the rabbinic methods of interpreting Scripture. Not even anti-Jewish apologists could wholly escape it, as may be also seen in Justin Martyr's *Dialogue* and Theophilus' *Altercation,* which is sometimes considered as antedating Justin. In later generations the Christian claims to spiritual descent from Abraham became such a stereotype in patristic literature that Augustine became alarmed lest it blur the distinction between Jews and Christians.[12]

  Without entering into direct polemics, the rabbis strongly emphasized the humanitarian aspects of Abraham's missionary successes and his early trials and tribulations. They also stressed circumcision as a major expiatory ritual which obviated the need of sacrifices. Provoked both by Christian attacks and Roman prohibitions, they glorified this "covenant of Abraham" more than ever before. With complete abandon R. Levi declared, "In the world to come Abraham sits at the entry of Gehenna and allows no circumcised Israelite to descend into it." Only as an afterthought an explanation was added as to how Jewish evildoers could be specifically made to enter. The old debate as to whether one might convert a Gentile without circumcision was totally silenced, and ultimately some rabbis taught that "heaven and earth are held together only by the fulfillment of this covenant." If Christians claimed atonement by Jesus, the Jewish sages extolled the *zekhut abot,* the merits of their patriarchal fathers, which were helping Jews of all generations to secure forgiveness for sins and to overcome every great crisis. Perhaps because of its similarity with the passion of Christ, the rabbis now dwelt with increasing persistence on the theme of Isaac's sacrifice and composed a number of *'aqedahs* for liturgical use. The Beth Alpha synagogue illustrates the use of this motif in graphic arts. The sages also emphasized that the ram which ultimately took Isaac's place on the altar had been prepared for that role from primordial days and associated with it the ritual of blowing the ram's horn on New Year's Day as an element in the cosmic expiation of Israel's sins. According to R. Abbahu, the Lord says to Israel, "Blow before me a ram's horn so that I remember in your behalf the sacrifice of Isaac the son of Abraham and count it to you as if you had sacrificed yourselves before Me." [13]

  Most of all, the sages emphasized the binding force of every detail in Mosaic law, contending, for example, that the three daily prayers (the early second-century Christian author of the *Didache* demanded that Christians, too, recite the Lord's Prayer three times a day) had been successively instituted by the three patriarchs. To undermine the Christian contention that the law had been invalidated by the prophecy of Jesus, the rabbis interpreted the Scriptural statement that the Torah "is not in heaven" to mean that "You shall not say that another Moses will arise and bring us another Torah from heaven; for no part of it has been left behind in heaven." They also frequently emphasized the cessation of all genuine prophetic inspiration in the days of Zechariah and Malachi in the early years of the Second Commonwealth. Moreover, commenting on the last verse in Leviticus they insisted, in frequent reiteration, that Moses had enjoined Israel that "from now on no other prophet shall be entitled to impose upon you any new commandment." One rabbi exclaimed, "By God! were Joshua the son of Nun to tell me something in his [Moses'] name, I would not listen to him." At a decisive moment R. Joshua controverted a statement by R. Eliezer, supported by a divine voice, by insisting, "It [the Torah] is not in Heaven," that is, the Torah had already been given and law now follows the majority rule, rather than new revelations. Ultimately another rabbi exclaimed, "Not only have all prophets received their message from Sinai, but also the sages arising in every generation receive their lore from Sinai." [14]

More recent events loomed equally large in the debate. Curiously, in contrast to the Church Fathers, the Jewish spokesmen rarely referred to the Maccabeans, either as heroes or as martyrs. Not because the subject was essentially noncontroversial, nor because the rabbis wished to stress less the idea of religious martyrdom—which was, in fact, now exalted more than ever—but rather because of the anti-Hasmonean heritage of the last generations before 70. On the other hand, the more the political power of the Jewish people declined, the more did Christian polemists see in its loss of national independence a divine retribution for its repudiation of Christ. Since the main controversy now concerned the question as to whether or not the messiah had already come, Justin Martyr and his successors pointed to Jacob's blessing of Judah as definite proof for their affirmation. "The sceptre shall not depart from Judah . . . as long as men come to Shilo" was translated "until the coming of Shilo," that is, Christ. The very fact that the sceptre had departed from Judah showed that the promise had been fulfilled. So certain was, for instance, St. Chrysostom of the force of such arguments that, in a homily on Isaiah, he assured his listeners that, had the Jews paid sufficient attention to biblical chronology, they would not have left Christ for Antichrist. "You see," he added, "how serious an error arises from the ignorance of dates." At the same time

Jews were also depicted as the most dangerous enemies of Christianity. Although in addressing Jews the Christian controversialists (for example, Justin) gloated over their political impotence and inability to hurt Christians, in most writings aimed at the pagan world these apologists found it convenient to appeal to pagan anti-Jewish prejudices and to pretend that pagan-Christian relations would have been most amicable were it not for constant Jewish denunciations and malicious rumor mongering.[15]

Once again Jewish leaders either ignored these attacks or answered them obliquely. Occasionally they were prepared to pay back in kind and place Christians on a par with other sectarian "informers"—with far greater justice, it appears, in the light of the historic record. But on the whole they imposed upon themselves extraordinary restraint. Whether the various fables concerning Jesus' descent, his study of magic in Egypt, his leadership of a gang of licentious brigands and the theft of his body by his disciples, included in the later apocryphon, *Toledot Yeshu* (Life of Jesus), go back to the second or third century, or were the outgrowth of the overheated medieval popular fantasy, they clearly betray their origin in the folklore of masses. To an astonishing degree, these tales were ignored by the spokesmen of the Synagogue. Some rabbis were even ready to accept the traditional pre-Christian identification of Shilo with the king messiah. But others interpreted the whole passage to mean, " 'The sceptre shall not depart from Judah,' that is, the Sanhedrin which punishes and rules, 'nor the ruler's staff from between his feet,' that is, the two court scribes standing on its right and left, 'until Shilo comes,' the majority [of rabbis] decided that it refers to Hillel" and his patriarchal house, which was of Davidic descent. Babylonian patriots had no difficulty in transferring the identification of Shilo to the even more directly Davidic house of the prince of captivity.[16]

Long before Chrysostom censured the Jews for their alleged errors in biblical chronology, talmudic sages tried to review the time sequence of the major events in their history in a way which permanently influenced all subsequent Christian, as well as Jewish, historiography. For practical and national reasons they first compiled the so-called *Megillat Ta'anit* (Scroll of Fasts), in which they curiously listed in succession the days (in our texts thirty-five in all) in the Jewish calendar year on which one *must not fast* because of some major events which had occurred on those days. Certainly this list, amplified and commented upon in later generations, helped infuse in its readers the conviction that the Jewish people was a specific object of the divine guidance of history and that, in ultimate emergencies, it may always count on God's direct intervention. In the middle of the second century R. Simon ben Gamaliel had to warn against further additions to the list resulting from man's natural proneness to exaggerate events occurring in his own lifetime. "Were we to list," he declared, "[every miraculous deliverance], there would be no end to it" (Shabbat 13b)—a statement wholly understandable after the calamities of the preceding decades.

R. Simon's colleague, R. Jose ben Halafta, went further. Revealing, in other connections, a healthy historical curiosity, and apparently having access to many old traditions (such as underlay the chronological computations of Demetrius four centuries earlier), he compiled a *Seder 'Olam* (World Chronology), listing the dates of all major events from Adam to Alexander. The extant texts conclude with a brief summary of events from Alexander to Bar Kocheba which, however, may be but the epitome of a longer section cut down by some later editor uninterested in "postbiblical" history. On the whole, this chronicle is dry as dust. Even the occasional homiletical extensions may largely be later interpolations. Nevertheless, to most of its pious readers it must have appeared as a paean on the immortality of the Jewish people. R. Jose himself voiced this keynote elsewhere: "The children of Israel accepted the Torah only in order that the angel of death should have no control over them." [17]

LANGUAGE AND EXEGESIS

So much in the entire Judeo-Christian controversy depended on the proper reading and interpretation of Old Testament texts that the debates also had far-reaching exegetical and linguistic effects. The eager response of Hellenistic Jewry to the new religion naturally provoked widespread suspicion as to the value of Greek studies for Jews. As long as Jewish leaders were confronted mainly by a pagan world, they could remain confident of ultimate spiritual victory by the very use of the Greek language and letters. As late as the end of the first century Rabban Gamaliel II could, with perfect *sang froid*, bathe in a Greek bathhouse adorned by a statue of Aphrodite, use a pagan looking seal, and even, according to his son's testimony, maintain at his patriarchal court a school for a thousand children, of whom "five hundred studied the Torah and the other five hundred were trained in Greek wisdom" (Soṭah 49b).

In the second century, however, when the Christian inroads became more marked, R. Joshua, himself a fine linguist and student of Greek, allowed a father to instruct his son in Greek culture only "at a time which is neither day nor night." After the Bar Kocheba disaster some extremists wanted all Greek culture (*hokhmat yevanit*) banished from Jewish intellectual life, finding strong support in the general repudiation of Hellenistic ingredients by the reawakened East. To eliminate the Greek language, the main medium of communication throughout the empire, was impossible. But a sharp line was drawn between the study of the language and the study of Greek literature and thought. That preventive measures against spoken Greek were necessary even in Palestine (at least in the vicinity of the Decapolis) is clearly shown, for example, by the fifth-century synagogue inscriptions of Ḥammath near Gadara, which reveal a high degree of Hellenization of the Jews in that district. Even rabbis living in Greek cities, as for example, R. Abbahu of Caesarea, remained rather friendly to Greek studies. Some undoubtedly even preached in Greek, perhaps like the Christian preacher Procopius in Scythopolis, using an interpreter to translate their sermons for the Aramaic-speaking villagers. Like their medieval and early modern successors, however, they recorded their most significant homilies only in Hebrew or Hebrew-Aramaic. Others, especially some new arrivals from the non-Hellenistic dispersion, wished to see Greek culture completely eliminated from the curriculum of young Jews. R. Johanan (according to one version) pithily explained, "On account of the informers," probably referring to Christians.[18]

Against the Septuagint, the traditional Greek version, which by its numerous messianic implications and its deep roots in Hellenistic Jewry had served as an eminent vehicle of Christian propaganda, hostility was even sharper. Originally, to be sure, the Greek translators seem to have been in close contact with the contemporary developments of Palestinian hermeneutics. The Septuagint is not only permeated with Jewish traditions later incorporated in rabbinic lore, but a recent student could even contend that it substantially anticipated the thirty-two heremeneutic rules formulated at the end of the second century by R. Eliezer, son of R. Jose the Galilean. The accelerated pace of reinterpretation, however, in the schools of Hillel and Shammai, and the new adjustments made necessary by the loss of state and sanctuary, left it far behind in the evolution of Jewish biblical learning. It completely outlived its usefulness to Jews when Christians started quoting it as a canonical authority, even where, in Jewish opinion, it was clearly at variance with the Hebrew text. No more characteristic change in the rabbinic attitude can be found than that portrayed in the two statements juxtaposed in the first chapter of the much younger *Masekhet Sopherim*. While one passage reflected the traditional reverence for the ancient version, reiterating the myth of how "God gave counsel to the heart of each one [of the seventy-two translators] and their minds agreed upon one opinion," the passage immediately preceding it renders most sharply the new view that "that day was as fateful for Israel as the day on which the [golden] calf was made, because the Torah could not be satisfactorily translated." According to a later tradition, that day was followed by three days of darkness which enveloped the whole world, and the Jews were enjoined to commemorate it by an annual fast day on the 8th of Tebet.[19]

Unable, however, to check the use of a Greek version in both home and synagogue, the rabbis of the generation following the destruction encouraged Aquila, the proselyte, to undertake a new, more literal translation. Incidentally, for similar reasons some Judeo-Christian sectarians were apparently dissatisfied with both these versions. The Ebionites, at least, found in Symmachus a cultured and less pedantic but also less accurate translator. Symmachus was able, moreover, to make use not only of the Septuagint and Aquila but of still another Greek translation, prepared by Theodotion, probably a Jewish proselyte. All three translations were apparently made in the course of the second century. Since at that time almost all the Jews in the Roman Empire knew Greek, Rabban Simon ben Gamaliel, to arrest further deviations, declared that the rabbis "had investigated and found that the Torah could not be adequately translated into any language except Greek." This statement may well have deterred western Jews from translating Scripture into Latin and other western tongues for centuries to come.[20]

To be sure, the very continuation of this statement in the report of the Palestinian Talmud seems to indicate the existence at that time of a Latin paraphrase from the Greek Bible. It had been prepared by either a Roman soldier or some "barbarian" Oriental, if we accept S. Lieberman's emendation of the text. It is possible, however, that this paraphrase was made for Christian rather than Jewish use. The Latin-speaking Jews of Rome and other western provinces must also have translated into Latin those Scriptural sections which they were teaching in their schools. Long restricted to oral transmission, such renditions doubtless developed, as elsewhere, certain peculiarities which affected all subsequent translations of the Bible and prayer book not only into Latin but also into Italian and, possibly, other Romance languages as well. A fine connoisseur like U. Cassuto believes to have detected such ancient vestiges in many peculiar phrases still used in Bible teaching in all Italian-Jewish schools during the present century. Of course, as in the preparation of the Vulgate and probably also the Vetus Latina, Jewish aides may have played a certain role. Even unfriendly Eusebius commented that among the Jews were so-called "Deuterotists," who "were grown grey in mind." Such men "were permitted to dive into the deeps and test the meaning of the words." Jerome did not hesitate to make good use of a Jewish assistant who, apart from his familiarity with the Hebrew text, may have possessed some knowledge of Latin. Pointing out that, in four of seven references to his Jewish assistant, Jerome "followed the Hebrew instructor against all the Greek versions," W. L. Newton rightly concluded that "this instructor's influence was greater than might at first appear." [21]

Together with the Septuagint, the rabbis repudiated the allegorical interpretation of Scripture. Not that the Midrash was given up altogether, but a sharp distinction was made between plain and homiletical exposition of a canonical sentence. Faced by necessarily allegorical Christian arguments, Judaism clung more and more to the simple meaning of the text. Instead of reading certain passages as containing messianic forebodings (for instance, Ps. 110:1; cf. Matt. 22:43–45), Jews interpreted them as but historical reflections of past events. That Scripture never loses its plain meaning (en miqra yoṣe mide peshuto) became a fixed principle. In the linking up of four major offenses, rabbinic ideology of the first century reveals most plainly its anti-Christian bent. Time and again the rabbis proclaimed the definite breach with all "who throw off the yoke of the law, break the covenant [circumcision], insolently interpret the Torah and pronounce the Divine name as it is written." [22]

Christian appropriation of Jewish Scriptures added impetus to the progress of their canonization. Such belligerent declarations as

Justin Martyr's, "Your Scriptures, or rather not yours, but ours,"
egged on the rabbis to differentiate sharply between their own "authentic" Bible and alien accretions. The text began to be definitely
established and the foundations of the *Masorah* were laid down
through the minute toil of generations. Certain books were definitely included in, others excluded from, the Hebrew Canon, a
peremptory line of demarcation being drawn between those endowed with scriptural authority and the inferior "external" works
(Apocrypha and Pseudepigrapha). The refusal of the rabbis to
repudiate such "worldly" but beautiful writings as the Song of
Songs and Ecclesiastes is not only a mark of their great aesthetic
sense of responsibility. The Song was soon elevated to a nationalist
ode on the chosenness of Israel, the beloved bride of the Lord, and
"Solomon's" skepticism in *Kohelet,* mitigated by a few pious interpolations, could well serve as a dam to the rising gnostic tide in
which the shade of the royal master of magic arts was frequently
invoked. Far from acting on Irenaeus' hypothetical suggestion that
Jews would have burned their Scriptures if they had foreseen their
use by Christians, talmudic Judaism, armed with the "twenty-four"
books of the Hebrew Bible, interpreting them both literally and
homiletically and stressing above all their legal sections, was ready
to defy an overwhelmingly inimical world.[23]

Even more curious was the reaction against the Aramaic tongue.
Aramaic, the third universal language of the Mediterranean world,
especially prominent in the eastern provinces, had been used extensively by Christian propagandists in and outside the empire.
Some Jewish teachers began to suspect even that language, in which
the Jews of Palestine and Babylonia had been born and raised for
centuries. The nationalist revival, combined with the defensive
fight against Christianity, began to bar Aramaic from synagogues
and higher schools. We recall, how soon after the Bar Kocheba revolt, R. Meir placed Hebrew speech on a par with residence in the
Holy Land among the foremost duties of a conscientious Jew.

Several decades after R. Meir, R. Jose ben 'Aqabiah pointed out
the juxtaposition of Deut. 11:19–21 and taught, "From here it is
said that as soon as an infant begins to talk, his father speaks to him
in Hebrew and teaches him the Torah. He who fails to speak
Hebrew with him [the infant] and teach him the Torah acts like
one who buries him." Even before the Christian menace loomed
seriously on the Palestinian horizon, Rabban Gamaliel I once
symbolically discarded an Aramaic translation of the Book of Job,

apparently in use for several generations. Official proceedings, particularly in the Palestinian academies, were always conducted exclusively in the neo-Hebraic dialect of whose deviations from biblical Hebrew, the result of centuries of slow growth, the rabbis themselves were perfectly aware. R. Johanan once disdainfully rebuffed a puristic affectation of a Babylonian disciple, because "the language of the Torah is one thing, the language of the sages another." In the synagogue, particularly, prayers remained predominantly Hebrew, the *Qaddish* being the most important exception throughout the talmudic period. The Palestinian R. Johanan and the Babylonian R. Judah agreed completely that a man must not use the Aramaic language, even in his personal prayers. The former added significantly, "because the ministering angels are not familiar with the Aramaic tongue." [24]

Inscriptions, too, reveal an increasing return to the ancient national language. On tombstones, from the fifth century on, in the Italian city of Venosa, there appear Hebrew words (in the Hebrew alphabet), instead of the previously customary Greek, or Latin in Greek characters. The Torlonia catacomb, for example, had sixty-three Greek and five Latin inscriptions, but none in Hebrew. Antagonism to Aramaic reached its climax in the famous pronunciamento of R. Judah the Patriarch, "Why should the Syriac language be used in Palestine? Either Hebrew or Greek!" (Soṭah 49b.) A faithful partisan paraphrased this utterance two generations later in Babylonia, in favor of the alternatives of Hebrew and Persian.

Realities were too strong, however, and the Jews, like other Western Asiatic nations, clung to the Syriac-Aramaic language, at least in daily life. All business documents, marriage contracts and letters were written in Aramaic, which finally subjugated the whole domain of law, as evidenced by both the Palestinian and the Babylonian Talmud. Compared to their proficiency in Aramaic, the rabbis' knowledge of Greek and Persian was frequently very slight indeed.

Aramaic influence, even in the synagogue, had to be acknowledged eventually. The need of an Aramaic version of the Bible, in particular, had to be recognized, the rabbis themselves soon insisting that a pious Jew should read on every Sabbath the weekly portion "twice in Hebrew and once in translation [*Targum*]." The existence of such a version throughout the talmudic period is not subject to doubt, even though recurrent attempts to revive the long-abandoned identification of Onkelos of the Aramaic, with

Aquila of the Greek version written about 100 C.E. cannot be said to have been successful. Our Onkelos may date from any time between the second and the sixth century; he certainly had more than one predecessor, probably reaching back to the Maccabean age or earlier.[25]

In short, long after the fall of Jerusalem the vast majority of Jews spoke either Aramaic or Greek. Only a minority seems to have been fully bilingual, combining the knowledge of both these languages or of either with Hebrew. A tiny group may have been genuinely trilingual. Even the ordinary Palestinian or Syrian Jew, however, seems to have acquired a smattering of Greek, while many of the western Jews doubtless understood some Aramaic or Hebrew, or both. At the same time the local dialects in the various eastern provinces mattered less and less, as the other ancient oriental languages were slowly dying out. We possess no Akkadian tablet or Phoenician inscription dated after the rise of Christianity. Egyptian, far more tenacious, survived, if not in hieratic, in a number of hieroglyphic writings until the third century, and in demotic works even longer. Some rabbis specifically permitted the recitation of Esther in *Giptit* to Egyptian-speaking Jews. Nevertheless the language played a far greater role among the later "Coptic" Christians than among Jews. Only Latin in the West and Persian outside the borders of the Roman Empire seem to have been gaining ground. But none of these languages represented serious obstacles in the way of mutual understanding among the dispersed communities. The linguistic problem, therefore, which was to plague the early churches and so significantly to contribute to their sectarian divisions, proved to be but a minor hindrance to the universal acceptance of the talmudic letters, written in a remarkable blend of Hebrew and Aramaic.[26]

PROSELYTISM

Perhaps the most important practical effect of the anti-Christian reaction was the new ambivalent attitude toward proselytism. Pharisaic Judaism which, in its triumphant march through the Graeco-Roman world, had become a missionary religion of prime import, now became apprehensive of all propagandist activities. The overwhelming success of the early Christian mission in the proselytic and semiproselytic appendages of the Jewish communities in the Diaspora was more than discouraging. Josephus remarked that many Greeks "have agreed to adopt our laws; of them some have remained faithful, while others, lacking the necessary endurance, have again seceded" (*Ag. Ap.* II, 10.123).

Jewish leaders must have become much concerned lest such experiences recur too frequently. So convinced was, for example, R. Eliezer ben Hyrcanus of the unreliability of converts that, rather than being impressed by the reiteration of the biblical safeguards in behalf of the stranger (*ger*, also meaning proselyte), he taught, "It is because there is a bad streak in the stranger that Scripture warns about him in so many passages." While most of R. Eliezer's colleagues disagreed, suspicion grew after the Bar Kocheba revolt. Rumor had it that numerous spies, masked as converts, were being planted by the Roman authorities at the Jewish academies. Later, during the fateful third century, was coined the bitter saying of R. Ḥelbo, "The proselytes are as troublesome to Israel as a tumor." To be sure, this may have been but a bad pun (*sapaḥat*, tumor, vs. *ve-nispeḥu*, "shall cleave" of Isa. 14:1) by an irate individual. But the old vigorous drive for conversion now decidedly gave way to a distinct *malaise*. No absolutely uniform policy could be adopted. The force of tradition on the one hand, and individual sympathies on the other, frequently tempered missionary, as well as antimissionary, zeal. The official tannaitic attitude is perhaps best summed up in the rule, "In general the left hand should repel and the right should attract, not like Elisha who pushed away Gehazi . . . nor like Joshua ben Peraḥiah who dismissed Jesus the Nazarene with both hands." [27]

Aversion to proselytism naturally affected the relations of Jews and Gentiles. The process of mutual segregation made rapid advances. Even regarding cultural contacts with the outside world, opinions differed widely. R. Meir, himself apparently a descendant of proselytes (according to a later legend, of Emperor Nero), declared that "even a Gentile who studies the Torah is equal to a high priest"; but many rabbis insisted on closing the avenues of Jewish learning to non-Jews. R. Johanan, apparently reacting to the new wave of persecutions, exclaimed that "a Gentile who studies the Torah deserves capital punishment"; and his colleague and friend, R. Simon ben Laqish, echoed him in the statement that "a Gentile who rests on the Sabbath deserves capital punishment." So poignant was the disillusionment with the God-fearing of the previous generations! [28]

The Mishnah's advice to Jews not to be closeted alone with Gentiles, since "they are suspected of murder" ('A.Z. II, 1) reflects intense mutual hostility. On the Sabbath especially, Jews were to remain among Jews exclusively. The sectarians of Damascus stated this in terms of an outright prohibition (11:14). No greater encouragement to the development of a voluntary ghetto was needed.

Environment, as well as national experiences of subsequent generations, greatly modified this caution. In Babylonia, particularly, where the Jews long lived in relative peace and prosperity, and where Christianity never made deep inroads into Jewish communities, a moderate missionary policy was revived. Raba and Rab Ashi, the great teachers of Babylonian Jewry in the fourth century, were outspoken advocates of proselytism, and at times the number of proselytes seems to have been considerable. Whole villages, it appears, asked Rabbah ben Aboah for admission into the fold of Judaism, while the ranks of the leading Jewish community of Maḥoza were swelled by proselytes ('A.Z. 64a; Qiddushin 73a). Despite the superficial assumptions of some modern scholars, it should be noted that the greatest advances of Judaism were made through the appeal of Jewish ceremonial law. The Jewish Sabbath and dietary laws seem to have attracted the Gentiles more than did Jewish monotheism and ethics. Consequently Aphraates, the leading Christian bishop in Persia, among others, vigorously assailed Jewish ceremonial law, because people were sadly disturbed, as he said, "over what enters their mouth" (Homil. XV, 1).

Under these circumstances semiproselytism, consisting in the partial adoption of Jewish mores, began to flourish once more. This time, however, taught by experience, the rabbis combated incomplete conversion with all means at their disposal, eventually accepting a Palestinian sage's hyperbole, "The *ger toshab* [at that time the Hebrew equivalent for *sebomenos*] existed only when the Jubilee year was in force." To test the genuineness of the conversion, the rabbis introduced a new ritual. In a tannaitic source, evidently dating after Bar Kocheba, we read:

A man, who in these days wishes to undergo conversion, is being asked, "What has made you come to be converted? Don't you know that Israel is today suffering, downtrodden, beaten, persecuted and afflicted with many sorrows?" If he answers, "Yes, I know, and although unworthy [I wish to share their fate]," they immediately admit him. Then they instruct him in some of the lighter and some of the more stringent commandments . . . and tell him about the punishments for their transgression. They say to him, "Until now you could eat [prohibited] fat without suffering extirpation, you could break the Sabbath without becoming liable to stoning, from now on [you will be subject to these penalties]." But just as he is warned about the punishment for breaking commandments, he is also told about the rewards for their fulfillment. They say to him, "Know that the world to come is prepared only for the righteous and that today, too, Israel cannot receive too much good, but neither shall it suffer excessive punishment. . . ."

It required a stout heart for a would-be proselyte to persist after so many warnings. It also stands to reason that no candidate could acquire full familiarity with the whole system of Jewish observance, which he had to keep from the first day after his conversion, through such a single lecture, however long. In fact, the rabbis warned in the same context that the lecture not be too long. One must assume, therefore, a fairly lengthy period of preparation and testing before the final rites were administered.[29]

Even in Babylonia, however, missionary gains were extremely limited. Parsiism, itself a missionary creed, naturally checked the expansion of other religions. The Roman Empire after the time of Constantine was even more intolerant of Jewish religious propaganda. The conversion of heathens to Judaism, once prohibited by Septimius Severus, was now apparently permitted, but imperial legislation, prompted by considerations of both state and ecclesiastical policy, prohibited the adoption of Judaism by Christians under severe sanctions. Constantine himself threatened in 335 a proselyte "from among the [Christian] people" with "deserved penalties." In order to encourage Jewish conversion to Christianity in the face of possible severe reprisals, he enjoined the Jewish elders that any attempt on their part to stone such renegades would be punished by death through burning (C. Th., XVI, 8, 1). Later laws became more specific. In 357 c.e. apostasy from Christianity was declared a crime, punishable by property confiscation. In 382 the disability to dispose of property by will was added. Jews responsible for such conversions were subject to the same punishment. Finally, by the laws of 409 and 438, the empire established capital punishment for the proselytizing Jew, if not for the Christian apostate. Since this prohibition covered slaves, male or female, and since imperial legislative and administrative measures greatly encouraged conversion to Christianity, it is easy to gauge the numerical insignificance of surreptitious proselytism. External and internal forces thus united to reduce the missionary and to increase the nationalist ingredients in the life and thought of the Jewish people.

CHRISTIAN SUCCESSES

Quite apart from its equivocal attitude toward proselytism the Jewish people was bound to lose out in the three-cornered struggle with paganism and Christianity which raged until 313 C.E. and beyond. The synthesis of Judaism and the Graeco-Roman culture, in its religious reformulation by Paul and his successors, was a great historical necessity. The increasing homogeneity of the vast empire, the mixture of races and cultures resulting in ethnic symbiosis, needed an appropriate religious expression, especially in an age so religious minded. Mommsen says rightly that Christianity "merely expressed in the religious field what had already been accomplished in the political." For a time, however, the Mithraic religion originating as a syncretistic creed in the Anatolian centers of Mediterranean piracy appeared as a dangerous competitor. It captured the imagination of the Roman soldiers by its warlike appeals, and spread rapidly all over the West. Even Diocletian and Julian hoped, by aiding it, to stem the Christian mission. It may be said without exaggeration that it was Hellenistic Jewry which, living in the economically and culturally more advanced eastern half of the empire, decided the struggle in favor of Christianity. With the erection of a new capital in Constantinople and the increasingly oriental character of the absolute monarchy, the Hellenistic provinces of the eastern Mediterranean, which had been conquered by Roman legions, now conquered Rome itself. This conquest without legions was as much religious as political.

In its basic negation of the idea of empire as well as in its worldwide attachment to the Palestinian homeland, orthodox Judaism could not serve as the factor cementing the new unity. It could not possibly subscribe to the theory expounded by such Roman patriots as Pliny the Elder that Italy had been selected "by the providence of the gods to make heaven itself more glorious, to unite scattered empires . . . and in a word to become throughout the world the single fatherland of all the races [gentium]." Paul and his successors had no such compunctions. In answer to pagan strictures why Jesus had not appeared earlier, Origen pointed out that Augustus' establishment of a universal monarchy uniting diverse races and nations was a necessary prerequisite for the coming of Christ and the success of his apostles. The more the Christian apologists gloated over the fall of Judaea, as did Justin, "that your land may be desolate, and your cities burned with fire," the more they were driven to the spiritual acceptance of the Roman Empire as an instrument of the divine will. Undismayed by the governmental persecutions, they could, by boring from within, cling to the hope of taking over the imperial machinery—as they ultimately did. Constantine and his successors doubtless realized that, by promoting Christianity, they would weaken the local autonomy based upon local worship and enhance the central powers of the growingly absolutist regime. Indeed, Roman imperialism readily lent itself to being translated into Christian imperialism.[30]

No such choice was available to Jews. Even at the height of Diaspora Jewry's close collaboration with Rome, Philo, though extolling the empire's great achievements in bringing unity, peace and prosperity to the civilized world, insisted that the time is yet to come when "the whole of our world should be as a single state enjoying that best of constitutions, democracy." Now after the sanguinary wars and ever-increasing fiscal exploitation Rome became the symbol of "oppression" and the Jewish people's hereditary enemy, Edom. This curious identification may have begun under the reign of Herod, the Idumaean. Perhaps impressed by the symbol of a pig on the flag of the Tenth Roman Legion stationed in Jerusalem in the crucial years 70–132, Jews also began alluding to the oppressive regime under the disguise of this unclean animal. In a noteworthy homily on Deut. 32:13, a second-century preacher combined it with the psalmist's complaint, "the boar [ḥazir] out of the wood does ravage it," to describe in considerable detail the various Roman agents of exploitation. "These are the oppressors who have occupied the land of Israel, and it is as difficult to extract from them a penny [peruṭah] as it is from a stone." The preacher concluded consolingly, however, by repeating, "But tomorrow Israel will inherit their possessions which will be as sweet to them as honey and oil." From the Roman Empire the pig symbol was readily transferred to its Byzantine heirs. Possibly with reference to the Czarist claim to the succession of Byzantium, it was transferred again to the Russians in modern Yiddish folkore.[31]

A gentle soul like R. Johanan, living in the midst of the anarchical conditions of the third century, could voice friendly sentiments toward the Gentile nations, enjoin his disciples never to talk evil of Gentile neighbors, stress that God was angry when the Israelites rejoiced over the Egyptians drowning in the Red Sea ("My creatures are drowning in the sea and you sing a song!") and hold out some ultimate hope even for the Roman destroyers of the

Temple. But he could not help interpreting the "fourth beast" in Daniel which "shall devour the whole earth, and shall tread it down, and break it in pieces," as referring to "criminal [ḥayyevet] Rome whose ill repute has spread all over the world." He and other rabbis did not hesitate to use for Rome the standardized designation of the "kingdom of wickedness." If imperial propaganda stressed above all Rome's invincibility and eternity, the rabbis not only emphasized the only genuine invincibility of their Lord, but also the ultimate Jewish victory over Rome—not through Rome— in the messianic age and the eternity of the Jewish people. Doubtless relating to the contemporary gnostic lucubrations concerning the cosmic succession of worlds, R. Eleazar ben Pedat, R. Johanan's disciple, speculated on the meaning of Moses' plea before the Lord,

"Remember Abraham, Isaac and Israel, Thy servants, to whom Thou didst swear by Thine own self," . . . Moses said to the Holy One blessed be He, Lord of the universe, "If Thou hadst sworn to them by heaven and earth, I should have believed that just as heaven and earth will pass so will Thy oath pass. Now that Thou hast sworn to them by Thy great name, just as Thy great name will live and persist for ever and evermore, so will Thy oath persist for ever and ever more."

To understand the import of R. Eleazar's teaching one must bear in mind that to a Palestinian sage heaven and earth were the equivalent of the universe. Trying to explain the meaning of the psalmist's reference to "inhabitants of the world [ḥaled]," a rabbi found no better formula than its equation with earth.[32]

Somewhat later R. Isaac paraphrased Ecclesiastes, "A kingdom cometh, a kingdom passeth away, but Israel abideth for ever" (Eccles. r. I, 9, on 1:4). True, the position of the Jewish people was low and depressed now. But did not Aquila the proselyte, in his imaginary conversation with his "uncle" Hadrian, remind the latter of the instability of all human affairs? "I have merely followed your advice," Aquila was quoted as saying, "when I informed you that I wanted to go into business you told me to pick up some low-priced and depressed merchandise which would ultimately go up, so I have wandered among the nations and I have found none in such a lowly state in the world as Israel, which will ultimately go up" (Tanḥuma, Mishpaṭim, V). Shortly after Bar Kocheba R. Judah bar Ilaʻi, taking a clue from the doubling of the verb *napol tippol* in Zeresh's warning to Haman, preached, "This people [Israel] is compared to dust as well as to stars. When they fall, they

fall down to dust, but when they rise, they rise up to the stars"
(Megillah 16a).

With such rationalizations of political inferiority there was no
compromise for Rome and its imperial traditions. We shall see that
even when Julian the Apostate tried to enlist Jewish support in his
hopeless battle against the victorious Church by the promise of
rebuilding their Temple (362 C.E.), he realized before long that,
despite all concessions, his approach was irreconcilable with the
basic beliefs of Judaism and turned away with disgust.

Christian attitude to graphic arts, even when used for worship,
was likewise far more flexible than the rigid Jewish repudiation of
all "idolatrous" forms. No matter how many concessions the rabbis were prepared to make to the growing use of paintings in synagogues, they had to reject sculptures and the representation of any
human figures for adoration. In Paul's speech on the Areopagus we
find a less severe condemnation of images than in the equally hellenistic Wisdom of Solomon or Philo. The Christian populace
went much further. Before long "shrines were built for the Saints,"
notes M. P. Nilsson, "votive offerings brought, and even animals
slaughtered just as for the heroes, food was placed and drink poured
out on their graves and banquets held on them just as on the graves
of pagan dead." Together with many contemporaries the Mani-
chean Faustus assailed the Christians for being but a "schism of the
Gentiles" with minor adaptations of the pagan ritual. "The sacrifices you change into love-feasts," he exclaimed, "the idols into martyrs, to whom you pray as they do to their idols." Even two and a
half centuries after Constantine, Pope Gregory the Great cautioned
Abbott Mellitus on his mission to England of the need of minor
compromises with established folkways and of imbuing some pagan
ceremonies with Christian meaning. The subsequent evolution of
English Christianity, as that in many other lands, showed that life
enforced far greater compromises than had been envisaged by the
pope. Nevertheless starting from the more restrained Jewish artistic motifs, Christian art soon began its triumphant progress against
the then fashionable oversophisticated and ornate products of the
Graeco-Roman epigoni. "It is a question," cautiously observes
Clark Hopkins, "whether one of the great appeals of the early
Christian church was not the calm and peace on one side, and the
austerity and discipline on the other, expressed in the symmetry
and strict convention of Eastern art, compared with the restless-
ness, the elaboration and the lack of order offered by Rome." [33]

In music, too, the increasingly simplified psalmody of the Diaspora synagogues, with its mournful undertones, could not effectively compete among the pagans with Church music which, even when it exercised utmost restraint, superimposed upon it tunes borrowed from a more joyous environment. To be sure, commenting on a Christian hymn of the late third century, E. J. Wellesz, a fine student of Byzantine Church music, found that, "this kind of cantillation is typical of the Early Christian liturgical singing, derived from the singing of the psalms in Jewish liturgy; it came down to us virtually unchanged, both in the practice of Jews in the Middle East and in the Eastern and Western Churches." None the less, the general rabbinic condemnation of hilarious singing as unfitting to a people in exile, even if not wholly lived up to in practice, and suspicions that Greek instrumental music might entice one to heresy, were not likely to appeal to the non-Jewish masses. Did not the rabbis explain the apostasy of the distinguished scholar Elisha ben Abuyah by the fact that "Greek melodies never departed from his lips"? In the decisive Syro-Anatolian areas, particularly, the Eastern Church permanently absorbed melodies, supported by instrumental music, from both the mystery religions and its own gnostic sects which, even in the midst of third-century anarchy and depression, loved to sing of the joys of life and spiritual-military victory. Little as we know about Jewish music and even art of the period, it can hardly be doubted that it could not as readily, as its Christian counterpart, swing back and forth from the adoration of "victors," in terms of religious martyrs, to that of Christian rulers who, since Constantin, used the military arm as an elongation of their religious, now pro-Christian policies.[34]

Jewish animal sacrifice might have given the Jews an edge over their Christian rivals in a world increasingly engrossed in the mysteries of the sacrificial ritual. But this advantage disappeared with the destruction of the Temples of Jerusalem and Leontopolis and the sacrificial self-abnegation of the Jews of the dispersion. Emperor Julian's anti-Christian praise of the Jewish sacrificial system and his luckless attempt to reëstablish it in Jerusalem had, as we shall presently see, no lasting effects.

On the other hand, though sharing with Jews a certain general aversion to conviviality with Gentiles whose food might previously have been offered in idolatrous "libations," Christians suffered from none of the other ritualistic deterrents of Jewish law. Nor can we overlook the availability of an ever-increasing body of Christian letters in Greek and Latin, contrasted with the diminishing supply of new Hellenistic Jewish writings. Aided by the new technique (mentioned by Martial in 84 C.E.) of distributing books in handy codices rather than the accustomed clumsy scrolls, Christian sermons and lives of saints and martyrs often became regular bestsellers. Small codices could more readily be carried around and concealed. They could also be used as magic talismans, like the fourth-century papyrus (now in Oslo) containing the beginning of Psalm 90, which was extremely popular as a protective amulet. We recall how widespread was the demand for such magical texts, with their foreign terminology, among the heathen masses. While in this area Jewish vendors could successfully compete with Christians (even St. Chrysostom tried to explain the success of Jewish magicians), no Greek homily of a Palestinian rabbi, however popular, with its obvious nationalistic overtones, could exercise as wide an appeal as did Christian homilies and epistles, often directly aimed at Gentile audiences. Jews faced, therefore, from the outset serious handicaps, even if they had still wished to missionize and even if most Jewish preachers had not preferred to circulate epitomes of their Greek sermons in their peculiar Hebrew-Aramaic dialect, which precluded use by non-Jews.[35]

PAGAN COUNTEROFFENSIVE

Pagan intellectual counterattacks against the Judeo-Christian outlook on life decreased in effectiveness, as they increased in number. More, in combating the monotheistic religions, the pagan writers increasingly accepted certain basic premises of their opponents—an invariable symptom of an approaching revolutionary upheaval. Gone was the serenity of the Augustan age and the Virgilian preachment of mankind's ultimate salvation through the power of Rome. Ever more frantic denunciations of Jews and Christians as the *odium generis humani* and the use of force to repress the Christian menace to the existing order proved the less effective as fewer and fewer people believed in the stability of that order. Even before the anarchy of the third century there was widespread acceptance of an approaching end of days. A Roman patriot like Annaeus Florus spoke in his epitome of Livy of the *senectus civilisationis* in the days from Augustus to Trajan. If, by dubious reasoning, he postulated that with Trajan a new cycle had set in and led to the complete rejuvenation of the empire, this clearly sounded like wishful thinking.

Most pagan writers, to be sure, even in the second century still evinced little real concern about Judeo-Christian doctrines. Epictetus, for example, rather calmly mentioned the "man halting between two faiths" (apparently the semiproselyte) about whom "we are in the habit of saying 'He is not a Jew, he is only acting the part.'" Although the obscurity of this and a preceding much-debated passage is probably owing to Arrian, the rapporteur, rather than to the philosopher himself, their detached tone is the more revealing, as Epictetus must have been fairly well acquainted with basic Jewish attitudes. As a native of Hierapolis in Phrygia, he doubtless knew something about its large Jewish community, while as a slave of Josephus' patron, Epaphroditus (himself perhaps a semiproselyte) he had probably met the Jewish historian and read some of his works. Going further, the Platonist, Numenius of Syrian Apamaea, praised the Jews for belonging to the peoples worshiping an incorporeal God and declared that Plato had been but a "Moses in Attic garb." In fact, in his "Appeal to the Orientals" Numenius expounded such strong syncretistic beliefs as to induce some such modern scholars as Charles Brigg to count him among Jewish proselytes. While outright conversion or even the status of *sebomenos* is highly unlikely, Numenius' sympathetic attitude to Judaism contrasted sharply with the alarm evinced by many pagan writers before the Jewish military defeats and, again, after the great Christian advances of the third century.[36]

The first full-fledged anti-Christian polemist Celsus, writing in the Antonine age (about 178 C.E.), still accused the Christians of being, like the Jews, merely a destructive and subversive force. Just as the Jews had begun their history as rebellious Egyptians, so did Christianity arise among rebellious Jews; "a revolt was the original commencement of the ancient Jewish state and subsequently of Christianity." Penetrating the main issues more deeply than his predecessors, however, he opposed the static Graeco-Roman view of an eternally moving, but essentially unchangeable *kosmos* in which man and his history play but a minor role, to the Judeo-Christian dynamic conceptions of a perfectible anthropocentric universe. In his opinion, Jews preferred to believe in angels rather than in the sun or the moon, because they thought that "they enjoy God's favor . . . and that angels were sent from heaven to them alone." This conceit of chosenness also made them assume that the course of nature would be altered to enable them to rise from the dead, as, in turn, it made Christians believe in God's incarnation. Even in these arguments, however, Celsus leaned heavily not only on Hellenistic Jewish critics of Christianity, but also on Philo's allegorical interpretations which often implied objections to the literal meaning of Scripture. He recalls, for example, Philo's query as to how the world could be created at the "beginning," if "time there was not before there was a world"; or, according to the Stoic definition, if time itself is but "the interval of the movement of the world"—a query which was to perplex believers in creation *ex nihilo* for centuries thereafter. Quite inconsistently, however, Celsus, being a child of his age, believed in miracles, "wicked" demons and oracles, and hence in the unpredictable irruption of supernational forces into the static universe. He who did not believe in anthropocentrism nevertheless was most deeply concerned about the survival of his civilization and came close to ascribing cosmic importance to the Roman Empire. In behalf of this political unity he was prepared to sacrifice even the uniqueness of his own faith and to admit, as we have seen, that all faiths in the empire essentially worshiped the same God under different names.[37]

A century later Porphyry, the "most learned of philosophers" (Augustine) and ingenious critic of the Bible, was even less sure of the values of the Graeco-Roman religion. Although a native of Phoenicia, he was apparently unable to read even the Aramaic portions of Daniel in the original and, following Theodotion's arrangement, was prepared to ascribe to its author also the story of Susanna. But he immersed himself deeply in the study of the Greek Old and New Testaments and, approaching both with eyes sharpened by hatred, showed an extraordinary critical acumen. He considered the Pentateuch as the work of Ezra rather than Moses and had the brilliant insight that Daniel's historiosophy, so influential in Judeo-Christian visions of the future, was expounded during the revolt against Antiochus. Nevertheless, without being too deeply committed to any particular pagan religion, he preferred the Greek mythology as subject to the greatest variety of interpretations and accepted, at best, monarchical polytheism rather than strict monotheism. He also argued that only the sublunary world might be subject to change and ultimate perdition, whereas the beautiful heavens were eternal. In fact, he believed that not only did the Old Testament itself recognize the existence of other gods, but the Judeo-Christian belief in angels was essentially a belief in subordinate deities under another guise. Porphyry also accused the Christians (and implicitly the Jews) of double loyalty. He reproached Paul, in particular, of having pretended to be both a Jew and a Roman, and in fact being neither. Outside his voluminous anti-Christian treatise, however, he could speak sympathetically of both Jews and Judaism, and in his old age he even married a Jewess, Marcella.[38]

Neither Celsus nor Porphyry were wholly representative of Graeco-Roman opinion, however. Celsus apparently wrote his work in Alexandria, the ancient focus of Greek antisemitism, within two generations after the bitter struggle under Trajan. Despite centuries of progressive Hellenization, Porphyry's Phoenician environment had retained much of its ancient Phoenician heritage and, with it, considerably less indifference toward anything affecting its Jewish neighbors. Similarly, Hierocles who, according to Eusebius, attacked Christianity some two decades after Porphyry, seems to have been that elder of the famous oasis of Palmyra whose name appears in contemporary Palmyrene inscriptions. There the Jewish and Christian issues constantly loomed large, because of large-scale local conversions and extensive religious syncretism. On the other hand, intellectual spokesmen living in the imperial capital seem to have taken the Judeo-Christian agitation much more calmly. Perhaps representative of their relative impartiality is the distinguished scientist Galen. Living in the less turbulent second century, Galen referred casually to Judaism and Christianity in a few passages which R. Walzer has culled from his numerous scientific works, partly extant only in medieval Arabic translations. His main objection to the Judeo-Christian outlook was the latter's excessive reliance on revelation, rather than on scientific proof. "They compare," Galen wrote, "those who practice medicine without scientific knowledge to Moses, who framed laws for the tribe of the Jews, since it is his method in his books to write without offering proofs, saying, 'God commanded, God spoke.'" On the other hand, he admitted that "one might more easily teach novelties to the followers of Moses and Christ than to the physicians and philosophers who cling fast to their schools."[39]

As time went on, Neoplatonists and Christians, especially of the gnostic variety, increasingly influenced one another, so that similarities in basic approaches soon began transcending dissimilarities. By the time Julian seized power, he betrayed in every step the deep impact of his early Christian training. In fact, some of his major objections to Christianity were based on its deviations from Judaism, which he respected and whose doctrines, in a characteristically syncretistic manner, he tried to equate with the basic concepts of the Graeco-Roman world outlook.

I wished to show [he reiterated] that the Jews agree with the Gentiles, except that they believe in only one God. That is indeed peculiar to them and strange to us; since all the rest we have in a manner in common with them—temples, sanctuaries, altars, purifications, and certain precepts. For as to these we differ from one another either not at all or in trivial matters.

Even in the worship of other gods, Jews might have listened to their truly wise king, Solomon, who "trusting in his own judgment and intelligence and the teaching that he received from the God who had been revealed to him, served the other gods also." We recall that Julian also extolled the Jewish sacrificial worship because of its essential similarity to that of Rome. That is why he was prepared to rebuild the Temple in Jerusalem so that the Jews might resume the offering of sacrifices. At the same time, of course, he knew well enough that he would thereby also administer a heavy blow to the hated Christians. Even in his extreme opposition to the institutional aspects of Christianity, however, Julian bowed to the superiority of Judeo-Christian ethics and tried to emulate the Christians' effective organization and propaganda. During the "pagan revival," finally, of 393–94, the adherents of the old Roman cult had little more to offer in its justification than its great antiquity.[40]

Jews remained rather cool to the emperor's advances. This is the less astonishing as they had been unprepared for this sudden change in Roman policy. It required a greater psychological readjustment than was possible in the brief span of Julian's reign for them to conceive the "kingdom of wickedness" itself, rather than a supernatural redeemer, hastening to restore their sanctuary. Julian was doubtless aware of that difficulty, and, having carefully studied the Septuagint in his youth, tried to appear to the Jews as a new Cyrus who, without departing from his own faith, could evince deep sympathy for related features in Judaism and the untold sufferings of the Jews. Why should not he, too, be hailed by another Deutero-Isaiah as the Lord's "anointed," entrusted with the mission of erecting the Third Temple? If in some of his other epistles he may have proved to be, as O. Sehl claims, "more diplomatic than the diplomats and more juristic than the jurists," his lengthy epistle "To the Community of the Jews" reveals both extraordinary care and skill. None the less, his insincerity was unmistakable, and the Jews refused to be made tools of his political manoeuvres. The whole enterprise was cut short by the spear of a Persian (or possibly a Roman-Christian) soldier, which eliminated this dangerous adversary of Christian rule after the reign of but a year and a half.[41]

Under the challenge of these external debates, as well as of endless sectarian controversies within the Church, Christian theologians, particularly those living in the Alexandrian center of Hellenistic theosophy, Clement and Origen, had to go on refining their doctrines of godhead until they developed their complicated, often paradoxical ideas of the trinitarian dogma. Despite their incipient antinomianism they also had to evolve an elaborate ritual, which they increasingly imbued with mystic meaning. To create for it the necessary sanctions of antiquity they also appropriated to themselves, as we have seen, the finest aspects of Jewish history which could be made to rival in antiquity the competing Egyptian and Chaldaean religions. In Eusebius, finally, Christianity became the direct heir of the pre-Abrahamite "Hebrew" religion.

Judaism, at least in its orthodox Palestino-Babylonian wings, required no such radical adjustments. Calmly and serenely the rabbis invoked the antiqutiy of their heritage, which impressed even such informed pagans as Porphyry and Julian. At the height of the tension in the latter part of the third century R. Simon ben Laqish taught that everything in Jewish tradition was part and parcel of the original Sinaitic revelation. Interpreting the Lord's saying to Moses, "And I shall give thee the tables of stone and the law and the commandment, which I have written, that thou mayest teach them," he declared, "the tables stand for the Ten Commandments; the law, for the Pentateuch; the commandment, for the Mishnah; 'which I have written,' for Prophets and Hagiographa; 'that you mayest teach them' for the gemara; to demonstrate that all of them were given on Sinai." So convinced was R. Simon of the eternity of Jewish law that, harping on the theme of the Torah's preëxistence, he figured out that it had been given by God some two thousand years before creation. He was evidently little disturbed by the philosophic problem of Time and its creation. He also disputed R. Johanan's contention that after the coming of the Messiah only the five books of the Torah would retain their validity. "Nor will [the recitation of] the Scroll of Esther," he exclaimed, "and the oral laws be abrogated." Both scholars, incidentally, thus repudiated the Christian assertion that even the written law had been abrogated by the coming of Christ. Their younger contemporary, R. Isaac, synchronized major events in Roman and Jewish history to show that the very foundation of Rome coincided with, and essentially was but the penalty for, Solomon's marriage with the Egyptian princess.[42]

Nor did the rabbis hesitate to broadcast their anthropo- and Judeocentric views and their insistence upon pure monotheism. To cite only another sage of R. Johanan's circle in Tiberias, R. Eleazar ben Pedat expressed the prevailing view hyperbolically when he taught that Adam's body extended from one end of the world to the other, or that "even ships plying from Gaul to Spain [at the other end of the Mediterranean] receive the divine blessing only on account of Israel" (Gen. r. VIII, 1, 55; b. Yebamot 63a). The rabbis also tried to impress upon their listeners that the Bible nowhere admitted the existence of "two powers," or any form of dualism, trinitarianism, or polytheism. They took particular pains to explain such questionable phenomena as the plural *Elohim* for God or the plural "Let us make man in our image" in the story of creation. Showing that these discrepancies can be understood only through their context, R. Simlai generalized, "Wherever you find [in Scripture] an opening for heretics, you find the answer beside it" (j. Berakhot IX, 1, 12d; Gen. r. VIII, 9, 62 f.). Simlai's questioners seem to have been Judeo-Christians who saw in phrases like "God, God the Lord He knoweth" (Josh. 22:22) proof of the Trinity, while the rabbi insisted both on the verb used in the singular and on the three divine appellations being mere titles like Basileus, Caesar, Augustus, applied to the same person.

HELLENISTIC JEWRY'S NEW RELIGION

All these apologias, of which only a very small selection can be given here, largely stem from one Palestinian group a generation or two before Constantine. They could readily be duplicated and amplified from other Palestinian, as well as Babylonian, sources of the third and fourth centuries. Unfortunately, however, our information concerning the thinking of Jews of that period in other countries of the dispersion is practically nil. Not only Babylonia, which lay outside the empire, but also Palestine with its fairly compact and self-administering Jewish settlements, its ever weak Christian minority and intellectually none too robust Samaritan and pagan populations offered only few of the challenges confronting the Jewish communities in Syria, Asia Minor, North Africa, or Rome. After the great catastrophe of Egyptian Jewry in 115–17 had all but extinguished its great intellectual center in Alexandria, the Hellenistic Diaspora has become for us the less articulate, as neither the Church Fathers nor the Palestinian rabbis had any genuine interest in perpetuating the memory of its intellectual efforts.

No one can ascertain, therefore, to what extent unconverted Hellenistic Jews continued to influence the intellectual and spiritual growth of Christianity from the second century on—not only indirectly by the way of challenge, but also directly. Nor can we hope to establish the numerical relation between Christians of Jewish and Gentile descent. True, the most prominent Church members recorded after the days of Paul seem to have been of Gentile stock. It must be borne in mind, however, that the leaders may not in this respect have represented the masses. They were, as a rule, educated men, either of the prosperous upper middle class or slaves, who often had more opportunity to acquire a good education than did free proletarians. On the other hand, we may well look for the majority of the early Jewish converts to Christianity among uneducated, poor free Jews (cf. I Cor. 1:26 f.).

That descendants of Jews in the third or fourth generation hardly ever mentioned this fact was no doubt owing to the general animosity toward their people. The majority, moreover, doubtless consisted of Jewish proselytes or *sebomenoi,* or their immediate offspring, who certainly could not be expected to count themselves among the descendants of Jews after their conversion to Christianity. Justin's apologetical exclamation that "the Christians from among the Gentiles are both more numerous and more true than those from among the Jews and Samaritans" (*First Apol.,* LIII) need not reflect exact statistical knowledge. Similarly, if close to the middle of the third century Origen speculated on the figure of 144,000 Christians of Jewish descent in the preceding generations (*In Joh.* I, 2; *PG,* XIV, 24), he was undoubtedly swayed by the mystic figure in Revel. 14:1–4, rather than by any realistic estimate of even the members of Judeo-Christian sects alone. Neither he nor his sources were racialist enough to estimate the ethnic origins of converts to Catholic Christianity. Almost to the end of the second century, the pagan world did not feel threatened by large-scale conversions to the new faith. Even when Celsus finally took up the cudgels against the Christian propaganda, we recall, he drew most of his arguments, not from any previously crystallized informed pagan opinion, but from Jewish sources.

Hellenistic Jewish influences must have been particularly strong in the northeastern corner of the Mediterranean. Havet exaggerates somewhat in saying that no real Gentile was converted to Christianity as long as Paul lived. Yet even later, Jewry was a major factor. When we compare the results of Harnack's famous investigations into the mission and expansion of Christianity in the first three centuries, with Cumont's equally renowned study of the spread of Mithraism in the same period, we see how definitely Christianity was rooted in the Hellenistic and Latin Jewish communities before it came to dominate the empire. During the first centuries after Christ, Christianity spread primarily in countries where large Jewish settlements of partly Jewish ethnic character were in existence. Wherever Jewish groups were ethnically pure, or wherever Jewish propaganda had made only feeble advances, Christianity took root but slightly. On the one hand, Palestine "offered stout resistance to Christianity"; Galilee, the cradle of the new religion, refused to follow the lead of Jesus and Paul. In later centuries Galilee became more and more the center of Jewish life and learning. Tiberias, Sepphoris, Capernaum, places that had achieved their greatest fame through the New Testament, had no Christians at all. In addition to the formerly Greek cities, only Jerusalem, whence the Jews had been banned since the time of Hadrian, represented an artificial settlement "in a hostile sea of Jews and heathens." [43]

The same is true of Babylonia, where Christianity had made only slight advances by the fourth century. Only when the intolerance of the Catholic Church, by that time dominant in Rome, forced the Nestorians to emigrate to Persia did Christianity become an important factor in those regions. Even in Egypt and southern Syria, where Judaism had had ancient strongholds, Christianity advanced relatively slowly, at first probably among the large groups of fully or half-converted Jews. In Harnack's list they are, therefore, classified under Group Two. The decline of Egypt's Jewish population after Trajan was as much of a hindrance to, as the weakening of Jewish communal control was an advantage for, Christian missionary efforts. H. I. Bell, who made a careful search of all extant papyri, came to the conclusion that "in the second century Christians formed only a small minority and even till late in the third century were probably not a large one." [44]

On the other hand, almost all countries classified by Harnack under Group One, as largely Christian at the beginning of the fourth century, namely Asia Minor, Thrace, Cyprus, Armenia, and Edessa, had earlier had Jewries of mixed racial composition. In Cyprus, Christian propaganda was doubtless aided, as it was in Jerusalem, by the imperial outlawry of Judaism there after 117. Whatever Jews may have surreptitiously survived the Roman reprisals were doubtless prepared to join the daughter religion or at least hide behind her cloak. Edessa, a Roman protectorate close to Parthian borders, may have found it politically expedient to join the new faith. When its ruler, Abgar IX, became in 202 the first Christian monarch in history, he may have thereby wished to declare a sort of political neutrality between the two rivaling empires, as did also King Tiridates of Armenia later in that century under Persian pressure. When Rome became a Christian power, other kings (in southern Arabia or Khazaria) were stimulated by similar considerations, as we shall see, to adopt Judaism. Between the fall of Adiabene, however, in the days of Trajan, and the days of Constantine, Judaism was decidedly less alluring to would-be neutrals.

In the West, Rome was not so thoroughly Christian as Africa, southern Spain, or southern Gaul. These three provinces obviously represented former Carthaginian settlements in which Jewish propaganda had been particularly successful. In Rome itself, Jews of pure Jewish origin, especially descendants of prisoners of war, were much more numerous. Thus is explained the almost complete failure of Paul's mission in that city and the slow growth of its early Church. The leading spirits of Latin Christianity in the following three centuries came mostly from North Africa rather than Italy. Northern Italy and other western countries not previously permeated by strong Jewish propaganda resisted all advances of Christian missionaries effectively and for a very long time. According to Harnack's estimates, the total number of Christians shortly before Constantine's conversion, in middle and northern Gaul, Germany, Belgica, and Rhoetia, amounted to no more than 10,000 in a population of some 5,000,000.[45]

These conclusions from the comparative study of population figures are largely confirmed by independent results achieved in other fields of investigation. Since the work of Strzygowski, the peculiar position of Syria and Asia Minor in the evolution of early Christian art has become an acknowledged fact. It has been further confirmed by the Dura discoveries. Similar results with respect to music have been reached by E. Werner and others. The researches of Reitzenstein, Bultmann, and others have proved that an equally unusual religious situation prevailed in these countries before and after the rise of Christianity. It seems, therefore, that to speak of Hellenistic Jewry generally as having given birth to the new religion is justified only with the geographic limitation to the northeastern corner of the Mediterranean and the former Carthaginian areas.[46]

Even in countries where Christianity spread rapidly, its growth, down to the fifth century, was largely restricted to urban areas. The *paganus*, the Latin equivalent for peasant, became for the Christians a synonym for heathen. This is another indication that the native population offered stubborn resistance, while in the cities, where Jews had often amounted to one-third of the population and more, this, so to speak, new variety of Judaism marched triumphantly ahead.[47]

Taken as a whole, Pseudo-Clement, a Roman Christian writing about 170 C.E., may have been right in asserting that in his day the number of Christians already exceeded that of Jews. But he doubtless disregarded the large Jewish masses of Babylonia and other countries outside the *oikumene*. Even at the end of the third century Christians probably did not exceed 10 per cent of the empire's population which had been the ratio of Jews in the first century. In the meantime the total population, which had increased considerably in the age of the Antonines, had fallen below the mark of the Augustan age. It may well be that at the beginning of the fourth century, Jews and Christians together did not amount to much more than 7,000,000, our estimate for Jews alone in the middle of the first century. The rhetorical exclamation of Augustine that the marvelous expansion of Christianity must have been "a miracle, because it would be the greatest miracle of all, had it happened without a miracle" and even the statement of a modern historian (De Broglie) that it must have been "a miracle of its own kind, a miracle of history" lose their edge when we examine the condition of Jewish society in that age.[48]

Of course, there were also many Gentile Christians, and they became more numerous as time went on. The wars under Trajan and Hadrian decimated the Judeo-Christian communities and decidedly strengthened the hold of the Greek Church, in which Gentiles soon outnumbered the Christians of Jewish origin. It was from

Gentile ranks primarily that the great direct and indirect losses, resulting from the persecutions of the third century, were made up. Naturally some Gentile Christians resented the preponderance of Jewish elements in their religion. In the early stages they had to repel all Judeo-Christian sects (Ebionites, Nazarites, and others) which, by identifying the two creeds, constituted a source of disturbance. It was against such leanings that the author of the Epistle of Barnabas warned the Christians:

Take heed to yourselves now, and be not made like unto some, heaping up your sins and saying that the Covenant is both theirs and ours. It is ours; but in this way did they finally lose it, when Moses had just received it [IV, 6; cf. X, 9; the text is somewhat dubious].

This sentiment was echoed by Ignatius (*To the Philadelphians*, VI, 1; *PG*, V, 701) and others.

Professing Jews were frequently accused of denouncing Christians to Roman authorities. To the Church of Smyrna describing the Martyrdom of Polycarp, one of the most ancient specimens of its genre, Jews and heathens were equally guilty of the saint's death (156 C.E.). When his time approached to be burned alive, we are told, the assembled crowd collected logs and firewood. "The Jews, too, as is their custom, were particularly zealous in lending a hand" —all that despite its being the day of their "great Sabbath" (*Sabbatou megalou*). Justin Martyr went a step further, bluntly accusing the Jews, "For other nations have not inflicted on us and on Christ this wrong to such an extent as you have, who in very deed are the authors of the wicked prejudice against the Just One, and us who hold by Him." Acrimony necessarily rose to a high pitch during the great persecutions of Christians in the third century, when Christianity was declared illicit, while Judaism remained a *religio licita*.[49]

The most formidable opponents of Judaism were the Palestinian Christian gnostics. Perhaps because of propinquity and greater spiritual affinity and indebtedness, they hated the mother creed more wholeheartedly than did more distant Christians. The Mandaeans included in their prayers three daily recitations of vindictive curses against the Jewish people. It was, however, again a man from Asia Minor who drew the sharpest line of separation. The philosophically and theologically trained Marcion of Pontus recognized the many contradictory Jewish and Hellenistic components in the Christian theology of his day. In his hatred of Jews and

Judaism, he went so far as to try to eliminate the Old Testament from the Christian Scripture (to quote Irenaeus), "blaspheming shamelessly Him who is proclaimed as God by the law and the prophets, saying that He is the author of evils and a lover of wars, inconstant in purpose and inconsistent in Himself." The Jewish God, whom he calls "Cosmocrator," a title normally given to Roman and other earthly rulers, was only the "maker" of this imperfect world, full of wretchedness and corruption; above him towers God, the Father of Christianity.[50]

While the official Church, under the influence of its strongly Jewish traditions, rejected such extreme formulations, it had to give way to the pressure of heathen conceptions. Not only did it become more and more a political organization, not only did it increase its dogmatic and sacramental constituents, but it was led to make great concessions to the popular religions. Gradually mediators in the shape of the revered saints crept between the transcendent God and the people. Another mediation was offered by the elevated position of the priesthood. The division drawn between the clergy and laity in the Catholic Church surpassed in sharpness anything known in Judaism, even when the Temple existed. The very designation of "Mother Church" was a borrowing from the Anatolian cult of *Magna Mater*. Nor were the age-old ethnic divisions completely submerged, despite the centuries-long operation of the imperial "melting pot." To preserve their identity many ethnic groups took refuge in religious sectarianism. Hence came, for example, the great success of Monophysitism in both Egypt and Armenia.[51]

As a result, in part, of these outward struggles and internal divisions the Church not only retained many Jewish elements but permitted the Jewish people to go on. Although no longer Israel in spirit, Jews still were Israel in the flesh. Some Christian descendants of Jews could not wish to see their people vanish altogether. Paul himself, notwithstanding his deep and ever-increasing animosity toward everything Jewish, occasionally reminded his hearers that "as concerning the gospel they [the Jews] are enemies for your sakes; but as touching the election, they are beloved for the fathers' sakes," and pointed out that Christians as a whole were but a branch springing from the Jewish tree (Rom. 11).

Four centuries later Jerome and Augustine repeated this formula which, particularly in its Augustinian formulation, became stereotyped in subsequent ages.

Now that they [the Jews] are dispersed through almost all lands and nations [Augustine wrote], it is through the providence of that one true God; that whereas the images, altars, groves and temples of the false gods are everywhere overthrown, and their sacrifices prohibited, it may be shown from their books, how this has been foretold by their prophets so long before; lest, perhaps, when they should be read in ours, they might seem to be invented by us.

Unlike his predecessors, moreover, Augustine saw in the Jewish dispersion not only a God-inflicted punishment for the rejection of Christ, but also a necessary element in the divine guidance of history. Perhaps unwittingly taking a clue from the rabbinic rationalization of Exile as an instrumentality of acquainting Gentile nations with Judaism, the Bishop of Hippo stressed the importance of the Jewish dispersal for the expansion of Christianity. Ultimately, of course, he, like other Christian leaders, expected the Jews to give up their blind resistance and join, or rather rejoin, the new, "true" Israel. This expectation, long an integral part of the Christian outlook, also penetrated the liturgy, finding expression in a special prayer, *Pro Judaeis*. As formulated in the *Gelasian Sacramentary* (ascribed to Pope Gelasius, 492–96 C.E.), it read in part, "We pray also for the unbelieving [*perfidis*] Jews that our God and Lord should remove the veil from their hearts, and they should themselves recognize our Lord Jesus Christ." [52]

On this basis the victorious Church harmonized the numerous contradictions in its attitude to the Jewish people, which had accumulated in the preceding three centuries of its uphill struggle. What is more, when Christianity became dominant in the empire, the principle of tolerance of Jews and Judaism was not only preached by the official Church, but maintained by state legislation. This tolerance was extensively qualified at all times, but it was an exception, based on principle, to the medieval rule of exclusion of unbelievers from Christian countries.

THREE-CORNERED STRUGGLE

When the failure of the Bar Kocheba uprising put a stamp of finality on their loss of national independence and central sanctuary as well as on the total separation of Christianity, the Jews faced one of the greatest crises in their history. Although long accustomed to life in Exile amidst more or less hostile neighbors, they were now confronted with an internal foe who either denied or tried to arrogate to himself all those traditional doctrines which had made Jewish minority existence worth living. They were told that the observance of the law which, whatever its hardships, had hitherto distinguished them from the Gentiles and lent them certain feelings of superiority, was now abrogated by the advent of the messiah. Their belief in chosenness, which had long kept up their spirits in the midst of untold adversities, was not as hitherto roundly denied, but said to have been transferred to the new, spiritual Israel. Even their claims to historic priority over the other contemporary religions and their glorification of the martyrs for their faith was now appropriated bodily by the new group of ardent believers. Although not literally contradicted, the Old Testament and later traditions were so reinterpreted as to lose all their validity for the bodily descendants of the Hebrew patriarchs or Maccabean martyrs. Perhaps most irritating was the fact that these feats were accomplished by constant invocation of the testimony of the Jewish Scriptures themselves, with the aid of twisted hermeneutics, in substance developed earlier by Palestinian and Hellenistic Jewish exegetes and preachers. One could dispute the details of the new exegesis, but not the validity of its hermeneutic method as such.

At the same time, the Gentile world, increasingly aroused by the Christian agitation, began to reformulate its own fundamentals in a way which must have attracted many Jews who had lost their strong Jewish loyalties and found no satisfaction in the preachment of the Church. Gone was the indiscriminate, bloodthirsty anti-semitism of an Apion, Seneca, or Tacitus. Perhaps realizing the greater danger threatening them from the ethnically indifferent Christian propaganda, the molders of Graeco-Roman opinion began evincing a greater, and certainly calmer understanding of the Jewish point of view. Objections, such as raised by Celsus in behalf of a cosmic, against the Judeo-Christian anthropocentric order, or by Galen in the name of scientific evidence against revealed truths, must have appealed to a great many rationally minded Jews, particularly in the dispersion. So did the new humanitarianism, which undermined all belief in the chosenness of particular groups, and the widespread religious syncretism, which claimed to absorb the best of all religions. Even in their decline, the beauty of Greek art and music, the magnificence of heathen temples and the colorful pageantry of their ceremonial, so sharply contrasting with the increasing self-imposed austerity of Jewish

life and worship, must have exerted a strong attraction on the
aesthetically refined tastes of some Jews.

Confronted by two such powerful enemies and evidently sustain-
ing great losses in manpower, not only on battlefields but through
defection, the Jewish people responded by the more closely con-
centrating on the traditional mainsprings of its spiritual evolution
and by the more rigidly adhering to its accustomed way of life.
Not that it became petrified, as its enemies accused it. The old dynamism of the Jewish faith reasserted itself. By way of challenge
and counterchallenge, rabbinic Judaism made ever new adjustments to the demands of the new age. Although outwardly trying
to ignore the new forces which were shaping the destinies of mankind and to steer clear of public debates particularly with the missionaries of the new faith, it nevertheless betrayed great awareness
of what was happening in the outside world and, accordingly, ad-
justed its own teachings. In this way it developed the possibility
of more or less peaceful coëxistence with the pagan world in the
second and third centuries. Essentially these compromise solutions
held true also when the mantle of imperial Rome descended upon
the Christian Church, which could no longer be artificially ignored.

XIII

INCIPIENT MEDIEVALISM

CONSTANTINE'S conversion to Christianity, however incomplete, must have stunned the Jewish leaders. They doubtless realized that, even in its gradualness and avoidance of extreme, the legislation initiated by him and Constantius differed in kind from the anti-Jewish measures of the earlier emperors to which they had become inured. For the first time since the brief outburst under Hadrian, their inner life, religious observance, community organization, and nonpolitical public utterances became an important concern of the central government. As is usually the case, the lesser bureaucrats in the provinces, with whom most Jews were in direct contact, tried to outdo the authorities in Rome in their zeal for the new policies.

Moreover, both in the capital and in the provinces, there appeared an entirely new factor, with which from now on the Jews had to count heavily: the Christian clergy. Unlike their pagan predecessors who, as servants of the various state temples, as a rule merely followed the lead of state authorities, the Catholic bishops and clerics considered it their duty to set the pace for the state, particularly in all matters having any bearing on religion. Already a bishop (St. Ambrose) had informed the emperor that "civil law [censura] must bow before religious devotion" (Epistulae, XL, 11; PL, XVI, 1152). The Jewish question clearly was of religious concern to the Christian state. With its universality and hierarchic discipline, the Christian clergy became a decisive force on both the local and the imperial levels. Even emperors and local officials, who bitterly fought some of its excessive political ambitions, often more readily made concessions with respect to Jews, who appeared as a legitimate object of ecclesiastical solicitude and for whom the political rulers themselves evinced ever diminishing sympathies.

Many Jews derived, therefore, great comfort from the rise of Persia. In accordance with R. Simon ben Laqish's dictum that "the Holy One blessed be He never strikes Israel without preparing a remedy in advance" (Megillah 13b, with reference to Hos. 7:1), they undoubtedly saw in the rise of the Sassanian monarchy, nearly a century before the edict of Milan, such an anticipatory remedy.

Even before 313, the economic and social decline of the Roman Empire was forcing many of its Jewish subjects to emigrate to Persian Babylonia. In the fourth century perhaps the majority of the world Jewish population, and certainly that of its intellectual leaders, lived under the somewhat milder Sassanian regime.

In essence, however, the Sassanians, too, were believers in an exclusive faith. They, too, sooner or later had to come under the sway of the (Zoroastrian) clergy and generally pursue far more intolerant religious policies than had their pagan Arsacid predecessors. Fourth-century Jewry, increasingly despairing of any truly satisfactory relations with neighbors and rulers, emphasized the old doctrines of segregation and wholly concentrated on the development of its inner resources. Invoking prophecies of Isaiah and Zechariah, it considered itself more and more the "third communion" (*kat shelishit*) destined to outlast pagan or Christian Rome and dualistic Persia alike, just as its ancestors had outlasted Isaiah's Egypt and Assyria.[1]

DECLINE OF HELLENISM

Such gradual alienation of Jews from the outside world and their increasingly segregated inner life was greatly enhanced by general developments both in the Roman and Persian Empires. On the one hand, disparate races and religious groups were increasingly developing into homogeneous nations. The Jews, unassimilated and as it appeared unassimilable, remained more saliently than ever outside this process. They were assured by their sages that the reason God had called their people "a leafy olive-tree, fair with goodly fruit" was, first, because the latter yields oil only after a succession of terrific pressures and, secondly, because oil does not mix with other fluids, but remains apart. "Thus Israel does not mix with Gentile nations," but always retains its identity. Moreover, if Israel shall do the will of the Lord, it will, like oil, always rise to the top.[2]

On the other hand, the individualism of the Hellenistic and the early Roman empires which had its basis in the capitalistic factors of the economic system and in the democratic trends of the political life of the various city states, now gave way to a universalist, authoritative social structure, under a despotic government foreshadowing feudalism. In the Orient, particularly, the reaction of native cultures against Hellenism progressed steadily. In fact, as early as 50 B.C.E. Hellenism began to die out beyond the borders of the Roman Empire. Parthia, especially, rid itself of its Hellenistic veneer more and more. As an outward sign there appeared on the Parthian coins of the second century, Pehlevi inscriptions side by side with the Greek. Even the Greek contract concluded in 121 C.E. between a high Parthian official and an Aramaean peasant, found in Dura, merely reveals the persistence of official usage. The literary Greek of the document certainly was understood by neither of the contracting parties. With the destruction of Seleucia by the Romans in 164, the last great stronghold of Hellenistic culture disappeared from those regions. The final blow was administered by Ardashir I, who, in 226, established on the ruins of Parthia the truly oriental Sassanian Empire.

Even in the eastern provinces of Rome, Hellenism steadily receded before the combined influences of the resurrected native cultures and those emanating from imperial Persia. Outwardly, to be sure, Greek speech and mores were often gaining ground. In Palestine itself, the Jewish population declined after Hadrian opened the gate to the influx of a mass of hellenized orientals and facilitated the conversion of many Jewish townships into "Greek" cities. Excavations in Gerasa (Jerash) have shown that "the Jews were eliminated from the life of the city to such an extent that not long afterwards [after the Great War] the stones from their buildings could be used as the interior fill of a Roman monument." The Jews themselves began assuming more and more Greek names. The rather local, lower-class necropolis of Jaffa shows a surprising number of Greek names, while in the more international Beth She'arim they reach the ratio of four out of every five. The inscription found in the fifth-century synagogue at Ḥammath near Gadara could onomatologically (except for one name) have fit equally well in a Christian church or pagan temple.

And remembered be for good Kyris Hoples and Kyra Proton and Kyris Sallustius, his son-in-law, and Comes Phroros his son, and Kyris Photios his son-in-law, and Kyris Hanina his son—they and their children—, whose acts of charity are constant everywhere (and) who have given here five golden denarii. May the King of the Universe give his blessing in their undertakings. Amen. Amen. Selah!

The name Sallustius merely shows the incursion of Roman substitutes, as did, for instance, in the field of architecture that of the city of Philippopolis in Transjordan founded in honor of its most prominent native, Emperor Philip "the Arab." [3]

Nevertheless, under this Graeco-Roman veneer the oriental factor reasserted itself ever more vigorously. After describing the general layout of Philippopolis as reconstructed from its present-day ruins, A. T. Olmstead observed that no other Near Eastern site "shows more clearly Romanization in plan and architecture, yet the near-desert inhabitants of this Latin colony knew only enough of the imperial language to place S.C., 'by decree of the senate,' on their coins. It was irony enough when the coins bore the bust of Philip's ex-bandit father, the 'god Marinus,' carried to heaven by the imperial eagle; it was crowning irony of ironies when this Arab himself, on April 21, 248, celebrated the thousandth anniversary of the imperial city's foundation by those secular games which Augustus had inaugurated for the preservation of the Italian character." Although numerically the Jewish population declined further and R. Eleazar was undoubtedly right when he controverted R. Johanan by saying that only the minority of the Palestinian population was Jewish at the end of the third century, Jews penetrated into many older Hellenistic strongholds. Caesarea itself, that long-hated miniature Rome, early in the fourth century embraced a sizable Jewish community and became the seat of R. Abbahu's academy. If here the Jews seem to have been outnumbered by Samaritans (not by Christians and pagans who apparently were a small minority in the days of Eusebius), they now completely dominated the originally "Greek" municipalities of Sepphoris and Tiberias. Even during their decline in the fifth century, synagogue building took a new spurt all over the country.[4]

More, the "Greek" patterns of life themselves underwent a deep inner transformation along Eastern lines. This was not the result of conscious efforts. Even in the first century, Apollonius of Tyana —the real Apollonius, not that of Philostratus' "literary biography"—had willingly adopted Eastern mores without adopting an Eastern faith. He defiantly explained, "I have become a barbarian, not because I had long been away from Hellas, but because I had long lived in Hellas" (Epistle 54). In his day he doubtless was a fairly rare exception, particularly in his conscious "barbarization." But many more westerners unwittingly assimilated Eastern ways of life, while hellenized orientals, equally unconscious, sloughed off many of the original Greek elements in their cultural synthesis. Ultimately, the center of gravity moved from Rome to Constantinople, the despotic Roman emperors themselves soon emulating the administrative methods and court etiquette of the Sassanian "kings of kings."

BETWEEN ROME AND PERSIA

From its inception Persia organized a caste system with a privileged higher nobility, lower nobility, clergy, and bureaucracy, all of whom lorded over the fiscally oppressed urban and rural masses. The latter, who even under the Seleucids and Parthians had lived in permanent economic and political dependence, now sank deeper into official serfdom. While the system may not have been as rigid as the Indian caste system, transition from a lower to a higher caste became very difficult. The Roman Empire, with its extreme development of the *colonate* and its enforcement of a permanent and hereditary attachment to their localities of the *curiales* (the urban inhabitants), also broke up its society into rigidly separated classes. Within these semifeudal systems, the Jewish people, clinging to its identity and maintaining its own quasi-democratic communal structure, constituted a unique group.

Geographically, too, the Jews occupied a singular position between the two empires. There were densely populated Jewish settlements on both sides of the frontiers for hundreds of miles. In the constant struggle between the two powers, the Jews held something like a strategic position. That few immediate benefits accrued to them from this situation, and that indeed they suffered severe losses during the long and devastating wars, was partly the result of their nonpolitical attitude, which militated against definite alliance with one power or the other. Neutrality, as usual, aroused the ire of both belligerents.

On the whole, Jews were more favorable to Persia than to Rome, which they regarded as their hereditary enemy. There were not lacking, however, moments in which, suffering desperately from Persian outrages, they sought the victory of Rome. In the period of Ardashir's conquests (226–42), Rab hopelessly exclaimed, "Loosened is the tie [of government]." Later the sick Rabbah bar bar Ḥana, witnessing an act of violence committed by a Persian priest, prayed to God, "Either under Thy protection or under that of the son of Esau [Rome]!" On another occasion, however, the latter sage quoted R. Judah bar Ila'i, a Palestinian teacher of the second century, who foretold that "the destroyers [of the Temple] are going to fall into the hands of Persia [Parthia]"; while Rab, more consistently, announced that "Persia is going to fall into the hands of the destroyers." The Talmud gives us a clue to Rab's political theory by quoting still another of his epigrams, "The son of David will not come until the kingdom of Edom shall have spread over the whole world for nine months." These contradictory utterances reflected not only changing personal moods, but also some momentary situations during a period filled, according to a contemporary poet, with "many wars and battles, homicides, famines and pestilences." We are unable to date these homiletical outbursts, although Rab, a personal friend of the last Parthian king, Artabanus, seems never to have been wholly reconciled to the permanence of the Sassanian regime. His faith in Rome's power, observed during his lengthy sojourn in Palestine under the Severi, doubtless received new nourishment during Gordian III's successful campaign aimed at the Persian capital in 243, and the more questionable exploits of Philip the Arab in the next two years.[5]

Rab's colleague, Samuel, however, seems to have become quite early a staunch Persian patriot. Once again personal considerations may have played a certain role. Samuel may not only have wished to take revenge on the Roman captors of his daughters (who were ransomed in Palestine), but he also evinced genuine friendship for Shapur (Shahpuhr) I (243–73), Persia's real empire builder. That is probably why he refused to mourn for the Jews who fell in the defense of Caesarean Mazaca in Roman Cappadocia. His sentiments seem to have been shared by the populace of Palestine, where Rome's growing anarchy and fiscal exploitation further alienated Jewish public opinion, and Cappadocian refugees in Sepphoris were not accorded the usual brotherly reception. Persia's victories possibly brought back to Jewish patriots the memory of the lost Ten Tribes originally resettled in the northeastern regions. This association may well have been in R. Samuel ben Naḥmani's mind when he taught that Patriarch Jacob had foreseen that "the descendants of Esau will be vanquished only by descendants of Joseph." When in 260, Emperor Valerian was captured, Jewish hopes surged higher and higher. The sudden defeat of Persia a few years later through the intervention of Odenath of Palmyra, who had previously paid homage to Shapur, must have come as a distinct shock to these optimistic molders of Jewish opinion.[6]

Did these academic speculations truly reflect mass sentiment and lead to positive action? It is difficult to say. Our information is almost wholly based on rabbinic homilies, Rome's legal enactments, and patristic polemics—none of them interested in recording historic events as such. Except for Caesarea Mazaca, in whose defense Jews allegedly sustained 12,000 casualties, we know nothing about Jewish activities during Shapur I's ambitious campaigns, of which he boasted in his famous inscription. He conquered Antioch two or three times, but he never reached Palestine.[7]

Caesarea Mazaca seems to have been an exception, however. The relatively few individual Jewish soldiers enlisted in Roman armies doubtless did their duty in the defense of their country. But Jewish leadership could never again evince those pro-Roman sympathies which had determined its behavior before 70. Not even Diocletian's friendlier attitude fully appeased either the rabbis or the rank and file. On his visit to Palestine, the emperor restated sharply the old imperial policy that "all peoples must offer libations [to the Roman gods] except the Jews." In a letter addressed to one Judah in 293 (of which we have an obscure excerpt in Justinian's Code) Diocletian seems to have attempted to increase the jurisdiction and dignity of the patriarchal office over and above the arrangements made by private parties. The rabbis reciprocated at best with a few sympathetic comments. But if Diocletian wished thereby to gain the sympathies of Babylonian Jews for his imperial aims, he was disappointed. He may well have tried to counter in this way his opponent Narses' appeal to Manicheism for the purpose of undermining Roman power, although Mani himself had been executed by the Persians in 273. It is perhaps not too venturesome to suggest that even R. Abbahu of Caesarea, who was generally on good terms with Roman authorities and once obliquely expressed admiration for Diocletian's newly stabilized gold coin, was so impressed by reports, probably exaggerated by popular rumor, of Narses' great victory at Callinicum (296) as to exclaim, "Who will repay Edom for you? Naṭrona." Naṭrona (or Neṭirata, both meaning the Avenger) may well have been a pun on some misspelling of the name Narses or Narseh. Considering the awkward mistransliterations occurring in the *official* Greek version of Shapur's great inscription, some such mispronunciation in popular usage is decidedly possible. Of course, Narses' ultimate withdrawal brought to naught all such hopes.[8]

We may reasonably assume that, after the time of Constantine, Jews were generally regarded by the Persians as spiritual allies, while Christians were suspected of leaning toward Rome. Rome herself nurtured these suspicions by her frequent interventions in behalf of the Persian Christians. In 563, Justinian actually concluded a formal treaty with Khosroe I, safeguarding the latter's extensive religious freedoms. Although there were no comparable

Sassanian interventions in behalf of Roman Jewry, the Romans long distrusted Jewish loyalties. Even the great favors bestowed by Julian the Apostate upon the imperial Jews failed to weaken the fealty of the Babylonian Jews during the tragic emperor's Persian campaign. About that time the Babylonian rabbis enacted (or at least tolerated) some regulations in favor of the Persian army. Despite the tannaitic prohibition of the sale of arms to Gentiles, Babylonian Jewish artisans apparently furnished all sorts of weapons to the Persians. R. Ashi rationalized this deviation by declaring that the Persians who "defend us" were in a different category.[9]

Especially in defensive warfare, however, the Jews fought on the Roman side as often as they did on that of the Persians. As late as 502–3, the Jews of Tella offered stout resistance to the Sassanian armies which, however, did not prevent their opponents from accusing them of contemplated treason. One must also remember that the Jews fought here after having been excluded from military service by Roman law. The Jews continued to participate in the local militia and sometimes excelled in defending their cities (for example, Arles in 508) against barbarian invaders. On the other hand, even a hostile writer like Procopius paid grudging recognition to the Jewish defenders of Naples against the Byzantine army in 536. They "kept fighting stubbornly," he wrote, "although they could see that the city had already been captured, and held out beyond all expectations against the assaults of their opponents." [10]

Only when life became unbearable in Palestine under the cruel and fanatical regime of Constantius and his Eastern lieutenant Gallus did a Jewish revolt break out in Galilee (352–53), probably sustained by the hope that Shapur II would invade the Roman Empire while the latter was preoccupied with western rebellions. But this uprising, which led to the total destruction of Beth She'arim, a partial burning of Sepphoris and perhaps of other Jewish communities, had decidedly a local character. Nor had it been sanctioned by the official leaders, the rabbis completely glossing over this incident.[11] More significant were the Jewish uprisings under Emperor Heraclius, which greatly facilitated Persian occupation of Palestine in 614–28 and helped prepare the ground for the great Arab conquests a few years later. These rather exceptional episodes, however, merely put into bolder relief the Jews' political and military reticence after 135 and their customary fealty to their respective rulers.

In retrospect, one may assert, this persistent refusal to make a conclusive commitment to any one empire eventually helped them to survive in both. Only thus could the persecutions in one region fail to affect simultaneously the entire people.

NEW LEGAL STATUS

On the whole, the legal situation of the Jews was much more favorable in the Persian Empire than in the Roman. After the time of Constantine, especially, the Christian state religion was less tolerant than was the Zoroastrian during the first two centuries of Sassanian rule. And yet the two legal systems essentially resembled each other far more than either resembled the structure of the Augustan Empire. The Jewish status, in particular, was affected as much by the new socio-economic and political developments as it was by the growing influence of purely religious, even ecclesiastical factors.

Both Christianity and Zoroastrianism had proclaimed the principle of nonconversion of Jews by force, the Parsees especially frowning upon such methods as causing the wrath of Ahuramazda. However, both encouraged conversions, even by worldly means. In Persia, for example, tax exemptions were granted for lip service to the Zoroastrian gods. The Christian empire went only a few steps further in excluding Jews from rights enjoyed by all other citizens. The old principle of equality of rights, never formally proclaimed and hence never formally abrogated, was in practice dishonored more and more. The *De altercatione ecclesiae et synagogae dialogus,* written after 404, speaks of the elimination of Jews from the *militia armata* and from several other offices. In 439 Theodosius II proclaimed the general exclusion of Jews from all civil and military posts of honor *(honos militiae et administrationis).* This may not have been as sharp a break with the previous practice as it might superficially appear. Even in the Augustan age, we recall, Jews played but a minor role in the imperial administration. With the rise to power of the bureaucracy and the military, exclusion was much more general. Nevertheless, by being enacted as an overtly discriminatory constitutional principle, such disqualification underscored the new legal inferiority of Jews with respect to all positions of power and prestige.[12]

The only exception was their enforced participation in municipal offices, whose occupants, selected by rotation, had to discharge many irksome and onerous administrative tasks. Jews had shunned these offices not only as reluctant taxpayers, but also because of their religious scruples. Now that the pagan rites associated with them had been discontinued, Constantine insisted on their equal participation (321). With this exception, the later emperors strictly applied the general principle that no Jew should exercise authority over a Christian—a principle which soon infringed even upon civil relations, Jews, for example, not being allowed to own Christian slaves. To prevent Judaism's further expansion, legislation was also gradually enacted forbidding the erection of new synagogues and the enlargement or improvement of existing structures. Imperial legislation, as we shall see, penetrated even the inner life of Jewry by abrogating the compulsory jurisdiction of Jewish courts, regulating Jewish marriages to conform with certain principles of Canon Law, suppressing the patriarchate, and, finally, in Justinian's *Novella* 146 of 533, interfering with synagogue ritual and the study of Oral Law (*deuterosis*). Its basic aim was to reduce to a minimum the appeal of the "Jewish perversity" and "abominable superstition," terms now freely applied by the otherwise linguistically still rather restrained and dignified Roman lawgivers.[13]

In Persia, too, the Jews were, as a rule, excluded from governmental positions, almost the entire civil service being in the hands of an hereditary "nobility of the robe." In principle, however, exclusion from this caste, along with the overwhelming majority of the population, was less derogatory than a specific disability inflicted upon a small group. What was in Persia a natural consequence of the social structure divided into the four estates of priests, warriors, officials, and the rest of the people, and which was, in part, welcomed by the rabbis themselves, was in Rome a special and willfully offensive regulation.

Nor did the Persian administration for a long time interfere with Jewish religious and communal life, although it did not always effectively protect Jews against intolerant acts of the Persian *magi*. There is no evidence that, like the Christians, the Jews were forbidden to erect new houses of worship. Neither did Shapur II's persecution of Christians, partly because of his suspicions of their loyalty, affect the Jews who, on the contrary, were accused by Christian writers of having instigated it. Later on Yazdegerd I (399–420) was so friendly toward both Jews and Christians that rumors were spread that he was married to the exilarch's daughter.

In the second half of the fifth century, however, certain fanatical currents in Persian society gained the upper hand. Yazdegerd II

(438–57) is reputed to have declared to the Christians of Armenia, "Whatever religion your master professes, you ought to profess, too." This adumbration of the sixteenth-century maxim of *cuius regio eius religio* now became dominant on both sides of the border and is curiously reflected even in Jewish liturgy. Apart from the restrictions imposed by Hadrian (if, indeed, these were directed against public worship in synagogues), pagan Rome had evinced little official interest in Jewish rituals. We have, to be sure, some traces of an obscure third-century provision aimed at the observance of the Day of Atonement. But its nature can hardly be surmised from R. Johanan's cryptic reference. It probably was a special move by some local administrator, dictated by purely local considerations. More plausible are the governmental measures against Jewish fasts generally, mentioned in the early fourth century by R. Ze'era. We know that many Church Fathers and Councils (for instance, that of Laodicaea) evinced great hostility to Jewish fasts because of the latter's great appeal to the Christian masses. But whatever these measures and the ensuing liturgical adjustments may have been, they were clearly of a transitory nature. But there also was a most interesting permanent modification, namely the incorporation of the *Shema'* ("Hear, O Israel") in the *Qedushah,* still recited three times daily by orthodox Jews today. Appearing at first in Babylonia about 450 C.E., it doubtless was the result of some Persian prohibition against the recitation in its usual place of this chief monotheistic credo, so offensive to the dualistic Parsees. Such enforced changes were sufficiently numerous for the rabbis, especially of the post-talmudic age, constantly to explain liturgical deviations by a stereotype phrase, "They changed it in the time of a religious persecution" *(bi-she'at ha-shemad shinnu),* even when there was no historical record to support this nexus.[14]

Conditions worsened further during the anarchy in the latter part of the fifth century, when Exilarch Huna Mari was executed (471). Thereupon his son, Mar Zutra II, revolted against Persia, established a small Jewish principality over which he reigned for seven years, but was ultimately defeated and executed (about 491). These disturbances were part and parcel of the great Mazdakite upheaval. Although we know of this significant social movement only through the writings of opponents, it is evident that the Jews were affected more by its underlying religious fanaticism than by its avowed communistic principles. But the general social turmoil must also have affected the Jewish community adversely. Mazdak's preachment of the community of women, especially, which all his opponents understandably stressed above all other points in his program, was fiercely resisted by Jewish leadership. Whatever gains might have accrued to Jews by the undermining of the power of the nobility and the Zoroastrian clergy—for this reason King Kavadh I (488–531) at first supported the revolutionary leader— quickly evaporated as a result of the revolutionary excesses which played havoc with the established ways of life of the minorities as well. After the restoration, especially under Khosroe I Anushirvan (531–79), conditions became more stable. At the same time, however, the *magi* became more powerful than ever before. The well-informed sixth-century Byzantine historian, Agathias Scholasticus observed,

Everybody reveres them [the *magi*] and views them with much veneration. Public affairs are arranged according to their advice and their predictions. They also direct in part the business of all those who have a litigation by carefully supervising all that happens and ultimately rendering the decision. Nothing seems among the Persians to be legitimate and just, unless it is approved by a *magus*.[15]

One of the most noteworthy features of Persia's domestic evolution was that, as under other oppressive regimes, Jews and Christians, although subjected to substantially the same discriminatory treatment, consistently refused to make common cause. While the rabbinic literature preserved its customary silence on the subject of their religious controversies and personal relations, Christians clearly carried over from imperial Rome their deep-rooted antagonism to their Jewish fellow sufferers. This held true not only for orthodox Church members, but also for those heretical groups which had to escape from Rome because of orthodox intolerance. In their missionary zest, too, Christian leaders tried to convert Jews as they did many other neighbors including even, despite express Sassanian prohibitions, some of the Parsees themselves.[16]

The impact of the two fiscal systems upon the life of the Jews was even farther reaching than that of the strictly political factors. After the anarchy of the third century, Rome never fully recuperated financially. Combined with pestilence, birth control, and the fall in the marriage rate, fiscal oppression brought about a steady decline in its population. In a vicious circle each decrease in population resulted in a decline of production, from which followed further increase of taxation. The Jews suffered with all others, perhaps more than any others. More than contemporary Christian and pagan literature, the talmudic sources are filled with complaints about the yoke of Roman taxes. To the direct imposts in money and kind (in the Talmud, *arnunia* equals *annona*) were added many indirect tolls. For instance, the so-called *quadregesima*, or 2½ per cent customs duty, levied at each of the numerous provincial boundaries, may already have affected the Jews, as merchants, out of all proportion. No less objectionable was the transportation *corvée*, or *angaria*. To obtain full information, the Roman tax collector frequently resorted to torture. Many a Jew was forced to sell his children into slavery in order to pay his taxes. Typical of a great many others is the following homily of R. Simon ben Laqish:

It is written: "As if a man did flee from a lion and a bear met him; and went into the house and leaned his hand on the wall, and a serpent bit him" [Amos 5:19]. Come and I shall show you the like of it in this world: When a man goes into the field he is met by a bailiff, which is like meeting a lion; he enters the city and is met by the tax collector, which is like meeting a bear; he returns to his home and finds his sons and daughters in a state of starvation, which is like being bitten by a serpent [Sanhedrin 98b].

But when confronted by similar complaints of the Palestinian population, visiting Pescenius Niger, we recall, replied sarcastically that he was sorry not to be able to tax their air. It is small wonder that, although the Roman Empire, to prevent tax evasions, increasingly attached the population to fixed places of settlement, numerous Jews fled abroad, finding refuge especially in Babylonia and the other provinces of the Persian Empire.

In Persia, too, the state claimed unrestricted sovereignty over the financial resources of its subjects. It declared all land to be royal domain. Jewish taxpayers were placed in an unenviable position by an annual capitation of the non-Parsees (in the sixth century, Khosroe I extended this to all his subjects, with the exception of the three privileged classes), amounting to from 4 to 12 dirhems (equivalent to from $1.20 to $3.60), coupled with a land tax (as a rule ranging between one-sixth and one-third of the produce) and with numerous "gifts" deliverable to the king at stated periods. Here, too, the evil was aggravated by Draconian methods of collection. Land on which payments were in arrears could be simply transferred to another proprietor. The Jewish taxpayer could be converted into a slave, without any protracted legal process, by any capitalist who deposited his overdue poll tax for him. Although such cases must have been very infrequent, several are recorded in the Talmud (B.M. 73b). Doubtless bribes alone served as a corrective.

Owing to the higher level of prosperity, however, taxes in the Persian Empire were much less excessive than under Rome. Although the Persian exchequer frequently suffered from a shortage of cash it was, for the most part, far better provided than the Roman. At times it was really prosperous. His Roman compeer must have deeply envied Khosroe II's accumulation, about 626 C.E., of a treasure equivalent to $460,000,000, with an annual revenue of no less than $170,000,000.

All in all, the effects of the Persian system upon the economic status of Babylonian Jewry was evidently much less damaging than was Roman fiscal pressure upon the western Jews. Hence arose the difference in the attitudes to the tax collector or tax farmer in the two regions. In Palestine a publican had for ages been regarded as an oppressor. A Jew who participated in this semiofficial and semicommercial occupation was almost a social outcast, often reckoned on a par with robbers. "There is no family that has a publican in its midst which does not consist entirely of publicans . . . because they defend him," said R. Simon (Shebu'ot 39a). Because the publican's money is derived mainly from robbery, the Palestinians taught, one must not accept charitable contributions from him (B.Q. 113a).

Even in Palestine, however, the new fiscal system, developed by Diocletian and his successors, practically eliminated the private tax farmer and, with it, much of the antagonism to the tax collector. But in Babylonia there was, from the outset, some enforced participation of the Jewish community in tax collecting which helped remove the opprobrium. The Persian administration frequently imposed upon a Jewish community a tax of a lump sum, based upon the approximate number of its members. Sometimes it collected the entire amount from one wealthy Jew, leaving to him the problem of reimbursing himself from his coreligionists. The leaders of the community frequently had to take part in the assessment and collection of dues. A delightfully naïve talmudic story is that of R. Ze'era's father, who secretly warned the Jews of the town to hide from the tax inspector and thus obtained a general lowering of the Jewish contribution.

Rome soon followed suit. Here the tax was originally a matter between the individual citizen and the state, the Jewish Diaspora community assuming no responsibility for its members. However, with the intensification of despotic rule, fiscal oppression, and corporate organization, the common liability of the group constantly increased. Naturally the Jewish community became an instrument of tax gathering. One curious illustration may suffice. The special Jewish fiscal tax, established by Vespasian and collected directly by the Roman administration, seems to have declined in importance from generation to generation. The storms of the third century apparently swept it away, since the progressive inflation of currency, with the concomitant devaluation of the prescribed two drachmas, made this revenue of little value. Probably the administrative outlay of the special *procurator* exceeded his income. That is perhaps why the last record of such collections is no later than 236 C.E. This tax was formally abolished when Emperor Julian officially destroyed the lists of Jews subject to it.[17] When in 429, Theodosius II used the extinction of the Palestine patriarchate as an occasion to introduce a new Jewish tax, he made its payment a matter of common concern to the entire community. He thereby made its collection both more secure and less expensive to the treasury.

The growing similarity between the two imperial systems is also illustrated by their new encouragement of denunciations of tax defaulters. Just as Persian citizens were urged to appropriate land by paying its accumulated tax arrears, the Roman administration promised to hand over to each delator a part of the revenue thus recovered. Irksome to all citizens, such denunciations could become doubly dangerous to members of minority groups. With increasing communal responsibility for tax collection, they could at times embroil the whole community in serious difficulties. We may understand, therefore, why "informing," for fiscal or other reasons, became such a major preoccupation of ancient and medieval rabbis.[18]

All this was a clear adumbration of the future medieval corporate system. Persia's blend of a feudal and bureaucratic state in many ways set the pace for the Roman Empire as well. Here, too, the growing economic feudalism, causally interrelated with the third-century inflation, was combined with the political control by an imperial bureaucracy, strongly influenced by the clerical spokesmen of the state church. Neither officialdom was strong and efficient enough, however, to manage the multitude of reluctant taxpayers and had to place increasing responsibilities for taxgathering on the shoulders of local communal organs. Thenceforth the Jewish community in Rome and Persia also became an important fiscal agent of the state, thus laying foundations for an evolution of primary importance in subsequent Jewish history.

INTERGROUP RELATIONS

Hand in hand with legislative and fiscal medievalism went also the newly developing "medieval" relations between Jews and Gentiles. Jews had long suffered from popular hostility, particularly in such turbulent cities as Alexandria. The imperial administrations, however, Hellenistic or Roman, had bent their efforts upon leveling down these group distinctions and amalgamating all their subjects into fairly homogeneous nations. Under the Christian Empire these policies were reversed. While Persia merely perpetuated an existing caste system, Constantine and his successors now initiated a conscious policy of segregation between the various groups of believers, lest the faithful Christians be contaminated by the "errors" of their pagan, heretical, or Jewish neighbors. This policy was, in part, both the effect and cause of the growingly regimented social order, which generally fostered the formation of corporate bodies, including those drawn along religious lines. The rabbis, on their part, welcomed the segregation of the Jewish people from its neighbors as an eminent safeguard for the retention of its identity.

It is doubly remarkable, therefore, that there were continued amicable personal relations between Jews and non-Jews. Under the Church's double-edged attack, pagans and Jews, in particular, seem to have been drawn more closely together. Julian's pro-Jewish, because anti-Christian, attitude undoubtedly was shared by many of his heathen subjects. Even such earlier emperors as Antoninus Pius and members of the Severan dynasty evinced friendly interest in Jews. Whether we identify the "Antoninus," frequent interlocutor of R. Judah the Patriarch, with any one of the Antonine or Severan rulers, or consider him altogether a figment of the people's fertile imagination, these dialogues nevertheless reflect the actuality of some such friendly exchanges. Alexander Severus was such a liberal donor to Jewish congregations that he received the nickname "archisynagogus." A full-fledged Roman "synagogue of Severus," so named in his honor, is recorded at least in a somewhat dubious medieval source.[19]

A more reliable and significant illustration of friendly relations is found in the correspondence of the distinguished Syrian Hellenist Libanius with Patriarch Gamaliel ben Hillel, a correspondence which extended over the last four decades of the fourth century. On the other hand, the bitter exclamation of Claudius Rutilius Namatianus, about 416–17, "Would that Judaea had never been subdued by the wars of Pompey and the reign of Titus. The contagion of the uprooted evil spreads further, and the conquered nation oppresses its conquerors," is primarily due to an unpleasant personal experience with a Jewish innkeeper. At its worst, it reflected a literary reminiscence of Poseidonius, to whose philosophy Rutilius was greatly indebted, and the latter's anger over the spread of Christianity, facilitated by Palestine's incorporation in the Empire.[20]

More remarkably still, even the Christian masses got along very well with their Jewish neighbors. Not only did opponents call such sectarians as the Arians and Nestorians "Jews" (the former, by denying the equality between Christ and God the Father, had indeed some Jewish affinities and apparently received at least the political support of Alexandrian Jews), but many orthodox Christians themselves chose to assume the romantic name of "Israelites" or "Jews." Warnings sounded by Augustine and others against such practices did not prove altogether effective. Many Christians continued to attend synagogues particularly on Saturdays. So widespread was the reverence for the Jewish Sabbath in Christian circles that the strongly anti-Jewish Council of Laodicaea had to concede them the right of reading in their churches from "the Gospels and other portions of the Scripture" on that day. Numerous Christians continued to celebrate Easter on the Jewish Passover (the Council of Nicaea and the ensuing imperial law to the contrary), asked Jews for medical and agricultural advice, had Jews bless their crops, and even intermarried with them. In many communities, particularly in North Africa, Christians were buried in Jewish cemeteries, the rabbis themselves enjoining their coreligionists to open their burial grounds to strangers in case of need, "for the sake of peace." Conversely, some Jews came to rest in Gentile cemeteries.[21]

Indeed, the main tenor of the canons adopted by Church Councils, beginning with that of Spanish Elvira before Constantine, was to outlaw these practices. The very violence of St. Chrysostom's anti-Jewish sermons of 387 was doubtless owing to the great friendliness of the Christian Antiochians toward their Jewish compatriots to whom the Arian emperor Valens himself had given "gardens . . . for their worship." It was poetic justice that, with the Church's new legalistic and ceremonial emphases, Antioch, the scene of the earliest breach between antinomian Christianity and Judaism, now witnessed the great appeal of the Jewish ceremonial to the city's Christian population.[22]

Much of this friendliness, to be sure, already had a suspicious coloring. It foreshadowed, in part, the growing belief among medieval Christians that the Jew was endowed with superior powers of healing and blessing crops because of his intimate association with demons. This belief was rooted in the old classical tradition and made realistic by the professional Jewish magicians who were found in many eastern communities. Because of their strange forms and Hebraic texts or symbols, even Jewish implements of worship were often considered endowed with magic powers. Many Christian women, St. Jerome informs us, wore Jewish phylacteries as talismans, although they sometimes replaced the Hebrew texts with pocket gospels or small crosses.[23]

These normally friendly masses were, nevertheless, easily swayed by a rabble-rousing preacher or any unsubstantiated rumor to attack Jews and synagogues. Burning of Jewish houses of worship and their conversion into churches became a frequent occurrence. Mobs and their ecclesiastical leaders effectively defied the imperial will, expressed in an endless reiteration of protective laws for synagogue property. In the *cause célèbre* of the burned synagogue at Callinicum, St. Ambrose of Milan, a leading statesman of the Church, forced Theodosius I, in 388, to retrace his steps—an adumbration of the future attempts at papal supremacy over the Western Empire. By 489 Emperor Zeno himself, informed of the burning of the Antioch synagogue together with the bones of Jews buried in its vicinity, exclaimed, "Why did they not burn the living Jews along with the dead?" [24]

In 414, Bishop Cyril of Alexandria, allegedly in retaliation for a Jewish assault, staged a miniature pogrom and expulsion of the Jews from their ancient center of learning—the first recorded expulsion of Jews from any city. Cyril's unprecedented action may have had many extenuating circumstances. Although Theodosius I had forbidden all pagan celebrations in 391, half the population of the turbulent city still was pagan and resisted the bishop's missionary efforts in bloody street battles. Internally, too, the Christian community was torn by the Athanasian-Arian controversy and other sectarian struggles, the Jews allegedly siding with the

Arian faction. It is possible, although unsupported by any direct evidence, that the antisemitic tradition was still the only uniting link between these warring parties. By appealing to the atavistic instincts of the masses, the bishop, elevated to the patriarchate in 412, may have hoped to restore peace in the community and to establish the full control of the orthodox Church. It should be borne in mind, however, that after its tragic eclipse following its uprising against Trajan, the Jewish community had become so greatly weakened that it was no longer the object of envy. In any case, when Caracalla on his visit to the city in 215 was confronted with a series of extremist demands harking back to the old imperial-municipal controversy (these negotiations are recorded in a replica of the old Acts of "Heathen Martyrs"), the Jewish issue was no longer under debate. Be this as it may, Cyril thus established a fateful precedent for the solution of local difficulties, which ran counter to the professed doctrine of the Church that Jews must be tolerated until the second coming of Christ—an evil augury, indeed, for all future Judeo-Christian relations.[25]

We possess considerably less information about intergroup relations in the Persian Empire. To begin with, unlike the patristic literature, the religious writings of the Parsees pay little attention to daily contacts with unbelievers, except for indirectly trying to stem them through tight ritualistic segregation. Most of this documentation, moreover, relates primarily to Iran proper, rather than to the western provinces where the bulk of Persian Jewry resided. On the Jewish side, we have the Babylonian Talmud, but no midrashic collections of the kind compiled in Palestine, which give us many more insights into the daily life of the people than the more rigidly normative sources. In general, the Babylonian Amoraim were on this score even less specific than their Palestinian colleagues.

It is certainly remarkable that, for example, Rab, whose real name, Abba Arikha seems to indicate that he was native of Arik (Khorazan?), never referred to Jewish life in the remoter eastern provinces. In Babylonia, on the other hand, the few resident Persians or Parsees largely consisted of government officials, soldiers, or *magi,* whose inveterate caste consciousness militated against simple human contacts with any members of the "fourth estate." With most of their lower-class neighbors, the Babylonian Jews seem to have established relations friendly enough for some Gentiles to repair on occasion to Jewish courts. With the Christians, to be sure, and even the Nestorians, whom the Roman lawgivers from Theodosius to Justinian considered non-Christians or outright "Jews," relations seem to have been more strained at least on the upper levels. But if we are to give credence to Aphraates and other polemical writers, here, too, the Christian masses were often attracted to Jewish ceremonies. No matter how friendly, however, these contacts always were sporadic and self-conscious on both sides —in other words, typically "medieval." Since the feudalization of the Persian Empire had progressed further than that of contemporary Rome, mutual segregration of all corporate groups, and particularly the ethnic-religious communities, doubtless was far more complete.[26]

BROAD SELF-GOVERNMENT

Segregated living became, indeed, the watchword of the new age. Insisted upon by Christian emperors and churchmen, as well as by Zoroastrian purists, it was doubly welcomed by the rabbis in this period of Judaism's extreme concentration on its inner resources. One cannot begin to understand even the legal and political position of the Jews in the two empires without taking full account of their extensive autonomy in most walks of life, both religious and secular. Whether under Roman or Persian domination, they lived primarily as Jews, and only secondarily as imperial subjects. Notwithstanding the increasing administrative centralization in both realms, the basic units—municipalities, districts and provinces— retained in general a large degree of self-government. For the Jews this was a matter of national life or death. No pagan Roman emperor after Hadrian dared interfere seriously with their autonomous life. Alexander Severus, we recall, directly supported it and is said to have paid for the construction of a number of synagogues.[27]

Christian emperors were less friendly. Under the impact of the constant denunciations of Judaism by the Church Fathers, the empire began to impose restrictions upon Jewish self-government, too. So long as it adhered, however, to the principle of basic toleration of religious disparity, it also had to grant the Jewish people the means of controlling its own religious affairs. The principle that no outsider could or should pass judgment on Jewish religious matters, or even such secular activities as price control, was clearly enunciated by such hostile rulers as Arcadius and Honorius in 396.

Their decree was subsequently incorporated in the *Theodosian Code* (XVI, 8, 10). Honorius also sufficiently respected the Jewish Sabbath and holidays to uphold (together with Theodosius) the prohibition of summoning Jews to court or forcing them to perform *corvée* labor on those days (409, 412; *C. Th.*, II, 8, 26, XVI, 8, 20). In view of the broad compass of religious functions in antiquity and the strenuous Jewish efforts to stretch their scope as widely as possible, this recognition meant in substance the preservation of traditional Jewish autonomy.

Indirectly, in fact, the empire's new segregationist policy and the new rulers' use of essentially the same religious idiom, however tinged with hostile undertones, reinforced both Jewish solidarity and communal control. The more successful, moreover, the Christian clergy was in wresting from the empire special privileges and immunities, the more it also strengthened the claim of Jewish sages to tax exemption and jurisdictional autonomy. The extensive use of anathemas by ecclesiastical courts enhanced the effectiveness of this weapon for Jewish law enforcement, too, and silenced whatever popular opposition to it may have existed before. We may understand, therefore, that the very persons who prohibited, for example, the erection of new synagogues, always tried to protect existing Jewish houses of worship, even if they sometimes denounced them as "sacrilegious assemblies." Five years after his dramatic controversy with St. Ambrose (393), Theodosius I wrote to the *comes* of the Orient:

It is sufficiently evident that the Jews' sect has not been prohibited by any law. Hence we are seriously aroused over the fact that their assemblies have been forbidden in various places. Your sublime Excellency will, therefore, upon receipt of this order, check with appropriate severity the overzealousness of those who, in the name of the Christian faith, arrogate to themselves illegal [powers] and attempt to destroy and despoil synagogues [*C. Th.*, XVI, 8, 9].

For more than a century the Christian empire continued to recognize the Palestinian patriarchate as both the supreme office of imperial Jewry and a high office of the state. Perhaps more than ever before the patriarchs now enjoyed the so-called *praefectura honoraria* and, in official correspondence, were styled *viri clarissimi et illustres*. If we may take a clue from a single recorded draft, the patriarch's letters to the emperor were couched in the traditional Jewish, rather than in the Graeco-Roman epistolary style (Gen. r. LXXV, 5, 883; cf. *ibid.*, note 1). According to Jerome, a Roman of high standing, Hesychius, was executed by Theodosius I because he had violated some papers of Patriarch Gamaliel (V?; see *Epistolae*, LVII, 3, in *PL*, XXII, 570).

Political and fiscal reasons largely accounted for this extraordinarily benevolent treatment of an institution which to Jews and their Christian opponents alike appeared as a symbolic residuum of Jewish sovereignty and a sign that the sceptre had not yet wholly departed from Judah. It seems that already Antoninus Pius had decided formally to recognize R. Simon ben Gamaliel as patriarch (the term had apparently been coined by the Greek translator of Chronicles) as an eminent means of pacifying and better controlling the recalcitrant province. He was not mistaken. Whatever grievances his successors may have had against such patriarchs as Gamaliel VI (in 415) arose from differences between the requirements of Jewish and imperial laws (cf. *C. Th.*, XVI, 8, 22). But none had any reason to suspect the loyalty of the Palestinian leaders with respect to his domestic or foreign enemies.

Even powerful Judah I allowed himself only such mild criticisms as when he homiletically commented on the phrase, "The voice is the voice of Jacob, but the hands are the hands of Esau" (Gen. 27:22), by saying, "The voice of Jacob [Israel] cries out against what the hands of Esau [Rome] have done him at Bethar" (j. Ta'aniot IV, 8, 68d). But far from being an incitement to a new revolt, it may have served as a reminder of its mortal dangers. In fact, according to one report, the patriarch wished to abolish the annual day of mourning on the Ninth of Ab, doubtless because it lent itself admirably to the delivery of subversive sermons. But he was overruled by the majority (j. Yebamot VI, end, 7d). From the Roman viewpoint it certainly seemed wiser to have imperial Jewry pay allegiance to a chief within the reach of imperial authority than to have it pay complete obeisance to a foreign head, the Babylonian prince of captivity.

In tax matters, too, the patriarchate was a much simpler organ to deal with than scores of more or less important Jewish communities in Palestine. During the great fiscal terror of the third century, Judah II had to absorb much of the popular resentment against the imperial treasury. Rabbinic literature has preserved two, closely related, versions of a noteworthy revolutionary homily by one Jose of Ma'on, near Tiberias. Taking a clue from Hosea (5:1), the preacher attacked the "house of Israel" for its refusal to pay priestly dues. He conceded that Israel had the legitimate excuse that the government was "taking everything away," but this also meant that Hosea's "house of the king" had become derelict of its duty. He concluded by exclaiming in the vein of an ancient prophet that, therefore, the Lord "will sit in judgment over them, pronounce their sentence and make them vanish from the earth." Owing to R. Simon ben Laqish's intervention, the bold preacher escaped punishment, although he proved quite unregenerate at the next meeting with the patriarch. But before long R. Simon himself had a serious altercation with Judah II over the latter's fiscal administration. To be sure, Judah's explanation, "Is not everything that I ask for being taken away from me?" was far more justified than R. Simon's stricture, "Take nothing and you will have nothing to give [to Rome]" (Gen. r. LXXX, 1, 950 ff., j. Sanhedrin II, 6, 20d). The discussion highlighted, none the less, the patriarch's precarious position as a buffer between the ever more exacting Roman treasury and his own impoverished people.

Reciprocally, the empire supported the patriarchate in collecting revenue for its own benefit as well. From the outset, it appears, the patriarchs tried to revive the ancient self-imposed tax of all Jewry for the support of its Palestinian center. The more the original substitution of the Temple's half shekel by Vespasian's "fiscal tax" had gone into oblivion during the third-century monetary and administrative anarchy, the readier were the Jews of the dispersion to bestow of their bounty upon their spiritual chief in the homeland. This revenue, later called the *aurum coronarium,* or *apostolé* varied according to the prosperity and charitableness of the donors, and the persuasiveness and fund-raising propensities of the patriarchal *apostoloi* (messengers). While lagging far behind the tremendous amounts sent annually to the Herodian Temple, it nevertheless helped maintain the patriarchal court in its accustomed princely style.

Since the patriarchs used these funds also for the support of academies and needy students (no lesser a leader than R. Johanan was on the patriarchal payroll), they readily secured some outstanding messengers. R. Ḥiyya bar Abba himself solicited the job. Equipped with a fine letter of authorization, which read in part, "We are sending you a great man, our messenger, who ought to be treated on a par with ourselves until he returns to us," this first recorded Jewish professional fund raiser visited Tyre, Emesa, Laodicaea, Gebalene, and Rome. Before long, however, the collections began to tax the patience and generosity of many communities.

While evidently trying to secure Jewish good will, Emperor Julian held out the hope of early discontinuation of the *apostolé*. It lasted for another half a century, however. Except for a temporary suspension under the Western Empire (399 to 404), which at that time frowned on any shipment of gold to the Eastern Empire, it was collected until the suppression of the patriarchate (about 425), to be converted thereafter into an additional special Jewish tax for the state (429). This was merely symptomatic of a general trend. In other areas, too, the ever revenue-hungry emperors tried to convert voluntary offerings into official imposts. "In this incessant struggle," comments C. Lacombrade, "indefinitely pursued, they were, we believe, but rarely victorious." But whatever the yield of the *aurum coronarium* was to the imperial treasury, the patriarchal office had by that time lost all its practical utility to the hostile emperors. Ineffectual as a fiscal agency, it was likewise no longer needed as a counterpoise to the Babylonian exilarchate which had begun to show symptoms of rapid disintegration. Decimated Jewry, on its part, was too weak and perhaps unwilling to put up a staunch defense of an institution which had outlived its usefulness.[28]

In Sassanian Persia the exilarchate long enjoyed even greater authority. The available evidence does not allow us to answer the intriguing question as to whether Persia merely continued a state institution well-established in Parthian times, or whether it was Shapur I who, for political as well as religious reasons, first wove it into the imperial fabric. The persistent claims of the exilarchs themselves, even if supported by documentary genealogical evidence, need not have been any more historically reliable than were the parallel claims of the Christian catholicos in newly rebuilt Seleucia to independence of the patriarchate of Antioch on the basis of forged "Letters of Occidental Fathers." On the other hand, Josephus' failure to mention the very existence of princes of captivity may be explained by his extreme apologetic preoccupation with Western political affairs. Certainly such silence is by itself not sufficient reason to deny the deep-rooted tradition, acknowledged by the rivaling Palestinian patriarchs themselves, about the unbroken continuity of the exilarchic regime since the ancient royal exile, Jehoiachin. The latter's elevation at the Babylonian court, we remember, asserted by the author of Kings, has been confirmed by a Babylonian tablet. However, the clue supplied by the genealogical list of fifteen generations from Zerubbabel to Nathan Uqban (Mar Uqba I), found in the ninth-century *Seder 'olam zuṭa* (in A. Neubauer's *Mediaeval Jewish Chronicles*, II, 70 f., 74 f.), is much too brief and altogether too dependent on the biblical sources to inspire any confidence.

There is no way of ascertaining, therefore, what role these reputed direct descendants of the royal house of David played in Achaemenid Persia and its Eastern successor states down to Arsacid Parthia. But there is no question that under the Sassanians they represented the Jewish people before the king, and in this capacity ranked high among the imperial councilors. The talmudic reference to the exilarch as placed just below the king, the *argabadh* (archduke), and the generalissimo hardly fits the complicated hierarchy of Persian officialdom. His position as a sort of Jewish vassal prince more nearly resembled that of the semi-independent provincial governors, who lived with a large retinue of courtiers and slaves in "towns" of their own. These governors, too, were largely recruited from native princely dynasties, particularly the seven privileged families, inherited from the Arsacid regime. Like them, the exilarchs doubtless controlled directly the close Jewish settlements in Babylonia. But owing to the peculiar ethnic and religious character of Jewish communities all over the empire, they also exercised considerable influence on all Persian Jewry and, hence, played a role in the central administration at Ctesiphon as well.[29]

On the whole, the few meager sources concerning the administrative structure of the Sassanian Empire reflect the conflicting trends between bureaucratic centralization promoted by the new rulers and the traditional feudal divisions taken over from the Parthians. Under these circumstances there were great opportunities for strong-willed and ambitious individuals among the princes of captivity and their scholarly adherents or opponents to display their ingenuity in exploiting existing circumstances for their own and their people's benefit. At the same time there were many temptations for the exilarchs to go beyond the confines of their Jewish constituency and to become involved in the general political struggles at the Sassanian court. Perhaps it was such a mixture of defense of Jewish rights and escapade into general politics which cost Huna Mari his life and later led to Mar Zutra II's short-lived experiment in political sovereignty. The latter's son, Mar Zutra III, emigrated to Tiberias to head the local academy which, even in its decline, had retained some of its former glory. In this way, half a century after the patriarchate, the exilarchic office, too, fell victim to the political storms of the fifth century, not to be fully revived until the Muslim era.

It would be a mistake, however, to ascribe the rise and decline of both institutions exclusively to external factors. Their fate was intimately bound up with the gradual ascendancy of the scholarly class to exclusive leadership in the Jewish community. At first the patriarchs themselves owed their preëminence only to the fact that they presided over an academy of scholars which, even in the days of R. Johanan ben Zakkai, had arrogated to itself the multifarious attributes and rights of the Sanhedrin. As long as the patriarchs themselves were distinguished scholars and headed the leading academy in its successive abodes, they held undisputed sway. Occasional revolts among the members, which led, for example, to the temporary deposition of Gamaliel II, were reduced to mere verbal criticisms after the official Roman recognition in the days of his son, Simon, and grandson, Judah I. Under the latter the office achieved the acme of its power and prestige.

Judah himself, however, sensed the rumblings of discontent and, on his deathbed, enjoined his son Gamaliel, whom he entrusted with the patriarchate but not, because of insufficient learning, with the presidency of the academy, "Conduct your office with high dignity, and impose austerity [*marah*, literally bile] on the disciples." Judah's successors, no longer eminent scholars themselves, had to allow the prominent rabbis of each generation to preside over the academy, issue ordinances, and exercise the main spiritual authority. In vain did R. Ḥiyya and R. Johanan try to buttress Judah II's waning prestige by insisting that, on all occasions, he appear in public in his official toga and that everyone, except mourners and sick persons, arise at his approach. Not even the patriarch's apparently exclusive authority to annul bans imposed by predeceased or otherwise unavailable judges could salvage the office from its spiritual oblivion. Before long the rabbis arrogated to themselves the patriarchal prerogative of appointing local judges and R. Abbahu of Caesarea often acted as the people's spokesman before Roman authorities. With all his reverence for the office, R. Abbahu also had to "restrain" his contemporary, Gamaliel IV, whom he considered "a small man." [30]

In Babylonia, too, exilarchic authority shrank gradually because of the rise of the rabbinate to power even more than because of external influences. In the days of Rab and Samuel, the hegemony of the prince of captivity was uncontested, but in the next generation, a faction led by quarrelsome Geniba made life miserable for Mar Uqba. Before appealing to the Persian authorities, which he knew would antagonize Jewish public opinion, the exilarch repeatedly sought the advice of R. Eleazar ben Pedat in Palestine. The latter, quoting the psalmist, counseled him to suffer quietly. We do not know how long the exilarch adhered to that advice, but ultimately Geniba was executed by the Persians. At that time, R. Naḥman, a son-in-law of the exilarch, already claimed supreme jurisdiction in legal matters. The academies, rather than the exilarch, now issued the proclamations concerning the calendar in accordance with Palestinian regulations. Soon the prince came to the learned gatherings (the so-called *Kallahs*) at the seat of the academy, instead of convoking such assemblies at his own residence. Finally, R. Ashi assumed the title Rabbana, apparently theretofore reserved for the exilarch alone. It was he who, together with two other rabbis, appeared as an official delegation "at the gate of King Yazdegerd's court." Many a rabbi must have felt, as did R. Ḥiyya's inebriated sons in the very presence of Judah I, that "the Messiah will not come until the two families in Israel, those of the exilarch in Babylon and the patriarch in Jerusalem, shall have ceased." [31]

LOCAL AUTONOMY

While Babylonian Jewry was ruled by central authorities, whether exilarchs or heads of academies, the other communities of the dispersion underwent a steady process of decentralization. The progressive decline of the Palestinian center was no less responsible than the gradual economic dissolution of the empire into its provincial constituents. To be sure, even in far-distant Stobi, the founder of the local synagogue stipulated in his will (dated about 165) that every attempt to alter its provisions should be punished by a fine of 250,000 denarii, for the benefit of the patriarchal treasury in Jerusalem (Frey's *Corpus*, I, No. 694). In practice, however, the individual Jewish community became increasingly independent.

Even provincial authorities seem to have lost their hold over the Jewries of their province. The ethnarch of Egyptian Jewry, as the title indicates, occupying a princely position during the Ptolemaic regime, disappears from the records after Augustus who, according to Philo, displaced this office by a council of elders in 11 B.C.E. Although Claudius is said to have denied that Augustus had ever issued such a prohibition and, hence, allowed the Jews to re-instate their supreme chief, the Jews apparently did not avail themselves of that opportunity. The *exarch* or *archon alti ordinis*, recorded on several Roman inscriptions, seems to have been from the beginning a decorative figure with little real authority. Power rested exclusively with the council of elders, the so-called *gerousia*, apparently elected by the various congregations of the city. On the other hand, the community rather than the congregation was the basic unit. In large cities the Jews would erect sufficient synagogues to accommodate the worshipers in all quarters; but the community, embracing all congregations, controlled the administration of justice, tax collection, and charity on a city-wide scale. In Rome, where we are able to examine the matter in greater detail, the cemeteries did not belong to the thirteen or more congregations, but to the community as a whole. The inscriptions reveal unmistakably that in one catacomb there might be buried the very officers of various synagogues.[32]

Individual congregations performed useful functions of their own and retained, within their particular sphere, a great measure of self-determination. Apart from the convenience of having a synagogue in the proximity of one's residence, Jews at all times organized congregations also on the basis of their country of origin. Despite the relative absence at that time of well-established ritualistic differences—a major factor in later congregational differentiation—the social cohesiveness of *émigrés* hailing from one locality or province fostered, and was mutually reinforced by, the possession of their own permanent meeting place. Seven of the thirteen Roman congregations bear names betraying their common place of origin. In Jerusalem before 70 flourished, side by side with the Temple and many native synagogues (according to legend a total of 394 or 480), various congregations of foreign Jews. Similarly the thirteen synagogues recorded in third-century Tiberias included a "Babylonian," "Tarsian" and "Antiochian" congregation, as well as probably one of neighboring Ma'onites. An Arsinoe papyrus of 113 C.E. mentions a synagogue of Theban Jews in that city. There apparently also was a "Cappadocian" congregation in Jaffa, an "Antiochian" congregation in Syrian Apamaea and possibly also a "Pamphylian" congregation in Caesarea. Rabbinic literature refers to another "Babylonian" congregation in Sepphoris as well as to a congregation of "Roman" Jews in Babylonian Maḥoza. Without infringing on the unity of communal

administration in matters transcending purely congregational interests, these subdivisions of larger communities greatly helped
new Jewish arrivals to adjust themselves to the strange environment and permanently nurtured the pride of members in their
self-governing institutions.[33]

In short, Judaism and Christianity evolved in diametrically opposed directions: Jewish autonomous life became ever more de-
centralized in favor of the basic unit, the community; Christian
communal life tended to develop an increasingly rigid hierarchi-
cal system under the supreme authority of the bishop of Rome.
Perhaps Roman statehood, operating behind the Church, was responsible for its centralization, just as Jewish opposition to this
state strengthened decentralizing factors in their case.

Life within each community was basically "democratic." Commenting on the Deuteronomic reference to the presence before the
Lord of "your heads, your tribes, your elders, and your officers,
even all the men of Israel" (29:9), the rabbis read into it the meaning: "Although I have appointed for you heads, elders, and officers,
you are all equal before me" (Tanḥuma, ad loc.). Another homily
on the same verse (ibid.), however, made it clear that it was neither
mechanical egalitarianism that was preached here, nor equality of
rights without a corresponding equality of duties. Scripture wished
to convey this idea, the second version asserted, that "you are all
responsible for one another. If there be only one righteous man
among you, you all will profit from his merits, and not you alone,
but the entire world will profit from his merits. . . . But if one of
you sins, the whole generation will suffer."

True, both patriarch and exilarch frequently arrogated to themselves semimonarchical prerogatives, and the granting to them by
the community of certain honors seemed to support their claims.
For instance, the sacred scroll, approached with reverence and awe
by every other Jew called on to recite a portion of Scripture, was,
in their case, carried to their seats. The whole people, cherishing
an inextinguishable and exaggerated memory of the glory of national independence, seems to have played at having a king. Legally, however, neither the patriarch nor the exilarch was treated
as a king. The principle of talmudic law, academic though it be,
that "a king can neither judge nor be judged," that is, cannot be
held responsible for his actions, was never intended for them.
Judges invested by the exilarch occupied a special position in the
Babylonian-Jewish judicial administration, but such investiture

was by no means a prerequisite for judicial office. In Babylonia as in Palestine, it was the teacher who usually conferred the title Rab or Rabbi upon his disciple. Even for Palestinian "ordination," bearing almost a sacred character, the principle prevailed that "everyone ordained may ordain." The ascendancy of this "aristocracy of learning" was not pure democracy, of course. But it had many democratic as well as aristocratic and even theocratic features, which placed it in a class by itself.

There is no telling what real authority the patriarch or the exilarch possessed, outside of the country's boundaries. Unfortunately, constitutional law governing the Jewish communities was neither clearly defined nor rigidly adhered to, even in Palestine and Babylonia. In the other provinces of Jewish settlement, the form of government seems to have been extremely ambiguous. In this formative, one might say experimental, stage of Jewish autonomy, many remedies were tried out. Everywhere, however, a governing body, evidently elective, seems to have exercised all rights in the name of the whole community. This local board at times carried in Palestine the distinguishing title *ḥeber ha-'ir*, reminiscent of the *Bet-ḥaber* of Proverbs, and of a still more ancient, though equally dubious, Ras Shamra inscription.[34]

Communal councils varied in size in accordance with local needs. In many cities there was a board of seven elders. In some others, especially in the smaller ones, there were only two officers, one in charge of religious, the other of secular matters. Sometimes, to prevent abuses in the administration of charity, the Talmud prescribed the appointment of two collectors and three distributors of the charitable contributions, all independent of one another. If this provision was designed to prevent excessive concentration of power and personal favoritism, rabbinic leadership made no effort to inhibit more innocuous human weaknesses which often crept into communal policies. There was, for example, a plethora of bombastic titles, more than twenty-four of which, mostly describing honorary offices, have been found in Roman inscriptions alone. Among the titleholders appears a *mellarchon* (prospective *archon*), who died at the age of two years and ten months.

We know very little about the electoral processes in the ancient Jewish communities. Fragmentary evidence seems to indicate that annual elections were often held after the Jewish New Year and that names of candidates were announced well in advance. Even in Palestine and Babylonia where local elders were often appointed by the national leadership or its rabbinic deputies, R. Isaac advised that "one shall not appoint an elder over a community without first consulting that community" (Berakhot 55a). Where elections took place, voters were evidently free to choose any qualified candidate, although the rabbis with their penchant for heredity in all occupations often seemed to favor the retention in office of members of the same family. In his well-known Jerusalem inscription, Theodotos, son of Vettenos, prided himself on being an *archisynagogus* (synagogue warden), as his father and grandfather had been before him. Roman inscriptions mention officers appointed for life (*dia biou*), but theirs may have been purely honorary titles conferred upon them for some congregational benefactions. Most others seem to have served only for a year or two. That somebody had been "twice an archon" was mentioned as a special mark of distinction on nine monuments. Only once do we hear that the deceased has served as "thrice an archon."

As far as one can judge on the basis of stray, often undatable, records, there occurred a marked change in the Jewish attitude to public office. There always existed shy and peace-loving persons who shunned communal responsibilities. The expense connected with honorary offices was also discouraging. Not only did the rabbis demand that charity supervisors make up deficiencies from their own pockets (B.B. 11a), but in an inscription found at Aegina near Athens an archisynagogus claimed to have served for four years and built the synagogue "from its foundations. Revenues amounted to 85 pieces of gold, and offerings unto God to 105 pieces of gold" (Frey's *Corpus*, I, No. 722). Such personal contributions by honorary officers were, moreover, widespread practice throughout the Graeco-Roman world. Therefore, the two rabbis whom R. Gamaliel II had to scold into accepting office (Horayot 10ab) need not have been rare exceptions.

On the whole, however, there probably was no dearth of public-spirited or ambitious individuals, prepared to run for office. The famous Berenice inscription discovered more than two centuries ago and much-debated ever since, gives us a touching example of public recognition for services rendered to the Jewish community, this time by a Roman official. This North African community, in public assembly during the Feast of Tabernacles (October 22, 25 B.C.E.), decided to inscribe the following vote of thanks:

Marcus Tittius, son of Sextus and Aemilia, a splendid and good man, having been called to the management of public affairs, has discharged his executive duties kindly and well and, while in this post, was found to have shown a peaceful disposition during the entire period of his administration. His behavior has been irreproachable not only in these matters, but also in those affecting the individual citizens. Discharging, moreover, in the best possible manner his executive duties for the Jews of our community [politeuma] in general as well as in individual matters, he did not fail to take the measures appropriate to their welfare. In consideration of all these circumstances the archontes and the community of the Jews in Berenice have resolved to honor him and, by naming him at every assembly and new moon, to decorate him with a wreath of olive branches and an honorary badge. The archontes are to inscribe this resolution [psephisma] upon a stele of Parian stone and place it at the most prominent spot of the amphitheatre. Unanimous consent.

A similar resolution, likewise inscribed on a stele of Paros marble (now extant in Carpentras), was somewhat later adopted with no less fanfare in honor of a devoted Jewish benefactor, Decimus Valerius Dionysius, son of Gaius. This benefactor was praised for "doing all the good he can both in public and in behalf of each individual citizen." He had, in particular, helped build an "amphitheatre" (apparently a general auditorum for communal use) and decorated it with murals.[85]

As time changed, however, and the Roman administration began imposing ever new burdens on the local elective officials and converting them into hated tax collectors, able leaders tried to steer clear of political entanglements. We may thus understand R. Johanan's blunt advice to flee the country rather than accept election to the city council (j. M.Q. II, 3, 81b). Now rabbinic theory gradually shifted from open discouragement of ambitious office seekers to emphasis upon everyone's communal responsibilities. Shemayah's well-known saying, "Hate public office," was now provided with a gloss, "that is to say, one must not place the wreath on one's own head, but others shall do so" (M. Abot I, 9; ARN XI, p. 46). Finally, a preacher exclaimed, "If someone says: 'Why should I concern myself with communal troubles, bother with men's controversies and listen to their voices? Peace be unto you, my soul!'— such a one is destroying the world!" (Tanḥuma, Mishpaṭim, II, on Exod. 21:1, with reference to Prov. 29:4).

In addition to these elective officials most communities had a larger or smaller salaried personnel. There also were in many cities and towns rabbis of distinction who, even if they had no formal appointment or authorization from the patriarch or exilarch, often exerted great influence on all communal affairs. Although living as private citizens and hence subject to neither election nor recall, they had spiritual weapons at their disposal which made their voice carry great weight, whether or not their advice had been solicited. Their excessive demands sometimes antagonized even members of their own guild. No lesser a champion of rabbinic supremacy than R. 'Aqiba enjoined, in his "ethical will," his son Joshua never to "reside in a city whose elders are scholars" (Pesaḥim 112a). We shall see, however, how, despite its frequent friction with the lay elders, rabbinic leadership proved in the long run beneficial to the Jewish people as a whole, on the local as well as the national level.

BABYLONIAN SUPREMACY

During the third and fourth centuries the center of gravity of Jewish life gradually moved from Palestine to Babylonia. The declining Roman Empire, forcing many subjects to emigrate, offered little attraction to Palestinian Jews. The Sassanian monarchs, on the other hand, encouraged immigration because the new arrivals brought technical skills for industrial projects and experience in commercial undertakings. Faustus of Byzantium tells us that Shapur II transplanted a large body of Jews (Faustus enumerates a total of more than 86,000 Jewish families) from Armenia to the Iranian provinces. His statement is essentially corroborated by Moses of Khorene, who speaks of Armenian Jews settled in Isfahan and Susiana. The Jewish population in these two cities in the interior of Iran became so large and influential that legend ascribed the rebuilding of Susa to Yazdegerd's Jewish wife. Isfahan became at least in the Muslim period an important center of Jewish life.[36]

Elsewhere in the Persian Empire, too, and particularly in Babylonia, the Jewish population increased and made steady progress economically and culturally. The Persians early recognized Babylonia's agricultural and intellectual superiority and, calling it "the heart of the Iranian empire," maintained their capital in Ctesiphon, despite its vulnerability to Roman attacks. In the vicinity of the capital, older and newer Jewish settlers often outnumbered their Gentile neighbors to such an extent that their rabbis seriously debated as to whether unidentifiable objects found there should carry the presumption of Jewish ownership with them (B.B. 24a). So overwhelmingly Jewish was, for example, the city of

Maḥoza, that the question arose whether the gates in the city wall did not require a *mezuzah* ('Erubin 6b).

Babylonia also had a vast *hinterland,* whose economic and intellectual resources greatly enhanced the power of its leadership. Media, especially, was even in Parthian times so intimately associated with it that their combination became stereotyped in Palestinian parlance. We recall R. Gamaliel's proclamation addressed to the "dispersion of Babylonia, the dispersion of Media and other lands." When R. Tarfon insisted upon the use of olive oil for Sabbath lights, R. Johanan ben Nuri objected by pointing out that the Jews of Babylonia had only sesame oil, of Media only nut oil, of Alexandria only radish oil, of Cappadocia only naphtha. The order is certainly illuminating. Josephus, too, speaks glibly of Ezra's "countrymen who were in Media." Median Jewry's intellectual achievements, to be sure, seem to have declined under Persian domination. While in the Parthian period Nahum, "the Mede," played in Palestine a coördinate role with similar Babylonian arrivals (late first century), several generations later Rab complained of the intellectual poverty of these neighbors or, as he phrased it, of Media being "sick." Some of this decline, however, may have been merely relative to the higher standards now set by the Babylonian academies.[37]

Since simultaneously the status of Palestine Jewry deteriorated, there gradually arose a certain rivalry between the two communities. No longer was there a Temple, a Hasmonean or even a Herodian dynasty to rule Palestine, and, indirectly, world Jewry. There were patriarchs in Palestine, of course, but Babylonia boasted of its exilarchs. These "princes of captivity" had a superior claim to distinction, as they were supposedly direct descendants of David, while the patriarchs of the house of Hillel (incidentally also a Babylonian) were regarded as progeny only of the female line. If Judah the Patriarch combined "learning and prestige in one place," had extensive estates, and employed a vast retinue of courtiers and a "Gothic" (Galatian or Teuton) bodyguard, the exilarch occupied a far higher position at the royal court, and his residence resembled a township of its own.

Nor was Babylonia devoid of most ancient traditions in a world obsessed with a quest for ancient origins. Even the Palestinian R. Johanan ben Zakkai, always with an eye to contemporary conditions, explained by a homely simile why the Jews had been exiled to Babylonia, rather than to other countries: "Because their ancestor Abraham had come from there. It is like a woman misbehaving toward her husband. To whom does he send her? He sends her back to her father's house." The Euphrates valley was dotted with ancient monuments, cherished by local Jews. The ancient community of Nehardea genuinely believed that its synagogue had been founded by the exiled King Jehoiachin. Another synagogue was ascribed to Daniel. Babylonian Jews also pointed with pride to a building which had allegedly housed Ezra's original academy and to other noteworthy biblical sites. Nor were these claims purely fictitious. After studying the Persian loan words in the Talmud, S. Telegdi reached the significant conclusion that most of these borrowings antedated the Sassanian period. This observation bears out not only the unbroken continuity of Babylonian Jewish life from the days of the Achaemenid Empire, but also its sufficient consolidation, before 226, for the Jews successfully to resist the incursion of new Iranian elements under the powerful Sassanian regime. More remarkably, the Palestinian R. Simon ben Laqish himself stressed the great historic achievements of Babylonian learning: "At first when the Torah was forgotten in Israel, Ezra came from Babylonia and restored it; it was forgotten again, when Hillel the Babylonian came and restored it; once again it was forgotten, when R. Ḥiyya and his sons came and restored it." Here and there Palestine adopted even Babylonian customs, such as "the beating of the willow branch" during the Feast of Tabernacles.[38]

Nevertheless, Palestine retained uncontested hegemony as long as Rome flourished to the end of the Antonine age. Sporadic attempts at independence, arising in Babylonian Jewry, were quashed without much difficulty. Not even when the high priest Hyrcanus II fled to Babylonia, and the throne of Jerusalem was occupied by a stranger like Herod, was any greater Babylonian self-assertion possible. After 135, we recall, the Palestinian leaders, combining persuasion with threats, frustrated R. Ḥananiah's attempt to proclaim independent regulations concerning the calendar and festivals. This prerogative, based on the observation of the new moon each month, had long been cherished by the ancient Babylonian kings. It was now tightly controlled by the Palestinian patriarchate, despite the availability of such reliable astronomic computations as were compiled by Mar Samuel.

As time went on, however, the rise of Babylonia to a leading position could not be checked. With the conclusion of the Mishnah by Judah the Patriarch, whether or not it was confined to writing, an instrument was created whereby the Babylonian study of Jewish law was to win greater independence. Of course the Mishnah contained only a minor fraction of the legal matter current in the Palestinian academies. Many additional collections of tannaitic law were issued afterwards, frequently exceeding R. Judah's fundamental compilation in size. Indeed for two or three generations Babylonian students migrated to Palestine, often under great personal hardship, to satisfy their thirst for knowledge from the living source of tradition. R. Johanan, in particular, attracted numerous disciples from the Euphrates Valley. Gradually, however, the influence of local traditions, many reaching back to the exilic age, became more marked. It is not far-fetched to assume that ancient Babylonian institutions had survived under cover from the days of Hammurabi and Assyria (we possess an Akkadian tablet of the first century B.C.E.), now to furnish novel ingredients for the religious and legal teachings of the Babylonian Amoraim. Mar Samuel, taking due cognizance of these innovations, declared almost immediately after the redaction of the Mishnah that some of its statements refer exclusively to Palestinian conditions, whereas Babylonia is to pursue her own way (B.B. 26a).

Samuel's equally distinguished colleague, Rab, seems to have thought differently. Although a born Parthian, he had spent most of his life in Palestine, whence he returned to his native land to found there, perhaps in connection with the internal strife and territorial divisions under the last Arsacid rulers of Parthia, a new academy in Sura (219 C.E.). Apparently few Jews had theretofore lived in this old military post which, owing to its connections across the desert with both Palmyra and Damascus, now developed into an important trade center. It has plausibly been suggested that thenceforth the permanent dividing line between the two renowned Babylonian academies of Sura and Pumbedita consisted in their relation to Palestine. Pumbedita, the heiress of ancient Nehardea, carried on the old tradition of native Babylonian Jewish learning. That is why the school of Mar Samuel favored independence from the Palestinian Halakhah. Rab, on the other hand, who founded his new academy "in a place where there had been no Torah before," transplanted much Palestinian learning and adopted many Palestinian customs, with which he had familarized himself at the school of Judah the Patriarch.[39]

The anarchy prevailing in the Roman Empire during the second half of the third century and, even more, the growing intolerance of the Christian Empire, decided the struggle in favor of Babylonia. Although Jerusalem was still theoretically the "navel" of the earth, the increasing supremacy of Babylonia could not fail to be reflected in rabbinic teachings. In the tannaitic age was proclaimed the principle that "under all circumstances a man should live in Palestine . . . , because whosoever dwells in Palestine is like one who has a God and whosoever dwells in the Diaspora is like one who has no God." Even later, R. Eleazar, himself a native Babylonian, declared that "whosoever dwells in Palestine lives without sin." The Babylonian rabbis thought differently, however. Not only did Raba reject R. Eleazar's teaching and his homiletical interpretation of a verse in Isaiah but, as early as the third century, Mar Samuel formulated the maxim that "just as it is forbidden to leave Palestine for Babylonia, so one must not emigrate from Babylonia to other countries." His disciple, R. Judah, who preserved this pronunciamento for posterity, was much more radical. His tart apothegm, "Whosoever emigrates from Babylonia to Palestine breaks a positive biblical commandment, because it is written 'they shall be carried to Babylon, and there shall they be until the day that I remember them, saith the Lord' [Jer. 27:22]," greatly disturbed his pro-Palestinian colleague, R. Ze'era.[40]

The two Jews, of the next two generations, who sold all their immovables in order to emigrate to Palestine, demonstrate the power of inextinguishable memories, but cannot conceal the gradual eclipse of the Palestinian center in the realities of Babylonian life. Soon Babylonian hegemony was so definitely established, even outside Babylonia proper, that the district of Mesene, for example, ceased to follow Palestinian regulations, and adopted those of Babylonia. Mesene was undoubtedly typical of the numerous Jewish communities in the border lands between Rome and Persia.[41]

In Palestine itself Babylonian students often became heads of academies and leaders of their generation. Among the outstanding rabbis of the late third century were the Babylonians Ḥiyya bar Abba, Ammi, and Assi, who traveled from one Palestinian town to another, establishing schools and appointing teachers. Ammi and Assi were also responsible for a new series of anti-Samaritan enactments, the better to preserve the orthodoxy of their coreligionists in that crucial period. Some supercilious Palestinians still spoke of the "foolish Babylonians"—this almost proverbial phrase merely reflected the usual regional superiority complex—and R. Jeremiah (himself a native Babylonian) actually asserted, "These foolish

Babylonians, because they live in an obscure country, express obscure thoughts." To which wholly unwarranted quip Raba sharply retorted, "Heretofore they have called us fools, now they are fools of fools, because we have taught them and they have failed to learn" (Yoma 57a). That such sentiments were expressed in a debate over a detail of the sacrificial ritual at the Temple added poignancy to the new self-assertion of the Babylonian schools.

Under the increasingly intolerant Christian Empire, finally, the patriarchs found it more and more inexpedient to exercise even their supreme authority over the Jewish calendar. The Church viewed with disfavor every public broadcast of the Jewish months which made it easier for Christian sectarians to set their Easter in accordance with the Jewish Passover. At the same time the customary dispatch of Palestinian messengers to inform Persian Jewry of the dates set for holidays appeared the more suspect to the Roman authorities, the more their own bad conscience made them fear Jewish espionage in behalf of the Sassanians. When such half measures as the advance proclamation of a whole cycle in the calendar failed to remedy these shortcomings, the patriarchs themselves decided in 358–59 to make public a permanent astronomic computation, and thus gave up their most significant function for world Jewry. That the patriarchate, as such, could not much longer pursue its shadowy existence, must have been clear to perspicacious observers.

SPREADING THINNER

Palestine's decline was intensified by biological developments. It is well known that the population of the Roman Empire decreased rapidly after the second century. The usual reasons adduced—racial degeneration and recurrent pestilences—are questionable. The first has yet to be proved; the second is contradicted by the general experience that losses from contagious diseases in an otherwise healthy society are made up by increased procreation within a very short time. Roman society, however, with its wide practice of birth control and even abstention from matrimony, was fundamentally sick. Perhaps in no other period of history was there such a high percentage of unmarried men and women. Few complaints are recorded against the practice of birth control by Jews. Social factors, such as the great poverty of the Jewish masses and the prevalent unfamiliarity with natural science, were enormously strengthened, as we shall see, by the rabbis' vigorous insistence upon procreation as the first commandment mentioned in the Bible, and by their vehement injunctions against any waste of human semen. Whether or not the hygienic precepts of talmudic law had already begun to build up in Jews an abnormal power of resistance to contagious diseases, we cannot say. Nevertheless, the demographic structure of Palestinian and Roman Jewry in general could not but be adversely affected.

As a whole, the Jewish population must have decreased considerably in the six centuries preceding the rise of Islam. The severe losses from wars and from the Christian mission were intensified by the negative biological and economic factors. Jerome's vindictive assertion, "In comparison to their previous multitude there hardly remained a tenth part of them" (*In Isa.* 6:11–13; *PL,* XXIV, 103), may be exaggerated even with respect to Palestine, which he had principally in mind. Nevertheless, it reflects the enormous shrinkage in Jewish manpower throughout the empire.

At the same time, the geographic basis of the Jewish people was steadily widening. In both the East and the West, Judaism took root in regions where the name of Israel's God had never been heard before. Not only the provinces east of Italy but the whole Roman Empire was now dotted with Jewish settlements. We recall that in Spain, about 300 c.e., the Council of Elvira found it necessary to admonish the Christians to desist from their friendly, even intimate relations with the Jews. That there were organized Jewish communities on the Rhine is shown not only by Constantine's edicts of 321 and 331, concerning the obligatory participation of Cologne Jewry in municipal offices, and the liberation of the Jewish communal officers from personal services, but also by recent archaeological investigation in southwestern Germany. The synagogue of Stobi (now Yugoslavia), a third-century Hebrew tombstone inscription in Gran, Hungary, and another in Bulgaria (after 250) are more recent confirmations of the spread of Jewish settlements to the northern limits of the empire.[42]

In the Orient there were the mass migrations from Palestine to Syria and Babylonia after 70, and later the transplantation of Jews over the entire Iranian Plateau. The districts neighboring on Syria and Babylonia, such as Palmyra and Kurdistan, absorbed a tremendous admixture of Jewish blood. Palmyrene Jewry, especially, has long intrigued scholars because of its commercial and political importance, particularly during the third century, and of the availability of a great many Aramaic inscriptions reflecting Jewish influence. No less than a hundred such inscriptions were dedicated "To Him Whose Name is Blessed." This description is sometimes amplified by the adjectives "The Good and Merciful" and decorated with two or four hands stretched out in prayer. The municipality itself prepared such a monotheistic legend in a bilingual (Greek and Aramaic) inscription dated 114 c.e. Few of these epigraphic monuments, to be sure, stem from orthodox Jews, who may, however, have been responsible particularly for the biblical texts inscribed on two Palmyrene door posts. In an inscription of 162, recently reinterpreted, one Bolai son of Zebida is commended to "the good remembrance by the Lord of the universe." The family tombstone inscribed in 212 by Zebida and Samuel, sons of Levi, son of Jacob, son of Samuel, reveals the presence there of a Jewish family using biblical names for several generations, as well as the adoption of the local name, Zebida, by one of the two brothers. This family probably worshiped in the third-century synagogue, remains of which have likewise been unearthed. Some other Palmyrene Jews were buried, quite expensively, in Beth She'arim. Most inscriptions, however, reflected only the various syncretistic mixtures (*Ba'al Shamen* = Lord of Heaven = Hypsistos = Zeus) characteristic of that age and region into which Jewish monotheism had injected strong ingredients of its own. Even the beautiful queen Zenobia supposedly evinced considerable sympathies toward Judaism.[43]

Equally important was the expansion of Judaism in the Arabian Peninsula, which culminated in the conversion of the southern Arabian king Dhu Nuwas to the Jewish faith in the early sixth century. In another context we shall see how great a role the Jewish tribes in northern Arabia were to play in the epochal transformations concomitant with the rise of Islam. From time immemorial southern Arabia also maintained relationships with neighboring Ethiopia, where Jews, probably coming down from Upper Egypt, seem to have settled in very ancient times. As elsewhere they were joined by native proselytes and together formed the community of Falashas, a designation probably indicating their origin from Hebrew exiles. Gradually pushed back into inaccessible mountain recesses, particularly by the persecutions of the Christian Church, for whose victory they had prepared the ground, they resisted conversion and assimilation through untold generations. Thenceforth they lived in almost total isolation from the rest of Jewry until their

discovery by nineteenth-century European travelers. They considered themselves descendants of Israelites brought back by the
Queen of Sheba from her visit with King Solomon, around which
the Christian Abyssinians, too, wove many romantic legends. The
Falashas staunchly adhered to Judaism as they understood it and
rigidly observed the Jewish commandments, modified by many
rituals and customs peculiar to themselves. Neither the meager
remnants of their literature, including their much revered apocryphal books of Enoch and Jubilees (none of them in Hebrew), nor
the legends still current among the surviving 50,000 to 100,000
Falashas today have been able to elucidate much of the long and
tortuous story of this stray branch of the Jewish people. But there
seems to be little doubt about its reaching back to remote antiquity, probably even to the days of the Second Commonwealth.
Only so can we explain, for example, the fact that, while they still
strictly observe the Sabbath commandment and celebrate the usual
biblical festivals, they seem to have preserved no recollection of
either Ḥanukkah or Purim.[44]

In this period the Jews may have reached out even to the Far
East, perhaps penetrating both India and China. The influx from
Persia to India, under Yussuph Rabban in the fifth century, though
more likely later, seems to have laid the foundations of a semi-
independent Jewish state which lasted into the sixteenth century.
A Hindu proselyte, Rab (!) Judah, living in Babylonia in the fourth
century is apparently mentioned by a talmudic writer as a matter
of course.[45] Even less reliable are the local legends tracing back the
origin of the Chinese Jews to the Palestinian exiles after 70. Both
these areas will be treated, therefore, more fully in their medieval
setting.

As against this expansion east and west, that in the southern and
northern directions encountered great natural and ethnological
barriers. Nevertheless, the impact of the Jewish religion upon the
Berber tribes on the extended fringe of the Sahara Desert, and on
the primitive peoples north of the Black Sea, becomes ever more
clearly discernible as we approach the Muslim era. With more right
than Pseudo-Sibylla, Philo, or Josephus, a rabbi now asserted,
"Truly you find Israel inhabiting the world from end to end"
(Pesiqta r. XXVIII, fol. 134b). In short, Judaism for the first time
became a "world religion" geographically, while in each particular
country it was more intensely than ever before the "national religion" of a struggling minority.

STRATEGIC RETREAT

Rise and decline of the Roman and the Partho-Persian empires during the first six centuries c.e. thus deeply affected the destinies of the Jewish people now progressively scattered from the Atlantic to the Pacific. After the great debacles the vast majority of the Palestinian Jews, whatever their messianic dreams, became basically reconciled to Roman rule and accepted, in principle, the sociopolitical *modus vivendi* previously developed by their coreligionists in the dispersion with a succession of Hellenistic and Roman rulers. The Babylonian community, never having enjoyed full political sovereignty, despite Adiabene and the small principality of Asinaeus or Mar Zutra II, readily came to terms with its Iranian conquerors. The new arrangement, harking back to Achaemenid precedents, for a time suited both parties perfectly.

These compromises were upset, however, when both empires came under the rule of religious fanatics. From the beginning faithful Zoroastrians, the early Sassanians were faced by a vast majority of unbelievers superior to their own "Aryan" people both culturally and economically. They followed the successful policy of religious toleration, once before laid down by Cyrus and Darius. Only after more than two centuries of internal consolidation did such new rulers as Yazdegerd II and Kavadh I feel strong enough to demand a measure of conformity from all their subjects, which spelled serious trouble for the Jews. The Roman emperors, on the other hand, once having surrendered to the implacably expansionist Christian Church were speedily driven into a policy of ruthless suppression of "heretics" and sharp discrimination against pagans and Jews. The Church thus finally secured the opportunity of realizing its ramified anti-Jewish program, laid down by its Fathers and teachers in the three centuries of its hard struggle for a place in the sun.

It is small wonder that Jews began spreading into ever new lands, some beyond the reach of both intolerant empires. Despite their deeply ingrained pacifism and legitimate apprehensions for personal safety, many Jews must have shared R. Ḥama bar Ḥanina's satisfaction over Rome's fear of the Berber and Teuton tribes. Most of all, they were interested in the continued rivalry between Rome and Persia. They knew, in particular, that whatever hopes they might have for regaining their national independence through their own efforts—Palestinian Jewry revealed considerable irredentist strength to the days of Heraclius and beyond—depended on this two-world system. Or, as R. Eleazar bar Abina phrased it, "When you see empires fighting one another, watch for the footsteps of the King Messiah" (Gen. r., XLII, 4, 409; LXXV, 9, 881).

Just as early Christianity had learned, therefore, through bitter experience that Roman statehood could not be decreed out of existence by an ideal postulate, so did Rome's new Christian rulers and their ecclesiastical advisers reach the inescapable conclusion that neither could the strong reality of Jewish nationality be wiped out by a theory, however alluring. Wherever real Jews had lived in masses, they had remained essentially Jewish. Their enormous war losses during the seven decades from Nero to Hadrian; the deterioration of their legal and political status; the decrease in their national power caused by the separation of Christianity; and the stupendous pressure exercised by the new Church against its mother creed—all these transformations contributed materially to the decline of the number of Jews. But they were not strong enough to suppress Judaism. On the contrary, the necessity of overcoming one national catastrophe after another tended in a sense to increase the cohesive power of the Jewish people and to strengthen the bonds of their religion. Out of this situation, so full of dangers and calamities, was born the Talmud.

XIV

WORLD OF THE TALMUD

JEWISH survival in the face of terrific external pressures and equally powerful lures to desertion has often appeared enigmatic to philosophers and historians. Wilhelm von Humboldt was not the only one to assert that the entire historic position of the Jewish people is "such an extraordinary phenomenon in world history and the history of religion that many a fine mind has doubted whether it can at all be explained in merely human terms" (*G.S.*, X, 97 ff.). However, such escape into the irrational and miraculous is merely a profession of intellectual lassitude. It certainly does not absolve the serious student of historic developments to inquire into the more overt human mainsprings which have shaped the destinies of mankind and the Jewish people during the last two thousand years.

Frequent reference has already been made to the various rationalizations which, whether inherited from ancient Israelitic prophets and lawgivers or newly developed during the struggle against Graeco-Roman paganism and nascent Christianity, helped thoughtful Jews to grasp the deeper *raison d'être* of their continued existence as both a people and a faith. The staunch messianic hope, undaunted by recurrent frustrations and the ensuing postponement to a dim and unpredictable future, remained the permanent lifebuoy against the recurrent waves of adversity. The doctrine of the Hereafter with its glorified celestial rewards, increasingly elaborated by homilists and teachers, helped reconcile even the unsophisticated masses with suffering in this world and aided them in resisting the strong outside temptations. Their leaders did not minimize these sufferings, but on the contrary made them the keynote of their interpretation of their people's history and destiny. The doctrine of Jewish martyrdom and the inescapability of persecutions during Israel's Diaspora existence became in itself a major source of communal solidarity. External temptations could not be decreed out of existence, but they were artificially ignored and thereby greatly neutralized.

Such rationalizations, however, could not possibly satisfy the rank and file of the people and give it the feeling of worthwhileness of life in general and Jewish life in particular. The man on the street needed more than mere assurance of celestial rewards, or fear of dire celestial punishments, to make him go on living his daily life as a normal and healthy human being. Whatever hopes he may have entertained for the messianic era, he must have found his actual Jewish life sufficiently appealing to carry on despite all handicaps. Here lay indeed the crux of his whole problem. Living as a Jew in the midst of an increasingly segregated community, he was affected by overt persecutions only on a few dramatic occasions. Many an individual doubtless lived all his life without encountering more than some milder form of discrimination, to which he had long become inured and of which he often was not the sole victim. Even if the hands of governmental taxgatherers lay heavily on his shoulders, the ordinary Jewish farmer, artisan, or trader often regarded it merely as just another obstacle to overcome in his generally hard economic struggle. Moreover, in practice he found that even here he had to deal increasingly with his own communal organs who were collecting state taxes as well. While he undoubtedly realized the great inimical force behind them, he personally seldom came face to face with it directly.

On the other hand, his Jewish forms of living were of daily, even hourly concern to him. From the moment he awakened in the morning until he came to rest at night his behavior was not only governed by the multiplicity of ritualistic requirements concerning ablutions, prayers, the type of food he was allowed to eat and the time he should set aside for study, but also during all his long and arduous working hours he constantly felt the impact of Jewish law and custom. It was in this vast interlocking system of observances and institutions, more and more fully elaborated by his rabbinic teachers, that he found his most integrated way of living as an individual and as a member of society. For the most part, he found this all-encompassing Jewish way of life so eminently satisfactory that he was prepared to sacrifice himself—here his indoctrination in martyrdom played a decisive role—for the preservation of its fundamentals.

In his choice of this irreducible minimum he was somewhat arbitrary and guided by instinctive feeling, rather than formal juristic logic.

Every commandment [complained an ancient rabbi] for which Israel have suffered martyrdom in a period of persecution (as in defying idolatry and observing circumcision) is still strictly adhered to, whereas every commandment for which Israel have not suffered martyrdom (phylacteries, for example) has remained of dubious observance.[1]

The prohibition of idolatry negatively embraced a great variety of assimilatory factors and could include general avoidance of imitating any of "the laws of Gentiles." Moreover, in addition to circumcision and the positive observance of Sabbaths and holidays, the ritual food requirements and mutual responsibility of all coreligionists were strongly ingrained in the Jewish public at large. For all these reasons, the continued existence of the people was never in doubt. Only the simultaneous marshaling of all hostile outside forces throughout the world—an intrinsic impossibility in a world divided against itself—might conceivably have destroyed this well-knit group. Otherwise, such hostility only helped cement its internal unity, which was fostered also by the general corporative developments and segregationist policies under both Rome and Persia. Whatever losses in manpower the Jewish people may have sustained, that large segment which remained Jewish was able to devote itself wholeheartedly to the cultivation of the mores of its forefathers. These found their most telling expression in the ramified institutions of talmudic Judaism, particularly those governing family and economic relations, providing for an effective judicial and social welfare system, furnishing education both to the masses and the intellectual elite, and regulating religious life from birth to death, at home as well as in the synagogue.

MARRIAGE

The regenerative forces of the Jewish people were greatly enhanced by the institution of Jewish marriage. The whole life of the Jew, including his sexual instincts, was subjected to the rigid supervision of religion. Social factors, such as the increasing concentration of the Jewish masses within the lower middle class, stimulated the exercise of sexual self-control. In this respect, too, the rabbis chose the middle path. Far from condemning, with Paul, the sexual appetite as an evil in itself, they effectively fought all forms of licentiousness. Marriage was for them a necessary social institution. As the foundation of ethnic life, it was especially vital for Judaism. In one remarkable passage, a Babylonian rabbi defended even sensual passion (*yeṣer ha-ra'*) as a positive good, because without it "no one would build a house, nor take a wife and beget children, [nor engage in business]" (Gen. r. IX, 7, 72). Hence the talmudic legislators neither elevated marriage to the position of a sacrament, a supernatural sanction of what otherwise would be an unforgivable sin, nor did they regard it as a mere contract in civil law.

Characteristically, while the Old Testament has no specific term for marriage, classifying it under the different types of "covenant," the talmudic *ishshut* distinctly reflects the attitude that this relationship is unique. Indeed the act establishing the communion between husband and wife was termed *qiddushin,* or "sanctification." Without receiving the indelible character of a sacrament, married life, as a whole, was regarded as sacred and under the direct control of Providence. Such ascetic trends as ran through talmudic Jewry had no bearing upon marriage. Even documentary evidence as to the sexual abstinence of the Essenes is contradictory.

After the destruction of the Temple, certainly, all such antisocial forces were banished. Rabbi Simon ben Zoma, with his gnostic inclinations, remained unmarried, but regarded his state as anomalous. "A Jew who has no wife lives without joy, without blessing, without good!" or "A Jew who has no wife is not a man" are two of the many sharp utterances of the rabbis condemning this destructive idiosyncrasy. Women were, unlike men, not subject to the commandment of procreation, but R. Joshua included a "sanctimonious woman" among those who undo the world. So intent were the talmudic sages on promoting marriage that, for a while, they upheld the "uncivilized" though most ancient institution of acquiring a wife by mere mutual consent (expressed in an appropriate formula) and actual consummation. Such marriages, too, had instantaneous effect and did not depend on long-term living together, as did Anglo-Saxon common-law marriages or Roman possession for at least one year. Only in the third century was there a sufficient revulsion against this sort of informality for Rab to outlaw it and to penalize transgressors by public flogging. Even he, however, did not dare to annul such marriages. To protect offspring of free and not otherwise legally prohibited relations, rabbinic law treated illegitimate children almost on a par with legitimate issue, granting them, especially, full rights of inheritance in their fathers' estates. Only relations with a prostitute were considered punishable by flagellation. Because her promiscuity raised the spectre of incestuous relations, a prostitute's children were also considered as likely "bastards." But, of course, the rabbis severely discouraged free love of any kind. Josephus correctly summarized their view by saying that "the Law recognizes no sexual connections, except the natural union of husband and wife, and that only for the procreation of children." [2]

As a rule, both men and women married so early and, as long as the agricultural economy prevailed, a wife was so much of an economic asset that the Talmud could afford to indulge in the legal "presumption that a man does not make his cohabitation illicit," wherever he can help it. Avoidance of temptation was an additional reason for the sages to advise early marriages. Most boys seem to have been married at the age of eighteen, some starting their marital careers at sixteen or earlier, while girls were often given away by their fathers at the age of twelve or less. In Graeco-Roman Egypt, too, most boys married at fourteen and girls at twelve years of age. Among the Parsees an unmarried girl of fifteen was considered rather anomalous. To assure procreation, moreover, the rabbis sharply condemned unions between very young and very old persons. They also elaborated the biblical prohibition for eunuchs to marry any but specified lower-caste Jewesses on the fringe of the community. Only when Roman legislation against castration and Persian aversion to this practice all but eliminated this formerly important social class, could Mar Samuel and his successors be somewhat more lenient, particularly toward men impotent from birth. [3]

Even in metropolitan Rome, Jews seem to have married quite early and stayed married for most of their lives. From one inscription we learn that one Domitia, who died at the age of nineteen, had lived with her husband for seven years. Another lady, Junia Sabina, at the age of eighteen had behind her three years of marital life. To be sure, several inscriptions commemorate "virgins" aged fifteen to nineteen, but this very designation indicates that they were considered of marriageable age. Nor was the young man Anteros exceptional when, at the age of twenty-two, he left behind a widow to whom he had been married for almost six years (Frey's *Corpus*, I, Nos. 45, 105, 168, 242, 302, 381; cf. *ibid.*, pp. cxvi f.).

We understand, therefore, the undertone of legitimate envy in Tacitus' remark that the Jews "take thought to increase their numbers; for they regard it as a crime to kill any late-born [*agnatis*, not desired] child." That the rabbis attached so great importance to orderly family life and intensive procreation is the less astonishing, as they lived in the midst of a civilization which from the second century on showed increasing signs of biological decay. When the third-century anarchy engulfed Palestine, too, we frequently learn even there of men marrying at the age of thirty or forty. But the biological balance was soon fully restored, and unfriendly Jerome conceded that, in his day, Jews were multiplying "like vermin." Life expectancy, too, in the ancient world was generally very low. Epigraphic and other data seem to indicate that a child born in the Roman Empire had no reasonable grounds to expect survival beyond his twenty-fifth birthday. Although, to quote Jerome again, Jews were "often seen reaching decrepit old age," the ideal age of one hundred and twenty years, attributed to Moses and some leading rabbis, must have been as rare in Palestine as was the parallel figure of one hundred and ten years glorified in Egypt. Certainly the tradition that Hillel, R. Johanan ben Zakkai and R. 'Aqiba reached Moses' age is vitiated by its all-too-neat division of every one of these lives into exactly three periods of forty years each. More realistically, Ben Bag Bag (or possibly Samuel the Small, who himself lived to a ripe old age of ninety) stopped his enumeration of the fourteen stages in man's growth at the age of one hundred, when "he is as though he were dead, and had passed away and faded from the world." On the other hand, Jews, too, must have had their share in the generally high mortality, particularly of infants and children. Only large families could help sustain a people which faced an additional drain on its manpower from assimilation and conversion.[4]

Economic considerations, to be sure, could not be totally neglected. The more urbanized the Jewish people became, even in Palestine and Babylonia, the fewer adolescents could afford to support a family and pay in advance the traditional *mohar* to the bride's father. In a transitional stage, it appears, the husband was allowed to substitute a pledge for cash, but even that obligation often proved so burdensome that many Jews "became old and did not marry." The author of the aprocryphal Testament of Issachar already sounded the complaint that his hero was financially in no position to marry until the age of thirty-five and then was too old and weary to enjoy his marital life. If in the earlier predominantly agricultural economy the bridegroom's father often welcomed a daughter-in-law into his household as an accretion to his working personnel, now it was the bride's father who sometimes had to play host to the newly betrothed couple. Before long the old *mohar* was converted into a marriage settlement for the bride to provide for her widowhood or divorce, and in addition her father had to give her a dowry (*neduniah*). We recall the fantastic sum allegedly bestowed by Naqdimon ben Gurion on his daughter shortly before the fall of Jerusalem. Even poor fathers were expected to supply a minimum dowry of 50 denarii; if they were unable to do so, the community chest took over. Charitable provision for needy brides became, as we recall, a major responsibility of the community particularly after the ravages of the Bar Kocheba revolt.[5]

Nor could conflicts of duties be avoided, especially when a man had to choose between married life and scholarly pursuits. The rabbis, touched in this most sensitive spot, were ready to compromise. If one's soul is longing for learning, they taught, one may postpone the assumption of marital relations beyond the stated age of eighteen. In more prosperous Babylonia, Mar Samuel preferred that "one should first marry a wife and then study the Torah," but R. Johanan, living in inflation and tax-ridden Palestine, countered, "What, with a millstone around his neck he should study the Torah?" Even a promised dowry at times depreciated here so fast as to create serious legal problems. In that period, we recall, Palestinians often postponed marriage to the age of thirty or forty. To encourage learning, some men of wealth selected promising young students for their daughters and saw them through their early difficult years. The rabbis soon advocated such preferential treatment as a matter of general policy. Their efforts seemed successful in so far as, apart from R. 'Aqiba, Ben 'Azzai and possibly R. Eliezer, cases of protracted celibacy among the talmudic sages are rarely recorded. When R. Hamnuna was introduced to R. Huna, the latter bluntly informed him, "Please do not come to see me until you are married." Their fellow Babylonian, R. Ḥisda, was far more typical. Married at the age of sixteen, he always regretted that he had not done so two years earlier.[6]

Rigid morality was demanded in married life. Maimonides, summing up the talmudic law in his code, discusses many extremely intimate details of marital relationships, recommending some, putting others under serious sanctions. Prudery was unknown to the rabbis and, while they declared obscene language to be ground for divorce, they were usually quite outspoken in their regulations and ethical expositions. Then and later there were strong tendencies toward prohibiting intercourse with a pregnant wife. Some sectarians, such as the Essenes, the Samaritan Dositheans, and 'Anan the Karaite, imposed a direct prohibition. The Talmud, however, after discussing this and related cases, fails to draw this logical consequence of its own justification of marriage exclusively as a means of maintaining mankind and the Jewish people (Yebamot 12b). It obviously regarded a legal injunction of this sort as beyond the power of the majority to sustain.

Marital fidelity was taken for granted, at least on the wife's part. Adultery still was counted among capital crimes. Although Jewish leaders were able to invoke similar provisions in Roman law, executions on this, as on any other score, became very rare in the earlier tannaitic period, and ceased altogether with the loss of capital jurisdiction by the Jewish court. If a late Babylonian rabbi (Ḥama bar Tobiah) once applied to a priest's dissolute daughter the old biblical penalty of death by burning, this was clearly an extralegal act, disavowed by other rabbis. It may have been but an emergency measure intended to discourage some Jewish followers of the Mazdakite sect, which had preached the community of women. Nor were the later tannaitic discussions of the ancient ordeal of the "water of bitterness," to be given women suspect of adultery, of more than academic interest. Nevertheless, there existed sufficient other deterrents in the numerous legal and social penalties inflicted upon transgressors. Such were, for instance, the adulteress' obligatory divorce, even against the wish of her husband, and simultaneous prohibition of her marrying the paramour. The offspring of adulterous relations was absolutely declassed, such "bastards" (*mamzerim*) being unable to marry a Jew or a Jewess even unto the thousandth generation.[7]

This exclusion of bastards had many significant consequences. Some rabbis wished to exclude such tribes as the Palmyrenes and Kurds from conversion to Judaism on account of a lingering suspicion that they were descendants of Jewish bastards whose ancestors had been absorbed by these two tribes. Of course, this may have been but a rationale for exclusion found desirable on other grounds. Ultimately, R. Naḥman bar Isaac decided that they be admitted. The Talmud engages in a curious speculation as to what eventually happens to a bastard and his progeny. One assumption, already adumbrated by Sirach and the Wisdom of Solomon, was that the disguised bastards were sooner or later removed from Jewish life by pestilence or some other cause of premature death. R. Ammi, after having exposed an honorable citizen to public contumely by discovering his descent from a prohibited relation, claimed credit for having saved this concealed bastard from impending disaster. There was only one legal escape for descendants of a male bastard. Over R. Eliezer's opposition, R. Tarfon advised such a person to marry a Gentile slave, whose offspring would then follow the mother in her status as a slave. Slaves, if liberated, could soon become full-fledged Jews.[8]

MONOGAMOUS TRENDS

Husbands were free from the obligation of marital fidelity. Needless to say that the legislators did not wish to encourage free sexual relationships on the part of men. Here was only the necessary corollary of polygamy, the recognized principle of talmudic law being that a man might marry as many wives as he could support. Only some sectarian wings preached monogamy. The New Covenanters of Damascus, for instance, pointed out that Noah took only one male and one female of each species into his ark and interpreted the biblical prohibition of taking "a woman to her sister" (Lev. 18:18) in the philologically perfectly tenable manner of outlawing any simultaneous second marriage (Schechter's *Fragments*, 4:20 ff.). The majority, however, agreed with Josephus (himself married to more than one wife) that "it is our ancient custom to have many wives at the same time" (*Antt.* XVII, 1, 2.14; *War* I, 24, 2.477). Justin Martyr was not wrong, therefore, in taunting his Jewish interlocutor about Jews "in all lands" taking as many wives as they pleased (*Dialogue*, 134, 1; 141, 4, in *PG*, VI, 785, 800).

Many independent developments, however, joined to make polygamy comparatively rare. In the first place then, as always, there were economic limitations. Most Jews, belonging to the proletarian or lower middle class, could not afford the luxury of maintaining more than one wife. Talmudic law, extending far-reaching protection to the wife, made the cost of indulging in such a luxury even more prohibitive. A second, equally vital, consideration was the lack of eligible women. In view of the practically total absence of unmarried men, only a relatively negligible surplus of women could have been available. Since Ezra and Nehemiah and, particularly, since the enactment of the "eighteen" separatist prohibitions, intermarriage with Gentile women encountered a serious obstacle in the talmudic insistence upon conversion to Judaism as an indispensable prerequisite. Even so, it seems the *amixia* of the Jewish people, as illustrated by the story of Tobit, always militated against such relationships. Did not Tacitus reproach the Jews for their "superiority complex" in this respect? Even where intermarriage was relatively more frequent, as in Egypt in the days of Philo, probably about as many Jewesses married Gentile husbands as Jews did Gentile wives. In 339, we recall, the Christian Empire prohibited the marriage of Christian women to Jewish husbands, apparently believing that the faith of the husband must prevail. In view of the speedy increase in the Christian population this law must have further reduced the available supply of Gentile wives.

Female slaves also decreased in number from generation to generation. Moreover, the rabbis prohibited free relations with them, prescribing liberation and marriage. Under these circumstances concubinage, permanently increasing in Roman society, seems to have vanished from Jewish life. At least as far as talmudic legislation is concerned, the biblical *pillegesh* (the Roman *pellex* is linguistically as well as institutionally related to it) appears to have been of but antiquarian interest. The discussion between R. Meir and R. Judah as to whether such a concubine was a wife without a marriage contract (providing for her widowhood and divorce) and other financial stipulations, or with a contract but without the latter, betrays their purely academic approach to an evidently obsolete institution. To all intents and purposes a woman was either somebody's legally wedded wife or his extralegal mistress. Nor could a woman entertain legally valid relations with her slave. She could either liberate him and then become his full-fledged wife, or else live in sin without any legal recognition whatsoever. The Roman practice of women (and men) of senatorial rank living in concubinage with persons of lower status and thus safeguarding their privileged position—a practice legalized even by Callistus, Christian bishop of Rome (218–23)—had no Jewish counterpart in either problem or solution. Nor did the Jews follow the Parsee example of having one main and a number of secondary wives, the latter with a concubine-like inferior legal status.[9]

Of course, rabbinic law and homilies reveal only some of the more superficial folkways in the ramified and obscure realm of sex relations. So long as there existed even a modicum of slavery, the temptation for the slaveholder often proved irresistible. The rabbis themselves expatiated on the extreme licentiousness of slaves and taught that "he who multiplies female slaves, multiplies fornication" (M. Abot II, 7). Even in the nearly all-Jewish city of Sepphoris under the strong control of both its rabbinic academy and orthodox public opinion there were Jews who begot children with their slave girls and raised them unceremoniously as Jews. According to law, these were to be treated as slaves until formally liberated. More, some women, like many Roman matrons, had children with their male slaves and, despite all opposition, seem to have succeeded in ultimately bringing them into the community. Many Palestinian towns had special "harlots' quarters," as did other Mediterranean cities, but we learn about them only through some incidental references. Extolling, for instance, the great piety of two priestly sages, R. Hananiah and R. Hoshaiah, the Talmud emphasizes that, although making a living as cobblers in the "harlots' quarter" (probably in Tiberias) and hence having prostitutes among their customers, the two rabbis never "raised their eyes to look at these" women (Pesaḥim 113b). The story was told, moreover, to pacify unmarried R. Safra as to why the sages esteemed so highly any bachelor living without sin in a big city. Nor do we hear of any cases where "zealots" made use of their exceptional right to lynch the Jewish transgressor caught in the act of cohabiting with a Gentile. How much more lax must have been the morals of Jews in the Greek cities of Palestine and the Roman dispersion! At its worst, however, Jewish sex morality seems to have towered high above the generally dissolute environment. Classical and patristic literature agree in depicting the anarchical conditions in the upper reaches of Roman society, which were probably duplicated or even exceeded among the masses.

Unfortunately, we know little about the daily life of the Diaspora Jews. Even inscriptions, at times quite eloquent among pagans, are as a rule emotionally rather inarticulate in the case of Jews, who limited themselves largely to the recording of names, dates, and occasional public activities. Only rarely do we find an outspoken husband like the one who, early in the second century after a happy marriage of over twenty-five years, erected a tombstone to his wife Regina in Rome. After describing his love for the deceased and her future resurrection, he added, "This would be assured to you by your piety and your chaste life, as it also would by your love of the people [generis], your observance of the law, your marital deserts, the care of which was your glory." It is not surprising, therefore, that Jewish epigraphy contributes practically nothing to our knowledge of the extramarital love life of ancient Jewry.[10]

Rabbinic discussions, too, center almost exclusively around wives, all being regarded as equals. The expressive technical term ṣarot (a term whose meaning may best be rendered by "jealous associates") shows the rivalry prevailing in such occasional "harems," a rivalry rather intensified by the absence of legal discrimination.

For this reason Rab advised that, if one insisted on marrying more than one spouse, one should take three, rather than two wives (Pesaḥim 113a). There was a slight idealistic preference for the "wife of one's youth," but legally it resulted, at most, in the advice of the Jewish sages (echoing Malachi) to refrain, as far as possible, from divorcing her. Pointing out the juxtaposition of Mal. 2:13–14, R. Eleazar exclaimed, "Even the [divine] altar weeps over a man who divorces his first wife" (Giṭṭin 90b).

The impact of monogamous Roman society also began to be felt. Although in the early Roman Empire the *peregrini* were expressly allowed to practice polygamy, there evidently was an increasing number of Jews enjoying the status of Roman citizens, for whom marriage of more than one wife constituted a crime. That the Herodians, notwithstanding their Roman citizenship, had many wives, merely shows how reluctant the Roman administration was to interfere with the established customs of subject nations. In 212, all Jews became Roman citizens and, as such, theoretically subjected to severe penalties for polygamy. Diocletian in 285 specifically extended the prohibition over all inhabitants of the empire. The Christian emperors reiterated it, for instance, in 393 with special emphasis. No matter how little Jews were inclined to obey Roman legislation when it differed from their own, public violation of imperial criminal law throughout a lifetime, open to denunciation from any quarter, necessarily became unusual.

In Babylonia, where the dominant group in the population, the Persians, were themselves extremely polygamous, the situation was quite different. One Persian king is recorded as having had not less than three thousand wives, far outstripping the legendary harem of King Solomon, whose memory, incidentally, kindled the imagination of polygamous Jews in subsequent ages. Indeed there are indications that Babylonian Jewish society had more polygamous features than did that of Palestine. Anecdotes like those current in regard to Rab and R. Naḥman, that after arriving in a foreign city they used to advertise for women ready to marry them for the time of their sojourn (*man havya le-yoma*), would have been impossible in Palestine. Indeed, the Babylonian Talmud notes the contrast between such proceedings and the Palestinian (tannaitic) prohibition of marrying two women living thereafter in different provinces, lest there result incestuous marriages between their respective children. It tries to reconcile the two statements by a dialectical subterfuge. In law, too, the Babylonian emphasis lay upon the Jew's right to "marry as many wives as he is able to support," while the Palestinians stated that "he who marries another wife is obliged to divorce his first wife [if she so wishes] and to pay her the amount agreed upon in the marriage contract." [11]

So strong, however, was the unity pervading all Jewish life, regardless of surrounding civilizations, that such differences as existed between Babylonia and Palestine were but nuances touching the periphery of the institution. In fact, from the days of the First Exile on, our records concerning actual polygamous families are exceedingly slight. Numerous prophetic passages presuppose an essentially monogamous society, despite the absence of legal enforcement; their very symbolism depicted Israel as the Lord's often unfaithful but much-beloved single wife. In the story of Job, we do not hear of his blessed life at the beginning, or at the end, as consisting of a large harem. According to R. Judah ben Batira's homiletical explanation, Job drew a lesson from Adam. Just as God might have given, he thought, ten wives to the first man, but created Eve alone, "my lot of one wife is enough for me, too." The rich biographical material concerning several hundred talmudic sages furnishes only two or three instances of rabbis actually living with two wives. In each case some exceptional circumstance accounted for the deviation (R. Eliezer, prompted by charity, betrothed a minor niece in addition to his distinguished wife, Imma Shalom; and Abba, whose first wife, the daughter of his brother Rabban Gamaliel was barren, took a second). The story, on the other hand, of Judah the Patriarch having ordered an inquirer to perform his levir's duty and marry all twelve wives of a deceased brother, was clearly intended only to drive home a legal doctrine. So was R. Tarfon's aforementioned betrothal of "three hundred" women to enable them to partake of priestly food. In fact, R. Judah himself, well cognizant of public opinion, counseled his son not to marry a second wife, for people would say that one "was his wife, the other his harlot." It may be taken for granted, therefore, that the consistently polygamous legal theory reflected reality only to a slight degree. Very likely the ratio of multiple marriages in talmudic Palestine was far below that in a modern Arab village, where H. Granqvist found that 199 men had married 264 women over a period of a hundred years.[12]

Possibly talmudic Judaism clung to this unrealistic legal theory in conscious opposition to Graeco-Roman monogamy. Trying to maintain the ancestral heritage against the influx of foreign ideas and institutions, the Jews insisted on the continued validity of the positive principle—man's liberty to marry more than one wife.

Similarly, Jews persevered in their long-established ability to sever marriage ties. If even in the formative stages of Israelitic divorce laws "outside influence was so slight as to be practically negligible" (Neufeld), the Jewish people now doubly adhered to its traditional customs, making but relatively minor adjustments required by its new social conditions. On the whole, it shunned the extreme latitude of the Elephantine soldiers, who, apparently influenced by Egyptian practice, had allowed women to secure the contractual privilege of asking for divorce at any time. But it also avoided the opposite extreme of outlawing all divorces, except on account of the wife's adultery, as demanded by the author of Jubilees, the Damascus sect, and, even within the rabbinate itself, by the house of Shammai and its heir at Yabneh, R. Eliezer ben Hyrcanus. Perhaps egged on by the growing Christian propaganda against divorce, the Hillelite school stressed the husband's freedom to divorce his wife even for some culinary deficiency or, as R. 'Aqiba taught, because he had found a better-looking woman. At times the court itself took the initiative and, in specified cases, forced the husband to issue a writ of divorce.[13]

In practice, however, one may readily assume, divorces were rather exceptional. Such moral considerations as voiced by Sirach ("Hast thou a wife, abhor her not"; 7:26) and echoed by rabbis, combined with strong material restraints (return of dowry, loss of income from the wife's property and payment of the stipulated marriage settlement), made unions far more lasting than one might expect. The growing complexity of rabbinic law likewise robbed the divorce proceedings of their original informality. With the text of the writ of divorcement elaborated to its minutest detail and the rabbis' insistence that any important deviation therefrom invalidated the whole act, it became increasingly necessary for divorce-seeking husbands to take recourse to experts. The need of explaining their motives to a rabbinic court and the accompanying publicity must have discouraged all but the most persistent claimants.

No wonder, then, that no divorcee appears in any Roman inscription, while several inscriptions mention specifically that the deceased woman had been an *unavira* (married only to one man), or that the deceased man had enjoyed a prolonged marital status.

A Capuan elder, for example, had been married for 48 years (Frey's *Corpus*, I, No. 553). There certainly were no Jewish counterparts to those Roman ladies who, according to Seneca (*De beneficiis*, III, 16, 2), counted their years "not by the number of consuls, but by the number of their husbands." Nor do we hear of rabbis who married four or five times as did, for instance, Caesar and Pompey, unless it be Josephus, whose long captivity accounted for some of his marital changes.

TALMUDIC EUGENICS

Even more pronounced was the rabbis' emphasis upon the prohibition of incest. While the permission of polygamy was by no means a commandment, incest was regarded as both a sin and a crime. The Greeks and the Romans likewise detested sexual relations between near relatives. But incest was widely practiced and even directly encouraged in at least two important countries of Jewish settlement. In Egypt the Ptolemaic rulers themselves, for the most part, married their own sisters. In Parthia-Persia, marriages between parents and children were valid, and those among brothers and sisters were quite customary. The Parsee religion, with its overemphasis on purity, as well as the caste structure of Persian society, encouraged such marriages as the fittest means of preserving family purity (cf. *Yasna* 12, 9). For example, the claim could be made that Artaxerxes II had married his two daughters and that Mithridates I had married his mother. Ardea Viraz is said to have married his seven sisters. Incidentally, this unique experiment in eugenics by the warlike Persian nobility did not, after four centuries of extensive inbreeding, result in signs of degeneration any more marked than those of similar ruling castes after an equal period.

Jews resisted to the extreme. The old biblical taboos may have originated from the conscious wish of keeping the Israelites apart from their neighbors, since Canaanite laxity in this respect is well illustrated by the marital ventures between close relatives at the pantheon of Ugarit. The biblical lawgiver thundered, "Defile not ye yourselves in any of these things; for in all these the nations are defiled, which I cast out from before you" (Lev. 18:24). In the course of time, however, this original motive was largely forgotten, and the prohibitions were now rationalized to fit the conceptions of the new age. Philo, in particular, viewing Ptolemaic realities,

tried to give them a philosophic motivation. He stressed bashful-
ness, which would disappear if sexual relationships were legalized
within the family, and reciprocal amity between men and nations,
which is best promoted by marriages between members of different
families and tribes (*De spec. leg.*, III, 4.25).

The rabbis, however, declared the prohibition of incest to be a
positive biblical law to which one must adhere with or without
reason. That is why only those degrees were prohibited which were
expressly mentioned in the Bible, although there were quite a few
minor amplifications through oral law (*sheniyot mi-dibre soferim*).
Once they had recognized the purely "positive" and even irrational
character of the biblical taboos, the rabbis had to offer just as stout a
resistance to the Roman computation of family degrees as to the
laxity of the Ptolemies or Persians. On one point, particularly,
Roman law differed from Jewish: marriages between an uncle and
a niece. The mother's brother was specifically excluded by Roman
law, while Jewish law regarded such marriages as highly meritorious. Whether or not we may see therein the survival of a pre-
Israelitic matriarchate, this insistence of official Judaism against
such sectarian currents as Samaritans and New Covenanters, as well
as against Roman law, in so far as it affected Roman Jewish citizens,
reveals again the enormous tenacity of Judaism's conservative
forces. We recall that both R. Eliezer and Abba married nieces, as
did also R. Jose the Galilean. Such marriages were placed on a par
with good neighborly relations and charitable loans to needy
friends. They had become frequent enough for the later sages to
explain on their account the necessity of dating the writ of divorcement. On one occasion, when a man specifically vowed not to marry
his niece (this seems to have been but one of many cases of popular
resistance to a custom no longer squaring with conscientious scruples), R. Ishmael made a special effort to overrule his vow and to
make the niece more attractive to him by improving her teeth.[14]

Of more theoretical interest are the rabbinic views on incestuous
unions among Gentiles, which Jewish courts were rarely, if ever, in
a position to enforce. Slaves, like cattle, were not subject to any
restrictions. Other "sons of Noah," however, were supposed to abstain from marrying their mothers or maternal sisters. Some rabbis
added stepmothers. As to descendants, R. 'Aqiba and R. Meir, by
outlawing all relations prohibited among Jews under the sanction
of capital punishment, evidently wished to include daughters,
granddaughters, and daughters-in-law, but the Babylonian R.

Huna, facing the facts of Sassanian life, taught that such unions were permitted to Gentiles.[15]

If the rabbis did not have the power of enforcing these regulations concerning Gentiles, and if, even in the case of would-be converts born from prohibited unions, they compromised under the legal fiction that proselytes were newly born children with no family relations of their own, the two imperial legislations on the whole abstained from seriously interfering with Jewish usages. Except in the case of the Mazdakite extremists' extralegal actions we do not hear of any Parsee moves to force their Jewish or Christian subjects to practice, for instance, *khvedhvaghdas* (marriage of close relatives). Zoroastrian teachers may have extolled marital unions between brothers and sisters as shining in divine splendor and keeping off demons, they did not seek to impose these concepts upon unbelievers. Pagan Rome, as we have seen, largely compromised with the Jewish mores, except in regard to polygamy. Even the extreme law enacted by the Christian Empire in 393, forbidding any Jew to "enter matrimony in accordance with his own law," was evidently aimed principally at polygamy and possibly uncle-niece unions. It may also have wished to outlaw levirate marriages, about which Roman legislation itself was far from consistent. But the Jews had long before devised an alternative for such unions with childless sisters-in-law through the ceremony of *ḥaliṣah*. However unsavory, this ceremony made it possible especially for men already married to refuse to take another wife. The imperial law certainly did not mean that the Jews could not perform weddings according to their ancient ceremonial. Under Persia, on the other hand, the general climate of opinion encouraged levirate marriages in order to perpetuate the memory of a predeceased brother. The Parsees themselves actually married off widows or daughters of those who died without issue to any close relative or even financed from their estates a "substitute marriage" of some male relative to a strange woman, so that the child might bear the name of the deceased. The rabbinic records, however, almost all of which antedate 393, do not allow for any generalization as to whether, because of these environmental differences, the *ḥaliṣah* gained ground more rapidly in Palestine than in Babylonia.[16]

Tribal endogamy lost its importance about the beginning of the Christian era. Under the pressure of Hellenism and the Nabataean-Arab expansion, the nations, eternally or temporarily excluded from "the community of God" by biblical law, disintegrated and then vanished. The Egyptians had largely been Hellenized. The Moabites and Ammonites now were so predominantly Arabian that Josephus could hardly distinguish between a Transjordanian Arab and an Ammonite. The Edomites had settled in a formerly Judaean district and, after their enforced adoption of Judaism, were finally absorbed by the Jews. In continuing to discuss the exclusion of the descendants of these tribes, the Talmud reflects its own conservatism rather than real legal practice. In Babylonia, in particular, such endogamous exclusion must have been extremely rare. When new antagonisms arose and the Jews wanted to break definitely, as, for instance, with the Palmyrenes, they were forced to base their action on the latter's questionable ancestry.

All these regulations applied, of course, only to converted Gentiles. Marriage with heathens remained strictly prohibited. Unlike the great empires of antiquity which, combining religious toleration with imperial interests, tried to overcome the ethnic heterogeneity of their subjects by lowering the barriers to mixed unions, the Jews (like Christians and Muslims after them) feared the influence of pagan spouses on the purity of their exclusive, monotheistic faith and observance. Experience taught them that a Jewess married to a Gentile was usually lost to the Jewish faith. Extremists, like the author of the Book of Jubilees, postulated therefore,

If there is any man who wishes in Israel to give his daughter or his sister to any man who is of the seed of the gentiles, he shall surely die, and they shall stone him with stones . . . and they shall burn the woman with fire because she hath dishonored the name of the house of her father and shall be rooted out of Israel.

Such penalty, derived from the combination of biblical sanctions on giving "any of thy seed to set them apart to Molech" and on a priest's daughter turning harlot, was rejected by the rabbis. The Mishnah specifically enjoined severe scolding for anyone relating the Molech passage to intermarriage. Nevertheless, R. Ishmael predicted direly that "he who marries an Aramaean [Gentile] woman and raises children with her will ultimately raise enemies of the Lord," sharpening the old biblical warning that Gentile women would "make thy sons go astray after their gods." R. Ishmael's warning had a realistic sound inasmuch as experience was to show that many an offshoot of mixed unions, in order to hide his Jewish descent, became an ardent Jew-baiter.[17]

Prohibitions did not always prove effective, however, as is evident from their very reiteration century after century. Just as the narrow confines of the Jerusalem community in the days of Ezra and Nehemiah had led many Jews to look for wives among the women of Ashdod and other neighbors (this sociological factor was not eliminated by these leaders' drastic measures), so did, at the other extreme, the overexpansion of the Maccabean era encourage indiscrimininate mixtures. Hence the pre-Maccabean author of the Testament of Levi already reprimanded his compatriots, "The daughters of the Gentiles shall ye take to wife purifying them with an unlawful purification" (14:6).

Diaspora Jews, particularly if living in small and scattered communities, must have found the selection of Jewish mates extremely limited. Intermarriage must also have increased in direct ratio with the intimacy of social contacts with Gentiles. Even in Philo's Alexandria, where the Jews lived in a compact mass apparently constituting the largest single religious and ethnic group in the city's cosmopolitan population, marriage outside the fold apparently was quite common. Philo himself, perhaps unwittingly, supplied an interesting rationale. Trying to justify to his Egyptian contemporaries the Jewish prohibition of incest, he exclaimed, evidently without fear of contradiction, "Why hamper the fellow-feeling and inter-communion of men with men by compressing within the narrow space of each separate house the great and goodly plant which might extend and spread itself over continents and islands and the whole inhabited world? For intermarriages with outsiders create new kinships not a wit inferior to blood-relationships." As against this perhaps consciously equivocal statement, Philo's defense of the Mosaic prohibition of intermarriage, doubly resented by his Egyptian neighbors, was obviously halfhearted and unconvincing. Understandably, the Jewish apologist also failed to mention here the biblical distinctions between the various nations and particularly the rigid exclusion of Egyptians.[18]

We must bear in mind, however, that, in the constant clash between the exclusive faith of the Jewish partner and the more tolerant, syncretistically often undermined beliefs of the non-Jewish mate, the former often won out. If conversion preceded marriage, as was probably the rule, Jewish leaders raised no serious objections. In fact, except for legal obstacles of marrying into the priesthood, female proselytes were treated on a par with native-born Jewesses and sooner or later were wholly absorbed by the Jewish community.

Legal equality did not connote full social equality, however. In the class gradation by descent, rather than by wealth, of talmudic Judaism, proselytes held an intermediary fifth place in a scale of ten. While permitted to marry into all groups above them, except the priesthood, they were also allowed to go down the line to bastards, hieroduls, and children of unknown fathers or foundlings, who were forbidden to the average Jew by birth (M. Qiddushin IV, 1). Josephus reflects prevailing practice more than formal law, when he asserts, that "young men, on reaching the age of wedlock, marry virgins, freeborn and of honest parents" (*Antt.* IV, 8, 23. 244).

Emphatic observance of family purity was, indeed, another eminently eugenic means of national preservation. While retaining its theocratic-democratic character, in this respect Judaism developed aristocratic features. Priestly families were obliged to keep detailed family records, and the lay aristocracy, too, prided itself on its descent. "Well-born, very well-born" (*eugenes, eugenestatos*) were Greek terms frequently used by distinguished Jewish citizens. Josephus reports in some detail as to how a priest, though free to "marry a woman of his own race, without regard to her wealth or other distinction," had first to "investigate her pedigree, obtaining the genealogy from the archives, and producing a number of witnesses" (*Ag. Ap.* I, 7.31). To a lesser extent the same was true in the case of other "noble" families (*meyuḥasot*).

In this respect there was a difference between Palestine and Babylonia. The increasing anarchy in Roman society partly affected the Jews, too, while Persian glorification of family purity and noble descent fortified Babylonian Jewry in its consciousness of social differentiation based on birth. Traditions reaching back to the First Exile helped to maintain family distinctions. The Palestinians recognized the high degree of reliability of Babylonian family records, admitting that only "pure sifted flour" had remained in Babylonia after the Return from Exile. Mar Samuel proudly asserted that, with respect to the purity of the Jewish family, "the whole world is leavened dough in comparison with Palestine, while Palestine is leavened dough as compared with Babylonia." So deeprooted was this Babylonian feeling of superiority that Ze'iri, one of R. Johanan's admiring Babylonian pupils, refused to marry the master's daughter, eliciting R. Johanan's caustic remark, "Our learning is good enough, but our daughters are not" (cf. the interesting fourth chapter of Qiddushin).

Needless to say that in both countries the complex motivations dominating sex relations often broke through this rationalistic façade. The rabbis themselves realized that most people, at least among the vast unlearned majority, were far more concerned about matters other than family purity. A typical rabbinic injunction used, therefore, a mixture of threats and suasion to counteract the purely worldly considerations.

Some marry out of lust [it read]; some marry for money; some marry for a career and some marry for the sake of Heaven. Concerning those who marry out of lust, the verse says [Hosea 5, 7], "They have dealt treacherously against the Lord, for they have begotten strange children." Concerning those who marry for money, the verse says [ibid.], "Now shall the new moon devour them with their portions." Those who marry for a career, will ultimately lose their position. Those who marry for the sake of Heaven, will ultimately have children who will deliver Israel [Masekhtot Derekh Eres, Tosefta, I, 6; ed. by Higger, pp. 246 f.: a variation of the English transl. p. 83].

Nevertheless, a nobility not of blood but of learning dominated the Jewish scene. For marriage, a scholar was regarded, at least by his fellow scholars, the talmudic legislators, as more eligible than the wealthy descendant of a noble family. The Tannaim did not tire of reiterating the advice that "under all circumstances should a man sell everything he possesses in order to marry the daughter of a scholar, as well as to give his daughter to a scholar in marriage." Only when he fails to find the daughter of a scholar to be his wife should he choose, in this order, the daughter of a magnate, an archisynagogus, a charity director, or an elementary teacher. Never should he marry the daughter of an illiterate man, because it is "an ugly thing and does not succeed" (Pesaḥim 49ab). There was even prejudice against marrying a priest's daughter, R. Johanan and other rabbis reporting that ill luck pursued such unions. No matter what his social origin, he who had acquired a high position in the Jewish world of learning was second to none in Jewish society. Thus family purity tended to direct natural selection into intellectual channels. Here the survival of the fittest meant primarily that of the best educated.

STATUS OF WOMEN

The rise of the Jewish woman's social status also contributed toward achieving eugenic balance. This evolution, which began in biblical times, continued during the Second Commonwealth and after. In Rome the legal development of the woman's marital rights had run the whole gamut from complete dependence on her husband, who actually had power over her life and death (*ius vitae necisque*), to fairly extensive legal and social equality under the empire. In Judaism she had never been so dependent in biblical times, nor so fully emancipated in the days of the Talmud. Josephus adequately described her contemporary position when he wrote, "The woman, says the Law, is in all things inferior to the man. Let her accordingly be submissive, not for her humiliation, but that she may be directed" (*Ag. Ap.* II, 24.201).

Her gradual advance was, nevertheless, incontestable. As early as the days of R. Simon ben Shetaḥ, we recall, it was decreed that the *mohar* should be converted into a settlement for the wife herself. Talmudic legislation elaborated the principle of the *ketubah*, which is considered in substance as of Mosaic origin. To Hillel and his associates those Alexandrian Jews who seemingly adopted the prevalent Egyptian system of *agraphos gamos* (unwritten marriage) appeared like "somebody from the street coming and seizing" the bride. The main purpose of this marriage contract was to safeguard at the time of the wedding the rights of the wife in case of divorce or widowhood. The minimum sum of 200 *zuz* for a virgin and 100 for a widow or divorcee was to be provided; without it the marriage act was null and void. A woman converted to Judaism, ransomed from captivity or freed from slavery before the age of three and one day, was placed on a par with a virgin; others on a par with a widow. This was substantial protection; for 200 *zuz* one could purchase two slaves or a one-family house. This amount was usually doubled in priestly and aristocratic families. The bridegroom often added a *tosefet ketubah* (supplementary provision) of a sum calculated by the bride's dowry. The dowry itself, as well as all other property which the wife acquired, were under the husband's exclusive managerial control (unlike imperial Rome, where married women often engaged independent *procuratores*) and were his for use for the duration of the marriage. But the wife retained the title to her possessions, for some of which (the so-called "property of iron sheep") the husband was held personally responsible.[19]

Talmudic literature seldom mentions business women; these may have been widows or divorcees. Discussing court sessions, for example, the rabbis took it for granted that the woman could almost always be found at home (B.Q. 113a). Certainly occupations requiring protracted absences, such as those of shippers, camel drivers, or sailors, are debated only in terms of males unable for this reason to comply regularly with their marital duties. On the other hand, women often assisted their husbands in business, sometimes taking over a distinct share. R. Huna's wife, for example, tended to the sheep while he cultivated the soil. More regularly, she attended to her household chores. A characteristic tannaitic enumeration lists:

These are the chores which a wife does for her husband: she grinds flour, bakes, launders, cooks, feeds her child, makes the beds, and works with wool. If she brought him one female slave, she is free from grinding, baking and laundering; two slaves, she does not have to cook or feed her child; three slaves she makes no beds and does no woolen work; four slaves she sits on the throne idly. R. Eliezer says, Even if she brought him a hundred slaves, he forces her to work in wool, for idleness leads to immorality. R. Simon ben Gamaliel says, Even if a man took a vow forbidding his wife to do any work whatsoever he must divorce her and pay her the marriage settlement, for idleness leads to boredom [M. Ketubot V, 5].

This was quite in line with the concepts of Roman aristocracy. Augustus himself is known to have worn almost exclusively cloth made by his wife, sisters, or daughters. On his part, the husband had to provide food, shelter, clothing, cosmetics, funeral services, and other necessities for his wife, in ratio to his ability to pay and her accustomed standard of life.

Cosmetics were considered necessities, in so far as cultivation of physical charm was incumbent upon each woman in order to retain her husband's affections. The leaders encouraged her efforts. We recall the dental work performed by R. Ishmael to make a niece attractive to her uncle-fiancé; this was only part of his general policy of embellishing Jewish womanhood. He believed that, by natural endowment, most Jewish women were beautiful and that only poverty diminished their charms. He tried, therefore, to supply them the necessary means for physical care. It is small wonder, then, that his death was widely mourned by women. Eugenic balance was further facilitated by R. Simon ben Laqish's advice to persons of marriageable age not only to be generally careful in the selection of their mates, but also to pay special attention to such physical features as height and color. The sages believed that a union between two very tall or very small, very fair or very dark-skinned persons might lead to undesirable further accentuation of these characteristics in the offspring.[20]

Like other rabbis a staunch believer in the "golden mean," R. Ishmael, who generally evinced great interest in physical beauty, also was extremely proud that Jews were neither as fair as Germans nor as dark as Negroes, but of an intermediate color "like an ebony tree." Although not racially conscious, the ancients at times indulged in such verbal displays of national superiority. In his *Res gestae* Shapur I, for example, played up the capture of many Roman, German, and other "non-Aryan" prisoners and their settlement "among our own peoples of the Aryans." On the other hand, a statement like that of the anonymous rabbinic preacher that one could expect a Teuton to sell a Negro slave, rather than *vice versa,* was the reflection of an historic fact, rather than of racial prejudice. In fact, Ethiopian slave girls were often considered dangerous rivals by Jewish women. Similarly, R. Isaac's exclamation that, were it not for the Romans, the Teutons would overrun and destroy the world only mirrored the awe with which the increasingly pacific civilian population viewed in the late third century the unbridled violence of the numerous Teuton mercenaries.[21]

All these rabbinic teachings, moreover, were but part of a deliberate campaign to counteract the general population decline. High on this program were efforts to reduce to a minimum the number of unmarried women. Not only did the rabbis discourage arbitrary or temporary divorces, but in the case of the unproved death of a husband they did all they could to mitigate the rules of evidence so as to enable his widow to remarry. For even more than a widow, an 'agunah (a woman tied to an absentee husband) was considered a hapless creature in need of communal protection. To make marriage more enduring, they also prohibited child betrothals without previous meeting and consent of the betrothed.

Moral injunctions went further than legal protection. Here is a typical tannaitic statement, "He who loves his wife as himself and honors her more than himself . . . is referred to in the verse, 'And thou shalt know that thy tent is in peace' " (Job 5:24; Yebamot 62b). Later R. Helbo explained that one ought to honor one's wife, because the home is blessed only on her account (B.M. 59a, with reference to Gen. 12:16). Several Palestinian rabbis vied with each other in describing the psychological effects of a wife's decease. "It is as if the Temple were destroyed in one's life-time," declared one; "The whole world is darkened for the widower," declared another; "His steps are shortened," said a third; "He loses his counsel," stated a fourth (Sanhedrin 22a).

Not that all rabbis were of the same mind. Probably there is an uneven balance of antifeminist utterances in the talmudic literature, particularly in its aggadic portions. Women were often considered easygoing, devoid of judgment, prone to excessive talk, indulging in sorcery, and setting their hearts on trinkets. "He who acts on his wife's advice," declared Rab, himself married to a shrew, "goes to hell" (B.M. 59a). Though not left uncontroverted, this utterance is typical of many irate exclamations.

At the same time, however, both preachers and jurists tried to buttress the woman's position within the family with all means at their disposal. They taught the essential equality of men and women before the law. Although conceding the father's primacy, they pointed out the reverse order in the biblical injunction, "Ye shall fear every man his mother and his father" (Lev. 19:3), and stated that the biblical lawgiver thus wished "to teach you that both are equal" (M. Keritot VI, 9). R. Eliezer praised even unreasonable extremes of filial piety, as when one Domna suffered calmly when his deranged mother threw slippers at him and spat in his face in the presence of strangers.

Woman's position in society at large also became more dignified. Although the Talmud reiterated the biblical apothegm, "All glorious is the king's daughter within the palace" (Ps. 45:14; Yebamot 77a), a woman could be moderately active in public life. Opinions as to the advisability of instructing girls in Jewish law were divided. Nevertheless many women achieved a high level of education. Beruriah, daughter of the famous martyr R. Ḥanina ben Teradyon and wife of R. Meir, and, to a lesser extent, Yalta, the wife of R. Naḥman, won high reputation as scholars. Jewish ladies, to be sure, had no opportunity of contributing as much to the artistic and literary life of their community, as did, for instance, the Roman patronesses. The rabbis frowned equally upon excessively jealous husbands, like Pappus ben Judah, who during his absence used to lock up his wife, and upon liberal husbands who allowed their women to appear in public places and mix with other men (Giṭṭin 90ab). There were, therefore, few Jewesses comparable even to those Graeco-Roman "matrons" who engaged the rabbis in philosophic conversations.

At home, however, the mother often taught her children how to read and write. By assuming all household responsibilities, she also enabled the husband to devote himself wholeheartedly to learning. Against rabbinic advice, many fathers appointed their wives as guardians of their minor children. Although having but restricted property rights, women appeared in court without the intercession of male attorneys, as was required by most Hellenistic laws. An amusing story is told about R. Naḥman's predicament when R. Huna's wife was to appear before him in a lawsuit. "If I should get up in her honor," he reflected, "the opposing party might become embarrassed. I could not remain seated, for a scholar's wife is like a scholar." He therefore arranged with his attendant at a moment's notice to bring in a flying duck. The ensuing disturbance gave him the opportunity to stand up unobtrusively. Women followed, in particular, their natural charitable propensities, at times embarrassing rabbis who suspected them of unlawfully giving away their husbands' funds. None the less the Babylonian Rabina unhesitatingly accepted precious jewelry offered for his collection by the women of Maḥoza. That scholars themselves were often the beneficiaries of such feminine liberality, is attested by St. Jerome. Occasionally a woman distinguished herself as a communal benefactress, several wealthy Roman patronesses being rewarded with the distinguished title *mater synagogae*. A few inscriptions commemorate a woman *presbytéres* (elder), but they may have referred merely to wives of elders.[22]

Within the synagogue proper, of course, the woman's role was negligible. She had neither the duties nor the rights of men with respect to regular prayers, wearing of phylacteries, and other liturgical functions. The Talmud laid down the general principle that women were exempted from "positive commandments which depend on stated times" (M. Qiddushin I, 7). Evidently the intention was to liberate them from recurrent duties, so that they might devote all their time to housework.

Nevertheless, some women attended daily services, the rabbis recognizing this participation to the extent of allowing women to be counted among the readers of the Torah at congregational services. "To safeguard the honor of the congregation," they were not allowed, however, to recite the lesson in public. The number of women congregants at Sabbath and holiday services was so large, as a rule, that architects of ancient synagogues had to provide special sections for them. Characteristically, the Mishnah nowhere refers to a separate "women's compartment" in the synagogue, such as had existed in the Temple court. But the same desire of counteracting licentiousness which had led to the separation of sexes in the Temple so "that women should look down from above and men look from below," also motivated the rabbinic leaders to set aside special sections for women in all houses of worship. Recent excavations of Palestinian synagogues have, indeed, demonstrated that most of them had such special galleries. For the Diaspora, this segregation of the sexes is well attested by as early an author as Philo. The austere philosopher actually taught that "a woman should not shew herself off like a vagrant in the streets before the eyes of other men, except when she has to go to the temple [synagogue], and even then she should take pains to go, not when the market is full, but when most people have gone home." Excavators of the synagogue of Dura, though unable to locate a formal partition, concluded that there were two sections accommodating some 52–55 men, and some 32–35 women, respectively.[23]

Separation was not very rigid, however. If we are to believe Ovid, Roman gentlemen often went to synagogues on the Sabbath day in quest of amorous adventures (*Ars amatoria*, I, 75). They evidently were able to meet worshipers in the feminine section. In the main demanded by the talmudic standard of morals, this separation nevertheless reflected the woman's inferior status in the synagogue. The concentration of woman's activities upon her home, however, while perhaps prejudicial to her general economic and social standing, had nevertheless great value for the preservation of the nation's physical and moral strength.

CHANGING ECONOMIC TRENDS

New economic developments greatly facilitated the process of Jewish consolidation. The profound social conflicts in Jewish society before the fall of Jerusalem, which had nurtured the intensive revolutionary spirit, now gave way to increasing solidarity. The cumulative force of anti-Jewish discrimination so seriously endangered the existence of the whole people, as well as of most individuals, that a common economic front became absolutely necessary. In those days R. Simon ben Laqish coined that portentous homily which, for generations after, was to be quoted in endless variations: "'Ye shall not cut yourselves [*titgodedu*],' this means ye shall not divide yourselves into separate groups [*agudot*]" (Deut. 14:1; Yebamot 13b f.). Before the battle for ethnic-religious survival, the inner class struggle receded.

Age-old antagonisms, to be sure, did not disappear overnight. The conflict between the scholarly class and the "people of the land" continued for several generations. Rabbis still insisted that "he who consumes his crops untithed is like one who eats carrion and other ritually forbidden meats." Fear of eating untithed bread, as we recall, had long been the main obstacle to conviviality between the two classes. At times students still echoed the old rabbinic denunciation of the 'am ha-ares. But when R. Eleazar tried to deny the "people of the land" the capacity for ultimate resurrection, he was severely reprimanded by R. Johanan. By teaching, moreover, in the name of an earlier sage that mere recitation of Shema' morning and evening sufficed to fulfill the biblical commandment that "this book of the law shall not depart out of thy mouth," R. Johanan to all intents and purposes removed the main barrier between the learned and the illiterate groups. The more the center of gravity of Palestinian Jewish scholarship moved to Galilee, the more closely could the rabbis observe the intrinsic piety of the neighboring farmers and their efforts, increasingly hampered by Roman taxation, to comply with all minutiae of Jewish law. In fact, in their struggle for communal control the rabbis now encountered greater opposition among the urban plutocrats of Sepphoris and Tiberias than among the rural populace.[24]

Class differences as such likewise receded into the background as the extremes of wealth and poverty were leveled down by the unrelenting pressure of Roman exploitation. Rarely do we now hear descriptions of such reckless display of wealth as characterized the generation of Martha, daughter of Boethos, before the fall of Jerusalem. Even the consciously exaggerated reports of the wealth of the patriarchal house in the days of Judah I fell far short of what we know about the conspicuous consumption of the Herodian court and aristocracy. It is characteristic that among the numerous pre-Islamic synagogues excavated in Palestine none was constructed by a single benefactor, although the country never lacked self-sacrificing and ambitious philanthropists.

In Babylonia, to be sure, economic differentiation seems to have been growing in time. In Maḥoza and other cities arose a wealthy class which, though generally observant and indulging in extensive patronage of Jewish learning, often bought up many landholdings of defaulting Jewish taxpayers and, at times, found ways and means to defy even the authority of the Jewish judiciary (cf. M.Q. 17ab; Giṭṭin 14ab; B.Q. 112b). It doubtless was under some such provocation that Rab uttered a curse on the "wealthy men of Babylonia." Even here, however, the Jewish minority community, placed on the defensive by a hostile outside world, could never develop those sharp internal conflicts which had characterized the declining Second Commonwealth. Talmudic Judaism, therefore, did not have to contend here with that awkward heritage of accumulated bitterness which had nurtured the sectarian divisions in Palestine before 70.

Tax exemption for scholars for a time injected a new source of discord into Jewish communal life in both countries. Ever since Antoninus Pius, to encourage scholarly pursuits, exempted philosophers from direct taxation, this prerogative seems to have been extended to ordained rabbis as well. Even the Christian emperors, at least until Justinian, maintained this rabbinic exemption. True, in 321, Constantine attempted to limit it to only two or three members of each community. But he soon retracted in the face of the Jewish leaders' determined resistance. The masses, however, felt differently at first. Since both persons and possessions of rabbis, wealthy as well as poor, were tax exempt, other taxpayers had to shoulder an increasing portion of the burden. That is why the populace of third-century Sepphoris clamored against the ordination of R. Hanina by virtue of which the income of this wealthy landowner would automatically have become tax free. In fourth-century Babylonia the government received a denunciation that no less than 12,000 Jews, presumably including a good many persons of means, had dodged their share under the guise of being scholars. The ensuing investigation caused the great teacher Rabbah bar Nahmani, whose authorization had probably been the source of their privileged treatment, to flee from Pumbedita and, after several changes of residence, die in exile.[25]

We must not forget, however, that communal responsibility for state taxation still was in its infancy then, particularly in Rome. For a long time tax exemption of individuals shifted the incidence on the whole population, Jewish and non-Jewish alike, rather than on the remaining Jewish taxpayers alone. The smaller the Jewish ratio in the population (it was declining throughout the Roman Empire, including Palestine), the more readily did the lower classes assume their slightly increased burden, in return for the principle of equal treatment of their rabbinic leaders. Moreover, daily observation had taught them that most scholars were really poor and eked out their existence by hard labor. When after Diocletian and Constantine the principle of communal responsibility assumed new significance, the extensive tax privileges now granted to the Christian clergy, both secular and monastic (the fifth century witnessed a mass flight of prospective taxpayers into the rapidly expanding monastic orders), made Jews, too, acquiesce in similar exemptions for rabbis and silenced whatever opposition had come down from the third century.

Outside of Palestine and Babylonia, the antagonism, first of the heathen Greeks and then of the Christians, as well as that of the Persians, put the entire Jewish group on the defensive, economically as well as politically and religiously. It is perhaps no accident that the records of Jewish agriculture become fewer as time goes on. In Egypt, where papyrological documentation of Jewish farming is fairly extensive for the period before 70, few such sources appear after 200—fewer, even, than one would be led to expect from the general paucity of Jewish papyri in that period. The estates confiscated from Jews after their revolt under Trajan, such as are mentioned in two Oxyrhynchus papyri (Nos. 500, 1189; III, 218 ff.; IX, 207 f.: "a list of property which belonged to the Jews"), evidently never reverted to Jewish owners. The antagonism generated by this revolt and later by the spread of Christianity must have discouraged new Jewish entries into farming. Then, as later, urban Jewry could more effectively resist the accumulated hatred of Gentile neighbors, whereas scattered settlements of Jewish peasantry were much more exposed. Certainly in this period of outspoken anti-Jewish legislative and administrative policy, the Jews could no longer secure effective protection from the central government.

Even in Palestine, Jewish commerce now began to play a far greater role than during the First and Second Commonwealths. Owing to the general economic decline, Greek merchants seem to have retired, leaving the Palestine trade to natives, primarily to Jews. Elsewhere, too, the age-old forces operating to urbanize and commercialize the Jews gained in strength through the intensified migratory movements, discriminatory legislation, and growing cohesion of the Jewish communities.

Nevertheless, there are reasons for believing that as long as the ancient world survived, everywhere a large number of Jews derived their living from agriculture. This is obviously true wherever Jews were in the majority, as in Galilee and in many sections of Babylonia. In all of Babylonia the Jewish peasantry was so numerous that no Jewish courts of justice functioned during the months of Nissan and Tishre, the seasons of intensive agricultural labor (B.Q. 113a). This concession had to be made despite the fact that already many Jews were exempted from court summons during the two preceding months of Adar and Elul, in so far as they attended the so-called *kallah* gatherings at the great academies.

Palestine's agricultural output underwent significant changes under the unfavorable political conditions. The country had hardly had a chance to recuperate from the deep wounds inflicted by the armies of Vespasian and Hadrian when the general anarchy of the third century ruined all prospects of renewed prosperity. Inflation was a double-edged sword. On the one hand, currency depreciation as such, particularly the more gradual one of ancient times in which the metallic content of coins always retained a certain minimum worth, encouraged the farmer to retain his land and to produce commodities commanding ever-increasing prices. He was also assured of most of his own basic necessities. In contrast thereto even before the onset of the rapid inflationary spiral, R. Johanan observed that grain was very cheap "and yet many persons died of starvation in Tiberias, because they did not even have one Roman *as*." As elsewhere, the recurrent famines were caused by difficulties of transportation much more than by a general failure of crops. Palestine's landlocked economy and absence of navigable rivers naturally aggravated such crises. On the other hand, the tax collector's hand lay heaviest on the tillers of the soil. The more cash revenue depreciated, the more the imperial bureaucracy and army depended on income delivered in kind by the peasants, in payment of both land taxes and enforced military supplies. The resulting land flight, however, was not limited to the rural population. On the approach of the taxgatherer, we are told in an undoubtedly exaggerated talmudic report, the whole population of Tiberias gradually disappeared. We can, therefore, understand the numerous apparently contradictory utterances of R. Eleazar, who lived at the height of the inflationary curve and fiscal pressure. On a single talmudic page R. Eleazar is reported as saying both that "there is no occupation inferior to agriculture" and that "he who owns no land, is not a man." Perhaps the best clue to the understanding of these epigrams is furnished by still another saying: "Land has only been given to strong-arm men" (that is, men who could forcefully resist bureaucratic violence).[26]

Inflationary and fiscal pressures also strengthened the forces of economic decentralization. Because each region, if not each locality or even homestead, now tried to produce all its necessaries, without depending on the exchange of goods, Palestinian agriculture, too, became more diversified. Many products which in the early more capitalistically minded Hellenistic and Augustan ages had been imported from neighboring lands were now grown locally. Names like Cilician or Egyptian beans, Egyptian cucumber or mustard, occurring already in tannaitic writings, clearly betray their foreign origin. Conversely, Palestinian grain no longer appeared in Western markets. Rome, for instance, received all its supplies from Egypt, Africa, Spain, and Gaul. Even Palestinian oil encountered insuperable competition from Spain in respect to quality, and from Africa in respect to price. Palestinian wine, according to the contemporary *Descriptio orbis terrae,* was still shipped to "every region of Egypt and Syria," but not much farther. Spanish, Italian, and other wines took their place on the tables of Western potentates. Palestinian economy thus became largely self-sufficing, incidentally another explanation of the advances of native merchants against their interterritorial Greek competitors.[26a]

Self-sufficiency and high taxation helped eliminate the ancient evil of absentee landlordism. No longer was Jerusalem the great center of attraction for the Jewish land-owning aristocracy from all over the country, while the general shrinkage of Jewish settlement brought everywhere owner and tiller of the soil more closely together. The new economic hardships deepened the conviction, underscored by many rabbinic homilies, that cultivating land was a full-time occupation demanding wholehearted devotion. R. Simon ben Laqish and R. Johanan complemented one another when they taught that "only if a man becomes a slave to his soil [a pun on *'obed* in Prov. 12:11] shall he produce sufficient bread" (Sanhedrin 58b) and that "he who inherits much money from his father and wishes to lose it expeditiously . . . shall hire workers [for his fields] and not live close to them" (B.M. 29b). The ancient system of living in a town, while working on one's field at some distance, continued by force of tradition rather than economic need, since sudden Bedouin raids had practically ended in Galilee and its vicinity. But close supervision of the workers by a landlord, even if he happened to be a busy student of the law or merchant, now became the rule.

Babylonian Jewish agriculture made even greater strides. True, as a frontier province, Babylonia was often called upon to supply the Persian or invading Roman armies, with little or no compensation. It also was subject to violent price gyrations, particularly in wartime. Losses of 50 per cent in land values within six months were not unusual even in ordinary years (B.Q. 7b). Nevertheless the ever growing population, swelled by Jewish immigrants from the Roman Empire, as well as improved methods of planting, greatly increased the productivity of the soil. Jews seem to have performed here one of their recurrent pioneering services, which characterized much of their entire migratory history. Just as during the First Exile they had helped develop new methods of credit and monetary circulation, so they now enriched their country of adoption by aiding in the introduction of the olive tree into the Euphrates Valley during the fourth century. Olive oil now began to replace the age-old extract of sesame as a primary foodstuff, cosmetic, and lighting fuel.

Only the extraordinary fertility of the Babylonian soil, however, can explain the landlord's exorbitant share in the tenant's crop (usually one-half but sometimes three-quarters of the entire harvest). There was much poverty, therefore, side by side with great wealth. At times a metropolis like Nehardea suffered pangs of hunger, while a few score miles away farmers and speculators hoarded their produce or found no means of transporting it. Hence Babylonian Jewry readily applied to itself the injunction of the Deuteronomist, preventing at least actual starvation by allowing any passer-by to consume freely from the abundance of wild dates. No wonder that envious Palestinians admired the low cost of living in Babylonia and, like R. Oshaya, spoke of the Babylonian barns always bulging with grain. An amusing story is told of Ulla who, on arriving in Babylonia, exclaimed with amazement, "A whole basket of dates for a *zuz* [28 cents] and yet the Babylonians do not study the Torah!" On overindulging in the inexpensive fruit, the rabbi upset his stomach. He then varied his epigram to say: "A whole basket of poison for a *zuz*, and yet the Babylonians study the Torah!" R. Ishmael ben R. Jose explained the prosperity of Babylonian Jewry by its devotion to the study of Torah, while R. Ashi was amazed that the Gentiles of Mata Mehasia, witnessing the great *kallah* assemblies in their glory, failed to become proselytes *en masse* and share the good fortune of their Jewish neighbors.[27]

At the same time, industrial and commercial activities steadily gained ground, with the increasing integration of the two centers of world Jewry into the vast empires. The competition of large-scale industry, employing hundreds and thousands of slaves, had previously been a great obstacle to Jewish industrial development.

As a result of the declining slave population and the Roman Empire's dissolution into smaller economic units, this competition diminished. Palestine, Syria, and Babylonia now had to produce almost all the industrial goods they needed, and Jewish craftsmen began to play a leading role in this field.

Palestinian industry, too, now produced an increasing number of cheap standardized wares which, particularly before the third-century inflation, made it uneconomical even for the farmer to produce them at home. Second-century Ben Zoma was not the only one to marvel at mankind's technical progress. While Adam, he reflected, had to go through the whole process from sowing grain to baking bread before he had something to eat, and from shearing sheep to sewing his own clothes before he had something to wear, "I merely get up and find it all prepared for me" (Berakhot 58a). Certainly, R. Papa's advice to his coreligionists in fourth-century Babylonia applied to the Roman provinces to an even higher extent: "Sow [your own agricultural produce] and do not buy it, even if it be of equal value, but cloth you should rather buy than weave" (Yebamot 63a, in R. Hananel's interpretation). In case of temporary shortages one could certainly hold out much longer without new clothing than without food. Difficulties in transportation, too, were less of a barrier to the clothing industry than to shipping grain from surplus to shortage areas.

Of course, among the many specialized crafts some were considered easier and more desirable than others. Odoriferous trades like tanning were usually banished outside city limits. Even wives could refuse to live with tanners, as well as with copper miners and collectors of dog dung, because of their intolerable smell. Certain craftsmen catering especially to feminine customers were suspect of moral laxity, although it hardly mattered to them that, according to the abstract rabbinic theory, they were ineligible for service as either kings or high priests. Temperamental R. Judah bar Ila'i vented his ire on other occupations by quoting another teacher's exclamation, "The best of surgeons belongs to Hell and the most conscientious of butchers is a partner of Amalek." But no one doubted the necessity of having all these craftsmen. Judah the Patriarch voiced popular sentiment when he taught, "The world cannot get along without either a perfumer or a tanner. Happy is he whose occupation is perfuming, and woe unto him who must earn a living as a tanner" (M. Qiddushin IV, 14; b. 82ab).

Before long Syria and Palestine excelled in some branches of industry. Scythopolis linen, we recall, was the highest priced linen in Diocletian's list. Modern excavations have brought to light an enormous mass of glassware used in Palestine during the first centuries of the Christian era. Jewish artisans were among the main producers of these goods. The flourishing Damascus silk industry must also have furnished employment to Jewish artisans and merchants. R. Abba (about 300) is recorded as a manufacturer or importer of raw silk (metaxa) who, for some reason, was denounced to the government (B.Q. 117b). Dyeing was another important Jewish industry, for skill in which Babylonian craftsmen have long been renowned. In late antiquity and again in the Middle Ages, the Jews thus played an important role in the production of textiles and glass. The brewing of beer, a popular national drink in the Euphrates Valley, enabled many Jews (among them the rabbis Huna, Ḥisda, and Papa) to accumulate considerable wealth. Because of their fine wines Palestinians apparently never cultivated a taste for beer, although "Median beer," brewed from a combination of dates and barley had been available to them as early as tannaitic times. R. Johanan actually explained the absence of leprosy among the Babylonians by their habits of frequent bathing, eating beets, and drinking beer (Ketubot 77b).

Despite the greater ease in communications under the *pax Romana*, travel and transportation still offered great hazards. Sea transport, especially, was imperiled by the caprices of weather and the residua of piracy. Nevertheless Palestinian and other Jews owned ships and, defying the advice of some more conservative leaders, went out on long journeys. Profits of up to 100 per cent on the original investment after the successful completion of a sea journey proved irresistible. A few rabbis themselves (like Judah the Patriarch or R. Dimi of Nehardea) are recorded as shipowners, although oriental fancy undoubtedly ran away with the talmudic narrators of stories involving 1,000 or even 10,000 ships. There was nothing fanciful, however, in the Alexandrian Jewish guild of *navicularii*, to whom even the antagonistic Christian emperors had to grant, in 390, numerous privileges. Alexandria being the main center of a flourishing international trade with India and China, Jewish merchants and shippers as well as industrialists must also have had a substantial share in the exchange and reconversion of goods for use in the Mediterranean world. For some reason, Jewish sailors enjoyed a much better reputation than their confreres engaged in land transport. In his aforementioned blanket appraisal

R. Judah bar Ila'i cited the saying, "Most of the donkey drivers are evildoers, most of the camel drivers are honest, most of the sailors are pious." [28]

Local commerce, too, including the money trade, yielded high returns. During the inflationary price rises, in particular, merchants could well keep a step ahead of their rising costs. Even Diocletian's price edict was extensively disobeyed throughout the empire, and blood frequently flowed when peasants and tradesmen resisted the imperial fiat. We have no information from Jewish sources, which, on the whole, are quite friendly to this emperor, but we may assume that Jewish merchants were hardly more subservient to a Roman edict than their pagan and Christian neighbors.

Most Jewish traders were but small shopkeepers, however. A Babylonian rabbi of the fourth century opined that a merchant with a capital of 100 *zuz* (the equivalent of $28) could afford meat and wine daily, while a farmer owning land of the same value had to be satisfied with salt and roots. Petty trade of this sort doubtless justified Emperor Theodosius I's derogatory statement, in 390, that "they [the Jews] are engaged in cheap trading." Acting from the standpoint of this petty bourgeois consumer and tradesman, talmudic legislation outdid the Bible in discouraging moneylending on interest. It proclaimed the general principle that a lender could charge interest even to Gentiles only when he had no other source of income. R. Jose observed, "Come and see the blindness of usurious lenders. If a man calls another an evildoer, the latter is angry enough to kill him. But these men here produce witnesses, a *libellarius*, pen and ink, to write [about themselves] and sign on the dotted line, to wit: So and so has denied the God of Israel." To call someone a usurer was considered a major insult. Jews were to be satisfied with such expectations of reciprocity in the case of subsequent need as were held out to the disinterested lender by Philo. Exceptionally a rabbi, like Gamaliel, consciously incurred losses. In lending grain to his tenants R. Gamaliel made it a practice to ask for repayment only at the price level of the lending or repayment period, whichever was lower. Nevertheless, the economic needs proved stronger in the long run. Certainly the 24 per cent interest rate prevailing for centuries in Hellenistic and Roman Egypt, often amplified by a stipulated penalty of 50 per cent in case of nonpayment on time, was a mighty incentive. Later, under the impact of the controlled economy the rates declined, but the legal maximum of 6–12 per cent was hardly observed universally even then. Babylonia never seems to have had such legal restraints. Rabbinic legislation itself, which, as we shall see, had already begun laying the foundations for the doctrine of "just price," inconsistently exempted bills from these general regulations, because of the risk involved. Such prominent rabbis as R. Papa and Rabina themselves extended large credits (12,000 and 6,000 denarii) to borrowers in distant regions.[29]

ECONOMIC POLICIES

Here, too, we may observe the tremendous influence of talmudic legislation upon Jewish economy. The rabbis constantly tried to maintain interclass equilibrium. They did not denounce riches, as some early Christians did, but they emphasized the merely relative value of great fortunes. Even their opposition to Mazdakite communism was religious more than social, for the latter propagated extremist Parsiism and demanded the community of women. The persistent accentuation of collective economic responsibility made the Jewish system of public welfare highly effective. While there was much poverty among the Jews, the community, through its numerous charitable institutions, took more or less adequate care of the needy.

Man's right, as well as duty, to earn a living and his freedom of disposing of property were safeguarded by rabbinic law and ethics only in so far as they did not conflict with the common weal. Extremists like R. Simon ben Yoḥai insisted that the biblical injunction, "This book of the law shall not depart out of thy mouth, but thou shalt meditate therein day and night," postulated wholehearted devotion to the study of Torah at the expense of all economic endeavors. But R. Ishmael effectively countered by quoting the equally scriptural blessing, "That thou mayest gather in thy corn, and thy wine, and thine oil." Two centuries later, the Babylonian Abbaye, who had started as a poor man and through hard labor and night work in the fields had amassed some wealth, observed tersely, "Many have followed the way of R. Ishmael and succeeded; others did as R. Simon ben Yoḥai and failed." Sheer romanticism induced their compeer, R. Judah bar Ila'i, to contend that in olden times people had made the study of the law a full-time occupation, and devoted only little effort to earning a living, and hence had proved successful in both (Berakhot 35b, with reference to Josh. 1:8; Deut. 11:14). R. Simon ben Yoḥai himself conceded, however, that day and night meditation had been possible only to a generation living on *Mannah* or to priestly recipients of heave-offerings (Mekilta, Vayassa, III, ed. by Lauterbach II, 104; Tanḥuma, Beshallaḥ, XX reads: ben Joshua). In practice the rabbis could at best secure, as we shall see, certain economic privileges for a minority of students, relying upon the overwhelming majority of the population to supply society's needs by economically productive work.

Private ownership, too, was hedged with many legal restrictions and moral injunctions in favor of over-all communal control. The special privileges for Temple property (*heqdesh*) lost their importance with the destruction of the Temple. Other communal property, though later designated by the same term, never enjoyed the same legal protection. But through various legal subterfuges, the rabbis succeeded in circumventing the extremes of unrestrained private control. By developing, in particular, the doctrines of *hefqer* (derelict property) and *reshut ha-rabbim* (public property), both going far beyond the Roman categories of *res nullius* and *res omnium communes,* they established the definite supremacy of public interest.

Rabbinic law also extended unusual protection to neighbors. Some rabbis wished to promote neighborly coöperation to the extent of forcing Jews to relinquish perfectly legitimate rights for the benefit of neighbors. "One who insists," these radicals taught, "that mine is mine and thine is thine [for which other sages made allowances] assumes the characteristic attitude of Sodomites." All sages agreed, moreover, that it was incumbent upon the courts to counteract unneighborly aloofness and to force parties to do each other any number of favors causing no harm to themselves. The right of expropriation by courts and communal leaders in cases demanded by public welfare was incontestable. Maimonides well summarized the general rabbinic view when he declared, "A judge may always expropriate money belonging to whomsoever, destroy it and give it away, if, in his judgment this would serve to prevent the breaking down of the fences of the law, to strengthen its structure and to punish a mighty offender." Even retroactively perfectly legal transactions could be invalidated by the legal fiction that the money used by a contracting party had a priori been confiscated (*hefqer bet-din hefqer*). So convinced were the rabbis of the validity of this fiction that they used it at times to explain serious departures from formal law.[30]

Nor did the individual enjoy complete mastery over testamentary dispositions. Family ties still were so strong that wills discriminating against one's close relatives were, in some cases, declared null and void, in others subjected at least to severe rabbinic censure. If R. Simon ben Gamaliel once commended the disinheritance of "misbehaving" sons (M. B.B. VIII, 5), he may well have had in mind a necessary communal safeguard against apostate children. The practice of transferring the portion of renegade children to more remote relatives became so prevalent in the period of increased conversion to Christianity that, in 426, an imperial decree called for the annulment of any Jewish will in which a baptized son, daughter or grandchild were left less than their intestate share (*C. Th.*, XVI, 8, 28). This provision, often repeated in medieval laws, was to prove a source of considerable annoyance to Jewish communities in Christian lands.

Apart from favoring discriminatory treatment of apostates, who were supposed to be dead to their families, the rabbis evinced great concern for the claims of minor children to support from their fathers' estate. Unlike Persian law, the Talmud recognized no legal differences between children of "privileged" or "secondary" wives, and extended protection even to a man's proved illegitimate offspring. In general, the sages were not only prepared to respect local customs more favorable to orphans, as did R. Simon bar Abba, but also, on their own, extended greatly the legal protection of orphan girls. Although biblical law, echoed also by Philo, had made no provision for the inheritance of daughters if there were surviving sons, the rabbis saw to it that each marriage contract should specifically pledge the bridegroom's estate for the support of his surviving minor daughters. Such a clause had early assumed the character of "conditions imposed by the court" and, hence, was automatically acted upon by the communal administration, even if a particular father had failed to spell it out. Ultimately the right of female orphans to support came to overshadow the claims of all other heirs and, if need be, the entire estate was used up for this purpose, leaving the sons with no inheritance whatsoever. "Let them go begging from door to door" was the melancholy alternative placed before them by the jurists.[31]

In a period of economic scarcity social interest demanded also communal control over wasteful practices even with one's own possessions. "Disregard of crumbs in a household," the preachers reiterated a popular proverb, "is conducive to poverty" (Pesaḥim

111b). Nor was one allowed spitefully to damage anybody else's property, even if willing to indemnify the owner. For that matter any willful destruction of a useful object in one's undisputed possession was considered as running counter to the biblical prohibition of "Thou shalt not destroy" (Deut. 20:19; Shabbat 129a).

An economy of scarcity, when combined with a strong feeling for social justice, naturally led also to manifold regulations and homilies aimed at speculative excesses. Although generally paying less attention to the realistic effects of a particular act than to the underlying intention, the rabbis were sufficiently familiar with the gnawing ills of the existing order to advocate a number of remedies. At times, they merely betrayed the usual antagonism of provincials to an advanced metropolitan economy. One may discount, therefore, such blanket condemnations as that of Raba who found "a great deal of robbery, licentiousness, vain and false oaths among the inhabitants of big cities" ('Erubin 21b). But some of the difficulties arose from the very reverence of the Jews for tradition. Certain commercial practices, for example, developed in the more prosperous periods of the Hellenistic and early Roman empires and found very useful at that time, had now become the source of social disturbance within the ever narrowing confines of the imperial economies of Rome and Persia.

It was relatively easy for the rabbis to insist on just weights and measures, since the Jewish community had retained much control over markets. In his decree of 396, often repeated thereafter, Theodosius I conceded that "no one outside the Jewish faith should fix prices for Jews" (C. Th., XVI, 8, 10). Such sages as Rab personally served as market supervisors. In fact, Rab was once arrested, because, as agoranomos, he had failed to hold down the prices (B.B. 89a; j. V, 11, 15ab). Hence even rhetorical exclamations like those of R. Levi had real meaning. "Punishment for [wrong] measures," this Palestinian teacher of the days of Diocletian's forceful regimentation declaimed, "is greater than punishment for incest. . . . Robbery committed on an individual is a greater crime than sacrilege." Neither was it too difficult to threaten "those who store up produce [to sell later at higher prices], lend on interest, make the ephah small, or raise prices" with Amos' words, "The Lord hath sworn by the pride of Jacob: Surely I will never forget any of their works" (Amos 8:4–7; B.B. 88b, 90b).

When it came, however, to devising practical methods of establishing a just price, just to both the "market" and the consumer, the rabbis who wrestled with this problem long before the Roman jurists or medieval scholastics, became involved in a maze of regulations, exceptions therefrom and exceptions from exceptions. Some of these were designed to meet a particular momentary situation, but proved to be a serious encumbrance under novel conditions and had to be interpreted away by some new legalistic, even casuistic twist. To give an idea of the ramified talmudic legislation on this subject, we need but quote the following summary of norms codified by Maimonides, which reflect fairly the view of ancient rabbis as well.

(1) Every community, if necessary with the coöperation of a great leader, may at its discretion fix the prices of all articles. (2) Every community should fix the prices of necessaries, allowing for a total profit of but one-sixth. (3) Wherever there are no communal fixed prices, the seller is wholly free to set his own price on land, slaves, free labor, and commercial paper. (4) A merchant may do the same with respect to movables, if he gives complete and candid information to the other party. (5) However, in case of failure to do so, he runs the risk that the injured party may choose to demand restitution of the balance of precisely one-sixth or complete annulment of the contract if the difference exceeds one-sixth of the market price. (6) An error in weight or measure merely calls for the restitution of the difference. (7) The merchant is entitled freely to sell below the prevailing market price and employ other "fair" methods of competition.

The main protective device of limiting profits to 16.66 up to 20 per cent on movables, particularly foodstuffs, must have proved even less effective than the maximum prices set by Diocletian. After all, the Jewish community did not have anything like Diocletian's vast army of officials and soldiers to enforce its will.

Even here, moreover, we note the rabbis' psychological-ethical, rather than purely practical, approach to fundamental economic problems. The very term used to designate the quest for just price, *Ona'ah*, really means "misrepresentation." Hence if the purchaser had been taken into the seller's confidence and frankly informed of the overcharge, he had no redress. Little attention was paid to his actual needs and temporary readiness to overpay. Similarly academic was the teaching of three rabbis, each giving a different reason, why verbal misrepresentation was worse than one involving financial losses. Despite its obvious exaggeration, therefore, the Mishnah's inclusion of shopkeepers among occupations known for robbery has a realistic, though rather resigned, ring.[32]

APPRECIATION OF LABOR

Above all, the talmudic sages stressed the value of honest labor. Contrary to the principle of the Essenes and the early Palestinian Christians, economic pursuits as such were glorified increasingly. Such utterances as "Skin carcasses in the market [the lowest occupation] and earn your wages," occur repeatedly. Even profanation of the Sabbath or outright idolatry is declared preferable to dependence on charity, a truly oriental hyperbole which conveyed the rabbis' high evaluation of labor. The high priest at Jerusalem had already included in his great annual supplication on the Day of Atonement the prayer "that thy people Israel not be dependent on one another." Later it became customary to offer public prayers, with the accompaniment of the ram's horn even on a Sabbath, whenever Palestinian wine or oil, or Babylonian linen fell in price 40 per cent or more. As times progressively worsened the rabbis commiserated more and more with their people whose "poverty at home is worse than fifty plagues." Taking a clue from R. Eleazar ben Azariah's homily that "earning a living is more difficult than the crossing of the Red Sea," R. Johanan added, It is "twice as difficult as childbearing" and "as difficult as [the messianic] redemption." The rabbis often personally learned the bitter lesson that, while excessive wealth was conducive to worry and led to distraction from the more important preoccupation with study, abject poverty (like pagan violence or the evil spirit of sex) made "a man lose his mind and the knowledge of his Maker." As responsible leaders of the community, they were also frequently guided in their legal enactments by the consideration of possible financial losses to the public. "The Torah has compassion with Israel's money," became a constant refrain, explaining many a deviation from an accepted legal norm.[33]

These citations, which could be multiplied many times over, will shed sufficient light on the rabbinic leaders' middle-of-the-road attitude toward wealth. If Jerome pointed an accusing finger at their "greed" (*In Ez.* 4:13 ff.; *In Os.* 2:20 f., *PL*, XXV, 50 f., 882 f.) his generalization was, if at all, justified only in relation to the patristic more other-worldly and ascetic theory. The recorded biographies of hundreds of talmudic sages show that many of them worked hard for a living, some serving in the menial occupations of "woodchoppers and water-carriers" (cf. Maimonides' *M.T.*, Talmud Torah, I, 9). True, ascetics were not lacking in ancient Judaism, even among the rabbis. But the majority believed in the legitimacy of pursuit of this-worldly happiness, including the enjoyment of material goods bestowed upon one by grace divine. They only insisted upon general moderation and the basic condition that such enjoyment would interfere with neither the welfare of neighbors or society at large, nor with the superior religious and ethical obligations of the persons concerned.

Under all circumstances, human life was valued more highly than wealth. In view of the combined pressures of landlord and tax collector upon the Babylonian Jewish farmer, the latter had frequently no recourse but to exploit the soil to the point of exhaustion. The rabbis cited with approval a popular proverb, "Let the soil become meager, but not its master" (B.M. 104b). No record of Hebrew slavery for debts or fines has been preserved, subsequent to Herod's sale of insolvent Jewish thieves abroad. In fact, the rabbis objected even to the employment of Jews in household chores, which, because of their old association with slavery, they regarded as degrading for men and as prejudicial to feminine morality. For purely economic exploitation of the workers, however, such as the payment of no wages, apart from food, for hard work, usually extending from sunrise to sunset, they found no words of condemnation. Once again what mattered most was verbal honesty. A typical anecdote relates how R. Johanan ben Matya reproved his son for hiring Jewish workers without specifying the kind of food he had promised them. "My son," he said, "even if you prepare for them a feast like that served by King Solomon you will not have fulfilled your duty toward them, for they are the children of Abraham, Isaac and Jacob. You better tell them before they start working that you are obliged to supply them only with bread and beans" (M. B.M. VII, 1).

We cannot discuss here at any length the ramified talmudic legislation affecting slaves, hired workers, and the various kinds of tenant farmers and sharecroppers. Land tenancy became the more important as the growth of feudalism under both Rome and Persia converted many small landholders into *coloni*. Bad as was the situation of the western farmers, who had become politically disfranchised and economically dependent on their masters, their Persian counterparts were even worse off. At the end of the fourth century, Ammianus Marcellinus commiserated with Persian peons living on the estates of the Parsee nobles. "They [the Parsees]," he wrote, "are boastful, harsh and offensive . . . claiming the power of life and death over slaves and commoners. They flay men alive, either bit by bit or all at once." It is doubly remarkable, therefore, that talmudic law discusses the respective arrangements between Jewish landlords and tenants almost entirely in terms of free contractual stipulations. Whether it be a farmer, renting land for a specified annual rental in cash or in kind (called respectively *sokher* and *hokher*), or a mere sharecropper, his relationship with the landowner was governed principally by the provisions of their contract. In fact, the technical term applied to the sharecropper, usually the most underprivileged farmer, is *meqabbel*, otherwise the equivalent of "contractor." Of course, custom, too, played a very great role. Even in Palestine during the more liberal period of the early Roman Empire there were enough regional variations for the Mishnah to state that "everything is governed by the custom of each district." Under these circumstances it would be astonishing if the rabbis remained totally immune to such fundamental outside changes as took place in the third and fourth centuries. That is why, for example, R. Hisda stated that, contrary to the express rules of the Mishnah, the Babylonian Jewish sharecroppers had no part in the hay and straw remaining after the harvest. The Babylonians generally went somewhat further than their Palestinian colleagues in protecting the rights of landlords. Nevertheless they, too, staunchly upheld the principle of contractual equality between the two parties, who acted as completely free agents under the law. There certainly was nothing in the rabbinic law of tenancy resembling the semibondage of the Roman colonate or of the still more restrictive Persian or medieval villeinage.[34]

Far more theoretical were the rabbinic debates on Jewish slavery. There certainly were but few Jewish slaves, although selling children into bondage to pay taxes sporadically occurred among Jews as among non-Jews. Despite its evident exaggeration, the talmudic saying, "One shall sell his daughter, rather than lend on interest" (Qiddushin 20a), reflects the availability of this desperate expedient. Nor were Jewish prisoners of war, especially as a result of the Perso-Roman conflicts, totally absent from the slave markets. However, rabbinic law placed increasingly serious deterrents in the way of would-be slaveholders. We recall the rabbinic extension of the Scriptural reference to the slave who "fareth well with thee" (Deut. 15:16), in itself hardly distinguished by economic realism, as the equivalent of an order to the owner to treat the slave on the basis of absolute equality. Rhetorical fulminations against even the casual employment of Jewish slaves, as well as the sale of any slave to Gentile masters, were reinforced by practical steps to secure the ransom of captive coreligionists. Apart from the ransom of Samuel's daughters, the release of Armenian or Persian Jewish prisoners by R. Aḥa "the fort commander" of Antioch (Yebamot 45a, according to Rabbinovicz's variant) is an early instance of the operation of this highly cherished commandment during the Perso-Roman wars.

Gentile slaves belonging to Jewish masters, on the contrary, seem to have increased rather than diminished after the third century. Here, too, protective laws, reinforced by the growing scarcity of slaves, lent plausibility to R. Naḥman's irate exclamation, "The slave is not worth the bread he consumes." But economic factors, particularly in the Roman dispersion, began forcing some Jews into the slave trade. They were sufficiently strong to overcome also the numerous obstacles placed in the way of Jewish slaveholding by the Christian Empire and its successor states. While for religious reasons, emperor after emperor tried to outlaw Jewish ownership of Christian slaves, most rulers realized that they could not afford to eliminate completely Jewish slaveownership by encouraging pagan slaves to turn Christian. If, according to Socrates, Constantius forbade Jews to acquire pagan as well as Christian slaves under threat of confiscation, such a prohibition was short-lived. Later emperors, until Justinian, allowed Jews to maintain even Christian slaves who had come into their possession through inheritance. Under Justinian, finally, Jews were permitted to hold and acquire pagan slaves, but had to give freedom to any slave turned Christian under capital sanction. But at that time the Western lands no longer were under imperial jurisdiction. These problems, becoming increasingly complex in the early medieval period, will be discussed more fully in connection with the economic developments following the fall of the western Roman Empire. Even in ancient times, however, Jewish ownership of slaves for resale, rather than domestic employment, started to become a branch of Jewish economy to which the rabbis had to lend grudging recognition. At times they had to oppose the excessive influence exercised by slaves, for example at the exilarchic court, which was somewhat reminiscent of the great power of freedmen in the Roman Empire.[35]

With the simultaneous strengthening of feudal tendencies and anti-Jewish discrimination in the two empires, Jews began to be slowly driven into certain peripheral occupations, like the slave trade, in which their far-flung dispersion gave them an edge over their competitors. Of course, the lure of quick commercial profits and relative immunity from governmental chicaneries also exercised great appeal. More farsighted leaders, however, taught by centuries of experience, realized the dangers inherent in the people's growing commercialization. They reiterated, therefore, R. Isaac's advice to the investor, "A man should always divide up his capital, [and invest] one-third in land, one-third in commerce, and retain one-third on hand" (B.M. 42a). They also quoted Rab who, probably taught by the ruin of many merchants which accompanied the transition from Parthian to Sassanian rule, had given his sons some sound business advice, but had wound up his peroration by coining this epigram, "Rather a *qab* from land than a *khor* [180 *qabs*] from profit!" (Pesaḥim 113a). Although land values frequently underwent sharp depreciation, agriculture offered partial security, compared to the sudden loss, through political upheavals, of entire mobile fortunes amassed during years of successful trading. Such losses must have become particularly numerous in Rome under Diocletian, whose regime was marred by wholesale confiscations and executions. Even a trained craftsman was better off. "There was a seven-year famine, but it did not cross the threshold of the craftsman"—ran a popular proverb in Babylonia (Sanhedrin 29a). No wonder many rabbis viewed with anxiety the abandonment of the ancestral agricultural and industrial pursuits in favor of the quicker and easier profits to be realized in commerce.

GROWING REGIMENTATION

This conservative attitude also found expression in the recurrent advice that a child should be instructed in the father's profession. The hereditary exercise of a craft, common during the First and Second Commonwealths was consciously stimulated by rabbinic teachings, as was the formation of artisans' guilds for mutual protection and support. From the third century on, general tendencies, both in Rome and in Persia, immensely favored this development. Perhaps nowhere is the transformation of Roman society more clearly shown than in the changing attitude of Roman law to the professional *collegia*. While the early empire looked with suspicion upon such organizations, which led an independent public life, the edicts of Diocletian and his successors made membership in such groups imperative.

Jews followed suit. Where possible, they organized their own professional guilds, for, in antiquity as well as in the Middle Ages, these associations combined socioreligious with economic interests. The second-century Jewish dyers' and carpet weavers' guilds of Hierapolis (Phrygia), and that of the shipowners of Alexandria in the fourth century, had counterparts in numerous cities of Palestine and Babylonia, as is recorded in the Talmud. The congregation of "Calcarienses" in Rome very likely was founded by a Jewish association of lime-kiln workers in that city. The medieval character of these guilds was emphasized by the evolution of customs and trade observances, peculiar to each branch of industry or commerce and fully acknowledged by talmudic legislation. The donkey and camel drivers and the shipowners of Babylonia had many peculiar usages sanctioned by prolonged practice. They even had a sort of insurance association strikingly similar to those of some medieval corporations.[36]

At the same time the Jewish community exercised general supervision over these corporate bodies. Roman officials in Alexandria actually tried to hold the community responsible for the state services required from members of the Jewish shipowners guild, but were checked by Theodosius I's order of 390. The rabbis actively participated in regulating corporate affairs. They assigned special streets to members of various crafts, and adopted incisive enactments concerning commissions and schedules of rates and fares. For instance, cloak and suit brokers were allowed a 4 per cent commission, while transportation costs were regulated by the rabbinical sanction of a drivers' zone tariff, based on a ten-*parasang* measure. Under rabbinical guidance, the community as a whole regulated prices and wages and mediated between employers and employees. In other words, it claimed the right to establish minimum wages and maximum prices—the very essence of economic medievalism![37]

Religious sanctions of talmudic law were also used for the protection of the national economy. The prohibition of Palestinian land sales to Gentiles, to be sure, could not easily be duplicated in Babylonia, although the title "Land of Israel" was occasionally conferred by an overzealous patriot on the Euphrates Valley as well. Yet even here the rabbis made the seller responsible for damages incurred by Jewish neighbors as the result of such a sale. According to R. Ashi, a neighbor might complain, "You have laid down a lion in my borders." In contrast to Palestine, too, the rabbis could not

completely outlaw here the sale of slaves abroad, although such restrictions had been imposed on the country as a whole by ancient
Babylonian law and existed also in Graeco-Roman Egypt and elsewhere. Rabbinic control over such phases of export trade as the
shipping of foodstuffs needed in the country must also have been
the less exacting, as Babylonia's greater fertility as a rule obviated
the need of sharp restrictions. One may doubt, in fact, whether
these efforts were completely successful even in Palestine, particularly after the Jewish population had become a minority and its
international trade was integrated in the larger Syro-Palestinian
economy. Many rabbinic regulations, moreover, had a decidedly
doctrinaire slant and were guided by other than purely economic
considerations. R. Judah ben Batira, for instance, advocated unrestricted exportation of wine "because it helps curtail lascivious-
ness." Even in the earlier period the rabbis themselves on occasions
had to check such patriotic excesses as when, in the days of Maccabean rule, R. Joshua ben Peraḥiah attempted to bar the importation of Egyptian grain by a halakhic subterfuge. Sometimes this
power of economic regulation was used by the rabbis to advance
internal, even separatist causes. According to R. Johanan, unspecified "younger teachers" (Samuel rather than the Palestinophile
Rab), seeking to promote Babylonia's independence, proclaimed
the liberation of Babylonian Jewish farmers from levitical dues.[38]

Reciprocally, there occurred a constant adaptation of talmudic
law to changing economic conditions. The most famous example
is the *Prosbol* enacted by Hillel. The biblical injunction canceling
all debts oustanding at each sabbatical year imposed heavy burdens
on the development in Palestine of a credit system suitable for the
growing capitalistic activities in the Herodian age. To encourage
lending, Hillel adopted a Hellenistic institution whereby the
lender could avoid cancellation by a specific declaration in court.
Hillel and his contemporaries thus consciously nullified an unequivocal precept of the Pentateuch. Even a progressive like Mar
Samuel denounced this abrogation of a biblical law as an "arro-
gance," because he himself was remote from the sphere of the
Palestinian sabbatical year and acquainted only with the less capitalistic Babylonia.[39] The people, however, accepted this innovation (*taqqanah*), and adhered to it for centuries to come. Indeed
the first complete document of this type is recorded by R. Judah
Al-Barceloni (about 1100), and one was written in Prague as late as
the beginning of the nineteenth century.

The abandonment of the law of fallowness during the sabbatical year soon followed. This commandment was emphasized in the earlier stages of the Halakhah as a paramount duty of Jewish land-owners, and was elaborated in minutest detail. It could hardly be adhered to, however, in a period when the Roman tax collector insisted upon the payment of the land tax every year. As long as the Roman Empire was favorably disposed toward its Jewish subjects, it followed the example of Alexander the Great in granting a gen-eral tax exemption for Jewish land during the year of fallowness. The antagonistic Roman rulers of the third century, however, tol-erated no such exemptions. Under the system introduced by Dio-cletian toward the end of that century, all the land and the inhab-itants of the empire were divided into fiscal units, each of which had to supply its share of the total tax. Jewish land and the Jews were incorporated into such *iugera,* with the rest of the population. Under these circumstances, the Roman collectors of revenue could not have granted tax reductions or exemptions to Jewish subjects, even if they had wanted to. About that time, R. Yannai publicly proclaimed the abolition of the sabbatical year because of the Ro-man tax (Sanhedrin 26a).

Another interesting example is the change in the attitude toward cattle raising. Before the Roman oppression, the dense population of Palestine necessitated intensive cultivation. The Tannaim therefore favored, we recall, intensive grain and fruit cultivation, as against the more extensive cattle raising. They prohibited the cutting of trees and plants which constituted the main source of nourishment for the major part of the population, simultaneously trying to discourage the raising of flocks as much as possible. In an excess of zeal some sages allegedly refused to visit a sick colleague (R. Judah ben Baba?) because for urgent medical reasons he kept a goat at his bedside to supply him with fresh milk. Forgetful that for health's sake one could violate even more serious prohibitions, the rabbis reputedly asked, "How can we call on him, if he has the gangster at his home?" (j. Soṭah IX, 10, 24a.)

After the conclusion of the Mishnah, however, the burdensome Roman taxes, primarily based upon the state's extensive share in agricultural produce, made agriculture as a whole ever less profit-able economically. The decrease of both the general and the Jewish population caused a labor shortage, thereby adding to landowners' difficulties. To transform farm into pasture land became more profitable and, in a sense, more beneficial to the whole people. Now the rabbis, too, changed their opinion; they began to advise land-owners to devote themselves to cattle rather than to grain. Not only did R. Johanan state that "he who wishes to get rich shall raise small cattle," but the biblical proverb, "The lambs will be for thy clothing and the goats the price for a field" (27:26), was interpreted as an advice to investors to sell a field and buy sheep, but never to sell sheep in order to buy a field (Hullin 84ab). In Babylonia, where from the outset there was no reason for discriminating against the raising of sheep, early attempts by Rab and other schoolmen to imitate these Palestinian laws broke down completely. R. Hisda enthusiastically repeated R. Johanan's advice, buttressing it by a quotation from Deuteronomy (Hullin 84ab; cf. the lengthy debates in B.Q. 79b f.).

More tenacious was the opposition to shepherds, although various homilists began to expatiate now on the theme of Moses' and David's appointment to positions of leadership after their honesty and ability as shepherds had been tested. The embarrassment of the Babylonian rabbis in the face of that inconsistent tannaitic legislation is clearly discernible. They drew a wholly artificial distinction between a hired shepherd, who is the full equal of any other Jew with respect to testimony, and the disqualified proprietor who tends his own flock. Ultimately Raba in fourth-century Babylonia indiscriminately admitted all sheepherders to testimony.[40]

The economic legislation of the Talmud thus presents a variegated and rich picture. It is an extraordinary combination of more or less liberal laws, emanating from semicapitalistic Palestine in the first century, and of those devised to regulate the life of the semifeudal fourth-century Jewish society of Palestine and Babylonia. By a process of constant adaptation, these contradictory elements were reconciled and integrated in a unique set of legal maxims. Equipped with such a law, the Jewish people could carry on its struggle for existence with great success in civilizations of either type. Hence the great influence of the Jew and his law on the Caliphate and, after the eleventh century, on Europe. Down to the eighteenth century, talmudic law represented a progressive factor, frequently enabling the Jew to perform pioneering services in the various countries of settlement. Only with the full development of modern capitalism after the Industrial Revolution did the more primitive talmudic patterns become a hindrance to Jews in the metropolitan centers of an advanced industrial civilization. At that time, indeed, as we shall see, powerful antitalmudic movements tried to liberate the Jewish capitalist and industrial worker from the shackles of this "obsolete" civil law.

JUDICIARY

All these legal enactments and academic interpretations would have remained dead letters without the general willingness of the people to follow its self-imposed rabbinic leadership and without some effective methods of law enforcement to batter down the resistance of recalcitrant minorities or individuals. Law enforcement was made possible by the Jews' enjoyment of an extensive ethnic-religious autonomy, which in the ancient world almost invariably included the right to live according to one's own law, as administered by one's own judges. The wide acceptance of the somewhat modified "personality principle," particularly by multinational empires, enabled many Jewish communities to secure from their rulers privileges resembling that enacted by Lucius Antonius, governor of Asia (50–49 B.C.E.) for the community of Sardes. The Jews had proved to his satisfaction, the Roman official wrote, "that from the earliest times they have had an association of their own in accordance with their native laws [of their forefathers] and a place of their own, in which they decide their affairs and controversies with one another." Lucius Antonius decided, therefore, to preserve these rights (*Antt.* XIV, 10, 12.235).

In mixed litigations with non-Jews, of course, both parties had to repair to some general courts, but even these, at times, seem to have taken cognizance of Jewish law. If some Jews, particularly when living in small and scattered communities unequipped with judicial facilities, preferred to make use of local courts, notarial offices or archives, this practice was frowned upon by their more orthodox leaders. Even the majority of Diaspora Jews doubtless shared Paul's sentiment of grieving over a brother going to law with a brother "and that before the unbelievers." The "archive of the Jews," attested by an inscription in Hierapolis, illustrates the existence of such institutions even in the smaller communities in the dispersion. True, Jewish leadership was not yet prepared to take stringent measures against deviations. The rabbis recognized, for example, the validity of deeds registered at Roman or Persian archives. Because of its apprehensions for family purity the majority invalidated writs of divorce and manumission thus registered, but curiously the otherwise intransigent R. Simon ben Yoḥai dissented even in this case. He probably wished to mitigate in this way the emergency created by the Hadrianic suppression of Jewish offices. Nevertheless increasing hostility on the part of the non-Jewish world, combined with the remarkable evolution of Jewish law during the talmudic period, must have induced many Jews, even outside of Palestine and Babylonia, to prefer their own courts of justice.[41]

With respect to Egypt, to be sure, there exists a remarkable dichotomy between the literary sources, which, beginning with Strabo, unanimously stress the extensive judicial autonomy of Egyptian Jewry, and the papyrological evidence. As pointed out by Tcherikover, all extant papyri, with but two exceptions, indicate that Jews used Greek deeds written wholly in the Hellenistic legal idiom (including even the customary deification of kings), registered them at governmental offices, and adjudicated controversies before non-Jewish courts. Beyond the qualifications suggested by Tcherikover himself, however, we must bear in mind that most of these documents come to us from smaller villages and date from the Ptolemaic rather than the Roman period. At that time the Jewish population still was relatively small. Many of these deeds, moreover, were written by Jewish soldier-farmers whose way of life was generally as atypical of the average Jew in the larger communities as had been that of the Elephantine colony in its day. None of the Berlin papyri, stemming in part from the fourth, predominantly Jewish, quarter of Alexandria, seems to record transactions between two indubitably Jewish parties. Of course, some of the Greek names on these and other documents from that collection may have been borne by Jews. Nevertheless the very paucity of reliable documentation from a populous and commercially very active community seems a clear indication that the bulk of its transactions was performed before Jewish authorities. One papyrus refers, in fact, expressly to a Jewish archive in Alexandria, as contrasted with the general city archive. The more rigidly statist Ptolemaic economy may also have encouraged business documentation before governmental offices, whereas the gradual relaxation of controls under the early Roman emperors doubtless fostered greater contractual freedom.[42]

Nor were the changes in the jurisdiction of Jewish courts enacted by the Christian Empire thoroughgoing. True, in 398, Theodosius I declared that the Jewish courts were to be regarded as courts of arbitration only, subject to a preliminary written agreement between the parties to accept the judgment of the court. But the excessive jurisdictional claims of ecclesiastical courts impelled the same emperor to impose far more rigid restrictions upon the Church, in the name of public order and the supremacy of the state. This limitation was least effective in the case of Jews because, with or without written agreements, the majority of Jewish parties doubtless continued to repair exclusively to Jewish courts, since rabbinic legislation now severely condemned deviations. Even after 398, imperial law itself acknowledged the validity of a Jewish court sentence and enjoined its execution by the provincial judges, whereas a judgment by an ordinary arbiter merely subjected the noncomplying party to the stipulated penalty. More, seventeen years later Theodosius himself found it necessary to forbid Christians in litigations with Jews to repair to Jewish courts, implying that Jews could freely do so. Even hostile Justinian merely took over the decrees of 398 and 415, which, in view of the changed status of ordinary courts of arbitration, doubly underscored the privileged position of the Jewish judges.[43]

In general, Jews retained even criminal jurisdiction. The rabbis scarcely resented their loss of capital sanctions, as they had long been reluctant to issue death sentences. Flagellation and heavy fines, combined with an extensive system of excommunication, were more than enough to uphold the authority of the courts. The officially "unordained" rabbis were, for a time, inclined to dispense with fines, but the extinction of official ordination in Palestine was speedily followed by the reintroduction of this penalty in Babylonia and elsewhere under another name. In short, Jewish law and judicial administration were much more decisive in the life of the Jewish masses than imperial or local legislation and judicial proceedings.

As both life and law became more complicated, there arose the need of a professional judiciary. Legal theory still adhered to the principle that in civil litigations each party should choose a judge and the two judges select a third impartial person. By constantly stressing their preference for a judgment reached on the basis of equity and mutual agreement, rather than formal law, the rabbis encouraged continued lay participation. In a characteristic controversy during the second century R. Eliezer, son of R. Jose the Galilean, insisted that the full severity of the law be applied regardless of consequences, or, as he phrased it, "Let the law bore through the mountain." But R. Joshua ben Qarha, homiletically quoting the biblical report, "And David executed justice and righteousness" (ṣedaqah; II Sam. 8:15) and Zechariah's injunction "Execute the judgment of truth and peace in your gates" (8:16), taught that the only way of combining justice with ṣedaqah (in the new meaning of charity) and truth with peace was for the judge to secure a mutually satisfactory settlement (T. Sanhedrin I, 3, 415; b. 6b). The majority followed R. Joshua to such an extent that less than a century later R. Johanan exclaimed, "Jerusalem was destroyed only because the judges had based their sentences upon the law of the Torah and failed to act inside the line of the law [according to the principle of equity]" (B.M. 30b; cf. 88ab). Only by allowing wide lay participation, moreover, could the rabbis hope to forestall both the overburdening of their own membership with judicial functions to the point of exhaustion, as happened to R. Ḥisda and Rabbah bar R. Huna (Shabbat 10a), and the professionalization of learning unavoidably resulting from such full-time concentration.

Nevertheless, the social forces favoring a professional judiciary became overwhelmingly powerful. Rather inconsistently, the rabbis themselves promoted this evolution by their doctrine of the judge's personal responsibility for damages resulting to either party from his errors in judgment or in fact. Curiously, errors in the interpretation of a clear-cut traditional law merely nullified the sentence without untoward consequences for the judge. If the latter provision by itself encouraged scholarly judges familiar with the entire domain of traditional law, the possibility of totally evading personal responsibility for errors by securing in advance an authorization from the exilarch (or patriarch) inescapably led to the evolution of a judicial bureaucracy. The rule that a court "superior in wisdom and numbers" could at any time annul a judgment of any other court likewise strengthened the hand of professional judges. Salaries were long masked by the pretense of being but compensations for the judges' time diverted from their occupational activities or, in smaller communities, by the combination of judicial with other more overtly remunerative functions. Levi ben Sissai, for example, served in the small Palestinian town of Simonias as preacher, ḥazzan (sexton), scribe, teacher of the Mishnah, as well as judge "and whatever else they might need." In the long run, a fully salaried class arose whose revenue was sufficiently large for some office seekers to invest money in securing appointment. Cases of "simony," reminiscent of the barter in the high-priestly office in the last years of the Temple, occurred quite frequently in the turbulent days of Judah II, arousing both popular disaffection and rabbinic resentment toward the patriarchal office. Even without such abuses, however, "authorized," that is practically appointed, judges began now to rival or exceed in communal influence the elective "best men" in most townships of both Palestine and Babylonia.[44]

The only effective method of perpetuating a nonprofessional class of scholars, namely through public and private charities of the kind then maintaining the growing monastic orders, was repugnant to Jewish recipients and the public alike. Only Jerome, perhaps oversimplifying the similarity between rabbis and clerics, mentions cases of such philanthropic aid.

According to usage [he writes] still persisting in Judaea, not only among us, but also among the Hebrews, those who meditate day and night on the law of the Lord and have no portion in this earth except God alone, are maintained by the services of the synagogues and the rest of the world. This is done out of sense of justice, lest some people live in well-being and others in care, but that the superfluity of the former alleviate the misery of the latter [*Contra Vigilantium*, 13; *PL*, XXIII, 365, with reference to Ps. 1:2; Deut. 18:2 f.; II Cor. 8:14].

We shall see that rabbinic law went far in trying to extend to students of the Torah a variety of economic privileges so as to enable them to devote themselves wholeheartedly to their studies. But in principle even a scholar was expected to make a valiant effort to be wholly self-supporting, in fact to help support others in great need.

SOCIAL WELFARE

Mutual responsibility for common welfare had deep roots in both the historic tradition of the Jewish people and in its social realities. From biblical times had come down the unbroken chain of prophetic preachment of social justice and the psalmists' exaltation of the lowly and downtrodden 'ani or 'anav. With the Greek Bible translators and apologists, the term πτωχός (mendicant), reminiscent of a charitable obligation, began to displace the more neutral πένης (poor) as the equivalent of the word 'ani. In the Septuagint their ratio is 35:11, while Sirach, Tobit, and the New Testament use almost exclusively *ptochos*. If Philo alone preferred the more colorless designation, it is he who helped transform the meaning of *philanthropia* from humanitarianism to charity. Finally came the crowning term *koinonia* to express the idea of mutual responsibility, via the support of the poor. So convinced were the rabbis of the superiority of their teachings in this domain that, during a remarkable discussion at Yabneh, disciple after disciple pointed out that the Graeco-Roman charities were dictated by pride, love for display, self-interest in the preservation of the existing order, and other extraneous aims, but not by the sheer compassion and loving-kindness characteristic of Jewish philanthropies. R. Johanan ben Zakkai himself, more generously viewing the expiatory function of even Gentile charities, now taught that, after the destruction of the Temple, charitable acts were going to take the place of sacrificial offerings in securing for the Jews forgiveness of sins. A third-century teacher adapted R. Johanan's thought to the conditions of his age. "When the Temple existed," he declared, "a man paid his shekel and secured expiation. Now that there exists no Temple, if a man gives charities it is well and good, if not, the Gentile nations come and take his money by force." Finally R. Assi late in that century exclaimed, "Charity is a counterpoise to all other commandments." [45]

Not that the element of self-interest was completely lacking even in the idealistically overdrawn picture of Jewish charities in both the Hellenistic and rabbinic writings. The people's increasingly defensive battle for survival nurtured an undying spirit of common responsibility of each individual for the whole group and of the group for the individual. The widely scattered interterritorial settlements called for expansion and a more urbane adaptation of the old Semitic traits of hospitality, as well as for a new emphasis on the ransom of captives. Moreover, the empire's growing instability brought home to every Jew the possibility that he himself or his children might come to depend on charity. R. Ḥiyya's wife thought that he had cursed their children when he had enjoined her to rush bread to beggars, "so that others may hasten to give it to your children." To pacify her he cited the school of R. Ishmael which had already expressed this thought by punning on a Deuteronomic verse (15:10: *gelal-galgal*): "It is a wheel which is turning in the world." In a constant refrain the rabbis quite convincingly argued with their compatriots that, if they "be filled with compassion for one another, the Lord blessed be He would be filled with compassion" for them. R. Joshua clinched the argument by stating, "More than the wealthy man does for the poor, the poor does for the wealthy." [46]

So ingrained had this feeling become that Jewish poor often vociferously demanded support as their God-given right. Had not Philo interpreted the sabbatical year as principally intended to convey the idea that the poor should "enjoy as their own what appeared to belong to others"? R. Eleazar of Bartotha consciously used such an equivocal phrase as "Give him [the poor] of what is His [the Lord's], for thou and thine are His." R. Eleazar himself used to give away all he had at any particular moment, so that, we are told, the charity collectors used to hide from him. When he once pinned them down and forced them to tell him that they were collecting funds to marry off a couple of orphans, he unhesitatingly gave them all his savings accumulated for the forthcoming marriage of his own daughter. To forestall such excessive zeal the rabbis advised that, while alive, one should not give away more than one-fifth of one's possessions so as not to become dependent on others, but that one might distribute the entire estate through charitable legacies. They thus toned down the decision of the Synod of Usha which, facing the difficult task of reconstruction after the Bar Kocheba revolt, demanded in an affirmative fashion that "everyone set aside a fifth of his property for pious causes." Probably more typical of the majority as well, was the rule promulgated by the Damascus sectarians that each man set aside "the wages of two days every month" for charity. This amount came closer to a "tithe," rather than *homesh* (fifth), which must always have been quite exceptional.[47]

At the same time, the rabbis insisted on every man's responsibilities toward his family, even toward more distant relatives. In the hierarchy of philanthropic values they taught, "Your own poor come before those of your city, those of your city before strangers." Occasionally Gentiles were to be supported from the Jewish chest, but a Jew was not to receive charity from non-Jews. Some Zealots like Eleazar of Modein believed that Gentiles supported Jews only in order to humiliate them. A Jew living publicly from non-Jewish charities was likened to a pork eater and disqualified from testifying in court. Orphans and widows, on the other hand, though far from forgotten, were no longer stressed with the same degree of urgency as in biblical times. Under woman's new economic opportunities and the newer emphasis on communal rather than clan or family responsibilities, fatherless children and solitary women no longer exemplified the acme of human misery. Beyond the alleviation of temporary needs, the sages emphasized constructive and timely charities enabling the poor to earn a living. A Tanna drew the homely lesson from a burden sliding from a donkey's back: "As long as it is still in its place, you can easily adjust it; but once it falls to the ground, not even five men are able to put it back." [48]

Characteristic of the rabbis' general psychological-ethical approach to charities, too, is their postulate that the sensitivities of recipients be carefully safeguarded and cognizance taken of their accustomed standard of life. When an impoverished man demanded from Raba funds for stuffed chicken and old wine, the rabbi asked him whether he had no compunctions about straining the resources of the community. "No," the petitioner replied, "I am eating not of their money, but of that of the Holy One blessed be He." Another Babylonian, Mar Uqba, customarily sent 400 denarii to a poor man on the eve of the Day of Atonement. He doubled this amount on learning from his son that the latter had found the recipient imbibing precious old wine. Hillel went even further. He once supplied a formerly wealthy man with a horse to ride on, but unable to locate a slave to run before the horse according to fashion, he himself ran for three miles (Ketubot 67b).

These exaggerations, intended to drive home a moral point, showed how far class distinctions were perpetuated in the very field of communal charities. But at least, on a pupil's stratagem, Judah the Patriarch discontinued during a famine the theretofore widely practiced discrimination against the 'am ha-areṣ. In fact, it now became accepted practice to give food to the poor on demand and to institute the necessary inquiries only before supplying them with clothing and other necessaries. At the same time to discourage mendicancy the rabbis taught, "He who is in business with a capital of 50 denarii shall not take charity; he who does not need and takes it, shall not die without really becoming dependent on other people; he who needs and refuses to take it, shall not die of old age without supplying others from his own bounty." They also discriminated sharply against beggars who went openly from door to door and in favor of the poor who concealed their misery. Anonymous donations to unidentifiable recipients were considered the acme of charity.

This is not the place to discuss the vast and ramified system of talmudic philanthropies which, beyond financial aid, extended to such active or verbal comforts as were given by visiting the sick, helping in funerals, eulogizing deceased members, and comforting mourners. To obviate, for instance, the existing inequalities between rich and poor, illustrated by the luxurious mausolea at Beth

She'arim, R. Gamaliel II set the example by ordering that his own corpse be buried in a simple linen shroud rather than the theretofore fashionable expensive attire (T. Niddah IX, 17, 651 f.; b. Ketubot 8b). Soon thereafter R. Meir condemned all conspicuous waste of this kind as falling under the prohibition of "Thou shalt not destroy" (Semaḥot IX, 23). Everyone was subject to special charitable levies, a tannaitic regulation providing that even strangers after a residence of but thirty days should contribute to the cost of maintaining a public kitchen. After three months they were taxed for the weekly distribution of food, and after further quarterly intervals also for clothing, funerals, and the city's defenses, respectively. While estates belonging to orphans were exempted from many imposts, rabbinic ethics demanded that even the poorest members contribute something to charity.

If collection of the necessary funds was very arduous, their distribution in the light of manifold claims must often have been an unbearable burden. Talmudic law, we recall, demanded the appointment of three dispensers of charity to impress upon them and the public at large their semijudicial function in deciding impartially how much to allot to each recipient. Many a harassed official must have echoed R. Jose's doleful wish, "May my destiny be to serve among the collectors rather than among the distributors of charities" (Shabbat 118b). Even more poignantly Rab described the following hierarchy of ruthless masters: "Let me live under Ishmael [Arab regime] rather than Edom [Rome], Edom rather than a *magus* [Persia], a *magus* rather than a scholar, a scholar rather than an orphan or widow" (Shabbat 11a). In order that prospective charity supervisors should not be completely discouraged, and also to obviate endless controversies over their administration, the rabbis demanded that they be treated with utmost reverence and trust, and not be held to strict accounting. More, R. Eleazar taught that "the merit of the charitable fund raiser is greater than that of the contributor himself."

How effective was this welfare structure in practice? Since our information is almost entirely limited to normative and homiletical expositions, the facts of ancient Jewish life can hardly be fully ascertained. Even recorded actions, such as the few mentioned here, are atypical in that, apart from possible exaggeration by subsequent narrators, they were often performed primarily in order to convey a lesson. There must have been many a wealthy person who, pointing to the healthy limbs of an approaching beggar, inquired why

he did not work for a living. The rabbis frowned upon such in-
quisitiveness. They reported God as scolding the recalcitrant donor,
"Not enough that you gave him nothing of your own, you cast an
evil eye also on what I have given him [his healthy limbs]." In an
irate mood Rab once condemned the entire wealthy class of Babylonia as "doomed to hell." On the other hand, actual starvation
seems to have been greatly mitigated in, if not completely eliminated from, Jewish communities even during the often recurrent
famines. Deeply impressed, Emperor Julian believed that Jews had
no beggars at all. Although the phrase "starved to death" appears
fairly frequently in rabbinic letters, it seems to have largely been a
figure of speech. Whether or not the idealistic picture presented by
the talmudic sources was in any way approximated in actual life,
there was enough power in communal leadership, buttressed by
public opinion and religious fears of retribution after death, as well
as by the enlightened self-interest of a strongly interdependent
community, to achieve the practical realization of at least a modicum of these postulates. Apart from its immediate effects, moreover, the theory became part and parcel of the Jewish legal-ethical
tradition, whereas the practical limitations of the day were, because
unrecorded, quickly forgotten. As such it was imbedded in the
Jewish heritage of ages, to exert an enormous influence on all subsequent generations.[49]

EDUCATION

Foundations of an extensive educational system were laid by the
Pharisees long before the talmudic era, and were built on antecedents going back to the schools of wisdom and priestly training of
ancient Israel. Whether we accept Bacher's hypothesis or the present version of the talmudic tradition, it appears certain that a program of primary and secondary education had been well formulated by the Pharisaic teachers of independent Judaea.[50] After the
destruction of the Temple, the rabbis intensified their efforts to
develop an efficient school system. They declared the acquisition of
a good education to be one of the primary duties of each individual,
and provision for it a major responsibility of the community. They
went into great detail concerning facilities for the instruction of
children and the outlining of a general educational program for
the entire Jewish world. They ruled, for example, that wherever
there were twenty-five children of school age, a teacher must be

supplied by the community. When the number increased to forty, an assistant teacher was to be appointed. Scholars were advised never to choose a residence where there was no elementary teacher.

Problems of pedagogy were likewise widely discussed in the Talmud. The majority of rabbis gave the preference to intensive and thorough studies within a limited range. They also believed that "a well-organized pupil is superior to an ingenious student." In truly oriental fashion, they encouraged oral study, however noisy, as a mnemotechnic help. When Beruriah found a pupil studying silently she kicked him and said: "Is it not written [that the Torah is] 'ordered in all things, and sure'? When it is ordered in all your two hundred and forty-eight limbs, it is surely preserved; if not, it is not preserved." A student of R. Eliezer (ben Jacob?) was cited as a horrifying example; having studied his lessons silently, he forgot them all within three years. Clearly, participation of all limbs involved gesticulation as well as articulation—an immemorial oriental habit carried down to modern times. To what extent tradition determined the methods of instruction is seen in another custom prevailing even today in orthodox Jewry. Children's lessons in the Pentateuch began with the third, and not the first, Book of Moses. The rationalization of R. Assi, "Let the pure come and study the laws of purity" is as unconvincing as is the modern hypothesis that the erotic passages of Genesis were avoided in the schools. Most likely the lay school of the Talmud inherited this approach from the priestly school of the First and Second Commonwealths, in which, naturally, great emphasis was laid upon Leviticus as the fundamental text for the training of young priests.[51]

Insistence on adult education was perhaps even more important. As long as he lives, every Jew must set aside for daily study as much time as he can possibly afford. In the first generation after the Great War, Samuel the Small and R. Joshua ben Hananiah outlined a well-known curriculum: at five a boy should be taught the Bible, at ten the oral law, at fifteen he should be guided toward his own interpretation of these traditional sources, to a kind of independent research. This threefold division of study should also be maintained throughout life. In Palestine and Babylonia great teachers often delivered public discourses for businessmen and farmers, and, after arriving in Babylonia, Palestinian scholars addressed the large crowds which usually assembled before the exilarch's palace.

The Babylonian rabbis set aside early morning hours for the instruction of those engaged during the day in earning a living, while farmers and artisans residing at a great distance had an opportunity to hear a distinguished leader during the Sabbaths preceding the holidays (*Shabbete de-rigla*). The semiannual *kallah* gathering enabled men of various walks of life, residing in distant parts of the country, to devote the month, or a part of the month preceding the high holidays or Passover, to concentrated study and exchange of thought with one another, under the experienced guidance of the greatest rabbis of the generation.[52]

To talmudic learning Judaism attached unique social recognition, in accord with its supreme evaluation of the all-human, indeed cosmic importance of Jewish education. Typical of endless encomiums are the epigrams broadcast by R. Simon ben Laqish in behalf of Judah II: "The universe is being held together only by the breath of schoolchildren. . . . One must not interrupt the study of schoolchildren even for the building of the Temple. . . . A city without schoolchildren shall be destroyed" (or "placed under a ban," according to Rabina's more realistic emendation; Shabbat 119b). Our information, of course, is based almost exclusively on rabbinic sources, which may not be without bias, and which are certainly filled with such other oriental exaggerations as the statement that "a bastard, if he be learned, takes precedence over an uneducated high priest" (M. Horayot III, 8). There is, however, no doubt that learning opened the road to the highest prestige in public and private life. A glance into the relatively well-transmitted biographies shows that many leading rabbis of the age rose from the lowest strata to win uncontested leadership in social as well as intellectual life. The biography of R. Joshua ben Ḥananiah may serve as an illustration. An artisan of limited means, he dealt with the patriarch on equal terms and boldly led his school of thought against that headed by R. Eliezer ben Hyrcanus, one of the country's richest landowners. In most of these controversies, moreover, the majority of the rabbis adopted his opinion as authoritative, incorporating it into the whole of Jewish law. There was more than a grain of truth in R. Joshua ben Levi's (?) assertion that "only he who is engaged in the study of Torah is truly free" (M. Abot VI, 2).

From Sadducean times a deep-rooted suspicion still lingered on that the rich were not really interested in learning. "Separate the children from the wealthy [*ba 'ale batim*]" was a favorite saying of

R. Johanan ben Zakkai, "because they keep people away from the words of the Torah." This explanation of the rebuilder of national life during the great crisis may have been but an irate response to the social antagonisms which had permeated Jewish society before the fall of Jerusalem. But we recall that in the following less class-conscious centuries Rab indulged in his resentful exclamation against the wealthy Jews of Babylonia. His angry outcry was reiterated by Raba, at least with reference to the upper classes of Maḥoza, whose corruption evoked many a sharp comment from other rabbis, too. In Palestine, R. Johanan speculated: " 'It [the Torah] is not in heaven,' this means that it shall not be found among the haughty; 'neither is it beyond the sea,' that is, that it shall not be found among the merchants and traders." Hence also the untiring reiteration, "Take heed of the children of the poor [or even of the 'ame ha-areṣ] because from them will issue forth the Torah." [53]

Material rewards of scholarship were indirect. In themselves they would hardly have compensated for the enormous sacrifices and tireless devotion necessary to win recognition. "That is the way of the Torah," insisted an anonymous, but probably very old saying of the fathers, "You shall eat bread with salt, drink water by measure, sleep on the ground and live the life of misery, and yet labor on the study of Torah" (M. Abot VI, 4). Not the least among the sacrifices was the student's frequent deprivation of ordinary family enjoyments, even total absence for months on end from one's family, however destitute. There was, indeed, much truth in R. Simon ben Laqish's famous pun on " 'This is the law: when a man dieth in a tent,' that is, the law endures only in the man who dies in its behalf" (Num. 19:14; Berakhot 63b).

By itself the economic position of the rabbi was little different from that of any other citizen. True, he inherited the priestly exemption from taxes, which seems to have been preserved in Palestine even after Diocletian's fiscal reform. Persia granted such exemptions also to visitors of the kallah during the two months of their attendance. In view of the crushing weight of taxation in general, such exemption meant a great deal to the few scholars who happened to be rich. On one occasion, we recall, the populace of third-century Tiberias staged a riot against the ordination of wealthy R. Ḥanina. Voluntary offerings to scholars, on the other hand, were much appreciated. They were at times compared with the daily sacrifices or the "first fruits" of the Temple. Furthermore, some businessmen regarded it a privilege to let scholars participate in their profits as silent partners. But there long was no financial benefit to be derived from academic teaching as such. Only at a later date was permission granted the teacher, as well as the judge, to charge a fee "as a compensation for the time diverted from one's work." Elementary teachers, to be sure, were allowed to receive regular tuition fees from parents or salaries from the communal chests. Otherwise the community could not possibly have recruited all the personnel needed to man the numerous elementary schools. But, unlike other professionals, the schoolmasters were not protected against unrestricted competition. In fact, we hear nothing of self-protective guilds of teachers, such as were to be found later in some larger communities.[54]

As a rule, the rabbi had to work hard for a living. No fewer than a hundred rabbis are recorded as earning a livelihood as artisans. One of the most prominent Babylonian teachers, Abbaye, worked so hard on his farm that his health suffered from too intensive labor and privation. When R. Simlai preached in Tiberias on R. Ḥanina's injunction that every Jew should have two suits of clothes, one for weekdays and another for the Sabbath, his colleagues lamented that they could not afford more than one suit (j. Pe'ah VIII, 8, 21b). In the generally more prosperous second century, we are told, "six pupils covered themselves with one blanket and yet they studied the Torah" (Sanhedrin 20a). This may, however, have been true only during the severe economic depression in the first years after the Bar Kocheba revolt. The talmudic rabbi thus was the true successor of the Judaean prophet and the Pharisaic scribe, retaining, despite all hardships, considerable financial independence.

Needless to say, the wealthy citizens did not always live up even to the more modest rabbinic expectations, which may in part explain the aforementioned fulminations of leading sages against the whole wealthy class. Apart from personal illiberality, many well-to-do persons may have resented the general rabbinic superiority complex and drive for power. Others may have disliked the starry-eyed "academism" of some teachers. Such sneers must have been heard frequently enough, at least in the Babylonian plutocracy, for R. Joseph to define an "Epicurean" as a man asking, "What have the rabbis done for us? They read and study for their own benefit." Raba illustrated this saying by the example of a physician Benjamin's family who contended that the rabbinic debates never had any such practical results as permitting one to eat a crow's flesh or forbidding him to eat that of a dove (Sanhedrin 99b f.). Of course, anyone familiar with the rabbinic literature knows how deeply concerned the sages really were with the pragmatic and activist effects of their teachings.

Equality of opportunity was perhaps greater in Palestine than in Babylonia. The increasing obliteration of social distinctions in all Roman civilization—"upstarts" could ascend even the imperial throne—worked in the direction of social leveling in Palestine, while Babylonia felt the influences of aristocratic Persian society, which made for family purity and social exclusiveness even more strongly than after the First Exile. But here, too, Jewish society was dominated by a new sort of theocracy, rather than by an aristocracy of birth or money—a theocracy, however, not of a professional or charismatic priesthood, but of rabbis recruited from all social classes, whose claim to leadership consisted exclusively in learning and personal piety.

That "the rabbis are called kings" (Gittin 62a) was almost proverbial. A teacher was frequently addressed as Abba (Father). A scholar always had precedence in the synagogue, in social gatherings and even in court proceedings. Once having won great distinction, he was assured of immortality. For centuries to come, disciples would recite his words orally and finally these would be included, in his name, in a sacred legal collection. Sometimes a rabbi's tomb, like that of R. Simon ben Yohai, was glorified next to that of a biblical patriarch or prophet, and some of these graves still attract pious pilgrims from many lands. To be uneducated was clearly a great social disadvantage—the rabbis were the last to refrain from pointing this out—and a certain measure of education became universal for men, if not for women. Josephus had boasted, with a good deal of apologetic exaggeration,

Should anyone of our nation be questioned about the laws, he would repeat them all more readily than his own name. The result, then, of our thorough grounding in the laws from the first dawn of intelligence is that we have them as it were engraven on our souls. A transgressor is a rarity; evasion of punishment by excuses an impossibility [*Ag. Ap.* II, 18.178].

In the talmudic period Jewish learning penetrated still deeper into the masses. This happened at a time when illiteracy was widespread throughout the Mediterranean world and when the Imperial City itself had only begun to establish public schools for the wealthy and the middle class.

SYNAGOGUE AND CEMETERY

With the elimination of the Temple and its sacrificial worship, the synagogue assumed a position in the Jewish cult more central than it had held even in the Pharisaic age in the Diaspora. But here, too, public instruction seems to have been the primary concern. Many synagogues were used as elementary schools during most of the day, and divine service itself had as many educational as devotional aspects. The reading of portions of the Torah in a triennial or annual cycle represented intellectual, rather than purely cultic, exercises. Josephus voiced a widespread opinion when he stated that Moses had introduced weekly readings of the law in order that the Jews might "obtain a thorough and accurate knowledge of it" (*Ag. Ap.* II, 17.175). The oldest extant description of a synagogue service, that of Philo, likewise stresses the educational value of reading "the holy laws" and their detailed interpretation.

Reading of Scripture was, indeed, often followed by a sermon devoted to instruction as much as to edification. Before the holidays, in particular, rabbis used homilies to explain to their audiences the laws and regulations pertaining to the ritual of those sacred days. Even purely exhortatory sermons often dwelt on the importance of study or, more indirectly, shed light on some intriguing academic problem. For example, when R. Ḥanina bar Abba, an itinerant fourth-century preacher, was asked to deliver a discourse on the Levitical injunction, "But that which is left of the meal-offering shall be Aaron's and his sons" (Lev. 2:10), he went far afield in what seems to have been a rather lengthy exposition. But he wound up by emphasizing Aaron's great contribution of "persuading sinners to study the Torah" (Lev. r. III, 6).

Most sermons consisted of a remarkable blend of legal and homiletical observations. We are told that when R. Meir's turn came to preach at his session "he devoted one-third of his sermon to law, one-third to Aggadah, and one-third to parables." So intent were the ancient preachers to drive home their lessons that they employed salaried interpreters to explain them to the audience in simple language. At the same time they made sure that the interpreters' rendition be accurate by insisting, as did Judah I, that "he who translates a verse with exact literalness is a falsifier, and he who makes additions is a blasphemer. Nor is an interpreter standing before a sage entitled to abbreviate, amplify and otherwise al-

ter anything, unless he happens to be the sage's father or teacher."
What could happen to a preacher who had an unscrupulous, or
perhaps overscrupulous, interpreter is illustrated by an incident
which occurred at a time when the imperial anarchy had weakened the regime of Judah II. One of the unworthy judges, who
had secured his office by purchase, had to preach. He appeared in
the synagogue with a learned interpreter hoping that the latter
would cover up his own insufficiency. The interpreter, however,
obliquely but unmistakably exposed his ignorance before the public. Philo was by no means wrong, therefore, when he likened the
synagogue to a school where Jews gather every Sabbath "in rever-
ent and orderly manner, and listen to the laws, in order that none
might be ignorant of them." [55]

Such merging of the house of prayer and the house of learning
was emphasized in later generations, and the phrase *bate kenesiot
u-bate midrashot* appears frequently as one unit in the phraseology
of Talmud and Midrash. Both together increasingly filled for the
Jewish people the place of political forms. Characteristically, the
rabbis ascribed even to a Greek thinker of the second century,
Oinomaos of Gadara, the statement that, as long as voices of children were heard chirping (words of the Law) in the houses of worship and of learning, the Jewish people was safe against all foreign
aggressors (Gen. r. LXV, 20, 734 f.).

Nor was the transition from study to prayer in the same building
readily noticeable. Just as study was conducted aloud, with the
pupils often reciting their lessons in unison, the recitation of prayers became a highly articulate congregational performance, in
which the reader, or "messenger of the public," merely served as
general guide and conductor. Trying to impress his listeners with
the importance of congregational services, Abba Benjamin, a first
or second-century rabbi, expatiated on the biblical phrase, "To
hearken unto the cry and to the prayer." This verse, he declared,
intended to convey the idea that "in the place where you cry and
sing [*rinnah*], there you shall pray." Even the sermon was not an
altogether solo performance by the preacher. It usually started
with questions from the public and probably led to extensive discussions thereafter. The unfortunate experience of R. Levi ben
Sissai in Simonias may serve as an illustration. Employed in a variety of communal functions, the rabbi was to deliver his first discourse at the synagogue. But he was so overwhelmed by the magnificent pulpit erected for him that he found no words to answer

one homiletical and two legal questions hurled at him from the audience. So articulate, indeed noisy, had the congregants become that, time and again, the rabbis tried to impress upon them the merits of silent prayers which, they admitted, were less, rather than more, conducive to concentration. But they apparently succeeded only in preserving the silent recitation of the *'Amidah*. Ultimately Pope Gregory the Great decreed in 591 that, if churchgoers found themselves disturbed by the *vox psallentium* from a neighboring synagogue, the latter be removed to another locality.[56]

Increasing congregational participation was but a facet in the growing democratization of synagogue services. Originally modeled after the Temple ritual, the synagogue liturgy was affected by the Temple's rigid separation between priests and laymen, even if sacerdotal functions had been reduced here to the recitation of the priestly blessing and a first call on the reading of the weekly lesson. Separation of a different kind was fostered by the continued enmity between scholars and *'ame ha-areṣ*. Because any layman called to the Torah was expected to recite his own lesson, such invitations were extended by the officials in charge only to men able to read well.

In time, however, Temple recollections grew dimmer, while the combination of outward pressures and internal educational reforms bridged the gap between the educated and unlearned groups. R. 'Aqiba already used the conclusion of the priestly blessing, "and I will bless them" (Num. 6:27), to impress upon the people that the blessing came directly from God, not from the priests. This egalitarian emphasis was underscored by the opposition of 'Aqiba's priestly colleague R. Ishmael (Sifre on Num. 43, ed. by Friedmann, fol. 13b; Ḥullin 49a). The recitation of the blessing itself became ever less frequent. Following the example of the Temple services, in which it naturally occupied a focal position, the synagogue at first assigned it a place of honor in the daily prayers. But apparently already in ancient times it was restricted to Sabbath services, to be later limited to major holidays alone in most orthodox congregations.

The concluding verse in the blessing was also utilized by the rabbis to stress its universal application. To counteract a possible restrictive interpretation of the injunction to the priests, "Ye shall bless the children [or even literally: sons] of Israel" (Num. 6:22), the sages pointed to the last sentence to show that the blessing included also women, slaves, and proselytes (Sifre, *loc. cit.*). The latter extension was doubly necessary as there were recurrent attempts to segregate converts as a separate class of worshipers. Such discrimination was practiced among the Damascus sectarians (17: 1–4) and was also advocated by R. Judah bar Ila'i (Qiddushin 73a). But the majority completely eschewed all manifestations of racial prejudice. More and more the congregants themselves (including proselytes), rather than their priestly leaders, conducted the services.

A price had to be paid for this welcome extension of popular participation, however. Since not all of those eligible for a call to the Torah were now able to recite it correctly, the custom gradually spread to employ official readers, leaving to the individual worshipers the recitation of simple benedictions. When the prayers grew longer and more complex, particularly through accretions of such liturgical poems on holidays as the "order of service" on the Day of Atonement, the congregation also required the guidance of a more or less professionally trained cantor. Such is recorded, for example, in the Palestinian *Sefer ha-Ma'asim*. Understandably, this custom seems to have begun in the Roman dispersion and thence spread to both Palestine and Babylonia. The taste in learned discourses likewise became less sophisticated. As R. Isaac Nappaha phrased it, "At first, when the penny was more readily available, man wished to hear something about the Mishnah or Talmud; now that the penny is scarce and government makes us ill, he prefers to listen to a discussion of Bible or Aggadah." Living in the period of military anarchy (he himself pathetically described how starving people ate unripe grain in the fields), R. Isaac clearly perceived the impact of economic and political pressures on what he considered a serious deterioration in the public taste.[57]

Some of R. Isaac's more fastidious colleagues now lost all interest in attending synagogue services. One generation earlier R. Simon ben Laqish had called a man failing to attend the synagogue of his locality a "bad neighbor." R. Johanan, too, had placed synagogue attendance in the dispersion on a par with living in Palestine, and thus explained the fact that so many Jews in Babylonia were enabled to reach ripe old age. But their immediate successors, R. Ammi and R. Assi refused to attend any of the thirteen Tiberian synagogues and preferred to pray in their own studies (Berakhot 8a). This example was followed by several Babylonian scholars, until Raba became so convinced of the superiority of study over prayer that, when he once saw R. Hamnuna unduly prolonging his prayers, he exclaimed, "They leave matters of eternity and busy themselves with the life of the moment"—a remarkably lopsided evaluation in the eyes of most modern theologians. To which stricture R. Hamnuna could but lamely reply, "There is a special time for prayer and another for study" (Shabbat 10a).

Behind the walls of the schoolhouse or synagogue or, as it usually was, a synagogue-schoolhouse, the Jewish people weathered all storms. This sense of security was enhanced by the essentially intangible character of the synagogue. The word refers primarily to the congregation, and only secondarily to the "house" of worship. Unlike the Temple, a synagogue could not be destroyed by an enemy. With the burning of the Temple, its entire sacrificial system was obliterated. The destruction of any number of synagogue buildings, such as at times occurred even in Persia (Yoma 10a), entailed no change in the established liturgy or mode of worship. Ten Jews assembled anywhere in public or in private were the real συναγωγή which could conduct a regular service like that held in the largest and most elaborate structure. No longer could the Romans obstruct the Jewish cult through minor chicaneries, as when they held the sacred vestment of the high priest in the tower of Antonia and handed it over to the Jews only eight days before the Day of Atonement. No matter how many scrolls of law were seized or burned, the Jewish congregation continued to worship God in the prescribed fashion. The loss of synagogue buildings or sacred objects having become a matter of financial rather than intrinsically religious concern, the community became more immune to strictly religious intolerance than it was to political and economic antagonisms.

The relatively secondary position of the *house* of worship bred a certain indifference to synagogue architecture. In fact, some rabbis resented the diversion of substantial building funds from educational budgets. When R. Ḥama ben Ḥanina pointed out to R. Hoshaiah II a beautiful synagogue in Lydda in which his ancestors had sunk a lot of money, the latter exclaimed: "And how many souls did they sink here? Were there no men willing to study the Torah?" R. Abin, on similar grounds, reproached a friend for installing a beautiful gate in his large schoolhouse and applied to him the verse, "For Israel hath forgotten his Maker, and builded palaces" (Hos. 8:14; j. Pe'ah VIII, 9, 21b). Handicapped, moreover, by their aversion to plastic presentations, the Jews of Palestine developed no specific architectural style. The oldest synagogue ruins, unearthed there, including the more recent finds at Beth-

Alpha and Jerash, reveal little that is distinctly Jewish. The orientation must be toward Jerusalem, a custom indicated as far back as
Daniel and religiously observed for many a generation, even by
Judeo-Christians. That the style be Greek, Roman, Byzantine, or
perhaps no "style" at all, was much less important. That the Jews
refrain from imitating the Temple too closely, that the candlestick
be not of seven but of five, six or eight branches, as a memento of
bygone days—these points were of concern to the legislators. The
rabbis insisted upon the prohibition of sculptured images, but were
rather lenient in respect to all other arts, even the painting of
human figures. Excavations have revealed several mosaics in the
Galilean and other synagogues, including one in Sepphoris donated
by a rabbi. Apart from prohibited forms, Jewish and Gentile synagogue builders and decorators could indulge in any fashion of the
day or any personal mood, simply because it did not matter. These
were outward expressions of the synagogue, not the synagogue
(*keneset*) itself, which, as the *keneset Israel*, symbolized the whole
Jewish people and its creed.

For the same reason the synagogue building was used for all
imaginable communal purposes. Most of the time it served as a
schoolhouse, but it was also the center of all charitable activities.
The expenditures for cult and philanthropy were usually defrayed
from a common exchequer (B.B. 8b). Private citizens often announced there their charitable contributions, calling forth the
evangelist's caustic remark about the "hypocrites" who "sound a
trumpet" in synagogues and streets, "that they may have glory of
men" (Matt. 6:2). When a stranger came to town he was sometimes
invited to come to the synagogue, where the preacher instituted a
collection for him (Lev. r. XXXII, 6). Ordinarily asylums for the
homeless and the aged were connected with the synagogue. Such a
"hospice" (or "chambers") is recorded in the ancient synagogue
of Theodotos in Jerusalem. A stone inscribed "the guest house"
(*bet orhota*) was found even in the small community of Ramah between Safed and Acco (*Sefer ha-Yishub*, I, 153, n. 1). Since, as at
Greek temples, the whole synagogue square was considered sacred
property, the protective laws extended also to those and other out-
buildings.

Most importantly, the house of worship was also used as a place
of general assembly for the discussion of public affairs. Here the
courts often sat in judgment, heard witnesses, administered oaths,
issued sentences, and, if the latter consisted of flagellation or bans,

saw to it that they be solemnly executed on the premises. An aggrieved citizen was once told to "call together an assembly" there for the purpose of exposing his ingrate son, thus apparently laying the foundations for the medieval institution of "interrupting prayers" in order to seek redress for extralegal wrongs. Excessive familiarity, to be sure, could also breed disrespect. The rabbis tried to forestall profanation of houses of worship by declaring that "one must not behave light-heartedly in synagogues; one must not enter them in the summer to escape the sun, in the winter to escape the cold, in rainy days to escape the rain, nor must one eat, drink, or sleep in them, nor use them for pleasure walks or physical culture, but one may read, study and preach there, as well as hold funeral services of communal concern." That is perhaps also why they resented the populace calling the synagogue a "house of the people," notwithstanding the venerable preëxilic antecedents of this designation. In the second century, R. Ishmael ben Eleazar sharply denounced the 'ame ha-areṣ on this score. Nevertheless, conviviality was not completely banished. Apart from helping feed strangers in the synagogue premises, the administrators seem to have held there festive meetings, similar to the Greek synodoi, particularly on New Moon festivals. On one such occasion R. Johanan supposedly appeared the next day at the synagogue of Sepphoris, ate crumbs left behind by the celebrants, and expressed the hope that he might share also their celestial rewards. The rabbis seem even to have permitted the pagan custom, prevalent in the Hellenistic Diaspora, of liberating slaves at a public ceremony in the synagogue; an act of social significance was quite naturally performed in the social center of the community. In a word, the synagogue focalized in itself the whole communal life of Jewry, and thus became the culminating expression of Jewish autonomy.[58]

Cemeteries were for the most part separated from synagogues; their close proximity in Antioch under Emperor Zenon doubtless was quite exceptional. Equally exceptional were the graves of kings and that of the prophetess Ḥuldah located within the walls of Jerusalem itself. Rabbinic law formally demanded that graves be removed to a distance of at least 50 ells from the city. The necropolis in Alexandria was, in fact, at the other end of town from the main Jewish quarter. The Roman catacombs, too, were both physically and administratively completely separated from the houses of worship, as apparently were also the necropoles of Jaffa and Beth She'arim.[59]

Historically, this separation doubtless sprang from the conviction that burial of the dead was a family, rather than communal, responsibility. The family could use its discretion in burying the deceased on its own land or in any one of the numerous Palestinian caves which, like the Makhpelah in the days of Abraham, had been set aside as family graveyards. Caves containing ossuaries have indeed been detected in many parts of Palestine. Since rabbinic law insisted upon speedy burial—it was considered undignified and perhaps unhygienic to let corpses lie overnight—any nearby plot seemed preferable to long-distance transportation. R. 'Aqiba was once severely censured by his colleagues for having dragged an unidentifiable corpse (a *met miṣvah*) to a cemetery, rather than burying him on the spot (j. Nazir VII, 1, 56ab; Semaḥot IV, 19, 125). Babylonia's geological composition, on the other hand, led to the early formation of larger communal graveyards. In time, more self-assertive Babylonians living in Palestine began voicing doubts about the permissibility of burial in caves.

Nevertheless, the community exercised general supervision, as when it prevented graves from obstructing traffic. It regulated and applied the elaborate ceremonial connected with funerals, the bewailing and eulogizing of the deceased and the comforting of mourners. Students were allowed to interrupt their studies to take care of burials. On hearing that his son Simon was gravely ill, even in a coma, R. 'Aqiba refused to suspend his teaching. But when a messenger came announcing the son's death, the master immediately "took off his phylacteries and tore his vestments." Any passer-by was supposed to join in a funeral cortège and pay homage to a deceased, though unknown person. Smaller communities often were so closely knit that all members behaved like mourners and did not greet one another. R. Aḥa bar Ḥanina demanded that "one should not bury an evildoer next to a pious man, . . . nor a great sinner next to a mild transgressor." Public rites were reduced to a minimum in the case of suicides or condemned criminals, except such as were sentenced by Roman courts for political transgressions. Such offenders often were but martyrs for their faith and were buried with full honors. Apostates and informers were not to be mourned at all; "their brothers and relatives wear white attire, eat, drink and rejoice over the perdition of the Lord's enemies." [60]

The community also tried to reduce the differences between rich and poor in regard to shrouds, although it could not prevent the wealthy from building imposing mausolea. The Babylonian Talmud quotes in succession a number of tannaitic sources attesting to this protracted struggle:

At first they carried to the mortuary the corpses of the rich in vase-shaped baskets of silver or gold, while the poor were brought in wicker baskets of pealed willow twigs. Since poor families were thus put to shame, the leaders ordained that everybody be carried in wicker baskets in honor of the poor. . . . At first the rich mourners in the mortuary were served drinks in white glasses, while the poor drank from [less expensive] colored glasses. Since this custom put the poor to shame, the leaders ordained that everybody be served in colored glasses in honor of the poor. At first they carried the corpses of the rich with their faces uncovered, while the poor men's faces, blackened by prolonged starvation, were covered. Since the poor were thus put to shame, the leaders ordained that everybody be carried with his face covered in honor of the poor. . . . At first the burial of a deceased person was more burdensome for his relatives than his last illness, until some relatives left the corpses behind and ran away. Then Rabban Gamaliel, disregarding his own dignity, willed that he be buried in a simple linen shroud, whereupon the whole people began using linen shrouds.

To which the fourth-century Babylonian R. Papa added, "Today people use even a rough cloth worth one *zuz*." The rigid class distinctions before the fall of Jerusalem thus gave way to the increasingly egalitarian structure of the Jewish community, promoted by the consistently democratic rabbinic policies. In fact, these excesses, though common throughout the Graeco-Roman world, could hardly be indulged in by the scholarly leaders themselves. Hence came the aforementioned rationalization that scholars did not need tombstones, for their words alone secured them immortality. The post-funeral meals, mentioned in our source, very likely were an immemorial heritage from pre-Israelitic paganism. They now also had to be carefully regulated. In R. Gamaliel I's days the customary ten cups of wine were increased by three (or four), one each drunk in honor of the city servants, city elders, (the Temple), and R. Gamaliel himself. The latter allegedly thus received homage for his successful struggle against expensive funerals. However, "when they began to imbibe [freely] and get drunk, the old system was restored." [61]

In all these matters the community was assisted by voluntary societies, prepared to aid fellow members on sad as well as joyous occasions. Our information about these ancient Jewish associations is very scanty, but it appears that they largely resembled the various

Graeco-Roman *sodalitates.* Although legally not recognized as artificial personalities, possessing independent corporate property —even in Roman law such recognition of the *piae causae* still was in its infancy—they played a great role in the community's social relations. R. Eleazar ben R. Zadok mentioned specifically old Jerusalem *haburot* which, among other functions, attended to the "house of mourning," while R. Ishmael considered funeral services superior to all their other duties. We cannot tell whether such multiple societies as observed by R. Hamnuna in the small community of Darumata divided their burial services among their members by catering to specific groups in the population, as suggested by Rashi, or what seems more likely, performed their functions in periodic rotation. It seems, in any case, that, without going the whole length of services rendered by the medieval *hebrah qadisha,* these ancient societies participated in a subsidiary, but important, fashion at all funerals. The extent of their collaboration obviously depended on time, locality, and the greater or lesser abilities of the mourners themselves. This fact is also borne out by a Beth She'arim inscription, which apparently recorded the seating in the synagogue of two respectable citizens distinguished by their performance of specialized functions at burials.[62]

All funeral rites were permeated with the idea of the Hereafter. To begin with, the cemetery was given the characteristic name *bet 'almin,* or house of eternity. Although its equivalent was found also among many other Near Eastern and Western peoples, this designation, having its roots in Ecclesiastes and Tobit, was imbued in Judaism with deep eschatological yearnings. Even the evidently assimilated Roman Jew, who after a quarter century of marital bliss erected a tombstone for his Regina, waxed eloquent in his expectation that "again she will live, she will return to the light again. For she may hope to arise for the age which has been promised—and this fate is true—to the worthy and the pious; she who hath deserved to have a place in that blessed abode." After the decay of their bodies even bones of executed criminals were preserved in graves in preparation for the day when the trumpets would call all the dead to arise. Collecting bones for these and other reasons is mentioned as one of the specific functions of the confraternities, and is attested today by the numerous ancient ossuaries. Since the sacred soil of Palestine held out the promise of immediate resurrection at the end of days, pious Jews from all over the world, including some exilarchs, made arrangements to be buried there. Of R.

Gamaliel II we are told that he had a temporary burial ground in Yabneh from which, after the completion of the usual rites, the corpse was transferred to Jerusalem for permanent rest.[63]

These difficulties were overshadowed by environmental complications in areas where burial was not generally practiced. Rome had long observed the custom of cremating bodies, and the new practice of burial may well have been promoted by oriental, particularly Jewish, influences. In Persia, however, the Parsees saw in the burying of corpses a defilement of the earth. Jews must have had a hard struggle in persuading the Sassanian authorities that their religion unequivocally required burial. On one occasion, we are told, King Shapur asked for scriptural proof of such requirement. He caused considerable embarrassment not only to his rabbinic interlocutor R. Ḥama, but also to later sages who had to admit the difference between an outright biblical commandment and mere records of an existing custom (Sanhedrin 46b). Jews also faced the hostility among zealous Parsee individuals, who at times resorted to forcible desecration of Jewish graves (Yebamot 63b). Nevertheless, considering it an essential part of their religion and familial piety they persisted and thus preserved another significant facet of their ethnic-religious self-determination.

ALL-EMBRACING COMMUNITY

Repulsed by the outside world, the Jewish people turned more and more inward. Not only did the average citizens (like their kind everywhere) attend to their daily chores, try to earn a living, habitually observe the law, and, at most, complain of fiscal and legislative pressures without being too deeply concerned about ideological implications, but this was essentially also the attitude of their intellectual spokesmen in Palestine and Babylonia. These leaders realized more clearly, however, than the masses that the traditional moorings of the Jewish community needed considerable strengthening now that the Temple lay in ashes and the territorial basis in the Holy Land was growing weaker and weaker.

As during the First Exile, there was a new accentuation of the ethnic-religious, rather than the territorial principle. It was too late in history, of course, to try to resuscitate the ancient clans. But one could undertake the reconstruction of the people's life by a new emphasis upon its family and communal structure. The sexual instinct was now placed under the strict control of each individual and the community at large. It was to serve principally the aim of raising good, law-abiding, and God-fearing children. The continuation of the aforementioned injunction to love and honor one's wife sounded a typical refrain of rabbinic homiletics. "He who guides," it stated, "his sons and daughters on the way of righteousness and marries them off soon after they reach maturity, of him it is written, 'And thou shalt know that thy tent is in peace.' " (Job 5:24; Yebamot 62b). Naturally, the children would in their turn raise offspring, train them properly and ultimately marry them off, so that the name of Israel would be perpetuated. For this reason any important deviation in laws governing marriage and divorce, which threatened to engulf the Jewish family in growing chaos, immediately stamped the deviating group as a sectarian movement to be peremptorily banished from the fold.

Family cohesiveness must not militate, however, against the broader loyalties to one's local community and the people as a whole. The entire domain of human life was to be conducted under the sanctions of the Law and was largely determined by the common weal. Not only were one's economic appetites to be curbed in behalf of the ethical golden mean, but even one's perfectly legitimate rights, arising, for example, from full-fledged legal ownership of an object, often had to be sacrificed to the welfare of the community. On the other hand, the community as such assumed full responsibility for its individual members, protecting their mutual interests, regulating the conditions of work, supervising prices, wages, and measures, and extending effective support to the sick and the needy. Fostered by the external developments toward a regimented economy and growing anti-Jewish discrimination, Jewish economic solidarity immensely strengthened the communal bonds.

These were further enhanced by the strong, and yet widely accepted, leadership of the rabbinic group, working hand in hand with the patriarchs and exilarchs, so long as these officials enjoyed the support of the imperial governments of Rome or Persia; or without them when the circumstances demanded it. Indoctrinated from early youth in the rabbinic ideals by a highly effective system of child and adult education, the people readily submitted to this guidance. Law enforcement was relatively easy, therefore, and could be secured by a small lay and professional judiciary with the application of a minimum of force. In the synagogue, finally, the community had a living center for all its public life, both religious and secular—if such a distinction meant anything to a Jew of that period—around which was focalized most of its life and thinking.

If the Jewish intelligentsia in other Roman provinces thought differently, it either found its way out of orthodox Judaism into one of the numerous fringe movements, or else kept silent and closed its ranks behind its rabbinic leaders in the Jordan and Euphrates valleys. Departing from Jewish orthodoxy now appeared even to many Diaspora Jews as outright apostasy. Religious syncretism, to be sure, had created so many intermediary movements, especially between Judaism and Christianity, that transition from the highway of orthodoxy to one of these by-paths was easy and often unconscious. In time, however, all such compromises were eschewed under the impact of the Palestino-Babylonian teachings. The syncretistic trends were now relegated to the fringe of Christian and pagan "heresies," while Judaism emerged, religiously as well as socially, a single, homogeneous and well-integrated faith.

TALMUDIC LAW AND RELIGION

R ABBINIC Judaism itself became so deeply concerned about the internal, rather than external, facets of Jewish life that, were one to eliminate from the talmudic literature all direct references to Romans and Persians, to Christians, Zoroastrians, and pagans, its size would be reduced but slightly. Most of these references, moreover, are to be found in the realm of Aggadah, that vast and uncontrolled domain of popular homiletics and folklore, whereas the more authoritative Halakhah rarely took overt cognizance of the non-Jewish environment. Behind these partly fictitious ramparts, erected by studiously ignoring the hostile outside forces, the talmudic sages tried to cultivate and develop their religious heritage in its various ramifications along its self-defined, by now well-trodden paths.

Appearances are often misleading, of course. Many students of talmudic Judaism, including some fine, critically trained, modern historians, were misled by them to treat of the talmudic evolution as if it had taken place in a complete vacuum. Only more recently has Jewish historical scholarship been able partially to overcome the shackles of this "isolationist" outlook. Much is yet to be done before the more hidden strains of social, cultural, and even religious interrelations with the outside world will be fully uncovered. As in the still more self-sufficient medieval ghetto, the influence of those external forces could more readily be ignored than decreed out of existence. We have already seen how many rabbinic teachings of the period can be understood only as responses, however oblique, to the prevailing climate of opinion.

Even these new teachings, however, were wholly in line with older traditions. They represented expansion, elaboration, and partial adjustment of doctrines which, even if previously unformulated, had been inherent in the world outlook of Pharisaic Judaism. It is this very process of constant elaboration and adjustment to meet life's ever-changing demands, which accounts for much of the vigor, richness, and charm of talmudic lore.

TALMUDIC LITERATURE

Out of the variegated patterns of the autonomous life of Palestinian and Babylonian Jewry, with its multiplicity of social and religious institutions, evolved that grandiose monument of ancient Judaism, the Talmud. Ranking almost as high as the Bible, claiming to represent, in its essentials, another form of revelation, the Oral Law, it influenced the subsequent history of the Jewish people perhaps even more than the Scriptures themselves.

The Talmud is not a book; it is a whole literature, the hoarded intellectual labor of centuries. If we restrict it to the Mishnah and the Palestinian and Babylonian Talmudim, it covers a period of at least half a millennium, but with its time-honored traditions, it embraces an even longer period. Together with the halakhic and aggadic Midrashim and the Tosefta, it is a prodigious depository of Jewish speculation and experience in Palestine and Babylonia. Reflecting the fullness of life, it necessarily contains as many contradictions, and he who seeks can find in it whatsoever he wishes. The Talmud has not only been a fecund source of inspiration for Jews through almost two millennia, but it has supplied weapons for enemies as well as for apologists. As a matter of fact, the logical categories employed by the talmudic thinkers, their outlook on life and the conditions of their age, differ from modern conceptions so deeply that much therein must appear incongruous and almost absurd to an outsider. Only one who has spent a lifetime exploring the Talmud, whose mind has been gradually molded to think in talmudic idiom, whose associations, even unconsciously, are those of a talmudic thinker, only such a one is qualified to lift statements from the Talmud with impunity, confident that he understands their true meaning with all its implications within the body of the whole.

Most obvious are the difficulties of dating. Even the Mishnah, the fountainhead of the entire talmudic literature, is not only a collection of sayings first formulated in various generations, but has itself been worked over many times before it reached its present form under the editorship of Judah I. Important variants between an earlier and a later recension by R. Judah himself, evidently shown in the conflicting traditions of the two Talmudim, have further complicated the task of isolating individual ingredients. On the one hand, there is R. Johanan's contention that "many laws had been told to Moses on Sinai, and all of them are intermingled in the Mishnah." We may, indeed, assume that the latter contains some traditions of immemorial antiquity. On the other hand, modern scholarship is in general agreement as to the fact, already intimated by Sherira Gaon in the tenth century, "that not only has a considerable part of the material of 'our Mishnah' been taken over from similar collections of the earlier Tannaim, but that also the structure, method and plan of Rabbi's [Judah's] compilation were in their main features fixed long before his time." The task of more precise dating is also aggravated by the existence of the great number of tannaitic sources both in the Tosefta and the two Talmudim which may date from the period *after* Judah I. The Talmud abounds with phrases like: Rab or R. Johanan "is a Tanna and may controvert" other tannaitic views. Not only have individual "tannaitic" statements been ascribed to R. Joshua ben Levi and other Amoraim, but even when the apparently obvious phrase *tana* occurs in the Talmud, it does not necessarily introduce a real tannaitic quotation. Moreover, even statements specifically attributed to a particular Tanna (or later an Amora) may not be original with him, but merely be quoted by him verbatim from his teachers. Much is yet to be done before the gargantuan task of unraveling the various strains in the Mishnah and other rabbinic writings, already tackled by many competent researchers during several generations, will be brought to a more or less satisfactory conclusion.[1]

Chronological and other difficulties beset with equal tenacity the student plunging into the "sea" of the two Talmudim and of the various midrashic collections. For a long time rabbinic scholars were wont to give preference to the Babylonian over the Palestinian Talmud, repeating a rationalization current among some geonim. "We rely on our *gemara*," said R. Isaac Alfasi in the early eleventh century, "because it is the later one. They [the Babylonian sages] knew better the western [Palestinian] *gemara* than we do, and unless they were certain that one was not to rely on a particular western statement, they would not have taken the liberty of deviating from it" (on 'Erubin end).

This rationalization was long supported in modern scholarship by the assumption that the Palestinian Talmud had been left unfinished under the impact of Roman persecutions during the fourth century, whereas the Babylonian Talmud had gone through several stages of careful revision since the days of R. Ashi (about 400). In recent years, however, scholarly opinion has veered away from this oversimplification. Not only have large-scale Roman persecutions in the mid-fourth century been seriously questioned, but the Babylonian Talmud itself has been shown, under critical scrutiny, to have been far less "finished" than it had long appeared to be. Even the attempt to relate the basic talmudic statement (B.M. 36a), "R. Ashi and Rabina mark the end of talmudic teaching [*hora'ah*]," to later, less renowned Amoraim who died in 476 and 509, respectively, failed to explain the mounting objections. Sociologically, too, the Zionist movement and the rise of Israel have created a deep interest in the *Yerushalmi*, as the most comprehensive source book for Palestinian Jewish life in the third and fourth centuries. For these reasons our generation has evinced ever greater appreciation of the Palestinian Talmud as the more genuine repository of ancient traditions in their unbroken continuity.[2]

Historical investigation of the vast midrashic literature, though studded with some magnificent achievements from the days of Zunz, still shows gaping lacunae. Since even such late medieval compilations as the *Yalqut Shime'oni* and the *Midrash Hagadol* include many indubitably genuine sayings of ancient sages no longer extant in any of our older collections, the difficulties of separating the wheat from the chaff are naturally enormous. Doubly so, if one wishes to ascertain the exact phrasing of the original statement, which even in antiquity may have undergone more than one alteration. Furthermore, by careful analysis of the underlying sources even the writings of such an ardent anti-Jewish controversialist as the Spaniard Raymond Martini have been shown to contain some real gems of ancient rabbinic learning, otherwise completely buried under the debris of ages. Nor is it enough to make sure that such and such a collection of sayings attributed to an ancient authority is apocryphal. For example, no critical scholars will venture today to uphold the authenticity of an overt apocryphon like the *Pirqe de-Rabbi Eliezer*, allegedly stemming from R. Eliezer ben Hyrcanus. But it still makes a great deal of difference whether we ascribe its compilation to the talmudic age and merely admit some later accretions, or consider the whole work, as is more likely, as being of early Muslin origin.[3]

Because of these staggering difficulties in dating, many scholars have been tempted to use indiscriminately tannaitic materials, particularly if handed down anonymously, as more or less dependable sources of information concerning views held by early sages, including pre-Christian leaders of the Pharisaic sect. This is of course a dubious, if not always avoidable, assumption. It is, therefore, with considerable misgivings that, even in our broad analysis of major socioreligious trends during the first five centuries, we had to have frequent recourse to "rabbinic teachings" in general, rather than to specific, chronologically fixed sayings by individual sages. Wherever possible we have attempted to avoid this "geological" treatment, against which Steinschneider has protested with much justification. But since the ancient compilers themselves were far more interested in the truth of a particular statement and its importance for law and morals rather than in its authorship, we shall probably never be able to ascertain the exact chronological setting of a great many talmudic sayings.

In considering the possible antiquity of a particular apothegm one must beware especially of using modern categories of thinking as an exclusive criterion. Far from being "prelogical," as other ancient oriental modes of thought are often styled in contrast to Greek logic, the talmudic categories have a logic of their own. Unconsciously pursued by talmudic students during the last fifteen centuries, these peculiar categories have been subjected to careful scrutiny from the standpoint of Western logic, though not always with complete nonapologetic detachment.[4]

As in many other areas of modern critical research, the relatively greatest progress has been made with the preparation of good editions of many rabbinic texts and with purely linguistic studies. To be sure, largely as a result of medieval Christendom's condemnation of the Talmud as an anti-Christian work and the ensuing wholesale destruction of the then extant copies, no reliable ancient texts have come down to us.[5] We consider ourselves fortunate in possessing a few twelfth to fourteenth century manuscripts of entire tractates of the Babylonian Talmud. Both the famous Munich manuscript of that Talmud (published in facsimile by H. L. Strack) and the Leiden manuscript of its Palestinian counterpart were completed in 1343 and 1289, respectively, and hence are some seven to twelve centuries posterior to most sayings recorded in them. Even the Cairo Genizah has not been too liberal in yielding substantial early transcripts of that literature, most fragments dating half a millennium or more after the compilation of either Talmud. Nevertheless by utilizing all of these extant manuscript resources and tirelessly comparing the variant readings found not only in the different parts of that literature, but also in the quotations given by early posttalmudic authors, the last two generations of scholars have brought out much-improved workable texts of many tannaitic and midrashic writings.[6]

SUPREMACY OF LAW

The Talmud is primarily *law*. This truism needs special emphasis, in view of tendencies in recent generations to elevate the aggadic or legendary part of it to a position of prominence which it certainly does not deserve in the perspective of talmudic doctrine. To the Talmudist, law really mattered, while the *Aggadah* represented an accession of often irresponsible, private and uncontrolled tales and opinions which, even if incorporated in the Talmud or Midrash, did not by any means become representative of the whole of Judaism. Even the reiterated saying, "One must not question an Aggadah" merely intended to convey the idea of the latter's irrationality, not of its indisputable authority.

Not that the interest in the Aggadah of modern scholars and laymen alike is without profound historic justification. Certainly the historian of ancient Judaism and of its linguistic, literary or social manifestations, will often find in the Aggadah more vital information than in the more restricted field of Law. To a secularized and frequently nonobservant generation the subtle dialectics of ancient rabbis concerning legal minutiae appear the more remote and inconsequential because they are clad in the form of debates so succinctly summarized that they require great ingenuity and concentration on the part of the reader. The non-Jewish student, on the other hand, even if he succeeds in completely overcoming his antinomian bias, is naturally more attracted to the world outlook, the ethics, the popular science and general folklore reflected in the Aggadah, than to the more technical areas of Jewish law. Viewed from the inside, however, of what really mattered to the compilers of these tomes themselves and their more serious students, the Aggadah decidedly was but a handmaid of the Halakhah —an important, even indispensable handmaid, but no more.[7]

Law's preëminence at the time also had its profound justification. Reacting tacitly to tendencies of Hellenistic Jews and of Paul in particular, talmudic Judaism insisted upon the rigid application of traditional law as the paramount national principle. Christianity claimed that the Law had been abrogated by the advent of the Messiah, that the Jewish nationality had died to give birth to the new universal religion. All the more did the Jewish people withdraw under "the yoke of the law," whose burden they did not regard as too heavy. Augustine himself could not refrain from admiringly, although resentfully, remarking,

The Jews, although vanquished by the Romans, have not been destroyed. All the nations subjugated by the Romans adopted the laws of the Romans; this nation has been vanquished and, nevertheless, retained its law and, inasmuch as it pertains to the worship of God, has preserved the ancestral customs and ritual [*Sermo,* 374, 2; *PL,* XXXIX, 1667].

This was, if anything, an understatement. The Jews retained their own customs and usages not only in religious and ceremonial matters. Even in purely secular and economic questions, the Talmud reveals amazing independence from both Roman and Sassanian law. Our information about the legal system of the Sassanian Empire may be too scanty to enable us to draw definite conclusions as to the influence of Persian law, but the Talmud itself, apart from making the evidently successful claim to exclusive validity, occasionally speaks slightingly of Persian legal doctrines and observances. The interesting antitheses drawn by several Babylonian Amoraim between Persian and Jewish law reveal an astonishing feeling of superiority. True, Frankel thought that he had discovered traces of Persian influence, but he could adduce only a few instances, all of legal procedure. The general unfamiliarity of Babylonian Jewish judges with the Persian language and institutions was amazing. They acknowledged proofs supported by Persian documents, but often had to employ Gentile interpreters.[8]

What is more astonishing, even Roman law appears to have been of small consequence in the evolution of the Halakhah. Despite more than a millennium of persistent scholarship and interpretation of all problems connected with Roman law and despite the fact that the specific question of the relation between Roman and talmudic law has engaged the attention of prominent jurists for three centuries, few indications of direct influence have been found. Jewish Halakhah was already well developed by the third century, the period of greatest achievement in Roman law. The conclusion of the Mishnah coincided with the period of the most intensive progress in the great controversies between the schools of Labeo and Capito. It appears that both the Roman and the Jewish systems were influenced by a common source, rather than by each other.

Since Mitteis and his followers have clarified so much of the accumulated mass of legal material of the Hellenistic East, we can pursue lines of development in both directions in the Roman *ius gentium* and in the Jewish Halakhah—with much more prospect of success. It has been pointed out that of the 62 legal terms (barring duplication) found among the Graeco-Roman loan words in the Talmud, fifty-eight are Greek, and only four Latin. These four are connected with the Roman court and its procedure, which were naturally of importance throughout the empire. The Greek terms, on the other hand, are used for most institutions in civil law pertaining to such higher economic activities as commerce and banking. This list, originally compiled by S. Krauss in 1899, has since been expanded, especially by S. Lieberman's ingenious detection and explanation of hidden allusions to popular practices. Here, too, the vast preponderance of Greek terms is unmistakable. There is no way of telling, to be sure, how many Latin terms, originally mentioned in Palestinian sources, were later dropped, replaced by more familiar Aramaic or even Greek words, or corrupted beyond recognition. Latin never was an important medium of communication in the Eastern provinces, outside the small circles of officials and the colonies of Roman veterans. After the division of the empire into an Eastern and a Western part and the transfer of the imperial capital to Constantinople, it practically disappeared from the daily life of the Eastern lands. Latin terms, therefore, even if originally adopted by Palestinian sages in the second or third century, now became meaningless to the compilers of the Talmud or midrashim and were readily replaced. Nevertheless, the paucity of reliable terminological borrowings from the highly developed Roman jurisprudence indicates little direct influence.[9]

Indirectly, however, such influence seems to have been quite considerable. While leaving most subject populations in the full enjoyment of their local laws, Roman administrators had a natural interest in acquainting themselves with the provisions of those laws, which they were at times called upon to help enforce. The need of the Roman officials to find their way through the maze of complicated and often controversial regulations stimulated the process of their codification in handy manuals which, at least with the aid of interpreters, could be readily consulted. We know that, owing to Roman initiative, both the native Egyptian laws and those of the Greek citizens in Egypt, the so-called *Astoi*, were codified in the course of the second century. That the Romans also evinced considerable interest in Jewish law at that time is shown by the reports of the two Romans who studied under R. Gamaliel II and allegedly expressed full satisfaction with the whole system of Jewish law, except its discriminatory provisions against Gentiles. It is quite possible that Roman curiosity thus added stimulus to the rabbinic efforts, in themselves prompted through the growing complexity of legal traditions, to review and reorganize the entire body of Jewish law along systematic lines. Hence, that great second-century creativity which led to the codification of Mishnah, Tosefta, and the halakhic midrashim.[10]

The ancient sources themselves are rather inarticulate with respect to this, as to most other aspects of intercultural relations. When within a century after the victory of Christianity the respective merits of ancient Jewish and Roman law became the subject of public controversy, they were debated from theological, rather than strictly juristic, angles. The *Collectio legum Mosaicarum et Romanarum*, whether written by a Christian or, what seems more likely, by a Jew, pursued not only overtly apologetic purposes, but was principally designed to persuade the Roman public of the priority and, in some respects, also superiority of the divinely instituted Mosaic law over any human law, even as close to perfection as that of the Romans.[11]

Once Jewish law had become definitely formulated in the age of the Tannaim, the pressure even of Roman law was felt only on the surface. Sassanian law was faced by a still more definitely organized body of Jewish jurisprudence, capable of resisting any outside influence. If by virtue of their royal appointment, the exilarchs seem at times to have adjudicated cases in accordance with Persian legislation (B.Q. 58b), the rabbis, as is evident from that very source, staunchly resisted the incursion of such foreign elements into their civil law. Occasionally a sage like R. Safra, a native Babylonian living in Palestine at the end of the third century, tried to draw at least a comparison between Jewish and non-Jewish law. But his rule contrasting the collectibility of debts under non-Jewish and Jewish law, respectively, was punched full of holes in the subsequent discussion, in which Palestinians and Babylonians indiscriminately referred to "their laws," as if there existed no differences at all between the legal systems of the two empires or their individual provinces (B.M. 62ab). Even where there is resemblance, real or apparent, it need not reflect mutual influence. Certainly the underlying socio-economic trends unfolding in the Western world doubtless led to similar regulations, however independently enacted by Jewish, Roman, or Sassanian authorities.

Some of the legal differences between the two Talmudim may actually be traced either to the persistence of local customs or to different social needs. If, for example, the Palestinian authorities, to meet the requirements of an expanding semicapitalist economy, tried to facilitate transactions in deeds and commercial papers, a progressive jurist like Mar Samuel, confronted with far more feudal conditions in Babylonia, practically eliminated all transfers of bills of exchange by teaching that, "if one sells a deed of indebtedness to his friend and subsequently foregoes his claim, the claim is forfeited. Even an heir can thus forego his [inherited] claim." The relationship between lender and borrower remained indissolubly personal, the former merely being obliged to compensate the purchaser of the deed for the ensuing loss. On the other hand, when the expanding Persian economy required greater facilities for credit transactions, Babylonian rabbis of the following century legalized those semifictitious "antichretic" sales, which allowed the parties legally to evade the prohibition of usury. In neither case, however, can these rabbinic teachings be traced back, with any confidence, to the impact of Sassanian law.[12]

More complicated is the problem of Jewish indebtedness to earlier Hellenistic laws. In itself very likely, it can be documented only in those relatively rare instances when the rabbis use a Greek term like *prosbol*. Even then, we recall, there is a considerable difference between the Greek and the Jewish institution, so designated. A. Gulak, to be sure, has shown that many formulas recorded in talmudic deeds closely paralleled those found in Egyptian papyri. He drew therefrom the conclusion that these and many other legal forms, hitherto ascribed by modern scholars to the period after the fall of Jerusalem, are in fact much older and may date back to Maccabean times or earlier. This argument is not altogether conclusive. Considering the religious conservatism of both the Sadducean and Pharisaic leadership, as well as the tenacity of legal customs, there must have been a considerable time lag between the evolution of certain Graeco-Egyptian patterns and their adoption by Jewish courts in Alexandria. A much longer period was doubtless required for their penetration, if such it was, possibly through Alexandrian-Jewish channels, into the legal structure of Palestine. Like most ancient jurists the rabbis evinced great reverence for existing customs and changed them with much caution and only in response to imperative needs. Even some of the customs repudiated or modified by them long continued to operate underground, to be revived much later by some sectarian groups. In other words, a legal institution attested, for example, by a papyrus of the second century B.C.E. may not have penetrated talmudic law until two or three centuries later and, even then, only in response to some imperative local need. Once such need existed, independent origin is just as possible as is any important modification in a borrowed pattern.[13]

Conversely, it is difficult to ascertain to what extent Jewish law influenced the other legal systems current under Rome and Persia. "We find Romans," observed R. Taubenschlag, "performing legal transactions hitherto peculiar to Hellenistic law alone. . . . And even when Romans transact business according to Roman law and use Roman forms the latter show Hellenistic influence" (*Law*, I, 36). Some such influence of Jewish legal concepts on Roman law, especially through the medium of Judeo-Christian jurists and their new outlook on life, is not altogether unlikely. Reference has already been made to the possible nexus between the Jewish law of "misrepresentation" and the overcharge in the *Code of Justinian*. Jewish legal concepts and practices may have affected particularly the evolution of the Syro-Christian laws and from there percolated into the imperial *ius gentium*.

By way of illustration we may cite here the changing regulations concerning the creditor's seizure of a debtor's property. In ancient Israel, we recall, as in most other ancient countries, an insolvent debtor was enslaved, often together with his family, until he worked off his debt or until the expiration of his six-year term. Such personal and family responsibility became repugnant to the basically individualistic postexilic society. Responding therefore to this profoundly felt social and ethical need, Jewish scribes some time during the Second Commonwealth replaced personal responsibility by the general "liability of one's real property" (*aḥrayut nekhasim*). They may have been encouraged in this respect by Hellenistic patterns, since mortgages of one's whole property (*omnium bonorum*) are occasionally recorded in Ptolemaic Egypt. At least the term *hypotheke*, used in the Talmud, was obviously borrowed from the Greek. The rabbis, however, went further. To insure, particularly, the collection of a widow's dowry and marriage settlement from her husband's estate, rabbinic law granted priority to her claims over all other civil obligations. It was only one logical step farther to the treatment of all creditors according to the chronological sequence of their claims. The rabbis also provided that a mortgage deed duly signed by two witnesses established a lien on the property, despite any later change of ownership, and that the widow's rights were fully safeguarded, despite a scribe's failure to insert the necessary protective clause into the marriage contract. If we find, therefore, in a fifth-century Syro-Christian lawbook the distribution of assets to creditors according to their chronological priority, rather than *pro rata;* if in 472, Emperor Leo introduced into Roman law the recognition of mortgage deeds signed by three witnesses; if in 530, Justinian extended to widows protection against scribal errors with a motivation paralleling that of the Talmud; and if generally in fifth and sixth-century Byzantium the mortgaging of all property became truly widespread—all these legal changes point to the adoption of Jewish provisions found more suitable to existing needs. On the other hand, if these needs were sufficiently urgent, they probably would have evolved parallel answers, even if no Jewish models had been available for ready borrowing.[14]

Not even in commerce, which now assumed new importance, did the Jewish leaders find it necessary to deviate from any essentials of their traditional law. This fact is doubly remarkable, as earlier laws had been entirely geared to an agricultural economy and as, with their usual conservatism, the rabbis maintained the original framework even in the later more mercantile society. In their anxiety, for example, to keep out any "usurious" gains from business transactions—a residuum of the older, more primitive economy— they reduced the penalty for breach of contract to the payment for losses actually sustained, but not for gains which might demonstrably have been realized (*lucrum*). In breaches of labor contracts the penalties were further minimized in favor of workers, thereby to underscore the difference between free and unfree labor, and later, for the sake of equality, also for the benefit of employers.

Such ethically determined doctrines could be sustained only because of the absence of a special commercial law in all ancient legal systems. Like Hellenistic, Roman, and Persian law, Jewish law was based on the principle of equity. It could thus easily apply civil regulations to that branch of civil relations encompassed by modern commercial codes. At the same time, the absence of large mercantile corporations—the Roman *societas* and the talmudic *shutefut* consisted of a definite, usually small number of partners—made superfluous any special corporation law. In extreme cases the rabbis, like other legislators and judges, could take recourse to that ultimate expedient, the legal fiction (as in the case of the *prosbol*) to bridge the gap between the dominant legal theory and new economic or social wants.[15]

Independence of Jewish civil law from the dominant legal systems in both empires was enhanced by the complete autonomy of Jewish legislation in such domains as marriage and religious observances in synagogue and at home, frequently affecting also ordinary civil relations. The essence of talmudic jurisprudence was that, to a degree surpassing even that of all other ancient religious law, it encompassed the whole of life. It regulated almost every detail of daily routine, as well as all extraordinary occasions. Law-consciousness pervaded the performance of such simple functions as eating breakfast. The prescribed washings before and after meals, the numerous benedictions, often amounting to whole prayers, converted each meal into a kind of religious function. R. Johanan and R. Simon ben Laqish, otherwise sturdy opponents, were in full agreement that "as long as the Temple existed the altar atoned for man, today man's table atones for him" (Ḥagigah 27a).

Talmudic law is, however, not dominated by pure ritualism. In fact, much more attention seems to be paid to social and economic than to purely ritualistic theory and practice. As is well known, the Babylonian Gemara does not comment on all six divisions of Mishnah. Characteristically enough, the sections omitted in the first and last divisions discuss mainly problems of agricultural law and of purity and impurity, all of comparatively little significance in the life of the Diaspora; whereas the Palestinian Talmud interprets the laws of the first division as extensively as all the others. Of a total of 2,920 folio pages of unequal length in the Babylonian Talmud, almost one-half (1,302) belong to the two divisions primarily devoted to civil and marriage laws. More than a quarter (785) are assigned to benedictions and the observance of holidays in synagogue and home. That a large space is also apportioned to discussions of the laws of sacrifices and of the Temple reveals the tenacity with which Judaism clung to the hope of immediate restoration, as well as the glorification of the Temple subsequent to its destruction, reminiscent of the First Exile. With the passage of time, however, these discussions lost their direct appeal to students of the Talmud, who continued to investigate them for underlying legal principles rather than for their own sake.

In other words, the laws concerning economic, family, and communal life, to which brief reference has been made in the preceding chapter, constitute the bulk and core of the Babylonian Halakhah. This is not merely a statistical coincidence. It is part of the this-worldly orientation of Judaism, and its ambitious attempt to link to the infinite each step in man's life.[16]

This wide scope of the Halakhah necessitated a many-sided education for rabbis. Of course, their training in natural sciences could not compare with that available in the heyday of the schools of Alexandria. The Jewish people was too poor and harassed to erect large well-equipped academies on the Alexandrian model. The rabbis were, as a rule, men of moderate means, too busy earning a living to devote much time or money to scientific experiment. The generally abstract and speculative character of talmudic studies also militated against full-fledged empiricism. There arose, however, certain strictly legal questions, in conjunction with the computation of the calendar, the laws governing the life of menstruating and child-bearing women and the ritual slaughtering of animals, which forced upon the Jewish leaders astronomical, mathematical, medical, and other scientific studies. W. M. Feldman is undoubtedly right in saying that "whilst the Greeks studied mathematics for its own sake and felt a strong craving to speculate and discover new mathematical facts, the ancient Jews do not appear to have taken any interest in the development of mathematical theory, and were satisfied with applying, with a variable amount of skill, what simple mathematical tools they possessed to the various practical problems with which they had to deal." The same may be said about medicine, geography, and other sciences.[17]

Even such fantastic Sindbad-like tales, however, as told by Rabbah bar bar Ḥana reveal a certain newly awakened scientific and historical curiosity. Some rationalistically minded rabbis may have frowned upon these incongruous tales and exclaimed, "All Rabbahs are asses and all Bar bar Ḥanas are fools." Later generations may have treated them seriously, with light amusement or with overt disdain. They nevertheless reflect the widespread popular curiosity about those distant lands of the East and West or about the Arabian desert, from all of which travelers and sailors reported strange, often equally incredible, tales. They certainly reveal both the widening of the geographic horizon and a certain newly awakened romantic longing for the glorious days of the biblical past.[18]

While talmudic medicine does not compare with that of Hippocrates and Galen, it goes much beyond simple folkloristic, popular medicine, and occasionally reveals a certain familiarity with the achievements of Hellenistic physicians. In mathematics and astronomy, the talmudic age seems to have produced a work of unusual significance. The so-called *Mishnat ha-Middot* (the Mishnah of the Measures), apparently composed by Rabbi Nehemiah about 150, has many an original approach to mathematical problems and, through Al-Khwarizmi, seems to have exercised great influence on Arabian and indirectly on European mathematical science. Mar Samuel, a leading rabbi and judge of Nehardea, combined especially well Jewish knowledge and the old traditions of Babylonian science. Without appearing ridiculous, he could declare, "Except for comets, I am as familiar with the celestial paths as with those of Nehardea." Indeed, he sent to the Palestinian R. Johanan an astronomic computation of the Jewish calendar for sixty years in advance, refraining from making it public only so as not to interfere with the prerogatives of the patriarch. In the great line running from Kidenas to Diophantus, Jewish astronomy seems to have contributed an element to the great synthesis of oriental and Greek science. How close Jewish scholars were to the pulse of their time is seen again in Mar Samuel, who derived much information about medical subjects from Western travelers and merchants. At the same time this crossroad of caravan routes must have received many stimuli from India and, possibly, China. But it was not science, as such, that interested the rabbis. Apart from its practical value, such as healing the sick, pure science was at best the "handmaid of theology" or rather of Jewish law.[19]

EQUALITY OF RITUAL AND MORAL LAW

Since the days of early Christianity the legalism of the Jewish religion has often been denounced. But whatever the practical abuses, in theory the principle of equality between ritual and moral law was by no means detrimental to the latter. Both were made intrinsic parts of a religious system whose primary concern was human action. On this point Judaism somewhat resembled all other thisworldly creeds of antiquity. But while the Greek and Roman religions were prone to overlook the element of creed, once actions were performed as prescribed, Judaism laid great stress upon the intention (*kavvanah*) behind each action. At the same time, the rabbis decided after lengthy discussion that absence of intention did not invalidate the action and preached that "not theoretical belief is what really matters but actual deeds" (*lo ha-midrash 'iqqar ela ha-ma 'aseh*). And even above the spontaneous good deed was placed the deed performed in fulfillment of an existing commandment.

Commandment (miṣvah) actually became also the equivalent of a good deed as such, not only cutting across the Roman distinction between the divinely ordained ritualistic regulation (the fas) and man-made law governing social relations (the lex), but blurring the very distinction between law and ethics. Not that the rabbis were wholly unaware of the practical advantages of such a distinction. In a remarkable decision concerning an administrative conflict between two contestants R. Joseph assigned to one the "affairs related to Heaven," while the other, an unlearned descendant of a proselyte, was placed in charge of the "affairs of the city" (Qiddushin 76b). Theoretically, however, there was no difference between the various categories of commandments, and Jews were frequently told that they must observe a "light" commandment with equal care and precision as the most "severe" regulation.

In fact, to make sure that the distinction between a "biblical" and a rabbinically enacted provision, which had important bearing on doubtful cases, would not lead to neglect of the latter, Raba, with the customary rabbinic overemphasis, insisted on paraphrasing Ecclesiastes, "My son, be admonished to observe the words of the scribes more strictly than the words of the Torah, for the latter includes positive and negative commandments [with their diverse sanctions] but he who transgresses the words of the scribes is liable to capital punishment." Their task was facilitated, however, by the public's willing response. So anxious were many pious persons to perform a legally enjoined positive commandment that the rabbis had to discourage interlopers from anticipating a good deed, thereby depriving its legitimate performer of the opportunity of adding it to his own record. Modern criticisms of the excessive "yoke" of the law would have appeared incomprehensible to a Jew of olden times, who was rather inclined to believe, with R. Ḥananiah ben 'Aqashia, that "God wished to bestow a favor on Israel and hence endowed it with so many laws and commandments." [20]

From this general attitude came the elevation of the idea of repentance, teshubah, to a supreme position in Jewish theology, until, second only to the Torah, it finally appears among the things preëxistent. The Pharisees had insisted upon this moral element, in addition to the actual performance of a rite. Building upon the foundations of the Priestly Code, which had spiritualized many sacrifices by making of them ceremonies leading to forgiveness of sins, the Pharisees demanded inner repentance as a prerequisite without which no sin against God could be forgiven. When another individual was adversely affected, his forgiveness was also necessary. The rabbis of the Talmud, witnessing, in these years of profound religious transformations, the apostasy of many who later returned to the fold, constantly elaborated the principle of repentance. Homiletically interpreting Ezekiel's warning, R. Simon ben Yoḥai drew a contrast between the righteous man who, by sinning at the end, "loses everything," and the evildoer who, by repenting at the end, "is accepted by God." This extension of Ezekiel's original formulation, though not quite in keeping with R. Simon ben Yoḥai's generally intolerant and impulsive character, is understandable in the period after Bar Kocheba, which undoubtedly witnessed the return to Judaism of many weak-kneed escapists. By another twist, the sages also taught that "if one was wicked all his life and then repented, he must not be reminded of his wickedness." The famous pronunciamento of R. Abba bar Zabda that an Israelite, even if he sinned, is still an Israelite received the necessary qualifications in the older sayings that one sinning in the expectation of making good by repentance and "he who induces many to sin shall not be given the opportunity to repent." This sharp distinction between leaders and followers was essential. Finally R. Abbahu, against strong opposition, assigned to penitents a position of honor above all true and just Jews, an extremist view, understandable only as an overemphatic rejection of fanatical tendencies to exclude such sinners, natural in a period of decisive struggle. Of such currents, however, we get few glimpses in the Talmud itself, owing to the controlling influence of the official opinion.[21]

Other theological elements of Pharisaism were also developed further. True to itself, Judaism persisted in emphasizing historical elements. Undeterred by the use of the term "God the Father" by Jesus and the apostles, the rabbis continued to view the relationship between God and man much as that of father and son. But while in the theology of the Church Fathers, as in that of Philo under the impact of Hellenism, the meaning of "father" became more and more that of the creator and maker of things, Judaism clung to the original meaning of a metaphoric family relationship with its lasting bonds of affection. Indeed this principle was much more reconcilable with the ethnic base of Judaism than with the universalist outlook of the Church Fathers.

ELABORATION OF PHARISAIC DOCTRINES

A chief characteristic of talmudic theology is, indeed, that while rich and colorful in its infinite variety of detail it contributed relatively little to the fundamentals of Judaism. All the essentials had been laid down by the Pharisaic scribes with an astounding finality, and talmudic Jewry adhered to them with unswerving fidelity. Whatever modifications became necessary affected details rather than fundamentals. Since many major adjustments, both theoretical and practical, made in response to the crisis of the second fall of Jerusalem and the rise of Christianity have already been discussed, we need give here but a few further illustrations of the religious outlook of talmudic sages.

In a world which "had more gods than men," the existence of God did not have to be discussed, although there seems also to have been some who "denied the very principle" of religion. Not even the "Epicureans," frequently mentioned by the rabbis, were outright atheists. Nor were they, for that matter, genuine philosophic followers of the Epicurean atomistic-hedonistic world outlook or, still less, persons concerned only with worldly pleasures. They were rather argumentative heterodox Jews, who voiced strongly antinomian views and spoke slightingly of the rabbis and scribes, whom they often annoyed with more or less embarrassing questions. Nevertheless faint echoes of the genuine Epicurean objections to a single act of creation may be detected in various alleged debates recorded in the Aggadah. When asked, for example, by a Roman matron as to what God was doing after He had completed His six days of creation, R. Jose ben Ḥalafta answered that He had been matching off pairs destined to enter wedlock. Another rabbi, in reply to a similar question put to him (anachronistically) by king "Ptolemy" in Rome, answered bitingly, "From that day on the fires of Gehenna are kept burning for evildoers; woe unto the world from God's judgments." It probably was also under some such provocation that R. Abbahu spoke of the successive universes created by God, thereby intimating the rabbinic belief in a continuous process of creation.[22]

Jews had greater difficulty in persuading the average idol worshiper of the invisibility, in fact immaterial existence, of their God. In the numerous imaginary debates recorded in talmudic literature, which doubtless approximated some real conversations, the rabbis used homely similes to illustrate to their pagan interlocutors their belief that, just as one's soul is invisible and as the sunrays penetrating one's house are but part of the sun shining all over the world, so is God's powerful, though invisible, presence permeating the entire universe. On the whole, however, they did not often engage in more detailed speculations concerning the relationships between God's transcendence and immanence. Only occasionally did a sage like R. Gamaliel drop a hint that "there is no place in the world devoid of the *shekhinah* [divine presence]." Similarly R. Ammi (echoing R. Jose ben Ḥalafta) explained why the Bible sometimes calls God *maqom* (place), "Because He is the place for [encompasses] the universe, but the universe is not a place for [does not encompass] Him." Contrasting Judaism's world view with that of the Greeks, L. Baeck rightly observed that in the former's doctrine of God

everything is in the tension between the infinite and the given, between the world beyond and this world, between the being other and being one. . . . The distance remains—the distance between the finite and the infinite, between the created and the Creator, between man and God; but it is, so to speak, an elastic distance, it becomes a dynamic, kinetic element in the world. Energy replaces art.

As a faint adumbration of the later ramified doctrine of attributes R. Abba bar Memel (third century) interpreted the various divine names in the Old Testament by the variety of God's active manifestations. "When I judge the creatures," the Lord is said to have informed Moses, "I am called *Elohim;* when I wage war on evildoers, I am called *Ṣebaot;* when I remember man's sins I am called *El Shaddai;* and when I have mercy over My world I am called YHWH." But evidently there existed as yet no widely felt need for the detailed elaboration of such maxims.[23]

Much more emphasis had to be laid upon the unity of God, to combat Graeco-Roman polytheism, Persian, and Marcionite dualism, and perhaps also Christian trinitarianism. But unity was the inherited creed of centuries. So was the belief in creation *ex nihilo.* Neither the Pharisees nor the talmudic rabbis seem to worry very much about Aristotelian eternality of matter. They may have admitted, with R. Abbahu, the existence of many worlds before the present universe took shape. But that God existed before any of these worlds and was the creator of all of them was little short of a truism. The consciousness of the rabbis that all these matters were settled long before their time appears even in the fascinating legendary discussions between Alexander the Great and the sages of the South. When they permitted this famous hero of folktales to ask how to overcome this world of perdition and attain the true life (Tamid 32a), they touched upon a problem which bothered them as much as it had their Pharisaic predecessors or Philo. They were, however, entitled to say that their answer had already been given in the Hellenistic era.

The same is also true of the belief in resurrection. The rabbis continued merely to adhere to a religious axiom firmly entrenched during the Second Commonwealth. They went so far as to assert that whosoever disbelieves in the resurrection of the dead will himself have no share in the world to come. Only occasionally did a teacher like R. Jeremiah (fourth century) dramatize his firm expectation to rise from the dead by the testamentary disposition that he be buried clad in a white bordered linen cloak, dressed in fine socks and slippers, with a staff in his hand, and placed on his side, so that at a moment's notice "when the Messiah comes, I shall be ready to follow" (j. Killaim IX, 4, 32b). The talmudic discussions do not, however, in any way point out clearly the essential difference between the Jewish belief in resurrection to come at a definite period in history, and the Greek and Jewish-Hellenistic acceptance of the immortality of the soul beyond all boundaries of time. In fact, when under changed conditions, the Jewish philosophers of the Middle Ages accepted the principle of immortality, they saw no difficulty in reconciling it with the talmudic belief in resurrection.

Once these and other fundamentals were accepted, their elaboration in detail could be left to the individual. It did not matter that the Bar Kocheba revolt, instead of strengthening the people's expectancy of an immediate coming of the redeemer, aroused the rabbis to counsel moderation and to dissuade the Jews from "forcing the end" and revolting against their oppressors. We recall R. Joseph bar Ḥanina's statement about the oaths imposed by God on the Jews not to rebel against the nations and on the latter not to oppress Israel too severely. These were amplified at the end of the third century by R. Levi through the addition of three other oaths, including one that Jews would not reveal the end of days and another that they would not postpone it (by their misdeeds) or, according to a more likely reading, that they would not unduly hasten its arrival. At the same time many pious individuals became obsessed with the fear of the preceding turmoil. R. Eleazar advised some such apprehensive pupils to escape the "birth pangs of the messiah" by the more intensely studying the Torah and by performing acts of loving-kindness. As long as a Jew believed that the messiah would eventually come, he remained a Jew. In the Talmud discussion of messianic annunciations and extravagant hopes of the most varied kind are much rarer than in the period before the destruction of the Temple. Nobody doubted that the messianic hope was an integral part of the Jewish creed, but Mar Samuel, the Babylonian, now uttered the famous aphorism, "The only difference between this world and the days of Messiah consists in foreign domination." Neither did it appear to make any real difference whether one believed that the redeemer would come in "a generation which is wholly righteous"—which seemed to imply something like the Zoroastrian doctrine of the individual's duty to accelerate the coming of the end through righteous living—or the opposite, in "a generation which is wholly sinful," indicating the conviction that history's course is predetermined.[24]

Indeed, a mere perusal of the messianic and eschatological utterances in the last chapter of Sanhedrin reveals the juxtaposition of layers of thought belonging to different periods and reflecting entirely contradictory attitudes. Often a statement was made which, if taken literally, would have appeared positively irresponsible. But the rabbi who made it, in order to bring home a salient idea, felt confident that the discerning listener or reader would himself discard the exaggeration. For instance, R. Abbahu did not really mean to say that "even a Gentile female slave, if living in Palestine, is assured of a share in the world to come"; he merely desired to praise superlatively the choice of residence in Palestine. This hyperbole reminds one of Sirach's more moderate assertion that "nobles will serve a servant that hath understanding, and a wise man will not complain." [25]

Were it a halakhic minutia, a decision would have been imperative. In the realm of theory and speculation, such contradictory opinions could constantly appear side by side without necessitating any authoritative settlement. Extreme liberty could be given the individual to adorn the few fundamental credos with a wealth of accessories derived from either personal experiences and passions or from the national experiences and passions of the age.

Such freedom could the more easily be conceded by the rabbis, inasmuch as dogmatic fixation, representing the eternal static element, was foreign to all rabbinic thought. In fact, the sages looked with a good deal of suspicion upon men whose minds were deeply involved in such abstract meditations. The scribes, to be sure, including at least two of R. Johanan ben Zakkai's most distinguished disciples, indulged in esoteric speculations. On one occasion R. Eleazar ben 'Arakh so impressed his master that R. Johanan "kissed him on his head and said, 'Blessed be the Lord, God of Israel, who hath given Abraham our father a son possessing so fine an ability to preach in honor of our Father in Heaven' " (T. Ḥagigah II, 1, 234; colorfully embroidered in b. 14b).

OPPOSITION TO GNOSIS

It appears increasingly clear that all the apocalyptic literature of the Second Commonwealth was not, as once assumed, the literature of the man on the street, but rather the esoteric Midrash of the intellectual élite. Before the written compilation of the Mishnah, the whole system of oral law was, in a sense, esoteric. Josephus, for instance, seems unable to quote any Pharisaic writings. But beginning in the second century, after the sad experiences with all the syncretistic, gnostic, and apocalyptic currents, there was a sharp reversal. Gnosticism and all mystic movements were explicitly frowned upon in the talmudic age. The well-known legend of the four who entered the "grove," of whom R. 'Aqiba alone "came out in peace" (Ḥagigah loc. cit.); the injunction not to inquire about things beyond one's reach; and the concrete laws, stating under what conditions a man may regard himself as qualified to ponder upon the problems of cosmogony and the prophetic visions of God's throne—all are typical of the views of representative leaders.

Of course, even in Babylonia, there were Jews whose personal inclinations made them prefer metaphysical speculations to the "dialectics of Abbaye and Raba" (as reported by the Talmud itself, Sukkah 28a). Some were greatly attracted by the magic power of the name of God, whose pronunciation, as time went on, was more and more forgotten. Even before Jerusalem's fall, the high priest himself uttered the "ineffable name" before the congregation assembled in the sanctuary but once a year. With the extinction of his office, the pronunciation of this name became the heritage of a small circle of students of the secret lore. New and even more esoteric names crept in, such as the name of 12, 42 or 72 letters. The rabbis, however, did everything in their power to restrict their knowledge to a chosen few. The Palestinian Abba Saul counted persons pronouncing the ineffable name among those who have no share in the world to come. R. Johanan stated that the *Tetra-grammaton* should be revealed by the sages to their disciples only once a week. The Babylonian Rab postulated that nobody be apprised of the name of forty-two letters, unless he be "discreet, modest and middle-aged, not irascible, temperate in drink and ready to forgive." Similar restrictions were imposed upon teaching and speculating on matters of cosmogony and the *merkabah* (Ezekiel's vision of the divine chariot), subjects of the most intense interest to the gnosis. A fairly typical warning is attributed to R. Eliezer the Great (ben Hyrcanus) in a later source. "Do not look for a glimpse of the vineyard of the Holy Blessed be He, if you have caught a glimpse do not enter it, if you have entered it do not derive enjoyment from it, if you have enjoyed it do not eat of its fruit, but if one has caught a glimpse, entered, enjoyed and eaten of it—such a one will ultimately be removed from the world." [26]

Rabbinic opposition was so successful in suppressing gnostic excesses that the very existence of a pre-Christian Jewish gnosis has become the subject of an extended controversy. O. Cullmann, who strongly affirms it and thereby explains many curious phenomena in early Christian writings, thus characterizes its main traits: (1) utmost secrecy; (2) freedom with respect to religious commandments; (3) rejection of the sacrificial system similar to that of the Essenes; (4) dualistic belief in the truth and the lie, or good and evil; (5) contrast between son of man and prophet; (6) ultimate salvation possible only through gnostic interpretation of the revealed truth. Be this as it may, there is no question that the rise of Christianity, including its increasingly anti-Jewish gnostic-Marcionite currents, added impetus to the rabbis' efforts to reduce esoteric speculations to a minimum. There was even a certain revulsion against the state of ecstasy per se. Highly extolled, as we recall, by Philo, ecstatic trance (*marmita*, or rather *mormotos*) was still counted by Rab alongside of ordinary sleep and prophetic vision, as a third important manifestation of the biblical *tardemah* (deep sleep). To which the majority retorted, "There also is deep sleep of stupidity." [27]

As long as these reveries were confined to the realm of theory and, at most, furnished spiritual exercises to a restricted group, the rabbis saw no harm in them. Even when they came to the fore as instruments of magic arts, enjoying much popularity among the masses, the leaders were inclined to treat them with greater tolerance than was vouchsafed by the stringent biblical injunctions.

Once, we recall, Judah the Patriarch himself sent a *mezuzah* to Artabanus of Parthia, assuring him that the biblical passages contained therein would guard him in his sleep. But it was left to each individual, whether scholar or unlearned, to cogitate about the meaning and implication of such spiritual exercises. In other words, they belong to the realm of folklore, rather than to that of authoritative rabbinic thought. Summarizing the impression of the numerous Judeo-Aramaic incantations extant from Babylonia of the talmudic and early posttalmudic age, J. Obermann concludes that, "in a manner which the sorcerers must have felt to be no more inconsistent than do the rabbis of the Talmud, their belief in the reality of spirits and in the validity of exorcism goes hand in hand with their inherited adherence to *God, the living and lasting, the Ruler and Creator*—although occasionally he may be referred to in terms more suitable to Ahura-Mazdah than to the God of Israel." While some rabbis may have frowned upon one or another of these folk practices, they could not, in view of their personal beliefs and the general climate of opinion, condemn them as outright pagan borrowings.[28]

It is truly astonishing how few of these folkloristic ingredients were incorporated into the official Babylonian Jewish theology. No matter how tremendous the pressure of the immemorial folkways of the Fertile Crescent or of the mystic teachings of the dominant Parsee religion, official Judaism deviated but little from its traditional outlook. In fact, Babylonian Jewry increasingly became the main cultivator of the Halakhah, relegating the Aggadah to a corner of intellectual life. Palestine, on the other hand, became the seat of the Aggadah, producing, even after the fourth century, those numerous homiletical compilations known as the *aggadic midrashim*. Apart from increasing poverty, as noted by R. Isaac, it was the decline of the academies and the patriarch's authority that induced the Palestinians to substitute more and more the picturesque homilies of the rabbis for the constant, disciplined elaboration of the Law. Babylonia, on the other hand, although possessing distinguished preachers of her own, such as Rab or Rabbah, contributed only a little to the Palestinian Aggadah. Although we know relatively few of these ancient homilies, it is safe to assume that the Babylonians did not emulate the example of R. Meir, who in his public lectures allocated two-thirds of his time to Aggadah and parables, and only one-third to Halakhah. The Babylonian Talmud, to be sure, contained large sections devoted to aggadic lucubrations; but, apart from incorporating much that was evidently of Palestinian origin, intrinsically it revealed its lesser appreciation of the Aggadah, as compared to the halakhic discussions. In fact, this very juxtaposition of the two in the Babylonian form could not but enhance the position of the Halakhah.

The relative independence of the Babylonian rabbis from the influences of the Babylonian and Persian environment, throws much light on that fascinating and still unsettled problem of the relations between Judaism and Zoroastrianism. Sources of information on the Persian religion are most abundant and reliable for the Sassanian period. In no other period of their history did the Jews and the Persians, the rabbis and the magi (*mobeds*), come into such close contact as during the four centuries after Ardashir I. Intolerant kings tried forcibly to inject Zoroastrian ideas into Jewish life. At the very beginning of the Sassanian regime the influential statesman Kartir, as revealed by his own inscription, set "his Mazdayasmian church on the path of foreign as well as internal missions" (Sprengling). Later, more tolerant rulers were induced, by political considerations, to foster an amicable rapprochement, from which, however, the Parsee side alone seemed able to gain. The erection of a royal statue (or bust) in the old synagogue Shaf ve-Yatib of Nehardea, for example, provoked no immediate Jewish revolt similar to that in Alexandria, only because the Persians themselves did not worship statues as divine representations. In fact, such pious scholars as Mar Samuel's father continued praying there, and subsequent generations insisted that it was the seat of the *shekhinah* (divine presence). Certainly, the double impact of the old Achaemenid and new Sassanian forces could not fail to influence Judaism.[29]

On the whole, there was, however, more clarification through resistance than genuine absorption of new ideas. Certain Parsee festive seasons (Naurard, Tirakan, Mihrakan, and Nauruz), for example, were observed by Christians, but sharply repudiated as idolatrous by the rabbis. Even the apparently Zoroastrian concept of God and the angels as a "heavenly family" (*pamalya shel ma-'alah*) is of Palestinian, not Babylonian origin, as is indicated by its Latin loan word. The first to introduce it apparently was R. Eleazar of Modein, at a time when Palestine was decidedly separated from Parthia. It was also another Palestinian, R. Johanan, who, by a curious inversion, placed denial of the heavenly family on a par with sorcery. In any case, contrary to Parsee convictions, the sages retained the doctrine that the Jewish people or even a righteous individual was superior to angels. In general, the bent of talmudic Judaism thus was to eschew competitive influences rather than to accept any original contributions from the Zoroastrian environment.[30]

It is still an unsolved question whether some of the central religious concepts such as the Kingdom of God, resurrection, and divine mediation, as found in exilic and rabbinic theology, arose under the stimulus of Parsiism. The consensus of scholarly opinion leans more and more toward the theory of independent origin. As these also constitute integral elements of the Samaritan creed, they must have been firmly grounded in Israel before the rise of the Samaritan schism. Indeed, the better our knowledge of the early phases of the Old Testament religion becomes, and the more consistently modern scholarship assigns earlier dates to the decisive passages in the Bible, the larger looms the independence and, in many ways, even the priority of ancient Israel. Hence students of ancient religions are now inclined to ascribe to Judaism a larger, and to Parsiism a smaller, share in this interchange of religious notions and practices, intermittently extending over more than twelve centuries.

As to the Talmud, the story about a Persian Jewish soldier discovering in Persian archives a Hebrew scroll where, in Hebrew script, it was written that the world would end in the year 4291 after its creation (531 C.E.) and that God would renew it only after an interval of 7,000 years seems to be borrowed from Persian eschatology. But the more generally held view that 6,000 years are assigned to this universe culminates in a truly Jewish sabbatical millennium. Both these computations may have sprung from early Babylonian astronomy. While Babylonian scientists conceded to the world another 50,000 years or more, the more sanguine Parsee and Jewish messianic dreamers shortened the period to something, so to speak, within the grasp of the popular mind. Eschatology certainly played a much more vital part in the Pharisaic and the Persian philosophies of life than in that of ancient Babylonia. This example must suffice to indicate that both religions may have been indebted to common sources, Babylonian and other, in a measure to which the latters' now extant debris give only an inkling. The fact that both Judaism and Zoroastrianism were sober and activistic, rather than mystic and contemplative, endowed them with certain essential similarities, unavoidable even had they been separated by continents.[31]

INTELLECTUALIZATION OF JEWISH LIFE

Overemphasis upon the Halakhah, the unparalleled law consciousness—or at least law subconsciousness—pervading Jewish life at every step, the Jew's great self-control in matters of sex, his increasingly anomalous economic status, and his abnormal political and segregated social life in autonomous communities, all bred an extreme and dangerous intellectualization of Jewish life. But, however artificial and contrary to nature this trend was, Jewish society as a whole in the lands of the dispersion was no less so. Artificiality, the logical expression of the existing social forces, was also the most effective means of preserving Jews and Judaism, a fact recognized by the intellectual leaders of Jewry. They saw their main task as the erection of a "fence around the Torah" by minute elaboration of its laws,[32] thus also building a fence around the people of Israel against all storms from without. Even so, the Jews did not live in seclusion. Everywhere their life received its special color from the surrounding environment. But wherever the talmudic "fence" remained erect, foreign ingredients were immediately absorbed and integrated into the total system of rabbinism.

That the Talmud could accomplish such a task at all, was owing both to its dynamic power and its enormous scope. The Pharisees had already found a formula for reconciling the divine origin of the Law, with its adaptation to the changing needs in life, through the never-ceasing flow of tradition. The talmudic sages proceeded further on the same road. They taught that the Torah was eternal and preëxistent, and that "nowadays no prophet is entitled to invent new laws." In his chronicle R. Jose ben Ḥalafta advanced the historical argument that until the days of Alexander "there were prophets who were prophesying through the Holy Spirit, from then on bend your ears and listen to the words of the sages." On the other hand, there were no bounds to interpretation. In a widely discussed legend, Moses is shown admiring the acumen of R. 'Aqiba, who succeeded in deriving from every stroke in the letters of the Torah many laws undreamed of by the great lawgiver himself. At the same time, Moses hears R. 'Aqiba quote him as the supreme authority and final source of all these new laws. In another remarkable passage, the Talmud tries to prove that the 613 laws of Moses were reduced by David to 11, and then by various prophets to 6, 3, 2 and 1, namely either Amos' "Seek ye Me and live" (5:4), or Habakkuk's "The righteous shall live by his faith" (2:4). Similarly four decisions made by Moses were reversed by the later prophets. Even for their own time, the rabbis adopted the progressive principle, "The law follows the last authority" (*halakhah kebatrai*).[33]

Reconciliation of all these changes with a belief in the preëxistence and eternal validity of the Torah was accomplished through an ingenious although artificial method of semiallegorical interpretation. The so-called Midrash in many ways resembles, in its aggadic form, the method employed by Philo, the Church Fathers and even Plotinus; with the distinction, however, that the rabbis paid less attention to philosophy and theoretical theology than to the concrete problems of law and behavior. Then, too, they viewed all life more in the light of national history than did any of their contemporaries. Through the application of this principle, they made the Talmud itself an important vehicle of history.

Once more Babylonia assumed intellectual leadership. In subsequent centuries the Babylonian and not the Palestinian Talmud became authoritative for world Jewry. No doubt the foundations were Palestinian; the originality of approach, the creative reinterpretation of old sources to suit new conditions, belong to the Pharisaism of independent Judaea. But this movement itself was nourished from sources in the Babylonian Exile, and it developed with reference to world Jewry rather than to the people of Palestine exclusively. For this reason the transplantation of Palestinian law into Babylonia met with little initial difficulty. But even the segregated and autonomous Jewish settlement of Babylonia soon evolved social features of its own. To adapt the law to these, it had to reinterpret the law of Palestine while retaining its method. As life became increasingly artificial, it tended to make reinterpretation more artificial too. At any rate, as in the times of Moses and Ezra, Jewish law received its authoritative formulation on foreign soil, but this time with a view to Jewish life in foreign lands.

BULWARK OF STRENGTH

Thus the Talmud became the main expression of a great crisis in the history of Jewish society and religion. At the same time, it served as a powerful instrument in overcoming the crisis. The progressive degradation of political and social life in the late Roman Empire; the still sharper drop in the Jews' legal and political status; the decrease in the number of Jews and the protracted falling off of whole sections of Jewry which joined the new religious movement—doubtless had far-reaching effects upon Jewish life. As a province of Rome, Palestine gradually lost its leadership, while Babylonian Jewry, happier under the rule of a rejuvenated, progressive, and relatively sympathetic Persia, took its place. Once again away from its soil, the Jewish people had, in one way or another, to live in defiance of nature. Conscious of the character of this new situation, Judaism reformulated its age-old ideology with still greater finality. In the Talmud it erected a much-needed, tremendously effective, and in many ways unique, bulwark between the Jews and the forces of nature.

NOTES

ABBREVIATIONS

AASOR	Annual of the American Schools of Oriental Research
Abhandlungen Chajes	Abhandlungen zur Erinnerung an Hirsch Perez Chajes. Vienna, 1933.
Abrahams Mem. Vol.	Jewish Studies in Memory of Israel Abrahams. New York, 1927.
Ag. Ap.	Josephus' Against Apion
AJA	American Journal of Archaeology
AJSL	American Journal of Semitic Languages and Literatures
Annuaire	Brussels, Université libre, Institut de philologie et d'histoire orientales et slaves, Annuaire
Antt.	Josephus' Antiquities
AOF	Archiv für Orientforschung
AR	Archiv für Religionswissenschaft
ARN	Aboth de-Rabbi Nathan. Ed. by S. Schechter
ASAE	Annales de Service des Antiquités de l'Egypte
ATR	Anglican Theological Review
'A.Z.	'Abodah Zarah
b.	Babylonian Talmud
BA	Biblical Archaeologist
BASOR	Bulletin of the American Schools of Oriental Research
B.B.	Baba Batra
BJPES	Bulletin (*Yediot*) of the Jewish Palestine Exploration Society
BJRL	Bulletin of the John Rylands Library, Manchester
B.M.	Baba Meṣiah
B.Q.	Baba Qamah
BSOS	Bulletin of the School of Oriental Studies (University of London)
CBQ	Catholic Biblical Quarterly
Cohen Mem. Vol.	Freedom and Reason: Studies in Philosophy and Jewish Culture in Memory of Morris Raphael Cohen. Glencoe, Ill., and New York, 1951.
C. TH.	Theodosian Code
CRAI	Comptes rendus de l'Academie des Inscriptions et des belles lettres
EJ	Encyclopaedia Judaica, Vols. I–X. Berlin, 1928–35.
Essays Hertz	Essays in honour of J. H. Hertz. London, [1942].
Festschrift Bertholet	Festschrift Alfred Bertholet. Tübingen, 1950.
Festschrift Breslau	Festschrift zum 75 jährigen Bestehen des Jüdisch-Theologischen Seminars. 2 vols. Breslau, 1929.
Festschrift Freimann	Festschrift Jakob Freimann . . . gewidmet. Berlin, 1937.
Festschrift Kaminka	Festschrift für Armand Kaminka. Vienna, 1937.

Festschrift Schwarz	Festschrift Adolf Schwarz. Berlin, 1917.
FJF	Forschungen zur Judenfrage
Gaster Anniv. Vol.	Occident and Orient . . . Gaster Anniversary Volume. London, 1936.
Ginzberg Jub. Vol.	Louis Ginzberg Jubilee Volume. 2 vols. New York, 1945. A volume each of English and Hebrew essays.
G.S.	Gesammelte Schriften
GSAI	Giornale della Società asiatica italiana
Gulak-Klein Mem. Vol.	Sefer Zikkaron (Studies in Memory of Asher Gulak and Samuel Klein). Jerusalem, 1942.
HJ	Historia Judaica
HTR	Harvard Theological Review
HUCA	Hebrew Union College Annual
HVLA	Kungl. Humanistika Vetenskapssamfundet i Lund Årsberättelse (Bulletin de la Société Royale des Lettres de Lund)
HZ	Historische Zeitschrift
j.	Palestinian Talmud (Jerushalmi)
JA	Journal asiatique
JAOS	Journal of the American Oriental Society
JBL	Journal of Biblical Literature
JE	The Jewish Encyclopedia. 12 vols. New York, 1901–6.
JEA	Journal of Egyptian Archaeology
JEOL	Jaarboek "Ex Oriente Lux"
JJGL	Jahrbuch für jüdische Geschichte und Literatur
JJLG	Jahrbuch der jüdisch-literarischen Gesellschaft, Frankfurt a.M.
JNES	Journal of Near Eastern Studies (continuation of *AJSL*)
JPOS	Journal of the Palestine Oriental Society
JQR	Jewish Quarterly Review (new series, unless otherwise stated)
JR	Journal of Religion
JRAS	Journal of the Royal Asiatic Society
JRS	Journal of Roman Studies
JSS	Jewish Social Studies
JTS	Journal of Theological Studies
Kohut Mem. Vol.	Jewish Studies in Memory of George A. Kohut. New York, 1935.
Krauss Jub. Vol.	Sefer ha-Yobel la-Professor Shemuel [Samuel]Krauss. Jerusalem, 1937.
KS	Kirjath Sepher, Quarterly Bibliographical Review
Lewy Mem. Vol.	Sefer Johanan Lewy (Commentationes Judaico-Hellenisticae in memoriam Johannis Lewy). Jerusalem, 1949.
Löw Mem. Vol.	Semitic Studies in Memory of Immanuel Löw. Budapest, 1947.
M.	Mishnah
Mahler Jub. Vol.	Emlékkönyv (Dissertationes) in honorem Dr. Eduardi Mahler. Budapest, 1937.

Marx Jub. Vol.	Alexander Marx Jubilee Volume. 2 vols. New York, 1950. A volume each of English and Hebrew essays.
Mélanges Dussaud	Mélanges syriens offerts à M. René Dussaud. Paris, 1939.
MGH	Monumenta Germaniae Historica
MGWJ	Monatsschrift für Geschichte und Wissenschaft des Judentums.
Miller Mem. Vol.	Essays and Studies in Memory of Linda R. Miller. New York, 1938.
Miscellanea Mercati	Miscellanea Giovanni Mercati. 6 vols. Vatican City, 1946. Studi e testi, CXXI–XXVI.
M.Q.	Mo'ed Qaṭan
M.T.	Moses ben Maimon's Mishneh torah (Code)
OLZ	Orientalistische Literaturzeitung
OS	Oudtestamentische Studien
PAAJR	Proceedings of the American Academy for Jewish Research
PEQ	Palestine Exploration Quarterly *or* Palestine Exploration Fund Quarterly Statement
PG	J. P. Migne's Patrologiae cursus completus, series Graeca
PJB	Palästina-Jahrbuch
PL	J. P. Migne's Patrologiae cursus completus, series Latina
PWRE	Pauly-Wissowa-Kroll, Realencyclopädie der classischen Altertumswissenschaft
Quantulacumque	Studies presented to Kirsopp Lake. London, 1937.
R	Rabbi or Rab
r.	Midrash Rabbah (Gen. r. = Bereshit rabbah; Lam. r. = Ekhah rabbati, etc.)
RB	Revue biblique (includes wartime *Vivre et Penser*)
REJ	Revue des études juives
RES	Revue des études sémitiques
R.H.	Rosh Hashanah
RHPR	Revue d'histoire et de philosophie religieuses
RHR	Revue d'histoire des religions
RIDA	Revue internationale des droits de l'Antiquité (II–V = Mélanges Fernand de Visscher, I–IV)
RR	Review of Religion
SB	Sitzungsberichte der Akademie der Wissenschaften (identified by city: e.g., *SB* Berlin, Heidelberg, Vienna)
Schorr Mem. Vol.	Qobeṣ madda'i (Studies in Memory of Moses Schorr). New York, 1944.
SH	Sefer ha-Shanah li-Yehude Amerika
Studies Robinson	Studies in Old Testament Prophecy Presented to Theodor H. Robinson. Edinburgh, 1950.
T.	Tosefta. Ed. by M. S. Zuckermandel
TZ	Theologische Zeitschrift (Basel, 1945–)
WZKM	Wiener Zeitschrift für die Kunde des Morgenlandes

ABBREVIATIONS

ZAW	Zeitschrift für die alttestamentliche Wissenschaft und die Kunde des nachbiblischen Judentums
ZDMG	Zeitschrift der deutschen morgenländischen Gesellschaft
ZDPV	Zeitschrift des Deutschen Palästina Vereins. Vols. LXVIII (1948) ff. are entitled Beiträge zur biblischen Landes- und Altertumskunde.
ZNW	Zeitschrift für die neutestamentliche Wissenschaft und die Kunde der alteren Kirche

NOTES

CHAPTER IX: NEW HORIZONS

1. *War* VII, 3, 3.46–53; Jones's *Herods of Judaea*, pp. 259 ff.; Philo's *De confusione linguarum*, II, 4–5, with reference to the *Odyssey*, XI, 305 ff. and Gen. 11; G. H. Macurdy's "Platonic Orphism in the Testament of Abraham," *JBL*, LXI, 213–26. Cf. also R. Meyer's "Ring des Polykrates, Mt. 17, 27 und die rabbinische Ueberlieferung," *OLZ*, XL, 665–70, "Geschichte eines orientalischen Märchenmotivs in der rabbinischen Literatur," *Festschrift Bertholet*, pp. 365–78 (explaining an obscure reference in Ta'anit 8a), and *Hellenistisches in der rabbinischen Anthropologie*; L. Wallach's "Alexander the Great and the Indian Gymnosophists in Hebrew Tradition," *PAAJR*, XI, 47–83, "Parable of the Blind and the Lame," *JBL*, LXII, 333–39; and, more generally, M. Braun's *History and Romance in Graeco-Oriental Literature*, and S. Lieberman's *Greek in Jewish Palestine*. This is, nevertheless, still a wide-open field and particularly its implications for religious syncretism would warrant careful reëxamination.

2. Plato's *Republic*, V, 16, 470a ff., W. W. Tarn's "Alexander: the Conquest of the Far East" in *Cambridge Ancient History*, VI, 437; Lysias' "Speech against Philon" in his *Works*, XXXI, 6, 638 f.; Tacitus' *Hist.*, V, 4. Cf. also I. Heinemann's *Poseidonios' metaphysische Schriften*, I, 35; his brief sketch of "Die Idee des Völkerfriedens im Altertum," *Der Morgen*, V, 3–17; and, more generally, M. Mühl's *Antike Menschheitsidee*; W. Nestle's *Friedensgedanke in der antiken Welt*; and M. Hadas's "Federalism in Antiquity" in the Conference on Science, Philosophy and Religion, *Fourth Symposium* on *Approaches to World Peace*, pp. 27–41 (with the additional comments by S. J. Case, *et al.*, pp. 41–53).

3. Pliny's *Hist. nat.*, II, 5, 16; Mekilta, Baḥodesh, VI, ed. by Lauterbach, II, 240. The variant "all donkeys in the world would not suffice [to carry the names of the idols]" conveys essentially the same idea. Cf. Sifre on Deut. 43, ed. by Friedmann, fol. 81b (ed. by Finkelstein, p. 97); and S. Lieberman's comments thereon in his *Hellenism in Jewish Palestine*, p. 115. Virgil's possible indebtedness to Judaism has intrigued many scholars. Cf. L. Herrmann's "Virgile a-t-il imité la Bible?" *Antiquité classique*, XIV, 85–91. Essentially, however, Virgil's messianism was eminently political. Cf. A. Alföldi's interpretation, on the basis of interesting numismatic materials, of "Der neue Weltherrscher der vierten Ekloge Vergils," *Hermes*, LXV, 369–84, and Y. Kaufmann's comparison between Virgil and Isaiah in his *Toledot*, III, 293 ff. Of course, this conflict between Rome's political-military world mission and the Judeo-Christian messianic ideal did not escape the attention of more critical minds. It was brought into sharp focus during the great expansion of Christianity and its ultimate victory over Rome's political power. Cf. the neat contrast between *Romanitas* and *Trinitas*, as it unfolded in the five centuries from Augustus to Augustine, in C. N. Cochrane's *Christianity and Classical Culture*.

4. J. Leisegang's Index to Philo's *Opera*, VII, 464, 820; Titus 3:4. Cf. F. Gregoire's "Messie," pp. 29 ff.; and Colson's remarks in his Introd. to Philo's *Works*, VIII, pp. xi ff. That Philo had retained, however, some residuum of the double meaning of *philanthropia*, akin to the Hebrew *ṣedaqah* (loving-kindness and justice), was rightly

pointed out by Wolfson in his *Philo*, II, 218 f. Cf. also H. I. Bell's review of the meaning of "Philanthropia in the Papyri of the Roman Period," *Hommages à Joseph Bidez*, pp. 31–37. On the interrelations between *humanitas* and *misericordia*, see H. Bolkenstein's "Humanitas bei Lactantius, christlich oder orientalisch?" in *Pisciculi. Studien . . . Franz Josef Dölger*, pp. 62–65. Interesting comparative data may also be gleaned from H. Pétré's detailed examination of the use of the term *Caritas* in early Latin-Christian letters. Cf. his French monograph under this title.

5. 'Arakhin 11b; Sukkah 53a; Philo's *Hypothetica* cited by Eusebius in his *Praeparatio*, VII, 7, 360a (Gifford's transl. III, Pt. 1, pp. 389 f.); Soṭah 30b. Although referring to the Song of Moses, the latter passage reflects more than a mere antiquarian debate. Cf. E. Werner's illuminating "Notes on the Attitude of the Early Church Fathers towards Hebrew Psalmody," *RR*, VII, 339–53, his "Conflict between Hellenism and Judaism in the Music of the Early Christian Church," *HUCA*, XX, 407–70; other literature listed in A. Sendrey's *Bibliography of Jewish Music*, pp. 47 ff.; and *infra*, Chap. XII, n. 34; and, more generally, A. Z. Idelsohn's *Jewish Music in Its Historical Development*. On the instruments recorded in the Bible, cf. C. Sachs's *History of Musical Instruments*, pp. 105 ff.; and *supra*, Chap. III, n. 24. Unfortunately there is no way of ascertaining to what extent the instruments mentioned in the Mishnah and Talmud (e.g., M. Kelim XI, 6; XV, 6) were used in synagogue services. Cf. Krauss's *Talmudische Archäologie*, III, 76 ff. Incidentally, according to K. G. Kuhn, rhymed prose, first found in the Christian liturgy of the third and fourth centuries, really goes back to Jewish prototypes. Cf. his *Achtzehngebet und Vaterunser und der Reim*.

6. T. 'A.Z. II, 5, 462; b. 18b. The Miletus inscription is reproduced and fully commented on in A. Deissmann's *Light from the Ancient East*, pp. 451 f. Even if it be translated with Deissmann, "Place of the Jews who are also called God-fearing," we have no reason to assume that it referred to the "god-fearing" semiproselytes only.

7. M. 'A.Z. III, 4; b. 44b. Much of the so-called "Sculpture du sud de la Judée" reproduced by F. M. Abel and A. Barrois in *RB*, XXXVIII, 580–92, consists of lintels with representations of candlesticks and other inanimate objects. This is certainly true of those which appear to have been located in the synagogue. Cf. L. A. Mayer and A. Reifenberg's preliminary and as yet incomplete report on "The Synagogue of Eshtemo'a," *JPOS*, XIX, 322 ff. (with some corrections in Hebrew, *BJPES*, IX–X).

8. Our knowledge of ancient Jewish art, as employed in the synagogues and cemeteries, has been revolutionized through the excavations of the last decades. Even the older material embodied in H. Kohl and C. Watzinger's *Antike Synagogen in Galiläa*, N. Müller's *Jüdische Katakombe am Monteverde zu Rom* and *Inschriften der jüdischen Katakombe am Monteverde zu Rom*, and, more generally, S. Krauss's *Synagogale Altertümer*, greatly qualified the prevalent assumption that the biblical prohibition of imagery had effectively checked all Jewish artistic creation. The discovery of several mosaics in the Palestinian synagogues, unearthed after the First World War, has given a new turn to investigation in this field. Cf., for instance, E. L. Sukenik's *Ancient Synagogue of Beth Alpha*, and "Ancient Synagogue of El-Hammeh," *JPOS*, XV, 101–80; C. H. Kraeling's *Gerasa*, pp. 234 ff., 318 ff.; and, more generally, Sukenik's *Ancient Synagogues of Palestine and Greece*; Watzinger's *Denkmäler*; and H. G. May's brief survey of "Synagogues in Palestine," *BA*, VII, 1–20. A fairly exhaustive list and classification of the older finds are found in M. Avi-Yonah's "Mosaic Pavements in Palestine," *QDAP*, II–IV. Avi-Yonah has also pointed out that much of what appears as Greek art in Palestine was in fact "its own blend of Hellenism with Canaanite decorative traditions." Cf. his "Oriental Elements in the Art of Palestine in the Roman and Byzantine Periods," *QDAP*, X, 105–51, XIII, 128–65, XIV, 49–80. Cf. also E. L. Sukenik's brief survey of "The Present State of

Ancient Synagogue Studies" in the *Bulletin* of the Hebrew University, Jerusalem, Museum of Jewish Antiquities, I, 7–23; and such monographic studies as C. Wendel's *Thoraschrein im Altertum.*

On the Diaspora synagogues cf. Sukenik's *Ancient Synagogues;* A. Plassart's "Synagogue juive de Délos," *RB*, XI, 523–34 (controverted, however, by B. D. Mazur in *Studies on Jewry in Greece,* pp. 15 ff.); Frey's *Corpus,* I, Nos. 694 (Stobi), 726–31 (Delos); A. Marmorstein's "Synagogue of Claudius Tiberius Polycharmus in Stobi," *JQR*, XXVII, 373–84; and Sukenik and M. Schwabe's "Ancient Synagogue of Apameia, Syria" (Hebrew), *Kedem,* I, 85–93. The oldest extant synagogue inscription still is that of Schedia, near Alexandria, which shows that that house of worship was dedicated under the reign of Ptolemy III Euergetes (246–221 B.C.E.). Cf. W. Dittenberger's *Orientis Graeci inscriptiones selectae,* No. 726.

9. These frescoes, which have opened "a new chapter in the history of art," have been subjected to close scrutiny in recent years. The outstanding works include a preliminary report by M. I. Rostovtzeff *et al.* on the sixth season of *The Excavations at Dura Europos,* pp. 309–96, and Rostovtzeff's *Dura-Europos and Its Art;* Count du Mesnil du Buisson's *Peintures de la synagogue de Doura-Europos;* A. Grabar's "Thème religieux des fresques de la synagogue de Doura," *RHR*, CXXIII, 143–92; CXXIV, 5–35; N. Schneid's *Ṣiyyure bet ha-keneset be-Dura Europos* (The Paintings of the Dura-Europos Synagogue); E. L. Sukenik's *Bet ha-keneset shel Dura-Europos* (The Synagogue of Dura-Europos and Its Frescoes); I. Sonne's "Paintings of the Dura Synagogue," *HUCA*, XX, 255–362; H. Riesenfeld's *Resurrection in Ezekiel XXXVII and in the Dura-Europos Paintings;* and R. Wischnitzer's *Messianic Theme in the Paintings of the Dura Synagogue.* Cf. also Du Mesnil's "Deux synagogues successives à Doura-Europos," *RB*, XLV, 72–91 (contrasting the synagogue built in 245 with its predecessor which was both primitive and conventional); G. Wodtke's "Malereien der Synagoge in Dura und ihre Parallelen in der christlichen Kunst," *ZNW*, XXXIV, 51–62 (emphasizing the importance of the Dura discoveries for the understanding of Christian art in the 9th to 12th centuries); M. Aubert's "Peintre de la synagogue de Doura," *Gazette des beaux-arts,* 6th ser., XX, 1–24; W. Stechow's "Jacob Blessing the Sons of Joseph," *ibid.,* XXIII, 196, n. 13; R. Wischnitzer-Bernstein's "Samuel-Cycle in the Wall Decoration of the Synagogue at Dura-Europos," *PAAJR*, XI, 85–103; M. H. Ben-Shammai's "Legends of the Destruction of the Temple in the Paintings of the Dura Synagogue" (Hebrew), *BJPES*, IX, 93–97; W. G. Kümmel's more general observations on "Die älteste religiöse Kunst der Juden," *Judaica,* II, 1–56; and other essays listed in Mrs. Wischnitzer's *Messianic Theme,* pp. 121 ff. Of considerable interest are also such related monographs as Du Mesnil's "Sur quelques inscriptions juives de Doura-Europos (Syrie)," *Biblica,* XVIII, 153–73; his "Parchemin liturgique juif et la gargote de la synagogue à Doura-Europos," *Syria,* XX, 23–34; J. Obermann's "Inscribed Tiles from the Synagogue of Dura," *Berytus,* VII, 89–138 (suggesting that the rebuilding of the synagogue occurred about 253, some three years before it went into disuse); and Rostovtzeff's "*Res gestae divi Saporis* and Dura," *ibid.,* VIII, 48 ff. Cf. also *infra,* Chap. XIV, n. 58.

10. Frey's *Corpus,* I, No. 109. Cf. N. Müller's aforementioned works on the catacomb at Monteverde and the useful survey of older discoveries in H. J. Leon's "Jewish Catacombs and Inscriptions of Rome," *HUCA*, V, 299–314. The outstanding find of the catacomb in the Villa Torlonia by R. Paribeni in 1920 was made known to scholarship by H. W. Beyer and H. Lietzmann in *Die jüdische Katakombe der Villa Torlonia in Rom.* Among the numerous interesting reviews of this work, cf. especially those by M. Schwabe in *Tarbiz,* III, 217–28; and by K. H. Rengstorf in *ZNW*, XXXI, 33–60 (in part controverted by P. Rieger, *ibid.,* XXXIII, 216–18). There are numerous studies of the religious and artistic implications of the various symbols. Cf., in particular, those by H. Gressmann, "Jewish Life in Ancient Rome," *Abrahams Mem. Vol.,* pp. 170–91; I. Zoller, "Il significato delle pitture nelle catacombe giudaiche

a Roma," *Studi e materiali di storia delle religioni*, VII, 144–52; K. Galling, "Die jüdischen Katakomben in Rom als ein Beitrag zur jüdischen Konfessionskunde," *Theologische Studien und Kritiken*, CIII, 352–60; A. Marmorstein, "Jüdische Archäologie und Theologie," *ZNW*, XXXII, 32–41; and H. J. Leon, "Symbolic Representations in the Jewish Catacombs of Rome," *JAOS*, LXIX, 87–90.

11. Cf. W. F. Albright's *Archaeology and the Bible*, pp. 161 f.; M. Kon's "Menorah and the Arch of Titus." *PEQ*, 1950, pp. 25–30; and, in general, J. Zwarts's data on *De zevenarmige Kandelaar in de Romeinsche Diaspora* (The Seven-Branch Candelabrum in the Roman Diaspora). Some Christian groups, particularly of the heterodox wings, likewise at times exhibited the seven-branch candlestick. Cf. M. Simon's judicious weighing of the evidence in "Le Chandelier à sept branches, symbole chrétien?" *Revue archéologique*, XXXI–XXXII (Mélanges C. Picard), 971–80. Decorations and inscriptions of this type were also found elsewhere in Italy and other countries. The Jewish community of Pompeii, for instance, seems to have been more thoroughly latinized than the majority of Roman Jews, who still used predominantly Greek letters and standardized Greek formulas on their epitaphs. Cf. J. B. Frey's "Juifs à Pompéi," *RB*, XLII, 365–84. An inscribed column discovered there in 1936 so clearly referred to Ezekiel's vision that one could merely debate as to whether the writer was a Jew or a Christian of Jewish origin. Cf. F. V. Filson's "Were There Christians in Pompeii?" *BA*, II, 14–16. It ought to be mentioned, however, that the presence of either Jews or Christians in Pompeii is questioned by A. Ferrua, who offers, in particular, a different interpretation of the inscription in Frey's *Corpus*, I, No. 563. Cf. his "Sull' esistenza di Cristiani a Pompei," *Civiltà cattolica*, III, 127–35. Similar questions of Jewish provenance, largely unanswerable with the evidence at hand, may also be raised with respect to some of the "Monumenti cristiani nell' Illirico," extensively documented by E. Condurachi in *Ephemeris Dacoromana*, IX, 1–118. Cf. also his summary of the available more or less certain Jewish data, *ibid.*, pp. 2 ff.; and *infra*, Chap. XIII, n. 42. On the other hand, the speedy Romanization of the Jews in the capital, too, in their daily life, if not in their more tradition-bound mortuary customs, is perhaps illustrated by a puzzling local inscription. If we accept M. Schwabe's division in the reading of Frey's *Corpus*, I, No. 535, it would appear that a family recently immigrated from Palestine included two daughters bearing good Hebrew names, while the youngest was already known under the Latin name, Cara. Cf. Schwabe's "Two Inscriptions from Rome on the Tombs of Persons from Eretz Israel" (Hebrew), *Zion*, IX, 46–47. Cf. also the name Regina on a second-century inscription in Frey's *Corpus*, I, No. 476; and many other Latin names listed in the Index, *ibid.*, pp. 618 ff.

12. Cf. E. R. Goodenough's "Crown of Victory in Judaism," *Art Bulletin*, XXVIII, 158. Goodenough points out that the crown had long played a great role in the Jewish iconography and ceremonial, being present, for example, on Jewish coins from John Hyrcanus to Bar Kocheba. His and Cumont's interpretation, however, of all winged angels as victories, with an implied promise of the Hereafter, seems strained. A more convincing explanation is offered by F. Landsberger in his "Origin of the Winged Angel in Jewish Art," *HUCA*, XX, 244 f. Cf., in general, C. R. Morey's *Early Christian Art;* Goodenough's discussion thereof in *JQR*, XXXIII, 403–18; and W. Lowrie's *Art in the Early Church.*

13. Philo's *Legum allegoriae*, II, 26.108, III, 23.74; M. *Middot*, III, 8; Josephus' *Antt.* XIV, 3, 1.34–36. Cf. H. Dantine's *Palmier-dattier et les arbres sacrés dans l'iconographie de l'Asie occidentale ancienne;* and H. G. May's "Sacred Tree in Palestine Painted Pottery," *JAOS*, LIX, 251–59. On the *asherah* worship and the seals of ancient Israel, see *supra*, Chaps. II, n. 38, IV, n. 17. Even the artist who decorated the synagogue in southern Judaean Eshtemo'a seems to reflect some such influence.

He packed into one decoration not only the traditional Jewish representations of a candlestick and a ram's horn, but also those of an incense burner, the palm tree, and a circular object which probably was the zodiacal circle symbolizing heaven. Together with the palm tree the latter may, indeed, have conveyed to the onlooker some mystical ideas of the Hereafter. Cf. Mayer and Reifenberg's comments on their Plate XXIX, in *JPOS*, XIX, 323 f.; K. Lehmann's "Dome of Heaven," *Art Bulletin*, XXVII, 1–27; and Goodenough's remarks, *ibid.*, XXVIII, 158. The incense burner, too, may reflect the growing importance of incense in the Hellenistic age, as emphasized, with special reference to the Syrian origin of the term *dendrolibanos*, in *Geoponica*, XI, 15–16, ed. by H. Beckh, pp. 334 f. Cf. also M. P. Nilsson's "Pagan Divine Service in Late Antiquity," *HTR*, XXXVIII, 65; and *supra*, Chap. IV, n. 32. Were we to assume that this particular artist was not Jewish, which is perhaps indicated also by his eight-branch candelabrum, the acceptance of such a decoration by the local congregation would none the less be revealing.

14. The Leningrad version of j. 'A.Z. II, 9, 41d–42a published by J. N. Epstein in his "Additional Fragments of the Jerushalmi" (Hebrew), *Tarbiz*, III, 20; M. Soṭah IX, 14; b. 49b; Giṭṭin 7a with reference to Ez. 21:31; Goodenough in *Art Bulletin*, XXVIII, 155. The explanation, once widely held, that Jews frequented synagogues donated to them, mosaics and all, by non-Jewish benefactors (such as are mentioned in Luke 7:5 or j. Megillah III, 2, 74a) had to be discarded in the light of the ever more accumulating evidence. Cf. S. A. Cook's *Religion of Ancient Palestine*, pp. 209 f.; and *infra*, Chap. XIII, n. 27. Cf. also S. Klein's "When Was Mosaic Pictorial Art Introduced into Palestine?" (Hebrew), *BJPES*, I, Pt. 2, 15–17 (identifying R. Abun as the Tiberian scholar, son of R. Abun the Elder, of the second half of the fourth century); J. B. Frey's "Question des images chez les Juifs à la lumière des récentes découvertes," *Biblica*, XV, 265–300; and Wischnitzer's *Messianic Theme*, pp. 8 ff.

15. J. J. E. Hondius's *Supplementum*, VIII, p. 14, No. 86; j. Sheqalim II, 7, 47a; Gen. r. LXXXII, 19 (according to some manuscripts cited by Theodor and Albeck in their ed., p. 988); M. Schwabe's "Greek Inscription from Beth-She'arim" (Hebrew), *Yavneh*, III, 59 (supplemented by his Hebrew note in *BJPES*, X, 79 f.). On the location of "The Sepulchres of the Kings of the House of David," see S. Yeivin's plausible reconstruction in *JNES*, VII, 30–45. Cf. also S. Krauss's "Sepulchres of the Davidic Dynasty," *PEQ*, 1947, pp. 102–11; Z. Wilnai's "Tombs of the Maccabeans: Hannah and Her Sons" (Hebrew), *Sinai*, XI, Nos. 128–30, pp. 89–93 (from a forthcoming volume on the sacred monuments in Palestine); M. Kon's careful archaeological study of the Jerusalem tombs of the kings of Adiabene in his *Kivre ha-melakhim* (The Tombs of the Kings); and M. Ish Shalom's anthropological investigation of *Kivre Abot* (Holy Tombs: a Study of Traditions Concerning Jewish Holy Tombs). Cf. also *infra*, Chap. XIV, n. 59.

The general acceptance, in Palestine as well as in Rome, of the formula "May he [or she] rest in peace" is also noteworthy. Cf. the two Jerusalem tombstones reproduced by Thomsen in *ZDPV*, LXIV, 217 No. 105A, 227 f. No. 185A. The orthodoxy of the inscribers is borne out by A. Deissmann's observation that the numerous Greek equivalents of this formula, although all based on Isa. 57:2, deviated from the Septuagint version. Roman and Palestinian Jews thus indicated their repudiation (at least in the third century) of that version which had in the meantime been appropriated by the Christian Church for its purposes. Cf. Deissmann's comment in Müller's *Inschriften*, p. 7. Nevertheless to have any meaning at all, this formula must have implied to any reader the belief in the deceased person's spiritual survival, even if it was not so blatantly stated as in the two Beth She'arim inscriptions published by M. Schwabe in his "Immortality in Beth-She'arim" (Hebrew), *Gulak-Klein Mem. Vol.*, pp. 187–200. Schwabe seems to exaggerate, therefore, the importance of the relative absence of such benedictions in the other inscriptions preserved in that locality. Not even the express invocation on the grave of another member of the same family, "Be comforted, no man is immortal" (cf. the full text of this interesting "Graeco-Jewish Inscription from Beth-She'arim" published by Schwabe in his Hebrew essay in *BJPES*, VI, 105–14, 159–77; VII, 17–21) is altogether conclusive. Although employing the adjective *athanatos* used by his more outspoken relative in the blessing of deceased parents (the latter's *biou* seems to make a difference), he may have wanted to convey the simple thought that, after all, everyone must die. Certainly there is no reason for assuming a basic dichotomy between the popular and the rabbinic views on the Hereafter several generations after Pharisaism's decisive victory. Cf. also Schwabe's "Peace upon Israel—in Caesarea and the Thessalian Diaspora" (Hebrew), *BJPES*, XII, 65–68.

Many other aspects of ancient Jewish art are treated in R. Krautheimer's *Mittelalterliche Synagogen*, pp. 27–75; H. L. Gordon's remarks on "The Basilica and the Stoa in Early Rabbinical Literature," *Art Bulletin*, XIII, 353–75, with R. Wischnitzer's comments thereon in *REJ*, XCVII, 152–57; S. Klein's "Fremdenhaus der Synagoge," *MGWJ*, LXXVI, 545–57, LXXVII, 81–84; J. Leveen's *Hebrew Bible in Art*; and, more generally, in A. Reifenberg's *Ancient Hebrew Arts*; F. Landsberger's *History of Jewish Art*; and R. Wischnitzer's "Studies in Jewish Art," *JQR*, XXXVI, 47–59.

16. Josephus' *Life* XII. 65–66; *Antt.* VIII, 7, 5.195; Philo's *De decalogo*, XIV, 70–71. On the interpretation of the latter passage, cf. Wolfson's *Philo*, I, 29 f., n. 22. J. Klausner's attempt to reconstruct "Jewish Art in the Maccabean Period" (in his *Ha-Bayit ha-sheni*, pp. 124 ff.) is vitiated by his highly conjectural and now often obsolete evidence. Reifenberg's *Ancient Hebrew Arts* is more restrained and up-to-date, but discusses only a few highlights. Our use of the term "Graeco-Oriental," rather than "Greek" art, as it appears in the rabbinic and other contemporary sources, requires little explanation, since even in this most intimate sphere of the Greek creative genius, there was much mutual borrowing. This is evident also in the building industry, "in which technical progress was much more rapid and achievements much more remarkable" than in most other industrial activities. Cf. Rostovtzeff's *Hellenistic World*, II, 1230 ff. Contemporaries, of course, could no more recognize the original oriental ingredients than they could, in using the Greek alphabet, instantly visualize its Phoenician-Hebrew background. It is less excusable for a modern scholar like C. Schneider to argue on the basis of such surface manifestations that the Eastern cultures had been completely overwhelmed by the Greek spirit, which on its part retained its unblemished integrity. Cf. "Die griechischen Grundlagen der hellenistischen Religionsgeschichte," *AR*, XXXVI, 300–47; and *supra*, n. 8.

17. Qiddushin 49b; Sanhedrin 67b. Cf. also, in particular, F. Cumont's *Egypte des astrologues*; the *Corpus hermeticum*, attributed to Hermes Trismegistus, edited by A. D. Nock and transl. into French by A. J. Festugière; and Festugière's comprehensive analysis of astrology and occult sciences in *La Révélation d'Hermès Trismégiste*, I. The first tract of this important *Corpus*, notes W. L. Knox, "is still trying to read Genesis and the *Timaeus* [by Plato] into one another, with a good deal of material drawn from other apparently incompatible sources." Cf. his "Pharisaism and Hellenism" in *Judaism and Christianity*, ed. by H. Loewe, *et al.*, II, 103.

18. Artapanus and Pseudo-Eupolemus cited by Eusebius in his *Praep. evang.* IX, 17.418d, 18.420b (in Gifford's transl., III, 450 ff.; cf. Freudenthal's *Alexander Polyhistor*, pp. 91, 98, 225); Josephus' *Antt.* I, 7, 1.156; B.B. 16b (with reference to Gen. 24:1); Testament of Solomon 20:16. Cf. also some other (mostly negative) rabbinic passages cited by L. Ginzberg in his *Legends*, V, 227, n. 108, VI, 283, n. 24; and B. N. Wambacq's comprehensive analysis of *L'Epithète divine Jahvé Ṣᵉba'ot*. On the widespread acceptance of the Jewish origins of astrology in ancient Jewish and Christian

circles, see J. Bidez and F. Cumont's *Mages hellénisés*, I, 41 ff. Some ancients, including Pseudo-Eupolemus, traced its origin farther back to Enoch, who had allegedly learned the astral sciences directly from the angels. This view was evidently stimulated by the book of Enoch, an entire section of which (Chapters 72–82), probably written before 110 B.C.E., is called "The Book of the Heavenly Luminaries." Cf. also Jub. 4:17–21; and, in general, R. Eisler's comprehensive study of *The Royal Art of Astrology*.

19. The later rabbis' ambivalent attitude to the rapidly accumulating apocalyptic literature is well reflected in L. Ginzberg's "Some Observations on the Attitude of the Synagogue toward the Apocalyptic Eschatological Writings," *JBL*, XLI, 115–36. It is likely that before the rise of Christianity and the ensuing need of tightening all controls there was even greater approval of accepted, and tolerance of rejected, patterns.

20. Cf. U. Cassuto's data in his "Aquila," *EJ*, III, 27–35; J. A. Smith's "Meaning of KYPIOS," *JTS*, XXXI, 155–60; Cardinal G. Mercati's "Note bibliche, I," *Biblica*, XXII, 339–54, 365–66, XXIII, 82; H. G. Waddel's "Tetragrammaton in the LXX," *JTS*, XLV, 158–61; and L. Cerfaux's "'Kyrios' dans les citations pauliniennes de l'Ancien Testament," *Ephemerides theologicae lovanienses*, XX, 5–17. Cf. also, from another angle, J. Z. Lauterbach's "Substitutes for the Tetragrammaton," *PAAJR*, II, 39–67.

21. Exod. 23:20–23; Dan. 12:1; Ethiopic Enoch 20:1–8; Jub. 2:2–3. That Enoch's mystic speculations were a fountainhead for both Jewish and Christian gnosticism has long been clearly recognized. See e.g., the keen analysis of "Mystique, gnostique (juive et chrétienne) en finale des paraboles d'Hénoch" by L. Gry in *Muséon*, LII, 337–78. However, even in such a far more prosaic and down-to-earth apocryphon as the Wisdom of Solomon, we recall, A. Dupont-Sommer seems to have detected some traces of "astral immortality." Cf. his essay cited *supra*, Chap. VI, n. 54.

22. Gen. r. VIII, 5, 60 f.; Midrash Tehillim VIII, 5, ed. by S. Buber, p. 78; II Macc. 11:9, 13–14; Pseudo-Jonathan on Gen. 11:7–8; Ḥagigah 12b, etc. Cf. Johansson's *Parakletoi*, pp. 37 ff.; W. Böld's dissertation, *Die antidämonischen Abwehrmächte in der Theologie des Spätjudentums*, pp. 11 ff.; A. Altmann's "Gnostic Background of the Rabbinic Adam Legend," *JQR*, XXXV, 371–91. The constant use by the Bible of the plural form *elohim* lent itself particularly well to angelological explanation. Cf., for instance, the sharp attack in Midrash Tanḥuma, Qedoshim, IV, on the "heretical" misinterpretation of the blatant plural in Josh. 24:19. Its reflection in the extant fragments of Symmachus' Greek translation of the Bible is stressed by H. J. Schoeps in his "Mythologisches bei Symmachus," *Aus frühchr. Zeit*, pp. 89 ff. Cf. such more recent studies as H. Odeberg's commentary on the Hebrew Enoch in his *3 Enoch or the Hebrew Book of Enoch*, and his "Fragen von Metatron, Shekina und Memra," *HVLA*, 1941–42, pp. 31–46 (with reference to a Yiddish work of 1735); L. Gry's "Quelques noms d'anges ou d'êtres mystérieux en II Hénoch," *RB*, XLIX, 195–204; A. Kaminka's analysis of "Die mystischen Ideen des R. Simon b. Joḥai," *HUCA*, X, 149–68; and, more generally, H. H. Rowley's *Relevance of Apocalyptic*. J. Daniélou has examined the relevant "Sources juives de la doctrine des anges des nations chez Origène" in *Recherches de science religieuse*, XXXVIII, 132–37. Interesting comparative data will also be found in S. Eitrem's *Some Notes on the Demonology in the New Testament;* and E. Schneweis's *Angels and Demons According to Lactantius*. Cf. also *supra*, Chap. V, n. 9; *infra*, n. 52; and Chap. XV, notes 27–28.

23. II. Macc. 12:40 ff.; *Antt.* IV, 8, 13.213; j. Pe'ah, I, 1, 15d; Gen. r. LXXVII, 3, 913 f. (cf. also Theodor's comment *ibid.*, p. 333); Berakhot 30b–31a. It may be noted

that Jesus' sharp assault on the Pharisees that "make broad their phylacteries" (Matt. 23:5) was not aimed at the latter's alleged protective qualities, but rather at the Pharisees' excessive public display of their ritualistic implements. Cf. also G. G. Fox's "Matthean Misrepresentation of Tephillin," *JNES*, I, 373–77. Some of R. Joshua ben Peraḥiah's formulas appear in J. A. Montgomery's *Aramaic Incantation Texts from Nippur*, pp. 225 ff. This valuable collection is to be read together with J. N. Epstein's comments in his "Gloses babylo-araméennes," *REJ*, LXXIII, 27–58, LXXIV, 40–72. Additional sources have been published, among others, by C. H. Gordon in his "Aramaic Magical Bowls in the Istanbul and Baghdad Museums," *Archiv Orientalni*, VI, 319–34 (with additional documents *ibid.*, pp. 466–74, IX, 84–106); his "Aramaic Incantation in Cuneiform," *AOF*, XII, 105–17 (with B. Landsberger's comments thereon, *ibid.*, pp. 247–57); his "Aramaic Incantation Bowls," *Orientalia*, X, 116–41, 272–84, 339–60; and J. Obermann in his "Two Magic Bowls," *AJSL*, LVII, 1–32. One of the latter offers, for example, an interesting text of "an amulet for muzzling, and for sealing, and for guarding, and for healing . . . against evil sorcerers, and mighty charm workers." Although for the most part belonging to the early Muslim age, these bowls and other texts shed considerable light also on the preceding period, and Obermann is perfectly right in advocating the publication of a comprehensive corpus, which ought to include, however, also some such Greek magic texts as that of the Paris papyrus, first ed. by Wessely. Cf. Deissmann's *Light*, pp. 254 ff.

Not even the protective curses over graves were totally absent. Though apparently far less frequent than among non-Jews, one such threat was deciphered by Schwabe in Beth She'arim. Cf. his text and comments in the *Gulak-Klein Mem. Vol.*, pp. 187 ff. (also A. D. Singer's further elaboration of the formula in *BJPES*, IX, 22–24), as against A. Parrot's *Malédictions et violations de tombes*, p. 60. Cf. also J. Irmscher's comments in *ZNW*, XLII, 172–84; and, more generally, I. A. Richmond's *Archaeology and the After-Life in Pagan and Christian Imagery;* and particularly F. Cumont's posthumous *Lux Perpetua*. Another imprecatory inscription, probably of Jewish provenance, is described in F. K. Dörner's "Ausserbithynische Inschriften im Museum von Bursa und neue Funde aus Eskişehir (Dorylaion)," *Wiener Jahreshefte des Oesterreichischen Archäologischen Institutes*, XXXII, 132, No. 12. More questionably Jewish are the "Two Curse Tablets from Beisan" (Scythopolis), dating from the third or fourth century and published by H. C. Youtie and C. Bonner in *Transactions of the American Philological Association*, LXVIII, 43–77, 128, although, e.g., the name Eua seems to be of Jewish (Eve), rather than Scythian origin. The editors' entire Scythian interpretation is the more dubious as the Scythian invasion in the days of Jeremiah may never have taken place. Cf. *supra*, Chap. III, n. 45.

24. Cf. C. C. Torrey's ed. of *The Lives of the Prophets*, pp. 21, 27 (Greek), 35, 41 f. (English); and C. Bonner's "Story of Jonah on a Magical Amulet," *HTR*, XLI, 31–38. Bonner rightly mentions also Jonah's great popularity in ancient and medieval art.

25. Josephus' *War* II, 7, 3.112; *Antt.* VIII, 2, 5.45–49, XX, 7, 2.142; Origen's *Contra Celsum*, VIII, 58; Lucian's *Tragodopodagra*, verse 173 in Reinach's *Textes*, pp. 159 f. It was widely believed that Noah had acquired the art of magic healing from the angels and had written "down all things in a book" which he bequeathed to Shem. Mentioned in Jub. 10:10–15, this belief created wide acceptance of a current literary concoction attributed to Noah. Of much later vintage are the various recensions of the so-called "Book of Noah," published by A. Jellinek in *Bet-ha-Midrasch*, III, 155–60, with brief comments, *ibid.*, pp. xxx–xxxiii. So widespread became the belief in the medical uses of magic arts that the Greek god of healing, Asklepios, soon became "one of the most popular deities in the Hellenistic world." Having entered Phoenicia through one of those facile identifications with the local deity, Eshmun, he finally

penetrated Palestine where he became associated particularly with the healing springs near Tiberias and Gadara. Cf. S. V. McCasland's "Asklepios Cult in Palestine," *JBL*, LVIII, 221-27; and, more generally, his "Religious Healing in First-Century Palestine" in *Environmental Factors in Church History*, ed. by J. T. McNeill, *et al.*, pp. 18-34. One must distinguish, however, between the worship of the god Asklepios and the reverence for a *hero* of that name. Cf. E. J. and L. Edelstein's comprehensive study of *Asclepius: a Collection and Interpretation of the Testimonies*. Cf. also, from another angle, the interesting data accumulated by W. B. McDaniel in "The Medical and Magical Significance in Ancient Medicine of Things Connected with Reproduction and Its Organs," *Journal of the History of Medicine*, III, 525-46.

26. Cf. j. Sanhedrin VII, 19, 25d; b. 65b, 67ab; B. M. 107b; Shabbat 67a, with reference to M. Shabbat VI, 10 (in the more correct version of j.); H. Loewe's "Ideas of Pharisaism" in *Judaism and Christianity*, ed. by him, *et al.*, II, 33; L. Wallach's "Jewish Polemic against Gnosticism," *JBL*, LXV, 393-96 (thus explaining M. Abot III, 7). The expression that someone "placed his eyes on him and he turned into a heap of stone" became almost a talmudic idiom. Cf. Berakhot 58a; Shabbat 34a; Sanhedrin 100a, etc. Cf. also the analysis of 28 rabbinic stories, as compared with those recorded in the Epidauros inscriptions and the Gospels, in L. J. McGinley's *Form-Criticism of the Synoptic Healing Narratives* (a critique of Dibelius and Bultmann's theories); and, more generally, L. Blau's survey of *Das altjüdische Zauberwesen;* and J. Trachtenberg's *Jewish Magic and Superstition* (though largely dealing with medieval Ashkenazic Jewry, the author often quotes talmudic sources). A more up-to-date comprehensive work on ancient Jewish magic, making full use of recent archaeological, epigraphic, and papyrological evidence, is urgently needed.

27. Origen's *Contra Celsum*, IV, 33 (also I, 22; V, 45); Justin Martyr's *Dialogue*, 85 (*PG*, VI, 676); Acts 19:13, 15, 19. On the magic bowls, cf. *supra*, n. 23. Cf. also J. Z. Lauterbach's "Belief in the Power of the Word," *HUCA*, XIV, 287-302; O. Eissfeldt's "Jahwe-Name und Zauberwesen," *Zeitschrift für Missionskunde*, XLII, 161-86; and M. Rist's data on "The God of Abraham, Isaac, and Jacob: a Liturgical and Magical Formula," *JBL*, LVII, 289-303. Rist is right in concluding that "the occurrence of the formula in Hebrew, Aramaic, Samaritan, Greek, Latin, and Coptic texts is a testimony of its wide currency in the Mediterranean world during the early centuries of our era." On the other hand, in his "Jao und Set," *AR*, XXX, 34-69, A. Procopé-Walter repeats Cumont's warning not to accept the numerous amulets and other magic implements found in the various museums at their face value, since many have been proved to be very skillful modern forgeries. While E. Meyer explains this prevalence of magic and superstition as concomitant with the growing ethical tendencies in the advanced stages of all ancient religions (cf. his *Ursprung*, II, 118 f.), Procopé-Walter ascribes it to the feeling of despair accompanying the dissolution of the Graeco-Roman slave economy. The acceptance of magic rites, nevertheless, cut across all class lines; and the magic papyri, gemmas, etc., were used as much by the great landowners and slave dealers as by the slaves and other proletarians. Cf. also M. Pieper's "Abraxasgemmen," *Mitteilungen des Deutschen Instituts für ägyptische Altertumskunde in Kairo*, V, 119-43; T. Hopfner's analysis of "Der religionsgeschichtliche Gehalt des grossen demotischen Zauberpapyrus," *Archiv Orientalni*, VII, 89-120 (especially p. 117; this famous third-century papyrus often refers to Jao, Adonai, Sabaoth, Moses, and Michael); M. P. Nilsson's "Religion in den griechischen Zauberpapyri," *HVLA*, 1947-48, II, 59-93 (somewhat overstressing Jewish influences on magic practices in fifth-century Egypt); his "Anguipede of the Magical Amulets," *HTR*, XLIV, 61-64; and, more generally, C. Bonner's *Studies in Magical Amulets*, pp. 26 ff. Although claiming that "almost every magical papyrus bears some marks of Judaism here and there, in its ideas or in the sacred names invoked, and so do scores of magical gems," Bonner admits that Egyptian influence was paramount (p. 28).

28. Origen's *Contra Celsum*, V, 45; W. Dittenberger's *Orientis gr. inscriptiones sel.*, Nos. 73–74; M. Giṭṭin VI, 5; b. Berakhot 54b. The phrase *sotheis ek pelous* or rather *pelagous*, seems to indicate escape from actual danger, but under the general conditions of ancient sea travel the rabbis could legitimately regard any prolonged voyage as tantamount to such escape. Cf. also R. Patai's *Ha-Sappanut*, pp. 59 f.

29. P. LeBas and W. H. Waddington's *Voyage archéologique en Grèce et en Asie Mineure*, III, 95, No. 294 (Inscriptions); III, 96a (Explications); W. M. Ramsay's *Cities and Bishoprics of Phrygia*, Nos. 550, 551, 559. Cf. W. H. Buckler and W. M. Calder's *Monuments and Documents from Phrygia and Caria*, No. 337 (a Torah scroll and seven-branch candelabrum); L. Robert's *Etudes anatoliennes*, pp. 409 ff. (showing that the "God-fearing" Capitolina was not a Christian *grande dame*, as hitherto assumed, but half Jewish and that she helped construct a synagogue in her home town of Tralles, Asia Minor); and the list of *ephebi* in Jasus, dating from the early imperial period and including one Joudas, published by Robert in *REJ*, CI, 85 f. Cf. also Schürer's *Geschichte*, III, 13 ff.; A. Reinach's "Noé Sangariou. Etude sur le déluge en Phrygien," *REJ*, LXV, 161–80, LXVI, 1–43, 213–45; various theories on the surname of Apamaea discussed by D. Magie in his *Roman Rule in Asia Minor*, II, 983 f.; H. Gressmann's somewhat overspeculative remarks in *Die orientalischen Religionen im hellenistisch-römischen Zeitalter*, pp. 115 ff.; and W. O. E. Oesterley's "Cult of Sabbazios" in *The Labyrinth*, ed. by S. Hooke, pp. 128 ff. Cf., however, W. L. Knox's forceful reservations with respect to the Bosporus inscriptions in *Judaism and Christianity*, ed. by Loewe, *et al.*, II, 89 f., n. R. Helbo was not altogether antiquarian when he blamed the loss of the Ten Tribes on the influence of Phrygian wine and the baths of Dimsit (probably another Anatolian locality, rather than Palestinian Emmaus). Cf. Shabbat 147b.

30. C. B. Welles's *Royal Correspondence in the Hellenistic Period in Greek Epigraphy*, pp. 266 f.; Oesterley's remarks in *The Labyrinth*, pp. 151 f.; and F. Cumont's "Pierre tombale érotique de Rome," *Antiquité classique*, IX, 9 f. In the light of that newly discovered inscription Cumont gave up his earlier interpretation of Vincentius' hedonistic advice in mystic terms and accepted its literal meaning. On the paintings in Vincentius' tomb, cf. M. P. Nilsson's "À propos du tombeau de Vincentius," *Revue archéologique*, XXXI–XXXII (Mélanges C. Picard), 764–69. Even in heathen Jerusalem after Hadrian, people drank from glasses bearing the inscription, "Enjoy yourself and be merry." Such glasses, found also in Cyprus, Italy, and elsewhere, seem to have been produced in large quantities in Syria during the second and third centuries. Cf. D. B. Harden's "Romano-Syrian Glasses with Mould-Blown Inscriptions," *JRS*, XXV, 163–86; and Thomsen's comments in *ZDPV*, LXIV, 232 f.

31. Cf. C. Roberts, *et al.*, "Gild of Zeus Hypsistos," *HTR*, XXIX, 39–88; P. Wendland's *Hellenistisch-römische Kultur*, pp. 194 f.; Moore's *Judaism*, II, 394. Even the splendid work of F. Cumont (cf. especially his *Oriental Religions in Roman Paganism*, preferably in the 4th French or 3d German ed.) and R. Reitzenstein, carried on by J. Toutain, W. Weber, O. Weinreich and others, is merely the beginning of a new, really scientific approach to this complex problem. Cf. also some of the studies by Eissfeldt mentioned in Chaps. II, n. 15, IV, n. 34, VI, n. 13; and such more recent essays as E. Visser's *Götter und Kulte im ptolemäischen Alexandrien*.

Research into the Jewish contributions to the various phases of the syncretistic evolution is still in its infancy. Comparatively speaking, the best, although in many points much too radical, survey of the interrelations between Judaism and the other religions of the time is to be found in the last chapter of Bousset-Gressmann's work (*Religion*, pp. 469–524). Another interesting sketch was drawn by Gressmann in *Die Aufgaben der Wissenschaft des nachbiblischen Judentums*, where the highly significant contributions of the half-Jews to the syncretistic and sectarian movements of the age are admirably summed up. Cf. also Isidore Lévy's "Cultes et rites syriens dans le Talmud," *REJ*, XLIII, 183–205; and M. J. Lagrange's "Cultes hellénistiques en Egypte et le Judaïsme," *Revue thomiste*, XXXV, 309–28.

32. Neh. 13:28–29; Josephus' *Antt.* XI, 7, 2.303, 8, 2–6.306–45; A. I. Silvestre de Sacy's "Correspondance des Samaritains de Naplouse pendant les années 1808 et suiv." in *Notices et extraits de manuscrits* of the Bibliothèque Nationale in Paris, XII, 63 (77), 173 (181); J. A. Montgomery's *Samaritans*, pp. 207, 236; Tractate Kutim II, 8, in *Sheba masekhtot qeṭanot* (Seven Minor Treatises), ed. by M. Higger, pp. 67 (Hebrew), 46 (English). The boundaries of Samaria at the end of the Second Commonwealth as well as its great fertility and population density are briefly described by Josephus in *War* III, 3, 4.48–50. Cf. the detailed analysis of Samaritan settlements in I. Ben-Zevi's *Sepher ha-Shomeronim* (Samaritans), pp. 61 ff. This work and other Samaritan studies by Ben-Zevi are distinguished by their documentation based in part on autopsy derived from the author's intimate relationships with leading Samaritans during more than three decades. Cf. also M. Gaster's *Samaritans, Their History, Doctrines and Literature*, which suffers, however, from his evident penchant toward excessively early dating of sources. On earlier attitudes of the northern population to the Temple in Jerusalem, cf. *supra*, Chap. V, n. 33.

33. Cf., e.g., A. E. Cowley's edition of *The Samaritan Liturgy*, II, 845 f.; Josephus' *Antt.* XVIII, 4, 1.85–87. This stress on orientation evidently induced a rabbi to forbid the circumcision of a Jew by a Samaritan "who circumcises only in the name of Mount Gerizim" (T. ʿA.Z. III, 13, 464; b. 26b–27a). The latter source reveals considerable hesitation on the part of the rabbis, mirroring the general ambivalence of the rabbinic attitude toward these sectarians. Cf. also J. Hershkovits's "Samaritans in Tannaitic Teachings" (Hebrew), *Yavneh*, II, 71–105; and G. Allon's "Samaritan Origins in Halakhic Tradition" (Hebrew), *Tarbiz*, XVIII, 146–56.

34. Cf. E. L. Sukenik's preliminary report on the "Samaritan Synagogue at Salbit," in the Hebrew University Museum of Antiquities' *Bulletin*, I, 29. Josephus' consistency in claiming for the Temple at Gerizim the duration of but two centuries (*Antt.* XIII, 9, 1.256; *War* I, 2, 6.63) should not blind us to his chronological weakness on this point. Cf. the literature listed *supra*, Chap. VI, n. 24; and J. Jeremias's *Passahfeier der Samaritaner*. More recently A. Spiro reinterpreted the account in the *Chronique samaritaine* (ed. by A. Neubauer in *JA*, 6th ser., XIV, 385 ff.) as an allusion to the Gerizim sanctuary destroyed by John Hyrcanus, combined it with the account of Abu'l Fatḥ and suggested, on that basis, the erection of that Temple in 388 B.C.E. Cf. the brief summary of his forthcoming paper, "When Was the Samaritan Temple Built?" in *JBL*, LXX, p. xi. To be sure, there existed also a second Samaritan temple, built some time after the Bar Kocheba revolt. It lasted for some three centuries, until it was destroyed by Emperor Zeno (474–91). But its only vestige now extant is, perhaps, the Leeds Decalogue, if we accept J. Bowman and S. Talmon's suggestion in their "Samaritan Decalogue Inscriptions," *BJRL*, XXXIII, 233 f. According to these authors all four inscriptions, here analyzed, may date from the period before Origen.

35. Cf. W. R. Taylor's "New Samaritan Inscription," *BASOR*, 81, pp. 1–5. Apart from pointing out (*ibid.*, 84, pp. 2–3) that he had previously published that "Beit Al-Almah Inscription," I. Ben-Zevi merely confirmed Taylor's dating of it in the pre-Islamic period. On the dating of *Asatir*, cf. M. Gaster's edition; his debate with B. Heller in *MGWJ*, LXXVII, 300–305; and Z. Ben-Haim's modern Hebrew transl. in *Tarbiz*, XIV, 104–25, 174–90, XV, 71–87, 128. How little reliance one may place

on the transmission of older sources by Samaritan scribes is perhaps best illustrated by the copy of Abu'l-Fath's chronicle prepared for Gaster by a recent high priest, Jacob ben Ahron. The latter not only completed that history down to his own day, but blandly inserted texts borrowed from elsewhere. "And yet the Ms. is still called the Chronicle of Abul-Fath, as if it contained nothing but what the old author had written" (Gaster's *Samaritan Oral Law*, I, 56).

Samaritan compilers also took greater liberties than their confreres of other faiths in reproducing accepted liturgical poems. They invaded the very domain of funerary rites which, because of the awe of death, usually belong to the most tenacious rituals. See M. Swarsensky's pertinent remarks in his *Begräbnis- und Trauerliturgie der Samaritaner*, pp. 14 ff. Cf. also P. Kahle's "Zwölf Marka-Hymnen aus dem 'Defter' der samaritanischen Liturgie," *Oriens Christianus*, XXIX, 77–106 (further illustrated by his pupils' dissertations, *Memar Marqa* by D. Rettig; and *Marqa-Hymnen aus der samaritanischen Liturgie* by I. Szuster); E. Robertson's *Catalogue of Samaritan Manuscripts in the John Rylands Library, Manchester,* and his "Notes and Extracts" from some of these manuscripts in *BJRL*, XIX–XXIII; and Z. Ben-Haim's "Samaritan Poems for Joyous Occasions" (Hebrew), *Tarbiz*, X, 190–200, 333–74 (publishing 28 poems from three manuscripts). According to P. Kahle's communication of 1949 (in *Theologische Rundschau*, XVII, 215; cf. *infra*, Chap. X, n. 12), John Bowman of Leeds was preparing a critical ed. of Marqa's chief work, a midrashic commentary of the Pentateuch.

Apart from more or less unconscious modifications one must beware of outright forgeries. An interesting example is furnished by the so-called Book of Joshua. Combining a fairly old midrash on Joshua with a legendary chronicle carried down to the fourth-century Samaritan revival under Baba Rabba, this important compilation has been widely known for over a century in T. W. J. Juynboll's edition. It has also been available for half a century in the English transl. by O. T. Crane, entitled *The Samaritan Chronicle*. The date of the main Arabic manuscript has been set somewhat more precisely at 1150–1260 by G. Graf in his "Zum Alter des samaritanischen 'Buches Josue,'" *Biblica*, XXIII, 62–67. But exactly because of its great importance and popularity it has stimulated ever new forgeries. Cf. I. Ben-Zevi's "Samaritan Book of Joshua and Its Recent Forgery" (Hebrew), *Keneset*, X, 130–53, describing in particular three manuscripts found in Damascus.

36. Ben-Zevi alone has analyzed five such manuscripts, including a particularly old and precious one now in the possession of the Hebrew University. Cf. his *Sepher ha-Shomeronim*, pp. 191 ff. E. Robertson has described in detail two other codices and commented, in particular, on the so-called Abisha Scroll in *BJRL*, XIX, 412 ff., XXI, 244 ff. Cf. also L. Goldberg's ed. of *Das samaritanische Pentateuchtargum;* and P. Kahle's *Cairo Geniza*, pp. 36 ff. Astonishingly, there are quite a few medieval Jewish manuscripts, the Masoretic text of which agrees in many details with that of the Samaritan codices. Cf. J. Hempel's detailed analysis of the book of Deut. in his "Innermasoretische Bestätigungen des Samaritanus," *ZAW*, LII, 254–74. The numerous Samaritan Bible commentaries, on the other hand, are of late medieval and modern vintage. Although doubtless containing kernels of ancient traditions (cf. J. Bowman's comparative study of "The Exegesis of the Pentateuch among the Samaritans and among the Rabbis," *OS*, VIII, 220–62), they have been overlaid with so many layers that they will more profitably be discussed in their medieval context.

Nor is it astonishing that the Samaritans early developed a peculiar postbiblical Hebrew dialect and pronunciation of their own, which deviated in many fundamentals from the postbiblical Hebrew current among Jews. Cf., especially F. Diening's philological study of *Das Hebräische bei den Samaritanern;* Z. Ben-Haim's plea for new approaches to "The Study of the Samaritan Language" (Hebrew), *Tarbiz*, X, 81–89, 113; and P. Kahle's brief remarks on "Die Aussprache des Hebräischen bei den Samaritanern," *Festschrift Bertholet*, pp. 281–86.

37. Josephus' *Antt.* XI, 8, 6.340–45, XII, 5, 5.257–64; II Macc. 6:2; j. 'A.Z. V, 4, 44d; Yebamot I, 6, 3a; Sifre on Deut. 56, ed. by Friedmann, fol. 87a (ed. by Finkelstein, pp. 123 f.); b. Soṭah 33b; Ḥullin 6a. Cf. *supra* Chap. VI, n. 33. On the dove cult, cf. Montgomery's *Samaritans,* pp. 168 f., 320 f. Although essentially dealing with later developments, E. F. F. Bishop's "Some Relationships of Samaritanism with Judaism, Islam and Christianity," *Moslem World,* XXXVII, 111–33, well illustrates the intellectual dependence of the Samaritans on their more powerful and dynamic neighbors, notwithstanding their stubborn adherence to the essentials of their faith.

38. Tractate Kutim, II, 8; Deut. 32:35; Marqah's *Memar,* cited in the English transl. by Gaster in his *Samaritan Oral Law,* I, 88. The authenticity of this passage need not be doubted, whether or not Marqah had a fully developed messianic doctrine. On the latter, cf. D. Rettig's remarks in *Memar Marqa,* pp. 31 f., where, however, the *argumentum a silentio* seems to be pressed too hard. Cf. also the impressive description of the Day of Judgment in the excerpts from an anonymous *Taheb* song, published by A. Merx in his *Messias oder Ta'eb der Samaritaner,* pp. 12 f. It may be noted in this connection that Philo rather consistently disparaged Rachel in favor of Leah, Joseph in favor of his brothers, and exonerated Judah for his affair with Tamar. All this may, indeed, have been derived from a Palestinian Midrash reflecting the contemporary Samaritan-Jewish controversy, as suggested by W. L. Knox in Loewe, *et al., Judaism and Christianity,* II, 92 f.

39. Acts 8:9–10; Justin's *Apology,* I, 26; Hippolytus' *Refutation of All Heresies,* VI, 2 ff., 14. In the note on his ed. of Justin's text (in the *Florilegium Patristicum,* II, 2d ed., pp. 50 f.) G. Rauschen explains the confusion by Justin of a statue dedicated to a Sabinian deity *Semoni Sanco Deo* (excavated in 1574) with one commemorating Simon Magus. Justin's mistake was repeated by Irenaeus, Tertullian, and others. Cf. also E. Meyer's *Ursprung,* II, 409 ff., III, 277 ff.; and L. H. Vincent's "Culte de Hélène à Samarie," *RB,* XLV, 221–34. Significantly, the Samaritans themselves retained but few memories of these heretical movements. The occasional references to them (e.g., by Abu'l-Fatḥ in his *Kitab at-Tarikh* [*Annales Samaritani*], ed. by E. Vilmar, p. 157; or by the author of the Samaritan chronicle, ed. by E. N. Adler and M. Seligsohn in *REJ,* XLV, 225 ff.) are greatly colored by the Christian tradition. Cf. Montgomery's *Samaritans,* pp. 265 ff. The Jews, too, retained but vague, if any, recollections about these sectarian movements among their neighbors. Cf. H. J. Schoeps's "Simon Magus in der Haggada?" in his *Aus frühchristlicher Zeit,* pp. 239–54.

40. *Antt.* XVIII, 2, 2.30; M. R.H. II, 2; Juynboll's *Chronicum Samaritanum,* XLVII. This story of the antecedents of the destruction of the Temple is typical of the ancients' delight in describing how slight initial episodes ultimately resulted in major disasters. It is no more far-fetched than the well-known rabbinic legend about the fall of Jerusalem because of a case of mistaken identity between two feuding individuals called Qamṣa and Bar Qamṣa (cf. Giṭṭin 55b–56a).

41. Sirach 50:25 f.; Testament of Levi 7; M. Demai III, 4; Berakhot VII, 1; T. Pesaḥim I, 15, 156. The generally more friendly Samaritan-Jewish relations since the later Middle Ages, will be discussed later.

42. Even in Egypt the Samaritan communities seem to have been sporadic rather than continuous. The village Samareia, for example, may well have been settled by Samaritan soldiers brought to Egypt by Alexander (Josephus' *Antt.* XI, 8, 6.345; cf. Marcus's note thereon). But the subsequent papyri discovered there indicate the presence of a mixed Jewish and pagan, rather than Samaritan, population. The existence of a Samaritan temple in Egypt rivaling that of Onias is extremely dubious. Josephus is undoubtedly right that the Egyptian Samaritans fought bitterly only in behalf of their sanctuary at Gerizim (*Antt.* XII, 1, 1.10; XIII, 3, 4.74–79). Cf. also A. Büchler's *Tobiaden,* pp. 204 f. In Rome, Samaritans are occasionally mentioned by Josephus, but they soon disappear from the records until we learn about a conflict over their local synagogue in the days of Theodoric the Great (about 507–11; cf. Cassiodorus' *Variae,* III, 45, in *MGH,* Auctores antiquissimi, XII, 101). It may be mentioned here, in passing, that a modern liturgical compiler of unknown date (in a manuscript copy of 1906 at the Prussian State Library) mentioned Samaritan settlements in Nablus (Shechem), Damascus, Gaza, Philistia, Egypt, Aleppo, Hamat, Safed, Tripolis, and Ḥaṣerim. Cf. Swarsensky's *Begräbnis- und Trauerliturgie,* p. 15. But there is no evidence that any of these medieval communities, except the first two, had endured for any length of time.

43. There is fairly wide agreement that the name "Sadducee" was derived from the priestly house of Zadok. As late as Sirach's prayer, often considered the prototype of the *'Amidah,* we find next to thanksgiving for the "horn to sprout from the house of David," one for God's choice of "the sons of Zadok to be priests" (51:12, viii–ix, Hebrew version). The name "Pharisees" may either be connected with their "exegetical" work on Scripture, or, more likely, express their "separation" from the nations. The latter point is strongly stressed by Schürer in his *Geschichte,* II, 465 ff., as well as by L. Baeck in his *Pharisees,* pp. 5 ff., with particular reference to Sifra on Lev. 20:26 (ed. by Weiss fol. 93d): "Just as I am a Parush, ye shall be Perushim. If ye are separated from the nations, says the Lord, ye belong to me; if not, ye belong to Nebukadnezzar, the King of Babylon, and his companions." All sorts of other explanations have been suggested, however. For example, in his "Sadducee and Pharisee: the Origin and Significance of the Names," *BJRL,* XXII, 144–59, T. W. Manson argued, with reference to a Palmyrene inscription, that "Sadducee" was derived from *syndikos* (member of Council), whose assistant (*boethos*) gave the name to the subsidiary group of Boethosians, while "Pharisee" originated from *parsaah* (Persian), i.e., a nickname given by opponents because of the Pharisaic acceptance of the Parsee belief in a future life, angels, etc. More recently, L. Finkelstein suggested that the original meaning was something like "heretics" and that the Pharisees were so styled by their opponents after the break during the Maccabean era. Cf. his *Ha-Perushim,* p. 33 n. 119. In any case, it is likely that at first they considered themselves but direct successors of the *ḥasidim,* and may long have preferred to use that designation. But as often happened in the history of party strife, an original name of opprobrium, coined by opponents, was ultimately accepted by the party in question and lost its derogatory meaning. That is why Josephus could pride himself on having governed his "life by the rules of the Pharisees, a sect having points of resemblance to that which the Greeks call the Stoic school" (*Life* II, 12). Nevertheless, even the talmudic sages had not entirely forgotten the old deprecatory connotation of this term.

44. Josephus' *Antt.* XV, 10, 4.368–71, XVII, 2, 5.42; Dessau's *Geschichte,* II, 760, n. 2, following Mommsen. Here seems to lie the solution of difficulties which have given rise to lengthy discussions. The figure of 6,000 Pharisees, probably taken by Josephus from Nicolaus of Damascus, a contemporary of the event (Meyer's *Ursprung,* II, 286, n. 2), appears authentic, notwithstanding Elbogen's objections (cf. his "Einige neuere Theorien über den Ursprung der Pharisäer und Sadduzäer," *Abrahams Mem. Vol.,* p. 136). As a total it is too low if compared, for instance, with the 4,000 Essenes recorded by both Philo (*Quod omnis probus liber,* XII, 75) and Josephus (*Antt.* XVIII, 1, 5.20). Acts (2:41; 4:4) speak of 3,000 to 5,000 Christians in Jerusalem during the early apostolic age. That the organized Pharisaic groups must have had, therefore, many more than 6,000 members is true whether or not we include the Essenes in the total.

As to the relation between the Pharisees and the rest of the people, it is well known that the New Testament writers single them out as a relatively small minority in the population, while rabbinic literature tacitly presupposes their identity with the people as a whole. Occasionally, to be sure, the Talmud speaks derogatorily of the *Perushim* as a group. But inasmuch as its own traditions largely follow those of the Pharisees it simply identifies them with those accepted by the entire people. Josephus, on numerous occasions, attests at least to the extraordinary popularity of his own, the Pharisaic group. While these contradictory attitudes have been re-echoed in modern investigations, the distinction here made between the minority of official Pharisees, or members of the fraternities (*ḥaberim;* this identification remains unimpaired by S. Zeitlin's contrary arguments in his "Am Haarez," *JQR,* XXIII, 45–61), and the unofficial majority which followed their lead, seems the most plausible. Apparently most of the official members belonged to the middle class, although many had come from the proletariat. That is why the sociological explanation of the chief Pharisaic teachings as "plebeian" ideologies, offered by M. Weber in his otherwise illuminating sketch on the Pharisees (*Religionssoziologie,* III, 401–42), has no historical foundation. Similarly, the main thesis of L. Finkelstein's comprehensive work on *The Pharisees* can be accepted only with serious reservations. The view that, like the prophetic movement before and rabbinic Judaism after it, Pharisaism was essentially but the product "of a persistent cultural battle, carried on in Palestine for fifteen centuries between the submerged, unlanded groups, and their oppressors, the great landowners," is a dangerous oversimplification. When narrowed down in the Maccabean and Herodian periods to struggles between plebeian traders and artisans living in the "slums" of Jerusalem and the landowning aristocracy and priesthood of the capital, as well as between the city and the countryside, it is clearly controverted by the relative absence of sharp urban-rural conflicts in ancient Palestine. Cf. *supra,* Chap. III, n. 14; the present writer's review of Finkelstein's work in *JBL,* LIX, 60–67, as well as the more severe, often exaggerating, strictures by S. Z. Zeitlin in *Horeb,* V, 27–42, and by G. Allon in his "Sociological Method in the Study of the Halacha" (Hebrew), *Tarbiz,* X, 241–82.

Equally obscure is the historic origin of these sectarian controversies. In "Der Prophet Maleachi und der Ursprung des Pharisäerbundes," *AR,* XXIX, 1–21, O. Holtzmann has suggested that in Malachi 3:16 we have the earliest record of such an association, out of which grew the Pharisaic order. Whether or not this hypothesis is correct, the Jewish tradition which claims Pharisaism as the direct inheritor of Ezra and the Men of the Great Synagogue, appears even more justified by recently acquired knowledge. The antecedents of its struggle with Sadduceeism, however, seem to go back to a much earlier age: to the conflict between the two priestly families of Zadok and Abiathar. This conflict became particularly sharp about 622, but was carried over into the exilic age and after. Cf., in particular, A. Bentzen's and other studies cited *supra,* Chap. III, n. 26. On the connections between the Pharisees and their immediate predecessors, the *ḥasidim,* cf. W. Förster's analysis of the pertinent passages in I Maccabees, the Ethiopic Enoch, and the Book of Jubilees in "Der Ursprung des Pharisäismus," *ZNW,* XXXIV, 35–51; L. Gulkowitsch's "Entwicklung des Begriffes Ḥasid im Alten Testament," *Acta et Commentationes Universitatis Tartuensis* (Dorpatensis), B: Humaniora XXXII, Pt. 4, pp. 5–38; and B. D. Eerdmans's essay on "The Chasidim" in *OS,* I, 176–257. Cf. also in general, B.-Z. Katz's *Perushim, Ṣedoqim, Qanna'im, Noṣrim* (Pharisees, Sadducees, Zealots, Christians). While replete with interesting insights in details, Katz's new approach to these complex historical movements has not persuaded the present writer to alter any of his basic views on the main trends in the history of the Second Jewish Commonwealth.

The literature concerning these religious movements is enormous. Most of the writings, however, still reveal much theological bias. Many Christian theologians, following the polemical attitude of the New Testament, severely criticize both movements. The Pharisees, especially, fare badly at the hands of—to mention only the greatest among their recent critics—Wellhausen, Schürer, Bousset, and Meyer. Their defense has been undertaken by R. T. Herford, in his *Pharisaism: Its Aim and Its Method, The Pharisees,* and *Judaism in the New Testament Period;* and still more successfully by G. F. Moore. Moore first attacked the prevailing treatment of Pharisaic Judaism among his coreligionists in his article, "Christian Writers on Judaism," *HTR,* XIV, 197–254. Then he proceeded to state the case in a positive fashion in his *Judaism.* Although slightly apologetical, this has become the standard work on Jewish theology of that period.

Among Jews the picture is the reverse. Everybody claims the Pharisees for himself. Not only has orthodoxy identified itself from time immemorial with Pharisaism, but Reform Judaism, too, sees in that movement a progressive, democratic current in the Jewish religion of the Second Commonwealth. Geiger was in this respect, too, Reform's pathfinder. Among contemporary scholars J. Z. Lauterbach reflected this theory in his study of "The Pharisees and Their Teachings," *HUCA,* VI, 69–139, while L. Baeck defended it by a positive restatement of Pharisaic lore. Jewish nationalist publicists and historians have likewise tried to claim the Pharisees for themselves. Especially S. Dubnow, in his *Weltgeschichte,* II, 187 ff., 571 ff., made of them the purest representatives of ancient nationalism. For a criticism of this and Meyer's theory, see I. Elbogen's remarks in *Abrahams Mem. Vol.,* pp. 135–48. All this merely shows how far we still are from general agreement even upon the fundamental problems. The very distinction between Jewish and Christian scholars, which had to be noted here, is indicative of the strong atavisms prejudicial to objective investigation.

45. Temurah 16a; Pesaḥim 66a; M. Pe'ah II, 6; Yadaim IV, 3; Sanhedrin, XI, 3, etc.; Josephus' *War* I, 5, 2.110. The context of the latter Mishnah, namely the laws concerning the treatment of an heretical elder which presuppose the existence of a Sanhedrin in Jerusalem, suggests that this passage originated before 70. Josephus, himself a Pharisee, on many occasions stressed the "accuracy" and "exactitude" of the Pharisaic interpretation of the law. Cf. *War* II, 8, 14.162; and other passages cited by Schlatter in his *Theologie,* pp. 204 ff. With what tenacity age-old traditions have persisted in the Palestinian environment even in modern times was shown by H. W. Hertzberg in his "Tradition in Palästina," *PJB,* XXII, 84–104. Cf. also J. Moffatt's *Thrill of Tradition;* N. Rotenstreich's "On the Notion of Tradition in Judaism," *JR,* XXVIII, 28–36; L. Finkelstein's "Transmission of the Early Rabbinic Traditions," *HUCA,* XVI, 115–35 (illustrating five major methods of transmission); and the literature listed *supra,* Chap. II, n. 10.

Of course, spokesmen for more conciliatory trends were not altogether absent. The author of the Book of Jubilees, for instance, seems to have attempted a reconciliation between the Sadducean insistence upon the written law and the Pharisaic emphasis on the oral commandments, by supplying revealed documentation for a large part of Pharisaic law. That he also synthesized Palestinian law with customs prevailing among Hellenistic Jewry has been pointed out by A. Büchler in his "Traces des idées et des coutumes hellénistiques dans le Livre des Jubilés," *REJ,* LXXXIX, 321–48. This appears more plausible than C. Albeck's assumption that the Book of Jubilees represents a distinct sectarian current opposed to both Pharisaism and Sadduceeism, or S. Zeitlin's suggestion that it was written in the early postexilic age by an author or authors opposed to many Pentateuchal laws. Cf. Albeck's keen analysis of *Das Buch der Jubiläen und die Halacha;* L. Finkelstein's reply, in his review of this work in *MGWJ,* LXXVI, 525–34, and the excursus on "The Date of the Book of Jubilees" in his "Pre-Maccabean Documents" in *HTR,* XXXVI, 19 ff. (175–167 B.C.E.); S. Zeitlin's "Book of Jubilees: Its Character and Significance," *JQR,* XXX, 1–31.

46. *Antt.* XVIII, 1, 3.14. Cf. Thackeray's *Josephus,* p. 96. Josephus, as a Pharisee, wrote the words "under the earth" for the benefit of his Greek readers. In another chapter he speaks quite openly of a "most holy place in heaven" allotted to the

righteous, and "the darker regions of the nether world [Hades]" assigned to the wicked (*War* III, 8, 5.373–75). On the Pharisaic distinction between the two groups, cf. the passages cited in Bousset-Gressmann's *Religion*, pp. 272 ff.; and Moore's *Judaism*, II, 298, 318. Josephus' treatment of this and other theological concepts of the age has been reëxamined and compared with rabbinic sources by H. Guttmann in his *Darstellung der jüdischen Religion bei Flavius Josephus;* and, from the standpoint of New Testament scholarship, by A. Schlatter in his *Theologie*. Cf. also S. Rappaport's *Agada und Exegese bei Flavius Josephus;* and *supra*, Chap. VI, n. 24.

47. Dan. 12:2; Enoch 25:6. Cf. also Sirach 10:9–11, 14:17–19, 28:21, 41:1–4; Enoch 22:3–4, etc.; and *supra*, Chaps. V, n. 5, VI, n. 53–54.

48. M. Sanhedrin X, 1, elaborated in b. 90 ff. To be sure, in the Cambridge manuscript of the Mishnah and some other texts the crucial words *min ha-torah* are missing and some scholars assume that the original sanction concerned only those who denied resurrection per se. However, their explanation that these words were added at a time when everyone acknowledged resurrection and that, therefore, the rabbis had to draw some line of demarcation (cf. H. Loewe's remarks in his *et al.'s Judaism and Christianity*, II, 25 f.) seems less plausible than the assumption that the formula originated at a time when the problem of scriptural backing was a major controversial issue. In this connection it is immaterial whether the early Sadducees or only their disciples negated resurrection (cf. Aptowitzer's *Parteipolitik*, pp. 264 ff.). Such negation was inherent in their whole attitude, which reflected their peculiar political and social position. It is even questionable whether they were ready to admit the immortality of the soul, which, as a Hellenistic heritage without scriptural support, probably also appeared obnoxious to them.

49. Cf. Elbogen's *Gottesdienst*, p. 44; Finkelstein's comments in *JQR*, XVI, 142; T. Berakhot III, 9, 7; b. 29a. Here the omission of God's might and his influence on rain is declared as nullifying the whole prayer, which must consequently be said over again. Since the farmer was more directly interested in rain than the inhabitant of Jerusalem and since as late as the days of R. Joshua and R. Eliezer (about 100 C.E.) the custom of adding the passage about rain on a particular day of the Feast of Tabernacles was not yet universally established (cf. M. Ta'anit I, 1), L. Finkelstein's interpretation connecting it with a controversy over the respective merits of wine and water (cf. his *Pharisees*, I, 110 f.) seems extremely forced. In fact, the whole problem of dating the '*Amidah* is still unsettled. In his recent "Structure and History of the *Tefilah*," *JQR*, XL, 331–57, M. Liber has attempted to superimpose what he calls the "liturgical" approach, which is admittedly "intuitive," upon the customary literary criticism. His general conclusion is that the initial three benedictions, representing "three episodes of the Messianic drama," best fit into the period of the Maccabean revolt, even if most of the other more neutral benedictions had originated in the more quiescent Persian or early Hellenistic periods; this will meet with the approval of many scholars who generally place their reliance only on more objective criteria.

50. Testament of Gad 5:3; M. Abot I, 3; 'Eduyot V, 7. If Meyer's dating, followed by R. Eppel (in *Le Piétisme juif dans les Testaments des douze patriarches*), that the Testaments were written not later than 198 B.C.E. in the Syrian Diaspora (which then also included Galilee) be correct, Gad's utterance is evidently chronologically as well as geographically removed from the scene of the raging sectarian controversies, but this and other views of the "Testaments" quoted in the following remarks can also be documented by later Palestinian sources. Cf. also E. J. Bickerman's "Date of the Testaments of the Twelve Patriarchs," *JBL*, LXIX, 245–60 (the first quarter of the second century or, possibly, the last decades of the third century). It should be

noted, however, that 'Aqabiah's statement in Abot, because of its possible implications for the doctrine of resurrection, may have undergone some editorial alterations. Cf. L. Finkelstein's "Introductory Study to *Pirke Abot*," *JBL*, LVII, 33 f. Cf. also his *Mabo le-Massektot Abot ve-Abot d'Rabbi Natan* (Introduction to the Treatises Abot and Abot of Rabbi Nathan), pp. 53 ff., 64 ff., and in general, G. F. Moore's "Fate and Free Will in the Jewish Philosophies According to Josephus," *HTR*, XXII, 371–89.

51. II Macc. 15:11–17; Testament of Gad 1:9, 3:1; of Asher 1:5. Cf. also A. Marmorstein's *Doctrine of Merits in Old Rabbinical Literature*. The controversy between the Pharisaic teachers Shemayah and Abtalyon as to whether the miracle of the Red Sea had been the effect of the Israelites' own merits or of those of their progenitor, Abraham, is turned by L. Finkelstein into a patrician-plebeian issue. But this interpretation is controverted by the context. Precisely the same contradictory views were echoed several generations later by two such staunch Hillelites as R. Eleazar ben Azariah and R. Judah the Patriarch. Cf. Mekilta, *Beshallaḥ*, IV, ed. by Lauterbach, I, 219 f.; and Finkelstein's *Pharisees*, I, 255 f., II, 680, n. 10.

52. Sirach 15:14–15, 21:27; T. Ḥagigah III, 35, 238; j. R.H. I, 2, 56d; M. Ḥullin II, 8, as compared with T. II, 18, 503 and b. 40a. The text of Sirach 21:27 is here given according to the Greek version. On its connection with sin, cf. Box and Oesterley's introduction to their translation in Charles's *Apocrypha*, I, 311 f. In j. Ḥagigah III, 8, 79d, the reading is "Watch the Pharisees purify the orb of the sun." On the relation between the seven branches of the *menorah* and the seven planets, cf. Philo's *Quis rerum divinarum haeres*, XLV, 221; Josephus' *Antt.* III, 6, 7.146.

53. Sifre on Num. 119, ed. by Friedmann fol. 40a; Targum on Exod. 19:6; M. Ḥagigah I, 8. Pseudo-Jonathan amplified Onkelos' description by adding "Kings adorned with crowns." He may have wished to emphasize that the people would wear the crown of the Torah and, *qua* scholars, resemble kings. Cf. the concluding sentence of the letter of the Jerusalem authorities to Egypt concerning the Feast of Dedication in II Macc. 2:18; and Baeck's *Pharisees*, pp. 21, 41. If we are to accept Sonne's brilliant reconstruction, the theme underlying the entire series of the Dura synagogue's paintings is that of the three crowns. Here, too, the crown of Torah, personified by Moses, clearly overshadows the other two in importance. Cf. *HUCA*, XX, 255 ff. The development of the educational and other institutions by Pharisaic Judaism will be treated more amply in Chap. XIV.

54. C. C. Torrey, following the more widely accepted view, that the Assumption was written soon after Herod, suggested that the central figure in the expected redemption, Taxo of the tribe of Levi (9:1), was a camouflage for "Hasmonean" (both words have the same numerical value in Aramaic and, one may add, also in Hebrew: *hashmona'i*). But this expectation did not necessarily imply any revolutionary upheaval. Cf. Schürer's *Geschichte*, III, 294 ff.; Torrey's " 'Taxo' in the Assumption of Moses," *JBL*, LXII, 1–7, and his debate with H. H. Rowley, *ibid.*, LXIV, 141–43, 395–97. On the other hand, G. Volkmar in his edition of the text in 1867 insisted that the book was written after the Bar Kocheba revolt. Cf. also S. Zeitlin's "Assumption of Moses and the Revolt of Bar Kokba," *JQR*, XXXVIII, 1–45.

55. Josephus' *War* II, 8, 1.118; 13, 3.254–57; 17, 8–9.433–48. The Christian apostle, Simon Zealotes, as he is called in Luke 6:15 and Acts 1:13, seems to have been a typical zealot of native stock. The designation, "Canaanite," given him in Matthew 10:4 and Mark 3:18, undoubtedly is but a mistranslation of *qananaios*, a derivative of *qananaia* (Zealots, in Aramaic), which appears in several manuscripts. Cf. H. Alford's note in his edition of *The Greek Testament*, I, 72. On the whole the rabbis re-

tained the memory of Zealotic violence rather than patriotism. J. Klausner's more sympathetic treatment of some of their leaders (John of Gischala and Simon son of Giyoras) and his assumption that there was a basic cleavage between *Sicarii* and Zealots are based on a rather subjective evaluation of Josephus. Cf. his *Ke-she-umah nilḥemet 'al ḥerutah* (When a People Fights for Freedom), 3d ed., pp. 297 ff.

56. Josephus' *War* II, 8, 7.139–42; *Life* II.11–12; *Antt.* XVIII, 1, 5.18–20; T. Demai II, 2 ff., 47; b. Bekhorot 30b–31a; Philo's *Quod omnis probus liber*, XII, 80. According to the Slavonic Josephus, the Essenian initiates swore by "invoking the living God and calling to witness His almighty right hand and the Spirit of God the incomprehensible [perhaps a corruption from: ineffable], and the Seraphim and Cherubim, who have insight into all, and the whole heavenly host." Cf. Thackeray and Marcus's ed. of Josephus' *Works*, III, 646.

57. Cf. K. Kohler's "Essenes and Apocalyptic Literature" in his *Studies, Addresses and Personal Papers*, pp. 20–36. The inherent difficulties of such investigations, which have already resulted in a "labyrinth" of contradictory explanations, are certainly discouraging. W. Bauer's thorough, though not unbiased, examination of the sources, in his monographic article, "Essener," *PWRE*, Supp. Vol. IV, 386–430, yielded more negative than positive results. His attempt, in particular, to eliminate as many Jewish components of Essenism as possible, misled him into negation after negation, without enabling him to offer any positive solution. F. Perles's "Hebrew Names of the Essenes and the Therapeutæ" (*JQR*, XVII, 405 f.) adds merely one more to numerous previous explanations of the two strange names. More significant is I. Heinemann's "Sektenfrömmigkeit der Therapeuten" (*MGWJ*, LXXVIII, 104–17), in which Philo's statements are thoroughly reëxamined. Heinemann reaches the following judicious conclusion: "Ancient mystics are usually reticent in revealing their secrets to visitors. Of whatever Philo may have actually known, he gives us only a small selection in accordance with the style of a Greek laudation. Even this he translates from the idiom of living piety into that of the popular philosophy and the quasi-religion of the metropolitan populace" (p. 113). Heinemann also points out the difference between the more practical Palestinian Essenes and their more philosophically minded Egyptian confreres. Cf. also F. Cumont's "Esséniens et Pythagoriciens, d'après un passage de Josèphe," *CRAI*, 1930, pp. 99–112; K. Friedmann's "Esseni," *Religio*, XII, 91–103; and J. J. Modi's "Who Were the Persian Magi Who Influenced the Jewish Sect of the Essenes?" *Festschrift Moritz Winternitz*, pp. 208–11, referring to a mystic sect, Maga, in ancient Persia and thereby incidentally explaining the name Essene as derived from the Avestan *ashavan*, or holy. Although this explanation agrees with Philo's statement that the Essenes "derive their name from piety" (*Quod omnis probus liber*, XII, 75; XIII, 91), it seems rather far-fetched.

58. Hippolytus' *Refutation of All Heresies*, IX, 20 (the sentence, "nay, some would not even rise from a couch" may, like the rest of the chapter, be a paraphrase of something Hippolytus read in his copy of Josephus); Philo's *Quod omnis probus liber*, XII, 75; Josephus' *War* II, 20, 4.567. Although in the latter passage Josephus seems unduly influenced by Philo (cf. Schürer's *Geschichte*, II, 656, n. 1), there is no reason to doubt their numbering more than 4,000. Cf. *supra*, n. 44.

59. Cf. Mekilta 'Amaleq, IV, ed. by Lauterbach, II, 187; T. Yadaim II, 20, 684; Sifre on Deut. 48 (cf. Finkelstein's note on his ed., p. 112, l. 5), etc. Cf. also M. Simon's "Sur deux hérésies juives mentionnées par Justin Martyr," *RHPR*, XVIII, 54–58 (with reference to Justin's *Dialogue*, LXXX, 4; *PG*, VI, 665). The comparative aloofness of contemporary scholars (until the discovery of the Dead Sea scrolls) toward the study of Essenism and its offshoots is the more regrettable, the more our eyes are opened to the great religious significance of the strange sectarian movements in

Palestine during the first centuries of the Christian Era. Between them and the Essenes run many unsuspected threads. For instance, the influence of the Essenes on the Sampseans (from *shemesh*, or sun) is clearly attested by Epiphanius (*Adversus Haereses*, XIX, 2; *PG*, XLI, 264). Not less evident are the Essenian ingredients in the work of Elchasai, early in the second century. His followers, the Elkasites, a Judeo-Christian and radically anti-Pauline sect, reached out a century later, characteristically enough, to Apamaea and Rome. Cf. especially W. Brandt's *Elchasai*. The study of the other early sects of Baptists, Hemerobaptists, Masbotheans, Nazarites, and Ebionites, in the light of modern research in the history of religion, would also yield considerable new data for the understanding of Essenism. Cf. J. Thomas's *Mouvement baptiste en Palestine et Syrie;* and H. Grégoire's brief "Note sur les survivances chrétiennes des Esséniens et des sectes apparentées," *Nouvelle Clio,* I–II, 354–59. In the case of the Mandaeans, at least, entirely new vistas have been opened through Lidzbarski's publications of their scriptures, and the ensuing discussions. But the problem has been inextricably complicated by the uncertainty in dating. While Lidzbarski and others accept Mandaism as a pre-Christian Baptist movement, some scholars (E. Peterson in his "Urchristentum und Mandäismus," *ZNW*, XXVII, 55–98; F. C. Burkitt in his "Mandaeans," *JTS*, XXIX, 225–35; and H. Lietzmann in his "Beitrag zur Mandäerfrage," *SB* Berlin, 1930, pp. 596–608) declare it to be a sect which sprang from the later Christian gnosis in the period after the rise of Islam. A middle road is chosen by I. Scheftelowitz in his interesting investigation into "Die mandäische Religion und das Judentum," *MGWJ*, LXXIII, 211–32. The sect originated, he thinks, in the second or third century, out of a Judeo-Christian group, and became inimical to both Judaism and Christianity. Cf. also W. Baumgartner's brief review of "Der heutige Stand der Mandäerfrage," *TZ*, VI, 401–10; S. A. Pallis's *Essay on Mandaean Bibliography;* A. Loisy's *Mandéisme et les origines chrétiennes;* and E. S. Drower's (Stevens's) anthropological study of *The Mandaeans of Iraq and Iran.*

60. Cf. especially S. Schechter's *Fragments of a Zadokite Work,* Hebrew text, pp. 1, l. 16; 2, l. 6; 4, ll. 13, 15, 20 ff.; 6, ll. 12, 19; and the corresponding passages in his English transl. or in that by R. H. Charles in the latter's *Apocrypha,* II, 785 ff. Since Schechter's publication, in 1910, of these fragments from tenth- and eleventh-century copies found at the Cairo Genizah, this sect has intrigued many investigators. The large crop which sprang up within the next two years alone may be gleaned from the list compiled by Juster in *Empire romain,* I, 26, n. 1. The basic contribution still is L. Ginzberg's *Unbekannte jüdische Sekte.* While one may regard the question of the Pharisaic, and not Sadducean, background of the sect as definitely settled, the problem of dating is still unsolved. Some (e.g., E. Meyer, in his *Gemeinde des Neuen Bundes im Lande Damaskus;* and again in his *Ursprung,* II, 47 ff.) believe that the formation of the sect goes back to the pre-Maccabean period, but others have dated it as late as the seventh or the eighth century (Büchler); or even the tenth or the eleventh century (Marmorstein). The question was reopened, but not settled, by G. Hölscher ("Zur Frage nach Alter und Herkunft der sogen. Damaskusschrift," *ZNW*, XXVIII, 21–46), who inclined to a later dating; and, especially, by R. Eisler ("The Sadoqite Book of the New Covenant: Its Origin and Date," *Gaster Anniv. Vol.*, pp. 110–43) who reached rather startling conclusions. In his opinion the *bene Ṣadoq* of our document "are the Ṣadukai of the Samaritan chronicles, the Sadducaei led by Dositheus of the Pseudo-Clementines and finally the 'disciples of Dostai' in Mesene, called 'Mandeans.' " Eisler also believed that the *moreh ṣedeq* and *yore ha-yaḥid* of the Damascus book was none other than John the Baptist of the Christian tradition whom the Mandaeans exalted in similar terms. These extremist views are not borne out by the existing sources. His dating, however, of the Damascus writings in the first century c.e., once considered the regnant opinion, has now become questionable. It largely depends on the dating of the new scrolls. See *infra,* n. 61–62. Cf. also F. F. Hvidberg's *Menigheden af den nye Pagt in Damascus* (The Community of the

New Covenant in Damascus); L. Rost's *Damaskusschrift neu bearbeitet;* J. Schousboe's *Secte juive de l'alliance nouvelle au pays de Damas et le christianisme naissant* (like Eisler, identifies the *moreh ṣedeq* with John the Baptist); B. I. Reicke's *Jewish "Damascus Documents" and the New Testament;* and K. G. Goetz's "Ist der *mebakker* der Geniza-Fragmente wirklich das Vorbild des christlichen Episkopats?" *ZNW,* XXX, 89–93. On the latter point, cf., however, *infra,* Chap. X, n. 45.

61. Cf. W. H. Brownley's ed. of the Habakkuk Commentary in M. Burrows *et al., Dead Sea Scrolls,* p. xix, and Plates LVIII and LX. Cf. also Brownley's earlier publication of "The Jerusalem Habakkuk Scroll," *BASOR,* 112, pp. 8–18; H. L. Ginsberg's early comments on "The Hebrew University Scrolls from the Sectarian Cache," *ibid.,* pp. 21 f. In his translation of "Le 'Commentaire d'Habacuc,' " *RHR,* CXXXVII, 129–71, A. Dupont-Sommer first suggested the identification of the Wicked Priest with Aristobulus II (67–63 B.C.E.). He has further elaborated this point in his *Observations sur le Commentaire d'Habacuc;* and his *Aperçus préliminaires sur les manuscrits hébreux de la Mer Morte.* Here he also suggested that the Righteous Teacher was none other than Onias who, according to Josephus (*Antt.* XIV, 2, 1–2. 21–25), was executed in Jerusalem in 65 B.C.E. R. Goossens went a step further. Combining Josephus' report with various talmudic legends (Ta'anit 23a, etc.) concerning the effective prayers for rain of Ḥoni ha-me'aggel, he collected and analyzed "Les Éléments messianiques des traditions sur Onias le Juste chez Josèphe et dans le Talmud" in the *Bulletin* of the Belgian Academy, 5th Ser., XXXVI, 397–426; and, finally, spoke with assurance of "Onias le Juste, le Messie de la Nouvelle Alliance, lapidé à Jérusalem en 65 avant J.-C." in *Nouvelle Clio,* I–II, 336–53. Cf. also his review article, "L'État actuel des recherches sur les manuscrits de la Mer Morte et sur la secte de la Nouvelle-Alliance," *ibid.,* pp. 634–71. Dupont-Sommer and Goossens have made such a strong case for the dating of the Habakkuk "commentary" in the first century B.C.E. that even P. Kahle is prepared to accept it, despite his general penchant toward considering the various Dead Sea scrolls as having been written several centuries apart. Because of an assumed addition in Column 28, he insists, for example, on dating the Isaiah scroll as late as the third or fourth century C.E. Cf. his "Age of the Scrolls," *Vetus Testamentum,* I, 38–48. On the other hand, B. Reicke's attempt to advance the Habakkuk scroll to the pre-Maccabean age and to equate the Wicked Priest with Joseph son of Tobiah (of *Antt.* XII, 4, 5.180–85) has little to commend itself. Cf. his otherwise very meritorious study of what he calls "Die Ta'āmire-Schriften und die Damaskus-Fragmente," *Studia theologica,* II, 45–70. Cf. also, from another angle, G. Kuhn's "Zur Bedeutung der neuen palästinischen Handschriftenkunde für die neutestamentliche Wissenschaft," *Theologische Literatur-Zeitung,* LVII, 72–86; and the literature listed *supra,* Chap. III, n. 27. None of these scholars, however, has paid sufficient attention to the social motivations which are quite evident throughout the booklet. Even where Habakkuk spoke of scoffing at "kings" and of "princes" becoming a derision (1:10), our author blames the regime of the Wicked Priest for "deriding the many" and making fun of a "large multitude." Cf. Plate LVI. These few hints must suffice here.

62. Cf. Sukenik's *Megillot genuzot,* II, 28 ff.; and Burrows's *Dead Sea Scrolls,* II, Plates I ll. 9 ff., V ll. 1 ff., 9. Sukenik's attempt to interpret away the crucial word *honam* in ll. 12–13 and to lend it a purely spiritual connotation, seems rather farfetched. The pledge is, moreover, a clear reminiscence of the injunction in *Shema'* to love God "with all thine heart, and with all thy soul and with all thy might" (Deut. 6:5), the latter obviously likewise referring to material goods. The similarities of this sect not only with the New Covenanters but also with the Essenes and Therapeutae is strongly stressed by Brownlee in his "Comparison of the Covenanters of the Dead Sea Scrolls with Pre-Christian Jewish Sects," *BA,* XIII, 49–72. Brownlee thus explains Josephus' failure to mention these marginal sects, because in the lat-

ter's opinion they merely formed a part of the Essenian group. While this is possible, one must not overlook the differences particularly between Essenian quietism and the political activism of the New Covenanters and their closer associates. On the other hand, such activism did not necessarily involve taking sides in the Sadducean-Pharisaic controversy. Hence, Onias the Just, if he be the Righteous Teacher, may indeed have maintained a position of neutrality on this issue, as described by Josephus. He may have anticipated therein the early Christians' opposition to both groups as falling equally short of meeting squarely the grave social problems of the country.

CHAPTER X: THE GREAT SCHISM

1. A Messiah ben Joseph, or ben Ephraim, is mentioned clearly only in such later sources as the Targum on Cant. 4:5 (comparing the two deliverers of the house of David and Ephraim to Moses and Aaron). However, C. C. Torrey has made a good case for the existence of this belief for several centuries B.C.E., although his interpretation of some passages seems rather forced. Cf. his "Messiah Son of Ephraim," *JBL*, LXVI, 253–77. Cf. also G. R. Beasley-Murray's and M. H. Segal's mutually independent analyses of "The Two Messiahs in the Testaments of the Twelve Patriarchs," *JTS*, XLVIII, 1–12; and "The Descent of the Messianic King in the Testaments of the Twelve Patriarchs" (Hebrew), *Tarbiz*, XXI, 129–36. Apparently dating from the pre-Maccabean era (cf. *supra*, Chap. IX, n. 50), these Testaments are particularly revealing. Segal has pointed out, in particular, the affinity of the messianic doctrine of the author of these Testaments, looking forward to a redeemer from the combined houses of Levi and Judah, with that of the New Covenanters of Damascus.

2. IV Ezra 5:4–7, 7:28–30; II Baruch 29:5. The term *aeon* is not used here in its technical Platonic sense which basically differed from the Jewish concept of the world to come or even of the messianic era. Cf. *infra*, Chap. XV, n. 31. The Baruch Apocalypse, or possibly some independent Aggadah, was the source of similar expectations, only with still more inflated figures, cited in behalf of unnamed Christian "presbyters" by Irenaeus in his *Contra Haereses*, V, 33, 3 (*PG*, VII, 1213). Of the vast literature on these writings cf. B. Violet's German reconstruction of *Apokalypsen des Esra und des Baruch;* C. G. Montefiore's *IV Ezra: a Study in the Development of Universalism;* and particularly L. Gry's *Dires prophétiques d'Esdras*, and his "Date de la fin des temps selon les révélations du Pseudo-Philon et de Baruch," *RB*, XLVIII, 337–56. Gry goes too far, however, in trying to identify the author of IV Esdras with R. Eleazar ben Azariah, who accompanied R. Gamaliel II on his journey to Rome, and fixing the date of its original composition in the second year of Trajan's reign (p. cxi). But he admits numerous subsequent revisions and interpolations down to 264–65. The titanic struggle which was to precede the ushering in of the messianic era assumed, in the Christian outlook, the shape of the final combat between Christ and Antichrist. On the Jewish antecedents of this important motif and its subsequent variations, cf. B. Rigaux's data in *L'Antéchrist et l'opposition au royaume messianique dans l'Ancien et le Nouveau Testament*.

3. This is not the place to discuss in detail the nuances in the messianic teachings of the different movements in Palestinian and world Jewry during the Second Commonwealth. A few indications are given in various other connections. In any case, Y. Kaufmann is right in stressing, perhaps slightly overstressing, the uniqueness of the Jewish messianic idea even in the Old Testament period. Cf. his *Toledot*, I, 418 ff.; III, 626 ff. The peculiarities of this concept became even more pronounced in the Graeco-Roman era, notwithstanding its constant absorption of new and partly alien ingredients. For more detailed analyses, cf. among more recent publications, J. Klausner's *Ha-Ra'ayon ha-meshiḥi be-Yisrael* (The Messianic Idea in Judaism), 3d ed.; M. Zobel's *Gottes Gesalbter, der Messias und die messianische Zeit in Talmud und Midrasch;* Moore's *Judaism*, II, 323 ff., III, 199 ff.; and Bousset-Gressmann's *Religion*, pp. 202 ff. Very stimulating also are Aptowitzer's *Parteipolitik*, pp. 82 ff., and Gressmann's *Messias*, in so far as the latter also refers to developments posterior to the Old Testament. An interesting collection of relevant rabbinic texts in French

transl. is offered by J. J. Brierre-Narbonne in his *Prophéties messianiques de l'Ancien Testament dans la littérature juive, en accord avec le Nouveau Testament*. Cf. his *Messie souffrant dans la littérature rabbinique;* W. Küppers's dissertation on *Das Messiasbild der spätjüdischen Apokalyptik;* J. B. Frey's "Conflit entre le messianisme de Jésus et le messianisme des Juifs de son temps," *Biblica*, XIV, 133-49, 269-93; the comprehensive analyses by P. Volz in his *Eschatologie der jüdischen Gemeinde im neutestamentlichen Zeitalter*, 2d ed.; M. Buber in his *Königtum Gottes;* and, from the comparative anthropological standpoint, W. D. Wallis's *Messiahs; Their Role in Civilization.* Cf. also *infra* n. 17, and Chap. XV, n. 24.

4. Josephus' *War* II, 13, 4.259; *Antt.* XX, 8, 6.170. On the "Herodians" cf. Mark 3:6, 12:13; Matthew 22:15-16; St. Jerome's comment on the latter passage, "Qui Herodem Christum esse credebant" (*PL*, XXVI, 168); and E. Bikerman's somewhat strained argumentation in "Les Hérodiens," *RB*, XLVII, 184-97, with reference to several other Church Fathers and the Slavonic Josephus. Although these sources are all of later vintage, there is no reason to doubt the use of messianic arguments by the pro-Herodian party in the defense of their embattled dynasty during the early first century.

5. Cf. E. Lohmeyer's *Urchristentum*, I (on John the Baptist); C. C. McCown's "Scene of John's Ministry and Its Relation to the Purpose and Outcome of His Mission," *JBL*, LIX, 113-31 (stressing the nationalist aspects of John's agitation and hence also Herod Antipas' right of suspecting a revolt); E. Bikerman's "Jean Baptiste au Désert," *Byzantion*, XVI, 1-19; and E. W. Parsons's "Significance of John the Baptist for the Beginnings of Christianity," in J. T. McNeill *et al., Environmental Factors in Christian History*, pp. 1-17. Cf. also H. L. MacNeill's "*Sitz im Leben* of Luke 1⁵-2²⁰," *JBL*, LXV, 123-30 (stating that this pericope was written not long before 60 and showing how in the subsequent Gospel tradition the Baptist was increasingly overshadowed by Jesus "until in the Fourth Gospel, John becomes merely a voice crying in the wilderness"). It is far more difficult to ascertain what significance John's preaching had within the inner Jewish messianic movements. Cf., however, *supra*, Chap. IX, n. 60.

6. Among the numerous surveys of recent literature concerning early Christianity cf., especially, S. J. Case's *Bibliographical Guide to the History of Christianity;* M. Jones's *The New Testament in the Twentieth Century*, 3d ed.; the annual surveys in *Biblica;* and the annotated periodic bibliographies of *New Testament Literature*, ed. during recent years for the New Testament Club of the University of Chicago by W. N. Lyons, or M. P. Parvis, or both. Interesting sketches of various approaches are to be found in O. Linton's *Problem der Urkirche in der neueren Forschung;* L. Salvatorelli's "From Locke to Reitzenstein," *HTR*, XXII, 263-367; H. J. Cadbury's "Present State of New Testament Studies," in *Haverford Symposium*, ed. by E. Grant, pp. 79-110; C. T. Craig's "Current Trends in New Testament Study," *JBL*, LVII, 359-75; M. M. Parvis's "New Testament Criticism in the World-War Period," in H. R. Willoughby's *Study of the Bible*, pp. 52-73; C. C. McCown's methodological essay in *HTR*, XXXVIII, 151 ff.; and T. S. Kepler's anthology of *Contemporary Thinking about Jesus*. A good general reference work is now available in *Theologisches Wörterbuch zum Neuen Testament*, ed. by G. Kittel, Vols. I-V. The *Reallexikon für Antike und Christentum*, on the other hand, an even more ambitious undertaking by T. Klauser and his associates, has not progressed beyond its early six instalments published in 1941-44.

7. The best known and, indeed, the most painstaking work done by a Jewish scholar in the New Testament field was that of C. G. Montefiore. But it clearly was only the expression of individual opinion with practically no following among Jews.

More typical for Reform Jewry in Anglo-Saxon countries was the attitude of K. Kohler (see especially his *Origins of the Synagogue and the Church*), and that of H. G. Enelow (*A Jewish View of Jesus*). Cf. also I. Abrahams's *Studies;* and L. Baeck's *Evangelium als Urkunde der jüdischen Glaubensgeschichte.* The most representative treatment from the Jewish nationalist standpoint is J. Klausner's *Jesus of Nazareth;* and his *From Jesus to Paul.* Cf., however, the serious scholarly objections raised, for instance, by M. Guttmann in "Die wissenschaftliche Talmudpflege der neueren Zeit, II," *MGWJ*, LXXV, 241–68, and, from a Catholic viewpoint, by C. Lattey in his "Professor Klausner and the New Testament," *CBQ*, X, 349–59. E. Fleg's *Jesus: Told by the Wandering Jew*, although imaginative rather than historical, is likewise typical of a contemporary trend among nationally minded Jews. One may also mention in this connection Sholem Asch's best-selling novels, *The Nazarene, Mary*, and *The Apostle*, against which Jewish scholars have raised manifold objections; cf., e.g., R. Gordis's "Jesus, Paul and Sholem Asch," *Reconstructionist*, X, Pt. 5, pp. 10–16. Of some relevance is also B. Danniel's extensive documentation (in his *Jesus, Jews and Gentiles*) of the widely held view that Christian teachings about Jesus' treatment by Jews are at the root of antisemitism. Nor is it at all astonishing that Christian scholars have frequently evinced great interest in such Jewish writings on Jesus. Cf. T. Walker's *Jewish Views of Jesus*, and, particularly, G. Lindeskog's *Jesusfrage im neuzeitlichen Judentum*, which reviews the literature since Jost and Salvador. Cf. also J. Jocz's "study of the relationship" between *The Jewish People and Jesus Christ.*

8. Cf. E. L. Sukenik's "Earliest Records of Christianity," *AJA*, LI, 351–65 (referring in particular to Nos. 7–8 and interpreting the dubious word *Iov* as a lamentation on the crucifixion); H. R. Willoughby's and J. Simons's comments thereon in *JBL*, LXVIII, 61–65, and *JEOL*, XI, 74 ff.; and C. H. Kraeling's "Christian Burial Urns?" *BA*, IX, 16–20. The crosses seem, in any case, to represent a much later form and may have been drawn several generations after the actual burial. See *infra*, Chap. XII, n. 12. Cf. also, more generally, M. Burrows's *What Mean These Stones?* and S. L. Caiger's *Archaeology and the New Testament.*

9. J. S. Kennard, Jr.'s "Was Capernaum the Home of Jesus?" *JBL*, LXV, 131–41, followed by his debate with W. F. Albright, *ibid.*, LXV, 397–401, LXVI, 79–81; H. M. Shires's "Meaning of the Term 'Nazarene,'" *ATR*, XXIX, 19–27 (in favor of the traditional equation with "one of Nazareth"); G. E. Elderkin's *Archaeological Papers*, VII: *Golgotha, Kraneion and the Holy Sepulcher;* A. T. Olmstead's *Jesus in the Light of History*, and his "Chronology of Jesus' Life," *ATR*, XXIV, 1–26. Cf. C. H. Kraeling's critique thereof, *ATR*, XXIV, 334–54; and such other chronological studies as S. I. Feigin's "Date of the Last Supper," *ibid.*, XXV, 212–17; Grace Amadon's "Ancient Calendation," *JBL*, LXI, 227–80 (in favor of Friday, April 27, 31; also citing George Ogg's inconclusive review of the vast earlier literature on the subject), further elaborated in her discussion with R. A. Parker, *JBL*, LXIII, 173–90, and her "Important Passover Texts in Josephus and Philo," *ATR*, XXVII, 109–15. Cf. also E. A. Cerny's review of "Recent Studies on the Date of the Crucifixion," *CBQ*, VII, 223–30.

Even the geographic data of the Gospels often reflect, as was said, the "collective memory" of later Christians rather than contemporary facts. Cf. M. Halbwachs's *Topographie légendaire des Evangiles en Terre Sainte*, the truth of whose main thesis remains unimpaired by L. H. Vincent's strictures in *RB*, LII, 45–76. In fact, New Testament topography has been for many years a choice target of such exponents of form criticism as K. L. Schmidt. Cf. also the more balanced appraisal of "Gospel Geography: Fiction, Fact, and Truth" by C. C. McCown in *JBL*, LX, 1–25; and "Die Stätten des Wirkens Jesu in Galiläa territorialgeschichtlich betrachtet" by A. Alt in *ZDPV* (Beiträge), LXVIII, 51–71.

10. D. W. Riddle's "Central Problem of the Gospels," *JBL*, LX, 99 (with reference to S. J. Case's *Jesus: a New Biography* and Bishop A. C. Headlam's *Life and Teaching of Jesus the Christ*); T. Craig's "Biblical Theology and the Rise of Historicism," *JBL*, LXII, 294; C. C. McCown's remarks in *HTR*, XXXVIII, 151 ff.; K. Weiss's critical review of "Urchristentum und Geschichte in der neutestamentlichen Theologie seit der Jahrhundertwende," *Beiträge zur Förderung der christlichen Theologie*, XL, 191–226; *supra*, Chaps. I, n. 6, III, n. 51, and *infra*, Chap. XII, n. 17. Some scholars are even prepared to accept F. V. Filson's declaration that "there is no valid neutrality" with respect to Christian origins and that only "a personal response for or against the New Testament explanation" will furnish a satisfactory answer. Cf. "The Central Problem Concerning Christian Origins" in H. R. Willoughby's *Study of the Bible*, p. 344, and the reiterated criticism of the "objective" approach in his "Method in Studying Biblical History," *JBL*, LXIX, 1–18.

On the dangers of the two equally unhistorical approaches of either denying that Jesus ever lived (scholars like Arthur Drews and J. M. Robertson spent a lifetime on this unprofitable exercise) or reinterpreting his attitude to miracles and exorcisms, his religious healing or conception of God in a way suitable to modern tastes, cf. the pertinent warnings by R. Thibaut in his "Jésus-Christ n'a pu être inventé," *Nouvelle Revue Théologique*, LXVII, 280–95, and by H. J. Cadbury in *The Peril of Modernizing Jesus*, supplemented by his "Peril of Archaizing Ourselves," *Interpretation*, III, 331–39.

From the vast literature on the life of Jesus and the beginnings of Christianity we need mention here only the following comprehensive works (in addition to those referred to in other notes): K. Lake, F. F. Jackson and H. J. Cadbury's *Beginnings of Christianity*; H. Lietzmann's *Beginnings of the Christian Church*; M. S. Enslin's *Christian Beginnings*; F. V. Filson's *New Testament against Its Environment*; R. Bultmann's *Jesus and the Word*; M. Goguel's comprehensive trilogy, *Life of Jesus*, *La Naissance du Christianisme*, and *L'Eglise primitive*; C. A. H. Guignebert's *Jesus*; M. Dibelius's *Jesus*; G. Ricciotti's *Life of Christ*; T. W. Manson's "Life of Jesus: a Study [or Survey] of the Available Material," *BJRL*, XXVII–XXX. Cf. also R. Eisler's brilliant but controversial study, *The Messiah Jesus and John the Baptist*, together with such critiques thereof as are mentioned *infra*, Chap. XII, n. 2; E. F. Scott's earlier survey of "Recent Lives of Jesus," *HTR*, XXVII, 1–31; C. C. McCown's *Search for the Real Jesus*; J. G. H. Hoffmann's *Vies de Jésus et le Jésus de l'histoire* (a review of French "non-Catholic" writings from Renan to Guignebert); and S. G. F. Brandon's "Recent Interpretations of Christian Origins," *Modern Churchman*, XLI, 21–38.

11. Mark 5:17; Matthew 8:34; A. Loisy's *Birth of the Christian Religion*, pp. 72 f. Cf. also M. R. Schippers's analysis of the New Testament "witnesses" (in the original legal meaning of that term, rather than in that of martyrs) in his dissertation, *Getuigen van Jezus Christus in het Nieuwe Testament* (Witnesses of Jesus Christ in the New Testament); and that of "The Oxyrhynchus Sayings of Jesus" by L. E. Wright in *JBL*, LXV, 175–83 (finding in that late collection, first edited in 1920 by H. G. E. White, traces of hermetic influence). Cf. also J. Jeremias's "Zusammenstoss Jesu mit dem pharisäischen Oberpriester auf dem Tempelplatz," *Coniectanea neotestamentica*, XI, 97–108 (defending the genuineness of Pap. Oxyrh. V, 840 and connecting it with the later controversy over ritual ablutions).

12. A. Deissmann's *Light*, p. 65; Eusebius' *Hist. eccl.* III, 39, end; C. C. Torrey's "Aramaic of the Gospels," *JBL*, LXI, 84. Cf. also J. Jeremias's *Gleichnisse Jesu*; and his *Unbekannte Jesusworte* (trying to reconstruct Jesus' sayings from extracanonical Christian sources; he believes that twenty-one of these sayings, some one-fifth of the total, have equal historical value with those recorded in the Gospels). A fuller, brilliant defense of the theory of the essentially Aramaic origins of the Gospels is found

in C. C. Torrey's *Four Gospels, a New Translation,* together with his *Our Translated Gospels,* and his essay in *JBL,* LIV, 18–28. Cf. also J. de Zwaan's "John Wrote in Aramaic," *JBL,* LVII, 155–71; and J. Bonsirven's "Aramaïsmes de S. Jean l'Évangéliste?" *Biblica,* XXX, 405–32. Upon the publication of Torrey's *Four Gospels* in 1933, this theory was assailed by such critics as R. Marcus, J. A. Montgomery and Enno Littmann (in their reviews in *HTR,* XXVII, 211–39; *JBL,* LIII, 79–99; and *ZNW,* XXXIV, 20–34, respectively). It has also been consistently combated by E. J. Goodspeed and his pupils. Cf. particularly Goodspeed's *New Chapters in New Testament Study,* pp. 127 ff.; and his "Possible Aramaic Gospel," *JNES,* I, 315–40. Goodspeed admits in the light of Eusebius' testimony, that the earliest Gospel was Aramaic, but he believes "that it consisted of an oral rather than written narrative." His main argument, however, derived from the paucity of Aramaic writings of the period, contrasted with the wealth of contemporary Greek letters, was hardly convincing. It certainly did not controvert A. T. Olmstead's evidence in favor of an affirmative answer to the query, "Could an Aramaic Gospel be Written?" in *JNES,* I, 41–75. But, of course, the actual fact of it having been written is likewise far from proved. Cf. also H. Grimme's "Studien zum hebräischen Urmattäus," *Biblische Zeitschrift,* XXIII, 244–65, 347–57 (arguing for a rabbinic Hebrew, rather than Aramaic original); P. Kahle's "Das zur Zeit Jesu gesprochene Aramäisch," *Theologische Rundschau,* XVII, 201–16; J. Kutcher's careful "Studies in Galilean Aramaic" (Hebrew), *Tarbiz,* XXI, 192–205; XXII, 53–63 (sharply critical of Dalman's grammar); M. Black's *Aramaic Approach to the Gospel and Acts* (discussing the Aramaic substratum rather than original), and his "Aramaic Studies and the New Testament," *JTS,* XLIX, 157–65 (with reference to A. J. Wensinck); H. F. D. Sparks's study of "Semitisms" in Luke and Acts in *JTS,* XLIV, 129–38, and *ibid.,* n.s., I, 16–28 (pointing out that not all chapters are equally septuagintal). Perhaps D. Daube is right in counseling against a uniform solution and in suggesting that "the proportion of Aramaic, Greek and other elements (for there are others, among which Hebrew is prominent) varies from one pericope to the next and, quite often, one verse to the next." Cf. his "Concerning the Reconstruction of 'The Aramaic Gospels,'" *BJRL,* XXIX, 69. It is painful to contemplate, however, as to what might happen to the lower criticism of the New Testament if this suggestion were generally accepted. What a new hunting ground would open up for the reconstruction of individual verses and phrases and, perhaps even (*horribile dictu*), for the publication some day of a polychrome edition of the Gospels marking in different colors the individual linguistic components!

13. Cf. such works of the founders of the form critical school as M. Dibelius's *From Tradition to Gospel;* R. Bultmann's *Geschichte der synoptischen Tradition,* 2d ed., and his *Theologie des Neuen Testaments;* K. L. Schmidt's *Problème du Christianisme primitif;* and other studies, listed in the "Bibliographia Dibeliana atque Bultmanniana," in *Coniectanea neotestamentica,* Vol. VIII (to 1944). Sharp critiques of the "negativism" resulting from the application of the form-critical method were voiced by E. F. Scott in *The Validity of the Gospel Record,* and by F. Büchsel in "Die Hauptfragen der Synoptikerkritik," *Beiträge zur Förderung christlicher Theologie,* XL, 347–440. Cf. also F. C. Grant's *Form Criticism: a New Method of New Testament Research,* and his (admiring) review of Bultmann's *Theologie* in *JBL,* LXIX, 69–73; and E. B. Redlich's *Form Criticism: Its Value and Limitations.*

14. Mark 1:39, 6:52, 10:23–25 (there is a slight but noteworthy change in the formulation of verses 23–24). The type of sermon which Jesus usually delivered in the various synagogues is exemplified in the story narrated by Luke (4:15–32). This passage has given rise to numerous attempts at identifying the synagogue in Nazareth. However, the synagogue mentioned by Antoninus Martyr, the pilgrim from Piacenza about 570 C.E. (cf. *infra,* Chap. XIV, n. 20), probably was built in the

second century or later. See C. Kopp's "Beiträge zur Geschichte Nazareths, V: Die Synagoge," *JPOS*, XX, 29–42.

The social aspects of the rise of Christianity have also attracted much attention. Among the various works elucidating both the social background and the social teachings of the New Testament, perhaps the most widely known in the earlier decades of this century was K. Kautsky's *Foundations of Christianity*. Its popularity, however, owed more to the renown of its author as the leading prewar exponent of Marxism than to the book's intrinsic merits. Much more searching was E. Troeltsch's analysis of *The Social Teaching of the Christian Churches*. Among more recent investigations, cf. S. J. Case's *Evolution of Early Christianity*, his *Social Triumph of the Ancient Church*, and many of his other writings listed in the "Bibliography" compiled by L. B. Jennings in *JR*, XXIX, 47–58; E. F. Scott's *Man and Society in the New Testament;* and some studies listed *supra*, Chap. VIII, n. 1, 28. One must bear in mind, however, that the documentary evidence is extremely confusing. In approaching the social problem, moreover, modern scholarship suffers from the exclusively religious orientation of the sources, as well as from their preservation in Greek only. Even those factors which are clearly the outgrowth of Jewish social life of the period are frequently obscured by the purely religious nomenclature, different connotations of Greek terms or misinterpretations by later redactors.

15. Matt. 5:17; Shabbat 116b; Mark 2:27; Mekilta, Shabbata, I, ed. by Lauterbach, III, 199. Although R. Simon ben Menasya was a late second-century sage, he could hardly have been influenced by the Christian tradition or wished in any way to detract from the ever more glorified sanctity of the Sabbath. Moreover, in an earlier paragraph (*ibid.*, III, 198) his statement is cited in the context of justifying the breaking of the Sabbath for the purpose of saving lives, an issue which had already been decided at the outbreak of the Maccabean revolt. On the other hand, T. W. Manson's emendation of the text in Mark to read "The Sabbath was made for the Son of Man, not the Son of Man for the Sabbath," although fairly well fitting into the context, leaves open the question as to how this formulation was replaced by the more innocuous statement in the later overtly antinomian Christian tradition. Cf. Manson's "Mark II:27 f.," *Coniectanea neotestamentica*, XI, 138–46. At the same time, Olmstead's theory that Jesus attacked the Sadducean high priests only, and that all references to Pharisees are "interpolations of the First Evangelist, or perhaps rather of later gentile scribes," seems likewise far-fetched. Cf. *JNES*, I, 54 f.; and his *Jesus*, p. 179, n. 1. But there is no question that the evangelists wrote in an atmosphere of even more heated anti-Jewish debates. Cf. *infra*, n. 23.

On Jesus' general attitude to Judaism within whose fold he remained all his life —it has almost become a truism that one cannot speak of Christianity before the crucifixion—cf. the host of general works listed *supra*, n. 10. For more specific treatment, reference must be made here above all to (H. L. Strack and) P. Billerbeck's *Kommentar zum Neuen Testament aus Talmud und Midrasch*. Much less exhaustive are C. G. Montefiore's *Rabbinic Literature and Gospel Teachings;* and M. Smith's *Tannaitic Parallels to the Gospels*. Cf. also G. Kittel's *Probleme des palästinischen Spätjudentums und das Urchristentum;* D. W. Riddle's *Jesus and the Pharisees;* I. Zoller's "Discorso de la montagna e la letteratura biblico-rabbinica," *Ricerche religiose*, VII, 497–517; W. G. Kümmel's "Jesus und der jüdische Traditionsgedanke," *ZNW*, XXXIII, 105–30; W. O. E. Oesterley's *Gospel Parables in the Light of Their Jewish Background;* S. Zeitlin's "Pharisees and the Gospels," *Miller Mem. Vol.*, pp. 235–86; several studies in *Judaism and Christianity: Essays Presented to the Rev. Paul Levertoff*, ed. by Fr. Lev Gillet; and *supra*, n. 7.

This problem assumed new practical significance during the sharp Nazi onslaught on Judaism and, hence, also on the Jewish foundations of Christianity. W. Grundmann and other "German Christians" began speaking of *Die Entjudung des religiösen Lebens als Aufgabe deutscher Theologie und Kirche;* cf. his *Jesus der Galiläer und das Judentum*, 2d ed., and the series *Germanentum, Christentum und Judentum*, ed. by him for the Institut zur Erforschung des jüdischen Einflusses auf das deutsche kirchliche Leben. On the antecedents of this pseudo-scientific approach, see H. von Hintzenstern's dissertation, *H. St. Chamberlains Darstellung des Urchristentums*. The impact of Nazi propaganda made itself felt even in J. Hempel's address, "Der synoptische Jesus und das Alte Testament," *ZAW*, LVI, 1–34, and, particularly, in G. Kittel's writings since 1933. Cf. *infra*, Chap. XIII, n. 42. With far greater scholarly objectivity, and despite apologetic undertones, the problem of *De Overname van het Oude Testament door de christelijke Kerk* (The Reception of the Old Testament by the Christian Church) was treated in the comprehensive work by J. L. Koole, and, more briefly, by W. Eichrodt in his *Worin gründet die unzerreissbare Einheit von Altem und Neuem Testament?*, by R. V. G. Tasker in *The Old Testament in the New Testament*, and by J. Coppens in *Les Harmonies des deux Testaments*. Cf. also J. Klevinghaus's *Theologische Stellung der Apostolischen Väter zur alttestamentlichen Offenbarung*.

16. Mark 1:14–15; Matthew 4:17. Although the phrase "kingdom of Heaven" occurs only in Matthew, but here no less than thirty-one times, it has the more authentic ring. Both Mark and Luke, who consistently use "kingdom of God," are nevertheless perfectly familiar with this circumlocution for the divine name which no conscientious Palestinian Jew wished to utter. Mark, for example, quotes Jesus as asking, "The baptism of John, was it from Heaven or of men?" (11:30). Similarly in the parable of the prodigal son, Luke twice quotes his confession, "Father, I have sinned against Heaven" (15:18, 21). Judging from the rabbinic sources, "kingdom of heaven" must have been a fairly common phrase in first-century Palestine. On the other hand, Greek readers, even if acquainted with septuagintal terminology, must have preferred the more direct "kingdom of God." For their benefit Mark and the author of the hypothetical "Q" source or, possibly, their Greek translator from Aramaic, substituted the more easily understandable idiom. Cf. S. V. McCasland's "Some New Testament Metonyms for God," *JBL*, LXVIII, 104 f.; and C. H. Roberts's comments on "The Kingdom of Heaven" in Luke 17:21 in *HTR*, XLI, 1–8.

17. Mark 13:32; Luke 17:20–37; F. W. Young in "Jesus the Prophet: a Re-Examination," *JBL*, LXVIII, 297. Cf. especially C. H. Dodd's *Parables of the Kingdom*; R. Otto's *Kingdom of God and the Son of Man*; H. B. Sharman's *Son of Man and Kingdom of God*; and P. E. Davies's "Jesus and the Role of the Prophet," *JBL*, LXIV, 241–54. Cf. also other interpretations from different angles by M. Goguel in "Eschatologie et apocalyptique dans le christianisme primitif," *RHR*, CVI, 381–434, 489–524; L. Baeck in "Der 'Menschensohn,' " *MGWJ*, LXXXI, 12–24 (stressing the importance of the term "Son of Man" in the Church's subsequent struggles against the Christian gnosis); J. Y. Campbell's "Origin and Meaning of the Term 'Son of Man,' " *JTS*, XLVIII, 145–55; E. Sjöberg's careful analysis of the pertinent Hebrew and Aramaic terms in *Acta Orientalia*, XXI, 57–65, 91–107; J. Pickl in *Messiaskönig Jesus in der Auffassung seiner Zeitgenossen* (also in English transl.); C. J. Cadoux in *The Historic Mission of Jesus*; H. Sahlin in *Der Messias und das Gottesvolk*; S. V. McCasland in "Christ Jesus," *JBL*, LXV, 377–83 (pointing out that the presence in the New Testament of 127 instances of "Jesus Christ" as against 91 of "Christ Jesus" militates against the assumption of an early acceptance of this double proper name); G. Santayana in his "critical essay" on *The Idea of Christ in the Gospels*; J. Klausner in his excursus on the differences between the Jewish and the Christian messianic idea in *Ha-Ra'ayon ha-meshiḥi*, 3d ed., pp. 312 ff.; and other studies analyzed in F. Holmström's fine review of modern Protestant theological approaches in *Das eschatologische Denken der Gegenwart*; supplemented by the more recent surveys by C. C. McCown, "Jesus, Son of Man," *JR*, XXVIII, 1–12, and by A. N. Wilder, "The Eschatology of Jesus in Recent Criticism and Interpretation," *ibid.*, pp. 177–87.

These publications, which could easily be multiplied many times over, show that on this crucial issue New Testament scholarship is as deeply divided as it is on the question of sources, and that there seems to be no prospect for the crystallization of some truly "regnant opinion" in the near future. Cf. also E. Werner's stimulating study of "'Hosanna' in the Gospels," *JBL*, LXV, 97–122, showing how much this "messianic password" (particularly according to Werner's Hebrew reconstruction of Matthew 21:9, 15, and Mark 11:9–11) became a subject of sharp controversy between the pro- and anti-Jewish forces in the early Church.

18. Cf. F. C. Grant's "Teachings of Jesus and First-Century Jewish Ethics" in H. R. Willoughby's *Study of the Bible*, p. 307. Jesus' pacifism and submission to Rome, an integral part of his eschatological and messianic teachings, has of course been discussed in most of the aforementioned literature. Of considerable interest are also the following comparative studies: W. S. van Leeuwen's *Eirene in het Nieuwe Testament* (Peace in the New Testament, comparing its use with that of the Greek equivalent of the Hebrew term, *shalom* in the Septuagint and other Jewish letters); A. Goetze's "Peace on Earth," *BASOR*, 93, pp. 17–20 (comparing Luke 2:14 with a passage in the Ugaritic poem on the goddess Anat, III, 10 ff.); L. Spitzer's "Classical and Christian Ideas of World Harmony," *Traditio*, II, 409–64, III, 307–64; and H. Loewe's somewhat emotional *"Render unto Caesar."* Cf. also *supra*, Chap. IX, n. 2.

19. Cf., in particular, the brief, but careful reëxamination of the sources by H. Lietzmann in *Der Prozess Jesu;* the subsequent discussion between Lietzmann, M. Dibelius, F. Büchsel, and M. Goguel, in *ZNW*, XXX–XXXI and XXXIII, and M. Radin's juridical treatment of the *Trial of Jesus of Nazareth*. Cf. also E. Bickermann's "Utilitas crucis: Observations sur les récits du procès de Jésus dans les Evangiles canoniques," *RHR*, CXII, 169–241; S. Zeitlin's "Crucifixion of Jesus Reëxamined," *JQR*, XXXI, 327–69, XXXII, 175–89, 279–301, and his *Who Crucified Jesus?* 2d ed. (both somewhat vitiated by the author's insistence on the particular functions of the two Sanhedrins; cf. *supra*, Chap. VII, n. 16); and other literature listed by U. Holzmeister in his "Zur Frage der Blutsgerichtsbarkeit des Synedriums," *Biblica*, XIX, 43–59, 151–74. Cf. also R. Delbrueck's "Antiquarisches zu den Verspottungen Jesu," *ZNW*, XLI, 124–45 (pointing out that what we know about the ancient costumes and observances confirms the realism, though it does not prove the historicity, of these scenes of derision). Perhaps the whole problem would have been discussed with less heat if it were more generally recognized that, as did I. H. Linton in attacking the "Arian Modernist" position, that either Jesus was a man and, hence, liable to capital punishment "for the most flagrant blasphemy in the world's history," or he was God and as such could not be affected by a trial; cf. his *Sanhedrin Verdict*, p. 24.

20. Acts 5:34, 38, 23:9; *Antt.* XX, 9, 1.200. The famous last words of Jesus on the cross (Mark 15:34; Matthew 27:46, with the well-known variation of *Eloi* and *Eli* respectively) and their relation to Psalms 22:2 have been reëxamined by several writers, including F. W. Buckler in his "Eli, Eli, Lama Sabachtani?" *AJSL*, LV, 378–91, and W. J. Kenneally in *CBQ*, VIII, 124–34. Cf. also V. Aptowitzer's "Eléments juifs dans la légende de Golgotha," *REJ*, LXXIX, 145–62. On the date and some other aspects of the crucifixion, cf. *supra*, n. 9.

21. IV Macc. 6:27, 17:21–22; M. Nega'im II, 1; Deut. 21:22–23; Targum Onkelos, *ibid.;* Gal. 3:13; Mark 14:10, 22–24; John 6:53. Cf. U. Holzmeister's "De Christi crucifixione quid e Deut. 21, 22s. et Gal. 3, 13, consequatur," *Biblica*, XXVII, 18–29; H. W. Wolff's *Jesaja 53 im Urchristentum;* J. Jeremias's "Zum Problem der Deutung von Jes. 53 im palästinischen Spätjudentum," in *Aux sources de la tradition chrétienne* (in honor of M. Goguel), pp. 113–19; C. T. Craig's "Identification of Jesus with the

Suffering Servant," *JR*, XXIV, 240–45; M. S. Enslin's "Atoning Work of Christ in the New Testament," *HTR*, XXXVIII, 39–61; and K. H. Schelkle's comprehensive form-critical and theological analysis of *Die Passion Jesu in der Verkündigung des Neuen Testaments*. The intriguing personality of Judas Iscariot, whose very name was to contribute so much to the poisoning of Judeo-Christian relations, has been reëxamined, among others, by R. B. Halas in a comprehensive "scriptural and theological study." His historicity is, nevertheless, as doubtful as ever. On the Last Supper and Resurrection, cf. F. L. Cirlot's *Early Eucharist;* A. S. C. Elliott's examination of the numerous conflicting theories in his unpublished Columbia Univ. dissertation on "The Lord's Supper in the New Testament"; P. Benoit's detailed critique of "Le Récit de la Cène dans Lc. XXII, 15–20," *RB*, XLVIII, 357–93; E. Lohmeyer's *Galiläa und Jerusalem* (emphasizing different traditions about Jesus' resurrection, but cf. N. Huffman's critique thereof in the *JBL*, LXIV, 209 ff.); and A. N. Wilder's "Variant Traditions of the Resurrection in Acts," *JBL*, LXII, 307–18. Cf. also J. Lebreton's interesting essay on the origin and development in early Christianity of "La Foi en Jésus-Christ vie du chrétien," *Science religieuse*, 1943, pp. 17–69, and A. Marmorstein's "Doctrine of the 'New Covenant' in the Jewish Aggadah and the Acts of the Apostles" (Hebrew), *Meṣudah*, III–IV, 134–51.

22. I Cor. 1:23; Mark 15:15; Matt. 27; Luke 23; John 19:4, 14, 19. Cf. E. E. Jensen's "First Century Controversy over Jesus as a Revolutionary Figure," *JBL*, LX, 261–72; C. B. Chawel's "Releasing of a Prisoner on the Eve of Passover in Ancient Jerusalem," *ibid.*, pp. 273–78 (the evidence from M. Pesaḥim VIII, 6; and R. Johanan's comment thereon in b. 91a is highly questionable); and, particularly, H. A. Rigg, Jr.'s "Barabbas," *ibid.*, LXIV, 417–56. On Pilate, cf. also the literature listed *supra*, Chap. VIII, n. 20; and *infra*, Chap. XI, n. 1.

23. Cf. R. M. Grant's "Bible of Theophilus of Antioch," *JBL*, LXVI, 173–96, and R. Meyer's *Prophet von Galiläa. Studie zum Jesusbild der 3 ersten Evangelien*. It is small wonder that the Gospel according to John so strongly appealed to modern German nationalists from Fichte to Rosenberg. Cf., e.g., F. C. Grant's *Earliest Gospel*, pp. 207 ff. (on Mark's attitude to the Jews); K. W. Clark's "Gentile Bias in Matthew," *JBL*, LXVI, 165–72; C. C. McCown's "Luke's Translation of Semitic into Hellenistic Custom," *JBL*, LVIII, 213–20 (with special reference to Luke 5:19, 7:38); and W. W. Sikes's "Antisemitism of the Fourth Gospel," *JR*, XXI, 23–30.

In postulating Mark's chronological priority we have followed what may be considered the regnant opinion among critical scholars over more than a century. Strong arguments in favor of Matthew's priority have been advanced, however, not only by traditionalists, particularly among Catholics, but also by F. C. Baur, one of the fathers of New Testament criticism. Cf. M. E. Andrews's restatement of his views in her "Historical Gospel," *JBL*, LXII, 45–57. The date and aims of John have been even more heatedly argued in recent years. The publication in 1935 of an early second-century Manchester papyrus containing a few verses of John 18, has merely assured us that this gospel could not have been written later (cf. C. H. Roberts's ed. of *An Unpublished Fragment of the Fourth Gospel in the John Rylands Library*). Contrary to regnant opinion, E. R. Goodenough tried to prove—in our opinion unsuccessfully—that the Fourth Gospel was "quite a primitive product from the very early church," independent of, and perhaps antedating Mark (see his "John a Primitive Gospel," *JBL*, LXIV, 145–82, and his debate with R. P. Casey, *ibid.*, pp. 535–44). The enormous pertinent literature has been reviewed by W. F. Howard in his *Fourth Gospel in Recent Criticism and Interpretation*, 2d ed.; and P. H. Menoud in *L'Evangile de Jean d'après les recherches récentes*, 2d ed. Cf. also E. Percy's *Untersuchungen über den Ursprung der Johanneischen Theologie;* R. Bultmann's extensive critique thereof in *OLZ*, XLIII, 150–75, and his own comprehensive commentary on *Das Evangelium des Johannes;* J. N. Sanders's *Fourth Gospel in the Early Church;*

E. C. Broome, Jr.'s "Sources of the Fourth Gospel," *JBL*, LXIII, 107–21; and H. A. Fischel's "Jewish Gnosticism in the Fourth Gospel," *ibid.*, LXV, 157–74.

Apart from the question of the Gospels' chronological sequence and the possible Aramaic originals and other linguistic aspects (discussed *supra*, n. 12), a host of critical problems concerning their textual correctness, their sources, written or oral, and their mutual indebtedness have engaged the intensive interest of scholars for many generations. Without wishing to restate any of the endless details which may be culled from any good introduction to the New Testament or from such general works as D. W. Riddle's *Gospels. Their Origin and Growth*, it may be asserted that all of New Testament research has been in flux in recent years. The publication of new papyri (Chester Beatty, Manchester, and others) has helped answer certain problems, but has also raised as many or more new ones. By adding, together with other newly discovered texts, to the mass of available readings—a decade ago a total of 52 papyri, 212 uncial, 2,429 minuscule manuscripts and 1,678 lectionaries was counted by Sir F. Kenyon in *Our Bible and the Ancient Manuscripts*, pp. 106, 124, 128—they increased the malaise of contemporary scholars with respect to the accepted texts. These had largely been based upon the Sinaiticus (Tischendorf) or the Vaticanus (Westcott-Hort), or some combination of both with the aid of some other, more or less arbitrarily selected, manuscripts (Soden, Legg). Cf. H. Pernot's devastating query, "Que vaut notre text des Evangiles?" in *Quantulacumque*, pp. 173–82, and E. C. Colwell's equally devastating critique of the "Genealogical Method" (*JBL*, LVII, 109–33), which, since Westcott and Hort, had served as a main instrument of selectivity among the manuscripts. Colwell's exclamation, "Our dilemma seems to be that we know too much to believe the old; we do not yet know enough to create the new" (p. 132), will strike a responsive chord among contemporary students. Cf. also K. and S. Lake's "De Westcott et Hort au Père Lagrange et au-delà," *RB*, XLVIII, 497–505; B. M. Metzger's repudiation of the so-called "Caesarean Text of the Gospels" (for three quarters of a century a widely held designation of a certain group of manuscripts), *JBL*, LXIV, 457–89, together with his comparative review of "Trends in the Textual Criticism of the Iliad, the Mahābhārata, and the New Testament," *JBL*, LXV, 339–52, and his brief survey of "Recently Published Greek Papyri of the New Testament," *BA*, X, 25–44; R. V. G. Tasker's no less hesitant "Introduction to the MSS. of the New Testament," *HTR*, XLI, 71–81; and W. G. Kümmel's rather pessimistic arguments about the "Notwendigkeit und Grenze des neutestamentlichen Kanons," *Zeitschrift für Theologie und Kirche*, XLVII, 277–313. It is small wonder that the Society of Biblical Literature and Exegesis appointed in 1945 a committee to study "The Need for a New *Apparatus Criticus* to the Greek New Testament," as explained in detail by M. M. Parvis in *JBL*, LXV, 353–69. Cf. also *The New Testament Manuscript Studies*, ed. by Parvis and A. P. Wikgren; and G. Maldfeld and B. M. Metzger's "Detailed List of the Greek Papyri of the New Testament," *JBL*, LXVIII, 359–70. On the Catholic side, cf. especially Père M. J. Lagrange's comprehensive *Introduction à l'etude du Nouveau Testament*, and other writings of this outstanding student of the Bible, listed in F. M. Braun's *Oeuvre du Père Lagrange*. Cf. also C. H. Moehlman's "Catholicism Revises Its New Testament," *RR*, VI, 384–91; and *infra*, n. 43, and Chap. XII, n. 35, 50.

24. Such a change of mind, originally postulated by A. Schweitzer, is ably defended by R. M. Grant in his "Coming of the Kingdom," *JBL*, LXVII, 297–303.

25. Acts 3:21; Jub. 2:33, 6:14; Niddah 61b; Shabbat 151b. On the complex meaning of the term, *apokatastasis* (3:21), cf. T. Klauser's *Reallexikon*, I, 511 ff., and F. Cumont's review thereof (in *Antiquité classique*, XII, 191) showing that the underlying idea was a Stoic borrowing from Babylonian astrology. With respect to the alleged invalidation of the law in the messianic age, it should also be noted that in

Pesaḥim 50a the rabbis speculated only on minor liturgical changes in the world to come. People would still recite benedictions, they were sure, but they would be able to drop a benediction provided for men hearing evil tidings, simply because there would be no bad news in the other world. Worshipers would also be allowed to pronounce fully the "ineffable" name, rather than continue using the substitute *Adonai*. Cf. also *infra*, Chap. XII, n. 13, 22; the sources cited by M. Zikier (Zucker) in "Studies in the History of Religious Disputations between Judaism and Islam," *Kaminka Jub. Vol.*, Hebrew section, p. 48, n. 46; and S. Lieberman's *Shkiin (Sheqi'in: On Jewish Legends)*, pp. 80 f.

26. Cf. F. W. Beare's "Sequence of Events in Acts 9–15 and the Career of Peter," *JBL*, LXII, 295; H. Hirschberg's "Simon Bariona and the Ebionites," *ibid.*, LXI, 171–91; and D. F. Robinson's "Where and When Did Peter Die?" *ibid.*, LXIV, 255–67. While admitting that one cannot definitely disprove the tradition of Peter's crucifixion and burial in Rome, Robinson hesitantly suggests that the apostle died in Jerusalem in 44 c.e. The much-debated "Cephas-Peter Problem" has been reviewed anew by D. W. Riddle, *JBL*, LIX, 169–80, without suggesting any definite answers, while the failure of the excavators of "Les Fouilles de Saint-Pierre de Rome" to publish the results with full documentation is deplored, among others, by P. Lemerle in *Nouvelle Clio*, I–II, 393–411.

27. Cf. James 2:10; *Antt.* XX, 9, 1.200–201; the Hebrew "Legend of Simon Kaipha," ed. by A. Jellinek, in *Bet ha-Midrasch*, V–VI; and J. H. Greenstone's "Jewish Legends about Simon-Peter," *HJ*, XII, 89–104. Except for occasional deviations explainable by special circumstances, Peter and James seem to have rigidly adhered to Jewish law (despite G. Kittel's reservations to the contrary in "Die Stellung des Jakobus zum Judentum und Heidenchristentum," *ZNW*, XXX, 145–57). Cf. A. Meyer's analysis of *Das Rätsel des Jakobusbriefes*. While both Meyer and Kittel agree on the approximate genuineness of the epistle of James, H. J. Schoeps has recently argued for its later origin from Judeo-Christian, though not Ebionite, circles; see his *Theologie und Geschichte des Judenchristentums*, pp. 343 ff. The chronological priority of the Fourth Gospel over Papias, long debated by scholars (cf., e.g., E. Meyer's *Ursprung*, III, 176 f.), has been definitely established by the aforementioned Manchester papyrus and other more recent evidence.

28. See Schoeps's *Theologie*, p. 258. Of course, in later transmission, even the strictly Jewish ceremony of baptism received a non-Jewish slant, as pointed out by J. Starr in "The Unjewish Character of the Markan Account of John the Baptist," *JBL*, LI, 227–37. Cf. L. Finkelstein's "Institution of Baptism for Proselytes," *ibid.*, LII, 203–11; H. H. Rowley's "Jewish Proselyte Baptism and the Baptism of John," *HUCA*, XV, 313–34 (overstressing, it appears, the differences with respect to John's *public* performance, intended for a complete change of life and filled with eschatological meaning); W. F. Flemington's *New Testament Doctrine of Baptism;* O. Cullmann's *Baptism in the New Testament;* J. Jeremias's "Proselytentaufe und Neues Testament," *TZ*, V, 418–28; and C. M. Edsman's comprehensive study of the eschatological significance of *Le Baptême de feu* (with special reference to Matthew 3:11).

29. The very complex "Pauline Chronology" is discussed by J. Knox in *JBL*, LVIII, 15–29, and, more fully, in such major biographical works as A. D. Nock's *St. Paul;* E. G. Goodspeed's *Paul;* and H. J. Schonfield's "unorthodox portrait" of *The Jew of Tarsus*. Cf. also R. M. Hawkins's somewhat extreme *Recovery of the Historical Paul*, and the critical surveys by A. Schweitzer, *Geschichte der Paulinischen Forschung;* R. Bultmann, "Neueste Paulusforschung," *Theologische Rundschau*, n.s. VI, 229–67; A. M. Hunter's "St. Paul in the Twentieth Century," *Expository Times*, LXI, 356–

60; A. M. Denis's "Saint Paul dans la littérature récente," *Ephemerides theol. lovaniensis,* XXVI, 383–408; and D. W. Riddle's "Reassessing the Religious Importance of Paul" in H. R. Willoughby's *Study of the Bible,* pp. 314–28.

30. Rom. 13:1–2, 5, 7; Acts 20:33–35. Contrast with this Pauline formulation the far more moderate statement in I Peter 2:13–15. Although not necessarily representing a genuine utterance of the leading Judeo-Christian apostle (cf. *supra,* n. 26), it is wholly in line with the quietistic policies of the leading Pharisees. The Christian leaders had the additional motive of silencing "the ignorance of foolish men," i.e., the denunciations of Jesus as a revolutionary agitator. Cf. also M. Dibelius's interesting analysis of *Rom und die Christen im ersten Jahrhundert,* pp. 6 ff.

31. Perhaps for this reason the problem of "conscience" (*syneidesis*) loomed so large in Paul's thinking. Of the thirty mentions of this term in the New Testament, fully four fifths are found in the Pauline epistles (eleven times in I and II Cor. alone). Cf. the data assembled by H. Osborne in *JTS,* XXXII, 167–79. That Paul used this term in its Jewish Hellenistic, rather than Stoic, connotations has been pointed out by C. Spicq in his "Conscience dans le Nouveau Testament," *RB,* XLVII, 67, 73 f.

32. Acts 16:3, 21:24; Gal. 2:19; 5:3, 6. Cf. E. B. Allo's keen analysis of "L' 'Evolution' de 'l'évangile de Paul,' " *RB,* L, 165–93, and the two complementary studies by P. Bläser, *Das Gesetz bei Paulus;* and C. Maurer, *Die Gesetzeslehre des Paulus nach ihrem Ursprung und in ihrer Entfaltung dargelegt.* Cf. also, more generally, C. H. Dodd's discussion of *Gospel and Law: The Relation of Faith and Ethics in Early Christianity.*

33. Acts 17:17 ff. The historicity of Paul's debate with the Athenian philosophers, long recognized as a turning point in Paul's missionary career, was denied by M. Dibelius in his *Paulus auf dem Areopag.* Although conceding its importance for the theological reformulations of the second century, Dibelius repudiated the entire speech in Acts 17 as a "strange element" in the New Testament and particularly foreign to Paul's way of thinking. However ingenious and refreshing, Dibelius's argument is vitiated by its exclusive stress on Old Testament concepts in Paul's thought, forgetful of the numerous interesting parallels he himself had adduced from Philo and other Hellenistic writers. Even the Palestinian Aggadah had reappraised many older teachings in the light of newer Greek popular philosophy which, as in the case of the Stoa, had itself grown out of the fusion of oriental and Greek ideas. Hence that frequent interdependence of Philonic and rabbinic teachings even where no positive influence can be proved. This is not to deny, however, that Luke may well have inserted in the *Acts* wholly or partly imaginary speeches in accordance with the widely accepted technique of ancient historians. At the least he doubtless interpolated many a passage into whatever record of a debate may have reached him. Cf. Dibelius's *Reden der Apostelgeschichte und die antike Geschichtsschreibung;* and M. Pohlenz's "Paulus und die Stoa," *ZNW,* XLII, 69–104.

On pre-Pauline Gentile Christianity, cf. Meyer's *Ursprung,* III, 167 ff.; and especially W. Bousset's *Kyrios Christos,* 2d ed., pp. 175 ff. Although the publication of the latter book provoked clamorous opposition, most of Bousset's conclusions have been buttressed by subsequent investigations. The progressive development of the Christian mission from the initial demand of full adherence to Judaism as a prerequisite of Christianity to the final dispensation even from circumcision, and the ensuing coëxistence of various types of converts in the first century, are briefly documented in W. Michaelis's "Judaistische Heidenchristen," *ZNW,* XXX, 83–89. Cf. also R. Liechtenhan's chapter on Paul in *Die urchristliche Mission; Voraussetzungen, Motive und Methoden;* D. Daube's "Jewish Missionary Maxims in Paul," *Studia theologica,* I, 158–69 (somewhat overstressing Hillel's opportunistic approach to would-be proselytes); and W. L. Knox's companion volumes on *St. Paul and the Church of Jerusalem* and *St. Paul and the Church of the Gentiles*. In the latter volume Knox rightly emphasizes that, although he attacked traditional Judaism and substituted Christ for the Torah, Paul couched his argument "in a form of thought with which the Jews were entirely familiar" (p. 96).

34. Tertullian's *Apology*, XIX, 1 (*PL*, I, 439 ff.; ed. by T. R. Glover, pp. 94 f.); J. Pedersen's "Auffassung vom Alten Testament," *ZAW*, XLIX, 161–81 (surveying the evolution of Christian attitudes to the Old Testament from Paul to the present). Among other more recent considerations of Paul's intrinsic Jewishness, cf. S. Belkin's "Problem of Paul's Background," *JBL*, LIV, 41–60; M. J. Shroyer's "Paul's Departure from Judaism to Hellenism," *ibid.*, LIX, 41–49 (with reference to W. L. Knox's pertinent study); Klausner's *From Jesus to Paul;* A. D. Nock's review thereof in *JBL*, LXIII, 55–63; and W. D. Davies's *Paul and Rabbinic Judaism*. Davies's general attempt to show what was distinctive in Paul rather than what he had in common with rabbinic Judaism is, from the standpoint of Paul's biographer, perfectly justified. However, for one interested primarily in the progressive alienation of early Christianity from its mother creed, the similarities are as important as the differences. Cf. also P. Bonsirven's detailed comparison of *Exégèse rabbinique et exégèse paulinienne;* J. J. Collins's briefer study in *CBQ*, III, 15–26, 145–58; H. J. Schoeps's "Sacrifice of Isaac in Paul's Theology," *JBL*, LXV, 385–92 (pointing up this link between the Jewish doctrine of atoning suffering and the non-Jewish doctrine of Jesus as Savior and God's son); H. Hirschberg's "Allusions to the Apostle Paul in the Talmud," *ibid.*, LXII, 73–87 (these allusions are often very dubious); and the various commentaries on Rom. 9–11, often with reference to contemporary antisemitism, including K. L. Schmidt's address on *Die Judenfrage im Lichte der Kap. 9–11 des Römerbriefes;* and the essays by R. M. Hawkins in *ATR*, XXIII, 329–35; and J. F. Walvoord in *Bibliotheca sacra*, CII, 280–90, 405–16. H. Windisch's learned *Paulus und das Judentum* is marred by his attempt to transform "Saul of Tarsus into a legitimate German Christian" (S. J. Case in his review, *JR*, XV, 376). Even Windisch admits, however, that there is no evidence of any admixture of Aryan blood in Paul's family background (p. 86). More extreme is G. Bertram's "Paulus, Judensendling und Christusapostel" in W. Grundmann's *Germanentum*, III, 83–136. On the other hand, whether the Greek mystery religions influenced Paul to the same extent is still a matter of grave doubt. While V. D. Macchioro answers the question strongly in the affirmative (cf. especially his *From Orpheus to Paul*), most other scholars are inclined to estimate that influence at a minimum.

35. Rom. 1:26, 2:27; IV Macc. 5:7. Cf. I Cor. 11:14. If we accept Dibelius's plausible reconstruction, we ought to translate the crucial passage in Paul's speech on the Areopagus (Acts 17:26) to read: "And hath made of one matter the whole human kind for to dwell on all the face of the earth. He hath determined for them the appointed times of the year and the bounded zones for their habitation." This argument becomes philosophic-naturalistic, rather than historical. Cf. Dibelius's *Paulus auf dem Areopag*, pp. 4 ff., 15. But such oscillation between historical and natural categories of thinking is so characteristic of Paul that it seems to favor, rather than militate against (as Dibelius believes), the apostle's authorship of this statement. It makes also more understandable Paul's interpretation of Dan. 11:35–45 as an eschatological prophecy, rather than the historical fact it appeared to be, e.g., to Jerome. Cf. J. B. Orchard's "St. Paul and the Book of Daniel," *Biblica*, XX, 172–79. Of course, under the existing conditions Paul could not help echoing the prophetic exaltation of "powerlessness." Cf. in particular, the "watchwords of the religion of redemption" which he formulated in I Cor. 1:26–31; and their analysis by J. Bohatec in *Theologische Zeitschrift*, IV, 252–71. Nor did Paul or any of his successors ever abandon Judaism's basic conception of the divine guidance of history. Cf., in particular,

H. D. Wendland's *Geschichtsanschauung und Geschichtsbewusstsein im Neuen Testament;* O. Cullmann's *Christ and Time;* and, more generally, S. J. Case's *Christian Philosophy of History;* R. Niebuhr's *Faith and History: a Comparison of Christian and Modern Views of History;* and G. Thils's "bibliographical note" on "La Théologie de l'histoire," *Ephemerides theol. lovanienses,* XXVI, 87–95.

36. Col. 1:13–20. That it was the adaptation, to Christian uses, of the Jewish-Hellenistic, particularly Philonian doctrine of the *logos,* which helped remove the historic personality of Jesus into a realm beyond time and space is stressed by S. Lyonnet in his "Hellénisme et Christianisme," *Biblica,* XXVI, 129 f. (with reference to G. Kittel's *Theologisches Wörterbuch*). Cf. also R. Asting's minute, though excessively Barthian, analysis of *Die Verkündigung des Wortes im Urchristentum;* and H. Ringgren's aforementioned comparative study of *Word and Wisdom.*

37. Acts 3:25; cf. 15:10. Pauline Christians, of course, emphasized Abraham's purely spiritual parentage. Cf. J. Cantinat's "Abraham à la lumière de l'Evangile," *Année theologique,* XI, 162–67. On the importance of this patriarch in subsequent Judeo-Christian debates, cf. *infra,* Chap. XII, n. 12–13.

38. Gal. 2:9–10. E. B. Allo goes too far, however, in seeing in this undertaking a conscious scheme on Paul's part to parallel the Temple collections and thus to proclaim both the Church's independence from Judaism and its world-wide unity. Cf. "La Portée de la collecte pour Jérusalem dans les plans de Saint-Paul," *RB,* XLV, 529–37. According to Paul's own report to the Galatians, the initiative came from the Jerusalem elders, who hardly would have had in mind any such grandiose projects, even if they had been less deeply attached to the Jewish people. Simple hunger may well have furnished them an additional incentive to come to terms with this spokesman of the large urban centers of the dispersion.

39. Isa. 66:1; Mark 13:2, 14; Josephus' *War* V, 11, 2.458; Acts 6:14, 7:48–50; John 2:19. C. H. Dodd contends that the Lucan oracle (19:43–44, 21:20–24) envisaged the final catastrophe in terms of the destruction of the Temple in 586 and, hence, was independent of the Markan tradition which linked that prophecy to that of Daniel in the days of Antiochus ("The Fall of Jerusalem and the 'Abomination of Desolation,'" *JRS,* XXXVII, 47–54). If so, we would have here parallel, rather than interdependent, traditions of Jesus' attitude to the forthcoming national disaster. An ingenious, though somewhat homiletical, explanation of "Le Signe du Temple," is given by A. M. Dubarle in *RB,* XLVIII, 21–44. Cf. also A. Feuillet's "Discours de Jésus sur la ruine du Temple," *ibid.,* LV, 481–502, LVI, 61–92 (commenting especially on Mark 13:24–27 and Luke 21:25–27); R. H. Bainton's "Early Church and War," *HTR,* XXXIX, 189–212; H. Wenschkewitz's "Spiritualisierung der Kultusbegriffe Tempel, Priester und Opfer im Neuen Testament," *Angelos,* IV, 71–230 (analyzing it against the background of Palestinian and Hellenistic Jewish traditions); M. Fraeyman's "Spiritualisation de l'idée du Temple dans les Epitres pauliniennes," *Ephemerides theologicae lovanienses,* XXIII, 378–412; and O. Cullmann's "Caractère eschatologique du dévoir missionnaire et de la conscience apostolique de S. Paul," *RHPR,* XVI, 210–45. The Jewish antecedents as well as the impact on early Christianity of "Retour du Christ et réconstruction du Temple" are discussed by Marcel Simon in *Aux sources de la tradition chrétienne* (in honor of M. Goguel), pp. 247–57. Cf. also T. W. Manson's keen analysis of the complex chronological problems arising from the account in Mark 10 and its contradictions with John 7:10–18, 12:12–19, in "The Cleansing of the Temple," *BJRL,* XXXIII, 271–82.

40. Col. 3:11. Recognizing the futility of all previous explanations of this omission, A. Deissmann thought he had found a new clue in Claudius' letter to Alexandria. He

interpreted the prohibition "not to introduce or invite Jews who sail down to Alexandria from Syria or Egypt" as the exclusion of foreign Jews even from temporary sojourn in the city. That is why, he thought, Paul did not venture to go there (cf. his *Paul*, p. 230, n. 8). This explanation, however, is equally unsatisfactory. Apart from the improbability that Paul would have been deterred by the relatively slight risk of expulsion, the prohibition itself, if read in context, obviously has an altogether different meaning. In this period of great mutual suspicion, Jews were not to draw reinforcements from abroad or even from the country itself. With the restoration of order, the usual commercial relations, including journeys of merchants and students doubtless were resumed several years before Paul's missionary journeys. Similarly S. Reinach's suggestion that Claudius' epistle contains "La Première allusion au christianisme dans l'histoire" (*RHR*, XC, 108–22) has long since proved untenable. It was speedily controverted by C. Guignebert, *ibid.*, pp. 123–32. In fact, when the editor of that papyrus, H. I. Bell subsequently made a valiant effort to assemble all the "Evidences of Christianity in Egypt during the Roman Period" (in *HTR*, XXXVII, 185–208), the results for the first two centuries proved to be very meagre. Cf. *infra*, Chap. XII, n. 44. Cf. also in general W. A. McDonald's "Archaeology and St. Paul's Journeys in Greek Lands," *BA*, III–V; supplemented by M. M. Parvis's data on Ephesus, *ibid.*, VIII, 61–73; and some of the literature listed *supra*, n. 9.

41. On the much-debated problem of Jewish influences on Christian worship cf. especially W. O. E. Oesterley's *Jewish Background of the Christian Liturgy*; F. Gavin's *Jewish Antecedents of the Christian Sacraments* and his "Rabbinic Parallels in Early Church Orders," *HUCA*, VI, 55–67; and C. W. Dugmore's more recent analysis of *The Influence of the Synagogue upon the Divine Office*. Cf. also O. S. Rankin's comments on the latter volume in *Journal of Jewish Studies*, I, 27–32; and, on the importance of the Old Testament canon (in contrast with the apocryphal literature) among the early Christians, E. Lichtenstein's careful analysis of "Die älteste christliche Glaubensformel" in *Zeitschrift für Kirchengeschichte*, LXIII, 1–74. The changing attitudes to art are well analyzed by W. Elliger in *Die Stellung der alten Christen zu den Bildern in den ersten vier Jahrhunderten*. This study must be somewhat modified, however, in the light of our enhanced knowledge of the artistic achievements of Diaspora Jewry. Cf. *supra*, Chap. IX, n. 8–10. Cf. also, more generally, R. Bultmann's *Urchristentum im Rahmen der antiken Religionen*.

42. I Tim. 1:3–4, 20; I Cor. 5:5. A. Schlatter is probably right in considering the transgression of the Corinthian sinner as but an extreme example of the teachings of the *pneumatikoi*. If, with the coming of Christ, Jewish law had to be abolished, they reasoned, why should one not freely satisfy one's sexual appetites, particularly if these could be given some mystic connotation? That is why Paul found it necessary to destroy the man, in order to stamp out a budding heresy. Cf. Schlatter's *Paulus, der Bote Jesu*, pp. 168 ff. Here, too, Paul may have been influenced by the rabbinic approval of lynching a man caught in the act of cohabitation with a Gentile woman. Cf. *supra*, Chap. VII, n. 36. Cf. also M. Goguel's "Pneumatisme et eschatologie dans le christianisme primitif," *RHR*, CXXXII, 124–69; CXXXIII, 103–61; and, more generally, A. G. Drachman's *Ktesibios, Philon and Heron: a Study in Ancient Pneumatics*.

43. Cf. Heb. 9; G. A. Barton's "Date of the Epistle to the Hebrews," *JBL*, LVII, 195–207; C. Spicq's "Philonisme de l'Epître aux Hébreux," *RB*, LVI, 542–72, LVII, 212–42; and O. Moe's "Gedanke des allgemeinen Priestertums im Hebräerbrief," *TZ*, V, 161–69. That Paul was often deliberately misunderstood goes almost without saying. His disciples were religious enthusiasts and not students bent upon the preservation of historically authentic sources. They chose from the Pauline teachings, by themselves often contradictory, those elements which best suited their particular purposes. Cf.

the data assembled by E. Aleith in her *Paulusverständnis in der alten Kirche*. On the spread and influence of the Pauline epistles, cf. especially A. E. Barnett's *Paul Becomes a Literary Influence;* the discussion between L. Mowry and E. J. Goodspeed in *JBL,* LXIII, 73–86, LXIV, 193–204; and several other studies by Goodspeed, listed in his brief *Biography and Bibliography* by J. H. Cobb and L. B. Jennings.

44. Cf. E. J. Bickerman's "Name of Christians," *HTR,* XLII, 109–24. Bickerman may be right in stating that at that time (40 C.E.) the Christians still were "a Jewish movement, who believed themselves to be the 'third order' called to enter the kingdom of Heaven, and who, as such, declared to the pagan world that they were officers of the anointed King in his kingdom which was a present reality" (pp. 123 f.). But it must be remembered that we deal here not with a Palestinian, but with an Antiochian group. It was not the Jerusalem community, not Peter and James, but Antioch, Paul and Barnabas who initiated this designation. Although Paul was only at the beginning of his ministry and his later ideas had not yet fully crystallized in his mind, he was from the outset a Hellenistic Jew and a talented organizer. He was evidently thinking in terms of the well-knit Jewish Diaspora community which, with all its spiritual underpinnings, had many semipolitical statelike features. That is why the Romans were not altogether wrong in sensing behind the term, "Christian," even if they themselves had not contributed to its original selection, an essentially political, conspiratorial movement. Cf. also E. Peterson's "Christianus," *Miscellanea Mercati,* I, 355–72. On the origin of the term "third order," and the question of its priority in Judaism or Christianity, cf. *infra,* Chap. XIII, n. 1.

45. Cf. A. Grenier's remarks cited by G. La Piana in *HTR,* XX, 330, n. 6; and R. Veillar's sociologically oriented *Recherches sur les origines de la Rome chrétienne.* On Paul's contribution to the formation of the Catholic Church, cf. L. Cerfaux's penetrating study of *La Théologie de l'Eglise suivant S. Paul,* 2d ed.; and the detailed analysis of the Epistles to the Colossians and Ephesians by S. Hanson in *The Unity of the Church in the New Testament.* Cf. also in general, T. G. Jalland's *Origin and Evolution of the Christian Church;* G. Johnston's *Doctrine of the Church in the New Testament;* E. Schweitzer's *Das Leben des Herrn in der Gemeinde und ihren Diensten;* J. Y. Campbell's study of the term *ecclesia* in *JTS,* XLIX, 130–42; S. E. Johnson's brief survey of a century of research on "The Emergence of the Christian Church in the Pre-Catholic Period" in H. R. Willoughby's *Study of the Bible,* pp. 345–65; and A. Oepke's more detailed review of the contemporary research on "Der Herrnspruch über die Kirche," *Studia theologica,* II, 110–65.

The quest for Jewish antecedents of the Christian Church has been vitiated, in part, by the inquirers' almost exclusive concentration on the more readily available Palestinian sources. Whatever one thinks of the respective ideological influences, however, emanating from Palestinian and Diaspora Jewries—here, too, the Diaspora was steadily gaining ground—there is no doubt that the Church had to adopt principally the patterns of communal living long developed in the dispersion. There was a basic difference between the majority communities in the homeland, which resembled municipalities organized on the basis of public law and with regular powers of law enforcement, and the more or less voluntary associations in the Diaspora. The Christian brotherhoods, commanding purely spiritual authority over their members, could utilize to their advantage the experiences of the pioneering Jewish communities in the Graeco-Roman world, particularly as these had already incorporated many features of the vast array of free associations of all types which had so greatly colored public and private life in the Hellenistic cities. Cf. my *Jewish Community,* I, 75 ff.; III, 13 ff. For example, the historic origins of the Christian episcopacy, extensively debated for practical reasons in contemporary England, decidedly ought to be sought in the communal officialdom of Diaspora Jewry. A. Guillaume may be right in suggesting an affirmative answer to his query, "Is Episcopacy a Jewish Institution?" *BSOS*, XIII, 23–26, on the basis of an emended reading in Prov. 29:18, "When there is no overseer [*ḥazzan* instead of *ḥazon*] people become disorderly." But it was not the humble first-century Palestinian *ḥazzan* (mainly a sexton and elementary teacher), but rather his Diaspora counterpart, the *hyperetes* (a communal factotum second only in prestige, but not in actual power, to the non-salaried *archon*), who served as a model for the increasingly authoritarian bishop of the Church. Cf. my *Jewish Community*, I, 104, III, 18, n. 32. It probably was with the view toward the contemporary *ḥazzan-hyperetes* of the Alexandrian synagogue (mentioned also in talmudic sources; cf. *ibid.*, I, 78) that the Septuagint translates the crucial term in Prov. by *exegetes*. Exposition of Scripture doubtless was one of that official's manifold duties. Cf. Philo's statement cited *infra*, Chap. XIV, n. 55.

CHAPTER XI: BREAKDOWN AND RECONSTRUCTION

1. Cf. Tacitus' *Hist.*, V, 6. Extent and duration of the Roman exemptions of Jews from military service (recorded by Josephus in *Antt.* XIV, 10, 11–17.223–40) are debatable. While T. Mommsen believed that these privileges permanently removed Jews, both Roman citizens and non-citizens, from the imperial armed forces, J. Juster has convincingly argued for their having had but a temporary effect on the Roman Jewish citizens of Asia Minor. Cf. Mommsen's "Religionsfrevel" (1890), reprinted in his *G.S.*, III, 404 n. 4, 417; and Juster's *Empire romain*, II, 275 f. Cf. also Dessau's *Geschichte*, II, 726, n. 3. In any case, however, Palestinian Jews seem to have enlisted in the Roman or Herodian armies only to a limited extent (despite Juster's efforts to prove the contrary). S. V. McCasland doubtless is right in asserting that the "rebels," deficient in military training, consistently betrayed the lack of discipline characteristic of haphazard crowds of farmers and slaves. Cf. his " 'Soldiers of Service,' " *JBL*, LXII, 68 ff. One must bear in mind, however, that the "brigands" who, like the Greek "klephts" of modern times, combined ordinary highway robbery with the popular struggle for national liberation, offered a strong and well-knit core of Jewish resistance. Moreover, the conflict with Rome had long loomed as an inescapable necessity in the eyes of many patriots. It might well have broken out not only in the days of Caligula, but even under Pontius Pilate who, apparently acting in unison with Tiberius' chief councillor Sejan, did everything in his power to provoke a widespread rebellion. These warlike designs of the notorious procurator have been plausibly demonstrated, on the basis of his own coins, by E. Stauffer in "Zur Münzprägung und Judenpolitik des Pontius Pilatus," *Nouvelle Clio*, I–II, 495–514. Cf. also *supra*, Chap. VIII, n. 20.

2. The individual stages in the long drawn-out campaign, interrupted by lengthy rest periods and particularly the retirement of the Roman army to its winter quarters, are fully described in Josephus' *War*, supplemented by a few sparse notices in Tacitus and other writers. Recent scholarship has been able to add but little to the large accumulation of critical literature on Josephus and the reliability of his eyewitness testimony (cf. *supra*, Chap. VI, n. 24). Archaeology has contributed some data on the walls of Jerusalem (cf. *infra*, n. 6) and localities in its vicinity. But perhaps because none of the other major centers of resistance have been excavated, it has furnished little of real significance for the elaboration of the long-accepted picture. Cf. I. Abrahams's brief survey of *Campaigns in Palestine from Alexander the Great;* and the latest summary in S. Yeivin's *Milḥemet Bar-Kokheba* (The Bar Kocheba War), pp. 1 ff. Of comparative value is M. Avi-Yonah's analysis, mainly topographical, of the "Battles in the Books of Maccabees" (Hebrew), *Lewy Mem. Vol.*, pp. 13–24. Cf. also his "Negev and Its Military and Strategic Importance in Antiquity" (Hebrew), *Ma'arakhot*, IX; N. Lewis's "New Light on the Negev in Ancient Times," *PEQ*, 1948, pp. 102–17 (relating to a later period); and the Latin inscriptions relating to Tiberius Claudius Fatalis, a Roman captain who participated in the Palestinian campaign, and to other Roman soldiers, published by Avi-Yonah in his "Greek and Latin Inscriptions from Jerusalem and Beisan," *QDAP*, VIII, 54–61, and his "Newly Discovered Latin and Greek Inscriptions," *ibid.*, XII, 84–102.

3. Cf. S. Tolkowsky's "Destruction of the Jewish Navy . . . in the Year 68 A.D.," *PEQ*, 1928, p. 157; F. W. Madden's *Coins of the Jews*, pp. 207 ff., 226 ff.; A. Reifenberg's *Ancient Jewish Coins*, pp. 28 ff., 33. In his *Institutio orat.* (X, 1, 91; cf. also Pliny's *Hist. nat.*, Preface, 5), Quintillian seems to indicate that Domitian even wrote a poem

extolling his brother's victory over the Jews. Vespasian had to punish two cynics for publicly criticizing Titus' affair with Berenice, according to Dio Cassius' *Roman History*, LXV, 15, 5. That this was not an innocuous game, but that this move had serious antimonarchical implications has rightly been pointed out by J. M. C. Toynbee in "Dictators and Philosophers in the First Century A.D.," *Greece and Rome*, XIII, 57. Cf. also P. Thomsen's "Römische Flotte in Palästina-Syrien," *ZDPV* (Beiträge), LXVIII, 73–89 (particularly pp. 76 ff.); and L. Homo's recent biography of *Vespasien, l'empéreur du bon sens*. Recent finds of coins also illustrate, on the one hand, the inspiration derived by the Palestinian "rebels" from their Maccabean predecessors. Some shekels resembling those of the early Hasmoneans have now been plausibly identified as struck in 67–68 C.E. Cf. A. Reifenberg's "Hoard of Tyrian and Jewish Shekels," *QDAP*, XI, 83–85; and, more generally, Sir G. Hill's "Shekels of the First Revolt of the Jews," *ibid.*, VI, 78–83. On the other hand, "Some Rare Coins from Transjordan," discussed by Sir A. S. Kirkbride in *BASOR*, 106, pp. 5 f., illustrate the growing independence of such Greek cities as Gerasa, which now ventured to issue their first local currency.

4. Tacitus' *Hist.*, II, 4; V, 1; Josephus' *War* I, 1, 1.1. The Nabataean Arabs' intervention in Judaea's domestic affairs had contributed greatly to the first Roman conquest of Jerusalem in 63 B.C.E. Cf. the description in Josephus' *Antt.* XIV, 1, 4.14 ff., and F. M. Abel's analysis of "Le Siège de Jérusalem par Pompée," *RB*, LIV, 243–55. This collaboration with the Romans did not save the Arabs, however, from the fate of their Jewish neighbors. In 106, Trajan incorporated their territory into the Roman Empire as the province *Arabia*—without unsheathing his sword.

5. Contrast Josephus' *War* VI, 4, 3.236–43; 6–7.254–66, with Sulpicius Severus' *Chronicle*, II, 30, 6–7 (*PL*, XX, 146; *Corpus scriptorum eccl. lat.*, I, 85) which is apparently taken indirectly from Antonius Julianus' description of the Jewish war, via a badly garbled excerpt by Tacitus. Cf. J. Bernays's "Ueber die Chronik des Sulpicius Severus" (1861) reprinted in his *Gesammelte Abhandlungen*, II, 158 ff.; and E. Norden's "Josephus und Tacitus über Jesus Christus und eine messianische Prophetie," *Neue Jahrbücher für das klassische Altertum*, XXXI, 664 f. Cf., on the other hand, the arguments in favor of Titus' responsibility advanced by G. Allon in his "Burning of the Temple" (Hebrew), *Yavneh*, I, 85–106; and, more generally, L. Gry's "Ruine du Temple par Titus," *RB*, LV, 215–26. Tiberius Alexander's high reputation not only in Roman official circles, but also among the Greek writers of the day, seems to be evidenced by the dedication to him of a contemporary philosophical work, *Peri Kosmou* (On the World), which was long to be attributed to Aristotle. Cf. M. Pohlenz's timidly advanced hypothesis in *Nachrichten . . . Göttingen*, p. 486. Cf. also *supra*, Chap. VIII, n. 20; and on Tiberius Claudius Balbillus, the anti-Jewish prefect of Egypt and friend of Nero, J. Schwarz's sketch in *Bulletin de l'Institut français d'archéologie orientale*, XLIX, 45–55.

6. Giṭṭin 56b. Unnatural death in connection with the desecration of the sanctuary is mentioned by II Macc. 9:9; *Antt.* XVII, 6, 5.169 (on Antiochus IV's miserable end). Cf. also Herodotus IV, 205; and P. Wendland's *Hellenistisch-römische Kultur*, 3d ed., p. 330, n. 6. In recent scholarly debates on the siege and other aspects of Jerusalem's history, the so-called Third Wall has played an important role. E. L. Sukenik and L. A. Mayer, who first unearthed it in 1925–27 (cf. their *Third Wall of Jerusalem*), have more recently found "A New Section" (*PEQ*, 1944, pp. 145–51). L. H. Vincent, on the other hand, has argued with considerable force for the identification of the new rampart with a portion of a fourth wall erected during the Bar-Kocheba revolt. See his "Encore la troisième enceinte de Jérusalem," *RB*, LIV, 90–126, and see also N. P. Clarke's general survey of "The Four North Walls of Jerusalem," *PEQ*, 1944, pp. 199–212; and J. Simons's "Three Walls of Jerusalem" (Dutch), *JEOL*, X, 472–

79; and C. N. Johns's more general review of three and a half decades of discovery pertaining to "The Citadel, Jerusalem," *QDAP*, XIV, 121–90. On the protracted defense of Masada, cf. A. Schulten's detailed archaeological study, "Masada, die Burg des Herodes und die römischen Lager," *ZDPV*, LVI, 1–185 (includes notes on Bethar, pp. 180 ff.). Cf. also M. Avi-Yonah's *Map of Roman Palestine*.

7. Cf. the Milan papyrus (especially col. IV, l. 1), published by I. Cazzaniga in his "Torbidi giudaici nell' Egitto romano," *Annuaire*, V, 159–67; the Bremen papyrus, No. 11 (40) in Wilcken's *Chrestomatie*, No. 16; *Oxyrhynchus Papyri*, ed. by Grenfell and Hunt, IV, No. 705, X, No. 1242, ll. 46–50; Eusebius' *Historia ecclesiastica*, IV, 2.4; Dio Cassius' *Roman History*, LXVIII, 32. The papyrological material bearing on the Jewish war under Trajan, in part published only in recent years, has been subjected to a careful, ingenious and, on the whole, felicitous reconstruction by Tcherikover in his *Ha-Yehudim be-Miṣrayim*, pp. 206 ff. Many crucial papyri are in bad state of preservation, however, and the ultimate determination of their meaning will depend on further research and new discoveries. But enough has been made available not only to bear out the facts briefly recorded by chroniclers, but also to show that the Jews, listening in their despair to the visionary preachments of a pseudo-messiah, were driven into a hopeless two-front war. Certainly, in so far as Egypt is concerned, K. Friedmann's contention (in his "Grande ribellione giudaica sotto Traiano," *GSAI*, n.s. II, 108–24, against Rachmuth and others), that the Jewish revolt was from its inception directed against Rome rather than against Greek compatriots, has been convincingly refuted. On its date (from late 115 or early 116 to 117), cf. S. Applebaum's "Notes on the Jewish Revolt under Trajan," *Journal of Jewish Studies*, II, 26–30.

8. Eusebius, *Hist. eccl.*, IV, 2, 4; Josephus' *War* VII, 5, 2.105; Cant. r. VIII, 11. On Turbo, see L. Leschi's sketch, "La Carrière de Q. Marcius Turbo, préfet du prétoire d'Hadrien," *CRAI*, 1945, pp. 144–62 (on the basis of a somewhat dubious restoration and reinterpretation of the Cherchel inscription). Cf. also, more generally, A. Schlatter's still valuable study, *Die Tage Trajans und Hadrians;* and following it rather closely H. Bietenhard's "Freiheitskriege der Juden unter den Kaisern Trajan und Hadrian und der messianische Tempelbau," *Judaica*, IV, 57–77, 81–108, 161–85.

9. Palestine Jewry's participation in the uprising against Trajan appears ever more questionable. The main source, a marginal note to a brief entry in *Megillat Ta'anit*, is of little value, since the entry itself is missing in the best manuscripts (see H. Lichtenstein's edition of "Die Fastenrolle," *HUCA*, VIII–IX, 272 f., 346). On the other hand, in his Syriac *Chronography*, ed. and transl. by E. A. Wallis-Budge, p. 52, Bar-Hebraeus merely reports that the Romans pursued Lukuas to Palestine and, after a brief encounter, executed him there. Whatever credence we give to this thirteenth-century record, it shows little of a genuine commotion in the Holy Land itself. To include, therefore, Pappus and Julianus among the celebrated "Ten Martyrs," as does L. Finkelstein in the *Miller Mem. Vol.*, pp. 29–55, seems far-fetched, despite the great variations in and generally late date of the rabbinic sources listing these martyrs. Cf. also A. Schalit's "Jews on the Eve of the War against Trajan" (Hebrew), *Sinai*, III, Pt. 6, pp. 367–81; and *supra*, Chap. VII, n. 28–29.

10. The great international importance of the Jewish uprisings of 66–70 and 115–17 in the struggle between East and West is ably pointed out by A. Schalit (Shallit) in his Hebrew essay on "Roman Policy in the Orient from Nero to Trajan" in *Tarbiz*, VII, 159–80. In his review of Tcherikover's *Ha-Yehudim be-Miṣrayim* in *JEA*, XXII, 106, F. M. Heichelheim has thrown out the suggestion that the revolt against Trajan, rather than owing its origin to internal Jewish affairs, "was probably encouraged by one of the leading Parthian commanders opposing Trajan, namely the

king of Adiabene, scion of a family with well-known Jewish contacts, who knew, in order to save his throne and life, how to use Jewish discontent and Messianic hopes effectively to menace Trajan's supply lines." Although evidently overstated, this suggestion deserves further elaboration. Cf. also, in general, F. A. Lepper's careful study of *Trajan's Parthian War*.

11. Cf. G. Manteuffel's remarks in *Journal of Juristic Papyrology*, III, 111 ff. Absence of Jewish names from the papyri during most of the second century probably proves the numerical decline of Egyptian Jewry, even if it does not evidence its complete disappearance from any particular region. Considering how few Christians are recorded in the papyri in the days of Clement and Origen, one must be cautious about drawing any definite statistical conclusions from papyrological evidence or lack of evidence alone. Cf. H. I. Bell's pertinent warning in the discussion mentioned *infra*, Chap. XII, n. 44. Neither is the survival of Cyrenaican Jewry in doubt. To be sure, the whole country was but slowly recovering from the shock. According to a newly published inscription of 134–35 C.E., Hadrian was still trying to restore normal conditions twenty years after the Jewish revolt. Cf. P. M. Fraser's "Hadrian and Cyrene," *JRS*, XL, 77–90 (with a note by S. Applebaum). Nevertheless quite a few Jewish names are recorded in inscriptions dating after 135 (see G. Oliviero's *Documenti antichi dell'Africa italiana*, II, Pt. 2, Nos. 333, 380, 383, 420, 436–37, 441, 448, 459). Cyprus, on the other hand, seems to have had no Jews for several centuries. The first reliable records of a Jewish synagogue there date from the fifth century. Cf. T. B. Mitford's "Religious Documents from Roman Cyprus," *Journal of Hellenic Studies*, LXVI, 36 (this essay includes also three newly discovered "ex votos" to *Theos Hypsistos*, which may be owing to Jewish influence).

12. Dio Cassius' *Roman History*, LXIX, 13, 2. A full account of the last great revolt is now available in S. Yeivin's *Milḥemet Bar-Kokheba*, with occasional sidelights also on the previous uprisings. In a lengthy appendix (pp. 138–91) the author subjects all available sources to careful, often incisive scrutiny; on Plate II he also reproduces, and on pp. 74 ff. carefully analyzes, all extant Bar Kocheba coins. Cf. also A. Reifenberg's *Ancient Jewish Coins*, pp. 33 ff., 60 ff.; B. Kirschner's "Mint of Bar Kocheba?" (Hebrew), *BJPES*, XII, 153–60; L. Mildenberg's "Numismatische Evidenz zur Chronologie der Bar-Kochba-Erhebung," *Schweizer Numismatische Rundschau*, XXXIV, 19–27, and his "Eleazar Coins of the Bar Kochba Rebellion," *HJ*, XI, 77–108; H. Strathmann's "Kampf um Beth-Ter," *PJB*, XXIII, 92–123; W. D. Carroll's "Bittir and Its Archaeolgical Remains," *AASOR*, V, 77–97; W. F. Stinespring's "Hadrian in Palestine, 129/130 A.D.," *JAOS*, LIX, 360–65 (referring in particular to inscriptions Nos. 30, 58, 143–45, published by C. B. Welles in Kraeling's *Gerasa*, pp. 390 f., 401 f., 424 f.); B. d'Orgeval's recent biography of *L'Empereur Hadrien* (chiefly concerned with legislative and administrative affairs); and *infra*, n. 30. It probably made little difference to the Jews that their conqueror, Lusius Quietus was an Ethiopian or a West-African Negro. Cf. the debate on this score between W. den Boer and A. G. Roos in *Mnemosyne*, 8th ser., III, 263–67, 336–43.

13. Cf. the interesting data from Cicero, the Stoics, and others assembled by A. Zwaenepoel in "L'Inspiration religieuse de l'impérialisme romain," *Antiquité classique*, XVIII, 5–23.

14. Cf. Berakhot 61b; Sanhedrin 12a; 'A.Z. 18a. The Samaritan chronicle (XLVIII; in a somewhat questionable context) mentions the crucifixion of 36 Jewish scholars at the gates of Neapolis (in Juynboll's ed., p. 52, and Crane's transl., p. 127). Not all of the sages, however, had been active supporters of the revolt. Some suffered martyrdom, as did R. Ḥanina, merely because they continued to teach the Torah in public. S. Krauss's suggestion that 'Aqiba was buried in Caesarea has been confirmed

by a reading of the Leningrad MS of the midrash on Prov. 9:2. Cf. S. Abramson's brief Hebrew note in *BJPES*, XI, 65. The complicated rabbinic teachings concerning the difference between a *milḥemet miṣvah* and *milḥemet reshut* (war in behalf of a commandment and one of one's free choice) are briefly analyzed in S. Federbusch's Hebrew essay on "Judaism and War" in *SH*, VII, 7–36.

15. Dio Cassius' *Roman History*, LXIX, 13, 2. For this reason Domitian was not altogether wrong in trying to stem the revolutionary movement even among the Zealots by removing all potential candidates for the messiahship. At least, according to Eusebius, he dispatched messengers to Palestine to track down and kill all members of the Davidic family, from which alone could come the Messiah ben David (*Hist. eccl.*, III, 20). How small a portion of Palestine's population followed the Zealot leadership in actively fighting Rome during the Great War may be seen by a glance at the active foci of resistance, which covered among them only a small fraction of the Jewish area; see the illuminating map in Yeivin's *Milḥemet*, p. 11. As to the Bar Kocheba revolt, A. Büchler made it clear that practically all the recorded battles took place within the Judaean area (see his "Schauplätze des Bar-Kochbakrieges und die auf diesen bezogenen jüdischen Nachrichten," *JQR*, o.s. XVI, 143–205). Yeivin (*Milḥemet*, pp. 60 ff.) has corrected some of Büchler's exaggerations, but has gone to the other extreme of accepting at its face value Dio Cassius' figure of 50 fortified towns and 985 "of their most famous villages" recaptured by the Roman legions during the campaign (cf. Dio Cassius' *Roman History*, LXIX, 14, 1). This number is evidently as exaggerated as is that of the Jewish fatalities mentioned by Dio in the same breath.

16. Josephus' *War* VI, 9, 3.420; Tacitus' *Hist.*, V, 13, and fragments thereof 1–3 in C. H. Moore's transl. II, 221; Dio Cassius, *loc. cit.* We ought to bear in mind that, in his description of the Jewish war, Tacitus did not merely follow Josephus, but utilized independent sources such as the aforementioned memoirs of Julianus, member of the Roman war council, and the official records of the Roman headquarters (mentioned also by Josephus as the "Commentaries of Vespasian" and the "emperors' own memoirs" in his *Life* LXV. 342,358; and *Ag. Ap.* I, 10.56). Cf. W. Weber's *Josephus und Vespasian*, pp. 103 f., 152 ff.; and *supra*, n. 5.

17. Cf. Mommsen's *G.S.*, III, 418 f.; and Gaius' *Institutiones*, I, 5, 14. Mommsen had originally suggested that this reprisal affected the Jews of the whole Roman Empire, all of whom were now considered *dediticii*. In the light of the obviously contradictory evidence, he later admitted that the Jews, though theoretically *dediticii*, were not treated as such in practice. L. Mitteis restricted the civic degradation of Jews to those living in the Holy Land. Cf. Juster's *Empire romain*, II, 21 ff., where other arguments are advanced to show the total futility of Mommsen's theory. On the generally complicated problems of the legal status of the Jews under the earlier Roman Empire, cf. *supra*, Chap. VII, notes 38 ff.; and on the specific status of *dediticii*, *infra*, n. 25.

18. Cf. Mommsen, *G.S.*, III, 418 f.; J. Wellhausen's *Prolegomena to the History of Israel*, p. 422; Herodotus, VIII, 144. Wellhausen's view is still echoed in the very title of A. Causse's *Du groupe ethnique à la communauté religieuse*, according to which this alleged transition took place during the First Exile. On the peculiarities of ancient nationalism, under which even such strictly political aspects as citizenship were never sharply enough defined or made mutually exclusive, cf. my *Modern Nationalism*, pp. 8 ff., 275 f.

19. Josephus' *War* VII, 6, 6.216. The "law of *siqariqon*," mentioned in several rabbinic sources (M. Giṭṭin V, 6, etc.), greatly complicated the legal problems of

landownership in Palestine, particularly after 135. It had to be gradually relaxed especially in Judaea. Because of its numerous ambiguities it has been extensively discussed in modern literature. Cf. the summary of the various theories hitherto advanced in A. Gulak's Hebrew essay on "Siqariqon," *Tarbiz*, V, 23–27. Gulak has made a strong case for considering this law as a principal safeguard for expropriated Jewish farmers by invalidating the governmental auctions of their property. That only a small minority of the country's farmers, however, had participated in the revolt is evident from the large sections of Jewish Palestine which had remained at peace. S. Yeivin's attempt to differentiate between the mostly belligerent agricultural and mostly pacific urban population (cf. his *Milḥemet*, pp. 9 ff.) is not only unsupported by any of the available sources, but also runs counter to the aforementioned fact that most of Palestine's town dwellers outside Jerusalem derived their livelihood from farming (cf. *supra*, Chap. IX, n. 44). The record also shows that the most protracted and heroic resistance came from the urban population of Jerusalem, which suffered by far the greatest casualties. Since few Jerusalemites owned land, they were evidently but little affected by its subsequent redistribution.

The new Roman administration of Palestine is fully discussed in A. Schalit's *Ha-Mishṭar*. Cf. also S. Krauss's "Gouverneurs romains en Palestine de 135 à 640," *REJ*, LXXX, 113–30; A. Alt's "Letzte Grenzverschiebung zwischen den römischen Provinzen Arabia und Palaestina," *ZDPV*, LXV, 68–76; F. M. Abel's *Géographie*, II, 141 ff., 162 ff.; and on Rome's provincial administration generally, T. Nöldeke's old, but still worth-while article, "Ueber Mommsens Darstellung der römischen Herrschaft und römischen Politik im Orient," *ZDMG*, XXXIX, 331–51; and G. H. Stevenson's *Roman Provincial Administration Till the Age of the Antonines*.

20. Josephus' *War* VII, 6, 6.216 f.; Suetonius' *Domitianus*, XII, 2. Cf. also Dio Cassius' *Roman History*, LXVII, 14, 1–2, LXVIII, 1, 2. Unlike the later period, when capitation taxes became universal, a head tax at that time had by itself a discriminatory character. No Roman citizen was otherwise subjected to it, while there is no record that Roman Jewish citizens were exempted from this fiscal tax. Cf. in general A. Déléage's *Capitation du Bas-Empire*. On the date, size, methods of its collection in Egypt, etc., cf. the papyrological material analyzed by Tcherikover in *Ha-Yehudim be-Miṣrayim*, pp. 102 ff. Cf. also A. C. Johnson's *Roman Egypt*, pp. 488 ff.; S. L. Wallace's *Taxation*, pp. 170 ff.; and G. Manteuffel's data in the *Journal of Juristic Papyrology*, III, 111 f. In any case there is neither evidence for special Jewish taxation under the Ptolemies nor for Egyptian Jewry's double taxation under Roman domination, apart, of course, from the superimposition of the *fiscus judaicus* on its regular, rather heavy taxes.

21. The connection suggested here between the Jewish "fiscal" tax and the rebellion in Gaul and Germany, is borne out by the information given by Tacitus (*Hist.*, especially IV, 54). Cf. also C. Jullian's *Histoire de la Gaule*, IV, 199 ff. According to St. Jerome, Vespasian began to rebuild the Capitoline temple in 73 C.E., apparently when the first substantial receipts of the Jewish fiscal tax, assessed also for the arrears of the previous two years, had begun to come in. See his transl. of Eusebius' *Chronicle* in *PL*, XXVII, 458. Glorified as the "conservator caerimoniarum publicarum et restitutor aedium sacrum" (*Corpus inscriptionum latinarum*, VI, No. 934), the emperor had the more reason to force, so to say, the rebellious Jews to rebuild that temple, as the Capitoline cult had long been considered the very symbol of Roman nationalism. Cf. U. Bianchi's "Disegno storico del culto capitolino," *Atti* of the Accademia Naz. dei Lincei, 8th ser., II, 349–415.

The general problem of the Jews as imperial taxpayers awaits elucidation. The work of Juster, S. Krauss, and their predecessors (especially L. Goldschmidt) has helped clarify many legal and philological questions respecting the Jews, but we are still in the dark on the most fundamental social and economic aspects. Not even the administration of the "Jewish fiscal tax," from the second century on, can be understood (cf. the summary of the known facts in M. S. Ginsburg's "Fiscus Judaicus," *JQR*, XXI, 281–91), as long as it is treated apart from the Roman tax system as a whole. We do not even know at what time it was suspended. Neither the older view still held by Juster and Ginsburg that it was abolished only by Julian the Apostate, nor Tcherikover's theory that its collections stopped in 116 C.E. have much to commend themselves.

22. Cf. Z. Zmigryder-Konopka's remarks in "Les Romains et la circoncision des Juifs," *Eos*, XXXIII, 334–50; and M. Auerbach's list (somewhat too broadly interpreted) of the Hadrianic prohibitions in his "Zur politischen Geschichte der Juden unter Kaiser Hadrian," *Jeschurun*, XI, 61 ff. S. Lieberman has far more plausibly argued, however, that many of these prohibitions were gradually enacted in reprisal for the revolt. Cf. his "Martyrs of Caesarea," *Annuaire*, VII, 424 ff. On Antoninus Pius and his possible identity with R. Judah the Patriarch's often quoted friend, cf. *infra*, Chap. XIII, n. 19. It should be noted that the Egyptian priests, too, continued their struggle for the right of circumcision. Cf. J. Schwarz's "Sur une demande de prêtres de Socnopéonèse," *ASAE*, XLIV, 235–42 (dated July–Aug. 171).

23. Cf. the pathetic description of these Jewish pilgrimages in Jerome's *Commentary* on Zephanaiah 1:15–16 (in *PL*, XXV, 1418 f.); and other patristic sources analyzed by [J.] R. Harris in his "Hadrian's Decree of Expulsion of the Jews from Jerusalem," *HTR*, XIX, 199–206. One must bear in mind, however, that the Church Fathers, bent upon proving to the Jews that they had lost their sanctuary because of their repudiation of Christ, are not impartial witnesses. Rabbinic sources, on the contrary, mention ever more frequent visits to the city. In the anarchical third century, law-enforcement seems to have broken down completely. Cf. the data assembled by M. Avi-Yonah in his *Bi-Yeme Roma u-Byzantion* (In the Days of Rome and Byzantium), pp. 47 f. However, the law remained on the statute books and the Christian Empire doubtless saw to it that it be more rigidly enforced. Cf. also W. D. Gray's "Founding of Aelia Capitolina," *AJSL*, XXXIX, 248–56; S. Krauss's "Did Hadrian Really Forbid Jews to Enter Jerusalem?" (Hebrew), *BJPES*, IV, 52–60 (answering in the negative); S. Klein's *Ereṣ Yehudah*, pp. 183 ff., 268 ff., and Yeivin's *Milḥemet*, pp. 123 ff. (both effectively combating Krauss's arguments); A. H. M. Jones's *Cities*, pp. 277 f. (on Sepphoris, Tiberias and Neapolis).

24. Cf. Josephus' *Antt.* XII, 3, 1.121 f.; *War* VII, 5, 2.110; and the aforementioned text published by C. H. Roberts in *JRS*, XXXIX, 79 f. The fact that Jews are not mentioned in this document does not militate against the nexus here postulated, since the Jewish question loomed in the background of all Alexandrian-imperial relations of that period.

25. Spartianus' *Severus*, XVII, 1. The full meaning and range of this significant *constitutio Antoniniana de civitate* have been extensively debated again in recent years. Cf., in particular, E. Schönbauer's "Rechtshistorische Urkundenstudien," *Archiv für Papyrus-Forschung*, XIII, 177–209 (based on the reconstruction of a Rhosos inscription published by P. Roussel in "Un Syrien au service de Rome et d'Octave," *Syria*, XV, 33–74); F. M. Heichelheim's "Text of the *Constitutio Antoniniana* and the Three Other Decrees of the Emperor Caracalla Contained in Pap. Gissensis 40," *JEA*, XXVI, 10–22; A. Segré's "Note sull' editto di Caracalla," *Rendiconti* of the Pontifical Academy of Archaeology, XVI, 181–214; H. I. Bell's reply thereto in *JEA*, XXVIII, 39–49, their further discussion, *ibid.*, XXX, 69–73; Bell's "*Constitutio Antoniniana* and the Egyptian Poll Tax," *JRS*, XXXVII, 17–23; A. Ranovitch's and H. (E. M.) Shtayermann's Russian essays in *Vestnik drevnei istorii*, XVI, 61–88; and V. Arangio-Ruiz's "Application du droit romain en Egypte après la constitution an-

toninienne," *Bulletin de l'Institut d'Égypte*, XXIX, 83–130. Cf. also, more generally, A. N. Sherwin-White's *Roman Citizenship;* and A. Berger and A. A. Schiller's useful "Bibliography of Anglo-American Studies in Roman, Greek and Greco-Egyptian Law . . . (1939–1945)," *Seminar*, III, 75–94. The full implications of these studies for the Jewish status after 212 would well deserve monographic treatment. On some communal aspects, cf. my *Jewish Community*, III, 19 f., n. 26.

26. Ulpian's statement is quoted in Justinian's code, *Corpus iuris civilis*, Dig. L, 2, 3.3. It is confirmed by another Roman jurist, Modestinus (quoted *ibid.*, XXVII, 1, 15.6) who, summarizing Marcus Aurelius' and Commodus' laws concerning Jews, emphasizes their admission to guardianship over non-Jews and other offices, "for these constitutions had only forbidden to force them into such occupations as would offend their religion [*threskeia*]." Juster's contention, however, that even before Septimius Severus the oath of office had been purified of pagan ingredients for the use of Jewish public employees (*Empire romain*, I, 344) is not necessarily implied in Modestinus' statement nor sufficiently supported by other sources. Severus' concession would be doubly remarkable if we were to assume with S. Lieberman that down to the age of Diocletian neither Christians nor Samaritans enjoyed similar exemptions in the oath of office or participation in the official cult. However, Lieberman's interpretation of two difficult talmudic passages (j. 'A.Z. I, 2, 39c; V, 4, 44d) in *Annuaire*, VII, 403 ff., is not altogether cogent. One could wish to be better informed, generally, about the various formulas of oath administered to Roman officials. Cf. E. Seidl's *Eid im römisch-ägyptischen Provinzialrecht*, I, 86. Cf. also S. Krauss's "Public Offices Held by Jews at the End of the Roman Period" (Hebrew), *Sinai*, X, Nos. 114–15, pp. 243–49.

27. Soṭah 49 ab; B.B. 60b. In *Die Agada der Tannaiten*, I, 2d ed., 159, n. 3, W. Bacher expressed the opinion that R. Joshua's original statement referred only to the impossibility of too little or too much mourning. He believed that the motivations, particularly those concerning the limits imposed by the endurance of the masses, are later additions, since this principle was unknown before Hadrian. One must bear in mind, however, that the fundamental aim, namely realistic idealism, is certainly in accordance with the whole world outlook of Pharisaism, even if it was not expressly formulated by R. Joshua in this particular wording.

28. Cf. j. Berakhot IV, 3, 8a; Sibylline Oracles, IV, 115 ff., V, 260 ff. Cf. also the complaint and comfort of Zion personified in IV Ezra 9:38 ff. The prayer *Raḥem*, reported by R. Ḥiyya, may, of course, have been much older, though it hardly antedated 135 C.E. On its vicissitudes, the variations in the first word, *raḥem* (pity) or *naḥem* (comfort), and the numerous elaborations until it reached the form included in our modern prayerbooks, see I. Elbogen's *Gottesdienst*, 3d ed., pp. 52 ff.

29. Yoma 57a; Sukkah 5a; Sanhedrin 111a; Soṭah 33b. Cf. Me'ilah 17b; A. Reeland's *De spoliis templi Hierosolymitani;* and Joh. Lewy's "Note on the Fate of the Sacred Vessels of the Second Temple" (Hebrew), *Kedem*, II, 123–25.

30. Mekilta, Baḥodesh, I, on Exod. 19:1–2 (in Lauterbach's transl., II, 193 ff.; with reference to Cant. 1:8; Exod. 38:26; and Deut. 28:47–48); Sifre on Deut. 305, ed. by Friedmann fol. 130a (ed. by Finkelstein, p. 325, listing also many variations of the story); b. Berakhot 3a. A capitation tax of 15 shekels is nowhere recorded. It may have been but a homiletical round figure (thirty times the half shekel), indicating that Roman taxation was so much heavier than that required by Jewish law. On the Arab participants in suppressing the Jewish revolt, cf. *supra*, n. 4. The talmudic and midrashic sources relating to "Rabbi Johanan ben Zaccai and His Disciples" have been reviewed once more by A. Kaminka in his Hebrew essay in *Zion*, IX, 70–83.

31. Mekilta, Baḥodesh, XI, on Exod. 20:22 (ed. by Lauterbach, II, 290; with reference to Deut. 27:5); B.B. 10b; Sifre on Numbers 42, ed. by Friedmann, fol. 13a; M. Abot III, 2; b. Ketubot 111a. It makes little difference in this respect whether the author of the last-quoted statement was the third-century Palestinian Amora R. Joseph (or Jose) ben Ḥanina, or his apparent second-century tannaitic namesake, quoted in such early sources, as T. 'Arakhin, V, 9, 550. One must also bear in mind that the prophetic doctrine of the "remnant," though less frequently stressed in order not to add to the people's discouragement, was still much alive in Judaism. It served as a spiritual lifebuoy at least against utter despair. As such it communicated itself also to the early Christians. Cf. J. Jeremias's study of "Der Gedanke des 'heiligen Restes' im Spätjudentum und der Verkündung Jesu," ZNW, XLII, 184–94.

32. Sifre on Numbers, fol. 12b; b. B.M. 59b; M. Yadaim IV, 4; T. II, 17–18, 683 f.; Qiddushin V, 4.342. Cf. also infra, Chap. XIV, n. 17. Certainly, there exists no valid reason for accepting L. M. Epstein's denial of the authenticity of R. 'Aqiba's sweeping declaration in T. Qidd. V, 4.342. Cf. his review of B. J. Bamberger's Proselytism in JQR, XXXI, 303; and the more cautious formulation in his Marriage Laws, pp. 207 f.

33. Mekilta, Baḥodesh, I, ed. by Lauterbach, II, 193 (this passage is here followed by the aforementioned homily of R. Johanan ben Zakkai, which strengthens the likelihood of his authorship, but it is greatly toned down in both Sifre on Numbers 64, ed. by Friedmann, fols. 16b–17a; and in j. R.H., I, 1, 56ab); M. Giṭṭin VIII, 5; L. H. Vincent's "Colonie juive oubliée," RB, XXXVI, 401–407; T. Reinach's "Inscriptions de Touba," REJ, LXXXV, 1–10; and A. Alt's "Zeitrechnung von Jerusalem im späteren Altertum," PJB, XXX, 71–79. The same double date as in Tuba is found also on the three inscriptions of that and a later period on the "Jewish Tombstones from Zoar (Ghor eṣ-Ṣafi)." Cf. E. L. Sukenik's Hebrew essay in Kedem, II, 83–88. Cf. also M. M. Kasher's discussion thereof in "A Tombstone Inscription of the Year 4000 of Creation" (Hebrew), Talpioth, III, 173–78. This system of dating persisted in Palestine and its vicinity down to the age of the Crusades. Cf. the Damascus documents dated in 933 and 1003 in S. Asaf's "From the Old Records of the Damascus Community" (Hebrew), BJPES, XI, 42–45. The pagan population's preference for dating according to the local era is attested, for example, by an Ascalon inscription of 362–63 C.E. Although prepared to exalt the reigning emperor Julian the Apostate —it read briefly: "God is one. Be victorious, Julian!"—, it is dated in the year 467 of the local era. Cf. M. Avi-Yonah's "Greek Inscriptions from Ascalon, Jerusalem, Beisan and Hebron," QDAP, X, 160 f. The Jewish era of Creation, on the other hand, although based on such accepted computations as those of R. Jose's Seder 'Olam (cf. infra, Chap. XII, n. 17) was very slow in penetrating the established usage. The oldest known inscription using it seems to be that detected by David Chwolson in the Crimea which, if his reading is correct, dated from 376 C.E. Cf. his Corpus inscriptionum hebraicarum, col. 248 f.; and, more generally, D. Sidersky's "Origine de l'ère juive de la création du monde," JA, CCXXVII, 325–29. Cf. also E. Mahler's Handbuch der jüdischen Chronologie, pp. 149 ff., 409.

34. Berakhot 32b (with reference to the juxtaposition of Isa. 1:11, 15); M. Sukkah III, 12; b. 41a; M. Pesaḥim X, 5–6; b. R.H. 31b; Berakhot 28b f. Cf. Elbogen's Gottesdienst, pp. 250 ff., with the literature cited there, pp. 555 ff., 582 ff. (the impact of the fall of both Jerusalem and Bethar on the evolution of Jewish liturgy seems decidedly understated here); and E. Levy's Yesodot ha-tefillah (Foundations of Prayer: a Study in the History of Prayer). Since no really ancient texts of the 'Amidah are extant, one must appreciate the new variants found in a Cambridge MS published in S. Assaf's "From a Palestinian Prayerbook" (Hebrew), Dinaburg Jub. Vol., pp. 116 ff. On the historic antecedents of the Jewish prayerbook and its theological im-

port, cf. also N. B. Johnson's *Prayer in the Apocrypha and Pseudepigrapha;* and H. J. Schoeps's "Zur Theologie des jüdischen Gebetbuches," *Judaica,* IV, 108–13.

35. Cf. j. Berakhot IV, 2, 7d. To be sure, R. Eliezer happened to oppose the standardization of prayers and allegedly was "reciting a new prayer every day." Cf. M. Berakhot IV, 4; j. IV, 4, 8a. But that chapter of the Palestinian Talmud is filled with prayers composed by rabbis who accepted liturgical uniformity, but none the less wished to combine with it the individual's free communion with his Deity.

36. M. Abot I, 2; ARN, IV, 5, 22; b. Gittin 56b; Josephus' *Life,* LXXV.418. Cf. *Ag. Ap.* I, 12.60; G. Allon's "How Yabneh Became R. Johanan b. Zakkai's Residence" (Hebrew), *Zion,* III, 183–214; and, for a somewhat later date, A. Marmorstein's "Importance of the Study of the Torah (in the Sayings of R. Simon ben Yoḥai)" (Hebrew), *Lewin Jub. Vol.,* pp. 160–70. Cf. also *supra,* Chap. VII, n. 16, and *infra,* Chap. XIV, n. 33, 53. In his Hebrew essay on "Johanan Ben Zakkai's Demand of Vespasian" (*Bitzaron,* XXIV, No. 137, pp. 34–45), A. Burstein advanced the daring hypothesis that R. Johanan had originally requested the Roman commander to recognize the supremacy of the Babylonian exilarchs over Palestinian Jewry. Only after Vespasian's rejection of this proposal as a dangerous invitation to some future irredentist moves, did the rabbi offer the milder, more "academic" alternative.

37. Lam. r. II, 5; j. Ta'aniot IV, 8, 68d (comparing Bar Kocheba with the "worthless shepherd" of Zech. 11:17); Midrash Zuṭa, ed. by S. Buber, p. 26; b. Sanhedrin 97a–98a (with reference to Ps. 95:7); Berakhot 32b (with reference to Ez. 4:3). The general effects of the fall of Jerusalem on Jewish life, faith, and learning have long intrigued scholars. Apart from the general histories by Graetz, Jawitz, and others, cf. W. M. Christie's "Jamnia Period in Jewish History," *JTS,* XXVI, 347–64; B. Z. Bokser's *Pharisaic Judaism in Transition* (illustrated by the life and thought of R. Eliezer ben Hyrcanus); H. J. Schoeps's "Tempelzerstörung des Jahres 70 in der jüdischen Religionsgeschichte," in his *Aus frühchristlicher Zeit,* pp. 144–83 (emphasizing the Jews' admission of their own guilt and the reaffirmation of their hope for the future, the *bittaḥon*); and the analysis, by S. G. F. Brandon, of *The Fall of Jerusalem and the Christian Church.* Biographical studies of individual rabbis of the period likewise shed much light on the significant transformations during that period. Cf., e.g., L. Finkelstein's *Akiba: Scholar, Saint and Martyr,* with the reservations thereon by G. Allon in *Tarbiz,* X, 241–82.

38. Cf. Avi-Yonah's *Bi-Yeme Roma,* pp. 2 ff.; Epiphanius' *Adv. Haer.,* XXX, 11 (*PG,* XLI, 425), with A. H. M. Jones's comments thereon in his *Cities,* pp. 277 ff.; j. Yebamot IX, 8, 3, 9d. The few archaeological excavations conducted in the vicinity of Jerusalem indicate that many settlements which had lost their Jewish population were not immediately resettled. In Gibeat-Sha'ul, for example, some two and a half miles from the capital, American excavators have detected signs of communal life between 70 and 135, but not thereafter. Three centuries later, Jerome still found that locality "destroyed to the ground." Cf. Yeivin's *Milḥemet,* pp. 12 ff.

39. T. 'A.Z. IV, 3–4.466 (with reference to Ruth 1:19); j. Sheqalim III, 4, 47c; b. Ketubot 112a; Berakhot 36b (with reference to Deut. 8:9); T. Ketubot XIII, 2, 275. Cf. also other passages listed by Avi-Yonah in *Bi-Yeme Roma,* pp. 17 f.; and, on the exaggerations of Palestine's fertility, the statements cited *supra,* Chap. VIII, n. 2. Although the economic transformations brought about by the fall of Jerusalem and Bethar and the ensuing population shifts have often been treated (cf. especially Büchler's brief analysis in his *Economic Conditions*), there is yet much to be expected from a careful reëxamination of all the sources.

40. Cf. Juynboll's ed. of the *Chronicon Samaritanum*, p. 52 (text; p. 190 transl.; Crane's transl., p. 127); Cant. r. II, 16 (5). In sermons delivered during the early meetings, R. Judah bar Ila'i took occasion to express his appreciation to the audience, some of which had traveled a distance of 30–40 Roman miles, and R. Nehemiah profusely thanked the local citizenry which had strained its resources to accommodate learned guests and pupils alike (*ibid.*). This so-called Synod of Usha adopted also a number of socio-economic regulations, which will be mentioned in their respective contexts (see Ketubot 49b f.). Only a few brief hints could be given here concerning the long-range impact of the loss of national independence on the inner life of the Jewish people. Much of it, and especially its institutional aspects, will be discussed more fully in Chapters XIV–XV.

CHAPTER XII: CLOSING THE RANKS

1. Compare Yebamot 63b with Sanhedrin 100b, both citing Sirach 26:1 ff. Cf. also G. H. Box and W. O. E. Oesterley's introduction to their transl. of Sirach in Charles's *Apocrypha*, I, 294 ff.; Zunz's *Ha-Derashot*, pp. 49 f., 280 ff.; and S. Liebermann's "Ben-Sira à la lumière du Yerouchalmi," *REJ*, XCVII, 50–57, which also shows how, reciprocally, talmudic phraseology helps explain some obscure statements in this pre-Maccabean work.

2. Shabbat 116a; *Antt.* XVIII, 3, 3.63–64. Cf. L. Wallach's "Textual History of an Aramaic Proverb (Traces of the Ebionean Gospel)," *JBL*, LX, 403–15; and *supra*, Chap. X, n. 15, 27, 34. The so-called "Christ passage," or *testimonium Flavianum*, in Josephus has given rise to much discussion since the sixteenth century. The older arguments against its authenticity are well reviewed in F. A. Heinichen's excursus to his edition of Eusebius' *Historia ecclesiastica*, III, 331 ff., 623–54; and E. Norden's essay in *Neue Jahrbücher für das klassische Altertum*, XXXI, 637–66. The suggestion, however, made by Heinichen and others, that it was Eusebius himself who interpolated that passage does not seem plausible. Generally unreliable as was the bishop of Caesarea in the use of his historical sources (see e.g., W. Völker's critique, "Von welchen Tendenzen liess sich Eusebius bei Abfassung seiner 'Kirchengeschichte' leiten?" *Vigiliae christianae*, IV, 159–81), it would seem too far-fetched to ascribe to him the diabolical scheme of first interpolating a lengthy passage in Josephus and then accusing the authors of the heathen "Acts of Pilate" of disregarding that testimony. Cf. his *Hist. eccl.*, I, 11, 9.

New impulses given the debate by the discovery and partial translation into German of the Slavonic Josephus by A. Berendts in 1906 quieted down after a few years, the overwhelming consensus of scholarly opinion being that the passage is an interpolation. The debate, reopened by R. Eisler, especially in his *Messiah Jesus*, has not changed the prevailing opinion that, except for a nucleus of at most two or three lines, the passage cannot possibly be regarded as authentic. Cf. the sharp critiques of Eisler's work by H. Lewy in *Deutsche Literaturzeitung*, LI, 481–94, and by J. W. Jack in his *Historic Christ*. Cf. also S. Zeitlin's *Josephus on Jesus;* and R. Eisler's caustic rejoinder, "Flavius Josephus on Jesus Called the Christ," *JQR*, XXI, 1–60. In his "Slavonic Version of Josephus' History of the Jewish War," *HTR*, XXV, 277–319, J. M. Creed, following Prince Mirsky and others, emphasized the enormous significance of the Slavonic translation, dating from about 1100 C.E., for the history of Russian literature; but denied its historical value as a source for the events of the first century. This conclusion is fortified by the evident unfamiliarity of the Church of Constantinople with such a text prior to 900 C.E., as demonstrated by A. C. Bouquet in his "References to Josephus in the Bibliotheca of Photius," *JTS*, XXXVI, 289–93. Any further doubts were dispelled by the publication of the Slavonic text, with a French translation, by V. Istrin, A. Vaillant, and P. Pascal under the title, *La Prise de Jérusalem de Josèphe le Juif*. Cf. also V. Ussani's "Giuseppe greco, Giuseppe slavo e Gorionide," *Rendiconti* of the Pontifical Academy of Archaeology, X, 165–75, and his and E. Bikerman's observations in *Annuaire*, IV, 53–84, 455–62. In any case, it is not astonishing that, on account of that passage, Josephus became extremely popular among the ancient Christian writers and that his works ranked next to the Bible among the most widely read writings in early modern England and America. On the former, cf. G. Bardy's "Souvenir de Josèphe chez les Pères." *Revue d'histoire ecclésiastique*, XLIII, 179–91. Cf. also J. Moreau's more general data on *Les Plus anciens témoignages profanes sur Jésus.*

3. Cf. Josephus' *Antt.* XX, 9, 1.200–203; Origen's *Contra Celsum*, I, 47, II, 2, 13; Eusebius' *Hist. eccl.*, II, 23, 4 ff.; and other patristic passages from Clement of Alexandria to Jerome cited by Schürer in his *Geschichte*, I, 581 ff., n. 45–46. Cf. also *supra*, Chap. X, n. 27; and M. Freimann's older, but still useful study of "Wie verhielt sich das Judentum zu Jesus und dem entstehenden Christentum?" *MGWJ*, LIV, 697–712; LV, 160–76, 296–316 (continued in the essay cited *infra*, n. 11).

4. Justin's *First Apology*, XXXI, 5–6. Cf. G. Rauschen's ed., pp. 60 f.; L. Williams's note in his transl. of Justin's *Dialogue*, p. 34, n. 1; and, more generally, M. S. Enslin's "Justin Martyr: an Appreciation," *JQR*, XXXIV, 179–205.

Pointing out that the official designation, *Syria Palaestina,* instead of *Judaea,* appears for the first time in a military document of 139, A. Schalit has plausibly suggested that the change was introduced by Hadrian at about the time he renamed Jerusalem. Cf. his *Ha-Mishṭar*, pp. 12 ff. To be sure, sporadically the name may have been used before, possibly as early as 117 (cf. L. Leschi's remarks in *CRAI*, 1945, pp. 152 f.). However, only the prohibition of Jewish settlement in Judaea's heartland around Jerusalem and the general depopulation of that region after 135 lent a realistic background to this alteration. For its antecedents cf. M. Noth's remarks in *ZDPV*, LXII, 125 ff. That the geographic term, Judaea, however, did not completely disappear even from official Roman lists of the third century is evidenced by Shapur I's famous inscription which, enumerating the origin of contingents led by Valerian, mentions it (in the Greek inscription: *Ioudaias;* and in the Parsic version under its Aramaic name, *Yvtaya = Yehudia*) together with Syria, Phoenicia, and Arabia. Cf. M. Sprengling's transliteration in his "Shahpuhr I, the Great: on the Kaabah of Zoroaster (KZ)," *AJSL*, LVII, 373 f., No. 23. It makes little difference in this connection whether this rather careless enumeration stems from an official Roman master roll, as suggested by A. T. Olmstead (cf. *infra*, Chap. XIII, n. 4–5), or was compiled in the Persian headquarters from the local archives found in captured fortresses and from titles of individual cohorts, as argued by Rostovtzeff in *Berytus*, VIII, 28 f.

5. Justin's *Dialogue with Tryphon,* 16 (*PG*, VI, 509; English transl. II, 107); T. Shabbat XIII, 5, 129; b. 116a (in the uncensored editions). Cf. R. Rabbinovicz's *Diqduqe soferim* (Variants on Mishnah and Talmud), *ad locum.* From the discussion (*ibid.*) it appears that among the later Babylonian sages the term *gilyonim* had lost its technical connotation, and they were much puzzled by the meaning of the tannaitic prohibition. Cf. in general, R. T. Herford's *Christianity in Talmud and Midrash;* J. Zurichadi's more recent summary of the ancient and modern Jewish criticisms of the New Testament in his *Ha-Berit* (The Testament); and M. Goldstein's *Jesus in Jewish Tradition.* It may be mentioned here in passing that the name Tryphon (of the Tanna or of Justin's interlocutor), rather than having, as is frequently assumed, a pejorative meaning, really connoted something reminiscent of living a better and more abundant life. Cf. J. Tondriau's "Tryphé, philosophie royale ptolémaïque," *Revue des études anciennes,* L, 49–54.

6. Ta'anit 27b (in uncensored editions). The matter is not simple, however. Against the usual explanation, supported by the *Masekhet Sopherim* (XVII, 4; cf. Higger's ed. p. 301, n. 22), that R. Johanan referred to a voluntary abstention from fasting in order not to offend the Christians, V. Aptowitzer argued with considerable success in favor of the one mentioned here. Cf. his "Bemerkungen zur Liturgie und Geschichte der Liturgie," *MGWJ*, LXXIV, 110 ff. On the other hand, both explanations take for granted that before the year 70, Sunday had been generally observed by Christians as the day of the Lord, which is possible but not definitely proved. Cf. P. Cotton's *From Sabbath to Sunday.*

7. Berakhot 12a; Mekilta, Baḥodesh, III, ed. by Lauterbach, II, 211. Cf. also Sifre on Deut., 34, ed. by Friedmann, fol. 74ab (ed. by Finkelstein, pp. 60 f.). Neither the

date nor the exact occasion of the elimination of the Decalogue from the daily service is known. The oldest authority to mention it is R. Nathan the Babylonian who lived after the Bar Kocheba revolt. But he seems to refer to a decision taken while the Temple was still in existence. G. F. Moore was unable to identify the specific Christian sect which "held that the Decalogue alone was the revealed law of God." Cf. his *Judaism*, III, 95 f. However, in his more recent study of "The Decalogue in Early Christianity," *HTR*, XL, 1–17, R. M. Grant presented unequivocal evidence that "by means of a careful and literal exegesis of the context of the Decalogue early Christian interpreters [not only sectarian] were able to show that it was only the Decalogue which God had spoken, and that the rest of the Law had been added for various reasons." The "cavils of heretics" which, according to R. Nathan, had brought about that liturgical change, may also have stemmed from such other antinomian circles as had already existed in the pre-Christian Diaspora, but of which Paul was the most effective, if not necessarily the most extreme, spokesman. Cf. *supra*, Chaps. VII, n. 27, X, n. 33, 42. To many allegorizing Jewish readers in the Hellenistic dispersion, which, one must always remember, had many representatives in Palestine as well, the ethical Ten Commandments certainly appealed more strongly than most other purely ceremonial biblical laws. Without specifying the precise object of that controversy R. Nathan may well have had in mind such arguments from ethics versus law which must have become a real menace as a result of the antinomian Christian propaganda. Cf. also, from another angle, V. Aptowitzer's "Usage de la lecture quotidienne du Décalogue à la synagogue et l'explication de Mathieu 19, 16–19 et 22, 35–40," *REJ*, LXXXVIII, 167–70.

8. Berakhot 28b; S. Schechter's "Genizah Specimens: Liturgy," *JQR*, o.s. X, 657; various passages by Justin, Epiphanius, and Jerome cited by Schürer in his *Geschichte*, II, 544, n. 161; T. Sanhedrin II, 6, 416 f. The original text of the antiheretical benediction can no longer be reconstructed. The formula recovered by Schechter from the Genizah does not necessarily carry greater authenticity than the other texts which, even in the Middle Ages, ranged from 22 words recorded by Maimonides to 45 words in a medieval manuscript. Cf. I. Davidson's succinct summary of the age-old discussions in his *Oṣar ha-shirah ve-ha-piyyut* (Thesaurus of Medieval Hebrew Poetry: From the Conclusion of the Bible to the Enlightenment Era), II, 192 ff., IV, 302, No. 322. Cf. also the phrasing in the Cambridge MS published by S. Assaf in *Dinaburg Jub. Vol.*, pp. 116 ff. On the much-debated meaning of the term, *minim* (heretics), cf. H. Hirschberg's recent discussion in *JBL*, LXVII, 305–18, defending his earlier thesis that "in talmudic literature [it] denotes Pauline Christians." But a good case has also been made for relating some references to the Judeo-Christian Ebionites, or even to non-Christian heretics. On the Ebionites, cf., in particular, H. J. Schoeps's comprehensive *Theologie passim;* and *supra*, Chap. X, n. 26.

9. Exod. r. XXX, 6; Berakhot 6a. On the early use of *paroikia* or *apoikia*, the Greek equivalent of *galut*, in III Macc., cf. *supra*, Chap. VII, n. 27. No letters concerning that benediction or Christians, in general, are recorded anywhere in the talmudic literature, but hints thrown out by Justin, Eusebius, and Jerome are too unmistakable, their intrinsic likelihood too great, for us to doubt the very historicity of that correspondence. Its content, however, is even more problematic than the original version of the benediction itself. A moderately plausible reconstruction of the substance of these letters is offered by J. Parkes in his *Conflict of the Church and the Synagogue*, pp. 79 ff.

10. Theophilus' *Letter to Autoclytus*, II, 33; III, 4 (*PG*, VI, 1105, 1125); Ignatius' *Letter to the Magnesians*, VIII–X (*ibid.*, V, 669 ff.); and Tertullian's *Adversus Judaeos*, II; *Apologeticus adversus gentes*, XXI (*PL*, I, 451, II, 637). In his "*Restitutio principii* as the Basis for the *Nova Lex Jesu*," *JBL*, LXVI, 453–64 (also in German in *Aus*

frühchristlicher Zeit, pp. 271 ff.), H. J. Schoeps traced this invocation of pre-Mosaic law back to the Gospels (Matt. 19:8, etc.).

11. Philo's *De posteritate Caini*, XI, 33–39; M. Sanhedrin IV, 5; b. 37b; Matt. 27:25. Cf. V. Aptowitzer's *Kain und Abel*; and H. Guttmann's "Kain und Abel Agadot in den Werken des Kirchenvaters Augustin," *Löw Mem. Vol.*, pp. 272–76. In his " 'Dialogues with the Jews' as Sources for the Early Jewish Argument against Christianity," *JBL*, LI, 58–70, A. B. Hulen has assembled much pertinent material. One must beware, however, of the great likelihood that many arguments were invented by the authors of these tracts in order the more effectively to demolish them, and that later writers merely repeated and embroidered the reasonings of their predecessors. Quite evident in most of the later treatises *Adversus Judaeos*, in which Jews and their pleadings very often serve as imaginary targets, this purely literary origin doubtless vitiates also much of the historical value of the earlier dialogues. When the occasion arose Christian apologists did not hesitate to borrow some teachings even from contemporary Jews. Minucius Felix, the elegant Latin writer and imitator of Cicero, whose associations with Jews probably were less intimate than those of the Greek writers in the eastern Mediterranean, clearly betrays such indebtedness. Cf. G. Quispel's interpretation of the "Jewish Source of Minucius Felix" in *Vigiliae christianae*, III, 113–22. Cf. also A. L. Williams's handy translation of many ancient and medieval texts in his *Adversus Judaeos*; J. Bergmann's *Jüdische Apologetik im neutestamentlichen Zeitalter*; and M. Freimann's analysis of "Die Wortführer des Judentums in den ältesten Kontroversen zwischen Juden und Christen," *MGWJ*, LV, 555–85, LVI, 49–64, 164–80 (chiefly concerned with Justin's *Dialogue*; and Origen's *Contra Celsum*).

12. The Letter of Barnabas, IX, 7–8, XII, 2–3, in *The Apostolic Fathers*, English transl. by F. X. Glimm, *et al.*, pp. 205, 210 f., with reference to Exod. 8:11, John 5:45–46 (this is an auspicious beginning of a new translation planned to cover, in 72 vols., the writings of Churchmen to the end of the seventh century; another equally ambitious and even better documented series, entitled *Ancient Christian Writers* by J. A. Kleist, *et al.*, has likewise been making good progress); Augustine's lengthy Epistle CXCVI in *PL*, XXXIII, 891 ff. (*Corpus script. eccl. lat.*, LVII, 221 ff.). Cf. also W. Völker's comparative study of "Das Abraham-Bild bei Philo, Origenes und Ambrosius," *Theologische Studien und Kritiken*, CIII, 199–207; and B. Kominiak's *Theophanies of the Old Testament in the Writings of St. Justin* (pointing out the importance of Justin's earliest recorded interpretation of the apparition of an angel of God at Mamre and the burning bush and the ensuing equation of that angel with Jesus). In his "Date of the Epistle of Barnabas," *JTS*, XXXIV, 337–46, A. L. Williams ascribes it to the last quarter of the first century under Vespasian or Nerva. Cf. also R. O. P. Taylor's "What Was Barnabas?" *Church Quarterly Review*, CXXXVI, 59–79 (the name means "Son of Paraclesis," because of gifts of understanding and counsel); G. Allon's "Halacha in 'Barnabae Epistulae' " (Hebrew), *Tarbiz*, XI, 23–38; K. Thieme's *Kirche und Synagoge . . . der Barnabasbrief und der Dialog Justins des Märtyrers*; and A. Marmorstein's "Juden und Judentum in der Altercatio Simonis Judaei et Theophili Christiani," *Theologisch Tijdschrift*, XLIX, 360–83. Innumerable examples of the general indebtedness of the early Christian preachers to the homiletical methods developed by the rabbis are assembled in L. Ginzberg's *Legends*, Vols. V and VI; and his "Haggada . . . bei den Kirchenvätern" (issued in parts). The subject has been briefly analyzed by A. Marmorstein in his "Synagogue Sermons in the First Three Centuries," *London Quarterly Review*, CXXVI, 227–40; and L. Treitel in his "Zur Entwicklungsgeschichte der Predigt in Synagoge und Kirche," *Festschrift Breslau*, II, 373–76. On the rabbis' reaction to the symbolic interpretation of the Greek T and Hebrew ת by the Church Fathers, cf. S. Lieberman's

Greek in Jewish Palestine, pp. 185 ff., 189, n. 30. The use of this symbol in lieu of a cross, or rather as a *crux dissimulata*, was the more important for the Christians as, living in a state of more or less perpetual outlawry, they appear not to have dared publicly to display regular crosses until the end of the second century and after. Cf. J. Carcopino's "Christianisme secret du 'carré magique,'" *Museum helveticum*, V, 16–59.

13. M. Abot V, 3, 6; Ta'anit II, 4; Qiddushin IV, 14 end; T. V, 21, 344; Gen. r. XLVIII, 1, 483, with Theodor's comments thereon; Nedarim 32a, etc.; S. Yeivin's "Sacrifice of Isaac in the Beth Alpha Mosaic" (Hebrew), *BJPES*, XII, 20–24. Most of these passages are tannaitic, even R. Abbahu's statement (about 300 C.E.) doubtless harking back to older traditions. Needless to say that circumcision had been a major issue long before Paul and Hadrian. Hence we find already in the book of Jubilees (15:26–27) such an evident exaggeration as that the very angels were circumcised. Controversialists in both camps had, therefore, at their disposal a considerable body of arguments pro and con. On Isaac as the prototype of the martyr and the redemptive powers of the ram's horn, cf. Shabbat 89b; R.H. 16a; Pesiqta de-R. Kahana, ed. by S. Buber, XXIII, fol. 153b ff.; and, more generally, S. Spiegel's "Legend of Isaac's Slaying and Resurrection," *Marx Jub. Vol.*, Hebrew section, pp. 471–547. Some rabbis, speculating on the symbolic meaning of the ram's horns having been "caught in the thicket" (Gen. 22:13), saw therein an adumbration of the future fate of Israel who, when caught in a thicket of sins, would find forgiveness through the blowing of the horn on New Year's day, and when caught in the claws of the four empires of Babylonia, Media [Persia], Greece, and Rome, would ultimately be redeemed when "the Lord God will blow the horn" in the messianic age (Zech. 9:14). Cf. Pesiqta, *loc. cit.*; j. Ta'aniot II, 4, 65d (with variations in Gen. r. LVI, 13, 605 f.); and *infra*, Chap. XIV, n. 33. The relative silence of Christian apologists on the sacrifice of Isaac is doubly remarkable when contrasted with the extensive use of this obvious theme by Paul, as well as in early Christian graphic arts. Cf. H. J. Schoeps's observations in *JBL*, LXV, 385 ff. (*Aus frühchristlicher Zeit*, pp. 229 ff.); J. Danielou's "Typologie d'Isaac dans le Christianisme primitif," *Biblica*, XXVIII, 363–93; and D. Lerch's *Isaaks Opferung christlich gedeutet*.

14. Berakhot 26b; Deut. r. VIII, 6, on Deut. 30:12; j. Megillah I, 7, 70d; b. Ḥullin 124a; B.M. 58b f.; Exod. r. XXVIII, 4. On the discussions concerning the cessation of prophecy, cf. the sources analyzed by E. A. Urbach in *Tarbiz*, XVII, 1 ff. Cf. also *supra*, Chap. V, n. 26. Although somewhat exaggerating the rabbis' suspicions of R. Eliezer's alleged pro-Christian leanings, A. Guttmann has rightly connected the rejection of the divine voice (*bat qol*) in legal controversies, as well as the rabbis' general caution with respect to miracles, with the reaction against Christianity's prophetic antinomianism (cf. his "Significance of Miracles for Talmudic Judaism," *HUCA*, XX, 363–406). On the *bat qol* and its generally unequivocal pronouncements, cf. also S. Lieberman's *Hellenism*, pp. 194 ff. The ambivalence of "The Talmudic Interpretation of Prophecy" comes clearly to the fore also in N. N. Glatzer's brief analysis in *RR*, X, 115–37. On the Christian arguments from prophecy, cf. A. Richardson's *Christian Apologetics*, pp. 177 ff.

15. Justin's *First Apology*, XXXII, 1–5 (*PG*, VI, 577 f.; ed. Rauschen, pp. 60 ff.); *Dialogue*, 133 (*PG*, VI, 784 f.); Chrysostom's Homily on Isa. 6:1 (*PG*, LVI, 111). The extent to which the Church, on its part, appropriated these "martyrs" is analyzed by M. Maas in "Die Maccabäer als christliche Heilige," *MGWJ*, XLIV, 145–56; and by E. Bickermann in his *Gott der Makkabäer*, pp. 36 ff. The importance of the fall of Jerusalem for the Christian argument of being the new "true Israel" is correctly stressed by H. J. Schoeps in his *Aus frühchristlicher Zeit*, pp. 144 ff. Cf. also A. Oepke's

comprehensive study of *Das neue Gottesvolk im Schrifttum, Schauspiel, bildender Kunst und Weltgestaltung.* On the mutual recriminations of "informing," cf. *infra,* n. 18, 49.

16. Gen. r. XCVIII, 10, 1259 (cf. *ibid.,* XCVII, 10, 1219 and Albeck's comments on both passages); Sanhedrin 5a, 98b. That the *Toledot Yeshu* in its present form is a medieval apocryphon can hardly be subject to doubt, but its ancient antecedents still await elucidation. While S. Krauss consistently espoused the theory that much of the material recorded in that apocryphon goes back to the third or even second century (cf. his *Leben Jesu nach jüdischen Quellen,* and his "Neuere Ansichten über 'Toldoth Jeschu,'" *MGWJ,* LXXVI, 586–603; LXXVII, 44–61), B. Heller has argued with considerable force in favor of its dating in the tenth century (cf. his "Ueber das Alter der jüdischen Judas-Sage und des Toldoth Jeschu," *ibid.,* LXXVII, 198–210). One of Heller's main arguments, however, namely the indebtedness of the *Toledot* to the tenth-century Hebrew *Yosippon,* loses much of its value when one considers not only the possibility of later accretions to the former's original text, but also the fact that both works undoubtedly derived some of their information from common ancient sources. On the other hand, Krauss's reiteration that the allegedly ancient author of *Toledot* wished to supply a Jewish answer to the Epistle to the Hebrews ("Nouvelle recension hébraïque du Toldot Yêšû," *REJ,* CIII, 65–90) has even less to commend itself.

17. 'A.Z. 5a. Unfortunately we do not yet possess a good critical edition of the *Seder 'Olam,* which came to be called *S. 'O. rabbah* (large), in contrast to a medieval compilation designated *zuṭa* (small). A. Marx's ed. with a German translation, which appeared nearly fifty years ago, covers only the first ten chapters dealing with the very early period, for which R. Jose possessed no independent sources of information. I understand, however, that a new, complete edition is now being prepared. Cf. also the still older ed. by B. Ratner, which is to be read together with his *Mabo* (Einleitung zum Seder Olam), containing valuable critical references.

Even remote and apparently wholly unrelated historical events appeared in a new light as a result of the Judeo-Christian controversy. For example, according to M. Ta'anit II, 1, it was the practice during Jewish fast days for a communal elder to exhort his coreligionists not to be satisfied with the externals of fasting but to repent sincerely, as the people of Nineveh had done in the days of Jonah. Under the pressure of Christian accusations, however, which frequently contrasted the readiness of the Ninevites to repent with the Jews' stubborn refusal to see the light of Christianity, some Palestinian sages now taught that Nineveh's repentance had not been genuine at all. Others declared that complete repentance was possible only to Jews and that, hence, Gentiles could become full-fledged repentant sinners only after their conversion to Judaism. Cf. E. A. Urbach's analysis of "The Repentance of the People of Nineveh in the Judeo-Christian Polemics" (Hebrew), *Tarbiz,* XX, 118–22.

The use of history in the ancient Judeo-Christian controversies merits far more detailed investigation. The available literature, by itself none too ample, deals with the one or the other side only. Cf., in particular, S. J. Case's *Christian Philosophy of History;* E. Seeberg's "Geschichte und Geschichtsanschauung, dargestellt an altchristlichen Geschichtsvorstellungen," *Zeitschrift für Kirchengeschichte,* LX, 309–31; and R. M. Grant's "Historical Criticism in the Ancient Church," *JR,* XXV, 183–96, as well as N. N. Glatzer's *Untersuchungen zur Geschichtslehre der Tannaiten.* The interrelations between the two lines of thought, however, and the mutual stimulation given by attack and counterattack could well become the subject of a fascinating monograph. Cf. also, more generally, M. Simon's comprehensive work, *Verus Israel. Etude sur les relations entre chrétiens et juifs dans l'Empire Romain (135–425);* R. Wilde's dissertation on *The Treatment of the Jews in the Greek Christian Writers of the First Three Centuries;* H. Bietenhard's address on "Kirche und Synagoge in den ersten Jahrhunderten," *TZ*, IV, 174–92; and other writings listed *infra*, n. 40, 46. There have been no comparable recent publications by Jewish authors.

18. Cf. j. Pe'ah I, 1, 15c; M. Soṭah III, 14; b. 49b; Eusebius' *History of the Martyrs in Palestine* (Syriac version), ed. by W. Cureton, pp. 3 f.; and some other passages quoted by M. Joel in his *Blicke in die Religionsgeschichte zu Anfang des zweiten christlichen Jahrhunderts*, I; and S. Lieberman in his *Greek in Jewish Palestine*, *passim*. Lieberman explains R. Johanan's compunctions about the informers as based on the possibility that students of Greek "could occasionally undermine the existence of the Jewish courts" (p. 24). This seems unlikely. Certainly a person wishing to disregard a Jewish sentence could seek redress before a Roman tribunal, whether or not he happened to know Greek. Much more serious was the use of Greek and Greek Scriptures by Christian missionaries who, if they were of Jewish origin, could readily be classified "informers" in the light of experience. Lieberman also seems to go too far in totally denying "the alleged ban on Greek wisdom" except in the instruction of children in his *Hellenism*, pp. 100 ff. Cf. also *supra*, Chap. VI, n. 19–21, and *infra*, Chap. XIII, n. 20.

19. Masekhet Soferim, I, 7, ed. by M. Higger, pp. 101 ff.; *Halakhot gedolot* by Simon of Kayyara(?) *Tish'a be-Ab ve-Ta'anit*, ed. by J. Hildesheimer, p. 194 (taken over in some eds. of Megillat Ta'anit, Appendix, but rightly discarded by H. Lichtenstein in *HUCA*, VIII–IX). Cf. L. Prijs's *Jüdische Tradition in der Septuaginta*, especially pp. xxii f.; H. G. Enelow's ed. of *The Mishnah of Rabbi Eliezer*; and *supra*, Chap. VI, n. 26, 37. One must bear in mind, however, that fast days were quite common in ancient Palestine and, perhaps, in connection with the generally lower food consumption were considered far less arduous than in our comfort-loving civilization. Not only were communal fast days frequently proclaimed to implore God to send down much-delayed rain, but pious individuals observed private fasting on every Monday and Thursday. Incidentally, to differentiate the more clearly between the new faith and the "hypocrites," the author of the Didache (VIII, 1–2) advised his readers to fast rather on Wednesdays and Fridays.

20. Cf. j. Megillah I, 11, 71c. On Symmachus, cf. L. J. Liebreich's "Notes," *JBL*, LXIII, 397–403; and H. J. Schoeps's remarks in *Biblica*, XXVI, 100–111, and in his *Theologie*, pp. 350–80. Cf. also S. Krauss's rather dubious theory of "Two Hitherto Unknown Bible Versions in Greek" (*BJRL*, XXVII, 97–105; these are supposedly alluded to under the name of "books of La'ana and Tagla" in j. Sanhedrin X, 1, 28a, and Eccles. r. XII, 13); H. Rost's extensively documented survey of *Die Bibel in den ersten Jahrhunderten;* and the respective chapters in *The Bible in Its Ancient and English Versions*, ed. by H. W. Robinson.

21. Cf. Lieberman's *Greek in Jewish Palestine*, p. 17; M. D. (U.) Cassuto's "Jewish Bible Translation into Latin and Its Importance for the Study of the Greek and Aramaic Versions" (Hebrew), *Lewy Mem. Vol.*, pp. 161–72; Eusebius' *Praep. evang.*, XII, 1, 3 (in Gifford's transl., III, 621 ff.); W. L. Newton's "Influences on St. Jerome's Translation of the Old Testament," *CBQ*, V, 30 f. Cf. also D. S. Blondheim's comprehensive work, *Les Parlers judéo-romans et la Vetus Latina*, with L. Blau's comments thereon in *JQR*, XIX, 157–82; and A. Marigo's study of the religious background of "Il Volgarismo" in *Studi medievali*, XIII, 108–40. On the numerous complex problems of the ancient Latin translations which, though produced by Christians, seem to be indebted to some Jewish prototypes, cf. the surveys by F. Stummer, "Hauptprobleme der Erforschung der alttestamentlichen Vulgata" in *Werden und Wesen*, ed. by P. Volz, pp. 233–39; and B. Bischoff, "Neue Materialien zum Bestand und zur Geschichte der altlateinischen Bibelübersetzungen," *Miscellanea Mercati*, I, 407–36. Cf. also J. O. Smit's comprehensive Dutch study, *De Vulgaat;* and such more

detailed monographs, as H. Schneider's study of *Die altlateinischen biblischen Cantica;* R. Weber's *Anciennes versions latines du deuxième Livre des Paralipomènes;* J. Ziegler's study of "Die jüngeren griechischen Uebersetzungen als Vorlage der Vulgata in den prophetischen Schriften" in the *Braunsberg Staatlich Akademisches Vorlesungsverzeichnis,* 1943–44; E. F. Sutcliffe's "S. Jerome's Hebrew Manuscripts," *Biblica,* XXIX, 195–204; C. M. Cooper's "Jerome's 'Hebrew Psalter' and the New Latin Version," *JBL,* LXIX, 233–44; and F. Stummer "Zur Stilgeschichte der alten Bibelübersetzungen," *ZAW,* LXI, 195–231 (on the Targumim as well as the Vulgate).

22. Shabbat 63a; T. Sanhedrin XII, 9,433. Cf. M. Abot III, 11; b. Sanh. 99b; and other passages quoted by A. Büchler in his *Studies in Sin and Atonement in the Rabbinic Literature of the First Century,* pp. 97 ff. Notwithstanding Büchler's discussion of various opinions (cf. *ibid.,* p. 103), the *megalleh panim ba-torah* probably refers as much to an allegorical interpreter as to one who ridicules the Torah. Only with this anti-Christian implication does the combination of the three transgressions make adequate sense, and only thus can we understand why they were "added" at a later date, namely after 70, to the list of those for which a Jew loses his share in the world to come. Of course, the rabbis themselves could not get along without their own system of semi-allegorical interpretation; cf. *infra,* Chap. XV, n. 4.

23. Justin's *Dialogue,* 29 (*PG,* VI, 537); Irenaeus, *Contra Haer.* III, 21, 1 (*ibid.,* VII, 946). The rabbinic reinterpretation of the Song of Songs as describing the specific relationships between Israel and the Lord, was to exert great influence on the subsequent exegesis, particularly by mystics, both Jewish and Christian. On the latter, cf. P. P. Parente's "Canticle of Canticles in Mystical Theology," *CBQ,* VI, 142–58. The lines between the Christian and Jewish exegesis were often blurred, however, not only by direct Christian borrowings from the large body of traditional Jewish interpretations but also by the indebtedness of both parties to the Hellenistic world, Jewish and pagan. Such indebtedness comes clearly to the fore even in the so-called *Testimonies against the Jews,* or collections of Old Testament passages in support of the Christian point of view. While the oldest extant collection by Cyprian (*PL,* IV, 705–810), citing over seven hundred passages, dates from the third century, traces of shorter compilations are found as early as Barnabas and Justin (cf. J. R. Harris's *Testimonies,* pp. 20, 25, 33). By closely analyzing the interpretations of Exod. 17:8–11 and Num. 21:6–9 in the Mekilta, Mishnah, Barnabas, Justin and Tertullian, L. Wallach has aptly illustrated the extent to which Hellenistic exegesis had colored both the rabbinic and patristic Bible studies. Cf. his "Origin of Testimonia Biblica in Early Christian Literature," *RR,* VIII, 130–36.

On the canonization of Scriptures, which need not be discussed here in further detail, cf. G. Östborn's *Cult and Canon* (somewhat overstressing the importance of cultic recitation for the process of canonization) and the vast older literature cited in the introductions to the Old Testament by Pfeiffer and others. The socioreligious aspects of the evolution of the Masorah, will be treated in the latter's better known medieval context. Only time will tell to what, if any, extent the newly discovered scrolls will affect the long-accepted views concerning this significant phase in the consolidation of talmudic Judaism.

24. Sifre on Deut. 46, ed. by Friedmann, fol. 83a (ed. by Finkelstein, p. 104); Shabbat 12b, 115a; 'A.Z. 58b. Cf. D. de Sola Pool's analysis of *The Old Jewish-Aramaic Prayer: the Kaddish;* and M. Black's "Aramaic Liturgical Poetry of the Jews," *JTS,* L, 179–82. Cf. also K. G. Kuhn's observations in his *Achtzehngebet, passim.*

25. Despite A. E. Silverstone's attempt (in his *Aquila and Onkelos*) to resuscitate the old identifications of the two translators, majority opinion still dates Onkelos' version in the Byzantine and that ascribed to Jonathan ben 'Uzziel in the Muslim

period. R. Marcus contends, however, that Josephus had before him an Aramaic translation which was almost identical with our *Targum Jonathan.* Cf. the Preface to his ed. of Josephus, Vol. V, p. viii. Similarly A. Baumstark has, in several studies, reiterated his conviction that "the Peshiṭṭa to the Pentateuch stemmed from a very old Palestinian Targum which had been adapted to Eastern Aramean, possibly in Adiabene, at the time of the conversion of its royal house to Judaism." Cf. his "Ps.-Jonathan zu Deuteronomium 34,6 und die Pentateuchzitate Afrahats," *ZAW*, LIX, 101. Cf. also P. Churgin's *Targum Jonathan to the Prophets;* his *Targum Ketubim* (T. to the Hagiographa); his "Law in the *Targum Onkelos"* (Hebrew), *Talpioth*, II, 417–30; A. Sperber's "Peschitta und Onkelos," *Kohut Mem. Vol.*, pp. 554–64; his "Targum Onkelos in Its Relation to the Masoretic Hebrew Text," *PAAJR*, VI, 309–51; S. Wohl's dissertation, *Das Palästinische Pentateuchtargum;* C. Peters's "Peschittha und Targumim des Pentateuchs," *Muséon*, XLVIII, 1–54; his "Pešitta-Psalter und Psalmentargum," *ibid.*, LII, 275–96; J. S. Noble's "Syriac Translation of Chronicles" (Hebrew), *Horeb*, X, 77–104; A. Vööbus's "Neuentdecktes Textmaterial zur Vetus Syra," *TZ*, VII, 30–38; P. Kahle's *Cairo Geniza*, pp. 117 ff., 179 ff.; V. Hamp's study of the "word" (*memra*) in the Aramaic versions; and particularly H. J. Kassovsky's *Oṣar ha-millim* (A Concordance to the Targum Onkelos); and D. Golomb's comprehensive work, *Targumno* (A Close Study of the Targums) which includes a detailed analysis of variants from the Masoretic text. Among recent text editions, cf., e.g., *The Targum of Isaiah*, ed. with an English transl. by J. F. Stenning. A good survey of two decades of Peshiṭṭa studies (1927–46) supplementing L. Haefeli's earlier listing is offered by J. van der Ploeg in *JEOL*, X, 392–99.

After the rise of Islam, Aramaic (or Syriac) was rather speedily displaced by Arabic, although it has survived in some isolated villages until the present day. Cf. S. Reich's *Etudes sur les villages araméens de l'Anti-Liban.* Cf. also R. Bowman's data in *JNES*, VII, 65–90; J. N. Epstein's analysis of two Aramaic words, as an additional sample of the much-needed dictionary of the Babylonian Talmud and geonic literature, in his "Babylonian Aramaic" (Hebrew), *Tarbiz*, XVI, 18–20; and, more generally, F. Rosenthal's *Aramaistische Forschung.* Cf. also *supra*, Chap. X, n. 12.

26. Cf. the rabbis' debates in Megillah 18a; and, by way of comparison, G. Bardy's *Question des langues dans l'Eglise ancienne.* The lesser familiarity of talmudic Jewry with the non-Semitic languages did not prevent the adoption by the rabbis of many Greek and Latin as well as Persian expressions current among the surrounding masses. An explanation of the former was attempted about half a century ago by S. Krauss (with the competent help of I. Löw), in his *Griechische und lateinische Lehnwörter im Talmud, Midrasch und Targum.* A serious obstacle then was the insufficient material available for the consideration of the contemporary Greek *koiné* from which the Jews appropriated their terms. The publication of abundant papyrological sources and especially of F. Preisigke's *Wörterbuch der griechischen Papyrusurkunden* (which ought to be supplemented from more recent finds; a revised ed. by E. Kiessling, begun in 1940, has not progressed beyond one issue published in 1944), now makes a thorough reinvestigation possible. The availability of improved editions of rabbinic texts should likewise prove very helpful. Cf. *infra*, Chap. XV, n. 1, 6. Cf. also the brief comparative study of P. Joüon, "Mots grecs de l'araméen d'Onkelos ou de l'hébreu de la Mishna qui se trouvent aussi dans les Evangiles," *Recherches de science religieuse*, XXII, 463–69. On the Persian loan words in the Talmud, cf. *infra*, Chap. XIII, n. 38.

27. Mekilta, Nezikin, XVIII, ed. by Lauterbach III, 138; Sifre on Deut. 344, ed. by Friedmann, fol. 143b (ed. by Finkelstein, p. 401); Yebamot 47b; j. Sanhedrin X, 2, 29b; b. 107b in uncensored editions (with reference to II Kings 5:27; cf. Rabbinovicz's *Diqduqe soferim ad loc.*). The reference to Jesus may, however, be a later interpolation, as it is slightly out of context in both these passages discussing only the rela-

tions between Elisha and Gehazi. Certainly the combination of R. Joshua ben Perahiah with Jesus is a gross anachronism. By making R. Helbo a contemporary of the Council of Nicaea (325), W. F. Braude sees in his statement merely "a political fact," namely a warning against converting Christians, which was frowned upon and soon outlawed by imperial legislation. Cf. his *Jewish Proselyting*, pp. 42 ff. Not only is the chronology dubious, however, but the rabbi could easily have found a less obnoxious way of warning his coreligionists than calling proselytes, by themselves perfectly innocent, a "tumor" (Braude translates "itch"). Moreover, in 325 the vast majority of likely converts still were pagans, rather than Christians. But we must be grateful to both Braude and B. J. Bamberger (in his *Proselytism*) for having marshaled an imposing array of evidence showing that, throughout the first five centuries C.E., rabbinic opinion was preponderantly friendly to the proselyte, although not necessarily to proselytism as a conscious communal effort. During the century following the Bar Kocheba revolt, the missionary zeal seems to have reached a low ebb, to be revived later particularly outside the reach of Christian Rome.

28. Sanhedrin 58b f. While somewhat overstressing the uniformly benevolent attitude of the rabbis toward the semiproselytes, S. Lieberman has correctly pointed out the existence of various kinds of "God-fearing" strangers. Cf. his *Greek in Jewish Palestine*, pp. 77 ff. The two alternative designations, however, of *gere ummot ha-'olam* (proselytes from the world's nations) and *gere ha-ares* (proselytes of the land) appear rather dubious. The former is an obvious tautology. If these manuscript readings in Lev. r. III, 2 and ARN XXXVI, 107 (a variant of *gere emet*, genuine proselytes) should prove authentic, one might perhaps suggest that the rabbis dealt here with Palestinian vs. foreign proselytes. That there existed a legal distinction between them is evident from the later tractate *Gerim* which states succinctly, "Beloved is the Land of Israel for it [automatically] absorbs the proselytes. He who says in the Land of Israel, 'I am a proselyte,' is immediately accepted. In other countries he is not accepted, unless he produces witnesses" (IV, 5, in M. Higger's *Sheba' masekhtot qetanot* [Seven Minor Treatises], p. 79). Be this as it may, we must clearly distinguish between rabbinic encouragement of semiproselytism, for which there is little evidence, and the rather friendly treatment of those already admitted.

29. 'Arakhin 29a; Yebamot 47ab. The emphasis on "these days" rather clearly indicates the date of the Baraita after 135. Christianity, on the contrary, at that time made admission fairly easy. "It appears," comments W. Robinson, "that all that was required before Baptism was faith and penitence. . . . Pre-baptismal teaching therefore seems to have been at a minimum." Cf. his "Historical Survey of the Church's Treatment of New Converts with Reference to Pre- and Postbaptismal Instruction," *JTS*, XLII, 42 f. Only in the third century do we hear of a more elaborate procedure. See Origen's *Contra Celsum*, III, 51.

30. Pliny's *Hist. nat.*, III, 5.39; Origen's *Contra Celsum*, II, 30; Justin's *Dialogue*, 16 (*PG*, VI, 509). A. Zwaenepoel furnishes further interesting illustrations for that religious inspiration of Roman imperialism (*Antiquité classique*, XVIII, 5 ff.). In his "Church and State in the New Testament," *JRS*, XXXIX, 23–30, W. L. Knox has shown that most New Testament authors were strongly pro-Roman and, hence, probably non-Palestinian Christians. Of the vast literature on the subject of church-state relationships in the early centuries and the underlying ideological conflicts, cf., e.g., E. Peterson's *Monotheismus als politisches Problem;* U. Gmelin's *Auctoritas;* and J. Westbury-Jones's *Roman and Christian Imperialism*.

31. Philo's *Legatio*, 2.8–13; *Quod Deus immut. sit*, XXXVI, 176; Sifre on Deut. 317, ed. by Friedmann, fol. 135b (ed. by Finkelstein, pp. 359 f.). Cf. T. Reinach's "Mon nom est légion," *REJ*, XLVII, 175 ff.; and S. Krauss's *Paras ve-Romi ba-talmud u-ba-*

midrashim (Persia and Rome in Talmud and Midrash), pp. 177 f., citing further rabbinic sources.

32. Deut. r. VI, 4; Megillah 10b; 'A.Z. 2b, with reference to Dan. 7:23; Gen. r. LXXVI, 12, 903 f.; Berakhot 32a, with reference to Exod. 32:13; Midrash Tehillim on Ps. 17:14, with reference to Ps. 49:2. Cf. also other rabbinic passages cited by A. Marmorstein in his Hebrew essay on "The Belief in the Eternity of Israel in the Homilies of the Tannaim and Amoraim," in *Studies in Jewish Theology*, pp. 1–16. On the other hand, there is nothing intrinsically wrong with respect to Paul's alleged use of the term, *kosmos* (world), in his Areopagus speech (Acts 17:24), questioned by Dibelius because of the absence of an Old Testament equivalent. Cf. *Paulus auf dem Areopag*, p. 19. Dibelius forgets that there was nothing to prevent a Jew, particularly a Hellenistic Jew like Paul, from using the Greek equivalent of *'olam* in the latter's newer Palestinian meaning. It had long been so used by the Septuagint translators. On the other hand, R. Eleazar's contrast between the arbitrariness of the Roman rulers and God's adherence to his self-imposed laws could well be echoed by any Christian apologist. Cf. j. R.H. I, 3, 57a; and Lieberman's *Greek in Jewish Palestine*, pp. 38 f., 144, n. 2. Even in his panegyric on Constantine (*De laudibus Constantini*, in *PG*, XX, 1315 ff.) Eusebius reiterated that the mightiest emperor is bound to obey the divine law. Many other sources are cited by K. M. Setton in his *Christian Attitudes towards the Emperor in the Fourth Century*, pp. 94, 112, 133, 193 f. Cf. also, in general, the data assembled by N. Wasser in *Die Stellung der Juden gegenüber den Römern* (only to the Bar Kocheba revolt); and by H. Fuchs in *Der geistige Widerstand gegen Rom in der antiken Welt*, pp. 68 ff.

33. Acts 17:24–25, compared with Wisdom of Solomon 13:10 ff.; 15:7 ff.; Philo's *De decalogo*, XIV, 66 ff.; *De spec. legibus*, I, 4.21–22; Dibelius's *Paulus*, pp. 33 f.; Nilsson's remarks in *HTR*, XXXVIII, 64; Augustine's *Contra Faustum*, XX, 4 (*PL*, XLII, 370); Gregory's *Epistolae*, No. 76 (*ibid.*, LXXVII, 1215 ff.; *MGH*, *Epistolae*, II, 330 f.); C. Hopkins's "Antioch Mosaic Pavements," *JNES*, VII, 96. Among more recent studies on the pagan survivals, cf. F. P. Magoun, Jr.'s "On Some Survivals of Pagan Belief in Anglo-Saxon England," *HTR*, XL, 33–46; G. J. Laing's "Roman Religious Survivals in Christianity" in J. T. McNeill, *et al., Environmental Factors*, pp. 72–90; A. Badawy's "Persistance de l'idéologie et du formulaire païens dans les épitaphes coptes," *Bulletin de la Société d'archéologie copte*, X, 1–26; and such archaeological comparisons as J. Leibovitch's "Hellénismes et hébraïsmes dans une chapelle chrétienne à el-Bagaouât," *ibid.*, V, 61-68. Cf. also, more generally, W. Elliger's *Stellung der alten Christen zu den Bildern*.

34. Hagigah 15b; E. J. Wellesz in "The Earliest Example of Christian Hymnody," *Classical Quarterly*, XXXIX, 45, with reference to the fuller documentation in A. Z. Idelsohn's "Parallelen zwischen gregorianischen und hebräisch-orientalischen Gesangweisen," *Zeitschrift für Musikwissenschaft*, IV, 514–24. Cf. also Wellesz's comprehensive monograph on *Eastern Elements in Western Chant*. Unfortunately, our knowledge of ancient Jewish music must be largely derived from its survivals in Church music, and hence their mutual interrelations will necessarily remain hypothetical. Cf., however, E. Werner's penetrating studies of "The Doxology in Synagogue and Church," *HUCA*, XIX, 275–351; "The Conflict between Hellenism and Judaism," *ibid.*, XX, 407–70; and his remarks in *RR*, VII, 344. One should also bear in mind that "The Liturgical Singing of Women in Christian Antiquity," contrasted with the relatively passive role of Jewish women in the synagogue services (see *infra*, Chap. XIV, n. 23), became an effective missionary instrument in the hands of Christian leaders. Cf. J. Quasten's pertinent remarks in the *Catholic Historical Review*, XXVII, 149–65. Cf. also *supra*, Chap. IX, n. 5. On the changes in the adoration of "victors," cf. F. Rütten's *Victorverehrung im christlichen Altertum*.

35. Cf. E. J. Goodspeed's *Christianity Goes to Press;* C. C. McCown's "Earliest Christian Books," *BA,* VI, 21–31; B. M. Metzger's remarks, *ibid.,* X, 28 ff.; J. Finegan's *Light from the Ancient Past,* pp. 305 ff.; and L. Amundsen's "Christian Papyri from the Oslo Collection," *Symbolae Osloenses,* XXIV, 121–47 (with special reference to P. Oslo Inv. 1644). Amundsen quotes here thirty examples of the use of Ps. 90 for magical purposes. On the Jews in magic arts, cf. *supra,* Chap. IX, n. 23–27. That Jewish participation still continued in the fourth century is evidenced by St. Chrysostom's attempted explanation of their success as owing not to their invocation of Moses or Joseph, but to the fact that, having killed Christ, they had altogether given themselves over to the demons. Cf. his *Adversus Judaeos,* VIII, 6 (*PG,* XLVIII, 935 ff.). That is why, for instance, the fever amulet, now included in the Princeton papyri and considered Christian by the editors, may actually have been Jewish. Cf. A. C. Johnson and S. P. Goodrich's ed. of *Papyri in the Princeton University Collections,* III, 78, No. 159. On the other hand, there is hardly any question that the Christians used the codex earlier and far more extensively than did the Jews, perhaps out of opposition to Jews, as suggested by P. Katz in "The Early Christians' Use of Codices instead of Rolls," *JTS,* XLVI, 63–65. A. Spanier's arguments in favor of the early and extensive use of the convenient codex by Jews, too (cf. his "Rollenform der Bücher im Mischna-Zeitalter," *Soncino-Blätter,* III, 67–71), in themselves admittedly dubious, have not been confirmed by any recent find. Pre-Constantine Jewry, generally reticent and conservative in its literary output, had the less reason to deviate from the accepted methods of book production, as it had fewer occasions to hide its writings from the inquisitive eyes of intolerant rulers. Cf. also C. H. Roberts's comparison of "The Christian Book and the Greek Papyri," *JTS,* L, 155–68 (suggesting Western influences); the *New Testament Manuscript Studies,* ed. by M. M. Parvis and A. P. Wikgren; and S. Lieberman's *Hellenism* pp. 203 ff. (arguing for the early use of codices by Jews, but admitting that as late as the fourth century rabbinic letters circulated only in a few private codices).

36. Epictetus' *Discourses,* II, 9, 19–20, with N. Bentwich's comments thereon in "The Graeco-Roman View of Jews and Judaism in the Second Century," *JQR,* XXIII, 337–48; Origen's *Contra Celsum,* I, 15; IV, 51; *supra,* Chap. VI, n. 43; and H. C. Puech's analysis of "Numénius d'Apamée et les théologies orientales au second siècle," *Annuaire,* II, 745–78. On the other hand, a curious and generally well-informed pagan like Plutarch betrays considerable ignorance concerning Jewish customs. Not only is his naturalistic explanation of the Jewish aversion to hogs and of the alleged Jewish donkey worship absolutely farfetched, but his general discussion of the kind of Deity worshiped by Jews consists of a series of half-truths or outright misrepresentations. Cf. his *Symposiaca,* IV, 5–6 (in the English transl. by W. W. Goodwin, 6th ed., III, 307 ff.). While no documented study of Plutarch's attitude to Judaism seems ever to have been written, much can be learned from such related monographs as H. Almquist's *Plutarch und das Neue Testament;* and A. M. Pizzagelli's "Plutarco e il cristianesimo," *Atene e Roma,* XLV, 97–102. Cf. also A. Kaminka's study of "Les Rapports entre le rabbinisme et la philosophie stoicienne," *REJ,* LXXXII, 233–52; V. Stegemann's "Christentum und Stoizismus im Kampf um die geistigen Lebenswerte im 2. Jahrhundert nach Christus," *Welt als Geschichte,* VII, 295–330; W. Eltester's "Krisis der alten Welt und das Christentum," *ZNW,* XLII, 1–19; and P. de Labriolle's comprehensive analysis of *La Réaction païenne* during the first six centuries c.e. One must bear in mind, however, that religious syncretism as such need not have been a sign of deep pro-Jewish or pro-Christian sympathies. Alexander Severus, for instance, who is said to have maintained in his palace a museum for all important religions in the empire (including statues for Abraham and Jesus) and was even nicknamed "archisynagogus," was nevertheless a staunch upholder of the old Roman faith. Cf. F. Altheim's *History of Roman Religion,* p. 463. Of more incidental interest to our subject are the Christian polemics against the

Egyptian and other oriental religions, except in so far as Christian apologists used to good advantage some of the age-old arguments assembled in the Hellenistic-Jewish literature. Cf. S. Jannaccone's brief survey of "Polemiche nella letteratura cristiana contro le religioni d'Oriente," *Aevum*, XXII, 67–74.

37. Origen's *Contra Celsum*, III, 5–8, 31 ff., IV, 62 ff., 74 ff., V, 6, 41 f., VII, 3; Philo's *De opificio mundi*, VII, 26 ff. Unfortunately Celsus' *True Discourse* is extant only in the various excerpts reproduced by his opponent Origen which may not fully reflect the original line of thought. Cf. R. Bader's remarks on *Der 'Αληθὴς λόγος des Kelsos*. Celsus' indebtedness to Hellenistic-Jewish writings and, particularly, Philo has been demonstrated by E. Stein in his "De Celso Platonico Philonis Alexandrini imitatore," *Eos*, XXXIV, 205–16, *Alttestamentliche Bibelkritik*, pp. 15 ff.; and by M. Lods in his "Etudes sur les sources juives de la polémique de Celse contre les chrétiens," *RHPR*, XXI, 1–33. "It is instructive to notice," rightly observes H. Chadwick, "how Origen, an allegorist *par excellence*, will not allow the validity of the method when applied to Homer . . . ; and Celsus and Porphyry deny the right of Christians to allegorize the Old Testament, although they use the method freely themselves to interpret Homer" ("Origen, Celsus and the Stoa," *JTS*, XLVIII, 43). Cf. also his "Origen, Celsus and the Resurrection of the Body," *HTR*, XLI, 83–102; and A. H. Chroust's "Meaning of Time in the Ancient World," *New Scholasticism*, XXI, 1–70.

38. Porphyry's *Contra Christianos* is lost. It appears that of its fifteen books written in 270 C.E., Books III–IV were devoted to a critique of the Old Testament generally and Books XII–XIII to a detailed commentary on Daniel. Some excerpts have been reconstructed from fragments of the *Apocryticus* by a fourth-century Christian writer, Macarius Magnus, by A. von Harnack in his *Kritik des Neuen Testaments von einem griechischen Philosophen des 3. Jahrhunderts* (the reference to Paul is on p. 60). Harnack later recovered further fragments which he edited in the publications of the Prussian Academy. These and other older works are cited in A. B. Hulen's *Porphyr's Work against the Christians*. Cf. also P. Nautin's "Trois autres fragments du livre de Porphyre 'Contre les Chrétiens,'" *RB*, LVII, 409–16; P. Benoit's "Adversaire du christianisme au IIIe siècle: Porphyre," *RB*, LIV, 543–72; G. Cardinal Mercati's *Nuove note di letteratura biblica e cristiana antica*, pp. 49 ff.; and, on Porphyry's unfamiliarity with the Hebrew Daniel, Stein's *Alttestam. Bibelkritik*, p. 29.

39. Cf. J. Friedrich's "Griechisches und Römisches in phönizischem und punischem Gewande," *Festschrift Eissfeldt*, pp. 109–24 (showing how, despite ready acceptance of Greek or Latin names and institutions, the Western influences long remained on the surface); Eusebius' *Contra Hieroclem* (*PG*, XXII, 795 ff.), with W. Nestle's comments thereon in "Die Haupteinwände des antiken Denkens gegen das Christentum," *AR*, XXXVII, 69; R. Walzer's *Galen on Jews and Christians*, pp. 10 f., 14, 18. Cf. also *supra*, Chap. VI, n. 13.

40. Julian's *Against the Galilaeans*, 224E, 306B, ed. by Wright, III, 384 f., 406 f. Unfortunately this work, too, is lost and, like those by Celsus and Porphyry, has to be reconstructed largely from the polemical work of an opponent (Cyril, the anti-Jewish bishop of Alexandria). On the crucial developments during the fourth century, cf. W. Seston's "Opinion païenne et la conversion de Constantin," *RHPR*, XVI, 250–64; H. Bloch's "A New Document of the Last Pagan Revival in the West, 393–394 A.D.," *HTR*, XXXVIII, 199–244; Labriolle's *Reaction*; and, more generally, C. N. Cochrane's *Christianity and Classical Culture*, and W. W. Hyde's *Paganism to Christianity in the Roman Empire*.

41. Julian's *Epistolae*, 396D, ed. by Wright, No. 51, III, 176 f.; O. Sehl's "Verbannung des Athanasius durch Julian," *Klio*, XXXII, 188. Julian's praise of the Jewish sacrificial system and attempted restoration of the sanctuary in Jerusalem are explained in connection with the emperor's Neoplatonic views by Johanan Lewy in a fine Hebrew study of "Julianus and the Rebuilding of the Temple," *Zion*, VI, 7 ff. Cf. also M. Adler's still valuable older study of "The Emperor Julian and the Jews," *JQR*, o.s. V, 591–651; J. Vogt's searching analysis of *Kaiser Julian und das Judentum;* M. Hack's "Is Julian's Declaration a Forgery?" (Hebrew), *Yavneh*, II, 118–39, and his note on Lewy's essay in *Zion*, VI, 157 f.; and F. A. Ridley's *Julian the Apostate and the Rise of Christianity*. The often impugned authenticity of the emperor's letter "To the Community of the Jews" has been successfully defended by both Hack and Lewy. It is doubly regrettable, therefore, that so much of the emperor's correspondence is lost. Of his three other recorded letters addressed to Jews only a small excerpt of one has been preserved by Gregory Nazanzien. Avi-Yonah's *Bi-Yeme Roma*, pp. 136 f., decidedly overstates, however, both Julian's "Zionism" and the allegedly enthusiastic response of the Jewish people. We know about Jewish reactions almost exclusively from patristic reports, which were naturally interested in presenting the hopes of Jews as having surged higher and higher, in order to enhance the impact of their subsequent debacle. Certainly the fact that their pagan, often hostile neighbors in both Ascalon and Arabia fervently hailed the new emperor (cf. the inscriptions published by Welles in Kraeling's *Gerasa*, pp. 489 f., and by Avi-Yonah himself in *QDAP*, X, 160 f.) must have given pause to thoughtful Jewish leaders. If we are to accept Lieberman's interpretation of R. Aḥa's vision (Eccles. r. IX, 8) the rabbi, soon after Julian's death, expressed his joy over the Lord having "removed the shame of Julian" (*Annuaire*, VII, 412 ff., 435 ff.). This interpretation remains plausible despite W. Bacher's interpretation of another statement by R. Aḥa as a friendly gesture toward Julian. In this evidently earlier and more factual observation, the Amora merely predicted that "the Temple is going to be rebuilt before the restoration of the house of David" (j. Ma'aser sheni V, 2, 56a). See Bacher's "Statements of a Contemporary of the Emperor Julian on the Rebuilding of the Temple," *JQR*, o.s. X, 168–72; cf., however, I. Sonne's weighty reservations against Lieberman's identification in his "Use of Rabbinic Literature as Historical Sources," *JQR*, XXXVI, 163 ff., and his "Word and Meaning—Text and Context," *ibid.*, XXXVII, 318 ff. At any rate, R. Aḥa's rationalization after the event proves little in regard to Jewish public opinion in Julian's lifetime, when it undoubtedly was very much confused and divided. Cf. also A. Marmorstein's Hebrew essay on "Emperor Julian in the Aggadah of R. Aḥa" in *Melilah*, I, 93–120.

42. Berakhot 5a with reference to Exod. 24:12; Gen. r. VIII, 2, 57 (cf. Theodor's note 7 thereon); j. Megillah I, 7, 70d, with reference to Deut. 5:19, Esther 9:28, and Hab. 3:6 (reading *halakhot* in lieu of *halikhot*); Sanhedrin 21b. Later Jewish authorities tried to harmonize the views of both R. Johanan and R. Simon. Cf. Moses Margulies's citations in his commentary *Mar'eh ha-panim* on j. *ad loc.;* and R. Johanan's statement in Megillah 19b. In Shabbat 56b the synchronization is ascribed to the Babylonian Samuel and combined with the older saying that Magna Graecia was founded on the day when Jeroboam erected his two golden calves. These and the following examples of the oblique rabbinic reactions to the raging controversies of the day could readily be multiplied.

43. Cf. A. Harnack's *Mission and Expansion*, II, 317 ff., 324 ff. Galilee, in fact, never was an important center of Christianity before Constantine. Even in its earliest stages the mother church embraced some 39 non-Galileans for each Galilean, according to B. W. Bacon in his "Resurrection in Judean and Galilean Tradition," *JR*, XI, 506–16. Nor have archaeologists been able to detect any remnants of pre-Constantine churches there or elsewhere in the Holy Land. Even the Scythopolis church, recorded by

Epiphanius as destroyed by the populace in the days of Julian, was very likely not the one in which Procopius had preached before 303. Cf. L. H. Vincent's "Cathédrale antique de Beisân-Scythopolis," *Muséon*, LIX, 303–18. Certainly the church excavated at Dura-Europos and dating from 232 c.e. is older than any such remains found in Palestine. Cf. J. W. Crowfoot's *Early Churches in Palestine;* and J. Lassus's *Sanctuaires chrétiens en Syrie.*

44. Bell in *HTR*, XXXVII, 204. Even this estimate leans to the optimistic side. Direct papyrological evidence for Christians in Egypt before Diocletian is extremely meager. Bell (improving upon Ghedini's researches) found by 1944 only "four certain [papyri], one of them perhaps from the end of the second century, two definitely of the third, one which may belong to the fourth and so fall outside our period; three probable, two of third century, one second-third; and ten doubtful, for only two of which can a strong case be made" (*ibid.*, p. 198). His main reliance is, therefore, on extant Christian literary papyri, some 39 of which may be dated in the second and third centuries. He must admit, however, that this figure compares unfavorably with upward of 166 Homeric papyri of that period in P. Collart's computation of 1932. Moreover, one can hardly compare the use of Homer, even as a textbook in schools limited to the upper crust of the Greek-speaking population, to the daily use, both liturgical and educational, of the Bible by Christian congregations, however small. Cf. also the divergent statistics cited by C. C. McCown in *BA*, VI, 27.

45. Cf., e.g., M. M. Baney's *Some Reflections of Life in North Africa in the Writings of Tertullian;* and M. Simon's "Judaïsme berbère dans l'Afrique ancienne," *RHPR*, XXVI, 1–31, 105–45. In his attempt to prove the existence of a substantial body of Christianity at Rome in the Apostolic Age, A. S. Barnes had to resort to the conversion of many authentic Jewish, into Judeo-Christian, sources (pp. 78 ff.).

46. Cf. especially J. Strzygowski's *Ancien art chrétien de Syrie*, pp. 179 ff.; E. Werner's aforementioned essays; and the graphic picture of the expansion of Christianity up to 300 c.e. in K. Pieper's *Atlas orbis Christiani antiqui*. Cf. also D. Magie's comprehensive work on *Roman Rule in Asia Minor* (to the end of the third cent.). The later prominence of "Punic" Christianity in the West is discussed, for instance, in V. Ehrenberg's *Karthago;* S. Dickey's "Some Economic and Social Conditions of Asia Minor Affecting the Expansion of Christianity," in *Studies in Early Christianity*, ed. by S. J. Case, p. 416, n. 1; and the literature listed *supra*, Chap. VI, n. 13. Numerous other solutions of the puzzling problem of how these two regions acquired their preëminence in the early Church have been offered, but none seems as satisfactory as that suggested here. Cf. also in general the comprehensive works by K. S. Latourette, *A History of the Expansion of Christianity*, I; H. Lietzmann, *The Founding of the Church Universal;* and J. Lebreton and J. Zeiller, *The History of the Primitive Church*, I–II.

47. Even if we accept B. Altaner's conclusion that the term *paganus* first connoted only a civilian in contrast to soldier (cf. his "Paganus. Eine bedeutungsgeschichtliche Untersuchung," *Zeitschrift für Kirchengeschichte*, LVIII, 130–41), the use of this term in Christian circles doubtless originated from the equation of *paganus* and peasant. On the importance of urbanization in the earlier Jewish religious propaganda, cf. *supra*, Chap. VI, n. 8. Cf. also J. Ellul's "Urbanisme et théologie biblique," *Dieu Vivant*, 16, pp. 109–23.

48. Ps.-Clement (Bishop Soter) cited by Harnack in his *Mission and Expansion*, II, 4; Augustine's *Civitas Dei*, I, 6. Various estimates of the Christian ratio in the population about 300 c.e., ranging from 5 to 12½ per cent, are cited in K. S. Latourette's *History of the Expansion of Christianity*, I, 108, n. 278. Cf. also G. Bardy's *Conversion*

au Christianisme durant les premiers siècles. The entire demographic problem of late antiquity and its impact on the expansion of Christianity, as well as on the development of talmudic Judaism, has not yet received the necessary attention by specialists. In "The Ecclesiastical Age; a Demographic Interpretation of the Period 200–900 A.D.," *RR,* V, 137–47, J. C. Russell has raised some pertinent questions; many more could readily be added. But in the present state of our knowledge scholarship cannot yet offer any adequate answers. Even the number of Christian victims of persecutions can be estimated only with extreme difficulty. L. Hertling did it only on the somewhat tenuous basis of recorded Christian communities. Cf. his "Zahl der Martyrer bis 313," *Gregorianum,* XXV, 103–29.

49. Martyrdom of Polycarp, VIII, 1; XII, 2; XIII, 1 (*PG,* V, 1035 ff.; and in the English transl. by J. A. Kleist in *Ancient Christian Writers,* VI, 93 ff.); Justin's *Dialogue,* 17 (*PG,* VI, 512). Cf. Abrahams's *Studies in Pharisaism,* II, 67 ff. The large Jewish share in anti-Christian persecutions before Constantine, under Julian and later on, a recurrent literary theme in patristic letters, is often accepted by modern scholars. Apart from many contradictions and intrinsic improbabilities appearing in this record of accusations, it is utterly unsupported by any reliable neutral source. The often invoked testimony of Tacitus, for example, concerning the alleged Jewish role in the earliest Christian sufferings under Nero is extremely dubious. Cf. F. W. Clayton's pertinent remarks in his "Tacitus and Nero's Persecution of the Christians," *Classical Quarterly,* XLI, 81–85. Cf. also, more generally, Parkes's *Conflict,* pp. 125 ff.; and M. Simon's *Verus Israel,* pp. 149 ff., where the part played by Jews in anti-Christian persecutions is plausibly reduced to minor proportions.

50. Epiphanius' *Adversus Haereses,* XXIX, 9 (*PG,* XLI, 404); Irenaeus' *Contra Haereses,* I, 27, 2 (*ibid.,* VII, 688). This antagonism, however, did not prevent the Marcionites from calling their own place of worship a "synagogue," although most Christians by that time used the term *ecclesia.* Conversely, the rabbis applied the term *cosmocrator* (ruler of the world) only the better to contrast God's omnipotence with the limited authority of even the most powerful monarchs. Cf., e.g., j. Berakhot IX, 1, 13b; 'A.Z. III, 1,42c; and G. Kretschmar's "Gebrauch des Fremdwortes Kosmokrator im Rabbinat," *Judaica,* IV, 114–23. The Marcionite and anti-Marcionite fragments are now readily available in R. M. Grant's English transl. in his *Second-Century Christianity.* Cf. also M. Rist's "Pseudepigraphic Refutations of Marcionism," *JR,* XXII, 39–62. On the date of the controversy, cf. E. Barnikol's "Zeit Marcions und die Entstehung der Kirche im zweiten Jahrhundert," *Theologische Studien und Kritiken,* CIII, 208–29, asserting that Marcion's public activity extended over the years 128–44, while the establishment of a Marcionite church followed about 155. More recently J. Knox suggested that Marcion's career began as early as 110–20 and ended in Rome about 175 C.E. Cf. his detailed analysis of *Marcion and the New Testament* and, more generally, A. von Harnack's *Marcion.* The influence exercised by Marcion on the Jewish Aggadah has been investigated by A. Marmorstein, in his "Background of the Haggadah," *HUCA,* VI, 141–204. Cf. also E. C. Blackman's *Marcion and His Influence.* It appears more plausible, however, that the main doctrines became known to the rabbis from the general Palestinian and Babylonian Christian as well as Jewish gnosis, and not from the Marcionite group itself. On the former, cf., E. Percy's searching *Untersuchungen,* cited *supra,* Chap. X, n. 23, and *infra,* Chap. XV, n. 27.

51. Cf. J. C. Plumpe's *Mater Ecclesia: an Inquiry into the Concept of the Church as Mother in Early Christianity;* and, on the nationalist elements in these sectarian controversies, the literature cited in my *Modern Nationalism and Religion,* p. 275, n. 11; G. Bardy's "Patriotisme égyptien dans la tradition patristique," *Revue d'histoire ecclésiastique,* XLV, 77–96; and E. Peterson's "Problem des Nationalismus im alten Christentum," *TZ,* VII, 81–91.

52. Augustine's *Civitas Dei*, IV, 34 (in Dodd's transl. I, 176). This formulation is sharper than anything found in earlier patristic writings. Cf. B. Blumenkranz's *Judenpredigt Augustins, passim*. Cf. also P. Bérard's *S. Augustin et les Juifs*. The background and meaning of the prayer *Pro Judaeis* (in the Gelasian Sacramentary, *PL*, LXXIV, 1105, etc.) is analyzed by L. Canet in *REJ*, LXI, 213–21, and by J. M. Oesterreicher in *Theological Studies*, VIII, 80–96. On the Jews in Christian liturgy generally, cf. the learned notes assembled by Juster in *Empire romain*, I, 81 ff., 290 ff., 333 ff. A comprehensive up-to-date analytical study would, nevertheless, fill an important lacuna.

CHAPTER XIII: INCIPIENT MEDIEVALISM

1. Cf. Tanḥuma, Beha'alotkha, 9, on Num. 10:2; Cant. r. I, 22, on 1:3; with reference to Isa. 19:24 and Zech. 13:8 f., as well as other rabbinic passages cited by L. Baeck in " 'Das dritte Geschlecht,' " *Kohut Mem. Vol.*, pp. 40–46. Baeck's attempt, however, to establish the priority of this Jewish doctrine over the Christian claim to being a *tertium genus* is none too successful. Christians naturally had every incentive to call themselves the "third order," in opposition to both paganism and Judaism. Hence their concept can be dated back to the beginning of the second century and was fully developed by Tertullian. The rabbinic passages, on the other hand, except for an equivocal messianic reference to R. Johanan ben Zakkai's circle (j. Ḥagigah II, 1, 77a), are anonymous and found in later midrashim, and hence may belong to almost any period of antiquity. The crucial homily in Tanḥuma, particularly, referring to a dualistic faith almost certainly points to Sassanian Persia, whereas the enforced idolatry given as its alternative need not even refer to Rome's "imperial" worship. In any case, this homily hardly antedates the third century. None the less, direct Jewish borrowing from the Christians is also unlikely. It is easy to see how Zechariah's mysterious prophecy concerning the survival of the "Third" would prompt homilists of both faiths to apply it to their respective denominations. On the otherwise unquestionably old and deep-rooted Jewish belief in the eternity of Israel, cf. *supra*, Chap. XII, n. 32.

2. Exod. r. XXXVI, 1, on Jer. 11:16. An interesting analysis of Jewish nationhood, as envisaged by the sages, in many ways distinguished from biblical views, is offered by M. Kadushin in his "Aspects of the Rabbinic Concept of Israel," *HUCA*, XIX, 57–96 (with notes by L. Ginzberg). This study made on the basis of rabbinic statements in the Mekilta, if expanded to other tannaitic and amoraic collections, would show some noteworthy modifications in detail, but no change in fundamentals. Cf. also A. Marmorstein's brief survey of "The Struggle of the Talmudic Sages against Assimilation" (Hebrew), *Meṣudah*, V–VI, 207–15.

3. Cf. A. H. Detweiler's "Some Early Jewish Architectural Vestiges from Jerash," *BASOR*, 87, p. 17; Avi-Yonah's *Bi-Yeme Roma*, pp. 1 ff., 46, 84 f.; Sukenik's *Ancient Synagogues*, pp. 69, 82. On the progressive urbanization of Palestine and the entry of ever larger segments of its Jewish population into trade and industry, both conducive to superficial Hellenization, cf. *supra*, Chap. VI, n. 8.

4. Cf. j. Demai II, 1, 22c; Lieberman in *Annuaire*, VII, 402; and, on Philippopolis, A. T. Olmstead's "Mid-Third Century of the Christian Era," *Classical Philology*, XXXVII, 260 f. An obscure statement by Samuel in 'A.Z. 11b refers also to the *ludi saeculares* of 248, as suggested a century ago by S. J. L. Rapoport. It is ingeniously explained as the epitome of some veiled anti-Persian harangue delivered at that celebration, by S. Lieberman in his "Palestine in the Third and Fourth Centuries," *JQR*, XXXVII, 39 ff.

5. 'A.Z. 10b f.; Giṭṭin 16b f.; Yoma 10a; *Sibylline Oracles*, XII, 113–14. It is possible that the anti-Persian utterance stemmed from Rabbah bar Ḥana, rather than from the younger Rabbah bar bar Ḥana. On the frequent confusion of these two sages, cf. Jawitz's *Toledot*, VII, Appendix, pp. 9 ff. Rab's animosity to the Persians, perhaps nurtured from some earlier antagonisms in his native eastern community (cf. *infra*, n. 26), also found expression in a homily emanating from his school. Identifying the

Persians with the ancient Chaldaeans, the preacher believed that God himself regretted having brought them into the world; he paraphrased Isaiah's exclamation, "This is the people that was not" (23:13), to mean that the Lord wished "that it were not" (Yalqut Shime'oni, on Isa., No. 425). The political relevance of the thirteenth book of the Sibylline Poems to the contemporary Perso-Roman warfare has been convincingly demonstrated by Olmstead in *Class. Philology*, XXXVII; and, with reference to rabbinic utterances, by S. Lieberman in *JQR*, XXXVII, 31 ff. On the chronology of the "Early Sassanians," cf. S. H. Taqizadeh's essay in *Acta Orientalia*, XVIII, 258–311. Cf. also, in general, N. C. Debevoise's *Political History of Parthia* and A. Christensen's *Iran sous les Sassanides*.

6. Ketubot 23a; B.M. 119a; M.Q. 26a; j. Shebi'it IX, 5, 39a; B.B. 123b. Cf. J. Horovitz's "Mar Samuel und Schabur I," *MGWJ*, LXXX, 215–31 (with special reference to B.M. 119a). In a series of stimulating articles A. Marmorstein has accumulated much evidence in favor of his hypothesis that during the mid-third century Palestine had been the scene of serious Roman persecutions of Jews, which gave rise to anxious messianic expectations. Cf., in particular, his essays in *REJ*, LXXVII, 166–76; "Eine messianische Bewegung im dritten Jahrhundert," *Jeschurun*, XII, 369–83; XIII, 16–28, 171–86; "The Age of R. Johanan and the *Otot ha-Mashiah*" (Hebrew), *Tarbiz*, III, 161–80; and "Judaism and Christianity in the Middle of the Third Century" in his *Studies in Jewish Theology*, pp. 179–224. Although Marmorstein, in the accustomed manner of older historians, has confused here evidence of widespread Jewish suffering as a result of general economic depression and political mismanagment with one caused by a specific anti-Jewish animus (cf. *supra*, Chap. VII, n. 29), it is not at all surprising to find that the sudden rise of the new Persia, with its dualistic religion and its threat to the integrity of the Roman Empire, resuscitated the ever dormant messianic expectations.

7. The figure of 12,000 Jewish victims in Caesarea Mazaca is, of course, an exaggeration. The entire city seems to have had only a population of some 40,000. Even if swelled by refugees from neighboring towns and villages, the Jewish community was not likely to have had such a high ratio in the population, nor was all of it slain during the campaign. That the entire city was not completely destroyed during its first occupation by Shapur about 249 (alluded to in the *Sibylline Oracles*, XIII, 93; only this occupation could have come to the notice of Mar Samuel who died in 254) is evidenced by its renewed prolonged resistance in 260. Cf. Olmstead's remarks in *Class. Philology*, XXXVII, 261 f., 416. According to a recent report by R. N. Frye from his archaeological trip to Fars, "grafitti in Hebrew characters have been discovered on a window sill of the harem of Persepolis" (cf. A. Perkins's "Archaeological News: the Near East," *AJA*, LIII, 53). Although, according to Frye's own "Report" in *Oriens*, II, 204–15, "nothing could be made of" these finds, the grafitti may indicate the presence at Shapur's court of a Jewish wife or courtier and help explain the king's reputed familiarity with Jewish laws and customs. Cf., e.g., his alleged praise of rabbinic sexual morals in 'A.Z. 76b; cf. also *infra*, Chap. XIV, n. 15. But these characters may have been inscribed under Yazdegerd I or any other king. On Shapur's inscription found on the so-called Ka'aba of Zoroaster, which has come to be known as the *Res gestae divi Saporis*, cf. the interpretations offered by M. Rostovtzeff in *Berytus*, VIII, 17–60, and by W. Ensslin in his *Zu den Kriegen des Sassaniden Schapur I*.

8. Cf. j. 'A.Z. V, 4, 44d; *Code of Justinian* (Codex), III, 13, 3, ed. by Krüger, II, 128; Gen. r. XVI, 2.143; Pesiqta de-R. Kahana, V, ed. by Buber fol. 56a (here the name Natrona is spelled Netirata; cf. the editor's note 241). Cf. also B. Z. Dinaburg's "Diocletian's Rescript to Judah of 293 and the Rivalry between the Patriarchate and the Sanhedrin in Palestine" (Hebrew), *Gulak-Klein Mem. Vol.*, pp. 76–93; A. Mar-

morstein's more general study of "Dioclétien à la lumière de la littérature rabbinique,"
REJ, XLVIII, 19–43; W. Seston's "Roi sassanide Narsès, les Arabes et le manichéisme,"
Mélanges Dussaud, I, 227–34; and, more generally, W. Ensslin's *Zur Ostpolitik des
Kaisers Diokletian.*

9. 'A.Z. 16a. Cf. E. Sachau's "Von den rechtlichen Verhältnissen der Christen im
Sassanidenreich," *Mitteilungen des Seminars für orientalische Sprachen zu Berlin*,
X, Pt. 2, pp. 70 ff., 79.

10. Joshua the Stylite's *Chronicle*, on the year 814 Sel. era (ed. by W. Wright,
LVIII); Cyprian of Toulon, *et al.*, *Vita Caesarii episcopi Arelatensis*, I, 29–31 (ed. by
B. Krusch in *MGH*, Scriptores Rerum Merov., III, 467 ff.); Procopius' *De bello gothico*,
I [V], 10.25. As a native of Palestinian Caesarea, the Byzantine historian had long
been imbued with anti-Jewish feeling. As in Tella, the defense of Arles gave rise to
rumors of attempted high treason by the Jews, although their self-interest clearly
pointed to their supporting the friendly regime of Theodoric the Great, rather than
that of the attacking Catholic Franks and Burgundians. That these rumors may
have been fabricated by Bishop Caesarius, himself implicated in the projected surrender, has been plausibly argued by Juster in *Empire*, II, 213. It may also be noted
that Cyprian and his associates, forgetting their previous narrative, reported that
Caesarius' death was later mourned by the Jews, too. Cf. *Vita Caesarii*, I, p. 501. We
shall see how these suspicions of Jewish loyalty during the barbarian invasions were
to swell into a chorus during the centuries of Muslim-Christian struggles in western
Europe, to become almost a literary cliché among medieval chroniclers.

11. Although generally right in minimizing the alleged Jewish persecutions by
Romans during the third and fourth centuries, S. Lieberman seems to have gone
too far in underestimating the extent of the Jewish "sedition" under Gallus. Cf.
his remarks in *JQR*, XXXVI, 329 ff., 336 ff. He has not only disregarded the rather
impressive array of literary sources (conveniently listed by Avi-Yonah in *Bi-Yeme
Roma*, p. 221, n. 28), many of which, indeed, only reproduced statements by predecessors, but also the archaeological evidence of the destruction of Beth She'arim, from
which the city never recovered (curiously this fact is not mentioned by the Church
historians). Sepphoris, too, although certainly not demolished, seems to have suffered
from a major conflagration during that period. Cf. Yeivin's observations in L. Water-
man's *Preliminary Report*, p. 31. The rabbis' silence can best be explained by their
unwillingness to justify either the uprising or its unduly violent suppression.

12. On the date (439 rather than 438) of this crucial third "Novella" to the Theodosian Code enacted by Theodosius II, as well as the explanation of its extreme
anti-Jewish bias, see F. Nau's "Deux épisodes de l'histoire juive sous Théodose II
(423 et 438) d'après la vie de Barsauma le Syrien," *REJ*, LXXXIII, 184–206. Cf.,
more generally, Juster's comprehensive analysis in *Empire*, II *passim* (the dates of
the individual enactments incorporated in our main source, *C. Th.* XVI, 8–9, must be
revised, however, in accordance with O. Seeck's penetrating observations in his
Regesten der Kaiser und Päpste; cf. Index, p. 438); and the more recent, briefer survey of "Privilegi degli Ebrei nell' Impero romano-cristiano," by G. Ferrari dalle Spade
in *Festschrift für Leopold Wenger*, II, 102–17.

13. Without quoting his medieval Christian source, Don Isaac Abravanel claims
that the prohibition of new synagogues was first enacted by Constantine and, later,
abrogated by both Constantius and Julian. Cf. his *Ma'yene ha-yeshu'ah* (Commentary on Daniel), XI, 5. It is not likely, however, that such a prohibition emanated
from Constantine, who continued serving as *pontifex maximus* of the Roman state
religion and effectively resisted ecclesiastical encroachments. Only toward the end

of his reign he enacted his first, rather moderate, anti-Jewish laws aimed at proselytism among Christians and the protection of Jewish converts to Christianity. Cf. *supra*, Chap. XII, p. 150; and J. Vogt's "Zur Frage des christlichen Einflusses auf die Gesetzgebung Konstantins des Grossen," *Festschrift . . . Wenger*, II, 118–48. It is equally improbable that Constantius wished to abrogate an existing anti-Jewish law, or that Julian failed to boast about its abrogation in his letter to the Jews. Most likely the law was enacted first under Theodosius I, who may have simply imitated the Sassanian outlawry (seldom applied in practice) of new Christian churches. Cf. Sachau's remarks in *Mitteilungen des Seminars . . . Berlin*, pp. 77 ff., and my *Jewish Community*, I, 111 f.

14. Ḥullin 101b (on its background, cf. A. Marmorstein's "Persécutions religieuses à l'époque de R. Yohanan b. Nappacha," *REJ*, LXXVII, 166–76); Ta'anit 8b; Elbogen's *Gottesdienst*, pp. 36 ff., 516 f., 584 ff. and the literature quoted there. Among more recent discussions, cf. especially J. Mann's "Changes in the Divine Service of the Synagogue Due to Religious Persecutions," *HUCA*, IV, 241–310; V. Aptowitzer's "Geschichte einer liturgischen Formel," *MGWJ*, LXXIII, 93–118 (on the formula "Blessed be His glorious Kingdom for ever and ever," mentioned in M. Yoma III, 8, etc.), supplemented in *MGWJ*, LXXIV, 104–26, and his "Le-'Olam yehe adam," *REJ*, XCIII, 179–91; L. Finkelstein's "Kedouscha et les bénédictions du Schema," *ibid.*, pp. 1–26, and L. Ginzberg's notes thereon, *ibid.*, XCVIII, 72–80. Cf., however, *supra*, Chap. VII, n. 29.

15. Agathias Scholasticus' *Historiae* II, 26 (*PG*, LXXXVIII, 1388). The chronology of the Mar Zutra revolt is given according to Funk's *Juden in Babylonien*, II, 143 ff., while Graetz and others date it in 511–18. Cf. A. Christensen's *Règne du roi Kawadh I et le communisme mazdakite;* J. Denner's "Weltalter, Stände und Herrschaft in Iran," *AR*, XXXIV, 254–76; and, for comparative purposes, J. Labourt's older, but still valuable study of *Le Christianisme dans l'empire Perse sous la dynastie sassanide*. Needless to say that even the occasional friendly relations between the Persian and the Eastern Roman empires did not necessarily accrue to the advantage of the Jewish subjects of either. On the contrary, the close coöperation established between the emperors Khosroe II and Maurice at the end of the sixth century seems to have reinforced the anti-Jewish trends in both empires. Cf. the somewhat exaggerated evaluation of these "Rapports" by P. Goubert in *Byzantion*, XIX, 79–98. However, these developments came at a time when the great scholastic activity of the Babylonian academies was drawing to an end, in part undoubtedly as their effect. That is why only a few faint echoes of these crucial transformations can be detected in the Babylonian Talmud. On the effects of these new international constellations on the Jews of southern Arabia, see *infra*, Vol. III.

16. Cf. J. Darmesteter's "Textes pehlevis relatifs au Judaïsme," *REJ*, XVIII, 4. The religious controversies between the Jewish and Christian minorities of the Sassanian Empire are treated in G. Richter's "Ueber die älteste Auseinandersetzung der syrischen Christen mit den Juden," *ZNW*, XXXV, 101–14, partly vitiated by the author's unfamiliarity with F. Gavin's researches on *Aphraates and the Jews*.

17. H. I. Bell has shown that, for similar inflationary reasons, the collections of the Egyptian poll tax were likewise discontinued in the course of the third century. See his remarks in *JRS*, XXXVII, 17 ff.

18. Cf., for example, the pathetic plea of an heir to an estate claimed by such an informer in the days of Diocletian, preserved in a Princeton papyrus and published by A. C. Johnson and S. P. Goodrich in their ed., III, 16 ff., No. 119. As mentioned above there are no comprehensive studies of ancient Jewish taxation, whether under

the Second Commonwealth or under the rule of Rome and Persia. Apart from the literature already referred to (*supra*, Chap. VIII, n. 20; Chap. XI, n. 20–21), cf. G. Allon's Hebrew study of the *strategoi* in Roman Palestine in *Tarbiz*, XIV, 145–55 (considering them to be Jewish municipal elders in charge of its fiscal administration); and S. Lieberman's data in *JQR*, XXXVI, 344 ff. On the general economic situation and its interrelations with the fiscal maladministration, cf. *infra*, Chap. XIV, n. 26.

19. David Qimḥi's *Commentary* on Gen. 1:31. This obscure passage has been elucidated by an inscription first published by J. B. Frey in 1930. Cf. his *Corpus*, I, No. 501, and *ibid.*, p. lxxxi; and other data cited in my *Jewish Community*, I, 82, 96, 109; III, 17, 20. The identity of "Antoninus" in the talmudic anecdotes has been inconclusively debated ever since Jost. Cf. S. Krauss's summary in his *Antoninus und Rabbi*. More recently, the case for identifying Judah I's friend with Antoninus Pius has been restated by S. Klein (*MGWJ*, LXXVIII, 169); with Caracalla by M. Avi-Yonah (*Bi-Yeme Roma*, pp. 28 ff.); and with Marcus Aurelius by J. Zlotnik in "The Identification of Antoninus, Rabbi's [Judah's] Friend" (Hebrew), *Sinai*, XI, Nos. 124–25, pp. 136–57. The existence of such historical relations is not controverted by the indubitable fact that form and substance of the dialogues as such are a work of fiction. Cf. L. Wallach's "Colloquy of Marcus Aurelius with the Patriarch Judah I," *JQR*, XXXI, 259–86.

20. Cf. M. Schwabe's "Letters of Libanius to the Patriarch of Palestine" (Hebrew), *Tarbiz*, I, Pt. 2, 85–110, Pt. 3, pp. 107–21 (including a new document of 364); Claudius Rutilius Namatianus' *De reditu suo*, lines 395–98. That Rutilius was under the strong influence of both Poseidonius and the cult of Isis is stressed by G. Boano in his "Sul *De reditu suo* di Rutilio Namaziano," *Rivista di filologia classica*, LXXVI, 54–87. Cf. also Schwabe's "Chapters on Hellenistic Palestine at the Time of the Redaction of Talmud Jerushalmi, I" (Hebrew), *Tarbiz*, V, 358–69 (under the reign of Julian); and, from another angle, M. Hadas's "Rabbinic Parallels to Scriptores historiae Augustae," *Classical Philology*, XXIV, 258–62. One of the illustrations here cited may be more than a literary parallel, however. The story told about Maximinus by Julius Capitolinus and more anonymously in the Aggadah (Exod. r. XLII, 2; cf. Mekilta, Baḥodesh, VIII, ed. by Lauterbach, II, 262), namely, that a rebellious city deposed the emperor by overturning his statues and stoning his likenesses, may represent a dim historic recollection of the time when Palestinian Jews coöperated with their pagan neighbors in supporting one or another contender for the throne. For example, in 194, the Jews sided with Septimius Severus against the much-hated Pescennius Niger, whereas the Samaritans bet on the loser. Cf. also other rabbinic quotations in Avi-Yonah's *Bi-Yeme Roma*, pp. 54 f. It was also during such an interregnum before Diocletian that R. Johanan dared to order the destruction of all divine images, doubtless including some emperor statues, at the public baths of Tiberias. The excuse, later supplied, was that one Jew was "suspected" of offering incense there. Cf. j. 'A.Z. IV, 4, 43d. On the other hand, the existence of public baths in an almost all-Jewish city like Tiberias, is in itself revealing, unless we translate the passage somewhat awkwardly, "at the would-be public baths." In fact, an attempt to convert the old Adrianeion into baths was frustrated by the Tiberian Jews (perhaps in that very move initiated by R. Johanan), according to Epiphanius' *Adv. Haereses*, XXX, 12 (*PG*, XLI, 425 f.).

21. Augustine's *Epistolae*, CXCVI (*PL*, XXXIII, 891 ff.); Council of Laodicaea, Canon 16, in Mansi's *Sacrorum conciliorum collectio*, II, 567 (English transl. in C. J. Hefele's *History of the Councils of the Church*, II, 310); T. Giṭṭin V, 5, 328. The passage in Giṭṭin provides also for eulogizing deceased Gentiles and comforting their mourners, "for the sake of peace." On the meaning of this phrase, cf. J. Z. Lauterbach's "Attitude of the Jew towards the Non-Jew," *Yearbook of the Central Con-*

ference of American Rabbis, XXXI, 201 ff., which, however, somewhat apologetically ignores the strong separatist tendencies of the age. Cf. also Juster's *Empire*, I, 479, n. 2, and 480, n. 4; and M. Simon's *Verus Israel*, pp. 382 ff. The Council of Nicaea threatened with severe punishment Christians calculating Easter to coincide with Passover. Although, according to Eusebius and other Church Fathers, the Council's canons were confirmed by Constantine as laws of the Empire, many Christians, not only sectarians, adhered to the old tradition. In despair, Justinian ordered the Jews, in 543, always to observe their Passover *after* the Christian Easter, but there is no evidence that any effort was made to comply with this arbitrary rule. Three years later, on the very first occasion of such coincidence, Justinian himself postponed the Christian Easter. On the sources and dates, cf. Juster's *Empire romain*, I, 282 f., 308 ff., 356 f. For centuries thereafter some Christians continued to observe Easter according to the Jewish calendar. As late as 1538–39 Jewish influence made itself felt in the "Conflit sur la date des Pâques chez les Orientaux," described by M. Chaîne in *Revue de l'Orient chrétien*, 3d ser., IV, 436–40, although, in contrast to I. Guidi, Chaîne tries unduly to minimize the Jewish factor in this controversy.

22. Michael Syrus' *Chronicle*, VII, 7. In his "Polémique anti-juive de S. Jean Chrysostome," *Annuaire*, IV, 403–21, M. Simon aptly analyzes the forms and causes of the Judaizing movement among the Antiochian Christians which evoked the "golden-mouthed" preacher's fulminating eight anti-Jewish homilies of 386–87. Cf. also A. Moulard's comprehensive biography of *Saint Jean Chrysostome*, and, on the local background, G. Haddad's *Aspects of Social Life in Antioch in the Hellenistic-Roman Period*.

23. Jerome's *Commentary* on Matt. 33:6 (*PL*, XXVI, 175). Of course, Hebrew texts as such, apart from their scriptural origin, were supposed to possess magic qualities. If Porphyry once inquired why incantations were as a rule couched in a barbaric idiom, he was answered by Iamblichus that a translation would deprive them of all their power (*dynamis*). Cf. the latter's *De mysteriis*, VII, 4–5 (especially 5, 12). This was indeed the widely held opinion. Cf. also, in general, Simon's *Verus Israel*, pp. 394 ff.; J. Trachtenberg's *Devil and the Jews* (though largely concerned with medieval opinions, this work points up certain obscure roots of ancient antisemitism as well); and *supra*, Chap. IX, n. 23–27.

24. St. Ambrose's *Epistolae*, XL–XLI (*PL*, XVI, 1148 ff.); Johannes Asiaticus' *Hist. eccl.*, cited by F. Nau in *Revue de l'Orient chrétien*, II, 462, n. 2. The importance of St. Ambrose's victory over Theodosius in the synagogue controversy for the subsequent evolution of an independent Western papacy, as contrasted with Eastern Caesaropapism, is stressed by Setton in *Christian Attitudes*, pp. 109 ff. Cf. also F. H. Dudden's summary in his biography of *St. Ambrose*, II, 371 ff.; G. Figueroa's analysis of *The Church and the Synagogue in St. Ambrose;* and, more generally, A. Piganiol's *Empire chrétien, 325–395*, and P. Charanis's *Church and State in the Later Roman Empire* (chiefly on Anastasius I, 491–518). The thrice-told tale of the relations of the Church to the Jews after 313 has been conveniently restated by Juster in *Empire romain, passim*, and especially I, 43 ff.; J. Parkes in his *Conflict;* and M. Simon in his *Verus Israel*. Cf. also some data assembled by L. Gillet in his *Communion in the Messiah;* and more detailed studies such as L. Ginzberg's monographs on the Aggadah and the Church Fathers, L. Lucas's *Zur Geschichte der Juden im IV Jahrhundert*, and E. J. Jonkers's "Einige Bemerkungen über das Verhältnis der christlichen Kirche zum Judentum vom vierten bis auf das siebente Jahrhundert," *Mnemosyne*, 3d ser., XI, 304–20. Jonkers (*op. cit.*, p. 312) is wrong, however, in explaining that the constant reiteration of imperial prohibitions of intermarriage between Jews and Christians (cf. *C. Th.*, XVI, 8, 6 [339]; III, 7, 2 [388], repeated IX, 7, 5; *Code of Justinian* [Codex], I, 9, 6, ed. by Krüger, II, 61) was needed because the Jews evaded

the law more readily than the pagans. From what we know about ancient Jewry's attitude to intermarriage, this is an entirely gratuitous assumption. Cf., e.g., G. Kittel's account, however biased, of "Das Konnubium mit den Nicht-Juden im antiken Judentum," *FJF*, II, 39. There were many valid social forces, however, which promoted intermarriage and which, therefore, required special legislation in addition to the general exhortation by both the rabbinate and the clergy. These reasons became more apparent in the later Middle Ages. Cf. *infra*, Chap. XIV, n. 17–18.

25. Cf. E. Drioton's brief study of "Cyrille d'Alexandrie et l'ancienne religion égyptienne" in *Kyrilliana*, pp. 231–46; and P. Benoît and J. Schwarz's "Caracalla et les troubles d'Alexandrie en 215 après J.-C.," *Études de papyrologie de la Société Fuad I*, VII, 17–33. It is to be regretted that this crucial expulsion is recorded only (in the typical semi-anecdotal manner of Byzantine chroniclers) by Socrates Scholasticus in his *Historia ecclesiastica*, VII, 13 (ed. by R. Hussey, II, 753 ff.) and by other Christian writers largely dependent on him. Cyril's own writings, including the extant fragment of his *De synagogae defectu* (*PG*, LXXVI, 1421–24) merely repeat stereotype anti-Jewish arguments. It seems, however, that this action had already all the earmarks of later expulsions, such as permission for Jews willing to embrace Christianity to remain behind, the confiscation of synagogues and indiscriminate pillage of other Jewish property. It was, however, clearly unauthorized. The patriarch evidently acted without the consent of the prefect, Orestes, who realized the illegality of these proceedings. That is why the latter was styled a "Judaizer" by John of Nikiu. Cf. Juster's *Empire romain*, I, 63; II, 175 f. Perhaps for this reason the mob action was less effective than most subsequent, technically more legal decrees of expulsion, and hence we hear nothing about this new "exile" from any extant Jewish sources. In fact, Jews are recorded in Alexandria during the two following centuries and at the time of the Arab conquest they were a large and affluent segment of the population.

26. Cf. *C. Th.*, XVI, 5, 66; *Code of Justinian* (Codex), I, 5, 6 (ed. by Krüger, II, 51) and Novella 109; S. Krauss's *Paras ve-Romi*, 23 ff., 90 ff.; and *supra*, n. 5. Despite the meagerness and tenuous character of extant sources, a monographic study of the Judeo-Gentile social relations on the mass level in the later Roman and Sassanian Empires might yield new and interesting insights.

27. Cf. *supra*, n. 19. Before the discovery of the fine Palestinian mosaics and the Dura frescoes, scholars were generally inclined to accept C. Watzinger's theory which ascribed the presence of human representations in various synagogues to the latter's imperial benefactors. Cf. H. Kohl's and his *Antike Synagogen*, pp. 200 ff. We need no longer resort, to be sure, to such forced explanations of synagogue murals or mosaics. Cf. especially L. Blau's "Early Christian Archaeology from the Jewish Point of View," *HUCA*, III, 176 ff.; E. L. Sukenik's *Ancient Synagogues*, pp. 62 f.; and *supra*, Chap. IX, n. 14. But at least one Antonine emperor is reliably recorded as the donor of a candlestick to a Palestinian synagogue. Cf. j. Megillah, III, 2, 74a. This was, indeed, a time-honored procedure, going back to the Achaemenid and Ptolemaic rulers, which was probably adopted in Rome herself by Marcus Agrippa. The Roman Jewish congregation of Agrippenses doubtless owed its name to Agrippa's financial support. This synagogue was very likely located on the Campus Martius in the midst of many other buildings erected by this famous patron of arts and learning. Cf. S. Collon's remarks in *Mélanges* of the Ecole française de Rome, LVII, 83 f.

The subject matter of this and the next section has been treated more fully and with considerable documentation in the present author's *Jewish Community*, I, 75–156; III, 13–33. Our summary here is, therefore, amplified only either by aspects particularly germane to the present inquiry or by fruits of scholarly discoveries and researches during the last decade. The actual operation of Jewish autonomy will come more clearly to the fore in the various communal institutions, social as well as religious, which will be described in the next two chapters.

28. Cf. j. Ḥagigah I, 8, 76d; Nedarim X, 10, 42b; Julian's aforementioned epistle No. 51; *C. Th.*, XVI, 8, 29. Cf. *C. Th.*, XII, 13, 1–6; and C. Lacombrade's "Notes sur l' 'aurum coronarium,' " *Revue des études anciennes*, LI, 59. Cf. also H. Vogelstein's "Development of the Apostolate in Judaism and Its Transformation in Christianity," *HUCA*, II, 99–123; H. Mosbech's "Apostolos in the New Testament," *Studia theologica*, II, 166–200 (suggesting widespread use of this term first among the Christians of Antioch, but admitting essential Jewish institutional priority); and *supra*, n. 18.

29. Shebuot 6b; j. I, 1, 32d. By generalissimo (*Rufila*, corrupted from *Rab ḥela*) the Talmud doubtless referred to the *artashtaransalar* (chief of warriors), rather than the *Eran-spahbadh* (chief of the military class), while the office of *argabadh*, the supreme military commander was reserved for the royal family. Cf. Christensen's *Iran*, pp. 99, 107 ff., 131 f. For obvious reasons the rabbis failed to mention another high dignitary, the chief of the Zoroastrian priesthood. In his *Paras ve-Romi*, pp. 93 f., S. Krauss has correctly pointed out, in this connection, the importance of rank in Persia's rigid court etiquette which, as is well known, soon served as a model also for the elaborate Byzantine ceremonies.

30. Ketubot 103b; M.Q. 17a, 27b; j. Sanhedrin II, 6, 20c.; 'A.Z. I, 1, 39b. The first rabbi to hold undisputed leadership of the academy was R. Johanan or possibly his teacher R. Ḥanina soon after Judah I's death. Cf. Ta'anit 21a; and L. Ginzberg's *Perushim*, III, 192, 196. Ginzberg may be right in arguing here that Gamaliel II's temporary deposition from the chairmanship of the academy did not affect whatever other "patriarchal" functions he may have exercised, although the main argument that otherwise this revolt would also have been directed against an official recognized by the imperial authorities is very dubious. It appears that Rome first granted formal recognition to Gamaliel's son Simon after 135, and that the earlier leaders were at best tolerated by the authorities as the Jews' self-imposed chiefs. Cf. my *Jewish Community*, III, 28, n. 24. Of course, we must bear in mind that we hear only the rabbis' side of the story.

31. Giṭṭin 7a; Ketubot 61ab; Sanhedrin 38a. There exists a large literature on the history of the two "dynasties." Cf. in particular the comprehensive monographs by F. Lazarus, *Die Häupter der Vertriebenen*, with additional notes on the medieval period in *MGWJ*, LXXVIII, 279–88; and by J. S. Zuri, *Toledot ha-mishpaṭ ha-ṣibburi ha-'ibri* (A History of Hebrew Public Law; includes 2 vols. on the patriarchate, and one on the exilarchate in the period of R. Naḥman). Nevertheless the interplay of external and internal factors in the rise and decline of the two dynasties, and particularly the effect on them of the economic and administrative changes in both empires during the fourth and fifth centuries still await elucidation.

32. Cf. Philo's *In Flaccum*, X, 74; Josephus' *Antt.* XIX, 5, 2.283. Numerous suggestions have been made to reconcile these contradictory passages. Hazardous as is any emendation unsupported by manuscript testimony, T. Reinach's substitution of ἄρχωντας for ἐθνάρχας in *Antt., loc. cit.* seems most plausible. Claudius would simply have wished to emphasize that Augustus, in his desire to safeguard the autonomy of the Jews, allowed them to elect their own elders in lieu of an ethnarch. Cf. Reinach's "L'Empereur Claude et les Juifs," *REJ*, LXXIX, 124, n. 5.

33. Ketubot 105a; j. Megillah III, 1, 73d, IV, 5, 75b; Sanhedrin II, 6, 20d; Wilcken's *Chrestomatie*, No. 193 (that the local synagogue was called *eucheion*, in contrast to

the Theban *proseuché*, appears dubious, however); Gen. r. LII, 4, 543; b. Megillah 26a (according to Rabbinovicz's variant). The juxtaposition of j. Sanhedrin 20d with Gen. r. LXXX, 1, 950, shows that the Ma'onite synagogue was located in Tiberias, not Ma'on. Cf. Albeck's note *ibid.*, against S. Klein's remarks in *Sefer ha-Yishub*, I, 105. Cf. also *ibid.*, pp. 51 (on Tiberias), 84, No. 35 (on Jaffa); M. Schwabe's "Two Inscriptions from the Synagogue Area, Beth She'arim" (Hebrew), *BJPES*, IX, 27 f., and his epigraphic study "On the History of Tiberias" (Hebrew), *Lewy Mem. Vol.*, pp. 216 ff., 247. In inscription No. 7, Schwabe has here identified the *gerousiarches* (head of the council) of the "Antiochian" congregation in Tiberias, illustrating once again the use of this title for the head of a single congregation, as well as for the chairman of a community-wide council.

34. Prov. 21:9, 25:24. Cf. *supra*, Chap. VII, n. 31. There is considerable confusion with respect to this title in both the ancient sources and modern literature. The various explanations offered are cited in my *Jewish Community*, III, 26, n. 16. Cf. also L. Ginzberg's *Perushim*, III, 410 ff., which, after a careful review of nine pertinent passages, comes to the conclusion that the term *ḥeber* is invariably used for a collective group representing the community. More recently, P. Chertoff has suggested that the city council usually consisted of ten members (seven general and three fiscal administrators), following therein a pattern already established at the Temple. Hence, it was identical with the "ten men of leisure," whose functions have likewise intrigued scholars for some time. Cf. his remarks in *JQR*, XXXIV, 87–98.

35. The Berenice inscription, published in 1732 by Scipio Maffeius and commented on extensively by Peter Wesseling six years later, is now readily available in Schürer's *Geschichte*, III, 79, n. 20, and elsewhere. Because of its somewhat uncertain local era, the date has given rise to endless discussions. The weight of evidence now favors 25 B.C.E. Cf. J. and G. Roux's "Décret des Juifs de Bereniké," *Revue des études grecques*, LXII, 294. Apart from republishing this well-known inscription, the authors have ably reconstructed and commented on the Carpentras inscription in honor of Decimus Valerius Dionysius. Because of the questionable reading of a letter "K," however, they have hesitated to date it more definitely at 8 or 6 B.C.E. But the fact that Cyrenaican contemporaries of Hillel possessed an amphitheatre decorated with murals by one of their members who, like his father, bore a purely Roman name, is truly significant. If and when the few remaining lacunae in this inscription are deciphered and interpreted by specialists, some further interesting light may be shed on this remarkable Diaspora community.

36. Faustus' *Geschichte Armeniens*, pp. 137 f.; Moses of Khorene's *Chronicle*, III, 35, ed. by P. E. Le Vaillant de Florival, III, 80 ff. Of course, one cannot give full credence to Faustus' figures. But it is remarkable that, according to his sources, Jewish captives carried off from the various Armenian cities invariably outnumbered the non-Jewish deportees. Evidently the Persians evinced special interest in bringing Jews into their country. Cf. also in general R. Grousset's *Histoire de l'Arménie des origines à 1071*. Moses of Khorene's reliability, often disputed by such modern scholars as H. Lewy, has been upheld by A. O. Sarkissian in "On the Authenticity of Moses of Khoren's History," *Armenian Review*, I, Pt. 1, pp. 38–43. We do not have to accept as literal truth the report of a Pehlevi author reading, "The cities of Shus [Shushan] and Schuster were built by Shoshan-Dukht [?], wife of Yazdkart [Yazdegerd] I, son of Shahpuhr. She was the daughter of the Reshgaluta, King of the Jews; she was the mother of Bahram [V] Gor." Cited from the *Shatroiha-i-Eran*, XLVI–XLVII, by J. Darmesteter in *REJ*, XIX, 41 f.; and, following him, by L. H. Gray in his "Pahlavi Literature, Jews in," *JE*, IX, 465. But it reflects the sudden rise of Jewish communities in the interior of Iran during the Sassanian period, as well as the governmental promotion of Jewish immigration. This is also undoubtedly what the rabbis had in mind

when they reported the Lord as saying, "If I shall exile them [the Jews] by way of the desert, they are apt to die of hunger, so I shall exile them by way of Armenia, which has cities and villages, so that they will have food and drink." Cf. Cant. r. I, 44, on 1:14. Armenia appears here as an intermediate station in the Jewish migrations to Babylonia. The policy of Sassanian rulers, including Shapur II, to transplant Western populations for the purpose of stimulating industrial activities is attested also by other sources cited by Christensen in *Iran*, pp. 126 f.

37. Shabbat 26a; *Antt.* XI, 5, 2.131–32; Qiddushin 71b. Cf. J. Newman's *Agricultural Life of the Jews in Babylonia*, pp. 3 (n. 1), 101. The spread and density of Jewish settlements in the Euphrates Valley and neighboring lands may be studied in detail in J. Obermeyer's *Landschaft Babylonien im Zeitalter des Talmuds und des Gaonats*.

38. T. B.Q. VII, 3, 357; b. Sukkah 20a, 44ab; S. Telegdi's "Essai sur la phonétique des emprunts iraniens en araméen talmudique," *JA*, CCXXVI, 177–256 (includes a glossary of 130 Persian loan words). The most important researches on these talmudic borrowings from the Persian still are those of Alexander Kohut, especially as laid down in his large dictionary *'Aruch completum*, of which a new impression, prepared by S. Krauss, *et al.*, includes a supplementary volume entitled *Tosefet he-'Arukh ha-shalem*. In this connection one of the collaborators, B. Geiger, published a paper, "Zu den iranischen Lehnwörtern im Aramäischen," *WZKM*, XXXVII, 195–203. On the numerous ancient monuments in and around Nehardea, cf. the rabbinic traditions cited in Jawitz's *Toledot*, VII, 6 ff.

39. Cf. Sherira Gaon's *Iggeret* (Epistle), ed. by B. M. Lewin, p. 79. Chiefly on linguistic grounds, A. Berliner once argued that Sura, being poor and having fewer business connections with Palestine, had retained more authentic Babylonian traditions concerning the text of Scripture and Targum than did the more cosmopolitan Nehardea which had attracted numerous Palestinian settlers. Cf. the introduction to his *Massora zum Targum Onkelos*. He seems to have overlooked, however, not only the importance of the caravan routes which at that time easily connected Sura, *via* Damascus, with Palestine (cf. especially M. Rostovtzeff's map in his *Caravan Cities*, p. 2), but also the halakhic evidence of both the talmudic and the geonic periods. On the latter basis L. Ginzberg first suggested the opposite theory mentioned in the text. It was more fully developed by B. M. Lewin in the introduction to his edition of *Methiboth*. A detailed monograph on this important subject is still in order, however.

40. Cf. the lengthy discussion in Ketubot 110b f.; and *supra*, Chap. XI, n. 39. Extensive Jewish emigration from Palestine after 70, and still more after 135, is reflected in many rabbinic sources. Cf. T. Ḥallah II, 6.11, 99; and other data assembled by A. Büchler in *Der galiläische 'Am-ha-'Areṣ*, pp. 237 ff. So many rabbis ultimately found their way to Babylonia that the appointment of "elders" residing in foreign lands under the condition that they would promise to return to Palestine soon lost all meaning. Cf. j. Bikkurim, III, 3, 65d; Demai II, 3, 23a.

41. Qiddushin 49b f. Located on an island between the Tigris and the Euphrates, Mesene was early occupied by the expanding Arabs. (The history of the Jewish settlements in these increasingly significant Arab buffer states between the two great empires will be treated in connection with the rise of Islam.) Conquered by Ardashir, it was rebuilt under the name of Astrabadh-Ardasher. As usual, the rabbis ignored the new Persian designation and continued calling the city by its old Aramaic name, Meshan. That, even earlier, Mesene had used the Babylonian, rather than the Palestinian, Aramaic dialect is evidenced by a curious terminological discussion in

connection with the sale of ships between R. Nathan the Babylonian and Sumkhos (Symmachus) the Palestinian. Appearing at first as a serious substantive difference of opinion it was straightened out by Raba who pointed out this purely dialectal variation (Shabbat 101a; cf. B.B. 73a).

42. Council of Elvira, Canons 16, 49–50, 78, in J. D. Mansi's *Sacrorum conciliorum . . . collectio*, II, 8, 14, 18; *C. Th.*, XVI, 8, 3–4; Frey's *Corpus*, I, Nos. 661 ff., and *passim*. For the sake of both convenience and consistency we shall quote deliberations and decisions of the various ancient and medieval Church councils from Mansi's old and not altogether adequate collection; from time to time we shall also refer to C. J. Hefele's *Histoire des conciles*, or its English transl. A new, critical ed. of the *Acta conciliorum oecumenicorum* was begun, under the editorship of E. Schwartz, for the Berlin Academy. But only the first four vols. in many parts have appeared before the editor's death in 1940. On ancient Jewish settlements in southwestern Germany, cf. A. Altmann's data, mostly rather questionable, in *Das früheste Vorkommen der Juden in Deutschland*; P. Rieger, *et al.*, *Jüdische Gotteshäuser und Friedhöfe in Württemberg*; G. Kittel's highly colored description of "Die ältesten Judenkarrikaturen: Die 'Trierer Terrakotten,' " *FJF*, IV, 250–59; and his appeal for further investigation by race-conscious German scholars in "Die ältesten jüdischen Bilder," *ibid.*, pp. 237–49 (more significant for the data assembled to show that these pictures could be Jewish than for the proofs that they really were). Cf. also his and E. Fischer's equally racialist survey of "Das antike Judentum," *FJF*, VII, 1–236. (In general, the deterioration of this once reputable scholar under the Nazi regime is incontestable, despite the whitewashing attempted by J. R. Porter in his "Case of Gerhard Kittel," *Theology*, L, 441–46; cf. W. F. Albright's "Gerhard Kittel and the Jewish Question in Antiquity," *Cohen Mem. Vol.*, pp. 325–36). Cf. also H. Schmitz's comprehensive study of *Köln in römischer Zeit*, I. On Hungary, cf. Z. Balazs's "Introduction to the Study of the New Vestiges of the Jewish Settlement in Pannonia," *Löw Mem. Vol.*, Hebrew section, pp. 5–14.

A newly discovered Jewish marble plate in Roman Reggio is discussed by N. Putorti in his *Culti e religioni in Reggio romana*, p. 23. A fifth-century Christian inscription from Grado, in the vicinity of Trieste, mentions a Jew who "alone among his people" was converted to Christianity. Cf. G. Brusin's "Grado-L'Epigrafe musiva di 'Petrus' " in the *Notizie degli Scavi* of the R. Accademia Naz. dei Lincei, Rome, 8th ser., I, 18–20. On the other hand, in "La Supuesta sinagoga de Elche," *Archivo español de arqueologia*, XX, 392–99, J. Lafuente Vidal denies the Jewish character of the basilica. Built by pagans, he believes, it was later used by Christians but not by Jews. Cf. also J. Vives's *Inscripciones Cristianas de la España Romana y Visigoda* (chiefly interesting for comparative purposes); and on Western Europe generally, D. S. Blondheim's searching philological analysis in *Les Parlers judéo-romans*, which revealed an astounding influence of the Jews on the Romance languages and peoples in their formative period. Cf. also L. Blau's remarks thereon in *JQR*, XIX, 157 ff. On Oescus (now Gigen in Bulgaria), cf. M. Schwabe's "Roman-Jewish Inscription of Bulgaria" (Hebrew), *BJPES*, II, Pts. 3–4, 19–25. Cf. also E. Condurachi's "Juifs en Illyricum," *REJ*, CI, 87–93; as well as F. K. Dörner's essay cited *supra*, Chap. IX, n. 23. A good collection of the early Latin Jewish epigraphic material is found in E. Diehl's *Inscriptiones Latinae Christianae veteres*, II, 488–506, Nos. 4851–5000; and J. B. Frey's *Corpus*, with L. Robert's and A. Ferrua's supplements mentioned *supra*, Chap. VI, n. 27. Even among the 102 inscriptions considered by Frey as wrongly attributed to Jews (pp. 527 ff.), there probably are some belonging to Jews. After all, apart from Jewish names or such pronouncedly Jewish symbols as the seven-branch candelabrum, we have little to go by. Occasionally, we may be guided by a formula like *Eis Theos* (One God; or, rather, God is One), whose Jewish provenance has been proved by E. Peterson in his interesting studies under this very title, pp. 276 ff.

43. Cf. especially the inscriptions analyzed by J. G. Février in *La Religion des Palmyréniens*, pp. 120 ff., 127, 219 ff.; B. Maisler's *Beth She'arim*, I, 115 f.; and J. Starcky's "Récentes découvertes à Palmyre," *Syria*, XXV, 336. Février's effort to minimize Jewish influence because of the paucity of Jewish names is controverted in part by W. Goldmann's analysis of *Die palmyrenischen Personennamen*. We know, moreover, from experience in other areas of that period, that the adoption of non-Jewish names and even the acceptance of certain syncretistic forms was by no means inconsistent with conscious loyalty to Judaism. Of course, there must also have been semiproselytes of various degrees. For example, the influential president of the Palmyrene senate, Malko, in whose honor the city erected a statue, probably was not a full-fledged Jew. And yet, in 274, he rendered thanks to the "One and Only Merciful God." On the legends current among Jews and Arabs connecting the city's foundation with King Solomon, cf. *infra*, Chap. XIV, n. 17. Valuable new materials have been brought to light in the 1930's and published by J. Cantineau in his "Tadmorea," *Syria*, XIV, 169–202, XVII, 267–82, 346–55, XIX, 72–82, 153–71; H. Seyrig in various instalments of his "Antiquités syriennes," in the same journal, and H. Ingholt in his "Inscriptions and Sculptures from Palmyra," *Berytus*, III, 83–125, V, 93–140. Cf. also F. Rosenthal's *Sprache der palmyrenischen Inschriften* (includes a brief bibliography for 1926–34); Z. Ben-Haim's "Palmyren Inscriptions" (Hebrew), *BJPES*, XIII, 141–48; J. Starcky's *Palmyre. Guide archéologique;* his and M. Salahud'-din's *Palmyre, la fiancée du désert;* and, more generally, M. Rostovtzeff's *Caravan Cities.* The numerous references to Zenobia's Jewish sympathies in the Church writings from Athanasius to Barhebraeus, particularly in connection with the Christian missionary activities of Paul of Samosata, are analyzed in the latter's French biography by G. Bardy, pp. 172 ff.

44. The perplexing problems of Falasha history and religion have more recently been comprehensively reviewed in A. Z. Aeshcoli's *Sefer ha-Palashim* (The Book of Falashas: the Culture and Traditions of the Jews of Ethiopia). Cf. also his bibliography of the extensive older literature in *KS*, XII–XIII, his "Ethiopian Jews in Hebrew Literature" (Hebrew), *Zion*, I, 316–36, 411–35, and his *Recueil des textes falashas*. More recently a competent philologist, W. Leslau, has spent much time in Ethiopia, and one may confidently expect some new valuable data and insights. Cf. his forthcoming *Falasha Anthology;* and for the time being, his "Falasha Religious Dispute," *PAAJR*, XVI, 71–95, and "Religious Life of the Falashas" (Yiddish), *Yivo Bleter*, XXXIV, 209–20.

45. Qiddushin 22b. It must be admitted, however, that the reading here is uncertain. Equally dubious is the date of Yussuf Rabban's expedition. It depends on whether we date the old privilege of the Jews of Cranganore, inscribed on copper plates still in the possession of Jews of Cochin today, in 476, 750, or 1020. The middle date is perhaps the most probable. A fuller discussion of this problem must, therefore, be deferred to Vol. III.

CHAPTER XIV: WORLD OF THE TALMUD

1. Shabbat 130a. This statement goes back to a briefer apothegm variously attributed to Judah the Patriarch, his father Simon ben Gamaliel, and others. Cf. Sifre on Deut. 76 (on Deut. 12:23), ed. by Friedmann, fol. 90b (ed. by Finkelstein, p. 141); and the editors' notes thereon.

2. Yebamot 62b f.; M. Soṭah III, 4 (*ishshah perushah*); Qiddushin I, 1; b. 12b; Josephus' *Ag. Ap.* II, 24.199. The difference between rabbinic law concerning marriage by *bi'ah* (consummation) and the Roman idea of marriage by *usucapio* and similar Egyptian and Assyrian concepts is rightly emphasized by E. Neufeld in his *Ancient Hebrew Marriage Laws*, pp. 92 f. "The Inheritance of Illegitimate Children According to Jewish Law" is analyzed by C. Tchernowitz in *Abrahams Mem. Vol.*, pp. 402–15. Cf. also A. H. Freimann's "Support of the Child out of Wedlock According to Jewish Law" (Hebrew), *Ha-Peraklit*, 1945, pp. 163–73. Maimonides' attempt to construe the biblical prohibition, "There shall be no harlot of the daughters of Israel" (Deut. 23:18), as referring to any Jewess' illicit relationship, however non-professional, was successfully controverted by Abraham ben David. Cf. *M.T.*, Ishshut, I, 4, and R. Abraham's note thereon. Conceivably Maimonides had before him the reading *azharah le-muṭnah* (a warning to the unmarried girl) in Sifre on Deut. 260, mentioned in Friedmann's ed. fol. 121a (ed. by Finkelstein, p. 283). On the general rabbinic attitude, exemplified in its extreme form by R. Eliezer's equation of an affair between two unmarried persons with cohabitation with a mother and daughter (T. Qiddushin I, 4, 335), cf. L. M. Epstein's *Sex Laws and Customs in Judaism*.

3. Yebamot 75ab, 80b, 107a, etc.; Qiddushin 29b f.; Sanhedrin 76a. On the early marriages in Egypt, not only among the native masses, but also among its Greek-speaking upper crust, cf. the literature cited by R. Taubenschlag in his *Law of Greco-Roman Egypt*, I, 84, n. 34. On Iran, cf. the passage from the *Dinkard*, quoted by Christensen in his *Iran*, pp. 327 f. It is noteworthy that the Judeo-Christian sects insisted, like other Christians and some Jewish sectarians, on monogamy. But they sharply repudiated the gnostic condemnation of marriage—according to Irenaeus, the Marcionites called all marriage "whoredom"—and advocated early unions. Cf. H. J. Schoeps's brief study, "Ehebewertung und Sexualmoral der späteren Judenchristen," *Studia theologica*, II, 99–101.

4. Tacitus' *Hist.* V, 5; Cant. r. VII, 7 (a statement by R. Levi); Jerome's *In Isa.* 3:2, 48:17 f. (*PL*, XXIV, 59, 462); Sifre on Deut. 357, ed. by Friedmann fol. 150a (ed. by Finkelstein, p. 429); and M. Abot V, 24 (with Herford's comments in his ed., pp. 119, 144 f.). On life expectancy in ancient times, cf. in particular, W. F. Willcox's methodological observations on "Length of Life in the Early Roman Empire," in the papers submitted to the International Congress for Studies in Population, Paris, 1937, II, 14–22. Cf. also G. Lefebvre's "Âge de 110 ans et la veillesse chez les Egyptiens," *CRAI* 1944, pp. 106–19. On the different cycles (mostly seven) in man's growth which, taken over from the Greeks, played a great role in talmudic and medieval letters, cf. L. Löw's *Lebensalter in der jüdischen Literatur*. (Although no longer up to date and supplemented by later researches by M. Steinschneider and others, this work is still very useful.) As general depopulation progressed, the whole Graeco-Roman world also discontinued child exposure and generally accepted from the orientals their higher appreciation of life. Cf. A. Cameron's slightly apologetic review of "The Exposure of Children and Greek Ethics," *Classical Review*, XLVI, 105–14.

5. Ketubot 82b; *Testament of Issachar* 3:5; M. Ketubot VI, 5–6. The transitional stage resulting in delayed and fewer marriages doubtless reflected the gradual urbanization of Palestine after Alexander. Dimly remembered in the tradition antedating R. Simon ben Shetaḥ (who introduced the husband's pledge of all his possessions as security for the marriage settlement) and recorded in Ketubot 82b, it was so little understood that the crucial reference to widespread inability to marry was omitted in the parallel passage in j. Ket. VIII, 11, 32bc. The legal implications of the gradual transition from *mohar* to *neduniah* have in part been studied (cf., e.g., C. Tchernowitz's *Toledoth ha-halakah*, III, 238 ff.), but its sociological and historical aspects would merit further careful consideration.

6. Qiddushin 29b; Ketubot 54a. The Talmud itself is clearly aware of the economic difference between Palestine and Babylonia; Rashi's explanation that Babylonian rabbis studying in Palestine were less hindered by their marital status is palpably forced. On the controversial sources concerning R. Eliezer's marital life, cf. B. Z. Bokser's *Pharisaic Judaism in Transition*, pp. 14 f. It may be noted that R. Johanan merely restated an ancient Palestinian view that a man should first acquire a house and field and then marry. Cf. T. Soṭah VII, 20, 309; b. 44a, with reference to Prov. 24:27.

7. Sanhedrin 52b; j. Soṭah I, 1, 16b; T. IV, 16, 301. The connection between Ḥama bar Tobiah's death sentence and the Mazdakite revolt has been plausibly argued by Funk in his *Juden in Babylonien*, II, 123. A comparison of the tannaitic discussions on the "water of bitterness" ordeal of Num. 5:11–31 with Philo and Josephus is given in N. Wahrmann's careful *Untersuchungen über die Stellung der Frau im Judentum im Zeitalter der Tannaiten*, Vol. I.

8. Cf. j. Qiddushin X, 1, 65cd; Sirach 23:24–25; *Wisdom of Solomon* 13:16; Yebamot 78b; M. Qiddushin III, 12–13; b. 69a. The rabbis decided in favor of R. Tarfon's advice. A. Geiger, who, as we recall, equated the term *mamzer* with *me'am zar* (from a foreign people) may have been etymologically as wrong as was R. Abbahu in explaining it by *mum zar* (having the blemish of foreigners; cf. j. Qiddushin III, 14, 64c). But both were doubtless right in seeking its original meaning in the offspring of prohibited exogamous unions. Cf. his *Urschrift*, pp. 52 ff.; and *supra*, Vol. I, p. 147. As a residuum of this ancient origin we still find R. 'Aqiba insisting that a child born of a Jewess to a Gentile or enslaved father was to be treated as a *mamzer*. Cf. the discussion in Qiddushin 75b; j. 32cd. In talmudic times, however, the new delimitation of this term to issue of adulterous and incestuous unions displaced the old designation to such an extent that, by a curious inversion, alleged descent from such "bastards" now had to serve as justification for the new exogamous prohibitions. It is not surprising, therefore, that to be called *mamzer* was a superlative insult which the rabbis put under a more severe sanction (of thirty-nine stripes) than that of naming one a slave or evildoer. Cf. the tannaitic source in Qiddushin 28a, as well as Rashi's and the Tosafists' strained interpretations thereof. Cf. also B. Cohen's "Some Remarks on the Law of Persons in Jewish and Roman Jurisprudence," *PAAJR*, XVI, 12 ff. (pointing out the inconsistencies in the Mishnah and other talmudic sources with respect to the definition of *mamzer*) and 25 ff. (on the status of freedmen).

9. Cf. j. Ketubot V, 2, 29d; Christensen's *Iran*, pp. 322 ff.; and, more generally, L. M. Epstein's "Institution of Concubinage among the Jews," *PAAJR*, VI, 153–88; and his *Marriage Laws*, pp. 62 ff. Since it more readily accepted Graeco-Roman mores, the Church found it difficult to combat concubinage. Even the legislation of Constantine, which tried to reduce it by legal obstacles, and that of Justinian which, on the contrary, attempted to assimilate it more fully to regular marriage, owed much more to intervening socio-economic developments than to the impact of Christian teachings. Cf. E. J. Jonkers's dissertation, *Invloed van het Christendom* (The Influ-ence of Christianity on Roman Legislation Concerning Concubinage and Divorce).

10. Frey's *Corpus*, I, No. 476. Cf. A. Büchler's "Familienreinheit und Sittlichkeit in Sepphoris in 2. Jahrhundert," *MGWJ*, LXXVIII, 133 ff.; and L. Friedlaender's classical *Darstellungen aus der Sittengeschichte Roms*, I, 283 ff. Nearly four decades ago J. Juster planned to publish a monograph on Jewish marriage as viewed from the inscriptions (to parallel a similar work on Christian marriage by Otto Pelka; cf. Juster's *Empire romain*, II, 41, n. 1), but was prevented from doing so by his un-timely death. Obviously, this is an even more urgent desideratum today.

11. Yebamot 37b, 65ab. Rab and R. Naḥman's temporary marriages have long intrigued scholars. Cf. R. Margulies's and S. Krauss's Hebrew essays on " 'Who Will Be [My Wife] for a Day?' " in *Sinai*, XI, Nos. 124–25, pp. 176–79 (suggesting that this was but a ruse to forestall an honoring royal offer of temporary mates); XII, Nos. 133–34, pp. 299–302 (even more forcedly removing the entire passage from the realm of sex relations).

12. Ez. 14:16–18; Isa. 54:6, etc.; II ARN, II, p. 9 (cf. also Schechter's n. 6 thereon); j. Yebamot IV, 12, 6b; XIII, 2, 13c; b. 15a; Ketubot 62b; H. Granqvist's *Marriage Conditions in a Palestinian Village*, I. On the much-debated problem of Jewish polygamy, cf. Epstein's *Marriage Laws*, pp. 12 ff.; Neufeld's *Ancient Hebrew Marriage Laws*, pp. 118 ff.; Ernest (Abraham Naftali Zevi) Roth's "About the History of Monogamy among the Jews," *Guttmann Mem. Vol.*, Hebrew section, pp. 114–36 (a summary of an unpublished larger study); and *supra*, Chaps. III, n. 19, IV, n. 14. Despite the intensive interest of apologists and legal historians for over a century, the ambivalent attitude of the masses and their rabbinic leaders is still full of ob-scurities, wholly understandable in view of the paucity of other than largely norma-tive talmudic sources, with their geographic and chronological limitations. Even V. Tcherikover, who made a valiant effort to summarize the information yielded by Egyptian papyri on "the social status of Egyptian Jewry" (*Ha-Yehudim be-Miṣrayim*, pp. 35 ff.), has refrained from analyzing the few sidelights shed by these sources on the Jewish family of the period. Such a study would be doubly welcome, as Egypt itself seems to have been largely monogamous. Although Herodotus' assertion that the an-cient Egyptians did not marry more than one wife has been controverted by modern scholars, and although in Hellenistic Egypt only priests were required to live a monogamous life, whereas, according to Diodorus Siculus, "any other man takes as many [wives] as he may determine," the trend toward single marriages was never-theless much more pronounced in the Nile Valley than anywhere else in the ancient Near East. Cf. Herodotus, II, 92; Diodorus' *Library of History*, I, 80, 3.

13. M. Giṭṭin IX, 10. Curiously, this debate appears at the end of the tractate as if placed there on second thought. I. Sonne may be right in emphasizing the peculiar "atomistic-nominalistic" approach of the Hillelite school to the interpretation of the crucial passage in Deut. 24:1, as against the Shammaites' greater attention to its con-text. Cf. his "Schools of Shammai and Hillel Seen from Within," *Ginzberg Jub. Vol.*, pp. 287 ff. He clearly underestimates, however, the provocation of Christian propa-ganda, which assumed increasing significance concurrently with the victory of the Hillelite school. The bitterness of the Bar Kocheba period helps explain R. 'Aqiba's extremist formulation, which went beyond anything previously taught by other Hillelites. Cf. also L. Blau's comparative study of *Die jüdische Ehescheidung und der jüdische Scheidebrief*. On the endless debates concerning early Christian attitudes to divorce, cf. U. Holzmeister's review of several studies (by Ott, Vogt, Staab and Allgeier) in "Die Streitfrage über die Ehescheidungstexte bei Matthäus 5, 32, 19, 9," *Biblica*, XXVI, 133–46; and F. L. Cirlot's *Christ and Divorce*. The socio-economic

factors which contributed to the tightening of the divorce laws under the Christian Empire are discussed by E. J. Jonkers in his *Invloed*.

14. Cf. Schechter's *Fragments of a Zadokite Work* 5:7–9; Gen. r. XVII, 3, 154 f.; Yebamot 62b; M. Nedarim VIII, 7, IX, 10; and other data assembled by S. Krauss in "Die Ehe zwischen Onkel und Nichte," *Studies in Jewish Literature in Honor of Kaufmann Kohler*, pp. 165–75. L. M. Epstein's list of the rabbinic secondary prohibitions added thirty new types to the original sixteen relationships reconstructed by the sages from the Bible (see his *Marriage Laws*, pp. 258 ff.). But they included not only grandmothers and great granddaughters, but also such out-of-the-way relationships as a wife's mother's father's mother or a wife of mother's maternal half-brother. Unlike biblically prohibited incest, however, such unions were valid and their offspring considered legitimate, but the wife was penalized by the loss of most of her protective rights, and courts imposed compulsory divorce.

15. Sanhedrin 58ab. The extent to which incest was practiced in Parthia, Persia, Egypt, Syria, Phoenicia, and among the Nabataean Arabs is succinctly shown in O. G. von Wesendonk's "Zur Verwandtenehe bei den Arsakiden," *AR*, XXX, 383–88. Cf. also A. A. Mazahéri's *Famille iranienne aux temps anté-islamiques*, pp. 113 ff.; and M. Hombert and C. Préaux's data on "Les Mariages consanguins dans l'Egypte romaine," *Hommages à Joseph Bidez et à Franz Cumont*, pp. 135–42 (showing that, for instance, in Arsinoe the extant documents reveal a ratio of 17 marriages among relatives as against only 24 "normal" marriages).

16. *Code of Justinian* (Codex), I, 9, 7 (ed. by Krüger, II, 61); Christensen's *Iran*, pp. 323 f., 330 f. Cf., in general, Juster's *Empire romain*, II, 41 ff. With the dissolution of the ancient clan society, levirate marriage was, in any case, losing ground. Cf. the documentation in Epstein's *Marriage Laws*, pp. 77 ff., 123 ff.

This is not the place to describe in any detail the colorful ceremonies which characterized the ancient Jewish weddings. They usually extended over a long period before and after the actual wedlock. The Palestinian rabbis advised Wednesday or Thursday weddings, which would give even working bridegrooms a chance to enjoy the festivities over a three or four-day weekend. Cf. Ketubot 5a; and, more generally, the brief but well-documented surveys in S. Krauss's *Archäologie*, II, 34 ff., 454 ff., and A. S. Herschberg's "Betrothal and Wedding Customs in the Talmudic Period" (Hebrew), *He-'Atid*, V, 75–102.

17. Jub. 30:7; M. Megillah IV, 9, with reference to Lev. 18:21; Sifre on Deut. 171, ed. by Friedmann, fol. 107a (ed. by Finkelstein, p. 218); j. Megillah IV, 10, 75c; Exod. 34:16. Curiously, despite the Mishnah's repudiation, the old interpretation persisted down to the Muslim age, and the otherwise orthodox author of Targum Jonathan rendered Lev. 18:21 precisely in the forbidden meaning. Nathan ben Yeḥiel's harmonizing explanation (cf. *Aruch Completum*, ed. by A. Kohut, I, 289, s.v. *Aram*) is but a dialectical *tour de force*. On the much-debated "Levitical Impurity of the Gentiles in Palestine before the Year 70" and its bearing on marital eligibility, cf. A. Büchler's essay in *JQR*, XVII, 1–81. Cf. also *supra*, Chap. XI, n. 32. Once again our information on the important and ramified subject of intermarriage among ancient Jews in various periods and countries is vitiated by the normative character of most sources and the theological or apologetic bias of such modern literature, as S. Holdheim's *Gemischte Ehen zwischen Juden und Christen*. More than a century old, this essay is still worthy of study, although a new monograph dealing with all the ascertainable historical facts and their sociological implications is very much needed.

18. Philo's *De spec. leg.*, III, 4.25; 5.29. Cf. Belkin's *Philo and the Oral Law*, pp. 232 ff. That Diaspora Jewry was, in fact, anything but rigidly endogamous is also

illustrated by the Jewish mothers of several pagan converts to Christianity, recorded in the early Christian sources (e.g., Timothy) or of Origen. G. Kittel's "confession" that he had wrongly believed in the Jewish "Abstammung der Mutter des Origenes" (*FJF*, III, 235 f.) is too obviously colored by the author's and editors' Nazi biases to be taken seriously. By marrying an Egyptian, Origen's mother lost whatever superior type of citizenship she personally might have enjoyed and, like her son, too, became an Egyptian. Cf. Taubenschlag's *Law*, I, 13, n. 54. According to Jewish law, the converted spouse of a Jew of either sex and the offspring of the couple became full-fledged members of the Jewish community. Cf. also *supra*, Chap. XIII, n. 24.

19. M. Ketubot I, 2, 4, V, 1; T. IV, 9, 264; b. 10a, 12ab, 56a, etc. Tobit 7:13 (14) seems to refer to such a marriage contract. Cf. the variants cited by D. C. Simpson in Charles's *Apocrypha*, I, 222. If this apocryphon was written in Egypt (*ibid.*, pp. 185 f.), this would be another proof that the Jews of the dispersion rather speedily followed the lead of Palestinian legislators. Otherwise the Egyptian population entered wedlock as a rule on the basis of unwritten agreements. The written contracts that have been found all seem to have been concluded after the wedding for purposes of property settlement. Cf. H. J. Wolff's *Written and Unwritten Marriages in Hellenistic and Postclassical Roman Law;* and other literature listed by Taubenschlag in his *Law*, I, 84, n. 33–34. Conceivably the *syngraphé* mentioned in Tobit likewise was such a postmarital agreement, but the context rather indicates its similarity with the Palestinian *ketubah*. On the latter, cf. L. Blau's *Jüdische Ehescheidung;* and particularly the fully documented analysis of the talmudic and posttalmudic evolution in L. M. Epstein's *Jewish Marriage Contract*. This study ought to be supplemented, however, by more extensive use of comparative materials from neighboring civilizations. On the meaning and historic evolution of the curious term, "property of iron sheep," cf. S. von Bohlen's *Untersuchungen zur Tiermiete*, p. 171 (pointing out the similarity of certain Babylonian and Greek institutions, but not of the terminology, which was to recur in the medieval Teuton *Eisernvieh* and French *cheptel de fer* contracts).

20. Nedarim 66ab; Bekhorot 45b. Cf. also R. ʿAqiba's views in Sifre on Deut. 213, ed. by Friedmann, fol. 113a (ed. by Finkelstein, p. 246). Even the Christian pilgrim Antoninus Martyr, who visited Nazareth about 560–70, was greatly impressed by the beauty of Hebrew women. Cf. his *Itinerarium*, V (in A. Stewart's English transl., p. 5). Cf. also the data assembled by A. S. Herschberg in his "Woman's Beauty and Physical Culture in the Talmudic Period" (Hebrew), *He-ʿAtid*, IV, 1–53, V, 102–104.

21. M. Negaʿim II, 1; Gen. r. LXXXVI, 3.1055; Cant. r. I, 41 on 1:6; Megillah 6ab. Cf. the neat contrast between *Anarianon* and *Arianon* in Shapur's Greek inscription ll. 34 f. Somewhat blurred in M. Sprengling's transl. in *AJSL*, LVII, 374, 379, this passage was correctly interpreted by Olmstead in *Classical Philology*, XXXVII, 417 f. On talmudic eugenics in general, cf. the pertinent essays in *Hygiene und Judentum*, pp. 26 ff., 51 ff.; and the comprehensive works by J. Preuss, *Biblisch-talmudische Medizin;* and I. L. Katzenelsohn's *Ha-Talmud ve-ḥokhmat ha-refuah* (Talmud and Medical Science). Cf. also W. Feldman's "Ancient Jewish Eugenics," *Medical Leaves*, II, 28–37; I. Simon's study of "La Médecine légale dans la Bible et le Talmud," *Revue de l'histoire de la médecine hébraïque*, II, 46–61; III, 33–62; S. R. Kagan's "Bibliography of Ancient Jewish Medicine," *Bulletin of the History of Medicine*, XXII, 480–85; and, more generally, B. L. Gordon's *Medicine throughout Antiquity*, pp. 251–94 (Ancient Hebrew Medicine), 725–93 (Talmudic Medicine).

22. Shebuʿot 30b; B.Q. 119a; Jerome's *Adversus Jovinianum*, I, 26; *Contra Vigilantium*, 13, end, in *PL*, XXIII, 257, 365; Juster's *Empire romain*, I, 441, n. 8. Even more

remarkable than the title *mater* is that of *pateressa synagogae* in a Roman inscription. Cf. Frey's *Corpus*, I, Nos. 523, 606, 639. It is generally agreed, however, that both titles reflect patronage and other benefactions, rather than active participation in communal work. The aforementioned woman archisynagogus in Smyrna (*supra*, Chap. IX, n. 29), must either have been given another purely honorary title, or was the wife of the congregational warden. There were, indeed, no women *archontes* found in any European inscription, although boys were often designated as future elders. A lady treasurer of charities (*gizberit*) is mentioned, however, as a matter of course in fourth-century Palestine by R. Jeremiah (Shabbat 62a).

23. T. Megillah IV, 11, 12, 226; M. Middot II, 5; Sukkah V, 2, 4; j. 55b; Philo's *De spec. leg.*, III, 31.171. Philo's advocacy of extreme seclusion was, however, a reflection of conditions existing in his Egyptian environment, rather than of Jewish tradition, Colson's comment thereon (VII, 640) to the contrary. Women's part in the recitation of Scripture is not clearly reflected in the sources. From the phrasing in T. Megillah IV, 226, S. Krauss thought that originally a woman was forbidden only to serve as public reader for the uninitiated so as not to put to shame illiterate men. Cf. his *Synagogale Altertümer*, p. 174, n. 1. There is no evidence, however, for such early employment of public readers, cf. *infra*, n. 57. Probably the more correct reading is *be-rabim*, given by Zuckermandl in his note, which more nearly agrees with the quotation (not interpretation) in b. Megillah 23a. In other words, from the outset, women seem to have been included in the number of worshipers, but not allowed to recite their portions. Cf. also M. Friedmann's responsum on "Mitwirkung der Frauen beim Gottesdienste," *HUCA*, VIII–IX, 511–23; and *supra*, Chap. XII, n. 34. On the general position of women in ancient Jewish society, of which, in keeping with the available sources, a somewhat idealized picture had to be drawn here, cf. the older study by L. G. Lévy, *La Famille dans l'antiquité israélite;* S. Krauss's *Talmudische Archäologie*, II, 43 ff., 462 ff.; P. Dikshtein's modern analysis of *Ha-Maṣab ha-mishpaṭi shel ha-ishshah be-Yisrael* (Legal Status of Women in Israel); and, more tangentially, the works by L. M. Epstein mentioned in previous notes. Interesting comparative data may be found in E. Kornemann's brief survey of *Die Stellung der Frau in der vorgriechischen Mittelmeerkultur;* and, more specifically, in W. Schubart's "Frau im griechisch-römischen Aegypten," *Internationale Monatschrift für Wissenschaft*, X, 1503–38; and C. Bartholomae's *Frau im sasanidischen Recht*. Much can also be learned from H. Granqvist's anthropological studies of *Birth and Childhood among the Arabs*, and *Child Problems among the Arabs*.

24. Pesiqta de-R. Kahana, fol. 99ab; Ketubot 111b; Menaḥot 99b, with reference to Joshua 1:8. The changed attitude toward the 'am ha-areṣ came to the fore as early as the days of Judah the Patriarch. As usual, it is explained by an anecdote in B.B. 8a. The struggle for power in the all-Jewish city of Sepphoris has been described, on the basis of scattered talmudic sources, by A. Büchler in *The Political and Social Leaders of the Jewish Community of Sepphoris in the Second and Third Centuries*. Of course, as elsewhere, we hear little from the other side.

25. C. Th., XVI, 8, 2–4; j. Ta'aniot IV, 2, 68a; b.B.M. 86a. The story about Rabbah is told in connection with a simple attendance at a *kallah*. In his *Empire romain*, I, 408, Juster has raised the question as to whether, by his failure to renew the manifold protective laws in C. Th., Justinian intended to abolish the tax exemption of rabbis. A fuller answer to this query can only be given by the examination of the generally complex problems of Jewish taxation in the Byzantine Empire, which will be discussed more fully in their medieval context. One may mention, in passing, that Egyptian priests, too, fought hard for tax exemption and succeeded in securing it from Marcus Aurelius. Cf. E. H. Gilliam's "Archives of the Temple of Soknobraisis at Bacchias," *Yale Classical Studies*, X, 260 ff.

26. B.B. 8a, 91b; Yebamot 63a; Sanhedrin 58b. At times, of course, bureaucratic interference could also favor individual Jews. In the latter part of the fourth century Libanius vividly described his difficulties in collecting rent from some recalcitrant Jewish tenants abetted by a Roman officer. Cf. his *Epistulae*, XI, 327. R. Johanan himself clearly recognized the governmental origin of the evil when he denounced "that kingdom of wickedness which injects an evil eye into man's possessions" (Gen. r. LXXVI, 6, 904). In the traditional vein of Jewish self-accusation, however, he blamed these sufferings principally on the misdeeds of the Jews themselves, attributing, for instance, the extraordinary price rises of his day to God's anger over Jews feasting with choral accompaniment (Soṭah 48a). "The Economic Status of Galilean Jewry in the Generation of R. Johanan bar Nappaḥa and the Generation After" is briefly reviewed in a stimulating essay by A. Marmorstein in *Festschrift Freimann*, Hebrew section, pp. 81–92. Cf. also, in general, A. Segré's "Inflation and Its Implications in Early Byzantine Times," *Byzantion*, XV, 249–79; and G. Mickwitz's *Geld und Wirtschaft im Römischen Reich des vierten Jahrhunderts nach Chr.*

26a. Cf. T. Sinko's "Descriptio orbis terrae, eine Handelsgeographie aus dem 4. Jahrhundert," *Archiv für lateinische Lexikographie*, XIII, 551 (c. 29, 31). Long known under the title *Expositio totius mundi et gentium*, this geographic and ethnographic compilation was apparently written by an Egyptian about 350 C.E. for the use of merchants and travelers. Cf. E. Wölfflin's "Bemerkungen," *ibid.*, pp. 573–78.

27. B.M. 103b (note the Tosafists' explanation), 109b; Ketubot 97a; Ta'anit 10a; Shabbat 119a; Pesaḥim 88a; Berakhot 17b. Many rabbis themselves both owned and worked on farms. R. Joseph, for example, was reputed to be a foremost expert in viticulture (B.B. 26a). On the price gyrations, cf. also the doubtless exaggerated assertion (in 'A.Z. 9b) that at certain times a field worth 1,000 denarii might not be disposed of for 1 denarius. Cf., in general, J[ulius] Newman's interesting survey of *The Agricultural Life of the Jews in Babylonia (200–500 C.E.)*; and, from the legal point of view, A. Gulak's *Le-Ḥeker toledot ha-mishpaṭ ha-'ibri bi-tekufat ha-talmud* (On the History of Hebrew Law in the Period of the Talmud, I: Land Laws), together with G. J. Webber's comments thereon in the *Journal of Comparative Legislation*, 3d ser., XV, 100–11.

28. M. 'Arakhin IV, 3; b. 'Erubin 86a; *C. Th.*, XIII, 5, 18; M. Qiddushin IV, 14. Cf. also S. Chonowicz's *Arbeitsrecht im Talmud;* and the literature listed *supra*, Chaps. VIII, n. 10–11, XIII, n. 25. On the background and importance of Palestine's glass manufacture, cf. F. Neuburg's survey of *Glass in Antiquity;* and D. B. Harden's "Tomb-Groups of Glass of Roman Date from Syria and Palestine," *Iraq*, XI, 151–59, pointing out that "the Syrian industry concentrated on blown vessels, and there is no direct evidence of cutting and engraving of glass," except perhaps by imported Alexandrian craftsmen (p. 159). Cf. also *supra*, Chap. IX, n. 30.

29. Yebamot 63a; B.M. 70b f.; Nedarim 49b; Philo's *De spec. leg.* II, 17.74 ff.; M. B.M. V, 8; B.Q. 104b; M.Q. 10b. The extensive talmudic data on commerce and money trade have thus far been analyzed chiefly from the legal rather than economic point of view. Cf., especially, A. Gulak's "Banking in Talmudic Law" (Hebrew), *Tarbiz*, II, 154–71; R. Salomon's *Prêt en intérêt en la législation juive;* and J. Rappaport's "Darlehen nach talmudischem Recht," *Zeitschrift für vergleichende Rechtswissenschaft*, XLVII, 256–378. In his "Antichresis in Jewish and Roman Law," *Marx Jub. Vol.*, pp. 179–202, B. Cohen has shown how the Babylonian Amoraim, under the pressure of urgent needs of credit, had to legalize such "antichretic" use of mortgaged property by the creditor (the Greek term itself is cited once, j. B.M. VI, 7, 11a) under the guise of fictitious sales. Such evasions of the law prohibiting all forms of interest were to become commonplace under the prohibitive systems of medieval Christen-

dom and Islam. Only S. Ejges has made an initial attempt to come to grips with some of the economic data relating to *Geld im Talmud*. In my essay on "The Economic Views of Maimonides" in *Essays on Maimonides*, pp. 127–264, I have likewise tried to penetrate behind the legal façade to the core of economic realities, as well as to separate the underlying talmudic views from later medieval and, particularly, Maimonidean accretions. But a detailed investigation of the light shed by the talmudic sources on both economic theory and practice is one of the major scholarly desiderata. Of course, there is a deplorable lack of reliable statistical data not only in the Jewish, but in all economic history of the period, as was rightly stressed by A.H.M. Jones in his lecture on *Ancient Economic History*. But both areas still offer numerous clues to be pursued. Cf., for example, A. C. Johnson and L. C. West's recent economic studies pertaining to Byzantine Egypt; and some of the literature cited *supra*, Chap. VIII.

30. M. Abot V, 10; b. B.B. 12b f.; Sheqalim 3a; Giṭṭin 33a; *M. T.*, Sanhedrin, XXIV, 6. Cf. the fuller analysis of the rabbinic doctrine of private ownership in B. Safra's (pseud.) stimulating Hebrew essay on "Private Property in Jewish Law," *Ha-Mishpaṭ ha-'ibri*, II, 25–73; and my *Essays on Maimonides*, pp. 145 ff. Safra overstresses, however, the rabbinic teachings of *hefqer*. The intermingling of ritual and civil law is also evident in the rabbinic view that one could acquire ownership in ritually unusable objects (*asurim be-hana'ah*) even less than in those illegally appropriated from someone else. Cf. the sources quoted by B. Cohen in his "Essay on Possession in Jewish Law," *PAAJR*, VI, 134 ff. To dam up a source of endless litigation the rabbis even provided for the loss of ownership as a result of the thieves' major permanent alterations in stolen objects. Of course, the transgressors remained personally liable for such losses and were subject to the biblically stipulated additional penalties. Cf. M. Jung's *Jewish Law of Theft*, pp. 66 ff. The much-debated problem of talmudic origins of the medieval *Hehlerrecht* will be discussed in connection with the other facets of medieval economy.

31. Cf. j. Giṭṭin V, 3, 46d; Philo's *De vita Mosis*, II, 44.243 ff.; M. Ketubot IV, 11; XIII, 3; b. 108b. These examples of the rabbis' eager response to changing social needs at the expense of individual property rights could readily be multiplied. Nor need we see therein the influence of Graeco-Roman legal patterns as suggested by Juster (*Empire romain*, II, 88, n. 3), but rather similarities arising from essentially parallel social backgrounds. In fact, Graeco-Roman law often failed to go the whole length of Jewish legal adjustments for the maintenance of the desired social equilibrium. On the extent to which Philo's restatement of biblical law reflected contemporary Alexandrian practices, cf. *infra*, n. 42. Cf. also S. Asaf's "Discontinuation of the *ketubat benin dikhrin* [Stipulation in Favor of Sons]" (Hebrew), *Hazofeh*, X, 18–30; and, more generally, M. Mielziner's *Rabbinical Law of Hereditary Succession*.

32. B.M. 58b; M. Qiddushin IV, 14; and many other sources cited in my *Essays on Maimonides*, pp. 170 ff. In his Hebrew essay on "The Just Price and Misrepresentation" (*Ha-Mishpaṭ ha-'ibri*, I, 15–55), P. Dikshtein argues that rabbinic law, particularly in R. Johanan's formulation, influenced Diocletian's decrees of 285 and 293 (*Code of Justinian* [Codex], IV, 44, 2.8; ed. by Krüger, II, 179). This is unlikely. Apart from the improbability of such an almost instantaneous emulation, there are overt differences in the amount of overcharge (100 versus 16.66 per cent), Diocletian's main emphasis on land sales specifically exempted in talmudic law, and his desire to protect the seller rather than the purchaser. Once more we should see here unrelated, if similar, attempts to deal with essentially the same problems. Cf. also H. F. Jolowicz's "Origin of Laesio Enormis," *Juridical Review*, XLIX, 53–72; and H. Grünwald's detailed juridical analysis of *Die Uebervorteilung im jüdischen Recht*. On the other hand, except for occasional regulations by professional groups (see *infra*), we

find few records of private agreements on prices or other monopolistic practices. Neither did there exist large enough corporations to wield control over a significant economic area nor was the economy in general quite so free and competitive, particularly in the age of Amoraim, to allow for dangerous private restraints. Even in the wider and more fully documented Roman evolution, A. A. Schiller has succeeded in marshaling only a few instances of such restraints and of legal measures taken to combat them. Cf. his "Restraint of Trade in Classical Roman Law," *Mnemosyna Pappoulias*, pp. 233–44.

33. Shabbat 118a; B.B. 91a, 110a, 116a; j. Yoma V, 3, 42c; Pesaḥim 118a; 'Erubin 41b; R.H. 27a. The exclamation concerning idolatry sounded too extreme even to some rabbis inured to hyperbolic speech, and one corrected the epigram to read: "Hire yourself for work which is strange to you ['*abodah she-zarah lo*, in lieu of *la-'abodah zarah*], rather than be dependent on other people" (B.B. 110a). The anti-demonic power of the ram's horn and its use to underscore the solemnity of the services, is stressed, even overstressed, in S. B. Finesinger's "Shofar," *HUCA*, VIII–IX, 193–228.

34. Ammianus Marcellinus' *Res gestae*, XXIII, 6, 80 (relating to the year 363 c.e.); M. B.M. IX, 1–10; and the lengthy discussions thereon in j. and b. Ammianus had traveled widely before he wrote his *History* and had occasion to compare the conditions of the peasants in various parts. Even before the colonate, it seems, Jews also had long-term, even hereditary tenants. Talmudic sources distinguish between the rights of tenants who had leased the land for seven years or longer, and those who had acquired short-term leases. A tannaitic source (j. Bikkurim, I, 13, 64b) speaks of hereditary "family tenants," who must have become quite numerous during the spread to Palestine of the Ptolemaic "large estate." Cf. *supra*, Chap. VIII, n. 35, 39.

35. B.Q. 97a; Giṭṭin 7b f. It may be noted that the complaint was voiced against the exilarch's slaves, not freedmen. We recall that, because of the rabbinic opposition to the liberation of Gentile slaves (Giṭṭin 38b, 40a), evidently out of fear that, in this way, Jewish family purity might greatly deteriorate, there were relatively few freedmen in the Jewish community. Other reasons for that opposition are mentioned by S. Krauss in his *Talmudische Archäologie*, II, 98, 497 f. On the legislation of the Christian Empire cf. Juster's *Empire romain*, II, 71 ff. Because of many lacunae in the records and many ambiguities and contradictions in the extant laws, Juster's analysis leaves many vital questions unanswered. An amusing story of how a father living in the dispersion succeeded in preserving his estate for a son studying in Palestine by outwitting his slave-majordomo is told with much relish in Yalqut Shime'oni on Eccles. II, No. 968. It has an altogether medieval flair, however. Cf. also, in general, my *Essays on Maimonides*, pp. 229 ff., 248 ff.; A. Büchler's "Notes on the Religious Position of the 'Canaanite Slave' a Century before and after the Destruction of the Second Temple" (Hebrew), *Gaster Anniv. Vol.*, pp. 549–70; A. Gulak's "Deed of Sale of a Slave in Talmudic Law" (Hebrew), *Tarbiz*, IV, 1–10; B. Cohen's "Civil Bondage in Jewish and Roman Law," *Ginzberg Jub. Vol.*, pp. 113–32, and his remarks in *PAAJR*, XVI, 25 ff.; and the literature listed *supra*, Chap. VIII, n. 11, 13. It should also be noted that hierodules had completely disappeared from Jewish life and whatever slaves were owned by the Second Temple or local synagogues differed in no way from those privately held. Even if W. Otto should be right in contending that the first mention of that institution in Egypt occurs in the pre-Christian Greek Ezra Apocalypse (cf. his posthumous *Beiträge zur Hierodulie im hellenistischen Aegypten*, p. 10), such an antiquarian literary flourish would prove nothing for the contemporary realities of Jewish life. Cf. also W. L. Westermann's "Freedmen and the Slaves of God," *Proceedings of the American Philosophical Society*, XCII, 55–64.

36. W. M. Ramsay's *Cities and Bishoprics of Phrygia*, I, Pt. 2, p. 545, No. 411. The reference to Passover in the Hierapolis inscription makes it highly probable that we deal here with Jewish associations. On the importance of the city's wool industry and guilds, cf. also A. H. M. Jones's *Cities of the Eastern Roman Provinces*, pp. 73 f.

37. *C. Th.*, XIII, 5, 18; B.Q. 116b; B.M. 51b; Hagigah 9b; B.B. 8b. The solidarity of donkey drivers went to such lengths that the rabbis were inclined to distrust even their praise of one anothers' wares. Cf. M. Demai IV, 7. On the general deprecation of their morals, as compared even with other transport workers, cf. M. Qiddushin IV, 14. Our literary sources with their legalistic and ethical bent do not vouchsafe, however, such detailed answers concerning the organization of these *collegia* as have been gleaned, for instance, from the inscriptions relating to the transport associations which carried on the extensive Palmyrene caravan trade. Cf. also F. M. de Robertis's *Diritto associativo romano dai collegi della Repubblica alle corporazioni del basso Impero;* other literature listed by R. Taubenschlag in his *Law of Greco-Roman Egypt*, I, 47, n. 26; *supra*, Chaps. III, n. 10, VIII, n. 11, and *infra*, Chap. XV, n. 16.

38. B.Q. 114a; B.B. 90b; Gittin 45a; T. Makhshirin III, 4, 675; j. Hallah IV, 4, 60a. The latter section includes a number of statements by Mar Samuel. R. Johanan was also more likely to call him a "younger teacher" than Rab (as assumed by Funk in his *Juden in Babylonien*, I, 49 f.) who had died in ripe old age before the Palestinian sage achieved his preëminent position in Tiberias. On the other hand, j.'s own explanation that R. Johanan had in mind "the interpreters," i.e., the sons of R. Hiyya, is less plausible on both geographic and chronological grounds. The prohibition of selling slaves abroad is found in many laws from ancient Babylonia to Graeco-Roman Egypt and Syria. Cf. the literature cited in R. Taubenschlag's *Law*, I, 59, n. 56. Of considerable interest are also Mar Samuel's recorded threats of modifying some existing ritual laws according to a tannaitic minority opinion in order to force down prices. Cf. Pesahim 30a; Sukkah 34b. Some other rabbinic attempts to use legal authority to influence economic life have been ingeniously interpreted by L. Ginzberg in his *Meqomah shel ha-halakhah* (The Place of Halakhah in Jewish Studies). The intriguing theory of later geonim that each and every Jew had an ideal claim on four ells of Palestinian soil and its possible talmudic antecedents will be discussed in connection with the general geonic modifications of talmudic law.

39. Cf. the interesting discussions in the Babylonian schools, Gittin 36ab, culminating in Raba's justification of the new procedure by the court's unlimited powers over Jewish property. In his stimulating paper, "Prosbol im Lichte der griechischen Papyri und der Rechtsgeschichte," *Festschrift zum 50-jährigen Bestehen der Franz-Josef-Landesrabbinerschule in Budapest*, pp. 96–151, L. Blau has shed much new light on that institution. Even granting that the *prosbol* was originally only a Hellenistic writ of execution and that Hillel simply took it over into the religious law, which is far from certain (cf. L. Wenger's remarks in *Archiv für Papyrus-Forschung*, IX, 281 f.), it does not follow that Hillel was unmindful of his antibiblical innovation. The repeated emphasis upon the novel ordinance (*hitqin*, in M. Shebi'it X, 3; Gittin IV, 3), as well as the motivation—"for the welfare of the world"—clearly testifies to this awareness in the original sources. It seems that without a *prosbol* the debt was not completely canceled, but retained the character of a Roman *obligatio naturalis*, which was neither collectible nor, on the other hand, refundable if paid. The statement of the rabbis that "he who pays his debt in the Sabbatical year meets with the approval of the sages" (M. Shebi'it X, 9) obviously presupposes that, once payment was made, repayment could not be demanded. Cf. also the comprehensive collection of ancient and medieval sources and analysis of contemporary implications in I. Z. Kahana's *Shemitat Kesafim* (Lapse of Debts), pp. 89 ff., 161 ff., 191 ff.

There is no evidence, however, that before Hillel there had been widespread violation of the Sabbatical cancellation of debt. The talmudic sources make it clear that the main evil was the refusal of many creditors to lend money on the approach of the Sabbatical year, precisely because they saw no way of collecting their loans from recalcitrant debtors abetted by law. For similar reasons the rabbis introduced a number of other, less radical alleviations in favor of creditors. Cf. Sanhedrin 2b f.; Giṭṭin 49b. This fact disposes of V. Tcherikover's main argument against Adler and Heichelheim's theory that the renunciation of his loan by a creditor in the seventh year after the loan had been contracted in 100 B.C.E. (*Adler Papyri*, Demotic, No. 20; and Introduction, pp. 5 f.) showed Jewish influence. Cf. his debate with Heichelheim in *HTR*, XXXV, 28 ff., 38 ff.; and his *Ha-Yehudim be-Miṣrayim*, pp. 150 f. Cf. also *supra*, Chap. VIII, n. 15.

40. Exod. r. II, 2–3, on 3:1; Sanhedrin 25b (in R. Ḥananel's correct interpretation); and B.M. 5b. Cf. also the various other explanations suggested in the literature cited *supra*, Chap. VIII, n. 5. More recently, A. Gulak advanced the hypothesis that the disqualification of shepherds on a par with robbers sprang from the rabbis' realization that, as in Egypt and elsewhere, many shepherds had been fugitives from Roman justice. Even those who had come in conflict with the law for patriotic reasons often engaged in highway robbery on the side. By pursuing a "scorched-earth" policy toward the Romans they were also responsible for much tree cutting during the recurrent campaigns. Cf. Gulak's posthumous study on "Shepherds and Breeders of Domestic Cattle after the Destruction of the Second Temple" (Hebrew), *Tarbiz*, XII, 181–89. It is difficult to see, however, how a movement generated by Roman oppression could discredit in the eyes of Jewish leaders an entire, formerly honorable, class of citizens and lead to the outlawry of an entire branch of economy. Both the initial hostility to the raising of sheep and those who tended them, as well as its subsequent mitigation, clearly mirrored some more fundamental and enduring economic needs. Incidentally, a similar discrepancy existed also in regard to the sale of cattle to Gentiles. Here, too, economic differences between the two countries induced the Babylonian rabbis to interpret away a clear tannaitic prohibition. Cf. M. 'A.Z., I, 6; b. 16ab. Unfortunately, there is very little epigraphic evidence on shepherds in Palestine or elsewhere in the Graeco-Roman world. A Hierapolis decree, however, directed against their destruction of vineyards offers an interesting parallel. Cf. L. Robert's observations on an "Epitaphe d'un berger à Thasos" in his *Hellenica*, VII, 153 f.

Illustrations of such profound interrelations between Jewish law and economic evolution could easily be multiplied. For many others, cf. L. Ginzberg's *Meqomah shel ha-halakhah;* and S. Zucrow's *Adjustments of Law to Life in Rabbinic Literature.* In his "Hadrianic Persecution and the Rabbinic Law of Sale," *JQR*, XXIII, 211–31, H. Klein explained the modification of the older law in M. B.M. IV, 1, by the prevailing uncertainties of the Hadrianic age. But its retention long after the emergency had passed is undoubtedly owing to the gradual commercialization of Palestinian Jewry after 135.

41. I Cor. 6:6; W. Judeich, *et al., Altertümer von Hierapolis*, No. 212 (cited in Schürer's *Geschichte*, III, 17 f.); M. Giṭṭin I, 5; b. 10b f. The gradual stiffening of the rabbinic attitude is well illustrated by a comparison of that Mishnah with the earlier debate in T. Giṭṭin I, 4, 323 f., which caused some embarrassment to later sages.

42. Cf. Tcherikover's *Ha-Yehudim be-Miṣrayim*, pp. 137 ff., especially p. 143, n. 34; and *Aegyptische Urkunden . . . Berlin*, Griechische Urkunden, Vol. IV, Nos. 1131, 1151. On the other hand, in his *Jurisprudence of the Jewish Courts in Egypt*, E. R. Goodenough decidedly went too far in asserting that Philo's *De specialibus legibus* does not merely offer academic expositions of ethical and legal postulates, as previ-

ously assumed, but that it reproduces actual laws as applied in practice by contemporary Jewish courts in Alexandria. That, for instance, Alexandrian Jewry, which had no means of execution except lynching, should have extended capital punishment much beyond the biblical commandments at a time when Palestinian jurisprudence voluntarily restricted capital jurisdiction, is hardly likely. Other serious objections have been raised by I. Heinemann, N. Bentwich, Tcherikover, and others. But even if we disagree with Goodenough's enthusiastic conclusion that Philo's work "is one of the most comprehensive pictures of legal practice which we have of any people from that period" (p. 255), we must admit that it certainly is the greatest repository of Jewish law found anywhere outside Palestine and Babylonia down to the end of the first millennium. At least in minor points even the most purely theoretical legal discussion cannot but reflect some actual application. That is why Goodenough, as well as Ritter, Belkin, and Allon (in their studies listed *supra*, Chap. VI, n. 45) have succeeded in uncovering many a hint to legal practice in Philo's immediate environment. It should be noted, however, that, probably as a result of the community's decline after Trajan, R. Simon ben Eleazar in the latter part of the second century spoke of a Jewish court in Alexandria in past terms. Cf. T. Pe'ah IV, 6, 23; Ketubot III, 1, 263. But there is little doubt that, with the subsequent revival of the community, some Jewish courts began functioning again. Certainly a community which Roman officials wished to hold responsible for the obligations of its shipowning members must have had at its disposal sufficiently strong means of law enforcement. Cf. *supra*, n. 37.

43. *C. Th.*, II, 1, 10; *Code of Justinian* (Codex), I, 9, 8.15 (ed. by Krüger, II, 61 f.). Cf. Juster's keen analysis in his *Empire romain*, II, 103 ff., where, however, no reference is made to Theodosius' decree of 415, which, stating that a mixed litigation, "non a senioribus Judaeorum, sed ab ordinariis judicibus dirimatur," clearly betrayed the emperor's lack of confidence in the efficacy of his earlier regulation. One wonders whether Theodosius was familiar with the somewhat analogous system which had prevailed in Ptolemaic Egypt with respect to native Egyptian courts. Here, too, state law did not attribute full force to judgments of such courts, unless the parties concerned acknowledged them by a formal renunciation of contrary claims. Cf. Taubenschlag's *Law*, I, 19. We know that, despite this willfully discriminatory provision, Egyptian law continued to flourish for centuries thereafter and, before long, significantly influenced the Greek law itself. The Romans, who had themselves helped to rehabilitate the Egyptian law courts, now attempted the same method of undermining the authority of Jewish law, evidently with even less success.

44. Sanhedrin 33ab; j. Yebamot XII, 7, 13a; H. P. Chajes's "Juges juifs en Palestine de l'an 70 à l'an 500," *REJ*, XXXIX, 39–52; H. J. Bornstein's "Rules of Ordination and Its History" (Hebrew), *Hatekufah*, IV, 393–426; H. Albeck's Hebrew analysis of "Ordination and Appointment at the Jewish Court," *Zion*, VIII, 85–93; and J. Newman's comprehensive study of *Semikhah* (Ordination). It should be noted that even informal ordination conferred upon the ordained the title *rabbi* in Palestine and *rab* in Babylonia (that the original pronunciation may have been *rib* seems indicated by both a Beth She'arim inscription and a homiletical pun in j. discussed by Schwabe in *BJPES*, IX, 22 f.). We have no information about the type of supervision, if any, exercised by higher courts or the central Jewish authorities on the ordinary courts of amateur judges. The former doubtless possessed the power of "evocation" (summoning before themselves cases pending before lower courts), as well as of rendering judgments on appeal. But whether there was any more direct form of supervision is questionable. True, we learn from occasional talmudic references that many courts had an official called *mufla she-be-bet-din* (distinguished member of the court; M. Horayot I, 4; T. Sanhedrin VII, 1, 425; and other sources), whose presence conveyed a certain additional authority to their sentences. But that he was a sort of

Pharisaic commissar appointed to local courts in order to veto decisions by local Sadducean majorities, as suggested by Finkelstein, or for that matter the appointee of any central organ, is very doubtful. Cf. L. Finkelstein's "On the Phraseology of the Tannaim" (Hebrew), *Tarbiz*, XX, 104 ff. This and many other unsolved questions make it doubly regrettable that, compared with the vast literature on the ancient Sanhedrin or the trial of Jesus (cf. *supra*, Chaps. VII, n. 16; X, n. 19, 21), there has been no recent attempt to review carefully the available evidence for the story of the Jewish judiciary in the various lands of Jewish settlement during the talmudic period.

45. B.B. 9a, 10b; ARN IV, 5. The debate at Yabneh centered around the verse, "Righteousness exalteth a nation, but sin is a reproach to any people" (Prov. 14: 34). These rabbinic teachings of the expiatory function of alms are based on old traditions. Cf., e.g., Sirach's expressive simile, "A flaming fire doth water quench, so does almsgiving atone for sin" (3:30). The linguistic evolution of the Greek terms referred to in the text is well summarized by H. Bolkenstein on the basis of researches by J. J. van Manen and others. Cf. his *Wohltätigkeit und Armenpflege im vorchristlichen Altertum*, pp. 181 ff., 327 ff., 410, and his essay in *Pisciculi* in honor of F. J. Dölger, pp. 62–65. On Philo, cf. *supra*, Chap. IX, n. 4. Cf. also S. Lieberman's explanation of the evolution of the terms *miṣvah* and *entolé* in the meaning of alms in his "Two Lexicographical Notes," *JBL*, LXV, 69 ff.

46. Shabbat 151b; Gen. r. XXXIII, 3, 304; Lev. r. XXXIV, *passim*. The instability of conditions in the Roman Empire is illustrated by the fact that few imperial fortunes lasted more than two generations. M. Rostovtzeff reports that, according to a pupil's investigations of the situation in Trajan's colony Timgad, most aristocratic families there also retained their wealth only for two generations. That is why, apart from their own sterility, the ruling classes in Rome constantly had to replenish their ranks from upstarts, freedmen, and provincial nobles. Cf. Rostovtzeff's *Social and Economic History of the Roman Empire*, pp. 177, 544, n. 55. Despite the remarkable endurance of the patriarchal dynasty, the continued enjoyment of wealth by any Jewish family for more than a generation or two must have been quite rare in Palestine and even rarer in other parts of the empire.

47. Philo's *De spec. leg.*, II, 21.106; M. Abot III, 8; b. Ta'anit 24a; Ketubot 50a; j. Pe'ah I, 1, 15b; Schechter's *Fragments* 18:2. Historically, it appears, the tradition in j. stating the positive requirement of a self-imposed charitable impost of 20 per cent better fits the emergency situation at Usha than the report in b. Ketubot (repeated in 'Arakhin 28a) that that Synod had merely set a maximum of 20 per cent. The latter has all the earmarks of a later revision in more realistic and permanent terms.

48. B.B. 10b; Sanhedrin 26b (according to Rashi's and the Tosafists' interpretation); B.M. 71a; Sifra, Behar, on Lev. 25:35. That the biblical term "widow" referred only to a solitary woman and not to one who, after her husband's death, returned to her father's house, is rightly stressed in M. David's address on *Der Rechtshistoriker und seine Aufgabe*, p. 21.

49. Lev. r. XXXIV, 4; Beṣah 32b; Julian's *Epistles*, ed. by Wright, III, No. 22. The fullest rabbinic discussions on the problems of charity are found in j. Pe'ah VIII; and b. B.B. 7b–11a, from which were taken many of the above quotations in the text not otherwise identified. In essence these rabbinic views have been repeated, in endless reiteration, by medieval codifiers and moralists, as well as by modern apologists and historians, down to E. Frisch's *Historical Survey of Jewish Philanthropy*, and J. Bergmann's *Ha-Ṣedaqah be-Yisrael* (Charity in Israel; Its History and Institutions), pp.

13 ff., 19 ff. Cf. also A. Cronbach's aforementioned summary of similar views scattered through the apocryphal literature, in *HUCA*, XVIII, 119–56; and A. van Iterson's *Armenzorg bij de Joden in Palestina* (Care of the Poor in Palestine from 100 B.C.E. to 200 C.E.). No one has as yet come to grips, however, with the historically and sociologically more significant problem of the extent to which this theory reflected changing socio-economic situations and the degree of its immediate acceptance by the public. Such an analysis, though arduous and in many phases decidedly problematic, would not seem altogether hopeless, particularly if one were to draw cautious conclusions from the delayed effects of these talmudic teachings during the medieval period.

50. B.B. 21ab. Bacher's chronological revision, replacing Simon ben Shetah by Simon the Just, and Joshua ben Gamala by Joshua ben Perahiah, and thus pushing back both stages of that great educational reform by more than a century, is based on the unwarranted assumption that such a major reform could not have been undertaken in the midst of the turmoil after 66 C.E. Cf. "Das altjüdische Schulwesen," *JJGL*, VI, 48–81. One might argue, on the contrary, that during the initial stages of the revolt against Rome, the extension of educational opportunities to almost all Jewish boys would have been a fitting concession of the ruling classes to an aroused citizenry. It could stem from a mercenary high priest like Joshua ben Gamala, no less than from an outstanding rabbi.

51. Cf. j. Horayot III, 7, 48c; b. 'Erubin 53b f. with reference to II Sam. 23:5; Pesiqta r. XVI, ed. by Friedmann, fol. 83b; Lev. r. VII, 3. L. Blau has suggested that the well-known division of biblical commandments into 365 prohibitions and 248 positive commandments, totaling 613 (*taryag miṣvot*), originated in the schools for adolescents between thirteen and fifteen. Cf. his "Lehren und Gruppieren der Gebote in talmudischer Zeit," *Soncino Blätter*, III, 113–28. From the large (for the most part popular and apologetical) literature on the talmudic system of education, cf. especially, N. Morris's *Jewish School*; N. Drazin's *History of Jewish Education from 515 B.C.E. to 220 C.E.*; and Sir H. Gollancz's *Pedagogics of the Talmud and That of Modern Times*. On the dispersion, cf. W. Bousset's *Jüdisch-christlicher Schulbetrieb in Alexandria und Rom*, and R. Marcus's "Outline of Philo's System of Education" (Hebrew), *Sefer Touroff*, pp. 223–31. Here, of course, the Jews were more deeply affected by Hellenistic educational patterns, participated in gymnastic games, and even organized, as they apparently did in Hypaepa during the second or third century, special Jewish sportive associations. Cf. my *Jewish Community*, III, 16, n. 21; and, more generally, H. I. Marrou's *Histoire de l'éducation dans l'antiquité*, especially the concise chapter on Christianity and classical education (pp. 416 ff., 565 ff.); and M. Schwabe's Hebrew essay "On the Jewish and Graeco-Roman Schools in the Days of the Mishnah and the Talmud," *Tarbiz*, XXI, 112–23. Nor were the Palestinian schools as much devoid of physical education as were the later Jewish schools in the eastern ghettoes. Apart from dietetic rules and ritual ablutions, physical cleanliness was stressed as a religious obligation: "A man ought to wash his face, hands and feet daily in honor of his Creator" (Shabbat 50b, a remarkable variant of the more theologically minded T. Berakhot IV, 1, 8). With similar rationalization Hillel went to the bathouse after every academy session (Lev. r. XXXIV, 3). A father was also enjoined to teach his son swimming, at least as a life-saving precaution (T. Qiddushin I, 11, 336). Cf. also S. Krauss's "Outdoor Teaching in Talmudic Times," *Journal of Jewish Studies*, I, 82–84; and, on the ancient predilection for both reading and praying audibly, E. S. McCartney's succinct "Notes" in *Classical Philology*, XLIII, 184–87.

52. M. Abot V, 24 (most texts read Judah ben Tema, rather than Samuel the Small); b. Qiddushin 30a. The fact that at fifteen a boy was considered mature enough to be introduced to independent research is not at all astonishing. After all at thirteen

he was a full-fledged adult from the point of view of religious law. In fact, at fifteen many Jewish, Egyptian, and even Roman boys were already family fathers. In Persia, too, where the vast majority of the population received no formal education whatsoever, the upper-class minority completed its training at the age of fifteen. Cf. Christensen's *Iran*, pp. 415 ff. It is doubly remarkable, therefore, that R. Simon ben Shetaḥ so early evinced interest in providing schools for boys of sixteen and seventeen. The *kallah* months of Adar and Elul were, of course, entirely devoted to the rehearsal of accomplishments by adults in their private studies during the preceding five months. This institution and its unusual name have been the subject of lengthy debates. To the older literature listed in my *Jewish Community*, III, 33, n. 40, add S. Krauss's more recent Hebrew essay, "The Explanation of the Term 'Kallah Months' in *Tarbiz*, XX, 123–32. Krauss suggests its derivation from *kelala*, or those general principles of the Torah to which Rab himself, possibly the originator of the institution, had been introduced by his uncle, R. Ḥiyya (cf. j. Kilayim IX, 4, 32b). But this etymology is not likely to find any more universal acceptance than the same author's three earlier attempts. On the social life centered around the academies, cf. D. Judilovitz's two Hebrew studies of Pumbedita and Maḥoza.

53. II ARN, XXXI, p. 67; Beṣah 32b; 'Erubin 55a with reference to Deut. 30:12–13; Nedarim 81a; Sanhedrin 96a. Schechter's query (in his note on ARN, *loc. cit.*) on the meaning of *ba'ale batim* (literally, houseowners) reflects the transmutation of the term in the course of years. The original connotation of wealthy, as contrasted with poor persons, is illustrated by M. Shabbat I, 1, which, like R. Johanan's saying, may well go back to the period of Jerusalem's fall. With the subsequent weakening of internal tensions, this term, too, received a more neutral coloring.

54. Berakhot 10b; Ketubot 105ab. Curiously, to assure the necessary technical services for themselves as well as the public at large, the rabbis were rather glad that the professional scribes as a class did not fare too well economically. Said R. Joshua ben Levi, "The Men of the Great Synagogue observed twenty-four fasts in order that the copyists of books, phylacteries and *mezuzot* should not get rich; otherwise they would stop copying" (Pesaḥim 50b). Evidently the drudgery of that profession could not compare with the appeal of the great spiritual and social, though not economic, rewards of scholarship. Cf. also H. Z. Reines's analysis of "The Support of Scholars in the Talmudic Period" (Hebrew), *Sinai*, IX, Nos. 106–7, pp. 137–52; and for some interesting comparative data, F. V. Filson's "Christian Teacher in the First Century," *JBL*, LX, 317–28. It should also be noted that a school often was a very closely knit unit, the pupils regarding their teacher as their father. This relationship had ancient antecedents in both Egypt and Babylonia. Cf. L. Dürr's "Heilige Vaterschaft im Alten Orient," in *Heilige Ueberlieferung. Festschrift für Ildefons Herwegen*, pp. 1 ff. On the other hand, there frequently existed also physical continuity in scholarly families, as pointed out by G. Allon in his "Sons of Scholars" (Hebrew), *Tarbiz*, XX, 84–95.

55. Sanhedrin 38b (the term *pirqa* here actually designates a homiletical type); T. Megillah IV, 41, 228 f.; j. Bikkurim III, 3, 65d; b. Sanhedrin 7b; Philo's *Hypothetica* preserved in Eusebius' *Praeparatio*, VIII, 7 (in Gifford's transl. III, 389 f.). The importance of the legal ingredients in the rabbinic sermons has been stressed particularly by S. Maybaum in "Die ältesten Phasen in der Entwickelung der jüdischen Predigt, I," *Neunzehnter Bericht über die Lehranstalt für die Wissenschaft des Judentums*, pp. 1 ff. The crucial problem of the *Yelamdenu*, that introductory legalistic query which often set the tone for the entire homily, has been elucidated in a lengthy excursus by L. Ginzberg in *Ginze Schechter* (Genizah Studies in Memory of S. Schechter), I, 449–513. Cf. also S. J. Glicksberg's "The *Meturgemanim* [Interpreters] in the Talmudic Period" (Hebrew), *Sinai*, II, Nos. 16–17, pp. 218–21; S. K. Mirsky's "Sermon in the Period of Mishnah and Talmud" (Hebrew), *Horeb*, VII,

75–91; and particularly J. Mann's *Bible as Read and Preached in the Old Synagogue;* and L. Zunz's *Die gottesdienstlichen Vorträge der Juden* which, a standard work for over a century, has more recently appeared in a Hebrew translation carefully revised and brought up to date by C. Albeck under the title *Ha-Derashot be-Yisrael* (Sermons in Israel in Their Historical Evolution).

56. Berakhot 6a (with reference to I Kings 8:28), 24b, 31a; j. Yebamot XII, 6, 13a; Gregory I's *Epistolae,* II, 6 (*MGH,* Epistolae, I, 104). Two years before Pope Gregory, the Council of Narbonne had forbidden Jews to chant funeral psalms (Canon 9 in Mansi's *Concilia,* IX, 1016). Cf. also Juster's *Empire,* I, 368, n. 2–3; E. S. McCartney's remarks in *Classical Philology,* XLIII, 184 ff.; and L. Dürr's *Erziehungswesen im Alten Testament,* p. 22.

57. *Sefer ha-Ma'asim* in the fragment, ed. by J. Mann in *Tarbiz,* I, Pt. 3, p. 8, ll. 21 ff.; Berakhot 11b (cf. here the third-century debate on the "finest of benedictions"); Pesiqta de-R. Kahana XII, fol. 101b; Gen. r. XX, 10, 194. Although probably dating from the early Muslim, rather than Byzantine period in Palestine, the *Sefer ha-Ma'asim* (Book of Halakhic Practice), of which several fragments were published by Mann, B. M. Lewin, and J. N. Epstein, reflects many older Palestinian traditions not recorded in j. It will be discussed more fully, together with other significant halakhic collections under early Islam.

58. Cf. j. Pe'ah I, 1, 15d; Sanhedrin VIII, 2, 26b; T. Megillah III, 7, 224 f.; Shabbat 32a, despite Jer. 39:8. Cf. *supra,* Chap. IV, n. 30. On the complex problem of the origin of "interrupting prayers," cf. my *Jewish Community,* II, 32 ff., III, 112. The chief works on the synagogue still are I. Elbogen's *Gottesdienst;* and S. Krauss's *Synagogale Altertümer.* Cf. also E. Levy's *Yesodot ha-tefillah,* pp. 75 ff.; and the literature listed *supra,* Chaps. VI, n. 17; IX, n. 8; XI, n. 34; to which add N. Makhouly and M. Avi-Yonah's "Sixth-Century Synagogue at 'Isfiya," *QDAP,* III, 118–31; M. Schwabe's "Caesarea Synagogue and Its Inscriptions," *Marx Jub. Vol.,* Hebrew Section, pp. 433–49 (tentatively identifying it with the synagogue which, according to Josephus, played such a great role at the beginning of the Great War, and publishing four inscriptions largely dating from the fourth to the sixth centuries); and F. Mayence's "La Quatrième [*and* La Sixième] Campagne de fouilles à Apamée," *Antiquité classique,* IV, 199–204, VIII, 201–11 (reporting the discovery of the remains of a synagogue dated 391 C.E.; one wonders whether the synagogue gallery mentioned in VIII, 203, was not a woman's compartment).

59. ARN XXXV, 52b; T. B.B. I, 11, 399; Nega'im VI, 2, 625; j. Nazir IX, 3, 57d; M. B.B. II, 9. In this connection, II ARN XXXIX, 54a, refers also to the grave of the prophet Isaiah as having been located within the walls of Jerusalem. On the actual location of the sepulchres of the kings of ancient Israel, cf. the literature mentioned *supra,* Chaps. VIII, n. 19; IX, n. 15. In his "Halakhot Applied to Jerusalem," *Marx Jub. Vol.,* Hebrew section, pp. 351–69, L. Finkelstein has plausibly argued that the debates concerning the graves of kings and prophets took place during the Bar Kocheba revolt, when some of the Zealots tried to remove the remains to an extramural burial place. On the likely Jewish influence in the gradual replacement of cremation by burial in ancient Rome, cf. *supra,* Chap. VI, n. 32. Conversely, Roman Jews, and still more the Christians, were affected by local burial customs. Cf. A. G. Martimort's "Fidélité des premiers chrétiens aux usages romains en matière de sepulture," *Mélanges de la Société toulousaine d'études classiques,* I, 167–89; and, more generally, A. C. Rush's *Death and Burial in Christian Antiquity.* Unfortunately no complete *corpus* of Greek Christian inscriptions, although projected as early as 1898, has yet appeared. Cf. John S. Creaghan and E. A. Raubitschek's comments in their *Early Christian Epitaphs from Athens,* p. 24. Incidentally, some of these epitaphs

may be Jewish, rather than Christian. For example, the curious inscription No. 5, twice mentioning the word *koimeterion* (cemetery), is not adorned by the usual cross.

60. Cf. j. Nazir IX, 3, 57d; Semaḥot I, 7, II, 8, VIII, 13, ed. by Higger, pp. 99, 106, 159 f.; b. Sanhedrin 47a. Diaspora communities, to be sure, were far more tolerant and often accommodated Christians, including Jewish converts to Christianity. Cf. Juster's *Empire*, I, 480, n. 4; and *supra*, Chap. XIII, n. 21. The ramified talmudic funerary regulations and customs are summarized by Maimonides and other codifiers and analyzed in such modern works as S. Klein's *Tod und Begräbnis in Palästina zur Zeit der Tannaiten* and S. Krauss's *Talmudische Archäologie*, II, 54 ff.

61. M.Q. 27ab; j. Berakhot III, 1, 6a (13 cups); b. Ketubot 8b (14 cups). The tradition concerning the thirteen, rather than fourteen cups seems quite authentic. Cf. Ginzberg's *Perushim*, II, 63 ff. The rabbis introduced also various other egalitarian reforms designed to eliminate existing differences in funerary rites between chronically ill and healthy persons, and others. Cf. M.Q. 27ab.

62. T. Megillah IV, 15, 226; b. M.Q. 27b, with Rashi's comments thereon; and Schwabe's interpretation of the Beth She'arim inscription in *BJPES*, IX, 22 ff., 29 f. In his commentary on j. Berakhot III, 1, 6a (*Perushim*, II, 55 f.), to be sure, L. Ginzberg suggested that the Jerusalem societies were engaged only in comforting mourners, not in burying the dead. But it is difficult to see why R. Ishmael should have praised so highly a purely verbal performance. According to Prof. Ginzberg's explanation, moreover, the relatives' obligation ceased when they handed over the corpse to someone in a public mortuary or a street, or even to some "porters." The latter may well have been members of such a friendly society, as is admittedly mentioned in b. M.Q. 27b. Cf. also *supra*, Chap. IX, n. 10, 15. These and other questions point up the need of a new comprehensive study, based on the vast amount of archaeological and literary evidence now available, of ancient Jewish cemeteries, funerary arts and rituals, as well as the communal control over them.

63. Eccles. 12:5; Tobit 3:6; Frey's *Corpus*, I, Nos. 337, 476, 523; Semaḥot X, 8 (ed. by Higger, p. 182). Eschatological hopes must have been in R. Abin the Levite's mind when he warned that, in contrast to a person taking leave of a living friend, one should never part from a dead man by wishing him "Go toward peace" (*le-shalom*, as in Exod. 4:18), but "Go in peace" (*be-shalom*, as in Gen. 15:15). Cf. Berakhot 64a (in M.Q. 29a ascribed to another late Amora, R. Levi bar Ḥayta); and Maimonides' *M.T.*, Ebel, IV, 4. Evidently even if using the Greek formula of "resting in peace," the Jews did not envisage blissful, static eternity, but rather preservation toward dynamic resurrection. This idea is underscored by the Babylonian Talmud (M.Q. 29a), which concludes the discussion with Rab's statement that "scholars have no peace even in the world to come, as it is written, 'They go from strength to strength, every one of them appeareth before God in Zion'" (Ps. 84:8). The Greek-Jewish epitaphs, moreover, often included the entire community in their prayer for peace. Cf. Schwabe's observations in *BJPES*, XII, 65 ff.

CHAPTER XV: TALMUDIC LAW AND RELIGION

1. Cf. j. Pe'ah II, 6, 17a; L. Ginzberg's "Tamid: the Oldest Treatise of the Mishnah," *Journal of Jewish Lore and Philosophy*, I, 33. In his *Hellenism*, pp. 83 ff. S. Lieberman has shown conclusively that long after its "publication" the Mishnah was authoritatively transmitted only through the successive memorizing of its sections by specially designated *tannaim*. Even when it was later confided to writing, its few privately circulated copies enjoyed no authority whatsoever in the academic circles. Older critical investigations of the tannaitic as well as later talmudic and midrashic literature are listed in H. L. Strack's *Introduction to the Talmud and Midrash* and M. Mielziner's *Introduction to the Talmud*, 3d ed. Among more recent studies cf. especially C. Albeck's *Untersuchungen über die Redaktion der Mischna*, his *Untersuchungen über die halakischen Midraschim*, and his *Meḥqarim be-baraita vetosefta* (Studies in the Baraita and Tosefta, and Their Relation to the Talmud); J. N. Epstein's "On the Mishnah of R. Jehuda" (Hebrew), *Tarbiz*, XV, 1–13 (a study of sources) and his " 'The Sages Said' " (Hebrew), *Gulak-Klein Mem. Vol.*, pp. 252–61 (on a significant formula in tannaitic letters); E. S. Artom's "Studi mišnici," *Annuario di studi ebraici*, II, 23–64; A. Guttmann's "Problem of the Anonymous Mishnah," *HUCA*, XVI, 137–55; S. Lieberman's *Tosefeth rishonim* (Commentary on the Tosefta; detailed comments with extensive use of manuscripts and rare editions); B. Cohen's *Mishnah and Tosefta*, I (with notes by L. Ginzberg); A. Spanier's *Toseftaperiode in der tannaitischen Literatur;* M. Higger's "Yerushalmi View of the Authorship of the Tosefta," *PAAJR*, XI, 43–46; B. de Vries's "Mishnah and Tosefta Baba Metzi'a" (Hebrew), *Tarbiz*, XX, 79–83 (showing on the example of this tractate that the compiler of T. used a halakhic collection antedating, and often superior to, the sources of M.); L. Ginzberg's "On the Relations between the Mishnah and the Mekiltah" (Hebrew), *Schorr Mem. Vol.*, pp. 57–95; L. Finkelstein's "Studies in the Tannaitic Midrashim," *PAAJR*, VI, 189–228, his "Sources of the Tannaitic Midrashim," *JQR*, XXXI, 211–43, and his "Transmission of the Early Rabbinic Traditions," *HUCA*, XVI, 115–35.

The need for tightly controlling such transmission, in order to prevent far-reaching cleavages, is self-evident. It is also illustrated by Justinian's (none too successful) efforts to safeguard the integrity of his *Code*, even after its publication. In his much-debated *Constitutio Tanta* the emperor forbade outright that anyone "dare to annex commentaries to these laws" (cap. 21). Cf. the text and its latest detailed analysis by F. Pringsheim in *RIDA*, V, 383–415. An interesting attempt at applying form criticism to the Mishnah was made by F. Maass in his *Formgeschichte der Mischna*, with special reference to the treatise Abot. Because of greater difficulties in dating, other treatises should prove both more difficult and more rewarding. Much could also come from an up-to-date economic, social and *religionsgeschichtliche* investigation of the Talmud, in the light of the ever-increasing archaeological, papyrological, and epigraphic material and of recent Iranological researches. Though merely scratching the surface in his stimulating papers, *Papyri und Talmud in gegenseitiger Beleuchtung;* "Early Christian Epigraphy," *HUCA*, I, 221–37; and "Early Christian Archaeology," *ibid.*, III, 157–214. L. Blau noted the riches in store for the investigator.

2. In his *Perushim*, I, 84 ff., L. Ginzberg has shown that Alfasi's statement reflected the view of some, but not all, geonim and that it was the result of an historic conflict which had begun already in the eighth century. This problem will be more fully discussed in connection with the great halakhic literature created under the Caliphate by the Babylonian academies, which understandably carried on the tradi-

tions of their Sassanian predecessors. Apart from his valuable general introduction (also in an abbreviated English transl.) Ginzberg has supplied in this work many illuminating comments on selected passages of j. So broad, however, is his canvass that the three substantial volumes thus far published cover only four chapters of the first tractate, Berakhot. Significant contributions to the understanding of j. have also been made by S. Lieberman, especially in his *Talmudah shel Qaisarin* (The Talmud of Caesarea), and his *Ha-Yerushalmi ki-peshuto* (Commentary on the Palestinian Talmud), Vol. I. Cf. also Z. W. Rabbinovitz's more old-fashioned "Comments and Notes" entitled *Sha'are torat Ereṣ Yisrael;* and C. Tchernowitz's more popular comparison of *Ha-Babli ve-ha-Yerushalmi* (The Babylonian and Palestinian Talmudim), arguing for the superiority of the Palestinian Talmud in regard to the authenticity of earlier traditions and familiarity with their local background.

This new appreciation of the Palestinian Talmud has curiously been reinforced by some recent critical researches in the Babylonian Talmud as well. For example, after a searching scrutiny of the available, for the most part very equivocal, source material, J. Kaplan has suggested, against the regnant opinion, that neither R. Ashi nor Rabina was the actual redactor of the Babylonian Talmud, but that "the *gemara* [brief halakhic conclusions] of R. Ashi accompanied by Saboraic expositions, makes up the bulk of the present Talmud" (*Redaction of the Babylonian Talmud,* p. 307). Other important contributions in this field include C. Albeck's "Studies in the (Babylonian) Talmud, I–II" (Hebrew), *Tarbiz,* III, 1–14, IX, 163–78, his "On the Editing of the Babylonian Talmud" (Hebrew), *Gulak-Klein Mem. Vol.,* pp. 1–12, and *Tarbiz,* XV, 14–26 (on early compilations and sources, respectively); A. Weiss's *Le-Qorot hithavut ha-Babli* (Studies in the Development of the Babylonian Talmud; on two technical terms), and his *Hithavut ha-talmud bi-shlemuto* (The Babylonian Talmud as a Literary Unit). Going even further than Kaplan, Weiss, who had at first suggested the identification of R. Ashi and Rabina with later sages (cf. his "Problème de la rédaction du Talmud de Babylon par R. Aši à la lumière de la lettre de Šerira," *REJ,* CII, 111), ultimately came to the conclusion that, although we may identify a first collection of Amoraic statements in the school of Pumbedita under R. Judah (before 300), the Babylonian Talmud had not been fully edited by R. Ashi, Rabina, or any other redactor. Cf. also his "Critical Notes on Mishnah and Talmud" (Hebrew), *Schorr Mem. Vol.,* pp. 127–48; and, from other angles, S. Federbusch's *Ḥiqre talmud* (Studies in the Talmud); and J. J. Weinberg's *Meḥqarim ba-Talmud* (Studies in the Talmud), Vol. I.

A useful reference work is J. Umanski's alphabetical list of *Ḥakhme ha-Talmud* (The Sages of the Talmud) indicating all passages quoted in their names in the Babylonian Talmud. A comprehensive compilation of talmudic and geonic comments on the Pentateuch has been prepared by M. M. Kasher in his *Ḥumash torah shelemah* (The Pentateuch with the Commentary "Oral Law"). M. M. Guttmann's voluminous *Mafte'aḥ ha-Talmud* (Talmudic Lexicon) unfortunately bogged down in the first letter of the alphabet, but an even more comprehensive talmudic encyclopedia devoted to talmudic law is now being prepared by a number of Israeli scholars. Entitled *Enṣiklopediah talmudit le-'inyene halakhah,* and ed. by M. Berlin and S. J. Zevin, it has thus far been brought up to the end of the first letter. For more popular use one may mention A. Cohen's *Everyman's Talmud;* and the respective chapters in M. Waxman's *History of Jewish Literature,* Vol. I (with selected bibliography).

3. As we shall see, such apocrypha are particularly numerous in mystic writings. Continuing the tradition of the books of Enoch, Baruch, or Ezra, many ancient and medieval compilers of mystical lucubrations preferred to attribute them to such an outstanding ancient sage as R. 'Aqiba or R. Simon ben Yoḥai. But the transition from mystical to rationalist Aggadah is often blurred. In the general field of Midrash most of the energies have been absorbed in recent years by the detection and publication of new manuscripts (see n. 6). Among the more significant analytical studies

cf. Albeck's notes on Zunz's *Ha-Derashot* and his "Midrash Leviticus Rabbah," *Ginzberg Jub. Vol.*, Hebrew section, pp. 25–43; S. Lieberman's lecture on *Midreshe Teman* (Yemenite Midrashim), and his *Shkiin*. The debate over the authenticity of the rabbinic citations in Raymond Martini's work, here asserted, will be discussed in connection with the medieval religious controversies. An enormous mass of comparative material is assembled in the notes to Ginzberg's *Legends* (Vols. V–VI); cf. B. Heller's extensive review thereof in *JQR*, XXIV–XXV. The crucial question of the "Dating of Aggadic Materials" has been briefly analyzed by B. J. Bamberger in *JBL*, LXVIII, 115–23, with reference to Goodenough's critique of Wolfson (cf. *supra*, Chap. VI, n. 46). Bamberger seems to go too far, however, in assuming that, because few aggadic sources can be definitely dated and some may reach back to remote antiquity, one may readily accept ancient origins of most rabbinic teachings.

4. Although in his recent comparative study of "Rabbinic Methods of Interpretation and Hellenistic Rhetoric," *HUCA*, XXII, 239–64, D. Daube has made a strong case for Greek influences on the rabbis, particularly in the formative days of Hillel, he has not paid sufficient attention to the differences between them. Cf. also S. Lieberman's *Hellenism*, pp. 47 ff. Among earlier scholars, A. Schwarz, in particular, has devoted a lifetime to the scholarly exploration of the hermeneutic categories used in talmudic dialectics. Cf. his general summary of a number of detailed monographs in "Die Hauptergebnisse der wissenschaftlichen-hermeneutischen Forschung," *Scripta Universitatis atque Bibliothecae Hierosolymitarum*, Vol. I, No. ix. Among more recent contributions, cf., especially, M. Ostrowski's *Ha-Middot she-ha-torah nidreshet ba-hen* (The Logical Categories in the Hermeneutic Interpretation of Scripture); and M. A. Amiel's *Sefer ha-Middot le-ḥeqer ha-halakhah* (The Book of Logical Categories in the Study of Jewish Law; this work includes a lengthy introduction on the methods and history of research in this field). On the hermeneutics of the Midrash, cf. especially H. G. Enelow's aforementioned ed. of *The Mishnah of Rabbi Eliezer*. Cf. also E. Stein's "Homiletische Peroratio im Midrasch," *HUCA*, VIII–IX, 353–71.

5. Condemnation and burning of the Talmud was to contribute much to the poisoning of all Judeo-Christian relations in the Middle Ages. These medieval debates were continued also in modern times, finding expression, in particular, in Eisenmenger's compilation of anti-Christian and anti-Gentile passages, genuine as well as spurious, included in talmudic letters. As we shall see, Eisenmenger served as the fountainhead of a vast antisemitic literature, which was in turn extensively copied, particularly in the Nazi period. Alfred Rosenberg, chief ideologist of the Nazi movement, himself published a pamphlet on the *Unmoral im Talmud*. Cf. also A. Fasolt's *Grundlagen des Talmud* (frequently reprinted); and various other publications cited by B. Z. Bokser in "Talmudic Forgeries," *Contemporary Jewish Record*, II, Pt. 4, pp. 6–22; and by C. Bloch in his *Hechal l'divre chazal* (Concordance of Quotations from Talmud . . . and Medieval Hebrew Literature), pp. 39–110.

6. Cf. E. N. Adler's brief and rather incomplete survey of "Talmudic Manuscripts and Editions" in *Essays Hertz*, pp. 15–17. Even the best-versed talmudic scholar still suffers from the lack of a critical edition of the two Talmudim. The great, but incomplete, work of R. Rabbinovicz, *Sefer Diqduqe Soferim*, in 15 volumes, supplemented by H. Ehrentreu's Vol. XVI, shows how many important variants may be expected from a thorough collation of the much larger firsthand material now available. The impression is confirmed by H. Malter's critical edition of *Massekhet Ta'anit* (The Treatise Ta'anit of the Babylonian Talmud). On the grave obstacles to such an undertaking, however, cf. V. Aptowitzer's very competent discussion in his "Sous quelle forme une édition critique du Talmud est-elle possible et admissible?" *REJ*, XCI, 205–17. The Palestinian Talmud has fared even worse. There is not even an

edition comparable to that of Vilna for the Babylonian collection, prepared with great care by old-type rabbinic scholars. Among the extant manuscripts, that of Leiden, though it underlay the first printed edition, has retained some independent value. Cf. J. N. Epstein's remarks in *Tarbiz*, V, 257–72, VI, 38–55; and S. Lieberman's "Further Notes on the Leiden Ms. of the Jerushalmi" (Hebrew), *ibid.*, XX, 107–17. The Cairo Genizah has yielded a number of significant fragments, many of them published by L. Ginzberg in his *Seride ha-Yerushalmi* (Yerushalmi Fragments from the Genizah), Vol. I; and *Ginze Schechter*, I, 430 ff.; by J. N. Epstein in *Tarbiz*, III, 15–26, 121–36, 237–48; S. Wiedder, *ibid.*, XVII, 129–37 (a Budapest fragment, with notes by J. N. Epstein); and by S. Loewinger in *Marx Jub. Vol.*, Hebrew section, pp. 237–86 (likewise from the Budapest collection, with notes by S. Lieberman). These and other texts were utilized by Lieberman in his monographs mentioned in n. 3 and in his numerous "Emendations on the Jerushalmi" (Hebrew), *Tarbiz*, Vols. II–V; cf. also, from another angle, his analytical survey of "The Old Commentators on the Yerushalmi," *Marx Jub. Vol.*, Hebrew section, pp. 287–319. Perhaps the new edition, planned in Jerusalem as part of an ambitious venture of republishing both Talmudim, may yield, if not yet a truly critical, a more satisfactory edition than that of Krotoschin, heretofore the main reference text for scholars. Cf. in this connection, M. M. Kasher's discussion of the principles for "A New Edition of the Babylonian Talmud" (Hebrew), *Talpioth*, III, 475–96.

Greater progress had been made in recent years with the critical editing and textual investigations of some parts of tannaitic and midrashic literature. Among the most notable achievements is J. N. Epstein's *Mabo le-nusaḥ ha-Mishnah* (An Introduction to the Mishnah Text), Vols. I–II. Cf. also G. Beer's photographic reproduction of the *Mischnacodex Kaufmann*; P. Kahle's "Mishnah Text in Babylonia, I–II," *HUCA*, X, 195–222, XII–XIII, 275–325; and C. J. Kasovsky's *Oṣar leshon ha-Mishnah* (Concordance to the Mishnah) and *Oṣar leshon ha-Tosefta* (Thesaurus Tosephtae); and such critical studies as J. Goldin's of "The Two Versions of Abbot de Rabbi Nathan" in *HUCA*, XIX, 97–120; A. Guttmann's "Tractate Abot—Its Place in Rabbinic Literature," *JQR*, XLI, 181–93; and particularly L. Finkelstein's carefully documented *Mabo le-Massektot Abot* (Introduction to the Treatises Abot and Abot of Rabbi Nathan). Other important editions include C. Albeck's completion of *Bereschit Rabba* (begun by J. Theodor in 1912); I. A. Rabin's completion of the *Mekilta de-Rabbi Ishmael* (begun by H. S. Horowitz); J. Z. Lauterbach's edition of the same work; that of *Sifre* on Deuteronomy by L. Finkelstein; S. Lieberman's ed. of *Midrash Debarim rabbah* (Deut. r.); and those of the *Midrash Haggadol* on Genesis by M. Margulies (improved version of an earlier ed. by S. Schechter); on Leviticus by E. N. Rabinovitz; on Numbers [1–5] by S. Fish; and on Deuteronomy by M. Z. Ḥasidah in *Hassegullah*, Nos. 1–40 (incomplete). Cf. also Finkelstein's studies of "The Mekilta and Its Text," *PAAJR*, V, 3–54, his "Fragments of an Unknown Midrash on Deuteronomy," *HUCA*, XII–XIII, 523–57, and "Notes and Emendations on the Sifra," *Ginzberg Jub. Vol.*, Hebrew section, pp. 305–22 (listing, on pp. 317 f., 15 editions and 11 manuscripts preparatory to a critical ed. of this work); J. Mann's "Some Midrashic Genizah Fragments," *HUCA*, XIV, 303–58, and his *Bible as Read and Preached*. Some other midrashic manuscripts (chiefly medieval compilations) have also appeared in the periodical *Hassegullah*, ed. in the 1930's by Ḥasidah. M. Higger, who has done yeoman's service in publishing critically sifted editions (some with English translations) of lesser rabbinic writings (cf. his *Masekhtot Zeirot* [Small Treatises]; *Sheba masekhtot qetanot* [Seven Minor Treatises]; *Masekhet Semaḥot; Masekhtot Derekh ereṣ; Masekhtot Kallah; Massekhet Sopherim*), has also compiled and systematically arranged the voluminous quotations from tannaitic sources scattered through the Talmud under the title *Oṣar ha-baraitot* (Thesaurus of Baraitot). Although somewhat marred by frequent repetitions and dubious chronologies, this pioneering effort will facilitate future research in the early rabbinic traditions. Y. Yunovitch who, under the sponsorship of the American Academy for Jewish Research, had undertaken the compilation of a complete concordance of the halakhic midrashim, died before completing this task. Reference may also be made here again to H. Lichtenstein's critical edition of the *Megillat Ta'anit, HUCA*, VIII–IX.

For nontalmudists the task is somewhat facilitated now by the availability of some more or less adequate translations. The older German translation of the Babylonian Talmud by L. Goldschmidt (published in a larger edition with, and a smaller edition without the Hebrew text) has largely been superseded by the new English translation issued in 34 vols. by the Soncino Press under the editorship of I. Epstein. We are less fortunate with respect to the Palestinian Talmud. Its French transl. by M. Schwab chiefly has pioneering merits. Tannaitic sources have, naturally enough, been more frequently translated. An English transl. of the Mishnah by H. Danby, is now being superseded by a collective work under the editorship of J. D. Herzog. Combined with the Hebrew text, it is also more fully annotated. A Mishnah translation is, of course, much easier than that of the Talmud on account of the greater lucidity of the original, the numerous previous attempts at editing and translating it, the availability of some good manuscripts, and the aid of a concordance. Cf. also Lauterbach's transl. of Mekilta; P. P. Levertoff's selective version of *Midrash Sifre on Numbers; Midrash Rabbah*, transl. under the editorship of H. Freedman and M. Simon; and C. G .Montefiore and H. Loewe's *Rabbinic Anthology*. Needless to say that even the best Western translations cannot quite reproduce the flavor and depth of the original pithy rabbinic sayings and dialectical debates. Even the collective scholarly attempt at editing and translating the Mishnah by G. Beer, O. Holtzmann, S. Krauss, and others has met with many adverse criticisms. Cf. C. Albeck's strictures (in his "Aus der neuesten Mischnaliteratur," *MGWJ*, LXXIII, 4–25), which, while needlessly sharp in tone, are not without justification. Cf. also G. Kittel's "Grundsätzliches und Methodisches zu den Uebersetzungen rabbinischer Texte," *Angelos*, I, 60–64.

7. Needless to say that this dichotomy between Halakhah and Aggadah never seemed so sharp to an ancient talmudist. To begin with, he was a great believer in study for study's sake. He indulged therefore with equal zest in the hermeneutic elaboration of Scripture, whether the results shed new light on a legal or a homiletical problem. J. J. Neubauer goes too far, however, in placing the main accent on hermeneutics per se, neglecting the essentially pragmatic approach of the rabbis who untiringly emphasized the superiority of good works over abstract study. Cf. his otherwise stimulating Hebrew essay on "Halakhah and Halakhic Hermeneutics," *Sinai*, XI, Nos. 128–30, pp. 49–80. Cf. also H. Z. Hirschberg and B. Murmelstein's judicious analysis of *Yaḥas ha-aggadah la-halakhah* (The Relation between Aggadah and Halakhah). In view of the unity of the human mind, moreover, the two disciplines often indistinguishably blended in the mind of the preacher and teacher. That is why one may learn many legally relevant data from the rabbinic homilies, too. This age-old truism has been well illustrated by S. K. Mirsky's more recent attempt to analyze, in the sequence of Karo's major *Code,* the "Sources of Halakhah in Midrashic Literature" (Hebrew), *Talpioth*, Vols. I–III. Cf. also, more generally, A. Marmorstein's "Observations on the Historic Importance of the Aggadah" (Hebrew) in his *Studies*, pp. 77–92; his "Place of Popular Traditions in the History of Religions" (Hebrew), *Edoth*, I, 75–89, 138–50; and particularly I. Heinemann's comprehensive analysis of the *Darkhe ha-aggadah* (The Methods of the Aggadah).

8. B.M. 62ab; Gittin 19b. After a careful comparison of the relatively few direct talmudic references to Persian law with the fragments of a Sassanian lawbook, ed. in several installments by C. Bartholomae (cf. his *Ueber ein sasanidisches Rechtsbuch,* and other studies), H. Finkelscherer came to the conclusion that the Talmud must have had in mind some other, probably earlier, version of these laws. Cf. "Zur Frage fremder Einflüsse auf das talmudische Recht," *MGWJ*, LXXIX, 441. The numerous parallels, on the other hand, between these Persian laws and those of the Palestinian

Mishnah may, in part, reflect certain common roots in both ancient Babylonian and Hellenistic laws and, in part, merely have resulted from independent responses to similar wants. Cf. also S. J. Bulsara's fuller ed. and English transl. of the *Laws of the Ancient Persians;* and, more generally, A. Christensen's "Introduction bibliographique à l'histoire du droit de l'Iran ancien," *Archives d'histoire du droit oriental,* II, 243–57. In modified form the Persian law code was adapted to Christian uses by the Metropolitan Ishobokht in the eighth century. This adaptation was published with a German transl. by E. Sachau under the title *Syrische Rechtsbücher.* On Jewish influences thereon, cf. *infra,* n. 14. Only the surface of these complex interrelations has thus far been scratched. They urgently call for comprehensive reëxamination through the coöperation of competent talmudists, Iranologists, and legal historians.

9. Cf. S. Krauss's *Griechische und lateinische Lehnwörter,* II, 630 f.; S. Lieberman's *Greek in Jewish Palestine, passim,* and some of his essays. More recently, N. H. Torczyner has made a case for interpreting a rather incomprehensible statement of R. Johanan in j. Pesaḥim VIII, 1, 35d, as a corruption of a Roman legal term *regale* (or *legale*) *repudium;* see his Hebrew essay in *Lewy Mem. Vol.,* pp. 59–64.

10. The story of the two Roman soldiers studying the Torah under R. Gamaliel, as told in j. B.Q. IV, 3, 4b, winds up with the statement that, heeding these objections, Gamaliel proclaimed a prohibition of unlawfully appropriating Gentile property, "because of the desecration of the name" of the Lord. On the other hand, it allays the reader's apprehensions by saying that, by a miracle, the two soldiers forgot all they had learned before they reached Tyre and hence could not reveal the contents of Jewish law to the Gentile public. This was entirely in line with the rabbinic insistence that one ought not to teach Torah to Gentiles, a law incidentally adopted later by medieval Islam as well. None the less the Jews certainly obeyed other similar official orders. Whenever it was in their interest to solicit the intervention of Roman officials to execute the judgment of a Jewish court, they also doubtless acquainted these strangers with the provisions of their law.

Jewish isolationism reached its extreme form in this double standard of law and morals, when applied to Jews and non-Jews. While most ancient laws contained discriminatory provisions between group members and outsiders, some rabbis went to great lengths in legalizing proceedings against Gentiles that were otherwise generally prohibited by the Bible. They interpreted biblical phrases like "neighbor" or "brother" as applying to Jews alone. In a most flagrant instance, R. Ishmael is recorded always to have favored a Jewish party against any non-Jewish litigant who had the temerity to appear before him. "If Jewish law was favorable to the Jewish party, he applied it, but when Gentile law could be invoked to better advantage, he invoked the latter." To justify such arbitrary proceedings, he cited the Deuteronomist's injunction, "Hear the cause between your brethren and judge righteously" (1:16) as referring only to litigations among "brethren." To which R. Simon ben Gamaliel sharply retorted that one ought to judge parties by whichever law they wished to be judged and then strictly adhere to it (Sifre on Deut. 16, ed. by Friedmann, fol. 68b; ed. by Finkelstein, pp. 26 f.). Finally, R. Abbahu, echoing Rab, interpreted, in a philologically admissible fashion, Habakkuk's phrase (3:6), *va-yatter goyim* (usually translated, "maketh nations to tremble") to mean that God permitted (*ve-hittir*) the appropriation of Gentile nations' money by Israel. To appease his conscience, however, this Caesarean rabbi, freely associating with non-Jews, added the rationale that, since the sons of Noah had been derelict in the observance of the seven Noahide commandments accepted by them, they were no longer subject to the protective laws administered by righteous judges, which was one of these commandments. These and other discriminatory rabbinic laws reflecting the great intergroup tensions of the talmudic age, show the seamy side of the separatist talmudic legislation. This part has, of course, been exploited to the full by the antisemitic assailants of the Talmud. Cf. the far calmer "Note sur la responsabilité d'un Juif pour dommages causés à un païen" by B. Cohen in *REJ*, LXXXIX, 164–68.

11. The *Collatio legum Mosaicarum et Romanarum*, ed. with an English transl. by M. Hyamson in 1913, has been the subject of searching investigations, especially since its reëxamination in 1930 by E. Volterra in *Memorie* of the R. Accademia Nazionale dei Lincei, CCCXXVII, 5–123. Cf. especially G. Scherillo's review of Volterra's study in *Archivio giuridico Serafini*, CIV, 255–65; and that of E. Lewy in *Zeitschrift für Rechtsgeschichte*, L, 698–705. More recently N. Smits, in his *Mosaicarum et Romanarum legum collatio*, tried to prove again that the author was a Christian, who, although neither a theologian nor a jurist, undertook in the years 390–438 to demonstrate through this comparison the supremacy of Christianity. In his *Ursprung und Zweck der Collatio Mosaicarum et Romanarum Legum*, K. von Hohenlohe wanted to be even more specific and to identify St. Ambrose as the author. Cf. also his (rather lame) defense against adverse criticisms of this view in *Archiv für katholisches Kirchenrecht*, CXIX, 352–64. I. Ostersetzer, on the other hand, has advanced the theory that the author was a Jew (probably a member of the patriarchal family) who tried to weaken the recurrent attacks on Jewish law, which ultimately led to the edict of 398, by pointing out the similarities of the two systems. Cf. "La 'Collatio Legum Mosaicarum et Romanarum.' Ses origines—son but," *REJ*, XCVII, 65–96. Cf. also D. Daube's note on "Collatio 2.6.5" in *Essays Hertz*, pp. 111–29, simply taking its Jewish origin for granted. This entire problem awaits further elucidation. Of independent value is F. Schulz's reinvestigation of "The Manuscripts of the *Collatio*" in *Symbolae J. C. van Owen*, pp. 313–32.

Modern monographs on environmental legal influences on the Talmud include A. Gulak's "General Comparison between the Spirit of Jewish and That of Roman Civil Law" (Hebrew), *Madda'e ha-Yahadut*, I, 45–50; I. Jeiteles's "Fremdes Recht im Talmud," *JJLG*, XXI, 109–28; and S. Lieberman's "Roman Legal Institutions in Early Rabbinics and in the Acta Martyrum," *JQR*, XXXV, 1–57 (illustrating reflections of Roman practices, rather than their influence on Jewish or Canon Law). Cf. also S. Rubin's comparative study, *Das talmudische Recht auf den verschiedenen Stufen seiner Entwicklung mit dem römischen verglichen*, I–II. A brief sketch of the history of these comparative studies is given in B. Cohen's "Relationship of Jewish to Roman Law," *JQR*, XXXIV, 267 ff. Despite the vast array of writings on the subject, Cohen, with an overdose of diffidence, came to the melancholy conclusion that "a critical comparison between Roman and Jewish law has hardly been inaugurated" (p. 423).

12. Ketubot 86a; Qiddushin 47b f. On the legalization of antichretic transactions, cf. *supra*, Chap. XIV, n. 28. Persia, to be sure, had a developed law of antichresis, which may well have affected the rabbinic views. Cf. A. Pagliaro's "Anticresi nel diritto sāsānidico," *Rivista degli studi orientali*, XV, 275–315. However, since Jews were in the front rank of merchants and bankers in the generally backward empire, it would seem that it was they who set the pace in developing such new commercial facilities. Despite occasional nods of approval toward Persian customs, the Jews resisted new legal practices, just as they refused to borrow even new loan words from their neighbors. Cf. 'A.Z. 24b, 71a; and *supra*, Chap. XIII, n. 38.

13. Cf. Gulak's *Urkundenwesen im Talmud*. On the "Persistence of Rejected Customs in Palestine," cf. L. Finkelstein's illustrations in *JQR*, XXIX, 179–86. Cf. also A. Guttmann's "Stellung des Minhag im Talmud," *MGWJ*, LXXXIII, 226–38; and M. Vogelmann's "Local and Provincial Customs" (Hebrew), *Sinai*, IX, 362–73. Gulak's quest for Hellenistic parallels to Jewish law has, nevertheless, proved very fruitful, and it is to be hoped that younger scholars trained in jurisprudence, the Talmud,

and papyrology will carry on these researches, which ought to be extended, particularly, also into the field of demotic papyri. Cf. Gulak's own remarks in *Urkundenwesen*, pp. 159 f. Cf. also his "Aeltere talmudische Parallelen zur Novelle 97 des Kaisers Justinian," *Zeitschrift für vergleichende Rechtswissenschaft*, XLVII, 241–55.

14. Cf., especially, A. Gulak's *Toledot ha-mishpaṭ*, I, 49 ff., and R. Taubenschlag's *Law of Greco-Roman Egypt*, pp. 212, 228 f. The influence of Christian, and indirectly Mosaic concepts, on the Code of Justinian in the area of "natural law," which was to play an increasing role in medieval and early modern legal philosophy, is carefully reviewed by B. Biondi in "La Concezione cristiana del diritto naturale nella codificazione giustinianea," *RIDA*, IV, 129–58. More directly Jewish, indeed talmudic influences on (undoubtedly often merely parallels to) Syro-Christian law have been analyzed particularly by V. Aptowitzer in *Die syrischen Rechtsbücher und das mosaisch-talmudische Recht;* and his brief summaries of "The Influence of Jewish Law on the Development of Jurisprudence in the Christian Orient," *JQR*, I, 217–29; and, with modifications, in a more recent Hebrew essay in *Gulak-Klein Mem. Vol.*, pp. 223–51. On the other hand, continued influences emanating from ancient oriental, particularly Babylonian, laws on talmudic legislation in Persia and even Palestine have been more postulated than studied. Cf., e.g., H. M. Weil's "Cautionnement talmudique comparé aux institutions correspondantes de l'Ancien Orient," *Archives d'histoire du droit oriental*, III, 167–208.

15. "Fictions have been condemned," writes S. Goldman, "as 'fraudulents,' and defended as 'invaluable expedients for overcoming the rigidity of the Law.' The choice of judgment will vary with one's approach." Cf. his "Legal Fiction in Jewish Law," *Studia semitica et orientalia* (Presentation Vol. to W. B. Stevenson), II, 72. It is small wonder, then, that this expedient has troubled the conscience of many modern investigators of legal systems in which they had an emotional stake, and has therefore produced a variety of apologetically colored juridical reasonings. Among more recent discussions of the talmudic legal fiction, cf. also the Hebrew essays by J. S. Zuri in *Lewin Jub. Vol.*, pp. 174–95, and by S. Atlas in *Ginzberg Jub. Vol.*, pp. 1–24.

16. A most useful introduction to the whole system of talmudic law in modern terms still is, after more than a quarter century, A. Gulak's *Yesode ha-mishpaṭ ha-'ibri* (Principles of Jewish Law). Cf. also I. Herzog's *Main Institutions of Jewish Law*. Many of the innumerable monographs on certain phases have been listed here in various connections. A great many others are systematically reviewed in S. Eisenstadt's bibliographical guide entitled *En Mishpaṭ*. Cf. also E. Roth's *Etude du système juridique juif;* R. Sugranyes de Franch's *Etudes sur le droit palestinien à l'époque evangelique;* B. Cohen's "Canons of Interpretation of Jewish Law," *Proceedings of the Rabbinical Assembly of America*, V, 170–88, and "Contractatio in Jewish and Roman Law," *RIDA*, II, 133–56; I. Ostersetzer's "Research in the Spirit of Hebrew Law" (Hebrew), *Sefer ha-Shanah li-Yehude Polaniah* (Polish-Jewish Yearbook), I, 35–60, and "Parhedrin-Parertin," *Zion*, IV, 294–306 (on legal terms pertaining to the high priesthood, etc.); L. Fischer's "Urkunden im Talmud," *JJLG*, Vols. IX, XIII, XIX, XX; F. E. Laupheimer's study of "Die ausserpentateuchischen Quellen der Sabbatgesetze," *JJLG*, XXII, 161–211; D. Daube's "Zur frühtalmudischen Rechtspraxis," *ZAW*, L, 148–59; P. Dikshtein's *Dine 'Oneshin* (Criminal Law); S. Ladier's *Proces karny w Talmudzie* (Criminal Procedure in the Talmud); and S. Gut's dissertation, *Die Religionsverbrechen nach jüdischem Recht*.

17. W. M. Feldman in *Rabbinical Mathematics and Astronomy*, pp. 220 f. Although largely based on secondary and in part obsolete studies, this volume offers a useful summary. Galen's aforementioned objection (cf. *supra*, Chap. XII, n. 39) that Jews

followed accepted literary authorities rather than new scientific discoveries is doubtless true in the whole realm of science. None the less, practical needs often gained the upper hand.

18. B.B. 73–74. Modern scholarship, too, has been greatly intrigued by these stories. Nearly half a century ago, J. Z. Lauterbach counted some twenty scholarly essays on Rabbah and his tales. Cf. Lauterbach's article on that rabbi in *JE*, X, 290 f. Among more recent studies, cf. especially A. Karlin's "Fantastic Stories of Rabbah Bar Bar Chana" (Hebrew), *Sinai*, X, Nos. 116–18, pp. 56–65; and G. Szalem's "Rabbah bar bar Ḥana and the Travelers' Talk" (Hebrew), *ibid.*, XII, Nos. 141–42, pp. 108–11. As in many other areas of Jewish scholarship, diffused by countries and languages, many of these writers were unfamiliar with the works of their predecessors. On the earlier geographic knowledge of the ancient Hebrews, cf. *supra*, Chap. VIII, n. 8. Much can also be learned from sectarian sources, however much these may be overlaid with legendary and mythological materials. Even the Mandaeans, despite their deep-rooted hatred of Jews whom they styled the "creators of the works of darkness," accepted much of the world outlook of Judaism. Cf. G. Furlani's study of "I Pianeti e lo zodiaco nella religione dei Mandei," in *Atti* of the Accademia dei Lincei, 8th ser., II, 119–87 (especially pp. 179 f.). Cf. also, more generally, P. Gordon, *L'Image du monde dans l'Antiquité.*

19. Berakhot 58b. "The *Mishnat ha-Middot* teaches us two important lessons," writes S. Gandz, "first that in the time of the Mishnah there was a certain degree of Greek influence upon Jewish education in Palestine. And second that in the beginnings of Islam there was a certain degree of Jewish influence not only in the religious but also in the scientific aspects of Muslim life" ("Studies in Hebrew Mathematics and Astronomy," *PAAJR*, IX, 16). Cf. his edition of the *Mishnat ha-Middot;* his "Studies in History of Mathematics in Hebrew and Arabic Sources," *HUCA*, VI, 263 ff., 275; his more recent "Studies in the Hebrew Calendar, I–II," *JQR*, XXXIX, 259–80, XL, 157–72, 251–77, and "Origin of the Planetary Week," *PAAJR*, XVIII, 213–54; and other illustrations in S. Lieberman's *Hellenism*, pp. 180 ff. On talmudic medicine and eugenics, cf. the literature listed *supra*, Chap. XIV, n. 21. That Mar Samuel and other Babylonian Jewish scientists had access also to Eastern sources of knowledge is evident, since Shapur I had made a special effort to secure *pehlevi* translations of Indian as well as Greek scientific works.

20. 'Erubin 21b with reference to Eccles. 12:12; M. Makkot III, 16. Cf. M. Y. Guttmann's "Historic Foundations of the Definitions of Commandments" (Hebrew), *Sinai*, I, Pt. 2, pp. 373–87. On the much-debated relationships between the rabbinic ideas of justice and mercy, cf. E. Sjöberg's *Gott und die Sünder im palästinischen Judentum;* and, more generally, S. Federbusch's *Ha-Musar ve-ha-mishpaṭ be-Yisrael* (Ethics and Law in Israel); S. Z. Pines's *Musar ha-miqra ve-ha-talmud* (Ethics of Bible and Talmud); and I. H. Weisfeld's *Ethics of Israel.* Of considerable interest are also the more popular selections from ancient, medieval, and modern sources, cited in German translation in *Die Lehren des Judentums nach den Quellen*, ed. by S. Bernfeld and F. Bamberger.

21. Pesaḥim 54a; T. Qiddushin I, 14–15, 337, with reference to Ez. 33:12; b. 40b; Sanhedrin 44a, 107b; M. Yoma VIII, 8–9; b. 87a; Berkhot 34b. These extensions of Ezekiel's teachings are but another illustration of the fact that, the doctrine of repentance having long been accepted as one of the corner stones of Judaism, variations of personal temper and social situations found expression merely in nuances of emphasis, rather than in basic approaches. On the difference between the Jewish and Christian doctrine of "Original Sin," cf. also S. Cohon's comprehensive analysis in HUCA, XXI, 275–330; and, more generally, W. Hirsch's *Rabbinic Psychology*, and

A. Marmorstein's collected *Studies in Jewish Theology.* Cf. also H. Karpp's *Probleme altchristlicher Anthropologie.*

22. Cf. Sifre on Num. 112, ed. by Friedmann, fol. 33a (here an Epicurean is identified simply with a man who "hath broken his [the Lord's] commandment," Num. 15:31); j. Sanhedrin X, 1, 27d; Tanḥuma on Gen. 1:1 (ed. by Buber, fol. 1b); Gen. r. IX, end, 68, X, 2, 85. Cf. also other sources cited by J. Bergmann in his "Schicksal eines Namens," *MGWJ,* LXXXI, 210–18; and A. Marmorstein's older review of "Les 'Épicuriens' dans la littérature rabbinique," *REJ,* LIV, 181–93. One wonders whether in the saying attributed to R. Jose that "those who calculate the end of days . . . , haters of scholars and their disciples, false prophets, and those who spread slander have no share in the world to come" (Masekhtot Derekh ereṣ, Tosefta, VI, 13, ed. by Higger, pp. 313 f.; a variation of the English transl. p. 117), the second category does not refer to that permanent nuisance of scholars, the "Epicurean" skeptic. This type is, indeed, expressly barred from the world to come in M. Sanhedrin X, 1, and T. XIII, 5, 434. It is also against such "smart-alecky" debaters that the sages enjoined their pupils to be prepared with adequate answers (M. Abot II, 19).

23. Num. r. XII, 4; Gen. r. LXVIII, 11, 777 f., with Albeck's note thereon; Exod. r. III, 6; L. Baeck's *Pharisees,* p. 138. It was left to the medieval philosophers to articulate some of these and other paradoxes and to uncover their perplexing logical implications.

24. Shabbat 63a; Ketubot 111a; Sanhedrin 98a. Cf. *supra,* Chaps. XI, n. 37; XII, n. 16. Cf. also numerous other passages cited in M. Higger's *Jewish Utopia;* A. Marmorstein's "Participation à la vie éternelle dans la théologie rabbinique et dans la légende," *REJ,* LXXXIX, 305–20 (also in his *Studieȝ,* pp. 162–78), and "Ideas of Redemption in the Aggadah of the Amoraim" (Hebrew), *Meṣudah,* I, 94–105.

25. Ketubot 111a; Sirach 10:25. This frequently anarchical diversity of theologoumena, aggravated by the staggering difficulties in dating, offers a serious obstacle to modern investigators of rabbinic eschatology. Not only such synthesizers of a large range of talmudic theology as Schechter, Kohler, and Moore, but even authors of monographs on specific rabbinic doctrines are bound to proceed to a somewhat arbitrary selection of sayings and to integrate them into some system. Dissenting views are frequently ignored or haughtily shoved aside. Some modifications and even outright polarity of views may be explained by the type of "organic thinking" which M. Kadushin has emphasized as an outstanding feature of rabbinic teachings. Cf. his *Theology of Seder Eliahu,* Vol. I (with notes by L. Ginzberg); and his study of Mekilta in *HUCA,* XIX. But this method, too, opens as many questions as it helps answer. A remedy can be expected only from such intensive special researches into the attitudes of individual rabbis as Bokser's study of R. Eliezer or Finkelstein's *Akiba,* as well as into the environmental changes. Even then it will be difficult to construe a well-rounded system out of fragments of a consciously unsystematic folkloristic body of material.

26. M. Sanhedrin X, 1; b. Qiddushin 71a; Seder Eliyahu rabbah. On the date of this midrash cf. V. Aptowitzer's "Seder Elia," *Kohut Mem. Vol.,* pp. 5–39 (placing it in Babylonia during the first half of the ninth century; and C. Albeck's note on Zunz's *Ha-Derashot,* pp. 55 ff., 293, n. 134, 138 (in favor of an earlier dating). Cf. A. Marmorstein's *Old Rabbinic Doctrine,* pp. 17 ff. Samaritans continued using the divine name in their oaths (j. Sanhedrin X, 1, 28b) and, as late as the fifth century, Theodoret learned from them its pronunciation, *Iabe.* Cf. Moore's *Judaism,* I, 426 f., III, 128 f. According to R. Eisler (in "Le Mystère du Schem Hammephorasch," *REJ,* LXXXII, 157–59) the mystic names of forty-two and seventy-two letters seem to be simple

derivatives, by way of *gematria*, of the thirteen attributes of God, enumerated in Exod. 34:6–7.

27. Gen. r. XVII, 5, 156 f., with reference to I Sam. 26:12 (Rab); Isa. 29:9–10 (the sages). Cf. O. Cullmann's *Problème littéraire et historique du roman pseudo-clémentin;* and H. C. Puech's "Mormotos," *Revue des études grecques,* XLVI, 311–33. Cf. also J. Moingt's comprehensive analysis of "La Gnose de Clément d'Alexandrie dans ses rapports avec la foi et la philosophie," *Recherches de science religieuse,* XXXVII–XXXVIII; K. Stuermer's "Judentum, Griechentum und Gnosis," *Theologische Literatur-Zeitung,* LV, 581–92; and *supra,* Chap. VI, n. 48. The influence of the rise of Christianity on the rabbinic opposition to gnostic teachings and rites of all kinds is stressed by M. Guttmann in his "Gebot und Mysterienhandlung," *MGWJ,* LXXVI, 319–30. Moreover, even in borrowing terms and concepts from the gnostics, the rabbis succeeded in filling them with Jewish content. G. Kretschmar rightly pointed out that, though some Palestinian (not Babylonian) sages applied the loan word *cosmocrator* to God, they did not budge from the idea of his absolute unity and omnipotence, whereas the Christian Fathers were too much concerned with the independent origin of evil and the devil to be able so to designate Christ. Cf. his remarks in *Judaica,* IV, 114–23. Cf. also A. Altmann's comments in *JQR,* XXXV, 371 ff. Perhaps the large new collection of gnostic writings found at Nag-Hammadi, Upper Egypt, and being published (1951) by H. C. Puech, T. Mina, and J. Doresse will throw some light on the pre-Christian Jewish gnosis as well. Cf. Puech's "Nouveaux écrits gnostiques découverts à Nag-Hammadi," *RHR,* CXXXIV, 244–48; and other studies reviewed by J. Doresse in *Bibliotheca orientalis,* VI, 102–4. Cf. also the latter's essay in *Archaeology,* III, 69–73. L. Ginzberg's "Observations" in *JBL,* XLI, 115–36; G. Scholem's *Major Trends in Jewish Mysticism,* pp. 40 ff., 351 ff.; A. Omodeo's "Problema delle origini storiche dello gnosticismo," *Parola di Passato,* II, 129–48; and *supra,* Chap. IX, n. 22–23.
Another moot question is the relation of the talmudic sages to asceticism. To the numerous utterances in favor of renunciation of worldly pleasures and even of self-mortification scattered through Bible and Talmud (cf. J. A. Montgomery's "Ascetic Strains in Early Judaism," *JBL,* LI, 183–213) can be counterpoised, on even more definitive evidence, the rabbis' affirmation of this-worldly life.

28. Cf. Obermann's observations in *AJSL,* LVII, 29. On the rabbis' generally ambivalent attitude toward amulets, cf. e.g., the discussion in Shabbat 61ab, 116b f.; and *supra,* Chap. IX, n. 23–26.

29. Cf. M. Sprengling's "Kartīr, Founder of Sasanian Zoroastrianism," *AJSL,* LVII, 197–228 (especially p. 220); 'A.Z. 43b; Megillah 29a. According to a widespread legend the synagogue of Shaf ve-Yashib had been founded by the exiled King Jehoiachin. Realizing that such a statue ran counter to clear-cut tannaitic prohibitions, the rabbis exerted their ingenuity in finding for it some justification. Cf. the lengthy discussion in 'A.Z. 42b f.

30. 'A.Z. 11b (clearly misspelled; three of these seasons are somewhat better reproduced in j. I, 2, 39c); Sanhedrin 67b; S. H. Taqizadeh's "Iranian Festivals Adopted by the Christians and Condemned by the Jews," *BSOS,* X, 632–53. In trying to establish here the authorship of R. Eleazar ben Pedat in lieu of his elder namesake of Modein, A. Marmorstein had to resort to strained interpretations and—always a suspicious sign—to serious emendations of the text. Cf. his "Anges et hommes dans l'Agada," *REJ,* LXXXIV, 46 ff.

31. Sanhedrin 97b. Cf. O. G. von Wesendonk's *Weltbild der Iranier.* The Parsees' eschatological computations were based on a 12,000-year duration of the world, di-

vided in periods of 3,000 years. Zoroastrian theologians differed as to the apportion-
ment of these eras. Cf. Christensen's *Iran*, pp. 147 f., 151 f. In his essay in *AR*, XXXIV,
254–76, J. Denner suggested that the doctrine of the aeons in many respects reflected
the social structure of three [later four] estates and the drive for power on the part
of such kings as Darius I. None of that evidently carried great appeal to the Jewish
egalitarian and nonmonarchical society. For this and other reasons, moreover, the
Jewish concept of the world to come and the Irano-Greek idea of timeless eternity
are worlds apart. Cf. A. Altmann's interesting comparison of "Olam und Aion," in
Festschrift Freimann, pp. 1–15; and A. J. Festugière's keen analysis of the "Sens
philosophique" of that term in *Parola di Passato*, IV, 172–89. On the general relations between rabbinic Judaism and Parseeism, cf. works by Söderblom, Bölklen, and
Gaster and the more recent investigations by I. Scheftelowitz, *Die altpersische Religion
und das Judentum;* A. von Gall, Βασιλεία τοῦ θεοῦ; *eine religionsgeschichtliche Studie
zur vorkirchlichen Eschatologie;* A. Marmorstein, "Iranische und jüdische Religion,"
ZNW, XXVI, 231–42; A. Christensen's *Essai sur la démonologie iranienne;* H.C.
Puech's brief discussion of some more recent publications, "De la mythologie indo-
iranienne à la légende juive et musulmane des anges Azael et Šemhazai ou Hārūt et
Mārūt," *RHR*, CXXXIII, 221–25; and E. Langton's *Essentials of Demonology: a Study
of Jewish and Christian Doctrine*, particularly pp. 58 f., 70 f., 220 f. (on Persian influence). Since Christensen has shown how, because of the victory of Median *magi*,
the West Iranian deities had been declassed into demons, we may well understand,
why Babylonian Jewry, being in contact chiefly with the western provinces, was much
more familiar with Parsee demonology than with angelology. Notwithstanding these
and many other publications, the scholarly elucidation of the complex problems
involved still is in its early stages.

32. It is immaterial in this connection whether we consider this meaning as the
authentic reflection of the original maxim of the Men of the Great Synagogue (M.
Abot I, 1), or whether they had merely advised their disciples, "Make a hedge about
your words," as is indicated in the elaboration of that passage given in ARN I, 1, p. 3.
Cf. Finkelstein's "Maxim of the Anshe Keneset ha-Gedolah," *JBL*, LIX, 457, 463.
Certainly from the days of Judah the Patriarch and, very likely, much earlier, the
sages not only felt *entitled* to extend the range of existing laws via interpretation,
but also considered themselves in *duty bound* to do so for the sake of Israel and its
religion.

33. Shabbat 104a; Seder 'Olam rabbah, XXX, in A. Neubauer's *Mediaeval Jewish
Chronicles*, II, 65; Menaḥot 29b; Makkot 23b f. In fact, the rabbis were often disturbed
by the legal divergences between the Pentateuch and such prophets as Ezekiel. According to tradition, some rabbis had opposed on this score the canonization of the
book of Ezekiel, which was salvaged for posterity only through the arduous efforts
of Ḥananiah ben Hezekiah, alleged author of the *Megillat Ta'anit*. Supplied with
three hundred kegs of oil, we are told, Ḥananiah never left his attic until he succeeded in hermeneutically harmonizing the prophet's sayings with the law of Moses.
Cf. Shabbat 13b; and, more generally, E. A. Urbach's essays in *Tarbiz*, XVII, 1 ff.,
XVIII, 1 ff. On the influence of the Judeo-Christian controversies on the rabbinic
attitude to prophecy, cf. also *supra*, Chap. XII, n. 14.